Windows® 2000
Server Bible

Windows® 2000 Server Bible

Jeffrey R. Shapiro and Jim Boyce

IDG Books Worldwide, Inc.
An International Data Group Company

Foster City, CA ✦ Chicago, IL ✦ Indianapolis, IN ✦ New York, NY

Windows® 2000 Server Bible

Published by
IDG Books Worldwide, Inc.
An International Data Group Company
919 E. Hillsdale Blvd., Suite 400
Foster City, CA 94404
www.idgbooks.com (IDG Books Worldwide Web site)

ISBN: 0-7645-4667-8

Printed in the United States of America

10 9 8 7 6 5 4 3 2 1

1B/SW/QW/QQ/FC

Distributed in the United States by IDG Books Worldwide, Inc.

Distributed by CDG Books Canada Inc. for Canada; by Transworld Publishers Limited in the United Kingdom; by IDG Norge Books for Norway; by IDG Sweden Books for Sweden; by IDG Books Australia Publishing Corporation Pty. Ltd. for Australia and New Zealand; by TransQuest Publishers Pte Ltd. for Singapore, Malaysia, Thailand, Indonesia, and Hong Kong; by Gotop Information Inc. for Taiwan; by ICG Muse, Inc. for Japan; by Intersoft for South Africa; by Eyrolles for France; by International Thomson Publishing for Germany, Austria, and Switzerland; by Distribuidora Cuspide for Argentina; by LR International for Brazil; by Galileo Libros for Chile; by Ediciones ZETA S.C.R. Ltda. for Peru; by WS Computer Publishing Corporation, Inc., for the Philippines; by Contemporanea de Ediciones for Venezuela; by Express Computer Distributors for the Caribbean and West Indies; by Micronesia Media Distributor, Inc. for Micronesia; by Chips Computadoras S.A. de C.V. for Mexico; by Editorial Norma de Panama S.A. for Panama; by American Bookshops for Finland.

For general information on IDG Books Worldwide's books in the U.S., please call our Consumer Customer Service department at 800-762-2974. For reseller information, including discounts and premium sales, please call our Reseller Customer Service department at 800-434-3422.

For information on where to purchase IDG Books Worldwide's books outside the U.S., please contact our International Sales department at 317-596-5530 or fax 317-572-4002.

For consumer information on foreign language translations, please contact our Customer Service department at 800-434-3422, fax 317-572-4002, or e-mail rights@idgbooks.com.

For information on licensing foreign or domestic rights, please phone +1-650-653-7098.

For sales inquiries and special prices for bulk quantities, please contact our Order Services department at 800-434-3422 or write to the address above.

For information on using IDG Books Worldwide's books in the classroom or for ordering examination copies, please contact our Educational Sales department at 800-434-2086 or fax 317-572-4005.

For press review copies, author interviews, or other publicity information, please contact our Public Relations department at 650-653-7000 or fax 650-653-7500.

For authorization to photocopy items for corporate, personal, or educational use, please contact Copyright Clearance Center, 222 Rosewood Drive, Danvers, MA 01923, or fax 978-750-4470.

Library of Congress Cataloging-in-Publication Data

Shapiro, Jeffrey R.
   Windows 2000 server bible / Jeffrey Shapiro and James Boyce.
      p. cm.
   Includes bibliographical references and index.
   ISBN 0-7645-4667-8 (alk. paper)
   1. Microsoft Windows 2000 server. 2. Operating systems (Computers) I. Boyce, James
II. Title

QA76.76.O63 S535   2000
005.7'13769--dc21
                             00-024343
                             CIP

 is a registered trademark or trademark under exclusive license to IDG Books Worldwide, Inc. from International Data Group, Inc. in the United States and/or other countries.

ABOUT IDG BOOKS WORLDWIDE

Welcome to the world of IDG Books Worldwide.

IDG Books Worldwide, Inc., is a subsidiary of International Data Group, the world's largest publisher of computer-related information and the leading global provider of information services on information technology. IDG was founded more than 30 years ago by Patrick J. McGovern and now employs more than 9,000 people worldwide. IDG publishes more than 290 computer publications in over 75 countries. More than 90 million people read one or more IDG publications each month.

Launched in 1990, IDG Books Worldwide is today the #1 publisher of best-selling computer books in the United States. We are proud to have received eight awards from the Computer Press Association in recognition of editorial excellence and three from Computer Currents' First Annual Readers' Choice Awards. Our best-selling ...*For Dummies*® series has more than 50 million copies in print with translations in 31 languages. IDG Books Worldwide, through a joint venture with IDG's Hi-Tech Beijing, became the first U.S. publisher to publish a computer book in the People's Republic of China. In record time, IDG Books Worldwide has become the first choice for millions of readers around the world who want to learn how to better manage their businesses.

Our mission is simple: Every one of our books is designed to bring extra value and skill-building instructions to the reader. Our books are written by experts who understand and care about our readers. The knowledge base of our editorial staff comes from years of experience in publishing, education, and journalism — experience we use to produce books to carry us into the new millennium. In short, we care about books, so we attract the best people. We devote special attention to details such as audience, interior design, use of icons, and illustrations. And because we use an efficient process of authoring, editing, and desktop publishing our books electronically, we can spend more time ensuring superior content and less time on the technicalities of making books.

You can count on our commitment to deliver high-quality books at competitive prices on topics you want to read about. At IDG Books Worldwide, we continue in the IDG tradition of delivering quality for more than 30 years. You'll find no better book on a subject than one from IDG Books Worldwide.

John J. Kilcullen
John Kilcullen
Chairman and CEO
IDG Books Worldwide, Inc.

VIII
WINNER
*Eighth Annual
Computer Press
Awards ≥1992*

IX
WINNER
*Ninth Annual
Computer Press
Awards ≥1993*

X
WINNER
*Tenth Annual
Computer Press
Awards ≥1994*

XI
WINNER
*Eleventh Annual
Computer Press
Awards ≥1995*

IDG is the world's leading IT media, research and exposition company. Founded in 1964, IDG had 1997 revenues of $2.05 billion and has more than 9,000 employees worldwide. IDG offers the widest range of media options that reach IT buyers in 75 countries representing 95% of worldwide IT spending. IDG's diverse product and services portfolio spans six key areas including print publishing, online publishing, expositions and conferences, market research, education and training, and global marketing services. More than 90 million people read one or more of IDG's 290 magazines and newspapers, including IDG's leading global brands — Computerworld, PC World, Network World, Macworld and the Channel World family of publications. IDG Books Worldwide is one of the fastest-growing computer book publishers in the world, with more than 700 titles in 36 languages. The "...For Dummies®" series alone has more than 50 million copies in print. IDG offers online users the largest network of technology-specific Web sites around the world through IDG.net (http://www.idg.net), which comprises more than 225 targeted Web sites in 55 countries worldwide. International Data Corporation (IDC) is the world's largest provider of information technology data, analysis and consulting, with research centers in over 41 countries and more than 400 research analysts worldwide. IDG World Expo is a leading producer of more than 168 globally branded conferences and expositions in 35 countries including E3 (Electronic Entertainment Expo), Macworld Expo, ComNet, Windows World Expo, ICE (Internet Commerce Expo), Agenda, DEMO, and Spotlight. IDG's training subsidiary, ExecuTrain, is the world's largest computer training company, with more than 230 locations worldwide and 785 training courses. IDG Marketing Services helps industry-leading IT companies build international brand recognition by developing global integrated marketing programs via IDG's print, online and exposition products worldwide. Further information about the company can be found at www.idg.com. 1/26/00

Credits

Acquisitions Editors
John Read
Michelle Baxter
Judy Brief

Project Editors
Brian MacDonald
Laura Brown

Technical Editor
Jim Kelly

Copy Editors
Chandani Thapa
Julie Smith

Proof Editor
Patsy Owens

Project Coordinators
Linda Marousek
Danette Nurse
Joe Shines

Media Development Specialist
Jake Mason

Permissions Editor
Lenora Chin Sell

Media Development Manager
Stephen Noetzel

Graphics and Production Specialists
Robert Bihlmayer
Jude Levinson
Michael Lewis
Victor Pérez-Varela
Dina F Quan
Ramses Ramirez

Book Designer
Drew R. Moore

Illustrators
Mary Jo Richards
Karl Brandt

Proofreading and Indexing
York Production Services

Cover Illustration
Murder By Design

About the Authors

Jeffrey R. Shapiro is the author of *Computer Telephony Strategies* (IDG Books Worldwide) and has authored and contributed to several books on Windows NT, software engineering, networking, and so on. He has written numerous features for magazines such as *Call Center, Computer Telephony,* and *NetworkWorld,* and he is also the editor and publisher of the newsletter, *CRM Review.* A consulting engineer for more than 13 years, Jeffrey has worked with hundreds of companies such as Microsoft, Novell, and IBM, a number of public institutions, and several governments.

Jim Boyce is the author or co-author of more than 40 books on computer software, hardware, programming (VB), and system administration. Jim is a former contributing editor and monthly columnist for *Windows Magazine,* and has also written numerous features for magazines such as *Cadence, CADalyst,* and *PC Magazine.* Jim is also the Vice President of Minnesota WebWorks, a Midwest-based Internet development company.

To the late Dr. Michael Edwards for his contribution to the "science" of Enterprise Analysis, and to Lesley Kalish for being there for me.

Preface

Windows 2000 is much more than an upgrade to Windows NT. In many respects, it is a new operating system, which will present you with both exciting and daunting challenges. This book is the culmination of thousands of hours spent testing, evaluating, and experimenting with just about everything that Windows 2000 Server will throw at you.

Gone are the days when the Windows server operating systems could be covered in a single book, or a week's crash course at a training center. If we told you that this is the only book you'll need on Windows 2000 Server, we would be lying. Many of the features we cover warrant advanced treatment under separate cover. We have attempted to build as complete a hands-on reference as possible while still providing a broad scope of coverage to give you a detailed look at the most important aspects and implications of the Windows 2000 operating platform, specifically for Windows 2000 Server.

While the conventional wisdom is usually to wait for the first service pack to begin moving to new software, Windows 2000 presents some compelling reasons to convert sooner rather than later. In addition to expanded hardware support and support for Plug-and-Play, Windows 2000 incorporates numerous new technologies and improves on several existing ones, particularly for Windows 2000 Server, the focus of the *Windows 2000 Server Bible*.

Perhaps one of the most pervasive changes in Windows 2000 Server is Active Directory. This new directory service impacts most aspects of Windows 2000 Server, including the areas of security and user and group administration, network and domain topology, replication, DHCP and DNS, and more. Other important changes include incorporation of the Distributed File System (Dfs), which enables you to build a homogenous file system structure from shares located on various servers across the network. In a similar fashion, volume mount points, a new feature of NTFS 5.0, enable you to mount a volume into an empty NTFS folder, making the volume appear as part of the structure of the volume in which the NTFS folder resides. Mounted volumes do much the same for a local file structure that Dfs provides for a network file structure. Changes in DNS and DHCP enable DHCP clients to dynamically request updates of their host records hosted by Windows 2000 DNS servers, enabling you to maintain up-to-date host records for all systems in the enterprise, even if they are assigned IP address dynamically or their host or domain names change.

These changes are just a few of the many new features and modifications offered by the Windows 2000 operating platform.

Who Should Read This Book

Windows 2000 Server Bible is for anyone involved in network administration, server management, MIS, and so on. If the questions you have are along the line of "how do we handle this?" then this book's for you.

Granted, Windows NT administrators have a leg up on our UNIX and NetWare comrades, but Windows 2000 Server makes waves in all IS infrastructures. The audience covers a wide spectrum . . . as broad as the number of services the product offers. Not only do we cater to network or server administrators, but many chapters are aimed at people tasked with certain responsibilities, such as security, user account administration, service level, customer relationship management, e-commerce, and so on.

While we assume that you are familiar with the Windows environment (either Windows 9*x* or Windows NT), much of what we have written will be of value to administrators working in heterogeneous environments, even midrange and mainframe facilities. We have also focused on issues of concern to managers and information offices. This is very much an integration book, so you will find conversion tips aplenty, culled from an eagle eye cast on every process that might create problems for business systems and processes that are still in place.

Whether you're just trying to get a handle on what's new in Windows 2000 Server and the impact it will have, you're looking at installing new Windows 2000 systems, or you've been tasked with converting from Windows NT Server to Windows 2000 Server, you'll find a wealth of information between the covers of this book that will help you meet your goals.

Everything we discuss in these pages has been tested and deployed in a number of early adoptions, in one form or another. So step into our shoes and get a heads up on the road ahead. You will no doubt go on to learn a lot more about Windows 2000 Server, as will we. If there is anything you would like to point out, or add to, we value your contributions. You can write to us at `jeffrey.shapiro@mcity.org` or `boyce_jim@compuserve.com`.

How This Book is Organized

The *Windows 2000 Server Bible* is divided into several logical parts, each focusing on a specific feature area or technology in Windows 2000 Server. The following list summarizes the topics covered and how they are structured:

> ✦ **Part I: Windows 2000 Server Architecture** — Part I provides extensive coverage of Windows 2000 Server architecture in three key areas: system design, the Active Directory (AD), and security. Chapter 1 covers the system architecture to give you an understanding of how Windows 2000's components

function and interact with one another. Chapter 1 also covers several higher-level components such as Internet services, power management, Plug-and-Play, and so on. Chapter 2 focuses on Active Directory to give you an overview of the AD's purpose and design. Chapter 3 finishes the section with a broad look at security in Windows 2000 including Kerberos, certificates, encryption, and many other security-related topics.

✦ **Part II: Planning, Installation, and Configuration** — Part II is where you'll turn when you're ready to start planning your Windows 2000 Server deployment, whether on a single system or a wider-scale deployment. Chapter 4 helps you decide whether you need to upgrade your hardware, plan deployment across the enterprise, and several other pre-installation issues. Chapter 5 covers the actual installation of Windows 2000 Server and discusses machine or platform configuration, hardware selection, choosing services, and so on. Chapter 6 takes you to the next step after installation and explains how to configure services, the user interface, and other Windows 2000 options and properties.

✦ **Part III: Active Directory Services** — Active Directory represents one of the most significant additions in Windows 2000 Server over Windows NT. Part III provides a complete look at AD, starting in Chapter 7 with a look at AD's logical structure and what it really represents. Chapter 8 explores the physical structure of AD to explain it in the context of domains, sites, servers, and security. Chapter 9 covers AD planning, installation, and management. Managing users and groups is covered in detail in Chapter 10, and Chapter 11 finishes the section with coverage of change management, and how Group Policy facilitates change control over users, computers, security, and the workspace.

✦ **Part IV: Networking and Communication Services** — Part IV explores in detail several key networking and communications services in Windows 2000 Server. Chapter 12 lays the groundwork by covering the ubiquitous TCP/IP protocol, along with routing, troubleshooting, Network Address Translation (NAT), SNMP, and legacy protocols. You'll find detailed coverage in Chapter 13 to help you configure and deploy DHCP for automatic IP address assignment and administration. DNS and WINS server configuration and client management are covered in Chapter 14, and the Routing and Remote Access Service is covered in detail in Chapter 15.

✦ **Part V: Availability Management** — Windows 2000 Server builds on Windows NT for fault tolerance, storage management, recovery, and other availability issues. Storage management is covered in detail in Chapter 16 to include removable storage, fault tolerance, RAID, general file system management, and related topics. Chapter 17 helps you develop and implement a backup and recovery strategy and explores the new Windows 2000 Backup utility, configuring removable storage, and media pools. The Windows 2000 registry and registry management are explored in Chapter 18, with auditing explained in Chapter 19. Chapter 20 rounds out the section with a detailed discussion of Windows 2000's service level tools such as System Monitor, Performance Logs and Alerts.

♦ **Part VI: File, Print, and Web Services**—Part VI explores critical services in Windows 2000 Server with Chapter 21 detailing the various file systems available in Windows 2000 Server. Chapter 22 explains how to configure and optimize file sharing and security, and manage file sharing effectively. It also provides thorough coverage of the new support for file and folder encryption. Higher-end print topics such as Internet printing, printer management, and troubleshooting are covered in Chapter 23. Chapter 24 rounds out the discussion with a detailed explanation of Web, SMTP, and FTP services to include such topics as service configuration and security, certificates, SSL, and so on.

♦ **Part VII: Interoperation and Integration Services**—Chapter 25 is dedicated to the new Terminal Services that is now fully integrated into the operating system. This chapter kicks off with a reality check of client/server computing and explores the growing trend of thin-client deployment. The chapter also covers setting up Terminal Services, configuring application servers, and tips garnered from actual Terminal Services projects.

♦ You will find two bonus apppendixes on the CD-ROM: Appendix A: Command Line Reference, and Appendix B: Windows 2000 Resource Kit.

Conventions Used In This Book

Throughout this book, we've followed certain conventions to make the material clear and useful to you. New terms are presented in *italics*, followed by their definitions. Filenames, directories, URLs, and code are presented in `monospace` font, and any text that you should type in at the keyboard is presented in **bold.**

The following margin icons are used to help you get the most out of this book:

Notes are used to highlight information that is useful and should be taken into consideration.

Tips provide an additional bit of advice that will make a particular feature quicker or easier to use.

Cautions are meant to warn you of a potential problem that could adversely affect your system or network.

Watch for this icon to learn where in another chapter you can go to find more information on a particular feature.

Acknowledgments

God knows how hard it is to write a book . . . and then get it published. So we are thankful for the team that has helped us bring this baby into the world.

We would first like to thank our agent, David Fugate of Waterside Productions, for his effort in bringing us together with the team at IDG Books Worldwide. If there were an Olympic team for computer writers, David would be the head coach for sure. Special honors also go to the IDG Books editorial team. In particular, we would like to "flag" our production editor, Brian MacDonald, who seemed to become an expert in midwifery when this title landed on his desk. Brian gives new meaning to the word "push."

Technical editor "Oscar" goes to Jim Kelly for not only reading our lines, but for reading in between them as well. And we would have no doubt gotten no further than this Acknowledgements page without the expert red pencils of our copy editors, Chandani Thapa and Julie Smith.

For every hour spent writing these words, at least ten were spent testing and toying with Windows 2000 Server. So how do two authors get this far? Simple — you gather around you a team of dedicated professionals who help you build a killer lab and help you to test everything from the logon screen to the shutdown command.

The following members of the lab were invaluable to us: Jay "Hota" Morrison for his continuous efforts in obtaining the betas and early releases of Windows 2000 Server, securing hardware and testing installation, remote and unattended deployment, and so on. Jay was flanked by Piers "Bond" Brew who tested every shade of Windows and UNIX for integration with Windows 2000 . . . always looking for the missing "link." Omar "/s" Martinez takes the gold for continuous work at the CD burner and his expert advice on PC and server hardware.

Much of the dabbling would certainly not have been possible without the support, encouragement, and advice of the following teammates: Tim Ruiz, Craig Neeb, Carl Bethel, Chris Riling, Jill Petersen, Wil Rego, Anne Telander, and Michael Jones. And the slap on the back goes to Armando "Colada" Blanco for his endless supply of Coladas (the Cuban equivalent of a 1000MHz espresso), humor, and chicken wings . . . without which the deadlines would have been impossible to meet.

The "home" team always gets the last mention, but without their support, input, and love, the soul in this work would not have taken flight. Special thanks to Kim and Kevin Shapiro.

Contents at a Glance

Contents

Part II: Planning, Installation, and Configuration   95

Chapter 4: Planning for Windows 2000 Server 97

Part IV: Networking and Communications Services   413

Part V: Availability Management   603

Part VI: File, Print, and Web Services   745

Chapter 21: Windows 2000 File Systems 747

Chapter 22: Sharing and Securing Files and Folders 789

Part VII: Interoperation and Integration Services   913

Chapter 25: Terminal Services and Thin Client Integration 915

Appendix: What's on the CD-ROM 941

Windows 2000 Server Architecture

Windows 2000 is a complex operating system. Built on Windows NT, it has inherited the familiar preemptive multitasking kernel, the hardware abstraction layer (HAL) and various subsystems that support DOS, Windows, OS/2, and POSIX applications. Part I includes three chapters that explore the architecture of the OS, Active Directory, and Windows 2000 security, respectively.

Chapter 1 introduces the kernel modes of the operating system, the differences between the subsystems, and so on. If you are a seasoned NT administrator, the early parts of Chapter 1 will be a refresher course. The latter part of the chapter, however, introduces the important additions to the operating system and sets the scene for many of the chapters in this book.

The directory service has been under development for years. It is now very much a part of Windows 2000. Chapter 2 discusses directory services in general and Active Directory in particular.

Chapter 3 is an introduction to the complex and exciting world of Windows 2000 security. This chapter is the place to start to obtain a handle on the likes of Kerberos, the cryptographic services, public key infrastructure, certificate services, and so on.

Introducing Windows 2000 Server

Windows 2000 is a complex operating system and very different from Windows NT 4.0 and earlier. This chapter introduces the product's architecture and provides guidelines to begin creating your strategy to adopt and support it.

Welcome to Windows 2000 Server

When Windows NT 4.0 emerged in 1996, we wrote an article in a leading magazine describing the operating system in military terms. We called it the strike craft of operating systems. A strike craft is a small boat that packs a lot of punch and usually carries a few missiles on its back. But a strike craft is not a vessel you take to war with you. It does not have the ability to endure long journeys; its so-called availability period is short. At the time, Windows 3.51 had just been awarded C2 security rating by the U.S. government, so the naval analogy seemed fitting.

Over the years and several service packs later, Windows NT moved up the ranks. By Service Pack 4, we compared it to a destroyer. But it was still a down-fleet vessel, not the ship that would lead the fleet with the top guns. Windows 2000 changes all that. The operating system is more than just one ship; it is the whole fleet — aircraft carriers, submarines, destroyers, gun-ships, minesweepers, and more. In fact, Windows 2000 *is* the navy.

Granted, it has its shortcomings. In fact, it is the first operating system ever to have shipped a service pack before its launch party. While the analogy to a warship seemed amusing to many over the years, it is more applicable today than ever before. In the world of e-commerce and the Internet, we are all on the battlefield. This is the world war of commerce and e-sabotage, exploding onto the networks of the world.

Over the past few decades, only the big companies could afford the big iron mainframes from the likes of IBM and Digital Equipment Corp. Now that firepower is in the hands of everyone with enough money to register a dot-com. We are fighting a network war in which the competition is able to obtain weaponry and firepower never before thought possible in computer science.

Viral warfare is surging beyond belief with thousands of computer viruses released every month. Hackers are penetrating corporate networks all over the world. Business people are hiring geeks to bombard their competition with datagram attacks and denial-of-service bombs. And fraud is just around the next router. You need an operating system that can protect you at home and away from home, at every portal, and at every location. Today, no operating system competes with the vastness of Windows 2000 Server.

Note   According to McAfee, there are currently 47,000 known viruses, variants, and Trojan horses in the world . . . "this increases by approximately 1,000 per month."

Before we look into the weaponry and architecture that supports Windows 2000 Server, it is important to understand that it is not all guns and roses. Windows 2000 Server leaves a few oil spills here and there, and we will discuss these where appropriate. However, it is worth mentioning here that a huge hurdle to overcome, besides the long-winded name, is the learning curve. No version of Windows NT (in fact, no other server operating system) is as extensive, as deep, and as complex in many places.

While Windows 2000 Server has been created to cater to the demand for operating systems that cost less to manage and own, realizing the benefit will be a long and costly journey for many. Windows 2000 Server is not the only culprit; UNIX, NetWare, and the midrange systems also have a long way to go before they can truly claim to reduce the total cost of ownership, not only in terms of operating systems and software, but also in terms of all technology ownership and management.

There are two ways to decide what you want to do about Windows 2000 Server. For a start, know that all your competitors are in the same boat. Whoever takes the plunge and adopts first will be better off down the road. You can a) ignore Windows 2000 Server for the next 6 to 12 months on the premise or misguided advice that you should wait for the OS to ship at least two service packs, or you can b) take the plunge now and deploy it in labs and development environments and be ready when the inevitable "we need it now" memo arrives.

Throughout this book, we suggest the latter approach. Put the OS into controlled development and pilot projects and deploy selective components that provide better services than what is available under NT. You cannot learn the OS overnight, so it makes sense to get the evaluation copies and learn as much as you can now. This is where much of Windows 2000 Server will be for most of 2000, in phased implementation and development projects. After all, you have nothing to lose except a little time.

With ongoing systems to support, Windows 2000 Server typically requires a skilled network engineer or systems analyst to invest about six to eight months into the OS. And even after eight months of intense study, you still can't consider yourself an expert. Perhaps the best way to tackle the learning curve, besides spending a lot of money on courses where end-to-end training runs into five figures per administrator and without the cost of absence from work during the training, is to divide up the key service areas of the OS.

To a large extent, we have divided this book along the key service lines listed here:

✦ Windows 2000 Architecture

✦ Active Directory Services

✦ Security Services

✦ Network Services

✦ Availability Services

✦ File and Print Services

✦ Application Services

This chapter deals with Windows 2000 Architecture and introduces you to key services that fall under the Zero Administration Windows (ZAW) initiative.

Windows 2000 Server Architecture

Making the effort to understand the architecture of an operating system is a lot like making the effort to understand how your car runs. Without knowing the details, you can still drive and the vehicle will get you from A to B. But when something goes wrong, you take your car to the shop and the mechanic deals with it. He or she will tell you that you should have changed your oil earlier, or that your tires needed balancing, or that your spark plugs were loose. Had you known how the car operates, you would have taken more care of it and prevented excessive wear and tear. You could probably have serviced it yourself.

The same can be said about an operating system, although it is a lot more complex than a car's engine. If you understand the various components of the kernel (the OS), the file system, and how the OS uses processors, memory, hardware, and so on, you will be better at administering the machine.

Operating System Modes

Windows 2000, built on NT, is a modular, component-based operating system. All objects in the operating system expose interfaces that other objects and processes interact with to obtain functionality and services. These components work together to perform specific operating system tasks.

The Windows 2000 architecture contains two major layers: user mode and kernel mode. The modes and the various subsystems are illustrated in Figure 1-1.

Note   The system architecture is essentially the same across Professional, Server, Advanced Server, and Datacenter Server.

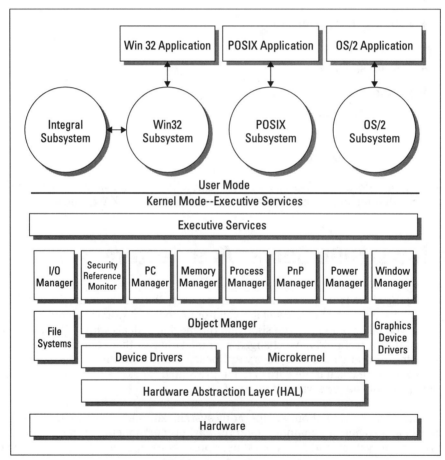

Figure 1-1: The Windows 2000 Server System architecture (simple)

User Mode

The Windows 2000 user mode layer is typically an application support layer, for both Microsoft and third-party software, consisting of both environment and integral subsystems. It is the part of the operating system on which independent software vendors can make operating system calls against published APIs and object-oriented components. All applications and services are installed into the user mode layer.

Environment subsystems

The environment subsystems provide the ability to run applications that are written for various operating systems. The environment subsystems are designed to intercept the calls that applications make to a particular OS API, and then to convert these calls into a format understood by Windows 2000. The converted API calls are then passed on to the operating system components that need to deal with requests. The return codes or returned information these applications depend on are then converted back to a format understood by the application.

These subsystems are not new in Windows 2000, and they have been greatly improved over the years on NT. There have been reports in some cases that the applications will run better on Windows 2000 than they do on the operating systems they were intended for. Many applications are also more secure in Windows 2000. For example, Windows 2000, without affecting server stability, terminates DOS applications that would typically crash a machine just running DOS. Table 1-1 lists the Windows 2000 environment or application subsystems.

Table 1-1 **Environment Subsystems**	
Environment Subsystem	*Purpose*
Windows 2000 Win32 (32-bit)	Supports Win32-based applications. This subsystem is also responsible for 16-bit Windows and DOS applications. All application I/O and GUI functionality is handled here. This subsystem has been greatly enhanced to support Terminal Services.
OS/2	Supports 16-bit OS/2 applications (mainly Microsoft OS/2).
POSIX	Supports POSIX-compliant applications (usually UNIX).

The non-Win32 subsystems provide a basic support for non-Win32 legacy applications and no more. There is no real demand for either subsystem, and they have been maintained only to run the simplest of utilities that make very direct and POSIX- or OS/2-compliant function calls, usually in C. The POSIX subsystem, for example, caters to the likes of UNIX utilities VI and GREP.

The POSIX subsystem is not retained as a means, for example, of advanced integration of UNIX and Windows 2000, such as running a UNIX Shell on Windows 2000. For that level, you need to install UNIX Services. More about this later in this chapter.

There are several limitations and restrictions imposed on non-Windows applications running on Windows 2000. This is demonstrated in the following list, which for the most part also includes user mode, Win32-based applications:

✦ Software has no direct access to hardware. In other words, when an application requests hard disk space, it is barred from accessing hardware for such information. Instead, it accesses user mode objects that talk to kernel mode objects, that talk down the operating system stack to the Hardware Abstraction Layer (discussed shortly). The information is then passed all the way up the stack into the interface. This processing is often known as handoff processing. The function in the Win32 code essentially gets a return value, and developers have no need to talk to the hardware. This is good for developers and the operating system. APIs that check the validity of the call protect the OS, and developers get exposed to a simple call-level interface, which typically requires a line of code, not 10,000 lines.

✦ Software has no direct access to device drivers. The philosophy outlined previously applies to device drivers as well. Hardware manufacturers build the drivers for Windows 2000 that access the hardware. The drivers, too, are prevented from going directly to the hardware, interfacing instead with abstraction objects provided by the device driver APIs. This is discussed later in this chapter, along with the new Windows Driver Model initiative.

✦ Software is restricted to an assigned address space in memory. This constraint protects the operating system from rogue applications that would attempt to access whatever memory they can. This is impossible in Windows 2000, so an application can only screw up in the address space it is assigned.

✦ Windows 2000, like Windows NT, will use hard disk space as quasi-RAM. Applications are oblivious to the source or type of memory; it is transparent to them. *Virtual memory* is a combination of all memory in the system; it is explained in more detail later in this chapter.

✦ The applications in the user mode subsystems run as a lower priority process than any services or routines running in the kernel mode. This also means that they do not get preference for access to the CPU over kernel mode processes.

Integral subsystems

The integral subsystems are used to perform certain critical operating system functions. Table 1-2 lists these services.

Table 1-2 Integral Subsystems	
Integral Subsystem	**Purpose**
Security Subsystem	Performs the services related to user rights and access control to all network and OS objects defined or abstracted in some way in the OS. It also handles the logon requests and begins the logon authentication process.
Server Service	This service is what makes Windows 2000 a network operating system. All network services are rooted in this service.
Workstation Service	The service is similar in purpose to the server service. It is oriented more to user access of the network. (You can operate and even work at a machine that has this service disabled.)

There is little you need to manage with respect to these systems. These services are accessible in the Service Control Manager and can be started and stopped manually.

Kernel Mode

The Windows 2000 kernel mode is the layer that has access to system data and hardware. It comprises several components, as illustrated in Figure 1-1.

The Windows 2000 Executive

The "Executive" is the collective noun for all executive services, and it houses much of the I/O routines in the OS and performs the key object management, especially security. The Executive also contains the Systems Services components (which are accessible to both OS modes) and the internal kernel mode routines (which are not accessible to any code running in user mode). The kernel mode components are as follows:

✦ **I/O Manager:** This manages the input to and from the devices on the machine. In particular, it includes the following services:

• **File System:** Translates file system requests into device-specific calls.

  • **Device Drivers:** Manages the device drivers that directly access hardware.

  • **Cache Manager:** Buried in the I/O manager code, it manages I/O performance by caching disk reads. It also caches write and read requests and handles offline or background writes to the hardware.

✦ **Security Reference Monitor:** This component enforces security policies on the computer.

✦ **Interprocess Communication Manager (IPC):** This component makes its presence felt in many places in the OS. It is essentially responsible for communications between client and server processes. It comprises the Local Procedure Call (LPC) facility, which manages communications between clients and server processes that exist on the same computer, and the Remote Procedure Call (RPC) facility, which manages communications between clients and servers on separate machines.

✦ **Memory Manager or Virtual Memory Manager (VMM):** This component manages virtual memory. It provides a virtual address space for each process that manifests and protects that space to maintain system integrity. It also controls the demand for access to the hard disk for virtual RAM, which is known as paging (see the section Windows 2000 Memory Management later in this chapter).

✦ **Process Manager:** This component creates and terminates processes and threads that are spawned by both systems services and applications.

✦ **Plug and Play Manager:** This component is new to Windows 2000. It provides the Plug and Play services and communicates with the various device drivers for configuration and services related to the hardware.

✦ **Power Manager:** This component controls the management of power in the system. It works with the various power management APIs and manages events related to power management requests.

✦ **Window Manager** and **Graphical Device Interface (GDI):** The driver, `Win32K.sys`, combines the services of both components and manages the display system.

  • **Window Manager:** This component manages screen output and window displays. It also handles I/O data from the mouse and keyboard.

  • **GDI:** This component, once the hardest interface to code against and keep supplied with memory in the days of Win16, handles the drawing and manipulation of graphics on the screen and interfaces with components that hand off these objects to printer objects and other graphics rendering devices.

✦ **Object Manager:** This engine manages the system objects. It creates them, manages them, and deletes them when they are no longer needed, and it manages the resources, such as memory, that need to be allocated to them.

In addition to these services, and as indicated in Figure 1-1, three other central core components complete the makeup of the kernel mode. These include the Device Drivers component, the Microkernel, and the Hardware Abstraction Layer (HAL).

Device Drivers

This component simply translates driver calls into the actual routines that manipulate the hardware.

Microkernel

This is the core of the operating system (some regard it as being the operating system, with everything else being services). It manages process threads that are "spawned" to the microprocessor, thread scheduling, multi-tasking, and so on. The Windows 2000 microkernel is preemptive, which means, essentially, that threads can be interrupted or rescheduled.

Hardware Abstraction Layer

The Hardware Abstraction Layer, or HAL, essentially hides the hardware interface details for the other services and components. In other words, it is an abstraction layer above the actual hardware, and all calls to the hardware are made through the HAL. The HAL contains the necessary hardware code that handles hardware-specific I/O interfaces, hardware interrupts, and so forth. This layer is also responsible for both the Intel-specific and Alpha-specific support that allows a single executive to run on either processor.

Windows 2000 Processing Architecture

Windows 2000 Server is built around a symmetric multiprocessing (SMP) architecture. This means that first, the operating system can operate on multiple CPUs, and second, it can make the CPUs available to all processes as needed. In other words, if one CPU is completely occupied, additional threads spawned by the applications or services can be processed on other available CPUs.

Windows 2000 combines its multitasking and multithreading capabilities with its SMP capabilities. Also, if the threads waiting for execution are backed up, the OS schedules the processors to pick up the waiting threads. The thread execution load is evenly allocated to the available CPUs. Symmetric multiprocessing thus ensures that the operating system uses all available processor resources, which naturally speeds up processing time.

Windows 2000 Server supports 4-way (4 CPUs) symmetric multi-processing. Advanced Server supports 8-way SMP, and Datacenter server supports up to 32-way SMP. And if you have the muscle, you can get the code from Microsoft, under hefty contract, to compile the OS to your SMP specifications.

Windows 2000 Memory Management

Windows 2000's handling of memory has been vastly improved over Windows NT. It consists of a memory model based on a flat, linear, albeit still 32-bit, address space. There are two types of memory used in the Windows 2000 operating system. First is *physical* memory, which includes the memory in the RAM chips installed on the system motherboards, memory accessible from platter space on hard disks. Second is *virtual* memory, which is a combination of all memory in the system and how it is made available to the OS.

The virtual memory manager (VMM) is used to manage system memory. It manages and combines all physical memory in a system in such a way that applications and the operating system have more memory available to them than is provided in the actual RAM chips installed in the system.

The VMM also protects the memory resources by providing a barrier that prevents one process from violating the memory address space of another process, a key problem of the older operating systems such as DOS and earlier versions of Windows.

Every memory byte, whether physical or virtual, is represented by a unique address. Physical RAM has limitations because Windows 2000 can only address the memory according to the amount of physical RAM in the system. But virtual addressing is another story. Windows 2000 can support up to four gigabytes worth of virtual addresses. This may sound confusing when you only have limited physical RAM in the system, but the VMM can map in so-called virtual memory from a hard disk. The VMM manages the memory and has two major functions:

1. The VMM maintains a memory-mapped table that can keep track of the list of virtual addresses assigned to each process. And it coordinates where the actual data mapped to the addresses resides. In other words, it acts as a translator service, mapping virtual memory to physical memory. This function is transparent to the applications, which continue to behave as if they have access to physical memory.

2. When RAM is maxed out, the VMM moves the memory contents to the hard disk as and when required. This is known as *paging*.

Thus, Windows 2000 basically has access to a 4GB address space, although the space is virtual and can be made up of both RAM and hard disk space. Even though we talk about a 4GB address space, this space is actually relative to how the system uses memory. In actual fact, the address space available to applications is only 2GB and is even less than that because the 2GB assignment is shared by all processes running in user mode, and the other 2GB assignment is reserved for kernel mode threads.

Note Windows 2000 Advanced Server and Datacenter Server can be configured to allow applications to access more than the default 2GB space.

We talk about an upper and a lower portion of the 4GB space, both containing 2GB addressing. The upper portion is reserved for kernel mode processes only, and the lower space is reserved for both user mode and kernel mode processes. The upper portion also reserves certain lower regions of its address space directly mapped to hardware.

The lower portion is also maintained in paging pools. There is a non-paged pool and a paged pool. The paged pool can be swapped out to disk and is usually assigned to applications. The non-paged pool must remain in physical RAM. The size of each page is 4K.

Paging in-depth

Paging is the process of moving data in and out of physical memory. When the physical memory pool becomes full and Windows needs more, the VMM will reallocate data that is not needed in the physical memory out to the disk in a repository known as the *page file*.

Each process is assigned address space in pages that are either identified as *valid* or *invalid pages*. The valid pages are located in the physical memory and are "online" to the application. The invalid pages are "offline" and not available to any application. The invalid pages are stored on disk.

When applications need access to data that has since been moved to offline memory in an invalid page, the system acknowledges this in what is known as a page fault. A page fault process is similar to a thread of execution that takes a different route in terms of routines when it encounters an error or exception. In this case, the fault is handled intentionally, and the VMM "traps" the fault, accesses the data in the page file that relates to it, and restores it to RAM. Other data that is now no longer needed is bumped out and sent offline to disk. This is one of the reasons why fast and reliable hard disks are recommended in data- and memory-intensive applications.

The VMM performs a series of housekeeping chores as part of the paging routines:

✦ The VMM manages the data in the page file on disk on a first in, first out basis. In other words, data that has been on disk the longest is the first to make it back to physical memory when RAM frees up. The VMM will continue to move the data back to RAM as long as RAM keeps freeing up and until there is no data left in the page file. The data that the VMM keeps tabs on in this fashion is known as the *working set*.

✦ The VMM performs what is known as *fetching* when it brings back data from the page file. In addition, the VMM also performs what is known as *page file clustering*. Page file clustering means that when the VMM fetches, it also brings back some of the surrounding data in the page file, on the premise that data immediately before and after the required data might be needed in the next instant as well, which speeds up data I/O from the page file.

✦ The VMM is intelligent enough to work out that if there is no space in RAM to placed fetched data, then it must first move out other recent data to the page file before attempting to place the fetched data back into faster RAM.

The parameters in which the VMM operates and the factors, such as the size of the page file, can be managed and controlled by you. We discuss this further in the performance management and troubleshooting techniques discussed in Chapter 20.

The Zero Administration Windows Initiative

The Zero Administration Windows (ZAW) initiative is a bold move to reduce the TCO and administration of Windows networks or environments. Take one look at the size of the Windows 2000 Resource Kit and decide if your administrative burden has been reduced in any way. Like us, you were probably wondering just whether ZAW was a figment of Microsoft's imagination.

However, ZAW is very much alive and apparent in Windows 2000. Consider the following to avoid having a heart attack. Understand and accept that you have a learning curve to climb, as discussed earlier, in comprehending Windows 2000 in general and Windows 2000 Server in particular. The ZAW technologies, which have been added by the boatload to Windows 2000, do in fact reduce administration. We know what you are thinking: "How many nights must I stay up armed with pizzas and dozens of cans of soda before I figure out how this all works?" Here's the comforting statement from our team that spent about 5,000 hours trying to make head or tail of Windows 2000 Server for this book. ZAW is here and now in Windows 2000, but you have to put it together now and suffer to achieve the long-term benefits.

Once you have put together all the pieces to your own satisfaction and understand how the new technologies come together, you begin to see ZAW emerge. Take it from us, Windows 2000 is the first operating system ever that is truly client/server. It can also be thin-client/server, fat-client/server (some call it rich-client/server), client/thin-server, and client/fat-server. Windows 2000 can also be client-client and server-server in many different variations.

When we say truly client/server, we mean that the client operating system processes, no matter if they are a remote workstation running on Windows 2000 Professional or a server operating system, are very tightly integrated and meshed with the server operating processes and features. This is true regardless of the physical location of the server. This is not only apparent in the ability of a user to log on to any computer running Windows 2000 and find his or her desktop exactly as he or she left it and with access to all resources required and used previously, but also in the transparent availability of these resources. This is made possible by several key technologies we will discuss here, the first of which is Active Directory.

Active Directory

Active Directory is extensively discussed in Chapter 2 and in Part III in this book, so we will not go into too much detail other than to say that all the configuration and preferences relating to the services we discuss in this section are stored in the Active Directory. If there is a learning curve, then Active Directory is where it starts. Unfortunately for larger businesses, there is more to Active Directory than what is apparent to small businesses.

Active Directory is the hub of the network, which is how Miami University executive Michael Gold explained the service to his IT peers. The term *hub* stuck, and we use it in other places in this book with his permission. Active Directory is very much the hub of the network. Without Active Directory, you really do not have a Windows 2000 network. We can find a lot of faults with Active Directory, and it is lacking in tools to prune and graft the trees in the domain forests, but that will come in time.

Microsoft Management Console

The Microsoft Management Console (MMC) was deployed on Windows NT to support BackOffice applications like Exchange, IIS, and SNA Server. In Windows 2000, the MMC is used system-wide for managing just about everything on Windows 2000 Server. A management module, known as a snap-in, exists or is created for each service. Each snap-in offers peculiar features and choices depending on the service targeted for configuration. We cover the MMC in Chapter 6.

Server and Client in Unison: IntelliMirror

Several technologies work to improve the integration between client and server. The IntelliMirror is a group of technologies that allows a user's settings, preferences, applications, and security to follow them to other computers on the network. Intelli Mirror also extends to laptops running Windows 2000 Professional and allows the user to maintain a disconnected state that is automatically restored seamlessly when the user reconnects to the network.

Group Policy, discussed in Chapter 11, is mostly responsible for the mirror and, of course, all configuration is stored in the directory. Clients access the data from the directory as needed. IntelliMirror is really an umbrella term that refers to the following technologies and features:

✦ *Offline folders.* This is further explored in Chapter 22. Offline folder technology allows you to obtain a copy of a file that is usually stored on the server and to work with that file when disconnected from the network. When you disconnect from the server, the file you were working on is managed as if it is still residing on the server. For all intents and purposes, your application thinks it is still connected to the server. You save normally as if saving to the network, but instead you are actually saving to an offline resource that is a mirror of the file and the folder on the server. When you reconnect to the network, the file is synchronized again, and the latest changes to the file are saved to the server's copy.

✦ *Folder redirection* is another IntelliMirror feature that makes a folder redundant. If the server disconnects from you but you are still connected to the network, the next time you save your file, you are redirected to another copy of the folder residing on another server. This is further discussed in Chapter 21.

✦ *Roaming profiles* were inherited from Windows NT profile management philosophy, but they are much more sophisticated under Windows 2000. The idea is that your user profile follows you wherever you go. This is further discussed in Chapter 11.

✦ *Remote Installation Services (RIS)* is a service provided by several components and services that makes it possible to remotely install Windows 2000 Professional to desktops and notebook computers. We describe several of the components that make this service possible in Appendix B, which covers the Resource Kit utilities.

✦ *Application Publishing and Software Installation and Maintenance.* With Active Directory Services, you can remove and install software remotely to user's workstations.

There is, of course, a lot of overlap between the IntelliMirror-cum-Active Directory services and System Management Server (SMS). SMS manages the deployment of software over multiple sites as part of its complex change control and change management services. It is also an extensive scheduling and inventory management system. SMS is a BackOffice product worthy of being between its own book covers, which is why we do not cover SMS in this book.

Group Policy

Managing Windows Networks and Windows 2000 Server just got a lot easier with the new Group Policy technology. Group Policy is used to manage user settings, security, domain administration settings, desktop configurations, and more. In short, most of the workspace is managed through Group Policy.

Group Policy is applied at all levels of the enterprise, in Active Directory, from domains down to organizational units, and so forth. The tool used for the job is the Group Policy Editor (GPE). GPE lets you create objects that are associated or referenced to organizational units (OUs) in Active Directory. Group Policy Objects (GPOs) can be secured with NTFS permissions in the same fashion as files and folders.

 Cross-Reference Group Policy is discussed in detail in Chapter 11.

Availability Services

Availability as it relates to information systems is the effort to keep systems and IS services available to users and processes all the time. We usually talk in terms of 24 × 7 availability, which if it were possible would be 100 percent availability. But 100 percent is only possible in a perfect world, so the target we strive for is 99.9 percent. Few systems are capable of 99.9 percent availability. Trust us, we work in an environment of mainframes, UNIX servers, NT clusters, AS/400s, and many other high-end servers, and no one can claim to have achieved perfect availability.

Availability is very important for companies that have service level agreements with their customers. *Service level* (SL) is an IT/IS term used to reference availability of host systems that customers depend on for service from their suppliers. But SL is no longer only applicable to host systems or supplier-customer relationships. It is important to all entities that depend on systems being available "all the time." Of particular importance are the Internet services because of the increased dependence e-commerce companies will place on Windows 2000 Server. If your server goes offline, it can result in mounting losses that can easily be calculated and related in hard-dollar amounts. Taking a server down on an Internet site is like closing the physical doors to the store, which would send your customers to the competition. Cyberstores cannot afford that.

It thus behooves every server administrator to zero in on this subject with the determination to maintain high availability of servers and services at all times. In fact, all services and components in Windows 2000 should be listed on an availability chart or a risk assessment chart. The following list enumerates several areas that have been built by Microsoft with high availability criteria on the agenda:

✦ Bouncing server syndrome

✦ Clustering and server redundancy

✦ Storage redundancy

✦ Disaster recovery

✦ Security

Bouncing server syndrome

We are not sure who first used the word *bounce* to refer to the act of rebooting a server. But the term has caused many good laughs. In mid-1999, we were joined by a good-natured but overly serious VMS administrator who took over the management of a nationwide network of DEC VMX machines. One day, he came over to network administration and told us that he had just received the strangest call from one of the remote centers. "They say they need me to bounce the Coral Gables VMX, but this is the first time I have heard such a term." And we replied: "Yes, you have to pick it up and drop it on the floor . . . do you need help?"

From that day on, our VMX administrator would often tease us about the number of times you have to "bounce" NT, a lot more than a VMX machine. Another term that is often used in IT circles is IPL, which stands for Initial Program Load (an operating system restart) and which is rooted in legacy host systems and midrange talk. All systems require you to reboot, bounce, or IPL. Availability is rated on how often you have to reboot.

Windows NT has a horrible availability rating. Just about any configuration change you make will demand a reboot. If you have administered NT for any number of years, you'll know that you just have to open the network configurations utilities and look at the settings and be told that you have to reboot. Often, we would just ignore the warning and hit Cancel. However, far too many changes require you to reboot an NT server. At times, we wondered if just breathing on the monitor would require a bounce.

Microsoft has improved the reboot record in the Windows 2000 kernel tremendously, both for new services and situations where applications and services crash. It is especially noticeable in areas where you typically make a lot of changes, such as the network configuration, and so on. Static IP address changes are, for example, immediate, as are reconfiguring network interface cards (NICs) and the like. There are a number of areas that have still to be improved. Installing software (like service packs) is a good example. While a service pack reboot might be forgiven, reboots while installing new user applications on the server devoted to terminal users is not. A reboot after promoting a domain controller is understandable, however. Still, we hope that later versions of Windows 2000 Server will require even fewer reboots.

Clustering and server redundancy

Windows 2000 Advanced Server now has clustering services built in, which is a big improvement over the Cluster Server product that was shipped as an add-on to Windows NT. Clustering is a form of fault tolerance that allows users connected to one server to be automatically connected to another server when the former server fails. This is technically known as a failover in clustering terms. We have not dealt with clustering in this book because our scope of coverage is Windows 2000 Server.

Clustering, however, is not only applicable to redundancy, but also to load balancing, particularly network load balancing, which clusters network resources. With technologies like IntelliMirror and Group Policy, your users need never know which server in a farm of 50 machines is currently servicing their needs. The distributed files system, folder redirection, offline files and folders, and more all play their part in clustering and availability.

Storage redundancy

Storage services in Windows 2000 play a critical part in availability. Windows 2000 supports RAID-1 (disk mirroring) and RAID-5 disk arrays. The distributed file systems and NTFS 5.0 have several key features that support the high availability initiative.

Disaster recovery

Disaster recovery is managed by using Windows 2000 remote and removable storage services to maintain reliable backup sets. The System Recovery Console is also a new feature that allows you to boot to an NTFS-supported command line that will allow you to access NTFS volumes. In addition, Windows 2000 also boots to a menu of "safe mode" choices in the event of serious system instability.

See Chapter 5 for a detailed discussion of troubleshooting a failed installation.

Security

Security services are critical to Windows 2000. In our opinion, you cannot have enough tools to protect the network. We discuss this further in the next section, in depth in Chapter 3, and in places in this book where security configuration is required. You would do well to take stock of the thousands of hacker sites on the Internet and join as many security groups as possible. The age of e-terrorism is upon us, and Windows 2000 servers are among the main targets.

Distributed Security

Microsoft has loaded Windows 2000 with security services unparalleled in any other operating system. Just about every port can be encrypted and protected in some way or form . . . all the way to 128-bit keys, which is now the world-wide encryption level in the wake of the e-business and e-commerce phenomenon. Windows 2000 also supports MIT's Kerberos version 5.0 protocol, now a de facto Internet standard that provides authentication of network logons using symmetric key encryption and digital certificates, and the *Single Sign-On* initiative (SSO).

We devote a whole chapter to a discussion of Windows 2000 security (Chapter 3). In addition, Chapter 9 investigates the deployment of certificate services.

Interoperation and Integration Services

A homogenous network in a large company is a pipe dream in our opinion, and Microsoft probably concurs despite evangelizing to the contrary before the advent of the World Wide Web. All large companies deploy a hodge-podge of interconnected systems running on different platforms. The aim is to reduce the number of different systems as much as possible. At best, we can get down to supporting just NT, Windows 2000 Server, UNIX, AS/400, and possibly some legacy stuff. NetWare, once king of the LAN, still manages a foot in the door (especially with attorneys), and OS/2 for most companies died on December 31, 1999, a legend of the twentieth century.

Microsoft has invested heavily in UNIX integration, which is very strong. Microsoft has recently acquired new technology that, once deployed into Windows 2000, will all but turn Windows 2000 into a UNIX box (okay . . . we are exaggerating just a little). Not only does Windows 2000 Server communicate natively with UNIX using TCP/IP, but it will also run the UNIX shell, giving administrators who work in both systems the best of both Windows and UNIX worlds.

File and Print Services for NetWare (FPNW) and Gateway Services for NetWare (GSNW) have been ported from NT to Windows 2000. We touch on both services in Chapters 6 and 12.

Hardware Support and Plug and Play

Do not try and count the number of drivers that have been made available to Windows 2000; you'll be at it for hours. Remember the bad old days when critics berated the first version of NT for not having support for a lot of the hardware that was being shipped on Windows 95? Now the hardware teams for Windows 2000 and Windows 98 share the device driver testing for all operating systems because they are the same drivers. For example, there are more than 2,000 printer drivers that already ship with Windows 2000 and many other drivers that are not even available to Windows NT.

Did we just say that Windows 2000 and Windows 98 device drivers are the same? Thanks to the long-awaited Windows Driver Model (WDM) initiative, all device drivers created for Windows 98, and its successor, that conform to the WDM can support hardware in both operating systems because they are the same drivers.

Hardware vendors will also be able to bring their products to market a lot faster because if they build device drivers to the WDM, they only have to add the final code to an extensive device driver template that has already been written by Microsoft.

The WDM also caters to media streaming and image architecture, allowing support for a wide variety of scanners, plotters, digital cameras, image-capturing equipment, and more.

Perhaps no other technology will be as welcome as Plug and Play in Windows 2000, which will be better felt by mobile and workstation users than by us server administrators. Of particular interest to server operators, however, is remote boot and power management, which is discussed in Chapter 5.

Storage and File System Services

Windows 2000 Storage and File Systems Services has been vastly improved over NT. Many new features have been added; some of them are mind-blowing to say the least. The following list highlights the key services that will impact your administration routines and how you will view both file and storage services in the future:

✦ Disk Administrator

✦ Removable Storage

✦ Remote Storage

✦ Microsoft Dfs

✦ NTFS 5.0

Disk Administrator

Windows 2000 now supports dynamic disks, which allow you to merge volumes or extend them over multiple disks. Software RAID support is built in to a much-improved disk management utility that is now a MMC snap-in. You have full control over RAID volumes and can manage the volumes for the most part without having to reboot the server. The MMC lets you connect to any remote server and manage its hard disk resources as if they were local. This is hard disk nirvana all the way.

Removable Storage

Removable Storage lets you manage removable storage media, such as tape drives and other removable media, to such an extent as is almost an art form. Tape drives are now no longer managed as part of the backup and restore services. NTBackup (NTBACKUP.EXE) is still there, but in a much-improved form (and labeled as Microsoft Backup) . . . though still not quite as professional and network-oriented as we would have liked. Removable Storage lets you create media pools that are assigned to various backup regimens and removable storage routines.

Remote Storage

Remote Storage is a service that takes files that are no longer accessed or used by the user or local process and moves them to removable storage media. An active file marker is placed in the place of the file with the data. This service thus frees up hard disk space on demand by looking at which files can be relocated. When the user requires the files, they are returned from remote storage. The access may be slow at first depending on the location or the technology used by the remote and removable storage service. This service is also known as Hierarchical Storage Management (HSM), which is discussed in Chapters 17 and 21.

Microsoft Dfs

Microsoft Dfs (named Dfs so as not to be confused with the DFS standard) works a lot like the UNIX NFS in which folders and the directory tree are local to the network and not to any particular server. In other words, you can locate the files and folders you need without having to browse to any particular server or having to map to a network drive from a workstation, as is the case with Windows NT. More about this in Chapter 21.

NTFS 5.0

The Windows NTFS 5.0 file system has been given extensive performance boost enhancements and supports mounted volumes, encryption, a folder hierarchy that extends multiple servers as earlier discussed, and so forth. Perhaps the most notable new service that sits between the storage services and NTFS 5.0 is enforceable disk quotas. Disk quotas are set on a per-volume basis and allow you to warn and deny access to hard disk space when or before the user has reached the quota level set. See Chapter 16 for an in-depth discussion on storage management services and Chapter 21 for a detailed study of NTFS 5.0.

Internet Services

Internet Information Server 5.0 is part and parcel of Windows 2000. There is now extended support for the SMTP and NNTP protocols besides FTP. In other words, when running the Internet Services, the server will also behave as a mail or news host, enabling relay support and more.

The fully integrated support for IIS allows you to host multiple Web sites on one server with only one IP address. Each site can also have its own user-related databases, which thus supports multiple DNS domains. We discuss IIS support in Chapter 21.

Communication Services

What is a network without the ability to communicate? Windows 2000 is loaded to the hilt with new and improved communications services. The Internet communications services have been highly optimized and advanced with e-mail, chat ability, and the wholesale support for the NNTP protocol, which is the pipeline to the newsgroups. For starters, Outlook Express, which is an Internet e-mail client with extensive support for security and attachments, is built into all versions of Windows 2000.

There is also new support for Virtual Private Networking (VPN) services, allowing connection to the enterprise network from remote networks like the Internet. These services fully support both the Point-to-Point Tunneling Protocol (PPTP) and the Layer Two Protocol (L2TP). The VPN services are secured with security services like encryption and IPSec, discussed in Chapters 3 and 21.

Terminal Services

Windows NT allowed a single interactive session from the console, usually some-one sitting directly in front of the monitor attached to the server. If you needed remote access to the server, you would usually have had to use pcANYWHERE or CarbonCopy. This is now completely obsolete with Windows 2000 Server. Terminal Services, inherited from the Terminal Server Edition of Windows NT 4.0 and the legacy of Citrix Winframe, is built in to all versions of Windows 2000 Server.

Terminal Services allows a user to establish a session on the server from a dumb terminal or with terminal emulation software running on just about any device that can connect to the network. The model, known as thin-client/server computing, works just like the mainframe model of a fat server to which many terminals can attach and obtain interactive sessions. The only difference here is that the "frame" sends back the Windows 2000 desktop to the user's terminal, and not some arcane and bland collection of green characters, typical of midrange and mainframe systems.

The Windows 2000 kernel now includes a highly modified Win32 subsystem to support interactive sessions running in the server's allocated process space. Looking at it from dizzying heights, you would essentially take the Win32 subsystem and "clone" it for each user attaching to the server and running a workstation service. Have a look back at Figure 1-1. Now just make numerous copies of the Win32 subsystem, and you have Terminal Services in action.

For the most part, Terminal Services are not managed separately from the rest of the server. There are a few user-specific settings to manage related to sessions and session activity. Terminal Services are extremely important and are expected to garner wide adoption. You just have to look at the Citrix Systems stock to decide if Terminal Services, described in Chapter 25, is important or not.

Summary

This chapter served as an introduction to Windows 2000. First, we looked at the Windows 2000 System architecture. It is the same architecture as Windows NT, and the same foundation, but with some dramatic changes.

There have been some major paradigm shifts demonstrated in Windows 2000. The most significant is the shift back to terminal-mainframe environments. However, the mainframe is Windows 2000, and the terminal gives you the Windows 2000 desktop and not a screen chock full of green characters and a blinking cursor.

We also introduced you to some of the key additions to the operating system. Almost all the topics that we introduced in this chapter are extensively covered in depth in the remaining 24 chapters and 3 appendixes.

We also warned that the learning curve you are about to face will be steep. Experienced NT administrators will have less of a climb than newcomers, but there is so much that is new to NT administrators as well, such as Active Directory, Certificate Services, Dfs, and more.

There is no time to waste in getting down to learning Windows 2000 Server and starting on the role to deployment and roll out.

The next chapter drops you into the deep end with the introduction to Active Directory.

✦   ✦   ✦

Introducing Active Directory

The directory service has become one of the hottest new technologies on corporate networks. Microsoft, a new member of the directory service club, has created a directory service on which almost its entire product line depends. Understanding Active Directory is thus a prerequisite to any management or deployment of Windows 2000.

In the 1970s, all the computing resources you needed, or could use, were on the same computer or the terminal you logged on at. In the 1980s, with the advent of the PC LAN, many files were located on remote machines, and there were definitive paths to these machines. LAN users shared the files and printers, and exchanged e-mail on the LAN. Before the end of the 1990s, we witnessed the beginning of the paradigm shift where all information *and* functionality could be accessed on any server on any network anywhere . . . and the user did not need to know where the objects were physically located.

This is the ideal computing model in which all network objects — servers, devices, functionality, information, authentication, and the transports — combine to become a single contiguous information system and computing environment. This environ-ment allows users, whether human or machine, to attach — or remain attached — to systems from a consistent user interface at any point of entry on the network. No matter what users require — be they functions of a device, communication, process, algorithms, or perhaps just information and knowledge — they must be able to access such an object without regard for its physical location.

The Active Directory is Microsoft's bold leap to realizing the dream of a truly distributed environment and IS architecture. It has been talked about for many years. Headlines in the technical trades were always gloomy. And thus, many network administrators and systems engineers forgot about the directory and worked hard to refine or improve what was already in place, at considerable investment. But now the directory is here. And you probably have little idea what it is and how to use it. You should not feel ashamed, because not only are you not alone, but also it is unlike anything you have ever used before.

Every day people ask us about the Active Directory (and these are not only Windows NT or UNIX and NetWare professionals, but also mid-range and mainframe engineers). The purpose of this chapter is to drill down to its core, to expose the elements, and to lay the foundations to bring what's precious to the surface, and then move forward. First, you must understand everything about the Active Directory (AD) before you can make the transition from the old ways of managing networks and computing environments to the promise that waits.

In this chapter, we discuss the elements of AD. We will kick off with a brief discussion of how and why we will use AD, and from whence it came. Then we break it down into its constituent components (its logical structure), and finally we discuss how the components work and interoperate with each other. You will notice that the subject of Windows domains and trusts is going to be left until a full discussion of the AD has been achieved.

This chapter also features the first appearance of Millennium City, or `mcity.org`, which is the example Windows 2000 network infrastructure we use throughout the book. It's a network that runs the infrastructure of an entire city, and its Active Directory is what we used to test the limits of what Microsoft says it's capable of. MCITY is essentially one huge Active Directory laboratory.

You don't need to be in front of your monitor for this chapter. Just curl up with some snacks and postpone any appointments you might have.

The Omniscient Active Directory: Dawn of a New Era

The Windows NT client-server architecture was a great improvement over other server and network offerings, both from Microsoft and other companies. However, it had a shortcoming that, had it not been resolved in Windows 2000, would have suffocated the advancement of this highly sophisticated operating system. On Windows NT — actually any network — resources are not easily distributed. The interoperation and scalability of numerous NT servers, printers, shares, devices, files, knowledge resources, functionality, and the sustained availability thereof, collapse when the ability for all network components and objects to share information is absent. As discussed briefly in Chapter 1, one of the most significant additions to Microsoft's technology is the Active Directory. There is perhaps no other aspect of Windows 2000 that will have the impact the directory service will, because just about every new feature or ability of this product depends on a directory service.

Before we haul out the dissecting tools, know this:

✦ The Active Directory service is critical to the deployment and management of Windows 2000 networks, the integration and interoperation of Windows 2000 networks and legacy NT networks, and the interoperation and unification of Windows 2000 networks with the Internet. Its arrival is a result of the evolutionary process of Microsoft's server and network technology. One way or another, the directory service is in your future.

✦ The Active Directory is a powerful directory service, either as part of a Windows network or as a standalone service on the Internet. In the latter role, it is an apt contender as a directory service in the same fashion Internet Information Server is an apt contender for a Web server. In other words, no querying client on the Internet needs to know the directory is Windows 2000 AD. Active Directory is 100 percent LDAP-compliant and 100 percent IP-compliant.

Why Do We Need Directories?

A directory provides information. At its most basic level, it is like a giant white pages, allowing a user to query a name and get back a phone number . . . and then possibly being connected to the person by automatically dialing that number. But a directory in the IT world is a lot more than a telephone book. Before getting into the specifics of AD, let's look at some reasons why we need directories. We kick off by placing AD at the center of all services provided by Windows 2000.

Single Sign-On and distributed security

Active Directory makes it easier to log in to and roam cyberspace. Imagine if you had to log in at every mall, highway, turnpike, newsstand, public facility, sports amenity, shop, fast food outlet, movie house, and so on, in the brick and mortar world we live in. Why then should we have to do this in cyberspace?

In every company today, it is almost impossible to get anywhere on the network without going through at least three logins. Everyday, we log into NetWare, the Windows NT domains, voice mail, the host system (to the AS/400 via Rumba), FTP, and then finally the Internet; we won't go into how many accounts and logins we have.

Not only do we have to log in dozens of times a day, and remember dozens of passwords and user or login IDs, but we also have to know exactly where information and resources are located on the network. The uniform resource locator on the World Wide Web has alleviated the resource location problem to some extent (it obviates having to know exactly where something lives on the Internet), but it is still not ideal and not very smooth. URLs are perishable, and for the most part unmanageable in large numbers, which means they often do not get updated. They are not managed in any sensible, cohesive system.

The ideal is some sort of badge that allows us to log in once and then flash it wherever we go. For starters, every application and service on our LANs, from e-mail to voice mail to data access to printer access, should be made available to us through one universal login, at home or at work. The type or level of access we have will depend on the attributes or "clearance level" of our badges. The access token provided by Windows NT security comes close to this, but it is not accepted by other technologies as a valid means of authentication. Figure 2-1 illustrates several systems that should be accessed and managed from a central login authority. In many cases, this is already possible with Active Directory-compliant applications such as SQL Server 2000 and Exchange 2000.

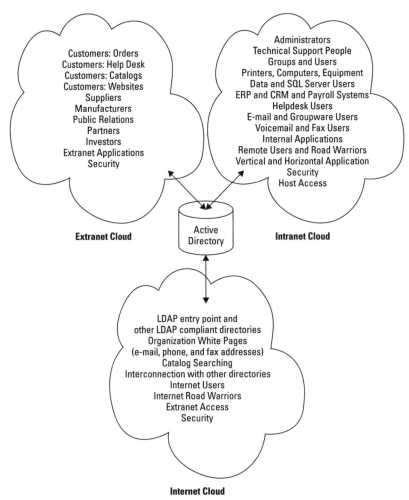

Figure 2-1: Active Directory as a central login authority

As you will learn in Chapter 3 and in the chapters in Part III, the single login dream is achieved using the services of AD and Windows 2000 support for MIT's Kerberos authentication. This service is known as *Single Sign-On* (SSO). SSO has become a quasi-standard among supporters of the Kerberos protocol, such as Microsoft, Apple, Sun, and Novell.

Once a trusted user is authenticated via the Kerberos protocol, all other services that support the Kerberos protocol can accept and allow access to the principal. This is made possible by the Kerberos use of tickets — the badge idea previously discussed — which are issued by the directory service.

In Chapter 1, we also told you that the Microsoft network domain architecture in Windows 2000 has been radically overhauled to seamlessly integrate with the AD and to extend out to the Internet. Imagine being able to log in to your domain from anywhere. We will be discussing this in much more depth in a later chapter.

Change management

Active Directory makes it easier to manage the roamers and users of cyberspace and corporate networks and the computers they use to attach to the network. We administrators want to be able to manage our users and computing resources in one central omnipresent repository. We don't want to repeatedly manage users in the voice mail directory, on the NetWare servers' directory, in the Host systems database, in our e-mail directory, on our Windows domains, and so on.

And we, as managers, need to be able to manage this information easier with change. Mergers, acquisitions, new products, and services need to be continually managed on a cohesive and consistent basis. Group Policy, the change control and change management service of Windows 2000, stores all user and computer information in AD (as discussed in the section on ZAW in Chapter 1).

Distributed administration

Active Directory lets you delegate administrative function and responsibility and lets you parcel out chunks of the network or domain for controlled administration. A distributed directory service makes it possible to delegate the administration of network resources and users throughout the enterprise. On legacy NT, you can create users and groups with administrative rights, but it is well nigh impossible to hide other network resources from these administrators.

Because Active Directory can be partitioned as a mirror of the structure or organization of the enterprise, it is also possible to partition the administration of the compartments. In other words, it makes more sense to appoint a member of a department to perform repetitive management of that department's resources.

You will see later how administration of the directory can be delegated to individuals who are only given selective access or right of passage to delegated areas of the directory.

Application management

Active Directory makes it easier to develop and distribute applications. Application developers need consistent, open, and interoperable interfaces and APIs against which they can code functionality that stores and manages information relating to applications, processes, and services in a distributed information store. We want to be able to create applications and store application and persistent data to an "invisible" repository through an open interface. This information should be available from anywhere and everywhere on the network.

Developers want to be able to create methods that install an application into a directory on the network for initial configuration and manipulation over the lifetime or use of the application. We do not want to concern ourselves with the inner workings of the directory. We want to create our information or configuration object, initialize, use it, and be done . . . no matter where the user installs or invokes our product. And wherever the object we created is moved to, it should always be accessible to the application.

With all of the above, the cost of access and management has in the past been high. We are looking for solutions that will, albeit in the long to medium term, reduce the cost of both management and operation of cyberspace and the information technology systems running our companies and our lives.

What Is Active Directory?

There are registries and databases that provide directory-type facility for applications and users. But not one is interconnected, share-centric, or distributed in any way. AD is a universal distributed information storehouse into which all network objects, such as application configurations, services, computers, users, and processes, can be accessed, in a consistent manner, over the full expanse of a network or internetwork. This is made possible by the logical structure of the directory. And before you start scratching your head, you should understand that without Active Directory you cannot log in to a *Windows 2000* domain, period. Chapters 7 and 8 discuss this and illustrate the control you have over AD's logical and physical structure.

We compare AD to a database later on in this chapter and in Chapter 7 in much more detail. Meanwhile, if you're keen to adopt this child, then you need to know something about its parents.

The Grandfather of the Modern Directory: The X.500 Specification

The directory service as we are coming to know it began with an interconnection model proposed by the International Standards Organization (ISO) little more than 20 years ago. This model is popularly known as OSI, which stands for *open-systems interconnection.* In the late eighties, OSI was given a huge boost by big business and government and quickly became the foundation for the information revolution we are experiencing today.

The OSI model and its seven layers lie at the very genesis of modern information technology. Without a fundamental understanding of OSI, it is difficult to be an effective systems engineer, software developer, network administrator, CIO, or Webmaster. OSI is to IT what anatomy is to medicine. While we assume that you are familiar with the OSI model, this brief discussion of X.500 serves to provide a common departure point for all systems engineers not familiar with a directory service.

The X.500 directory service can be found at the OSI application layer, where it sits as a group of protocols approved and governed by the International Telecommunications Union (ITU), formerly the CCITT. The objective of X.500 was to provide standards and interfaces to an open and interoperable global and distributed directory service.

X.500 is made up of many components (databases) all interoperating as a single contiguous entity. Its backbone is the Directory Information Base (DIB). The entries in the DIB provide information about objects stored in the directory. Figure 2-2 represents the information contained in the DIB.

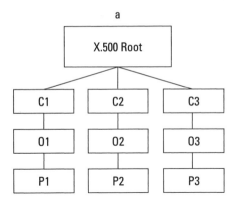

Entry Identifier	Classes	Attribute Values
P1	Country Organization Person	US MCITY Jeffrey Shapiro

Figure 2-2: The X.500 hierarchy (a), and the DIB and the information it contains (b)

In order to access the information stored in the DIB, both users and computers needed a structure or model that would make it easier to understand where data could be located. The model proposed was an object-oriented, hierarchical structure that resembles an upside-down tree, as illustrated in Figure 2-3. The root of the tree is at the top, and the branches and leaves hang down, free to proliferate. This model assured that any object in the tree is always unique as long as it is inherently part of the tree and can trace its "roots" to the single node at the top. Active Directory trees (and DNS) work the same way, as discussed later. The tree is read from the bottom to the top.

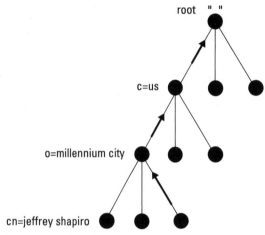

Figure 2-3: The X.500 tree structure

The objects in the X.500 tree represented containers for information representing people, places, and things. These objects would also be organized or grouped into classes (for example, groups of countries, companies, localities, and so on).

The X.500 standard included the following container objects:

- ✦ Countries
- ✦ Location
- ✦ OU or organizational unit

Unfortunately, X.500 suffered from several limitations in its early days. It became bogged down under its own weight (the specification was exhaustive), and in many respects it was ahead of its time (especially with respect to its ties to OSI). It made its appearance in the late 1980s at a time when most innovators could care less about managing information openly and globally, when we were all huddled in our garages inventing or writing code like crazy, and when we were all competing for market share at every turn.

X.500 was also born before the advent of the World Wide Web and the mass utilization of the Internet by both the public and businesses. And what really dragged it down was its ties to the OSI protocols (the datalink protocols — DLC — such as 802.2 and 802.3), which turned out to be its Achilles' heel, because the way of the Internet world was IP. Meanwhile, the Internet took off on the coattails of TCP/IP, leaving X.500 struggling in a protocol desert landscape.

Like so many innovations before it, X.500 provided nourishment for other inventions that followed. And much of the foundation for the modern directory service, especially Active Directory, can be directly attributed to the vision of X.500, as we will soon see.

The Father of the Modern Directory: LDAP

The X.500 specifications defined a protocol by which services would be able to access the information stored in X.500 databases. This protocol was known as the *Directory Access Protocol,* or DAP. It consisted of a comprehensive set of functions that would provide the ability for clients to add and modify or delete information in the X.500 directory.

DAP, however, was overkill and consisted of far more functionality than was required for the implementation of a directory service. Therefore, a simplified version of DAP was created, called the *lightweight directory access protocol* (LDAP). After several refinements, LDAP has begun to stand in its own right as a directory service. After adoption by the Internet Engineering Task Force (IETF), several important features of LDAP have garnered its widespread support:

✦ LDAP sits atop the TCP/IP stack rather than the OSI stack. This means that every client with an IP address, able to send and receive packets over IP, can access and exploit LDAP-compliant directory services. The client needs only to know how to "talk" to LDAP (IP). TCP, the transport, takes care of the rest.

✦ LDAP performs hyper-searching, which is the ability of a directory to refer to another for authoritative information. In other words, one LDAP directory can defer to another to chase information. An example of this is how Web-based search engines look to other search engines, via hyper-linking, for collateral information or information that does not exist in their own databases. Directory services on a worldwide Internet thus can become contiguous and distributed to form a transparent massive service, limited only by available servers and network resources.

 Note The replication mechanisms Microsoft is building into its products are so advanced that products such as SQL Server 2000 will become fully distributed before 2003.

✦ Early on its childhood, LDAP implemented a rich C-based API, making C the de facto programming language of the directory service. Using the most popular language of the day with which to call directory functionality ensured LDAP widespread support in the bustling developer community.

LDAP consists of the following components, which in some shape or form are the foundations of all modern directories, including the AD:

✦ **The data model:** This model represents how data is accessed in the directory. The data model is inherited directly from the data model of the X.500 specification. Objects are infused with information by way of assigning attributes to them. Each attribute is type-casted and contains one or more distinct values. The objects are classified into groups of classes, such as organizational units (OUs) or Companies.

✦ **The organization model:** This is the inverted tree paradigm we earlier discussed, which is also inherited directly from the X.500 specification. It is the structure adopted by all modern directory services. Of particular note is how the Domain Name System (DNS) of the Internet is arranged around inverted trees. The DNS consists of several trees, the root or topmost levels, that sprout downward and contain millions of leaves (or nodes). Figure 2-4 illustrates the DNS forest and the seven roots. It also illustrates the .com tree and how it has fired the Internet into the commercial juggernaut it is today.

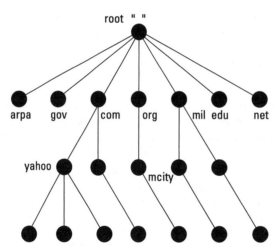

Figure 2-4: The organizational model revolves around the inverted tree, a hierarchical collection of objects.

✦ **The security model:** This model specifies how information is securely and safely accessed. LDAP adopted Kerberos password authentication and has since added additional authentication layers with the inclusion of the Simple Authentication Security Layer (SASL). This SASL provides a tiered architecture for a multitude of service providers. Version 3.0 of LDAP also supports the SSL or secure socket layer of TCP/IP, which was developed independently by the Internet community. Windows 2000 supports SSL in its browser, Internet Explorer.

✦ **The functional model:** This model specifies the methods for querying and modifying the directory objects. It includes operations to add entries and to edit, populate the attribute fields, delete, and query objects in the directory.

✦ **The topological model:** This model specifies how the directory services integrates or interoperates with other compliant directories. The ability of LDAP directories to refer or defer to other directories is inherent in this model.

LDAP's popularity flourished with the sudden popularity of the Internet. Today, many popular applications and server technologies support the protocol. It can be accessed from most e-mail applications, Web-based applications, and even embedded systems such as routers and gateway devices.

After X.500

A number of large technology companies are hard at work on directory services. The two of note who appear to have been at it longer than Microsoft are Banyan Systems and Novell. Others include Netscape and IBM (Lotus Notes).

Banyan perhaps has been at it the longest with its StreetTalk product that has been part of the Vines OS for more than a decade. Novell entered the market mid-way through the 1990s with a directory service aimed at its installed NetWare base, called the Novell Directory Service (NDS), and it has been working on versions of NDS that will be independent of the NetWare OS, including a version for Windows NT.

Note Despite its immaturity, AD has been built on proven technology. One area on which it heavily depends is replication, and the technology for this comes from Microsoft Exchange. The Exchange site integration and replication technology has been proven on millions of installations around the world.

From the ground up, Active Directory has been built on open, international standards. It is important to note that AD is not an X.500 directory, but it has borrowed heavily from the X.500 specifications. In particular, it uses LDAP as the access protocol, which opens it to everyone and everything. In short, Microsoft has taken everything that was great about X.500 and LDAP and combined it with proven technologies it has develop-ed for other purposes over the years (such as Microsoft's Component Object Model [COM]). AD can exchange information with any application or service that uses LDAP.

AD also relies on DNS as its locator service, allowing clients to transparently locate domain controllers (AD hosts) by merely connecting to a DNS server and looking up the IP addresses for the closest domain controller. (We will discuss this further in Chapters 7 and 8.)

The Open Active Directory

AD also provides a rich set of APIs to encourage the development of tools and applications. The AD will thus serve as a repository for application-specific information, particularly software that is group-driven. For example: We have developed a customer relationship management (CRM) system for several medical and dental clients. Our users typically log in to the application and become apparent as a community of active users to the rest of the practice or hospital, once authenticated in the AD.

The application is able to obtain enterprise-wide information about the state of the application at any given time, and we are able to group users according to service and access levels, governed by objects in the AD. In particular, the application publishes information about who is logged in and using the system, the files (data) they have checked out of the database management system (such as SQL Server or Oracle), and what they are currently doing.

We do not need to provide users with a second login just to use the application. Instead, when they run the CRM, it checks to see if the AD has authenticated them, the machine they are accessing the system from, and what they are allowed to access. Based on this information, we populate the GUI that drives the CRM with information the user is allowed to see or use.

What About the Registry?

Now that you can see why we need directory services, and where they came from, where does the registry fit in? In the early days of Windows 95 and Windows NT, Microsoft improved the information repositories of applications running on the Windows platform with the creation of the registry. It was a great relief from the mess created by initialization and configuration files, insecure text files that anyone could access.

The registry, however, was more a technology or system created to stabilize the platform or the OS and is a repository for managing information and the configuration of applications and computers. When users deleted their Windows 3.11 and earlier version .ini files in error, the application was, for better or worse, destroyed (if the .ini files were not backed up). The registry set out to change all that. Today, some of the largest software houses in the world still do not use it; I can't imagine why.

What's more, the registry also became the home for the so-called Security Account Manager (SAM). This database stores and manages all the security and access control authority of network resources.

There are some similarities between the registry and the AD. Specifically, the registry is:

✦ Also a database, somewhat cryptic and complex, but still a database.

✦ Open and accessible (except for the SAM part).

✦ Able to be programmed against.

✦ A replicating structure (single master), providing some vestige of a distributed system.

✦ A system of hierarchical structures, which contains records that hold configuration data.

For the most part, the similarities end here. Comparing the registry to Active Directory is like comparing a JetSki to the USS Kitty Hawk. AD is a completely different animal. Yes, you can still use the registry to store configuration data, and you would still use the registry on a standalone workstation or server, even a domain controller. Specifically, the difference is that AD is:

✦ A distributed multi-master database (peer directories update each other in real time, latency aside).

✦ Built on open, Internet-based standards.

✦ Object-oriented.

✦ Interoperable (almost coexistent) with the Domain Name System of the Internet.

✦ Able to service any network client using TCP/IP.

✦ Able to grow to gargantuan proportions.

Unfortunately, many applications today still store configuration information in unguarded flat text files, ignoring the registry for the most part. Ignoring both the registry and the AD will likely render your application incompatible with Windows 2000, from both a functional perspective and as a Microsoft logo requirement.

Note   AD does not set out to replace the registry. The registry still plays an important role in Windows 2000, as you will discover in Chapter 18 and in various other places in this book. In fact, even AD uses the registry to store some configuration-related information. Microsoft began working on a directory or distributed information storage facility some time ago, possibly even at the same time it was developing the registry.

From the outset, Microsoft believed it could only succeed with AD by ensuring it was based on open standards and interoperable with the Internet, period. In other words, any IP-based (LDAP) client will be able to access the AD, and like the Internet Information Server (IIS), FTP, and other services, this access is transparent (in terms of what OS it is sitting on).

✦ Active Directory supports and coexists with both DNS and LDAP. Both are modeled on the X.500 standard, especially with respect to its structural and organizational model.

✦ Active Directory supports open and interoperable standards, especially with regard to the widespread naming conventions in use today.

✦ Active Directory is seamlessly integrated into the Internet by virtue of Microsoft's total adoption and commitment to TCP/IP. All other protocols that Microsoft supports are essentially provided for backward compatibility with earlier versions of NT, other network operating systems, legacy transports such as SNA and the DLC protocols, and NetBEUI clients.

✦ Active Directory provides a rich set of C/C++, Java, VB, and scripting language interfaces, allowing it to be fully programmed against.

We have investigated which languages or programming environments should be used to program the Active Directory. For the speed required by complex code and advanced development, such as creating service providers, C++ is best. For RAD and the majority of component-based development, Visual Basic, using the Active Directory Services Interface (ADSI), is best. Java is useful when you need to make calls to the LDAP API, but we have found Microsoft's support for Java-based access to Active Directory lukewarm to say the least.

✦ Active Directory is built into the Windows NT operating system (still at the core of Windows 2000), making it backward compatible with earlier versions of Windows NT.

✦ Active Directory is a fully distributed architecture allowing administrators to write once and update everywhere from a single point of access, across any network.

✦ Active Directory is highly scalable and self-replicating. It can be implemented on one machine, or the smallest network, and can scale to support the largest companies in the world. Resources and adoption permitting, once the kinks (and it has a few) are worked out, it will likely become a pervasive technology within a short time.

✦ Active Directory's structural model is extensible, allowing its schema to evolve almost without limits. In this regard, Active Directory has to comply with the X.500 specification that extending the schema requires you to register the new class with a X.500 governing body. This compliance is achieved by registering an Object Identifier (OID) with the authorities. In the United States, the authority is the American National Standards Institute (ANSI).

AD has fully adopted the most popular namespace models in use today. It embraces the concept of an extendable namespace and marries this concept with the operating systems, networks, and applications. Companies deploying AD are able to manage multiple *namespaces* that exist in their heterogeneous software and hardware.

The Elements of Active Directory

Active Directory is a highly complex product that will no doubt become more complex and more advanced in future versions. At the core of the product, we find a number of elements that are native to directory services in general and AD in particular.

Namespaces and Naming Schemes

AD has adopted several naming schemes, which allows applications and users to access the AD using the formats they have most heavily invested in. These name formats are as follows:

RFC822 names

RFC822 is the naming convention most of us are familiar with, by virtue of our using e-mail and surfing the World Wide Web. These names are also known as user principal names (UPN) in the form of `somename@somedomain`, for example, `thepresident@thewhitehouse.gov`. AD provides the RFC822 namespace for all users. If you need to find a person's extension number at a company (if they publish it), you need only query the directory and look up `someone@somedomain.com` (your software will translate that into the correct LDAP query, as shown later). The UPN is also the login name or user ID to a Windows 2000 domain. Windows users can now log in to a Windows 2000 network by simply entering their user ID and password, like this:

```
User: jeffrey.shapiro@mcity.org
Password: *************
```

Tip   It is possible to assign any UPN to a domain for login. In other words, you might create a domain called MCITY but prefer users to log in as `someone@acmesales.com` so that they do not need to remember more than their e-mail addresses.

LDAP and X.500 names

The LDAP and X.500 naming conventions are known scientifically as *attributed naming,* which consists of the server name holding the directory (which we refer to as the *directory host*), user name, organizational unit, and so on. For example:

```
LDAP://anldapserver.bigbrother.com/cn=jsmithers,ou=trucksales,
dc=bigbrother,dc=com
```

LDAP names are used to query the Active Directory.

Active Directory and the Internet

It is possible to locate AD servers anywhere on the Internet or a private intranet. These AD servers can be full-blown Windows 2000 domain controllers, or they can serve the single purpose of being LDAP directory servers. The information and access that users and clients enjoy from these servers is transparent.

The client needs only resolve the closest AD server to it to get information. The closest server might be on the same site as the client, in which case the DNS server will resolve to an AD server on the same subnet as the client. Or it may be located on a site far away. This means that AD can and will be used as an Internet directory server without ever being accessed for domain authentication. Multiple AD servers will link together to provide a global directory service that spans the continent.

Active Directory Everywhere

Microsoft also set out to ensure that the AD was highly scalable and would become pervasive as quickly as resources permitted. AD, as you will discover in Chapter 8, is easy to install and set up on a simple server. It is also easy to set up and install AD as a single-user repository, and it carries virtually no noticeable overhead on the simplest configuration (we will discuss AD configuration in Part III). In other words, when AD needs to be small, it can be small, and when it needs to be big, it can grow at an astonishing rate.

This makes it ideal to use the AD for even the simplest of application information storage requirements. Although it is no substitute for database management systems that provide advanced information management services such as information analysis and data mining (or the management of corporate data), it may not be uncommon to find a single-user application deploying AD in the hope that later scaling up will be as easy as merely further populating the directory. AD even installs on a standalone 133MHz desktop machine with 64MB of RAM, and is easily deployable as a domain controller supporting a small company (this configuration is not what Microsoft officially recommends, and such a configuration should support little else but a directory with a small helping of user and computer accounts).

On the other hand, it is possible to deploy AD in such a way that it scales to astonishing levels. As a domain repository, Windows NT 4.0 maxes out at about 100,000 users, but AD can scale to the millions — it can grow as large as the Internet. All the replicas of the AD are synchronized (which itself is quite an administration feat, as we will soon see). All copies of an organization's AD system propagate changes to one another, similar to how DNS servers propagate domain records.

 Note   In practice, an NT domain becomes shaky at between 30,000 and 40,000 accounts, which is why many large companies create multiple resource and account domains.

The key to the scalability of AD is the domain tree . . . a data hierarchy that can expand, theoretically, indefinitely. The AD provides a simple and intuitive bottom-up method for building a large tree. In AD, a single domain is a complete partition of the directory. Domains are then subdivided or partitioned into organizational units, allowing administrators to model the domain after their physical organization structure or relevant business models. A single domain can start very small and grow to contain tens of millions of objects; thus, objects can be defined at the smallest corporate atomic structure without the fear of overpopulation, as was the case with Windows NT 4.0, and NetWare 3.*x* and 4.*x*.

Inside Active Directory

The core of the Active Directory is largely accessible only to geeks who see heaven in a line of C++ code (authors included). It does not ship with special viewer tools, like MS Access, that give you a feel for what exists in its structures or what these structures look like (a few Resource Kit tools provide some access). The following, however, describes the key components with the objective of providing an insight into the innards of this directory service.

If It Walks Like a Duck

One area seriously lacking in administrator education is database knowledge. Database 101 should be in every engineering course. All too often, we see administrators "reinitializing" databases to free up space, only to discover that they wiped out valuable corporate data in the process. Later on in this chapter, we will study the anatomy of the directory from a very high level. To fully understand how the AD engine works, the following is a mini-course on Active Directory, the database:

On the physical level, AD is two things: It is a database and a database management system (DBMS) . . . pure and simple. The data it keeps can be viewed hierarchically. A *database* is a repository for data. It is a software structure in which data is stored, manipulated, and retrieved by any process seeking to gain access to and exploit the information it contains. If you are not sure this is a valid definition of the AD, then let's apply the definition of a database (the rules) to the AD.

A database is a database if:

> ✦ It contains functional layers — which include a schema — that define the structure of the database: how data is stored, retrieved, reviewed, and manipulated. Other functional layers include an "engine" that comprises I/O functions, maintenance routines, query routines, and an interface to a storehouse for the data. This is often known as a storage engine.

> ✦ The data, properties, and attributes of a thing are stored in containers, which comprise collections of records, known as tables (such as in relational database) or some other cubby (such as in an object database).

The simplest definition of a DBMS is that it is a software application, on top of which sits a user interface, used to manage the data in a database and the database itself. A DBMS can be used to extract data (query), format it, present it to users, and to print or transfer it into a comprehensible form. Modern DBMS systems, like SQL Server, provide users with the technology to interpret or analyze data, as opposed to simple quantification.

Users of databases and DBMS include both humans and machines. Software used by machines and computers saves and accesses data because it is a means by which a process can gain access to persistent information. Persistent data can and should be shared by multiple users, both human and man-made. For example, an engineer puts data into a database so that a robot can perform repetitive work based on the data.

Active Directory is all the above and more, but you would not use it to, say, extract records of a group of individuals who pose a credit risk to your company because such support is beyond the purpose of a directory service. Whether AD is a relational database or an object database brings us to debateable levels in our discussion, so we won't go there. Our analysis of AD will help you to make that assumption on your own.

A relational database is made up of tables; it is made up of columns (collections) that represent things, such as a column or collection of first names. Information about each individual entry is stored chronologically (for example, the fifth *first name or fn* in the collection is David). Figure 2-5 represents a column of first names.

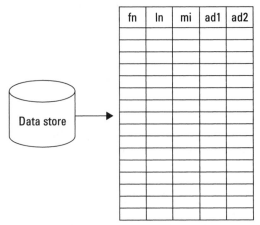

Figure 2-5: The column in a relational database contains records, which are members of collections or groups.

You can have multiple tables in a relational database. You can also have "things" in one table that relate to things in another table, not only by chance, but also by design and purpose. In relational tables, you access the properties of a thing, and the information that it represents, by referencing its place in the collection, as shown in Figure 2-6.

An object database is a little harder to define, mostly because many forms of object databases evolved from relational databases. An object model-compliant database might be more about how the information it contains is exposed to the users and how the underlying schema can be accessed than about the underlying makeup and technology or how it was created.

But an object database might also be best described as a database that conforms to the object model as opposed to the relational model. We do not know enough about how the AD works because at the very core, it is a proprietary technology. What we do know is that data is stored in the AD in a structure that resembles tables with columns and rows. In fact, Microsoft has used the very same database engine (Jet) it deployed in Exchange Server in the AD. It is thus a blood relative of Microsoft Access.

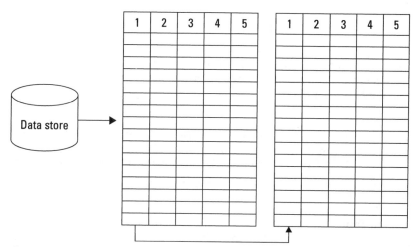

Figure 2-6: Two columns in a relational database contain records that are related to each other.

The Active Directory Database Structure

AD has been implemented as a layered system comprising the Core Directory Service Agent (DSA), the Database Layer (DB), and the Extensible Storage Engine (ESE). Above these layers lie the interfaces that comprise the replication service, the Security Account Manager or SAM (as with the NT 4.0 SAM), the LDAP interface, and the API (ADSI). The LDAP interface, as you will see later, provides the interface or access to LDAP clients. LDAP is supported in all 32-bit desktop and workstation environments. LDAP is also built into Outlook. SAM provides the security interfaces to the AD, and hooks in the access control technology. See Figure 2-7.

Note The time has come to dispense with the acronym SAM. The problem is that SAM stands for Security Account Manager, Security Accounts Manager, and Security Access Manager, and Surface to Air Missile fits as well. If Microsoft would simplify this to SM for Security Manager, the industry and Microsoft's people might then agree on what the acronym stands for.

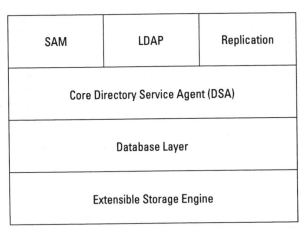

Figure 2-7: AD consists of three functional layers, on top of which lie the access and replication layers and the Security Account Manager (SAM).

The ESE comprises two tables: a data table and a link table. The ESE database is used to maintain data on the structure of the directory and is not apparent to clients. The AD database, NTDS.DIT, on the other hand, contains the following collection of database tables that users will relate to, either transparently, via some cognitive processing, or directly.

✦ **Schema Table:** The *schema* dictates the type of objects that can be created in the AD, how the objects relate to each other, and the optional and compulsory attributes applied to each object. It is important to note that the schema is extensible, and it can thus be expanded to contain custom objects that are created by third-party applications and services.

✦ **Link Table:** The link table contains the link information and how the objects relate to each other in the database.

✦ **Data Table:** The data table is the most important structure in the AD database system because it stores all the information or attributes about the objects created. It contains all the compulsory and optional information that make up the objects such as user names, login names, passwords, groups, and application-specific data.

Active Directory Objects

If Active Directory is a casserole, then the objects are its ingredients. Without objects, the directory is a meaningless, lifeless shell. When you first install AD, the system installs a host of user objects you can begin accessing immediately. Some of these objects represent user accounts, such as Administrator, without which you would not be able to log in and obtain authentication from the directory.

Objects contain attributes or properties — they hold information about resources they represent. For example: The user object of a Windows Network contains information (the attributes) of the user pertaining to his or her First Name, Last Name, and Logon ID. Figure 2-8 is an object-oriented representation of a user object in the Active Directory. (The actual data structure is a table of columns or fields.)

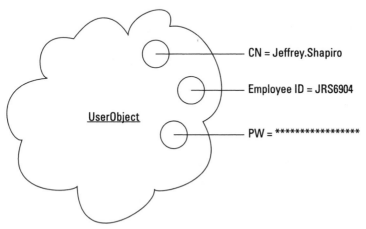

Figure 2-8: An Active Directory user object and three attributes or properties

There can be many different objects in Active Directory. Some hold exploitable information, and some are merely containers for other objects. You might conclude that the entire Active Directory is one big object, inside of which are container objects, which contain other objects, and which in turn contain other objects, as illustrated in Figure 2-9. Here, we depict a *container object,* technically represented by a triangle, a popular storage symbol, which holds other container objects. This nesting can continue until the last object is a *leaf object,* which cannot be a container.

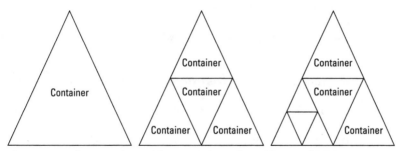

Figure 2-9: The container object contains other objects, which in turn may contain objects.

Objects that are not container objects, such as a user object, are known as leaf objects, or end node objects, as illustrated in Figure 2-10. When a leaf object is added to the container, the nesting ends there.

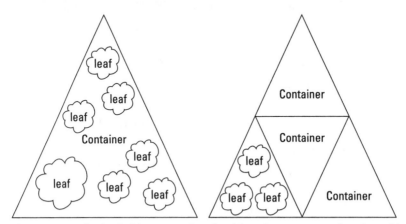

Figure 2-10: The leaf object or end node object does not contain other objects.

The AD is like one big babushka doll. Figure 2-11 provides a popular two-dimensional view of the container philosophy. However, the metaphor we are more familiar with in IT and Windows network administration is the object tree, which we will discuss shortly.

We also talk in terms of *object classes* when working with AD. The object class is less a class in the object-oriented technology sense and is more a collective noun for the type and purpose of objects organized as groups. Object classes can be user accounts, computers, networks, and more; actually any of the objects that AD currently supports.

Another way to look at the object class, or simply class, is that it is a definition of an object that can be created and managed by the directory. *Content rules* govern how an object can be attributed. Classes are also endowed with certain rules that dictate which classes of objects can be parents, which can be children, and which can be both.

We mentioned earlier that the AD schema is extensible. This means that programmers can code against the API and create and manage their own objects (refer to the discussion on ADSI earlier). This allows application developers to use the AD and save configuration and state information about applications. Of course, the registry is still a valid place to store information, especially for hardware settings, but the AD offers features such as replication, propagation, and a wider "gene pool" of objects, such as users, with which to interact and coexist.

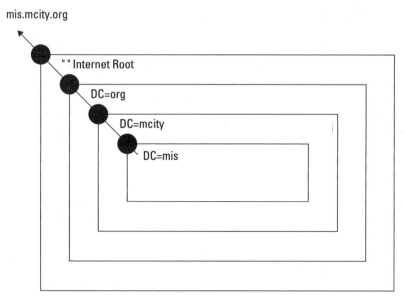

mis.mcity.org

" " Internet Root

DC=org

DC=mcity

DC=mis

Figure 2-11: If we join all the dots representing the ID of each box, a systematic, hierarchical collection of boxes begins to emerge.

Active Directory Schema

The *schema* is the Magna Carta of the AD. When you create an object in AD, you have to also comply with the rules of the schema. In other words, you have to supply all the compulsory attributes required by the objects, or the object cannot be created. The schema governs data types, syntax rules, naming conventions, and more.

As we just mentioned, the schema, which is stored in the schema table, can be extended dynamically. That is, a program can extend it with new custom classes and then provide the rules by which the schema can manage the classes. Once this has been accomplished, the application can begin using the schema immediately.

Extending or changing the schema requires conforming to programmatic and administration rules. That the schema is itself part of the directory means that it is an enterprise-wide service in the AD. And as such, a master schema has to be properly accessed before any peer schema receives propagated schema changes. We will not delve too far into this because it is a subject that belongs in a book devoted to programming the AD.

Object Attributes

Objects contain *attributes*. Some are essential to the object's existence, such as a password for a user object. Some are not essential, such as a middle initial.

Walking the Active Directory

The route to an object in AD is achieved by traversing a hierarchical path that resolves the object's name. This path includes all the container objects through which you can drill down to the end node. What might be a little difficult to grasp is that on the one hand, we talk about containership, while on the other, we talk about how you have to walk a long and winding road to discover the name of the leaf or end node object. The best way to try and understand this is by examining the diagram in Figure 2-11, which shows a system of boxes that contain smaller boxes, and so on. If we join all the left top corners of the boxes, we see the emergence of the hierarchical path about which we speak.

In AD, this full path name (the names of all the dots joined together) is known as the *distinguished name,* or DN, of the object. The name of the final object itself, apart from the path, is known as the *relative distinguished name,* in this case "mis."

We say the full path to the object and the object name itself is *distinguished* because it is unique in the AD. No other object contains the identical object DN. In other words, the object itself is unique. The purpose of this naming and tracing mechanism is to allow an LDAP client to rapidly track down an object and retrieve its information as quickly as possible.

The relative distinguished name (RDN) of the object is the object name itself. The RDN is an attribute of the object. The RDN is not necessarily unique, although it is unique in its container in AD, because such a name can exist at the end of another DN somewhere else in the AD, down some other path. Figure 2-12 illustrates how two objects can have the same RDN but somewhere up the chain the similarity will end, if finally at the root or the parent.

When we make a query to the AD, we naturally start at the root of the DN of an object and follow the path to the node. But in LDAP, we start at the RDN and trace the name parts to the root. In this fashion, the entire DN is constructed during such a query, such as:

```
cn=box1,root=,container5=,container6=,container7=,container8=..
```

It might help to clear things up for you at this point if you construct a DN on a scrap piece of paper. For the exercise, let's say that you need to construct a query to the user named jchang. To get to jchang, you need to start with the cn, which is jchang, then go up to office=232, floor=3, building=maotsetung, city=peking. LDAP works from the bottom up. Try not to think about an entry point into the AD, but to merely start at the object and parse your way up the path until a match is found when you hit the root object.

Naming Convention

Each section of the DN is an attribute of an object expressed as `attribute_type=value`. When we talk about the object name itself or the RDN, we refer to the *canonical* or *common* name of the object, expressed in LDAP lingo as `cn=`. If we are talking about a user, the common name takes the format `cn=jchang`.

Conversely, each object's RDN is stored in the AD, and each reference contains a reference to its parents. As we follow the references up the chain, we can also construct the DN. This is how LDAP performs a directory query. This naming scheme is very similar to the mechanism of the Domain Name System (DNS) of the Internet, as illustrated in Figure 2-12.

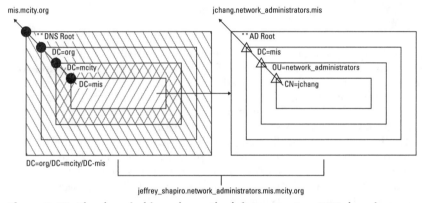

Figure 2-12: The domain hierarchy on the left represents a DNS domain namespace on the Internet. The domain hierarchy on the right represents an AD domain namespace.

Now that we have discussed the naming mechanisms of AD, you should know that Windows does not require everyday users to go through this exercise every time they access an object. The UI does all the work for you and hides this syntax. However, such attributes are required when you code directly to the Active Directory API (ADSI) or LDAP, or are using scripting languages or tools to query and work with AD in a more advanced fashion than the standard tools allow.

AD supports both LDAP v2 and LDAP v3 naming styles, which comply with the Internet's RFC 1779 and 2247 naming styles. This style takes the form of:

cn=common name

ou=organizational unit

o=organization

c=country

However, AD drops the c=country and replaces o=organization with dc=domain component.

For example: cn=jchang,ou=marketing,dc=mcity,dc=org

Note   The use of commas in the DN is a separation or delimiter mechanism. LDAP functions parse the DN and go by the delimiters to break the DN into its relative parts.

In *dot notation,* this would read `jchang.marketing.mcity.org`. An LDAP algorithm translates LDAP names to DNS format and vice versa.

By complying with the LDAP naming convention, any LDAP client can query the AD via an LDAP Uniform Resource Locator (URL) as follows:

```
LDAP://ldapserver.mcity.org/cn=jchang,ou=marketing,dc=mcity,
dc=org
```

Objects in AD are stored and tracked according to an attribute consisting of the object's globally unique identifier or GUID (pronounced *gwid* by some and *gooeyID* or *gooID* by others). The attribute is called the *objectGUID*. The object can thus be moved around and changed, even renamed, but its identity will always remain the same. The GUID is the 128-bit number that is assigned to the object upon its creation. An object cannot exist in AD without a GUID; it is one of the compulsory attributes that are automatically assigned when the object is created. The GUID is available to external process reference and programmatic function. In other words, you can reference the object in AD from an external program by its GUID. This mechanism assures that the object will always be accessible as long as it exists. Ergo, wherever it is moved, it is still accessible.

Objects are protected in the AD via the SAM access control mechanisms and security through the functionality of access control lists (ACLs). In other words, you need to be able to prove ownership and rights over an object if you want to edit or delete it.

Domain Objects

When you set up AD for an enterprise, your first exercise will be to create your root domain or, in AD terms, the root domain object. If this root domain will also be your Internet root domain, you should register it with an Internet domain administration authority as soon as possible. Such an authority is Network Solutions, Inc. If you already registered a root domain, you will be able to create an object that represents it in AD and link it to the DNS server hosting or resolving that name. (We will go into this later, in Chapter 7.) If you have not registered your domain, you might not be able to match it to your company name, because domain names are being claimed every second of the day. This root domain in fact becomes the first container object you create in your chain of objects that represent the "expanse" of your local network logon domain in AD. Under this domain, you create more container objects that represent the organizational units (discussed next) within your enterprise. For example, you might create a domain called `mcity.org` and register it with the InterNIC. There are also security considerations we will address later.

For now, know that the domains you are creating here are full-blown security and administration entities of your network, in the same fashion that legacy NT 4.0 and earlier domains are. How they work will just confuse you now, so we have left this discussion for the chapters in Part III. Note, however, that we will not discuss integration and migration of legacy domains until Part III.

Figure 2-13 represents a path (from the bottom up) of a user all the way up to the domain root. As you now know, you can only have a single domain parent in AD. It is entirely feasible and good practice to create sub-domains under the domain root that reflect sub-division of resources, departments, politically and geographically diverse divisions of an enterprise, acquisitions, resource entities, and more. Chapter 7 presents some reasons you would or would not partition the AD into several domains.

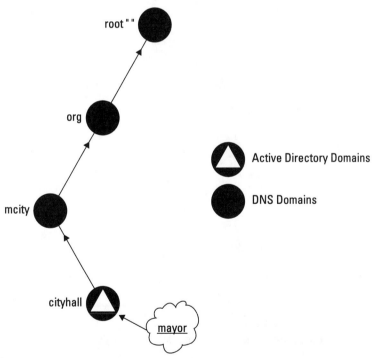

Figure 2-13: A user object (account) on an Active Directory local domain. There is a direct connection between the AD domain and the DNS domain.

For example, a root domain of ABC Company might be `abc.com`. You could then easily create a sub-domain of `abc.com` called `marketing.abc.com`. Note that the `.com` should not be your domain root, because the Internet authorities own that domain root. Keep in mind that we are still only creating objects from an AD point of view. These domain objects are container objects, with name attributes for easy lookup and management (and GUIDs for internal tracking and identity). What we are actually asking AD to do is to maintain the first domain as a root container object, which in turn contains subordinate domain objects.

Organizational Units

Organizational units (OUs) are key container objects in which you can group classes of objects. OUs can, for example, contain objects such as user accounts, printers, computers files shares, and even other OUs. Figure 2-14 illustrates the "containerization" of a group of user accounts into an OU.

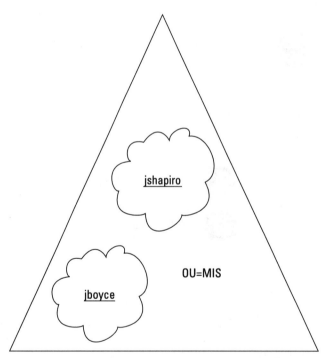

Figure 2-14: User accounts grouped in an OU container

The OU is a welcome addition to network management in Windows 2000. In AD, you can create these containers to reflect your enterprise or organization. To illustrate, we re-created the organizational chart of a major U.S. city and merged it into the domain of a cyberspace city called Millennium City. This will become the sample enterprise we will return to during later discussions of the AD.

The organization chart on the left in Figure 2-15 shows the hierarchy of departments and divisions in Millennium City at the time a directory for this organization was being contemplated. We also see that the chart shows a diverse collection of departments, both local and geographically dispersed, and various sites and services. On the right in Figure 2-15, the same organization chart is represented with OU objects in the AD.

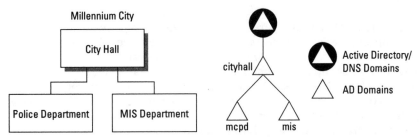

Figure 2-15: The left side of the figure represents an organizational chart. The right side represents the same organizational chart as an object hierarchy in Active Directory.

In any domain on the domain path, you can create organizational units, and inside these organizational units you can create group, user, and computer objects. You can also add custom objects to the domains and OUs. AD lets you also create any end point or leaf object outside the OU.

Trees

The AD refers to the domain structure we just studied as *domain trees*. Everything from the bottom of the object path is considered part of the domain tree — leading from the bottom up, all the way to the single domain parent at the top. The domain tree is unique in the AD, because no two or more parent domains can be the same. The schema does not allow it.

As demonstrated earlier, the domain tree is a systematic collection of AD domain objects that belong to a contiguous namespace. Remember that in AD, the root domain can be extended or partitioned into multiple subdomains that share a common single parent. Sub-domain names must also be unique; however they all share a common directory schema, which is the formal definition of all objects in the domain tree.

AD deploys the DNS naming conventions for hierarchical naming of AD domains and domain devices. In this regard, the AD domains and devices therein are both identified in DNS and AD. Don't worry, Windows 2000 takes full advantage of

Dynamic DNS, so DDNS names, like WINS, do not have to be created in AD and then manually entered into DNS. Although the two domain hierarchies have identical names, they still reflect separate namespaces. DNS manages your Internet name-space, while AD manages your enterprise namespace. The enterprise namespace is, however, resolved via the services of DNS, which provides a directory to the servers that hold your AD directories. This may seem confusing. It is, but it will become clearer for you when we set up DNS in Chapter 14.

Forests

It is possible to create another parent domain in the AD and create objects under it that may appear identical to objects in adjacent domain trees. These collections of domain trees are called *forests*. AD refers to a single domain tree as a forest of one tree. You can also set up trust relationships between these trees, and allow users of one tree in the forest to access the resources in another tree. You would find yourself adding trees to your forest, for example, when you acquire another IT department in a corporate takeover or merger, or when migrating objects from one domain to another, or integrating with legacy NT domains.

Trusts

Finally, we get to the issue of trusts. Like NT, Windows 2000 domains interrelate or interoperate according to trust relationships. In other words, the security principals of one domain are trusted by the security services of another domain according to the trust relationship between the two domains. This is illustrated in Figure 2-16.

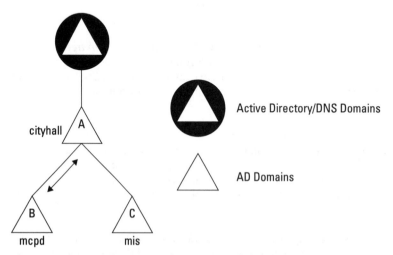

Figure 2-16: Domain A trusts domain B, and domain B trusts domain A . . . a two-way trust.

Figure 2-17 illustrates the three domains that are linked by transitive trust relationships. For those who are wondering about this new virtue, *transitive* essentially means that if domain A trusts domain B and domain B trusts domain C, then A also trusts C. Another way to look at it is by stating that a friend of my friend is also my friend. Figure 2-17 illustrates the transitive trusts.

 Note Transitive here really means that something is able to get from point A to point B by going via point *n*. Transitive can refer to the transient activity of other systems besides security. Replication is a good example.

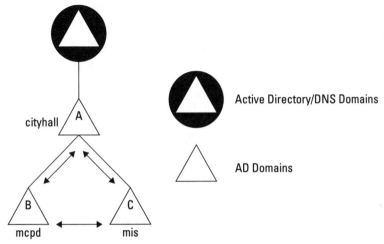

Figure 2-17: Transitive trusts: If domain A trusts domain B and domain B trusts domain C, then domain A trusts domain C.

You might be wondering why then Windows 2000 domains are automatically transitive while NT domains are not. There is no magic in this, no nifty trick performed by Microsoft other than the adoption of an established security standard long overdue, Kerberos. The ticket granting service that Kerberos and AD bring to Windows 2000 creates a distributed security network. Like the Single Sign-on initiative discussed earlier, Kerberos tickets issued by one domain can be used as good currency in another domain. The Kerberos ticket is like a multi-national visa or passport that allows the bearer to gain access to any territory that can accept the instrument.

The Global Catalog

As we discussed earlier, in LDAP, the mechanism for searching or parsing a domain tree is to start from the bottom and travel all the way up to the domain root. LDAP also works on a system of referrals in which a search that ends in a dead-end can be referred to other domain trees in the forest. However, LDAP searches only work when you know what you are looking for; in other words, if you already have the DN or object name and all you are hoping for are the attributes you will be allowed to see. But what if you want to find, for example, all the printers in the OU named Town Planning or all the users that have access to a certain folder? Enter the Global Catalog.

AD supports directory deep queries by means of a global catalog (GC). This GC is created as soon as the first domain root is created. It contains the attributes of all objects in the AD that are, by their nature, searchable. Last or first names are a good example; organization names, computers, printers, and users can be searched by supplying certain attributes as keywords. Applications and users are thus able to query the GC by using a known, or assumed, attribute as a keyword to find possible matches.

GC also allows you to find an object without knowing in which domain it resides, because the GC holds a subset of all the objects of all domains in a forest. For example, a domain member tells you that he or she is unable to log on to the domain. When you search the domain, you find no object that represents this user's name or logon attributes. You can then search the GC to find if the user has perhaps been assigned to another domain, if an account has not yet been created, or if it is disabled.

My Active Directory

Of extreme importance to domain administrators is the ability to program against AD. Custom access to account information has always been a limitation in Windows NT 4.0. Microsoft provided no easy way to access the SAM for customized administrative functions. Every organization has a particular need that cannot be satisfied by the base functionality alone. A good example is the desire to find out which Windows NT accounts have dial-in access enabled, and who has used this privilege in the past three months. To build a tool to query this against the NT SAM and generate a report for management is like trying to add another face to Mount Rushmore.

But Active Directory provides several APIs you can use to access its data for such custom needs.

✦ **ADSI:** The most important API Microsoft has released is ADSI or the *Active Directory Service Interfaces*. ADSI is a collection of COM (Component Object Model) objects that can be used to manipulate and access the directory. Since its release, Microsoft has added Java support (JADSI), which allows any Java tool to program against the ADSI interfaces, but given the litigious atmosphere around Java, you would be better off programming AD from the LDAP API using Java, as described in a moment.

✦ **MAPI:** The WOSA (Windows Open Services Architecture) Messaging API. One of Microsoft's oldest APIs, AD supports MAPI to allow mail-enabled directory applications to gain access to the MAPI address book provider.

✦ **LDAP API:** This is a C API, which is the de facto standard for programming against anything LDAP-compliant. The LDAP API can be programmed from C, C++, Java, and Delphi; essentially any programming language capable of calling C functions.

However, through ADSI, you can access any LDAP-compliant directory (the AD, LDAP repositories, and third-party directories such as NDS). This means that ADSI can be used by anyone looking to create applications that access any LDAP-compliant directory. In other words, write once to ADSI and support any directory (with MS Windows, naturally).

ADSI provides an abstract layer above the capabilities of the directory (it wraps the LDAP API). In this fashion, it provides a single set of directory service interfaces for managing or accessing LDAP resources.

Developers and administrators will use ADSI to access LDAP directories in general and AD in particular. This opens AD and LDAP to a host of possible applications. Consider this: Under NT 4.0 and earlier, it was cumbersome to work with APIs to duplicate the functionality of User Manager for Domains and Server Manager. Administrators were pretty much saddled with these applications, no matter how creative they believed they could be in managing network resources through code or scripting.

ADSI will see both ISVs and corporate developers developing tools to make their administrative tasks easier and cheaper. Using traditional languages and scripting tools, a developer might create functionality that automatically sets up groups of users, applications, network resources, tools, devices, and more. These "applets" can also be targeted to the Microsoft Management Console, which makes their installation and deployment a cinch. And developers will be able to easily "directory enable" their applications.

ADSI has been designed to meet the needs of traditional C and C++ programmers, systems administrators, and sophisticated users. But it is as easily accessed with Visual Basic, making it the most comprehensively accessible LDAP product on the market. ADSI presents the services of the directory as a set of COM objects. For example, an application can use the ADSI PrintQueue object to retrieve data and to pause or purge the print queue, leading to applications that coexist with the underlying technology (as opposed to applications that just run on the platform).

AD is also MAPI-compliant or, should I say, supports the MAPI-RPC address book provider. This support allows a MAPI-based application to look up the contact information of a user, such as an e-mail address or telephone number.

Bridging the Divide between NT and Windows 2000

One of AD's primary features is its accommodation of earlier versions of Windows NT. Most companies will not switch their entire operations to Windows 2000 overnight, but will instead run Windows 2000 alongside Windows NT for some time.

Many companies will adopt the AD domain controller or several controllers as the new "PDC" of legacy Windows NT domains. NT servers, workstations, and clients view AD servers as PDCs in mixed mode (NT and 2000 mixed) environments. To users, applications, and services, the authentication by AD is transparent, thus allowing NT domains to continue services oblivious that the PDC is in fact the proverbial disguised wolf, as Microsoft cunningly did with the File and Print services for NetWare, which made clients think the NT server was a NetWare server. (This requires a special upgrade to the NT registry and SAM to make it AD-compliant, which starts with Service Pack 5.)

AD achieves this magic by totally emulating Windows NT 3.51 and NT 4.0 domain controllers. In a mixed mode environment, the Windows 2000 domain controller acts and behaves like a Windows NT 4.0 domain controller. Even applications and services (including the ISV and third-party products) that are written to the Win32 API will continue to work without modification in an AD environment

A term you will encounter in chapters ahead is *down-level compliance.* This down-level compliance allows many IT and LAN administrators to plan gradual and safe transitions to Windows 2000 domains in which AD is the master logon authority. Thus, the transition in most cases will be evolutionary rather than revolutionary, while still guaranteeing that AD gets deployed right at the very beginning. Transition by phased implementation is the route we will primarily advocate to you in the chapters to follow, and we will also discuss routes to Windows 2000-Windows NT integration that do not require Active Directory.

AD provides or denies logon authority and access privileges to the network resources of a Windows domain. Before we proceed further with AD, we deem it necessary to get certain information straight about Microsoft domains. So let's define "domains" in the Windows network sense (as opposed to what you have been reading about earlier in this chapter) so we all know what we are talking about. Not only should we try to clear up the confusion about domain generations or versions, but also you will almost certainly have to integrate or migrate legacy NT domains into 2000 domains, and unless you understand the differences, you are likely to really foul things up. Philosophically, things are very different.

So now there are two types of Windows domains: the NT domain (now the legacy domain) and the Windows 2000 domain . . . a container object in the AD, a speck on the Internet, and conceptually the extent of your network. Both can be analyzed in terms of a logon "stack." And both share common traits.

Figure 2-18 represents the Windows NT and Windows 2000 local logon stack on the local machine, and the logical order (from the top down) of the process to authenticate access to the local services. At the top of the domain stack are client processes; these reside on local machines or on other client machines, workstations, and network devices. When the client process requires access to a service, the local Security Account Manager, using data stored in the local SAM, controls the access (this works the same for Windows NT and Windows 2000).

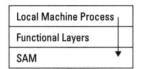

Figure 2-18: The Windows NT and Windows 2000 logon and authentication stacks

Figure 2-19 represents the Windows domain logon and authentication stack, which encompasses the Windows NT networking environment. The domain logon stack works in the same fashion, only the clients do not log on locally to a machine or network resource. Instead, the OS passes the access request to the Active Directory, in Windows 2000, or the domain (PDC or BDC) registry (where an accessible copy of the SAM resides), on NT domain controllers.

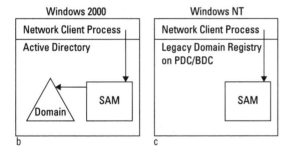

Figure 2-19: The Windows NT and Windows 2000 domain logon and authentication stacks

The Windows 2000 domain is a single collective, albeit extendable, unit that comprises all the network objects considered to be members. In many respects, the domain structure is one huge distributed container that embraces all your company's networking and IT assets. You can view a domain as a "collective," much like a fleet of ships comprises a flotilla or a navy, or a group of marines comprise a brigade or a corps. We'll go over the models in Chapter 7.

Before we discuss what's new about Windows 2000 domains, let's discuss some quick similarities, which for many will provide familiar turf. The NT domain begot the Windows 2000 domain, and that's probably the best way to compare them (even if the kid somehow came out very different).

Single Point of Access and Administration

NT domains allow an administrator to log on to the network and gain access to the administration tools at a server or workstation (even via scaled-down tools on Windows 95 and Windows 98). The tools include User Manager for Domains and Server Manager. Users, groups, network devices such as printers and drives, and resources such as folders and sharepoints are accessible to administrators who have been assigned the necessary rights.

Windows 2000 domains provide the same single point of access and administration, but with a lot more flexibility to manage resources and users. Organizational units (OUs), for example, is a new entity on the Windows domain that allows you to group users in administrative structures, compartments, or diverse organization divisions or management entities. This means it is possible to create units and assign administrative functions to departments. For example: The materials management department is managed under the Mat-Mgt OU. And a user in this OU is assigned administrative rights to manage the contents of this OU and only this OU. This obviates the need to assign everything to a single administrator, or having an admin group with dozens of users gaining access to blanket administration authority on the domain. (The differences between groups and OUs will become clearer in Chapter 7.)

Domains and More Domains

The NT (or Windows network) domain represents a logical grouping of computers and devices that are accessible to a group, or groups, of users and computers, no matter their logon place or position. The domain provides a means of containing and controlling users on the network, and also provides a defined boundary and a security shield behind which computers, users, and operators function in a secured environment. Windows 2000 domains perform an identical function, as described in later chapters.

If you are new to Windows networking, here's a quick explanation of the Windows network domain: Compare it to a workgroup. When Microsoft launched Windows 3.11 and Windows for Workgroups back in the early 1990s, it provided a means for computers to connect to each other as peers so that each computer could share its resources. You would have to specifically deny or permit access to the resources on a computer before anyone or anything could use it. This is already a pain to do at each computer in a small office of people, because each computer acts as a standalone server and has to be managed as such. Once your network begins to expand, it becomes impractical and well nigh impossible to manage.

The domain, on the other hand, was born of the ability to locate a central security, login, and access a permissions authority on a master server, called the primary domain controller, or PDC. The SAM database, which lives inside the registry, provided a global access to the users in the central security database, to the resources on all the computers, and to devices attached to the network, such as printers, backup drives, and CD-Rs.

Intra-domain Trust Relationships

The ability of NT domains to trust each other (bi-directionally) is very apparent in Windows 2000 domains, but you will uncover big differences. The inter-operation of flat NT domains (4.0 and earlier) is tedious. It seemed to make no sense under NT 4.0 to create separate domains for a small to medium company, even across wide area networks. Any company of, say, 100 people that requires the establishment of more than 100,000 domain objects is doing something very wrong. Yet often, small companies would create multiple domains for no apparent reason other than to organize their thoughts.

Note   Few follow the 100,000-object limit rule for a Windows NT domain because domains are in a constant state of change. It makes more sense to monitor the size of the SAM, which has a tendency to become unstable when it grows larger than 35 or 40MB.

The only time we have had to administer more than one domain in a company (70+ in one company is the record) was due to aggressive acquisitions, in which we inherited domains from the various takeovers. Daily, we would have problems trying to assign resources and absorb users. Nonetheless, many large companies ran out of registry space because they were so big, or they created separate resource domains where devices and other network services resided apart from "user" or "account" domains. These are typically companies with tens of thousands of users.

Windows 2000 domains are modeled on Internet domains, have depth and perspective, and can be partitioned almost infinitely. They inherently trust each other, in much the same way that a family trusts each other under the same roof, even though each member goes about his or her business in his or her own section of the house.

It makes sense to create multiple domains (actually domain extensions or partitions) on a Windows 2000 network, but for very different reasons, the most important, already mentioned, being devolution of power and delegation of management. As you will see later, you can create domains that encompass subnets, sites, departments, locations, and the like. And as long as your domains are attached to a common ancestor, the domain root, trusts between them are full-blown two-way. Although the term "transitive" relates to two-way trusts that exist between many domains, not only on the same tree, but also across trees in the forest, this naturally does not mean that two domain groups (the forests) can be somehow grafted into each other like you would two living plants. But it is a darn sight easier to migrate, move, and eventually eliminate orphan domains in a forest.

In short, Windows 2000 domains are modeled after Internet domains, have dimension, and can be partitioned. NT domains, on the other hand, are flat.

Access Control Lists and Access Tokens

When a user (human or service) logs into a domain, NT authentication and security management grants the user access to the network and resources it is permitted to use. This is done in the form of access control lists (ACLs) and access tokens. Seasoned or astute NT administrators will recall how it is possible to access and edit the ACL on a local machine. And if you do not know how, you will learn later. NT also provides the user (login) with an access token, which the user wears as it browses the network. The access token works like the security badge you wear to work. As you approach doors or devices, they either open for you or deny access. Windows NT domains and 2000 domains both control access using ACLs. In AD, the SAM ACLs (in the directory) control who has access to objects and the scope of that access.

All Windows 2000 services are referred to as objects. These objects are stored in either the local Security Account Manager (SAM), which is a registry tree, or else the AD is controlled by the ACLs. Each ACL contains permissions information, detailing which user can access the object and the type of access allowed (such as read only or read/write). ACLs are domain object-bound; they are not transient entities.

Reality Check

It goes without saying that Microsoft, with Active Directory and Windows 2000, is taking us to a point from which we will be unable to return. Of course, we asked for this in our quest to be liberated from the old norms to the promises of e-commerce, DNA, and an information-ruled network society.

While the technology presented herein is impressive, there are several caveats to consider. Firstly, small companies will be able to install Windows 2000 far quicker than larger companies because the IT infrastructure of smaller companies is far less complex. A small Windows NT network is easier to convert than peeling a banana skin (provided you have supported hardware and current drivers). So, installing Active Directory for domain authentication and security in a small business is a relatively painless procedure.

Small companies typically do not currently drive their internal networks on pure IP and DNS. They still use NetBEUI and NETBIOS, and rely on IP and DNS only when it is time to take a trip on the Web or get e-mail. Larger companies, especially those that have long ago seen the sense of pure IP networks, already have DNS servers and IP infrastructures in place. This means that existing DNS support is likely to come into conflict with two factors, UNIX-based DNS servers and UNIX-based DNS administrators (asking a UNIX administrator to adopt Windows-based DNS is like asking a cat to bark).

So, for some time to come, complex IT environments will likely run mixed networks (Windows NT, Windows 2000, NetWare, and UNIX). And as long as NT domains (and Windows 9x clients) need to be supported, not all the wonders of Windows 2000 (such as SSO) can be accessible or appreciated. The entities that can most use the advanced features of Windows 2000 will mostly be the entities that take the longest to adopt the operating system or at least convert their domains to native Windows 2000. It all depends on the boldness of the people and the IT management at many firms.

And despite the enthusiasm for Active Directory, you need to be careful in your adoption strategy. The wish list for this directory-elect's next version already runs into dozens of pages at many organizations. The chapters in Part III are thus designed with these realities in mind.

Summary

In this chapter, we introduced Active Directory (AD) as one of the most exciting new additions to Windows networking: that it is bound to be the technology that drives the transition from legacy NT domains, and probably from most other environments to Windows 2000 Server environments.

As applications developers, we need consistent, open, and interoperable interfaces and APIs against which we can store and manage information relating to applications, processes, and services. Many companies have risen to the challenge of providing directories. Directories and directory services will and must be free, open, accessible, and part of the network operating systems and technology we use. Active Directory is all this and then some.

Directories should not be seen as the next killer application; rather, they represent important evolutionary processes to support the existing and future revolutions in computing, communications, and information technology.

✦　　✦　　✦

Windows 2000 Security

In This Chapter

Encryption

Kerberos

IPSec

Microsoft Certificate Services

Logon and Authentication

T his chapter starts you off with a discussion on the need for powerful distributed security before introducing you to the specifics of Windows 2000 distributed security services. It also reviews the new Windows 2000 security protocols, and protection of services and data.

Windows 2000 Security

While the new era of computing and Windows 2000 will bring forth many benefits, it will also herald dastardly attempts to rob you, beat you up, and shut you down. There are many forces out there that have only one thing on their evil minds, and that is to find any way to break into your network to plunder and pillage.

Before you start building your new corporate infrastructure around Windows 2000, it will pay for you to become thoroughly versed in the security mechanisms the operating system offers and how to go about locking down your assets. Without a doubt, it is probably the most secure operating system available today. Not only has it inherited the Windows NT C2 security compliance, which was a ton of work for Microsoft and set the stage for a secure Windows 2000, but also, if there were showbiz awards for security, Windows 2000 would clean up at the Oscars, the Golden Globes, the Grammies, and more.

But before we get into Windows 2000 security specifics, let's look at the problem holistically, then you can evaluate your current security status before devising a security plan.

You have probably heard the term everywhere, so what does C2 security mean to you, the network or server administrator? Absolutely nothing. C2 security is nothing more than a U.S. government sanction. The United States keeps a series of "books" that grade the security levels of operating systems. Windows NT passed with distinction because it was able to demonstrate compliance of the C2 specifications. These specifications include object ownership, object protection, audit trail, memory protection, and user identification, all of which are discussed in various places in this book.

C2 is defined in the so-called "Orange Book," which is really titled the *Trusted System Evaluation Criteria.* C2 evaluation checks to see how secure a computer really is. However, C2 only applies to standalone computers. Microsoft is also testing to the specifications for network computers (Red Book and Blue Book). Microsoft has gone above and beyond C2 with Windows 2000. So the term is really meaningless.

Note   The operating system is not C2 out of the box. Everyone has access to everything. A vendor or security service provider has to set up a machine and the OS to be C2-compliant. This means locking down objects, setting up audit trails, creating user accounts with secure password philosophy, and so on. Only when a machine has been fully locked down can it be rated as C2-compliant . . . no matter if it's a washing machine or a file server.

C2 security meant a lot to Windows NT, and whatever hoops and hurdles Microsoft went through and over to gain C2 security is not lost in Windows 2000. However, we are now playing away from home . . . the field is the Internet, and the game is e-commerce. You have high-powered security protocols to configure, and you have lots more room to drop the ball.

Another reason that C2 is not important to you is that, as mentioned earlier, out of the box Windows 2000 is as locked down as the space above your head. You have to lock down every aspect of it; the network is only as secure as you make it. If Windows 2000 is not properly configured, claiming awards like C2 will not get you out of a jam when a hacker pulls your pants down on the Internet. We know we are being blunt, but security is part of the day-to-day life of a network administrator. If you don't have a security problem, you don't have a network.

The Need for Security

If you are new to network administration in general and Windows 2000 (and NT) in particular, then before you devise a security plan, you need to understand the risks to your network and yourself. Unless you plan to hire a security expert, you will probably have to come up with a plan yourself. Chances are your company will ask this of you . . . your superior will assume that you are well versed in the subject. If you are well versed in the security threat, you can skip this part and go directly to the section titled "Rising to the Challenge."

A company's data is its lifeblood, and it needs to be vigorously protected. As the network administrator, you will be required to ensure that data is kept confidential and that it can be relied upon. There are numerous mechanisms in place to assist you with respect to data integrity and confidentiality, and they range from sensible access control policy to encryption, backup, and availability.

Data Input

Data is vulnerable to attack and capture from the moment a person types in a user ID and password. How often have you had to enter a password while someone was standing over your shoulder? You try to type as quickly as you can, but spies will watch you typing and pick up your passwords quicker than you think. Then, when you are not at your desk, they will get your user ID from the memo field at the sign-in screen and masquerade as you from any computer, anywhere.

The new smart card technology has been introduced in Windows 2000 and is discussed later in this chapter. With a smart card, the user is authenticated without risking being compromised because the thief needs the card to complete the hack. Smart card readers offer one of the most sophisticated domain authentication solutions available to Windows 2000.

Data Transport

The PC's or input device's operating system must transport the information down the network stack to the transport, all the way to the domain controller's (DC's) network interface and up the DC's respective stack. All along this route, the data is vulnerable to interception. If the data is not encrypted, or is encrypted very lightly, there is a risk that a person tapping the network will be able to pick up conversations between your input device and the domain controller, or any other partner for that matter.

To counter this, Windows 2000 employs extensive encryption technology both in data and network communications, and in file storage and protection.

Why the Threat Exists

There are many reasons people threaten your security. Let's look at a short list of threats that you are most likely to encounter during your life as a Windows 2000 Server administrator:

1. **Espionage:** People need to break into your communications realm to learn company secrets, employee secrets, product plans, financial situation, strategy, and so forth. This level of threat is the most virulent. The attackers have strong motives to get the attack under way and to ensure they succeed. The attackers do not want to be discovered and will continue to hide in your environment as long as they need to. The damage is often irreparable if the attackers are undiscovered. This is the most difficult form of attack to counter because, for the most part, you do not know where they are hitting you or why.

    While bugging devices and spying are not usually the responsibility of the network or server administrator, espionage via the network is becoming more probable every day because it is so easy and it is where all the jewels are located.

Over the network, hackers will read files and e-mail, and try to log in to databases wherever they can to steal credit card numbers, bank account numbers, and so forth. An attacker can, for example, find out the password of your voice mail system and then listen to your messages.

2. **Denial of Service (DoS):** These attackers are intent on destroying you. They can attack your physical premises or locations, which is becoming harder to do all the time, or they can target your network, which is becoming easier to do because you are connected to the Internet or because you provide users with remote access. This is fast becoming the favorable means of attack for stopping your work: firstly, because of the dependency your company has on the network, and secondly, because the attacker does not need to be physically present for the attack.

   DoS attacks are made by flooding your network portal (targeting your gateway to the Internet) with massive floods of e-mail, or with *syn* attacks, which are the low-level communication barrages that suck up all the server's resources, finally causing it to crash. Sometimes the objective is to crash the server just to trigger backdoor code that spawns a process. There could be a million places on a network to hide a sliver of code that gets executed when certain files are loaded. Good examples are the boot files and startup files like AUTOEXEC.BAT.

3. **Hostile Applications:** Hostile applications are placed on the Internet for unwary surfers to download. Upon execution of the code on your internal network, the application can begin its dirty work, which for a while might be to do nothing that can cause it to be detected, but rather to find information that would be valuable to the attacker. Such applications are also called Trojan horses.

4. **Virus Attacks:** By far, the most visible attack on the network comes in the form of viruses. Contrary to the claims that there are tens of thousands of viruses, only a handful of virus writers can actually claim to have invented one from start to finish. Most virus authors are not as brilliant as you may have been led to believe; they are just copycats. However, this information does not provide any relief.

   A lot of virus code is available on the Internet to be freely downloaded, manipulated, and enhanced or packed with a payload. This is the reason we see so many variations of viruses every month. Some can be detected by anti-virus software such as NetShield and cleaned up; others are more sinister, such as Backdoor-G, which can only be picked up by the anti-virus software after it has delivered its payload. Not only does it wreck your PC before it can be detected, but it also first attacks the anti-virus software.

Threats emanate from two locales: the external environment and the internal environment. These two environments can be easily defined as follows:

✦ **The external environment:** The threat comes from people who have no contractual status with the enterprise. They are complete strangers. The attack comes from the outside.

✦ **The internal environment:** The threat comes from people who have a relationship with the company, from employees to contractors to customers. The attack usually comes from the inside. In some cases, it comes from the outside, with inside information. Other times, the threat is not born out of revenge or criminal intent, but ignorance.

The External Environment

Not too long ago, the only way to threaten or attack an organization, its people, or its business was through some sort of physical act. This is no longer the case. It costs far less money and is much safer for a hacker to stay in a safe haven and attempt to break into a network through a RAS portal or connection to the Internet. For many, it means the possibility of financial reward; for others, it has to do with some form of demented feeling of achievement.

Now that many small companies can afford dedicated connections to the Internet, the pickings have become very attractive. While we have not yet realized the paperless office, almost all data is placed on the network in share-points and databases. The network and server storage silos are thus loaded with valuable information.

Attackers also no longer need to proactively choose their targets. They create hostile code that gets inadvertently downloaded from the Internet and gets executed by a number of mechanisms, from rebooting to the mere act of unzipping a file. The code then can gather intelligence and send it to its master. It is therefore essential that you establish policy to ensure that code downloaded from the Internet is authenticated and signed with the digital signature (a public key) of a trusted software publisher.

E-mail is now very much tangible property, and it can be used in court cases as evidence and as a source of information that can be used to plan an attack on a person or an organization. We all communicate more by e-mail than we do by snail mail, yet e-mail is treated like a postcard. We do not enclose our messages in an envelope and seal it. We just put it in the mail for anyone to look at.

E-mail needs to be secured on two levels. We need to be sure that the people with whom we communicate are really who they say they are. And we need to be sure that our e-mail is not being read or changed as it traverses the net. It is very easy to trace the route a message takes over the Internet and penetrate e-mail systems. Securing e-mail is becoming essential and falls under the auspices of public key encryption, discussed shortly.

The Internal Environment

The internal environment threat comprises employees who are either malicious, stupid, or who make honest mistakes. Threats come in the form of outright misuse of privileges to total ignorance or stupidity. For example: The perpetrator of outright misuse of privileges has administrative rights on the network and provides him or herself access to sensitive data.

The ignorance factor often involves users failing to keep anti-virus software current, or downloading all forms of rubbish from the Internet, thereby introducing malicious content to the network from the external environment.

Outright stupidity and honest mistakes that often cause headaches for administrators are usually deleted files, corrupted databases, deleted mailbox folders, and the like. Deleted data can usually be recovered from backups, as long as the backup regimen is well practiced in your company. Most of the time, recovering deleted files is just a waste of time spent doing administrative work to have to keep recovering files. Often, the problems are not user-related issues at all, but just bad management on the part of a lazy network or server administrator.

Rising to the Challenge

Over the years, there has been a lot of discussion about the security capabilities of Windows NT. Microsoft has often been criticized for not delivering a more secure operating system when, in fact, the opposite is the case. But it has not been all Microsoft's fault. For starters, the U.S. government has for years not allowed the export of 128K-bit encryption algorithms . . . although that did not deter many organizations from smuggling out the software.

And as for the comparison with UNIX, UNIX systems are more at risk today than Windows 2000. Since the UNIX source code is open for all to see, many hackers can read the code to look for weak points and plot their attacks. Server for server, there are still more UNIX machines on the Internet than Window NT or Windows 2000 machines. On Windows NT, hackers resort to scanning network communications to look for information with which to replay attacks. Data interception was and still is a common form of attack against an NT network.

For Windows 2000 to compete and even excel over the competition in the risky and exposed world of e-commerce, it needed to be *the* most secure operating system. The following sections explore the standard Windows 2000 security mechanisms Microsoft has implemented in Windows 2000:

✦ Kerberos

✦ IPSec

✦ PKI

✦ NT LAN Manager (NTLM)

Note All the fancy encryption algorithms you use will be useless if your server stands in the middle of an open-plan office for anyone to plunder or sneak out. Unless a server or key systems and data storage are locked up behind secured barriers, you might as well forget the rest of this chapter.

Before you tackle the protocols, you need to get up to speed on the cloak-and-dagger stuff.

Encryption 101

This is a true story. A man walked into a diner one morning and ordered fried eggs. When the eggs were delivered, he changed his mind and advised the waitress that he had ordered scrambled eggs. The waitress, peeved at the cheek of the client, picked up a fork and with a quick whipping movement rendered the eggs into an unrecognizable heap. "There, now they are scrambled," she said, and stormed off.

The action of rendering the eggs into an unintelligible mess is known as scrambling. Data is scrambled in similar fashion; we call it encryption. At first, the data is in whole recognizable form, often called *plain text,* like the fried eggs. The motion to scramble them is known as the *algorithm* . . . and the result is often termed *cipher text.* In the anecdote, the algorithm is the technique, style, or "recipe" by which the waitress used her wrist and fork to turn a perfect pair of sunny-side-ups into a mound of yolk and white. If she only took a few stabs at the eggs, the patron might be able to claim he still had fried eggs (not a strong encryption algorithm).

Knowing the key that reverses the process is vital to the recovery of the data, but that is the only difference between egg scrambling and data scrambling. If we knew how to unscramble eggs, Humpty Dumpty might still be alive, and our world would be very different.

In computer science, the standard that governs the techniques and recipes for encryption of data is known as the Data Encryption Standard (DES). DES data encryption algorithms (DEAs) specify how to encrypt data and how to decrypt that data. A number of important bodies, such as ANSI and the National Institute of Standards and Technology (NIST), govern the specifications for DES. Each algorithm is rated according to the strength of its encryption ability (and resistance to duplication, attack of the encryption/decryption key).

DES, actually the DEAs, needs to be continuously improved because the codes are often cracked by encryption experts (for science and crime). New standards are on the horizon, and soon the Advanced Encryption Standard (EAS) will replace DES. Other standards governed by these bodies include the Digital Signature Standard (DSS) and the Digital Signature Algorithm (DSA). Incidentally, the U.S. government does not regulate encryption.

Note   For more information on encryption standards, see the RSA Laboratories Web site at `www.rsasecurity.com`.

Cryptography

Cryptography dates back more than 4,000 years. Over the past millennia, it has protected many a culture's communications and has brought them through wars, treaties with neighbors, and more.

In recent years, electronic data communications have escalated to such volume and importance in our lives that without electronic or digital cryptography we would not be able to continue on our logical course.

In fact, we owe our computerized environment to cryptography. If you have time during the locking down of your networks, you should read the biography of Alan Turing, who directed the British to build the first digital computers to break the German's Enigma code.

Pretty Good Privacy (PGP) is a software program written originally and distributed illegally for no financial gain by Phil Zimmerman, who believed that the cryptography algorithms that were being protected by patents should be made public property . . . worldwide. He created PGP back in 1991, and over the years, it was disseminated around the world on the "undernet." Even though its export was expressly forbidden by the U.S. government's International Traffic in Arms Regulations, which classified his software as a munition, it became available everywhere on bulletin board systems and the first pioneer sites of the World Wide Web. In the last decade, PGP was pretty much the only means of securing data and communications on the Internet and corporate networks of the world.

But encrypting data always required a user to make an effort to secure communications. Lethargy and lack of knowledge have always left room for error and holes. Only with the incorporation of the encryption algorithms in the very core of the operating systems and standards-based network protocols would encryption become as pervasive and as transparent as air.

We have come a long way since Phil Zimmerman risked detention to make the slogan *encryption for everyone* a reality. Today, Windows 2000 incorporates it extensively. Only you, the administrator, need to ensure that it is configured correctly, through security policy, and everyone on the network will be able to use it, without even knowing it exists. Before we look at this native support for cryptography in Windows 2000 and how it is used, here is some cryptography 101.

Keys

Cryptography is a lock, a means of securing information by rendering it undecipherable without a key. The key, or cryptographic key, is held closely by people sending and receiving the communication. The following is the simplest example of cryptography:

The communication: Package color baby burger

The Key:

Package = meet

color = same

baby = grand central station

burger = 14:00 hours

Deciphered: meet me at the same place at Grand Central station at 2 p.m.

Obviously, if you have the key, you can unlock the code and decipher the message.

Private Keys

Private key encryption is also known as *Symmetric Key Encryption* or just *conventional cryptography.* This encryption uses the same key to decrypt and encrypt the data. In other words, the key you use to lock the door is the same key you use to unlock the door. In the previous example, both the sender of the message and the receiver share a common codebook or key. The sender encodes the message with the key, and the receiver decodes the message with the same key. This form of encryption is not the most secure in the public domain, because for widespread communications, numerous parties must hold the key. As soon as the key falls into wrong hands, then all bets are off. But it can be used in network authentication where the compromising of a key is highly unlikely.

Public Keys

Public key encryption uses two keys. One key is public, and the other is private. Both keys can encrypt data, but only the private key can decrypt the data. To be pervasive, the technology depends on a public key infrastructure (PKI), which Windows 2000 now supports (more about PKI later).

A mathematical process is used to generate the two keys, and the keys are related to each other by the product of that mathematical process. So the message encrypted with one key can be decrypted only with the other. This is how it works:

You want to send an encrypted message. The receiver has a public key, which he or she makes publicly available for encrypting messages. You encrypt the message using the public key and send it. When the receiver gets your message, he or she can decrypt it using the private key, which is mathematically related to the public key. No one, including you, can decrypt the message with the public key.

It goes without saying that the private key must be closely held or your messages will be compromised.

Session Keys

The chief problem in making public keys widely available is that the encryption algorithms used to generate public keys are too slow for the majority of just-in-time communications (there are numerous algorithms used to create the keys, but the technology is beyond the scope of this book). For this reason, a simpler session key is generated, and it in turn holds the "key" to the encrypted data.

1. A session key is randomly generated for every communication that requires encryption. A *key distribution authority* (or the originator of the communication, or a vouchsafe process) creates the session key for the communication or message.

2. The data is encrypted with the session key.

3. The session key is then encrypted with the recipient's public key. The encryption of the data by the session key is a thousand times faster than the encryption of the data by the public key.

4. The encrypted data and the encrypted session key are then sent to the receiver, who can decrypt both by first decrypting the session key with the secret key and then decrypting the data with the session key.

Key Certificates

Key certificates are containers for public keys. Key certificates usually contain the public key of the recipient, the identity of the creator of the public key, the date the key was created, and a list of digital signatures.

Digital Signatures

We sign most things we do in the material world, so why not in the digital world? Most of us spend our working lives in cyberspace. Our customers deal with us on the net, they buy from us on the net, and they expect that when they send us confidential communications, they are sending it to the right people. We also want to know that when someone sends us a message, hits our Web site, or connects to our computers that they are who they say they are. We also need to use digital signatures to prevent repudiation. In other words, if someone places an order with you over the World Wide Web or via e-mail, or enters into some form of contract with you, they should sign the document so that they cannot turn around later and repudiate the transaction.

It is also not always necessary to encrypt a message, which taxes computer resources. Sometimes, the message or data content or information is not sensitive. Sending someone a publicly available encrypted price list would be an absurd idea. But what if someone intercepted that message and changed the content, which would affect the relationship? What if someone sent you a message saying, "Mary just had a little lamb," and a jokester intercepted the message and changed the content to read, "Mary just ate her little lamb?" The effects could be devastating.

Digital signatures are thus used to authenticate the sender, to legally bind parties in digital transactions, to authenticate content, and to be sure that content has not been changed or tampered with in any way.

Windows 2000 makes wide use of the encryption mechanics described above. One of the most important implementations is in the use of the Kerberos protocol, which is now the most important means of authentication and protection of data in not only Windows 2000, but also all major operating systems.

Kerberos

What if we told you that every time you come to work you have to go to a certain security officer who signs you in and issues you a clip-on tag that allows you to enter the building and go to your desk, but do nothing else? And that you had to check in with the officer every hour to renew your tag?

What if you then needed to go to this person for a new tag every time you needed to access a resource in the company, such as the file room or the copier machine? And then what would you think if we told you that you have to present this tag to guards that protect each resource so that they can verify that you are legitimate?

You'd say, "Wow, this is overkill. Why is security so tight here?" It would probably be hard to work in such an environment. But what if several companies, or a whole city, adopted such stringent security practices? Life in the city would be so secure that companies would be able to trust each other enough to share resources. But for all intents and purposes, it would still be hard to work in such an environment.

Yet, this is precisely how Kerberos works. The only difference is that the security check-ins and tag issues are handled transparently by the underlying protocols, and everything takes place in network transmissions. The user is oblivious to what is going on under the network hood.

Kerberos is based on a system of *tickets,* which are packets of encrypted data that are issued by a *Key Distribution Center (KDC)* — the security officer we just mentioned. This ticket is your "passport" and carries with it a myriad of security information. Each KDC is responsible for a *realm,* and in Windows 2000 every domain is also a Kerberos realm. Also, every Active Directory domain controller (DC) is a KDC.

When you log on to Windows, WinLogon and LSA kick in to first authenticate you to the KDC (see Chapter 2), which provides you an initial ticket called the *Ticket Granting Ticket (TGT),* which is akin to a right-of-way coupon at the fairground, or a passport. Then, when you need to access resources on the network, you present the TGT to the DC and request a ticket for a resource. This resource ticket is known as a *Service Ticket (ST).* When you need access to a resource, your processing environment presents the ST to the resource. You are then granted access in accordance with the ACL protecting the resource.

The implementation of Kerberos in Windows 2000 is fully compliant with the Internet Engineering Task Force's (IETF) Kerberos v5, which was originally developed by MIT. This specification is supported by many, which means that tickets issued in a Windows 2000 domain (now also known as a Kerberos realm) can be passed to other realms, such as networks running Mac OS, Novell NetWare, UNIX, AIX, IRIX, and so forth.

Trusts can therefore be established between the Kerberos Domain Controllers (KDCs) in the respective realms. The KDC trusts, for all intents and purposes, work just like trusts for Windows NT systems, which are set up between the primary domain controller (PDC) in each domain. And because Windows 2000 still speaks NT LAN Manager (NTLM), trusts are maintained to legacy Windows domains.

Kerberos, however, does require more tweaking and administration than you may be used to on Windows NT domains using NTLM. That's because users have to check in with the KDC several times a day. For example, if you are logged on for 12 hours straight, you will probably have to check in with the KDC about 12 to 15 times in that period. If the domain supports 1,200 users, that will result in about 18,000 hits to the KDC.

Also, trusts between heterogeneous networks are not as transparent as the trusts between Active Directory domains, in which the domain controllers can explicitly vouch for the users. Trusts between Windows 2000 forests, Windows 2000 and Windows NT, and Windows 2000 and other realms involve manual setup between each domain's or realm's respective administrator. The process that takes place in the UNIX or IRIX realm may be very different to the setup that takes place between Windows 2000 realms.

When planning the physical layout of the network, if you have multiple domains that communicate across a WAN, you will need to establish shortcuts or the best possible routes that ticket transmission can use to move from realm to realm. Shortcuts may be required so that authentication does not become bogged down in network traffic over a small pipe.

Note If authentication is slow due to slow links between networks, you may have a good reason to establish the site as a new domain. For more information on deciding when to create a new domain, check out Chapter 7.

Kerberos is, however, a very fast protocol and is an ideal environment for implementing the Single Sign-On paradigm in network authentication.

Kerberos and the Single Sign-On Initiative

Single Sign-On is long overdue. From a security angle, it provides tremendous benefits. If a user has six or seven passwords, it means he or she has six or seven more opportunities to compromise security. Many people are so sick of the different passwords they have to deal with that they would rather not have a password. This is a problem in systems where the password creation and application is in the hands of the user. A good example is a voice-mail system. Many, such as CallXpress for Windows NT, ask the user not to enter 1234 or to leave the password blank. But a review of the password history on the system usually shows that many passwords are left blank or are simply 1234.

Other users go to the opposite extreme and type their passwords into a password database or a spreadsheet, or worse, a simple text file. An intruder will go to town on a document loaded with keys. Password databases are the mother lode; it takes a few seconds to crack the password that locks the file.

With Single Sign-On, the user authenticates once, and that authentication is respected by other network applications and services. Made possible by Kerberos and Active Directory, Single Sign-On is supported in SQL Server 2000 and Exchange 2000, and is supported by trusts set up between realms implemented by other operating systems and Windows 2000. It is the very reason that Windows 2000 trusts — between domains that share a common root or forest — are transitive.

Psst . . . This Is How Kerberos Works

Kerberos is built around the idea of "shared secrets." In other words, if only two people know a secret, then either person can verify the identity of the other by confirming that the other person knows the secret. The shared secret in Kerberos is between Kerberos and the *security principal* (the human user or a device).

Here's an analogy: Two people send each other e-mail regularly and need to be sure that each e-mail cannot be repudiated by the other, or that someone else is not masquerading as the sender. So in order to be sure that the sender or receiver is who they say they are, both agree offline that something in the messages between them will confirm that each one is "the one." However, if someone is analyzing e-mail and spotting word arrangements, it will not take them long to discover the hidden confirmation message. On a network authentication mechanism, this can be quite a problem because it would not take long to intercept a message and fool an authentication service into thinking the user is genuine.

So how do the two correspondents devise a plan to be certain of their identities? The answer is symmetric-key cryptography. The shared key must be kept secret, however, or anyone will be able to decode the message. As discussed earlier, a symmetric key is a single key that is capable of both encryption and decryption. In other words, as long as the two corespondents share the same key, they can encrypt their messages and be sure that the partner is able to decrypt it.

Note The terms *secret key* and *symmetric key* are often interchanged when discussing the use of a single key to encrypt and decrypt text. However, it is entirely possible for a secret key to fall into the wrong hands.

The practice of secret key cryptography is not new and goes back to before the Cold War days when insurgents perfected secret key techniques and cipher science. In the Kerberos implementation, however, authentication is a done deal as long as the information is decrypted, or as long as one party can prove they are the real thing by being in possession of the decrypting key in the first place. But what if someone on the network steals the key, or manages to copy previous authentication sessions? Kerberos then makes use of an unalterable factor that goes back to the Big Bang . . . time.

Time Authentication

Kerberos authentication begins, literally, from the time a user tries to log on to the domain. When Kerberos receives an authentication request, it follows this series of steps:

1. It looks the user up and loads the key it shares with the user to decrypt the authentication message.

2. It then looks at the information in the message. The first item it checks is the time field, which is the time on the clock of the user's workstation or machine from where the user requested logon authentication. If the time on the sender's clock is out of synch by five minutes, Kerberos will reject the message without further ado (Kerberos will compensate for the different time zones and daylight savings time). However, if the time is within the allowable offset of five minutes, Kerberos accepts the message pending one more item.

3. Kerberos checks to see if the time is identical or older than previous authenticators received from the sender. If the time stamp is not later than and not the same as previous authenticators, Kerberos allows the user to authenticate to the domain.

However, it is also important to know that the authentication is *mutual*. Kerberos will send back a message demonstrating that it was able to decrypt the user's message. Kerberos sends back only select information, the most important being the time stamp that it obtained from the original authentication from the client. If that time stamp matches the client's information, then the client is sure that Kerberos, and not an imposter, decrypted the message.

Key Distribution

Authenticating to Kerberos works well for authentication to the domain, but what about accessing resources once the client has logged in? In that Kerberos is used for authenticating to domain resources, how does the client authenticate to other network resources?

Well, Kerberos is able to distribute keys. In other words, it acts as a broker. This, in fact, is where the name Kerberos comes from. In Greek mythology, you may recall that Kerberos was a three-headed dog that stood guard over the gates of Hades. Kerberos, the protocol, also has three heads: the client, the server, and a mediator or proxy. The proxy is known as the Key Distribution Center . . . it dishes out keys. In Windows 2000, the Key Distribution Center is installed on the Active Directory Domain Controller.

Okay, so now you are beginning to think one step ahead here, and you say, "Cool, that whole rigmarole of decrypting the message and checking the time stamps just has to be repeated between clients and servers." And you would be further correct if you assumed that the job of giving the network resources copies of every user's key would be that of the Key Distribution Center. However, you are correct in theory only, because so much key distribution would be a tremendous drain on resources. Every server would have to store keys from potentially thousands of users in memory. What, in fact, is implemented is quite ingenious in its simplicity.

Session Tickets

Instead of following the logical plan and sending the session key to the client and the server at the same time, the KDC in fact sends both copies of the key to the client and then gets out of the way. The client holds the server's copy of the key until it is ready to contact the server, usually within a few milliseconds. The illustration in Figure 3-1 may help you "decrypt" what is going on here.

The KDC invents a session key whenever the client contacts it to access a resource (A). The server sends the session key to the client, and embedded in the session key is the session ticket (B). Embedded in the session ticket, which really belongs to the server, is the server's session key for the client. All that really happens here is that the KDC acts as a domain broker or proxy for secret key negotiations that take place between a client and the resource to which it requires access.

When the client receives the communication from the KDC, it extracts the ticket and its copy of the session key. It stores both items in secure volatile memory. Then, when the client contacts the server (C), it sends the server a message that contains the ticket that is still encrypted with the server's secret key and a time authenticator that is encrypted with the session key. The ticket and the authenticator make up the client's credentials in the same fashion as the logon authentication process.

If everything checks out, the server grants access to the client (D) because the server knows that a trusted authority, the KDC, issued the credentials. As soon as the client is done using the server, the server can get rid of the session key that the client was using to communicate with the server. The client will instead hold the session key and re-present it to the server each time it needs to access it.

Session tickets can also be reused, and as a safeguard against ticket theft, the tickets come with expiration times. The time to live for a ticket is specified in the domain security policy, which is discussed later in this chapter. Typically, ticket life usually lasts about eight hours, the average logon time. When the user logs off, the ticket cache is flushed and all session tickets and keys are discarded.

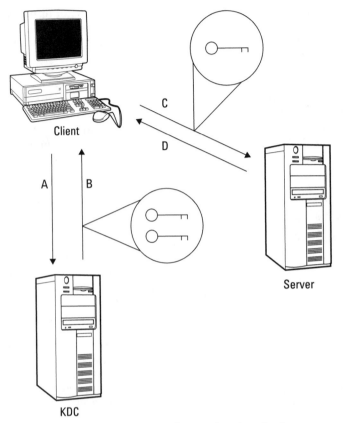

Figure 3-1: Key distribution and mutual authentication

Kerberos and Trusts

Kerberos trusts are made possible by extending the concepts we just discussed beyond domain boundaries. When a trust is established between two domains, which happens automatically between domains that are part of a contiguous namespace (an Active Directory tree), the two domains share an *inter-domain key,* and one KDC becomes the proxy for the other and vice versa.

Once this inter-domain key has been established, the ticket granting service in each domain is registered as a security principal with the other domain's KDC, allowing it to issue ticket referrals. Clients in their home or native domains still contact their local KDCs for access to the foreign resource. The local KDC checks to see that the resource needed by the client resides in another domain. It then sends the client a referral ticket for the resource in the other domain. The client then contacts the other domain's KDC and sends it the referral ticket. The remote KDC authenticates the user or begins a session ticket exchange to allow the client to connect to resources in the remote domain.

Locating KDCs

DNS is the locator service for Kerberos. The governing RFC (1510) specifies how DNS should resolve KDC hosts to IP addresses. Client computers need to send their messages to the IP address. If the IP address of the KDC cannot be resolved, it generates an error message to the client indicating that the domain cannot be located.

In a Windows 2000 domain, the KDC is usually installed on the Active Directory server. They are not connected in terms of application process space and run as separate services. However, since the KDC is always installed on the DC, it is possible to resolve a KDC by looking up the host address of a domain controller.

It is also possible to install Windows 2000 servers in non-Windows 2000 domains, and they can still participate in Kerberos authentication. You will need to ensure that they resolve to the correct host addresses, which will not be to Active Directory domain controllers. The utility called `ksetup.exe` (see Appendix B) is used to configure clients and servers to participate in Kerberos realms that are not Windows 2000 domains.

There is obviously a lot more to Kerberos than what we discussed here, but it exceeds the scope of this book. Numerous books have been written that deal exclusively with the subject. However, Kerberos security is the de facto pervasive security mechanism that protects Windows 2000 domains. Kerberos is a good reason to move to native domains as soon as possible. As ugly as it may sound, the three-headed hound guarding your network is a welcome addition to Windows 2000 domains.

IPSec

IPSec, which is a contraction of IP and Security, is an Internet Protocol (IP) security mechanism employed in Windows 2000 for maximum protection of network traffic. IPSec is mainly used for communication over an insecure IP network. One such network springs to mind — it's called the Internet.

The protection, encryption, is applied at the IP layer and takes place between two computers. The encrypted packets are not filtered in any way by firewalls or routers and simply pass through. It is also thus transparent to the users and applications deployed on either side of the correspondence.

IPSec operates on four levels: encryption and encapsulation, authentication and replay tolerance, key management, and digital signing and digital certificates.

The encryption is also known as *end-to-end,* which means that it remains encrypted en route to the other computer, and it can only be decrypted by the other computer. IPSec also uses public key encryption; however, the shared key is generated at both ends of the encryption, and it is not transmitted over the network.

The IP Encapsulated Security Protocol uses 40/56-bit DES or 112/168-bit DES to encrypt the IP address of the sender along with the datagram. This thwarts attempts to grab the packets in transit between hops and prevents the attacker from learning the source or destination address, which would be required in order to mount an attack. The original packet is also encapsulated in a new packet, along with the contents of the packet and the header information. The packet is still transmitted to the destination IP address, but that is not apparent during transmission.

In order to guarantee data integrity, the secure data encryption algorithm (SHA-1 or MD-5 of RSA) ensures that the data cannot be tampered with en route. This is called IPSec anti-replay. Each datagram is tagged with a sequence number. When the datagram reaches its destination, its sequence number is checked to verify if it falls within the predetermined range. If it does not, the datagram is discarded.

The key management component is supported by the ISAKMP (Internet Security Association Key Management Protocol)/Oakley key management protocol v8 used to enable the use of a single architecture to secure transactions with different vendor products that are IPSec-compliant. The Digital Signature Standard (DSS) and RSA provide the proof of authorship for signatures on digital certificates.

IPSec also supports the ability to import your company's unique x.509 v.3 digital certificate into IPSec-compliant hardware and software. This means that you are essentially integrating IPSec into your Public Key Infrastructure (PKI), which is discussed later in this chapter. The integration between IPSec and PKI provides even stronger network security.

This is how IPSec works:

1. Computer A sends data to computer B across an insecure IP network. Before the transmission begins, an algorithm on A checks to see if the data should be secured according to the security policy established on A. The security policy contains several rules that determine the sensitivity of the communication.

2. If the filter finds a match, A first begins a security-based negotiation with B via a protocol called *Internet Key Exchange (IKE).* The two computers then exchange credentials according to an authentication method specified in the security rule. The authentication methods can be Kerberos, public key certificates, or a predefined key value.

3. Once the negotiations are underway, there are two types of negotiation agreements called *security associations* that are set up between the two computers. The first type is called *Phase I IKE SA,* and it specifies how the two computers are going to trust each other. The second type is an agreement on how the two computers are going to protect an application communication. This is known as *Phase II IPSec Sec Sas,* and it specifies the security methods and keys for each direction of the communication. IKE automatically creates and refreshes a shared secret key for each SA. And the secret key is created independently at both ends without being transmitted across the network.

4. Computer A signs the outbound packets for integrity and also encrypts (or not) the packets according to the methods agreed upon in the earlier negotiation. The packets are then transmitted to B.

5. Computer B checks the packets for integrity and decrypts them if necessary. The data is then transferred up the IP stack to the application in the usual fashion.

Although IPSec was designed to protect data on insecure networks, it can also be deployed on an intranet, especially in light of the widespread implementation of TCP/IP in a Windows 2000 intranet. It has obvious application to protect against many of the threats discussed earlier in this chapter.

However, all encryption carries with it the burden of the actual encryption overhead on CPUs. So you need to test IPSec in various situations before you deploy it.

Note Network Interface Card (NIC) vendors are supporting IPSec, and using a Windows 2000 IPSec driver may go a long way in reducing CPU usage. The idea is much like a hardware-based RAID controller that employs a CPU on the interface card to perform striping, as opposed to giving that burden to the main system CPU.

Like Kerberos, IPSec is managed under group policy, which is discussed extensively in Chapter 11. You define it per site, per domain, or per organizational unit (OU). And it can also be defined for computers that are not affected by domain or OU security policy. Specifically, IPSec can be configured to provide variations of the following services:

✦ You can specify the extent of authentication and confidentiality that will be negotiated between the communicating parties. For example, you can specify the minimum acceptable level of security allowed between clients, which is sending clear text over the network but hiding both sender and receiver information.

✦ You can set policy that communication over certain insecure networks takes place using IPSec, or not at all.

IPSec is discussed later in this chapter in "Security Planning," and in Chapter 11 under Group Policy.

SSL/TLS

Secure Sockets Layer/Transport Layer Security (SSL/TLS) has been around in several Windows NT or BackOffice products for a while. It is a widely supported protocol both on corporate networks and on the Internet. SSL/TLS has been supported in IIS and Exchange.

Windows 2000 uses SSL/TLS and X.509 certificates (discussed next) to authenticate smart card users for network and data protection. SSL/TLS is used to secure a wide range of communications such as network traffic, IIS traffic (Web and FTP), e-mail, and client transactions created in browsers.

Microsoft Certificate Services

There are two levels of public key cryptography at work inside Windows 2000. One level is implicit and expressly built into the operating system. It is at work in Kerberos, IPSec, and the Encrypting File System (EFS), and does not require attention from you, other than some minor configuration management. The second level is explicit. It requires you to build a public key infrastructure to accommodate a pervasive use of public key cryptography throughout the enterprise.

Cross-Reference   See Chapter 21 for a detailed discussion of EFS.

Public Key Infrastructure

A *Public Key Infrastructure* or PKI is a collection of services and components that work together to a common end. It is used to build a secure environment that will allow you to secure e-mail communications both on the intranet and over the Internet, to secure your Web sites and your company's Web-based transactions, to enhance or further protect your Encrypting File System, to deploy smart cards, and more.

A PKI gives you the ability to support the following public key services:

✦ **Key Management:** The PKI issues new keys, reviews or revokes existing keys, and manages the trust levels between other vendors' key issuers.

✦ **Key Publishing:** The PKI provides a systematic means of publishing both valid and invalid keys. Keys can also be revoked if their security is compromised. PKI handles the revocation lists so that applications can determine if a key is no longer to be trusted (akin to the revoked and stolen credit card lists published by the banks for the benefit of merchants).

✦ **Key Usage:** The PKI provides an easy mechanism for applications and users to use keys. Key usage is key (no pun intended) to providing the best possible security for the enterprise.

Digital Certificates

As discussed earlier in this chapter, public keys are packaged in digital certificates. A good example of a digital certificate is the visa you are given by a foreign country permitting access. The visa number is the key; it is what allows you to get into a country and move around. The visa, issued by the country's consulate, and which is usually laminated or expertly printed so that it cannot be tampered with, is the digital certificate, an object of trust that proves that you received the visa or "key" from a trusted authority, in this case the consular general, and that the number is authentic. Although visas can be forged and the authorities are constantly working to come up with better certificates, passport control officers use verification equipment to check on the authenticity of the visa. If a visa is forged, the immigration authority at the port of entry will be able to detect the forgery and deny access. Digital certificates, however, rely on certificate authorities for verification.

But how do you verify a digital certificate? The answer is that a certificate authority (CA), the issuer of your key, or the equivalent of the consular authority in the previous analogy, signs the certificate with its digital signature. You can verify the digital signature with the issuer's public key. But who vouches for the issuer? The answer lies in a *certificate hierarchy,* a system of vouchsafes that extends all the way up to a group of root certificate authorities that have formed an association of vouchsafes. You can obtain the public keys for the CA from Microsoft, but it is all transparently taken care of in Microsoft Certificate Services.

Creating the PKI with Microsoft Certificate Services

A PKI is based on many different services and components all deployed in concert. For example, a Microsoft PKI depends on Active Directory for the publishing of information of issued keys. Also, certificates, revocation lists, and policy information are all stored in the directory. Knowing your directory service thus brings you closer to realizing the reality of the ultimate secured enterprise.

Managing a Microsoft PKI is not difficult and is even less time-consuming than managing users, printers, or the network. Actually, many tasks you perform in your day-to-day activities already encompass management of the PKI. Chapters 11 and 21 will thus offer pointers and guidelines specific to the management of your PKI on Windows 2000.

NTLM

The NT LAN Manager (NTLM) is a legacy protocol that Microsoft has included in Windows 2000 to support legacy Windows clients and servers. We will not be covering NTLM in detail here because our predecessors have published much information on it over the years. Also, NTLM support is not configurable to the degree that Kerberos is, and it does not support transitive trusts and the Single Sign-On initiative.

In Windows 2000, the default authentication and security protocol between Windows 2000 machines is Kerberos. By continuing to support down-level or legacy Windows technology, you obviously leave room for infiltrators to maneuver; but that does not mean NTLM is a weak protocol. After all, it has kept Windows NT networks together for many years and was key to the C2 award earned by the operating system back at version 3.51.

NTLM is omnipresent; it only stops working when the last process that needs it signs off. NTLM will be invoked under the following circumstances:

✦ You have legacy clients and servers that need to log on to the network or locally.

✦ You have UNIX clients that need to continue talking to NT servers.

✦ You have UNIX clients that are using the server message block (SMB) daemon that authenticates to NTLM.

Consider the following strategy for phasing out NTLM:

1. Move your legacy Windows NT and 9*x* clients to Windows 2000. Servers can be upgraded or replaced; clients can also be upgraded to support Kerberos or moved to terminal services (so the clients do not actually log on to the domain from a remote operating system).

2. Configure your UNIX services to authenticate to Windows 2000 domains using Kerberos. Phase out SMB usage.

3. Deploy Microsoft's services for UNIX package.

Smart Cards

A smart card is really dumb looking. It is no bigger than a credit card and is carried around like one. Smart cards work just like ATM cards; you slide the card into a slot, and then you will be prompted for a personal identification number (PIN).

The smart card contains a smart chip that is wafer-thin and embedded in the card. The chip holds a digital certificate, the user's private key, and a load of other information that can be used for Single Sign-On, e-commerce, access control, and data protection and privacy, such as securing e-mail and Web access.

In order to install smart card technology, you must have a public key infrastructure established. You must also install smart card readers, which can be a little expensive, but capitalized over many users, it will pay for itself in TCO and security.

 Note For further information on smart cards and Windows 2000, see the Smart Card White Paper "Smart Cards" at www.microsoft.com/technet/win2000/smtcard. asp. RSA Laboratories at www.rsasecurity.com is also a good starting point for smart card research.

Domains

Let's look at the basics. *Domains,* or network domains, are the logical containers of a network, which controls access to all the resources placed in the custody of a domain. The domain does not exist in the physical sense, yet it is accessible from anywhere in the world if it maintains a portal to the Internet or a remote access service; all you need is a computer and connection to a network or a modem.

A domain means different things to different technology vendors. The term *domain* is not exclusively used by Microsoft. It is used on the Internet and by technologies such as SNA (mainframe protocols and services still believed by many to be superior to the TCP/IP domain).

A domain is a loosely defined term, and it represents a collection of computer and data processing devices and resources collected together under one "roof" or security boundary. For the benefit of new administrators to both Windows NT and Windows 2000, let's look at some basic facts about domains. Undoubtedly, what makes a domain a domain is that it is held together by a security policy that dictates the protection of the resources within the domain.

You gain access to a domain at the application level of the OSI stack. Interactive software to let you manually present credentials to the domain is available on the computer or via a device into which you insert a token for your credentials, such as a smart card or magnetic card.

Domains are held together by *domain controllers*. These controllers are keepers of databases that can authenticate a user by asking him or her or it to verify identity by confirming a password. This is known as *authentication*. The databases in question are the SAM in Windows NT and the Active Directory in Windows 2000.

Logon and Authentication

When you logon to a network, you do not have access to network resources. You simply land in a holding area (for a few milliseconds) before being further authenticated to the network's resources. Logon is much like using the international airport in a country after you've landed from abroad. You get rights of passage around the airport. Heck, you can even spend money on duty-free items, set up a home, get married, and pass out; but that's about all. If you want access to the city, you have to go through passport control and customs.

Windows 2000 Logon

When a user or machine logs onto a domain, he or she or it interacts with a collection of functions that make up the Windows Logon service, better known in development circles as WinLogon. WinLogon is now fully integrated with Kerberos, which provides the initial Single Sign-On architecture now part of Windows 2000.

After the login, the user continues to be attached to the security protocol its client software best understands, which could be Kerberos, NTLM, or Secure Sockets Layer/Transport Layer Security. These protocols transparently move the user's identity around the network.

The authentication model of Windows 2000 is the same as Windows NT and almost every computer system in the world. (Refer to Chapter 10 for a discussion on the Local Security Authority.) But it is not so much the model that causes problems in network security, but the other missing or weak links in the chain.

Bi-factorial and Mono-factorial Authentication

Network login is a *bi-factorial* exercise, meaning that it requires the user or device to present two factors to the authentication mechanisms of the network:

✦ User ID (also known as account name or ID)

✦ Password (or what is also known in the secret service as the "cipher")

Every user ID must have a password. In order for the authentication system to validate the user, it asks for a password, and that is the only way it authenticates. But the authentication is really weak. The authenticator cannot guarantee that the user is in fact the correct user; it could easily be a masquerader pretending to be the user.

Besides the network login (user ID and password), other examples of bi-factorial authentication are ATM cards, smart cards, and the like. The user presents the card and either types in a user ID or a password. Two components have to match to unlock the door. However, it is still not 100 percent secure. ATM cards get stolen, passwords can be discovered, and so forth.

Mono-factorial identification is a far more secure and convenient form of authentication for two reasons:

1. It is more secure. There can be only one.

2. It is more convenient, both for the user and the authenticator.

The bottom line is that the user has to do less work to authenticate; he or she need not remember a password and does not have to type in a user ID. Examples of mono-factorial authentication include fingerprints, retinal scans, and voiceprints. These factors seldom require another factor of identification. A user has only one retinal pattern, voiceprint, and fingerprint in existence. In many cases, the password is not needed because the pattern itself is the cipher, and because it is attached to the user, there is no need to verify the user.

Trusts

For many reasons, it becomes necessary to beget new domains. With Windows NT, big companies spawn domains like frog eggs because they are physically restricted by the technology (the SAM becomes unstable at more than 40MB in size). In Windows 2000, we beget domains to compartmentalize or partition the directory, to represent distributed resources, corporate structure, ease of management (delegation), security, and much more.

It often becomes necessary for resources in one domain, such as users, to access resources in another domain. In order for this to happen, the domains, if "genetically" different, have to set up trust relationships. While domains that share a domain tree trust each other by default, domains on other trees in other forests, non-Windows 2000 domains, and realms from other environments do not, and you have to explicitly set up the trust. A domain that is trusted by another domain is known as a *trusted domain*. The domain that trusts the other domain is known as the *trusting domain*. This policy is the same in Windows NT as it is for Windows 2000.

If the trust is only one-way, we call it a uni-directional or one-way trust. In other words, domain A trusts domain B, but domain B does not trust domain A. This is illustrated in Figure 3-2.

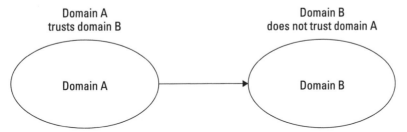

Figure 3-2: Uni-directional trust relationship between two domains

When the feelings of trust are mutual, the trust relationship becomes bi-directional or two-way. Bi-directional trust allows the users or devices in each domain to access resources in each other's domains (Figure 3-3).

Windows NT trusts are limited by the underlying database and security technology, which endows the operating system with a less than suitable "cognitive" ability. In other words, Windows NT domains are always mistrusting, and as such, whenever two domains need to interoperate, explicit trusts must first be set up between them.

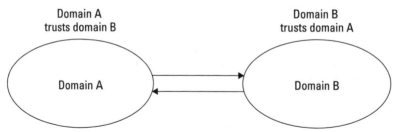

Figure 3-3: Bi-directional trust relationship between two domains

What's more, Windows NT trusts are not transitive, which means that just because Domain A trusts Domain B, and Domain B trusts Domain C, Domain C does not necessarily trust Domain A, or the other way around. This is illustrated in Figure 3-4.

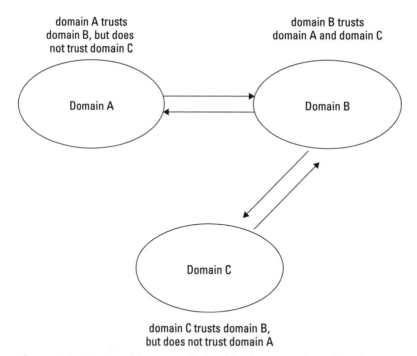

Figure 3-4: Non-transitive trust relationships between three domains

The domain container and security technology of Windows 2000 is very different. Enabled by a robust directory service, a hot security technology, such as the Kerberos v5 protocol, and a powerful policing ability, Windows 2000 domains that are part of the same namespace, or family, and even of the same tree in a forest, implicitly trust each other. Not only are the trusts already implied, but they are also transitive, as illustrated in Figure 3-5.

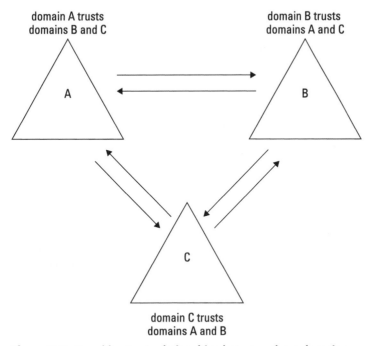

Figure 3-5: Transitive trust relationships between three domains in the same forest

However, domains from one forest do not automatically trust domains from another forest. Let's take the metaphor further. There are several domains in Sherwood Forest. All these domains fall under the auspices of Robin Hood (the root domain in Active Directory). This means that as long as you live in Sherwood Forest, you pledge allegiance to Robin Hood and can visit any domain (access control, however, still applies).

But a domain that is part of another forest in the British countryside is not automatically trusted by Robin Hood's realm, Sherwood Forest. The administrators of both root domains need to get together and formalize a treaty before the two forests and domains will be able to trust each other.

Windows NT does not have a treaty with Windows 2000, partly because it speaks the wrong security language; that is, NTLM. In order for Windows 2000 and Windows NT users to exchange vows, you have to set up a bilateral trust. Windows 2000 will talk to NT using NTLM.

Setting up trusts is awkward, and whenever mistrusting administrators from two domains try and set up trusts, it usually takes an assertive individual to lead the way. But you have to know how to set up trusts between NT and Windows 2000; it is the only way for the two operating systems to coexist, and it is key to any conversion effort. The steps to creating trusts are explained in Chapter 8.

Once authentication is successful, the user or application gains certain default rights to the network and its resources. The next level of protection steps in. It is called Access control.

Access Control

Once a user or device account is authenticated to the domain, it is given permission, through certain default privileges, to network objects. The objects represent files, devices (such as printers and computers), and the file system's structure. In Windows 2000, these objects are stored in the Active Directory and "point" to the actual network location (in Windows NT, they are stored in the SAM portion of the registry).

In order to gain access to an object, the object has an access control list (ACL) associated with it. This access control list is also stored in the directory. An analogy might be to think of your ACL as a bouncer standing at the door to a club. When someone tries to gain entry to the club, the bouncer makes a check on his or her ACL. If the dude is not on the list, entry is denied. The items on the ACL are known as Access Control Entries. You can view the ACL by opening the Security tab on an object's property sheet.

The property sheet lists the users and groups that have access to the object and the level of access they have, such as Read or Write or Execute. ACLs apply only to Security Principals — that is, user accounts, computer accounts, and security groups (as opposed to distribution groups). Security principals and ACLs are further discussed in Chapter 10.

Auditing

The word *auditing* strikes fear into the hearts of everyone. Even if you have nothing to fear, auditing is an ominous idea, a prying into your every move. But auditing is not only a practice defined within a security context, it is also an essential practice in troubleshooting and problem solving. An audit trail, a requirement for C2 security compliance, can not only lead you to the wolf's den, it can also lead you to a solution to a problem that was impacting network resources or causing users grief.

Auditing leaves a trail that you can follow to see what was done or attempted by network objects. If the network object has a user name attached to it, then your audit trail will be a history of what was attempted by whom.

A good example of an audit trail is on the RAS. When a user calls to say he or she cannot logon to the network remotely, you can check the audit logs and trace his or her attempts by searching for information related to his or her user ID. The audit trail will then tell you why the person was rejected and give you a possible remedy.

Auditing of objects is not enabled by default. It has to be enabled and applied to the object. Auditing is discussed in depth in Chapter 19.

Security Planning

Before you go jumping up and down shouting, "Whoop, whoop, IPSec, PKI, SSL, way to go!" you should know that unless you are running a native Windows 2000 network, you will not realize the full potential many of these protocols have to offer.

Windows 2000 security is also so extensive that it is possible to get bamboozled in your efforts to provide the *ultimate* security. As you learn more about the capabilities of Windows 2000, you'll discover that the adage "less is more" applies to many Windows 2000 Server components in general and Windows 2000 security in particular. The subject of security planning is therefore coupled to the subject of planning for Windows 2000 in general and is discussed in the next chapter.

Summary

This chapter provided an overview of the key security protocols and mechanisms available in Windows 2000. Perhaps no other subject related to networking is as important as security. You can offer your users all manner of features and performance, integrate to perfection (almost), and maintain a server room that hums like a Rolls Royce engine. But even the tiniest security breach can scuttle the entire boat.

The external environment of an enterprise is like an ocean of pressure, pushing and pushing until the rivets of your ship pop. Before you can plan your security strategy, you should first try to understand the technology that is at work in the Windows 2000 security subsystems.

In particular, this chapter covered security threats and risks, cryptography, the new authentication protocols, and the Microsoft certificate services, which are used to build a public key infrastructure to serve your enterprise.

Part II now takes you into planning for Windows 2000 Server, installing and configuration.

✦　　✦　　✦

Planning, Installation, and Configuration

We do not believe in "winging" a Windows 2000 installation, and therefore we stress the need for testing and planning. The chapters that follow here present strategies for evaluation, installation, deployment, and configuration. These chapters are the culmination of literally thousands of hours setting up and installing Windows 2000 on a myriad of machines, from the likes of Compaq, IBM, Dell, Hewlett Packard, and a few clones knocked together by the lab team.

Chapter 4 stresses the importance of testing and pilot projects. It goes into setting up a lab, communicating with management and obtaining the budget, formulating blueprints, and other topics. Chapter 4 also presents an outline for developing a rollout plan for new services. We also cover conversion strategies for integrating into Windows NT infrastructures.

Installation is covered in Chapter 5. This chapter explores the various services that can be installed on Windows 2000, machine configurations, hardware limitations, memory and processor requirements, and so on. This chapter is essential before you install Windows 2000 on any machine, no matter the service.

The Microsoft Management Console and the numerous applets and utilities in the Control Panel are explored in Chapter 6. Here we show you how to work with the Microsoft Management Console and how to configure the various snap-ins.

Planning for Windows 2000 Server

No matter how small your network or your needs, you should not install Windows 2000 without preparing an implementation and deployment plan. This chapter covers planning for Windows 2000 Server and takes you through the steps required to formulate and execute a deployment plan.

Steps to Implementation

Many of you are probably following the advice of your peers: Microsoft should release the first service pack or two to Windows 2000 before you touch it. Here's your wake-up call: You need to install Windows 2000 Server now. Not after one or two service packs. Now. Are we paid Microsoft supporters? No. We just want to make sure you get on the train when it stops at your station.

By "now," we do not mean you have to rush out and install it in a production environment. But you have to start testing now, understanding now, and learning now. You have to plan for Windows 2000 Server, and this advice is aimed at not only the multi-national company with 432,981 employees in 65 countries, but also at the single-person company that you'll find around the next corner.

Why the rush? Windows 2000 Server is a shocker. It is more stable at release time than NT 4.0 was, and in many cases, even without its advanced functionality, it is preferable to install Windows 2000 than Windows NT 4.0. It is not only years ahead of its time, it is also more stable without its first service pack than Windows NT 4.0 at service pack 5.0 and higher. However, there is something else you need to know. Don't be fooled into thinking that the competition, even another department in your company, is adopting the wait-and-see position.

Windows 2000 provides such a huge competitive advantage, when wisely adopted, that the early implementers could end up well ahead of you and their competition: on the Web, in office productivity, in security, in lowering TCO, in administration, and more. In fact, we have recently talked to administrators who are choosing companies they would like to work for based on their early adoption of Windows 2000.

Got the message? So if you are wondering, "Where do I begin?" this is the chapter that takes you down the Yellow Brick Road. Put your worries and neuroses behind you and get cracking.

Formulate a Plan

The first step you need to take is to formulate a plan of attack. You can be very scientific about your planning for Windows 2000 Server, and you can also overdo it. We urge you to keep the planning simple. The cliché that works for Windows 2000 Server is to make sure you can see all the trees *and* all the forests. If you already have a well-organized domain, you have lots of time; Windows 2000 is not going away.

You must come up with a formal document for management, proposing a project to evaluate and plan an upgrade or conversion to Windows 2000 Server. If you take the CEO or CTO a 1,200-page tome, he or she will freak out. Managers will want to know how Windows 2000 Server is going to save them money, make them more competitive, and keep them secure. Most executives need nothing more than an executive summary with which to begin.

Note   **Migrate.** This is the first and the last time you will see the term *migrate* in this book because it is a misnomer when referring to moving to Windows 2000 Server. We don't want you to use it because it has negative connotations. Migrating implies that you can go back to where you came from. Migrating is not possible with Windows 2000. If you're trying to go back, then you're in disaster recovery mode. Your domains can coexist, which most of you will be doing for a while, and you *will* convert. But if you follow the advice in this book and in the next few chapters in particular, you will not have to climb down from Windows 2000 and reinstall Windows NT.

If you think we are playing petty semantics, you are wrong. In many languages and cultures, migration is a temporary thing. Once you convert your last Windows NT Domain Controller, there is no reversion; you are done . . . dead or alive.

There are many ways to approach a project and a plan. And we do not intend to teach project science here, so whatever works for you, or is required by your organization, is fine with us. We are not going to offer you the best way to approach the conversion. We will give you some pointers culled from many years of doing needs analyses and syntheses.

Tip   It is important that in the early days of the planning and testing phase, you only choose a handful of energetic people to evaluate Windows 2000 Server. You don't want too many people doing their own thing and becoming unproductive and uncoordinated. In the beginning, there will be little time for managing all the egos and eager beavers. If too many people join the project or you have subsidiaries and divisions setting up their own projects, the company on the whole will lose out because you'll end up with disjointed installations everywhere and the project will drown under the weight of everyone's two ounces of input. Incidentally, there were five people involved in the Windows 2000 development project that this book is based on. Three were employed almost full-time in lab work.

The following is a suggested plan of attack. It is the one we followed when testing Windows 2000 Server for this book, and it is the plan we used to evaluate Windows 2000 for our own customers, clients, and companies, from our six-person insurance company to our huge multi-national distributors. Like you, back in early 1999, we knew very little about Windows 2000. We were too busy keeping our NT networks in check. Our respective clients wanted to wait until late 2000 before considering Windows 2000 . . . and then everyone changed their minds when they started seeing the fruits of our labor.

Phased Implementation

Phased implementation is a big phrase that represents a logical course to completing a difficult transition from one state to another. In the example here, our objectives are to move from state zero (no Windows 2000 Server) to tests in the lab, pilot project, conversion, and rollout. Depending on the nature of the implementation and your objectives, your project phases may vary or be very different from ours. Each phase may itself become highly nested with sub-phases, milestones and sanity checks.

Phased implementation allows us to stop at checkpoints along the way, assess results, and make changes, as required. Our Windows 2000 Server project consisted of several phases, illustrated in Figure 4-1. Some phases overlap and others are ongoing.

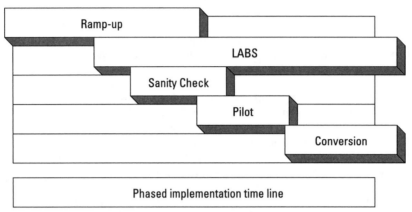

Figure 4-1: Phase implementation plan (drawing of plan)

There are also several steps within each phase. The conversion step is in itself a phased-implementation effort. However, take care not to over-nest your project with too many phases. Our suggested phase-implementation structure is as follows:

✦ Phase 1: Analysis and Ramp-up

✦ Phase 2: Labs

✦ Phase 3: Sanity Check

✦ Phase 4: Pilot

✦ Phase 5: Conversion

Here are the suggested steps that span all five phases, outlined in Table 4-1:

Table 4-1
Planning Steps

Phase	Step
Phase 1	Step 1: Establish a Timeline for Your Project
Phase 1	Step 2: Understand the Technology
Phase 1	Step 3: Understand How Your Enterprise is Currently Positioned
Phase 1	Step 4: Establish Budget
Phase 2	Step 5: Create the Lab

Phase	Step
Phase 2	Step 6: Design the Logical and Physical Structures
Phase 2	Step 7: Secure the Lab
Phase 2	Step 8: Test
Phase 2	Step 9: Position the Enterprise on Windows 2000 (Gap Analysis)
Phase 3	Step 10: Evaluate
Phase 4	Step 11: Create Pilot Projects
Phase 5	Step 12: Begin Conversions

Step 1: Timelines

Establish a timeline for your project. For the record, plan on at least six months for a team of about three people. The ideal length of time from assessment to rollout will be about 40 weeks. And that should cover everything to integrate or infiltrate Windows 2000 into core functions of your IT and telecom structures.

Note You might get away with a shorter timeline for a small company using Win32-compliant software or proven or ironed-out IT processes. By small, we are referring to not more than 20 people. Just because a company is small does not mean it is not performing mission-critical work comparable to a unit in a Fortune 500 company. Remember, if a unit in a large company goes offline for a few days, it might hardly be noticed. Take a small company offline for a few days, and it could go insolvent.

It will take a large company about two years to completely convert to a Windows 2000 Server, and Microsoft concurs. Smaller companies will require less time, but no less than 24 weeks. You may be able to rush it, but you'll be studying every day, seven days a week. You could also take classes and do an MSCE in the middle, but that would not get you anywhere faster. An MCSE is a good idea in parallel with this project, but take classes so you can interact with your instructors and clarify sticking points.

Step 2: Understand the Technology

If you have Windows NT experience, you can draw on that, and you can draw on any general IT/IS experience you have, but for the most part, you'll be learning a lot of new stuff. It is also not sufficient to say you now know all there is to know about Windows 2000 after six months of shining a flashlight under the covers; that's impossible, but it is vital that you understand the technology, what Windows 2000 is, and how it achieves its objectives.

Prerequisites

Windows 2000 architecture is highly complex. Our joke is "ZAW = Zero Administrators for Windows." Key to understanding the technology is having a good grounding in general computer science and network engineering, but be willing to specialize. You are going to need expertise on your team, and the members of the team should be prepared to show proficiency in several IT areas.

They will need a complete understanding and experience in all of the following: TCP/IP, DNS, WINS, DHCP, Server Hardware Platforms, Storage, Windows NT Server administration and deployment experience, NT and Windows *9x* workstation experience, Internet practices, and tons more.

After you have established the timelines and have picked a team of experts, you need to spend no less than two months, possibly four, understanding everything about the technology and the architecture, Active Directory (six to eight weeks). Trust us, we work with engineers all day long, and they are very good at what they do, but on some Windows 2000 subjects, they still have to scratch their heads.

Where do you start?

Besides this book to break ground, the best place to start is the Microsoft Web site. There are tons of white papers there and documents that will get you started on both the easy and difficult stuff. The Deployment planning guide in the Windows 2000 Resource Kit is also a worthwhile document to read, as long as you have lots of Alka-Seltzer handy.

Avoid books that are nothing but a rehash of the Windows 2000 Help Files. They may have worked in the past. But not only are the Help Files very thorough, they are also "mind-blowingly" vast, covering many different functions and features of the server. And, before you interject, you can take them "anywhere" you can take this book . . . on your Windows Pocket PC or CE handheld, which puts you directly on the server, as Chapter 25 explains.

Also avoid books that attempt to teach you about subjects not really germane to Windows 2000 Server or that have been covered more times than the Oscars. For example, you won't find instructions on how to format a hard disk in this book, or what constitutes an IP address, or a crash course on HTML. If you don't already know this stuff, you're not qualified to be involved in planning for and installing Windows 2000 Server.

You will also need new equipment, but more about that later. For the first few weeks, you need to read, read, read. There are going to be payoffs. You'll find that people caught off guard will start turning to you in desperate need of help to understand a complex Windows 2000 issue. Your peers who scoffed when you plastered your office with thousands of Windows 2000 white papers won't be laughing now.

Step 3: Understand How Your Enterprise Is Positioned to Exploit Windows 2000 Server

We know this is difficult to do in the early stages of the project, but it is very important to prepare yourself to take your early findings to management. Although many projects are sanctioned or sponsored by people high up in the management channels, unless you come up with specific reasons to make changes to or enhance the existing IT infrastructure, your project may come to an abrupt end.

No matter how big or small the organization, change is always difficult, and there is the risk of business or work stoppages resulting from unanticipated events that result directly from your conversion attempts. Believe it or not, many companies are doing just fine on Windows NT.

Management, especially the CIO/CTO or MIS, is focused on keeping the business systems running. Without the systems, the business fails. Nine times out of ten, most senior executives will cite the "wait until service pack 1" rule. Your job is to convince them to start testing now and then to get the initial sponsorship and budget for the project. And the only way to do that is to become an informed evangelist in less than two full moons.

Step 4: Establish Budget

You'll need several stages of financing for your project, so think like an entrepreneur. The early stages can probably be catered to out of existing equipment, unused servers, hard disks, and so on. If you don't have surplus hardware, you'll need to get a few servers. And we don't need to tell you that the best means of providing servers for a project like this is to buy the pieces and assemble the hardware in your lab. You'll not only learn about Windows 2000 hardware compatibility, but you'll end up saving a lot of money in the early stages.

Caution Older brand servers are as risky for Windows 2000 (if not more so) than flea market finds. We battled one failed installation for this book, discussed in Chapter 5.

Step 5: Create a Lab

With your initial budget, you need to set up a lab. This should be a secure area where you can set up a number of servers, workstations, printers, and a slew of network components, such as routers and hubs. Depending on the size of your organization and the project, you will want your lab to emulate an enterprise-wide domain structure, both physical and logical. In which case, you'll need to set up several domain controllers, role servers like DNS and DHCP, and so on.

Obtain a space in which you can comfortably fit about 12 full-tower servers and all collateral network equipment and printers. You might get away with a lot less, and you might need a lot more. One company we know built a test domain complete with domain controllers for 24 remote centers — that's 24 domain controllers. Follow Chapter 5 for specifics on installing the servers.

Step 6: Design the Logical and Physical Structures

Once you have a budget and you are ramped up on the technology, you can begin designing your logical and physical domain structures in the lab. You will need to set up key role servers such as domain controllers, certificate servers, license servers, DNS, and so on. In the next chapter, we discuss issues directly related to the domain controllers and role servers. The logical and physical designs are discussed in Part III, Active Directory Services.

Step 7: Secure the Lab

Pay particular attention to security during all phases of the test project. In other words, experiment with various levels of encryption and security practice (such as using smart cards). You will also be setting up initial user accounts for your administrators and a selection of mock users for your organizational units (OUs) and groups in Active Directory.

Step 8: Test

After you have designed and created a logical and physical structure and applied security, it is time to test. You will be testing authentication, policies, DNS, WINS, DHCP, storage, files and folder access, and so on. During your tests, you should also pay attention to the position your enterprise is currently in. Moving directly from Step 8 to Step 9 will allow you to perform insightful gap analysis. Gap analysis is used to determine the technology gap between the company of the present and the company of the future.

Step 9: Position the Enterprise on Windows 2000 Server

During your test project and lab work, you need to assess the position your organization now finds itself in and the position it can be in during and after conversion. Also, list all the situations the company would not like to be in during and after the conversion and phased implementation. The first situation we would not like to be in that comes to mind is being offline; another is being up but finding that users have lost access to their resources. This is discussed a little more, later in this chapter.

Step 10: Evaluate

You need to stop at predetermined intervals or milestones along the way for sanity checks and to evaluate how far you have come, how far you have to go, deadlines that may have been missed, and other problems. Towards the end of the project, you will need to make the decision with your sponsors and management to move forward with a test or pilot project in which you will be deploying servers in production environments.

Step 11: Create Pilot Projects

The pilot projects can take on many forms. They could be limited to the installation of a role server, many role servers, the beginnings of Active Directory in the organization, and more. More on this in a later section.

Step 12: Begin Conversions

On the basis of successful pilot projects, you will be able, with the blessings of management or your own confidence, to move forward with rollout and conversion. Our strategy for a phased implementation is discussed shortly.

 Tip   There is a lot of material floating around that covers planning. The material in the Windows 2000 Deployment Planning Guide is extensive. However, we found it too detailed in parts and too verbose for the majority of installations. Many sections call for teams of experts (a way of picking up the fallout from defunct Y2K projects?) that most companies would not be able to afford. Indeed, a team of such experts, even for a month, would be beyond the budgets of all but a few companies.

The previous steps are a starting point, something on which you can build. The following planning guide worked for us, suited our environment, and is based on many projects that came before Windows 2000. Each step along the way was fully documented and evaluated. Indeed, you are holding much of the research and lab work we did between these covers. Now let's kick our implementation into high gear.

Analysis and Ramp-up

There is a huge difference between learning about Windows 2000 Server and understanding what the technology means for the enterprise, and, as components of Phase 1 described earlier, analysis and ramp-up set out to achieve both in logical order. We touched on this a little earlier in this chapter, and in Chapter 1, where we placed Windows 2000 Server in the middle of Microsoft's architectural feast. Your planning efforts should thus be based on the following objectives:

1. Understanding how to use the technology
2. Installing and deploying Windows 2000 Server with that knowledge

Understanding the Technology

Only after you have a thorough understanding of the technology and the architecture will you be in a position to determine the benefits for the enterprise. Granted, you may have heard how wonderful Active Directory is. But you have probably heard rumors that it is "overkill for a small company." How do you know if that statement is invalid until you fully understand how Active Directory works and what it can do for your company, no matter what the size? Just because Active Directory can hold a billion objects does not mean it should not hold a hundred. It is also important to understand the various services that play domain roles. Official documentation, for example, refers to three roles a server can play. The server can be any of the following, and it is important to *understand* the differences:

1. A Windows 2000 server can be a *standalone* server, which means that it is not joined to any domain and stands alone in its own workspace. Understanding how this server interacts or participates on the network will provide you with the information you need to assess needs and cater to them with the establishment of standalone servers. A standalone server, for example, is an ideal bastion. And it can be used as a firewall or proxy server without having to be part of a domain. A certificate server, established for a public key infrastructure (PKI), is a good example of a standalone server.

   There are millions of Windows NT and 2000 servers on the Internet, and they are not part of any Windows domains. The machine is thus more secure as a standalone server than as a member server because standalone servers are not given domain accounts nor are they authenticated on the domain. They can also be print servers, and so on, but their resources cannot be published in Active Directory, short of mapping them to IP addresses (see Chapter 23).

 Tip   If you are in a hurry to install Windows 2000 Server, do not try to join it to any domain or promote it to a domain controller. Make it a standalone server that logs into its own workgroup.

2. Windows 2000 can be a *member* server, which means that it has an account in the domain. Now, that account can be in a Windows NT domain or a Windows 2000 domain. As long as it is a member server, you can access its resources via the authentication mechanisms of Windows NT and the NTLM authentication service (see Chapter 3), or via Kerberos on a Windows 2000 network. This means that the Windows 2000 member server can play certain worthwhile roles in an NT domain. We will discuss such roles shortly.

3. A *domain controller* loads the Active Directory support infrastructure. You can install a Windows 2000 domain controller when you are ready to begin learning about Active Directory, or when you are building your test domains in the lab. You can also install a Windows 2000 domain controller server into a Windows NT domain.

Good examples of understanding the technology are coming to the conclusion that Windows 2000 Server-DNS, Windows 2000 Server-WINS, and Windows 2000 Server-DHCP are ideal role servers to install in the existing environment, be it Windows NT or something else . . . and figuring out how to integrate them. In fact, this is the design technique that forms the basis of our evangelism in this book in general, and in Parts II and III in particular.

We call this technique "conversion by subversion." Sun Tzu would be proud. The process is straightforward:

1. Target the service that can be overthrown.
2. Move the role server into a position where it can perform the role of the target.
3. Take over the role.
4. Shut down the subverted server.

Let's look at this concept more closely. Take WINS. On NT, it's a stinker; causing more headaches for every new segment you have to roll out. Let's face it: It is a Band-Aid for a service that was not meant to be used the way it is being used, and we are talking about NetBIOS.

After years of complaints from thousands of IT managers, Microsoft has rolled out a new WINS. Managed behind the MMC, it's a new wave for a service that will not last more than a few more years.

We have zoomed in on all of the WINS servers at one of our clients (19 servers to be precise). That's 19 targets to take over. After tests proved that the Windows 2000 WINS servers would work well in their new environments, we began a conversion project to take the legacy servers out one by one. Why were we able to deploy in this fashion? Because WINS 2000 is not for pure Windows 2000 . . . it's for Windows NT, Windows 9*x,* and clients needed to resolve NetBIOS names to IP addresses (see Chapters 12 and 14).

Focus on Capabilities, Not Features

We take this understanding philosophy further and implore you to focus on capabilities as opposed to features. If you focus on features, you lose sight of your enterprise needs and become a royal pain to everyone on your team. Rather than coming up with "did you know...?" lines day in and day out, focus on, for example, why WINS 2000 should be implemented now, because it supports persistent connections.

If you support a large WAN with multiple sites, you'll be glad to know that your days of endless forced replicating between "sterile" WINS servers is over. Does this mean much for the enterprise? It does if your sites are interconnected over low bandwidth

WAN (56K circuits). It does not take much to fix broken WINS server services using the old WINS. But when users call because they cannot find their network shares and when automatic file transfers fail, WINS 2000 may be one of the first new servers you try to get into production and deployment, as we earlier explained.

Needs Analyses-Needs Syntheses

A needs analysis or need synthesis is a study of the needs of an enterprise for certain technology or solutions. This can and should be done during the planning phase and before testing efforts and pilot projects are complete. This is your opportunity to "sell" Windows 2000 Server to your enterprise.

Here is a good example of a needs synthesis. One of our clients is a large multinational that is about to embark on the complex process of merging the IT departments of two recent acquisitions into its own IT infrastructure. Mergers and acquisitions can collapse if IT cannot get it right, and merging the network infrastructures and domains of once-competing companies can cause your cholesterol levels to skyrocket.

For the foreseeable future, at least two years, the companies will have to operate as separate entities while IT converts key services and infrastructure into the acquiring, now parent, corporation.

Between the three companies, there are 9,000 employees. Each company has a collection of Windows NT domains. The domains between the three companies number about 45, many still from earlier acquisitions, and acquisitions of acquisitions, and all 45 need to be managed holistically. Many of the domains are NT account domains, collectively containing some 13,622 accounts. This is a daunting task. For starters, under Windows NT all the domains interconnect over a large WAN and thus all need to be related to each other with complex Windows NT domain bi- and uni-directional trusts.

Investigating the processes shows that several thousand folders need to be also shared between the entities. One of the biggest problems anticipated by all is the translocation of key employees, many of them from their old company to the new HQ. The translocated employees need to be given new user IDs and be able to log on to the new "HQDOMAIN." However, they still need access to their old folders and shares back at the old offices where they logged in (for example, EXDOMAIN).

This means that administrators from both domains will have to cooperate, long distance, to make the resources available to the users. The effort is made much more difficult because the administrators from the acquired domains do not trust their peers. So administrators in HQDOMAIN have to create user groups for the translocated souls, and the administrators from the old domains have to implicitly add the new groups to the resources, such as groups that need access to share-points.

The needs synthesis shows how Active Directory should be used to consolidate the file and folder resources and make them easier to access in a Windows 2000 domain hierarchy. This means that folders would be published in Active Directory and made available to the users no matter where they log on.

The project, as you can imagine, is extensive. So between now and Part III in this book, take some time to ponder how you would go about such a project, and where you would start.

Do Not Overlook Your Present Needs

It is important while planning that you do not lose focus of what brings in the bread and butter today. Many companies are so busy with current projects that they cannot spare anyone to work on a Windows 2000 Server planning project.

This can be either a minus or a plus, depending on your circumstances. The previous example in the needs synthesis indicates how Windows 2000 can cater to present needs. On the other hand, you should not suggest or deploy Windows 2000 without first ensuring that you are not risking present systems; your lab work and pilot projects will ensure that.

Assess Your Future Needs

Looking to the future will help you and the team, and especially the managers who need to come up with the money, understand where Windows 2000 technology will come in. If you can show, as we did in the previous needs synthesis, that investing in Active Directory will cut six to eight months off the merger process, you will make a lot of people sit up and take notice. If you can show how much you will save, and how you will pave the way for the next big acquisition, which is expected to add another thousand accounts to the absorption process, you will probably get double the funding you need to take your project to the next level.

Assess Your Strengths and Weaknesses

We cannot stress how important it is to assess your strengths and weaknesses before you take your planning project to the second phase. This assessment must be done on several levels, specifically:

- ✦ Support from management
- ✦ Available funds
- ✦ Available time
- ✦ Material resources

✦ Human resources

✦ Technical expertise

✦ Network infrastructure

✦ Technology or systems already in place

✦ Direction of the company

✦ What the competition is doing

Support from management

Without champions, you're dead. In one company, we know the project was blocked from higher up because of the investment in Novell Directory Services (NDS). Don't take that the wrong way. NDS has been out there a lot longer than Active Directory and is a fine product, but the company was not willing to change to Active Directory in the middle of an NDS rollout. In such a case, it would be prudent not to focus on competing technology, but to get support for other services, such as printing support, IIS, DNS, telephony, media, and so on (remember, conversion by subversion).

See Chapters 2 and 7 for information on the coexistence of NDS with Active Directory in particular, and about meta-directories in general.

Available funds

Microsoft has made Windows 2000 available for 120-day trials. We do not believe that this is sufficient time for a comprehensive project. Many companies we know have unused Windows NT 3.5 and 4.0 licenses lying around. If you need more time, a cost-effective option is to buy the Windows 2000 Server upgrade. Installing the upgrade, even on a virgin machine, is a painless process, as we explain in Chapter 5, as long as you have the original CDs.

You still have to invest in servers, hardware, and time. Make a list of everything you need and then estimate costs. Then ask management for twice the amount of money and work backward from there. Having money left over is far better than having to go back to management for another shot in the arm.

You may think this is "seat-of-the-pants" budgeting, and it is, but given that IT people can be terrible at costing and that you need to cater to unknowns, you must take care not to underestimate, even if you think it will all go smoothly. After all, even though Windows 2000 seems ahead of its time . . . Microsoft did promise it several years ago.

Also, if you are struggling with budget and need to buy a few months, consider making the leap to terminal services as opposed to buying Windows 2000 Professional. Microsoft gives you three months to deploy an application server before enforcing its licensing restrictions. See Chapter 25.

Available time

Be sure you have the time to be involved in such a project. If you are planning a comprehensive technology assessment, test lab, pilot project, the whole thing, then nothing short of full-time and a team of several souls will do. Work out how much time you need to complete the job, then double that and work backward from there. We understand this might not be realistic for many companies and individuals that often wish they could multithread all the work processes they have.

Material resources

You need space, a test lab, hub space, rack space, monitors, storage, workbenches, tape backup units, cartridges, CD burners (for cutting auto installation CDs), and so on. Many companies have a lot of stuff lying around, so before you put pencil to paper to get a budget, first see how much can be "borrowed" from the other departments or divisions.

You may still have to invest in new hardware, however, because Windows 2000 exploits new hardware services the major manufacturers are bringing out on their new platforms. These include Plug and Play, Advanced Configuration and Power Interface (ACPI), and the Boot Information Negotiation Layer (BINL), which is the service that enables remote booting.

Human resources

You cannot hope to complete a full-scale Windows 2000 Server test or planning project on your own. This is tough on smaller companies that do not have many employees to spare, and trust us, the MSCE on Windows 2000 will not prepare you sufficiently to convert a considerable infrastructure. You need hands on, all the time. Microsoft invested millions of person-hours on Windows 2000. Also, do not forget to allow for time off, sick leave, and so on.

Technical expertise

This is not the same as the previous (HR). Our projects would have traveled a lot faster had several peer technicians been available. For example, the mainframe and mid-range integration efforts had to be pushed back because people were tied up in Y2K efforts.

Network infrastructure

This one can be tough. Collateral operating systems, protocols, topology, legacy applications, and legacy Windows (there are still many copies of Windows 3.11 in use) will all have an impact on the design process. Your enterprise and gap analyses will need to "discover" all the components. For example, a so-called barrier to entry is the steep learning curve of DNS for many administrators who have never needed to touch it before.

If you support a highly complex network infrastructure, you should use products like Microsoft System Management Server (SMS) to help you discover what you have. If you have not worked with discovery tools, you need to factor in ramp-up time and learning curve to learn how to use such productivity or administration tools. By the time you are finished, you'll have an equation not even Pierre de Fermat can solve.

And now for some words on Windows domains: Windows NT domains are not easily merged into Windows 2000 domains. Due to the limitations of the earlier technology, many companies were forced to create several domains to avoid blowing up the SAM database. You might be tempted to upgrade the Windows NT domain to an Active Directory domain, but it is not an easy process and is risky because the NT domain controller is converted to an Active Directory domain controller and just not simply copied.

We have mixed sentiments about the conversion of Windows NT domain controllers (PDCs and BDCs) to Windows 2000, and we believe Microsoft should have provided more tools to import accounts to the Active Directory, as opposed to converting the whole primary domain controller. We go into this in some depth in Chapters 5 and 9, where you benefit from a first-hand account of a disastrous PDC conversion.

If you have large and complex domains, you should explore using ADSI (Active Directory Services Interface) to programmatically copy user accounts to the Windows 2000 domain. Your user accounts can be exported from the SAM database and then imported to Active Directory. You can also build a simple tool, using Microsoft's database technologies, such as the Active Data Objects (ADO) and the Active Directory OLEDB service provider to perform your import. This is much harder than it looks, especially if your network administrators do not write software, and most don't.

Regardless of how you plan to transfer user accounts to Active Directory from NT 4.0 domains, there is no getting away from the amount of work it will be. Thus, you should plan now with Active Directory in mind, even if your conversion project will only begin a year down the road.

If you have investigated Active Directory really well, you will notice that many attributes or properties of the user account objects are very different from the attributes of user accounts in NT (meaning all versions of NT). NT user accounts, for example, do not contain attributes for new services such as Terminals Services sessions, or new fields for properties such as User Principal Names (UPNs); and home directories, policies, profiles, and passwords are all radically different in Active Directory. You thus need to consider if your NT domain should be phased over, rather than converted by the promotion of the domain controller. While conversion may appear to be more desirable, there are caveats.

Many NT domains are a mess. They have thousands of accounts in them that are dormant, dead, or disabled, and which should have been deleted and purged from the SAM in the last millennium. At one client, for example, generations of administrators failed to stick to procedure and policy. And the domain had accounts created according to combinations of *firstname, lastname,* or *lastname, firstname,* or contractions, middle initials, and so on. We deemed it better to put the domain "down" than lose sleep . . .

It therefore may pay to start from scratch when creating user accounts in Active Directory because you may just end up with a huge list of user accounts that still require individual attention or may give you further headaches. Of course, you need to properly plan the installation of a parallel domain structure.

We, in fact, have declared several large clients we surveyed for Windows 2000 and Active Directory as "non-convertible." And we would rather walk away from the business than attempt the impossible (discussed further in Chapter 5).

Caution   If a small client does not have a BDC, and many do not, then do not under any circumstances attempt to promote or convert the domain controller unless you are sure you can restore, quickly, a failed conversion. If you find yourself faced with such a scenario, you have three choices: 1) Bring in a new machine and establish a BDC, 2) Bring in a new machine to be the Windows 2000 domain controller, or 3) Do nothing. As discussed in Chapter 5, we rate creating a DC from scratch to be the most logical choice in many situations.

Chapter 9, which deals with the installation and deployment of Active Directory, also provides guidelines for the domain conversion process. We have been to the "Promised Land," and we have returned empty-handed. The only way some of our Windows NT domains are going to be converted is to infiltrate the Active Directory domain controller into the user environment, and gradually, organizational unit by organizational unit, convert the users.

Tip   Microsoft has promised to deliver tools that help speed up the conversion process. But that does not mean you still do not have to manually clean up the accounts.

Technology or systems in place

This is closely related to the previous factor, but existing systems may not be flexible. At one client, for example, we were unable to move a certain application because it depended on Pathworks, Digital Equipment's protocol suite for VMS networks (now part of Compaq), to connect to the NT share-point, and the replacement that worked on TCP/IP was not ready. We had to wait for ten months for the replacement.

Direction of the company

You will need to do things like enterprise analysis (covered in Chapter 7), gap analysis, and needs syntheses. Chapter 7 delves into company types and philosophy, and what drives management. If you work for a progressive company or one that is driven by change, you will encounter a lot of support for the new era. If your company is stagnant or wavering, you might have to live with the status quo.

What the competition is doing

This is difficult to assess for obvious reasons. However, larger companies like to boast about their projects, and finding out that your competition is rolling out Windows 2000 Server *en masse* will either prompt you or your management to get moving or to defect.

Assessing the Risks

Document and fully understand the risks involved in conversion. Risk analysis will be more a factor in the pilot phase and the conversion or roll-out phase than in the lab or test phase. Before components of the project are ready to come out of the sandbox, make sure you have done your homework and that a disaster is not about to happen. Make a list of all the possible things that can go wrong; from systems being denied access to critical shares to users not being able to log in. Always have a counterattack ready. Have your logistics ready. Understand and identify the risks, and then decide if you are ready for anything.

Labs

This section comprises the components of Phase 2, which, in a sense, were launched in Phase 1. You no doubt managed to secure some space at the office or perhaps the company penthouse, and then began tinkering around with Windows 2000 Server on some old beat-up Pentiums. If you have not touched the W2K CD yet, then you are not ready to begin lab work. You should ramp-up with the other chapters and Windows 2000 documentation before you start any lab work, but please read on for reference only.

Note   The next chapter, Installing Windows 2000 Server, also caters to the ramp-up phase, the lab phase, and the pilot phase.

You cannot consider yourself ready to begin designing and testing until you have logged a hundred or more hours of study. And then not until you have installed role servers at least ten times, installed and trashed Active Directory at least eight times, stayed up until the wee hours trying to install over the network, created boot disks, cut unattended install CDs, and so on . . . all dozens of times.

The how-to material and extensive Help files on Windows 2000 have a point of diminishing return. You can't read all of the information, but you have to start somewhere. The number of document pages at Microsoft covering Windows 2000 runs into the millions and would take you much more than a year to read. Baptism by fire, as the saying goes, maketh a good network and Windows 2000 Server administrator.

Create the Network Infrastructure Plan

Before you begin laying out the lab, bring in a huge white board and begin sketching up the topology and network infrastructure you will be creating in the lab. The infrastructure might contain elements similar to the plan we created in our labs. You can use our plan as a guideline. It contains the following elements:

✦ A domain and network representing our Active Directory root domain or namespace placeholder. In this case, we called this domain GENESIS — after the first domain controller in the Millennium City forest, which Active Directory also calls GENESIS — (see Chapters 7, 8, and 9).

We touched upon this in Chapter 2, but deployment of the Millennium City Active Directory forest is covered in Part III.

✦ The CITYHALL domain and segment representing HQ, where most of our executive accounts and support staff live.

✦ The DITT (Department of Information Technology and Telecommunications) segment representing the third domain in the GENESIS forest. This is connected to CITYHALL and the GENESIS domain over a 100Kbps network.

✦ The MCPD (Millennium City Police Department) segment representing the third domain in the GENESIS forest. This network is running Ethernet and Token Ring networks, and is connected to the network via the 100Mbit network.

So if you count the domains, they are GENESIS, CITYHALL, DITT, and MCPD (four). The network infrastructure is further described in Chapter 8.

You will notice that our forest, GENESIS, currently goes down two levels. The levels cover three domains. To recap: We have a root domain, or namespace placeholder, which we finally called GENESIS (after the first domain controller in the forest). Then we installed CITYHALL, a first-level domain, to which is attached the DITT domain. Another first-level domain called MCPD is also attached to GENESIS.

GENESIS

In the examples given throughout the book, GENESIS (the forest) contains four domain controllers. In the GENESIS domain, we have a DNS server on one of the domain controllers, a separate WINS server, which also hosts DHCP, and an application server running terminal services in application mode (which will be tested from the Windows 95 and Windows 2000 machines). We also installed a RAS server to connect the GENESIS network to the DITT network. A print server was installed and a number of printers were connected to the network using Lantronix and HP JetDirect printer servers.

The clients include Windows 95, Windows 98, and Windows 2000 Professional. This is a mixed-mode domain (earmarked to go native mode). We also installed Windows NT 4.0 Server into the domain to test connecting the NT 4.0 server to the Windows 2000 server, and to test the ability of the Windows NT 4.0 server to obtain WINS information, name services, and account privileges from the Windows 2000 network.

CITYHALL

CITYHALL is the first-level domain. This network contains the domain controller for CITYHALL, a DNS server, WINS, DHCP, and a RAS server for the low bandwidth link to DITT. The RAS server is also multi-homed to provide a second test site for network address translation. We also installed several Windows 2000 Professional clients to test access to network resources and group policy. CITYHALL is a native-mode domain.

DITT

The DITT network was installed to test the domain hierarchy. This network contains the domain controller for DITT, a DNS server, and a RAS server for the low bandwidth link to CITYHALL. The RAS server is also multi-homed to provide a second test site for network address translation. We also installed several Windows 2000 Professional clients to test access to network resources and group policy. DITT is a native-mode domain.

MCPD

The MCPD network was installed to test the domain hierarchy and divergent network requirements such as routing IP to a token ring segment using RRAS, FTP access from an AS400, NetWare, and UNIX integration. The domain is running in mixed mode. We installed a Windows 2000-dedicated IIS server to cater to requirements for Web and FTP access. MCPD is a mixed-mode domain.

Setting Up the Lab

The first task, if you are starting a lab from scratch, is to secure your lab and make sure that you can keep intruders out. If you cannot secure it behind closed doors and you have to set it up in the corner of an open-plan office, then put up a sign warning unauthorized personnel to stay out.

Creating the network

Before you bring servers into the lab, you will first need to install the network. Lay down your hubs, routers, switches, network analyses, and network emulation and simulation tools according to the topological and network infrastructure plan you developed earlier. The mini-network infrastructure you create should represent, or clone, as far as possible the intranet in which you are eventually going to deploy.

Tip

To install Active Directory, you need to plug your domain controller machine into a hub even if there is no one else on the network yet. Windows 2000 refuses to install Active Directory and promote the machine if the NIC is deactivated and there is no network. If you encounter the error, do not cancel the setup, just click back and install the hub and plug in the NIC cable. Windows 2000 sees the network automatically and switches on the NIC. If you don't have an NIC installed . . .

List the number of servers that you will be installing in the lab, and then count the number of clients you plan to test in the lab. If you are going to install about 24 machines, you will need a hub that has a 48+ port capacity. If you are testing or interconnecting three domains as demonstrated in the GENESIS example, you will need three hubs (GENESIS and CITYHALL can run on the same segment). These hubs will then cater to network equipment such as routers and gateways and give you enough room to expand. Remember that you might need to multi-home machines and make them network routers to obtain the desired network simulation.

It is a good idea to invest in network simulation tools to mirror your WAN and the interconnection topology between sites. If you need to test replication between domain controllers, DNS servers, and WINS, but you cannot afford a network simulator and do not have access to a multi-site network, consider setting up two networks and then connecting them with RAS servers or services over a simple analog telephone network. If you use two 56Kbps modems (they should be the same brand), such as two 3COM-US Robotics V.90 modems, you will be able to simulate a 56Kbps DDS frame relay circuit, which is sufficient to test replication between the domain controllers.

There are a number of ways to set up a low bandwidth test WAN. You can create another lab at a remote office and use your existing network infrastructure. Or, if you cannot afford to intrude on business traffic, you can connect the two sites directly or via a Virtual Private Network (VPN) over the Internet. The latter gets you testing VPN solutions, however, so that is a consideration. But it is not ideal to split the lab over two or more locations because you lose some control of your test environment. You need to be present on two or more networks at the same time so that you can monitor what is going on and document your observations.

Cross-Reference

See Chapters 14 and 15 for information on VPNs.

An inexpensive solution is to invest in T1 or analog telephone circuit simulators. We used equipment made by Teltone Corporation (www.teltone.com), a company based in Bothell, Washington. Using this equipment, we were able to get one RAS server to dial the other RAS server and set up a link in excess of 56Kbps between the two networks. It is important to use identical modems on each network (one dials, the other answers) to obtain the maximum bandwidth. Later, you can throttle the bandwidth by forcing either of the two modems to V34 or lower, bringing the bandwidth down to 56Kpbs, 36.6Kbps, then 28.8Kpbs, and so on. The network diagram is illustrated in Figure 4-2.

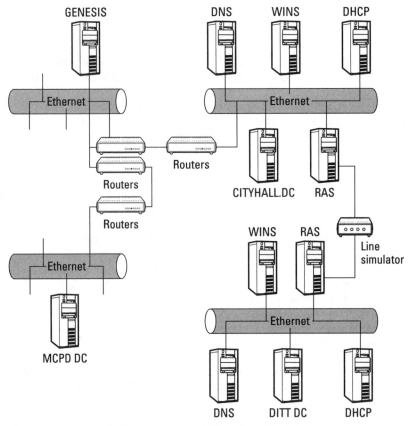

Figure 4-2: Network diagram for the Millennium City labs

Setting up two RAS servers in this fashion serves several purposes:

✦ You get experience in setting up RAS and routing services (see Chapters 12 and 15).

✦ You get experience in setting up Network Address Translation (NAT), which is covered in Chapter 12.

✦ You get experience in multi-homing Windows 2000 servers and routing IP between the networks.

✦ You can test replication between your domain controller, DNS, and WINS partners.

✦ You can test user logon to domains in remote networks.

✦ You get to do some nifty TCP/IP exercises (subnetting, routing, addressing, and translation).

In order to set up a RAS and routing server, you will need to install Windows 2000 Server on two machines and enable the remote access and routing services on both (RRAS). Servers will need to be multi-homed, and you will need to configure them to route IP between the NICs in each server. This is illustrated in Figure 4-3.

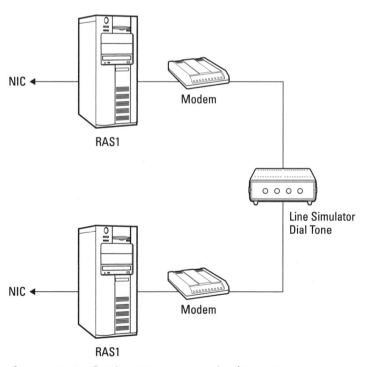

Figure 4-3: Configuring RAS servers to simulate a WAN

If you have Token Ring (TR) environments, you will need to test that in the lab as well, so it will save time if you add TR interface cards to the RAS servers as well (you only need to put a TR card in one machine really, the RAS-Router). The object of putting a TR card in the machine is to test the TR segment (access to the domain controller) and to investigate transitioning the TR network to Ethernet.

Installing servers and services

Assuming you have ramped up on theory, Table 4-2 is the list of servers and services you are advised to install in the lab (Chapter 5 discusses the steps to installing some of these servers). You can install many services on one server but, if you can afford it, you should install them on separate servers in the lab for a couple of reasons. First, the more times you install a server, the better you'll be when you get to the pilot phase and then the rollout or conversion phase. Second, you might screw up a server big time, only to lose a good domain controller in the process. And third, there will come a time when it is necessary to install the service on a dedicated role server.

Another point about domain controllers: To experience the Active Directory in full throttle, you should try to install as many domain controllers as you can. This will get you experience not only in installing peer domain controllers but also in additional domains. The servers you need to experiment with are listed in Table 4-2.

Table 4-2 Server Roles	
Role	**Description**
DC	This is the domain controller, the host server for Active Directory. It is recommended that this server be dedicated to directory services (flexible for small domains) and mirrored (see Chapter 9 for health tips for this server) with replication partners for redundancy.
DNS	This is the Domain Name System (DNS) server. DNS services should be installed on a dedicated server (although this is also flexible in small companies). DNS servers should be partnered with secondary servers in large or busy deployments. You only need to install one DNS server in the lab. Chapter 14 is devoted to DNS and WINS.
WINS	This is the WINS server, which is used to resolve NetBIOS names into IP addresses (see Collapsing the NetBIOS infrastructure discussed in this chapter). WINS can be installed on the DNS server for the lab work but should be a dedicated server on busy or large intranets. See Chapter 14.

Role	Description
DHCP	This is the DHCP server for assigning IP address leases. You can also install this service to the DNS/WINS server. However, it should be installed on a separate machine, especially on a busy network. Please pay attention to the specific health tips offered for this server in Chapter 5.
IIS	This is the Internet Information Server or IIS 5.0 that ships part-and-parcel of Windows 2000 Server (see Chapter 24). This server provides both Web and FTP services to the intranet and is an extremely powerful Internet server. IIS should most definitely be set up on a dedicated server, even in the lab where it can be used as a public relations tool for the project.
PRINT	This server is configured specifically to provide logical printers to the network and to cater to queues and print spools. See Chapter 23, which is dedicated to print services.
FILE	This server is configured for advanced file services and storage (it can also be the storage server); however, you can set it up for hierarchical storage management (HSM) and as a general file server for the enterprise. This server is usually configured for RAID-0 or RAID-5 arrays, fail-over and cluster arrangements, to provide high availability of file services to all users. In busy environments, this server should be dedicated, mirrored, or clustered, running on the Windows 2000 Advanced Server operating system.
MEDIA	This server provides media streaming services to the network. It should be a dedicated server.
TELEPHONY	This server is dedicated to telephony services; in other words, services that make full use of the telephony API (TAPI). You would typically dedicate this server to messaging, faxing, voice-over-IP (in tandem with media streaming services), and telephony services (such as switching, dial-tone access, and so on).
CLUSTER	Cluster servers can only be built on Windows 2000 Advanced Server and are not discussed in this book. However, setting up and running clusters in the lab is also essential, as is experimenting with network load balancing. Many of the services discussed in this book will find their way into high-availability requirement situations, which will require clustering or other methods of fail-over and load balancing, especially application servers.
DATABASE	This server can be set up to cater to database environments such as SQL Server 2000 and others. You do not need to install anything special, but we suggest architecture and configuration for base requirements of database servers in Chapter 5.
MAIL	The server can be set up to route and forward e-mail. See Chapter 24 for information on setting up SMTP services.

Continued

	Table 4-2 *(continued)*
Role	**Description**
BACKOFFICE	Windows 2000 Server is the base or host operating system for all Microsoft BackOffice products, such as Exchange, SQL Server, SMS, SNA, and so on.
RIS	RIS is the service that performs remote installation of Windows 2000 Professional. It should be set up as a dedicated member server. We discuss options for RIS server installation in Chapter 5 and in Appendix B.
BACKUP	A backup server is dedicated to backing up other servers and storage units over the network, and HSM or Dfs systems (see Chapters 17 and 21, respectively).
APPLICATION	The application servers are usually installed as dedicated member servers. They include component servers, terminal services, application servers, Indexing, and Message Queuing services. Terminal services installation is discussed in Chapters 5 and 25.
CERTIFICATE	Certificate services supply X.509 digital certificates for authentication. This is how you identify users on a non-secure connection, such as the Internet. This service is ideal for use with application publishing services using terminal services. It is also used to secure communications.
LICENSE	The license server was created to ensure compliance with Microsoft licensing requirements. It is used for services such as terminal services.

The number of services that are available from Microsoft and third parties is exhaustive. Depending on the application and the environment (number of users, networking, e-commerce, and so on), you might be able to get away with installing multiple services on one server. For example, it is feasible to deploy terminal services to a small office of, say, five people and also use the same server for Active Directory. Other services, no matter the size of the company, will require dedicated servers. A sophisticated firewall package is a good example. This is further discussed in Chapter 5.

The first server to install in the lab is the root domain controller . Only begin installing Active Directory on this server after you have installed everything you need on this machine and the machine is stable. You will not be touching the root host system again, other than to install networking services, such as DNS or WINS, and to manage senior administrator accounts. (See Chapters 8 and 9 for detailed information on installing the domain controllers.)

After the domain controller has been installed and you have promoted it to host Active Directory, you can begin setting up your administrator group and machine accounts. Consult Chapter 10 for information on setting up users and groups, and Chapter 9 for specifics regarding installation of Active Directory.

The next server to install is the DNS server, then DHCP, WINS, and so on. The flow charts in Figure 4-4 suggest the logical progression of installing these services or servers. Remember, as long as you are setting up a Windows 2000 domain, you will first need a domain controller before you do anything else.

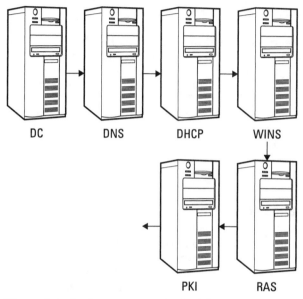

DC   DNS   DHCP   WINS

                    PKI   RAS

Figure 4-4: Setting up servers in the lab

Lab Management Pointers

The reason you set up a lab in the first place is so that you can test Windows 2000 without risking production systems. However, the lab in every way simulates the real thing and should easily be convertible to a production environment. Our GENESIS lab, for example, contained more equipment than most small businesses will ever need. And just because it is a lab does not mean you should not treat it as if it *is* a production network in full throttle. Consider the guidelines in the following sections.

Lab isolation and security

The lab must be a sandbox. In other words, keep it off the corporate network and completely isolated. By isolating the lab, you are not only protecting production systems from anything unforeseen, you are also protecting the lab from network intruders.

A good example of a why isolation is important: Back in July 1999, when we were still testing the Windows 2000 betas, eager beavers in the IT department installed Professional on the network and adopted it as their new desktops (it is very hard to resist). Next day, the helpdesk database crashed, and for two days we sat with the vendors trying to figure out what was chewing up our Btrieve files. After a lengthy process of elimination, the culprit turned out to be Windows 2000. We reported the problem to Microsoft, and new support was added by the next beta. After that, we made sure that no test systems were connected to the production networks. It cost us a lot of time and affected more people than we cared to know about in more than 25 U.S. cities, because it almost shut down the call center.

It is also very important to keep people who are not part of the lab team out of the lab and off the test network. This might be very difficult to do in an open-plan office where you have taken over a pit that anyone can walk into. In such a case, run screen savers that lock access to the computers if they are left alone for a few minutes.

Why is this so important? Your lab should be treated in the same way you treat a medical test laboratory. If someone does something unauthorized, and it causes a problem, how are you going to work out what caused the problem? If a server crashes, you could spend days trying to replicate the problem and determining the cause.

Documentation and change control

It is also highly important that you document everything that gets done in the lab. Make all members keep journals and have them write down everything they do. Deploy change control management (see Chapter 11) and documentation software in the lab so that information is sensibly recorded. One or two people should be tasked with keeping the documentation up to date. If members of your team do not update their documentation or forget to write down the steps taken to execute their test and the results, make them redo it.

Change control is a very important IT discipline to extend to the lab. For starters, make all the tests you intend to do separate projects. If you are testing group policy, then make a project and call it Group Policy Test (or Group Policy Security Test). List all the items you plan to test, determine how you are going to test, document the results, and manage the whole project in project management software, such as Microsoft Project.

As the team determines each project, list it in change control and have everyone sign off the change control documentation. Change control keeps everyone on the same page. It is also key in determining the cause of problems and being able to work back to restore a previously working condition. (There is a sample change control request form on the CD, and the subject is discussed with Group Policy in Chapter 11.)

Deciding what to test

You cannot test everything that Windows 2000 offers, so you have to decide what is important to test with respect to the environment you are planning to convert or integrate. It does not make sense to test things that Microsoft and thousands of other beta testers have already tested, unless you are on the beta program or learning about something specific.

One of the prime objectives of the corporate lab is to test how well Windows 2000 Server behaves in a production NT environment, or how NT behaves on a Windows 2000 domain.

There are two key segments to evaluate: applications and processes, and domain-wide integration. Applications testing is usually focused on the server; you need to test how a particular application functions in the Windows 2000 Server environment. For example: One of the things we tested was an AS400-based process that needs to open an FTP session to the server and copy and retrieve files from it several times a day. We also tested running batch files using the AT and SOON command line utilities (see Appendix B) to run a process that performs unattended transfers of data to another network.

We also used our lab to test automated and unattended installations, especially on test Windows NT servers, to see how they would fare when the time came to upgrade them.

Domain-wide integration testing has to do with how the new server, or domain controller, behaves on the network. For example, we tested how NT and other legacy systems fared resolving to the new DNS, or if there were any problems resolving NetBIOS names with the new WINS and if the DHCP clients were able to obtain IP address leases.

We also tested Windows 9x clients logging into network shares and how NTFS 4.0 systems and NTFS 5.0 systems coexist.

Note When we tested various flavors of UNIX with Windows 2000, we got mixed results. For example, when we removed permissions from a file, Corel Linux reported that a file it was trying access was "corrupted." Another version of UNIX reported that the file no longer existed. These are not ideal messages to send to sensitive users. UNIX is like a box of chocolates . . .

Table 4-3 is a collection of test projects to get you started:

Table 4-3 Typical Test Projects	
Aspect	**Components**
Active Directory	Logical domain structure, OU design, trusts, groups, publishing, Single Sign-On (SSO) (Chapters 2, 7)
Active Directory	Physical domain structure, sites, replication (Chapters 2, 8)
DNS	DNS namespace, zone replication, WINS integration, DHCP integration, standard replication, domain controller replication (Chapters 8, 14)

Continued

Table 4-3 *(continued)*	
Aspect	**Components**
DHCP	DNS integration, client access (Chapters 12, 13, 14)
WINS	WINS replication, client access, DNS integration (Chapters 8, 14)
Security	SSO, one-way trusts, Kerberos, NTLM, file systems, user access, Active Directory, RAS, IPSec, Encryption, Registry, Auditing (Chapters 3, 9, 11, 15, 19)
File Systems and	Mount points, Dfs, HSM, Encryption, RSS (Chapters 16, 17, 23, 24) Storage
Workspace Management	Policies and change control (Chapter 11)
Upgrading/Converting NT	Converting PDC, BDC, cloning (Chapters 5, 9)

Sanity Checks

Establish milestones and checkpoints along the way. While we have made sanity checks a component of Phase 3 described earlier, sanity checks should start at the beginning of the project. Once you have listed all the tests you plan to perform, you can establish checkpoints after each step or after each project or group of projects. The sanity checks will allow you and the team time to check in and determine progress made, areas that need to be revised, tests that need to be redone, new directions to take, and other directions to cancel.

Divide the entire lab phase into major checkpoints allowing everyone to report in, discuss and determine the next steps, and then to take R&R for a few days. The chart in Figure 4-5 is an example of how the GENESIS lab phase was divided up.

Pilot Projects

The whole idea of the lab phase is to provide you with a controlled, isolated environment in which to test systems and applications that need to be deployed into production environments, and to assess risks.

The lab projects need to be completed and operating with all the parameters that would be expected in the production environment. Only when the lab phase project is considered complete can you promote it out of the lab or hand it over to the pilot project team, which handles Phase 4. If you have any doubts about the success of a lab phase project, you cannot hand it over to the pilot project team.

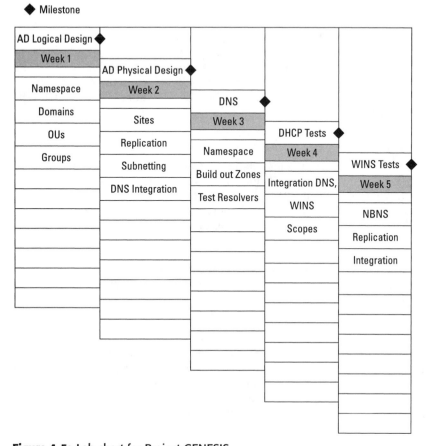

✦ Milestone

Figure 4-5: Lab chart for Project GENESIS

The pilot phase allows you to place new or changed systems into a controlled and monitored production environment. It is probably a good idea to start the pilot phase with only one pilot project. Naturally, you will have many different projects evaluating different things, but in the beginning, you should try and focus on one important or pivotal pilot.

There are several items that need to be considered in a pilot project:

✦ Pilot Scope

✦ Pilot Objectives and Timelines

✦ Participants or Users

✦ Disaster Recovery

✦ Communication

Pilot Scope

The scope of the pilot determines how much and what you intend to place into the production environment. Let's examine two pilots: Genesis pilot and Marine pilot (a marine insurance company). Both involved testing with the objective of deploying Windows 2000 Server into live production environments. In the case of Marine, the pilot was key to the company's existence because its entire IT infrastructure had reached the end of its life.

Genesis pilot

The scope of Genesis was the installation of the GENESIS domain controller into a production Windows NT network and to allow a select group of users to authenticate to the GENESIS domain. The pilot tested the GENESIS domain's ability to establish a one-way (out) trust with the NT domain. It also tested and monitored the GENESIS users, paying particular attention to the ability of the users to access their resources as usual.

In addition, the pilot allowed users to log in with their new User Principal Names (UPNs) from anywhere (SSO) and to access resources published in the GENESIS directory.

Marine pilot

The scope of the Marine pilot was to place a role Windows 2000 Server into a NetWare environment, which, using NetWare Services, masqueraded as a NetWare file server. Users in the Marine pilot continued to use legacy MS-DOS Database clients to access a Marine insurance application that resided on the NetWare server. The users currently log in to the NetWare server and can thus gain access to executables, the databases, and the NetWare print server services.

The databases currently installed on the NetWare volumes will be backed up and moved to the Windows 2000 Server. Phase 1 of this pilot will allow the users to access the databases on the Windows 2000 Server.

Pilot Objectives

The objectives should be clear and stated in the pilot documentation. The pilot group members also need to fully understand the reason for the pilot and what is required of them during the pilot phase. It is also necessary to determine how long the pilot will remain in force and the progression of one phase of the pilot to another.

Genesis pilot objectives

The objectives of the Genesis pilot are as follows:

✦ To ensure that the domain controller works properly in the NT domain environment

✦ That users can consistently log on to the Genesis domain

✦ That users can gain access to resources in the NT domain

✦ That the trust relationship between the Windows 2000 domain and the NT domain works as expected

✦ That using the UPN to log in does not cause any unexpected events to take place either on the Genesis domain or on the NT domain

Additional objectives for Genesis could also be to monitor how users adapt to using the UPN, assisting them with peculiarities of Windows 2000, and learning how to support them in the process. We also used the pilot to test Remote Installation Services.

Marine pilot objectives

The objectives of the Marine pilot are as follows:

✦ That the Windows 2000 Server behaves in a NetWare environment using IPX as the only protocol

✦ That it is possible to access the databases on a Windows 2000 Server, even though the server is disguised as a NetWare server to the application in the client workspace

✦ To reduce dependency on the NetWare-based volume for storage needs and to eventually begin a conversion of the applications to the Windows 2000 Server

Note that the objectives of the Marine pilot and the nature of the pilot suggest that much of what was taking place in the Pilot phase should have been signed off in the lab phase. It was, to some extent. The Pilot phase allowed us to test continually in a controlled live environment with users. The databases were not moved to the Windows 2000 Server in the production environment until the move was tested in the lab with a backup of the databases.

Pilot Users

You should use experienced users as far as possible in the pilot phase. With Genesis, we decided to test with members of our own IT team. These people appreciated the scope and objectives of our pilot and were more-than-willing participants. We asked them to note problems, and we received a lot of help. Sometimes, however, they caused a few problems for us by being overly inquisitive.

In the Marine pilot, the users were at first oblivious to the fact that the databases were no longer on the original server. While the users were presented with the scope and objectives of the pilot, they were not in the same camp as our willing Genesis users who were trained network administrators and support personnel. Marine users had a job to do and were concerned about finishing on time and were loath to be interrupted with network issues and training. In later phases, the Marine users were introduced to terminal services, which was a very delicate phase because they were being converted from DOS to Windows 2000 (a leapfrog over technology that spanned more than a decade).

Disaster Recovery

You need a disaster recovery plan with every pilot project. The disaster recovery plan should explicitly detail the steps to take in the event a problem occurs that will require rollback. In the case of Genesis, the disaster recovery procedures involved the clients logging on to the NT domain with their old accounts. In Marine, it was a little more complex. In fact, we encountered a disaster shortly after the database move.

Using backups we were taking of the new databases on the Windows 2000 server (employing the Backup utility on the Windows 2000 server), we were able to restore the database tables to the NetWare volume (on the NetWare server). The application kicked in, and the users were able to continue working after a two-hour break. We then proceeded to compare the two volumes and found a file that for some reason had not been copied along with the rest of the databases (it may have been locked at the time). We performed the move again, and the pilot continued forward.

Communication

Keep users and all pilot participants constantly informed of the progress of the pilot, the progression along the timeline given, and the expectations of all parties. Also provide feedback on how problems were resolved and the current status of the pilot.

Conversion

You are almost home. The conversion phase (Phase 5) is where rollout of your solutions begins. Conversion can only start once all problems encountered in the pilot project have been ironed out.

Using documentation culled from the pilot phase, you will be able to inform the new users, via e-mail, live conference, or conference calls, of the conversion and what is expected of them.

The conversion phase should contain the following elements:

1. **Introduction to the conversion project:** Get all your users together and introduce them to the conversion project. You will be telling them why they have been chosen for conversion, and so on.

2. **Training:** Users need to be grouped into teams and trained on the new systems. For our Marine users, the learning curve was extremely steep. Users had never clicked a mouse before and were now expected to use e-mail and applications like Microsoft Word.

3. **Support:** The helpdesk or support staff should be one of the first (if not the first) to be converted to any new systems or applications. After their training, you will rely on them to assist newly converted users with problems. Support staff should have access to documentation and the steps taken to resolve problems all the way back to the lab phase.

4. **Feedback and communication:** Users should be encouraged to report problems encountered and to make suggestions to the conversion team.

5. **Disaster recovery and change control:** Ensure that change control protocols are strictly adhered to, especially if your conversion project will extend to users in far-off remote sites. Continually review disaster recovery (which you should be doing anyway) and keep support staff, and conversion, pilot, and lab people on their toes. You never know when a very tricky problem has to be sent all the way back to the lab phase for a resolution.

Conclusion of Phased Implementation

There is no conclusion to implementation. New projects, lab work, pilots, and so on, need to be conducted all the time. Get ready for the next service pack.

Coming to Grips with Windows 2000 Server

You may not be ready for Windows 2000 Server for any number of reasons. You also might not be in a position to set up a lab to test variations in deployment and conversion. Does this mean you must sit around and do nothing? No. There is a lot you can do, especially if you have an existing investment in Windows NT, to prepare you for the future — be it in two months, ten months, or over the next two years.

Consider these options:

✦ Clean up your NT domains

✦ Standardize on TCP/IP

✦ Deploy DHCP

✦ Deploy WINS 2000

✦ Deploy DNS

Clean Up Your NT Domains

The smaller the company, the smaller the domain, and the easier it will be to upgrade. The tools are available in the Resource Kit, and they are discussed in Chapter 5, Chapter 9, and Appendix B.

However, if you are managing domains in a large company, the amount of domains you have and the complexity of the structure of these domains, as well as the size of them, will determine how risky the conversion will be . . . when it finally must come. We have found that converting a domain of a thousand or more accounts (and we did this several times in the lab) is easily handled by Windows 2000. The problem arises in the restructuring that has to take place once all the accounts have been imported. In many cases, you might be better off starting from scratch, as mentioned earlier in this chapter. We deal with more of this in Chapters 5 and 9.

Clean up account domains

This can be started now, even before you have a final decision on testing and investing in Windows 2000. Get rid of disabled or decommissioned accounts. You don't need to import them into Active Directory. By the way, Active Directory accounts contain much more information and thus can become untidy, quicker. If your housekeeping (or housekeeper) left a lot to be desired in the NT domain, start thinking replacement now.

Consolidate domains

Clean up your resource domains. If you have many resource domains, then investigate consolidating them into one domain. Also, investigate not converting your resource domains and devising a plan to decommission them before the conversion to Windows 2000. Perhaps you are going to replace a lot of equipment and it would make no sense to try to convert these old domains.

Trusts

Reduce the amount of manually configured trusts. Such trusts in Windows 2000 are for domains that are in other forests, which usually belong to other companies, partners, and associates. In Windows NT, trusts needed to be created between siblings, usually between resource and account domains. This is not the case with Windows 2000, and converting domains with trust relationships requires care.

User IDs

Start analyzing your user IDs. Windows 2000 user IDs can also be e-mail addresses. Jshapiro on the MCITY domain is also `jshapiro@mcity.org`, which anyone who sends e-mail on the Internet is familiar with. But js4po12 at MCITY does not make a good e-mail address . . . `js4po12@mcity.org` is hard to remember. Keeping to one User Principal Name (UPN) as the universal sign-on makes life easier for everyone. UPN-type IDs are also easier to convert in an upgrade effort.

Stay ahead in the service pack game

Windows NT gets a little antsy when it only has Service Pack 3 or lower and Windows 2000 arrives on the network. The best thing you can do to cater to NT's inferiority complex is to upgrade to the latest stable service pack as soon as possible. For the record, Windows NT needs to be upgraded to Service Pack 5 at a minimum before it can be considered "educated" enough to talk to Windows 2000.

Also, keep track of the new features that are coming out in the service packs for NT; they are not only fixes for past infractions, but they may also contain important Windows 2000 compatibility features.

Standardize on TCP/IP

No matter the size of your network, you need to plan a wholesale conversion to TCP/IP in everything you do. Windows 2000 without TCP/IP is like an eagle in a cage. As long as you maintain a hodgepodge of network protocols, such as IPX/SPX, NetBEUI, NWLink, AppleTalk, and the like, you will not be able to convert to native-mode domain.

Besides the features of the native domain, maintaining several protocols makes for more network management, slower applications (the overhead of supporting more multiple protocols on the network), opportunities to breach security, introduction of viruses, bugs, and so on.

Not only should TCP/IP be the network protocol of choice, but also your applications should be supporting it from one end of its stack to another. Begin binding the TCP/IP protocol to all network interfaces and start planning the logical design of a TCP/IP network, if you have not already started.

Take inventory of software and hardware that will not function on a TCP/IP network and devise the necessary plans to begin phasing them out. Work towards an end of systems' or applications' life dates for everything that does not support TCP/IP, just as you did with your Y2K systems and applications. In other words, standardize on TCP/IP and make it policy.

If you still need legacy applications that require support of the NetBIOS API, SNA, IPX, and so on, then you obviously still have to support protocols, at least at the network topological level; that is, on routers, interface cards, and so on. However, that does not mean you are required to support these protocols on the Windows network infrastructure unless you still have a huge investment in legacy Windows operating systems and applications, or in operating systems like NetWare (prior to version 5.0).

We have small (four PCs) clients to large (1000+ computers) clients beginning wholesale conversion to TCP/IP. The smaller the clients, the easier their conversions will be to Windows 2000 on TCP/IP.

As for NetBIOS support, you just have to use common sense. As soon as all NetBIOS-dependant applications and operating systems have been shut down, you can end your reliance on the API and begin to plot the end of life for your WINS services. The writing is on the wall for NetBIOS, so if you are planning development that will perpetuate the API on your systems, you are placing your bets on the wrong horse.

Deploy DHCP

The larger the network, the more important it is to deploy dynamic IP address assignment. So if you have not yet deployed DHCP, now is the time to start. Rather than invest in Windows NT DHCP, consider a Windows 2000 role DHCP server. Not only is it easier to manage than Windows NT DHCP, but it also gets you started in using the Microsoft Management Console, which is pervasive in Windows 2000. You only really get to use MMC in Windows NT with BackOffice products like SNA Server and IIS.

Deploy WINS 2000

If you are dropping NetBEUI, you will need to deploy WINS so that NetBIOS clients can resolve IP addresses to NetBIOS host names. If you already have a WINS presence, then consider deploying a role Windows 2000 WINS server. It is not only easier to manage, but it also has a lot of new features that make management a lot less troublesome.

Deploy DNS

Many companies do not use DNS, but they will have to when the time comes to start thinking Windows 2000. If you are in such a position, deploy Windows 2000 Dynamic DNS (DDNS) on a role server (discussed in Chapter 14). If you support intranet-based Web and FTP servers, that is all the more reason to begin converting these to Windows 2000 role servers.

Summary

This chapter provided an overview of the key planning steps to deploying Windows 2000 Server as soon as possible.

We first discussed the steps involved in putting together a phased implementation plan. Our plan consisted of several phases, essentially labs, pilot projects, and conversion. We also advised you to ramp up on the technology before testing and deployment. A good example of understanding the technology is understanding that Windows 2000 Server-DNS, Windows 2000 Server-WINS, and Windows 2000 Server-DHCP are ideal role servers to install in the existing environment, be it Windows NT or something else . . . and how to integrate them. Only when you know what you are dealing with, will you be able to move forward and test key solutions.

For example: One of the prime objectives of the corporate lab is to test how well Windows 2000 Server behaves in a production NT environment, or how NT behaves on a Windows 2000 domain. But it serves little purpose to just install the server and watch it sit on the network. You need to devise specific experiments that test the new technology you have learned about with applications and technology you currently have in place.

After the lab phase, you need to roll out a pilot project, which will give you the ability to test your solutions in a controlled production environment. And if you are not ready yet to test or deploy Windows 2000, now is the time to get your Windows NT infrastructure in shape so that your conversion will be a lot easier, when it must come.

✦　　✦　　✦

Installing Windows 2000 Server

This chapter reviews the installation of Windows 2000 Server. It discusses a number of hardware configurations and setup options, and reviews potential obstacles.

Installation and Configuration Strategy

If you have read Chapter 4 and have done your homework, you will now be ready to begin installing Windows 2000 in your lab. You may be tempted, or you may have an urgent need, to go directly to a working or production system, in a production environment. Perhaps your DHCP server died, or a new DNS server is needed urgently, and so on. Resist, or stick with what you know. If you have an NT network and need to raise a new service to fill an urgent need, stick with Windows NT.

On the other hand, if you are a seasoned administrator and you know what you're doing, you will probably have items like a hardware checklist, remote or unattended installation, hot standby, and so on, well taken care of. So only go directly to a production system if you know what you are doing and the production system is part of a conversion and rollout project.

For the most part, you should always raise servers in a lab. Then you should burn them in (run them continually) for about a week; hit them with work for at least another week. After that, and if all test items check off, then ship or go live. But no two environments are the same. Let's look at the various installation and configuration situations and then go from there.

Note A lot of people ask how you burn in a server that is standing idle and has no users connected to it. One simple way is to set up NTBackup to run continually. Running backup is great physical therapy for a server. It works the hard disks, memory, system buses, access control, permissions and the NTFS, remote and removable storage functions, and more. You can also configure NTBackup (or any other backup utility for that matter) to perform both pre- and post-backup routines, such as sending alerts, moving files around the house, and so on. Depending on your stress test, you may need to write a backup script to automatically overwrite media, and so on. See Chapter 17 for more information. And if you want to test disk I/O and other routines, you might have to write some custom software for the job.

Getting Psyched Up about Installing

This chapter takes you through the basic install routines, and then to rollout and sophisticated deployment strategy. We are going to help you cook up a variety of server meals. Microsoft has spent many millions on the installation and configuration process. So, for the most part, Windows 2000 rises well for the power that it wields. It is certainly a lot smoother and friendlier to install than any other server operating system in existence (other than the machine you receive pre-installed from the factory).

We have installed the operating system more times than you care to know and on about ten different platforms with a variety of hardware from scrap piles to brand names. We have also deliberately sabotaged our systems (like taking away drives, drivers, memory, and certain system files) and tried a variety of recovery techniques. What we have to report to you is as follows: If you experience any difficulty installing Windows 2000 Server, you must be using very unconventional methods, thrift store hardware, or not paying attention to details and recommended strategy.

Now sit back, close your eyes, and imagine you are in a class going through installation training. You'll feel good thinking that you spent no more than the cost of a nice dinner on this book, and did not have to mortgage your house for a five-day course.

Server Recipes

In evaluating the various needs in the enterprise, we classified our installation into various recipes of server installation, which are discussed in the following sections.

Low-road or bare-bones system recipe

This option consists of using minimum hardware requirements to raise the server. You can use a no-frills motherboard with one CPU, the minimum RAM (64MB), a single IDE hard disk drive, a CD-ROM, a 1.4MB floppy disk drive, a standard network card, and a mouse, keyboard, and monitor (MKM).

Tip Microsoft now ships the Server OS and the upgrade version with a note that 128MB is recommended. However, the installation will still get the green light if you only have 64MB.

We have raised servers (both Server and Advanced Server) on CPUs ranging from old Pentium 133s, 166s, 200s, Pro 200s, and 266s, to Pentium II and III 300s, 450s, 500s, 700s, duals (two CPUs), quads, and so on. You can raise a Windows 2000 server on 133MHz and 166Mhz Pentiums, but we don't recommend it for anything more than the smallest role server, discussed later. On the other hand, an old Pentium Pro with a lot of RAM will serve many of your needs. You can usually pick these servers up on the Internet for a song, and if they are good brands, they'll do well for many years.

Small file and print server recipe

A small file and print server caters to small business' file and print services. You should still use the bare-bones components, add a second large IDE hard disk drive for file and print services, the usual peripherals, and so on. The amount of RAM will depend on the number of connections and users. Printing services will require a lot more RAM than file services. If you are supporting a lot of printers, then go to 128MB of RAM and stick with no less than a Pentium Pro (a PII or PIII of 300Mhz and higher is better).

Don't be a chump and install 32MB RAM modules (unless they are lying in your top drawer gathering dust). In fact, it is almost impossible to buy anything less than 64MB nowadays. Check out the chapters on File Systems and Printer Services for further advice on hardware requirements (Chapters 21 and Chapter 23, respectively).

Your hard disk demands will be higher, and you should now consider adding a second drive. You can stick to a cheap IDE disk (even the cheap IDE or EIDE drives are good disks) or begin thinking about SCSI. But let's hold the thought about hard disks for later on in this chapter.

Note You may have read information elsewhere calling for more firepower in a Windows 2000 Server. We would preempt that question with the answer that our assessment is based on various experiments, projects, pilot systems, and deployment. Every situation is different, and the only way to really know what you need to throw at a situation is to test.

Application server installation recipe

Microsoft now uses the term *application server* to refer to a server running Terminal Services, but a server can still host applications without terminal users. You may want to install applications on servers for users who will load them into local memory at their workstations. The application is thus loaded across the network, but the "footprint" and ensuing resource consumption is local to the user's hardware.

You may also have applications that are server-based or server-oriented. These may include database front-ends, communications software, processing-oriented software, and network management applications. There may be hundreds of applications that are suited to server-side execution and that need no user interaction, such as process control applications and data processing.

You could use the recipe for file and print servers; it will take some testing to raise the ideal configuration for your purpose. Depending on the availability requirements, you might need to add RAID, hot-insert drive-bays, and so on, which are discussed later in this chapter.

Terminal Services installation recipe

A terminal service application server is a whole new ball game. The WinFrame licensing arrangement between Citrix Systems, Inc., and Microsoft (see Chapter 25) was the origin of Terminal Services. Terminal server, under the Hydra project name, first made its debut in Windows NT 4.0 in late 1997. It was then launched as a separate NT 4.0 operating system called Windows NT 4.0 Terminal Server Edition (TSE).

Terminal server is no longer a separate product under Windows 2000 Server. All servers come with Terminal Services built into the OS (see Chapter 1), and, as described in Chapter 25, you either configure Terminal Services as a remote Administration tool (which does not require licensing) or as an Application Server service (which does require licensing). This computing model is known as thin-client/server computing.

With Windows 2000 acting as a Terminal Service application server, all your users run all their applications on the server. There is no such thing as a local Terminal Service client. The client can be a browser, a fat client running a Terminal Service terminal application (like a TN3270 character-based terminal running on Windows and accessing a DB2 database on the mainframe), a dumb terminal (known as Windows-based terminals), or terminals running on the Windows CE or Pocket PC platforms. Your users' terminals can also be installed on any non-Windows platform, such as Macintosh, DOS, and UNIX, but these require the MetaFrame product suite from Citrix, which uses the ICA protocol.

Terminal servers can be raised with any of the recipes discussed so far. However, it is not what you start up with, but what the terminal users do when they are attached to the server that matters. We have tested these services and deployed them in vigorous real-life situations since 1997, and the following configuration pointers, which apply to a different configuration recipe we will shortly discuss, are key:

✦ Restrict your users from having more than four applications open at a time. For example, make sure they can comfortably open and run a database application, a word processing application, e-mail, and a Web browser.

✦ Configure the applications to run without fancy splash screens, animations, or any resource-intensive software. This may not always be possible (see Chapter 25 for further information).

✦ Assign and enforce hard disk quotas. This is important to do for all users, but especially useful when you are dealing with terminal users.

A server hosting no more than five terminal users should be running on a CPU of no less than 300MHz. Each user (depending on the applications and the type of processing) should be assigned no less than 32MB of RAM. You should also install fast SCSI drives and support them in hardware RAID configurations on fast controller cards. In short, there is no bare-bones situation when it comes to Terminal Services and application hosting. After all, if you were deploying to standard clients, they would likely each be above 266MHz with 32MB or more of RAM.

At 32MB each, the recipe thus calls for the following total server RAM:

✦ Operating system = 128MB

✦ Five users @ 32MB each = 160MB

✦ Total RAM needed = 288MB

You will probably have a hard time adding 32MB modules into a modern motherboard. Your configuration would thus be two 128MB modules and one 64MB module, or a single 320MB or larger RAM module.

We have actually succeeded with less RAM, and you could count on a 300MHz system with 128MB RAM and a couple of fast IDE drives to service three to five users. But you should know that this will work only if you can guarantee that the users keep no more than two apps open (say their e-mail and one work app, like a database front-end). This latter "easier" configuration should be your bare-bones recipe for Terminal Services (to give users a reasonable work environment).

 We talk about which applications work well on Terminal Services in Chapter 25.

Role server installation recipe

Role servers are servers running services like DHCP, WINS, DNS, and Active Directory. Your application and needs may vary widely, depending on the service and how many subscribers it has. A small company might get away with a light-weight configuration, like the small file and print server recipe offered earlier. In other cases, you may require much more firepower, especially on medium to large intranets. For the record, we've been running DHCP, WINS, and DNS on Windows NT Professional on Pentium 200s with 128MB of RAM in each, servicing several thousand users over a nationwide WAN for several years. But there is a lot more replication and dynamic configuration overhead with Windows 2000, and you might have to shell out for a Pentium II or III machine.

BackOffice, high-road, or mission-critical recipe

Mission-critical servers should have no less than 300MHz in CPU capability. For the most part, and if you have more than a handful of users, your CPU should be more than 400MHz. You might consider equipment running two-CPU configurations, or possibly deploy quad systems.

Hard disk needs may vary, but you'll need to configure a second drive letter running at RAID 5 under hardware control (in case you're wondering, these are SCSI devices, which we discuss later).

Redundant or stand-by system recipe

Any of the server recipes mentioned so far could be cloned to provide an offline or hot spare. These are obviously not cluster or automatic fail-over machines. If the primary server goes down, you could pull dynamic volumes out of the primary arrays and install them into the hot spares. But a better solution, if you can afford it and have the budget, is to install Advanced Server and run cluster services and network load balancing.

Large systems, clusters, and Datacenter server installations

Advanced clustering (high availability) and Datacenter Server solutions are beyond the scope of this book, although most of the configuration information in this book will apply to the high-end operating systems. As discussed in Chapter 21, there is not that much difference between the operating systems, at least not from the average user's point of view. Any large system will call for an external SCSI-based storage silo under hardware RAID-5.

The various recipes we've discussed so far are summarized in Table 5-1.

Table 5-1 Hardware Guide for Server Recipes			
Recipe	*CPU/MHz*	*RAM/MB*	*HDD*
Bare-Bones	200	64+	IDE
Small F&P	200-300	64+	IDE
App Server	300+	64+	IDE/SCSI
Terminal Service	300+	300+	SCSI-RAID
Role Server	266+	96+	SCSI-RAID
BackOffice	300+	128+	SCSI-RAID
Standby	300+	128+	SCSI/IDE
Large	450+	300+	SCSI-RAID

Hardware

Choosing hardware is not a difficult exercise at all for Windows 2000 Server. There is really not a lot that you will put into your system. The list of hardware we will discuss is as follows:

✦ Motherboards

✦ CPU

✦ Memory

✦ Hard disk drives

✦ HDD controllers

✦ Network interface cards (NICs)

The Hardware Compatibility List (HCL)

Before you go buying parts, review the Hardware Compatibility List (HCL) in the `\support` folder on the Server CD, for your own peace of mind. If your part is not listed, check out the HCL on the Microsoft Web site at `www.microsoft.com/hcl`. You will probably find the HCL a little amusing because Windows 2000 has already been available to the leading manufacturers for more than a year as of this writing, and they have a ways to go before their products will be logo-compliant. Some popular brands are not even listed as compatible, and some have even stated that they will not go for the logo . . . that in-house tests are good enough.

Also, according to Microsoft policy, Microsoft will not support you if the item is not on the HCL, but not many items are on the HCL yet. And if you spend $195 with Microsoft to figure out if hardware is the reason a server will not start, will they refuse to take your money? They never have to date. Microsoft's paid support team is very responsive and will help you determine if hardware is your problem. At least if they tell you that you have a hardware compatibility problem, that's probably all the advice you'll need.

The HCL aside, you should heed the following advice: Most large companies will buy brands from the likes of IBM, Compaq, Dell, or HP, and so on. And if the budget is there, a small company looking for one business server should go this route as well. The servers will be burned in and tested, and the manufacturer will stand behind the compliance of its product running Windows 2000 Server, logo-compliant or not. The servers will also come with warranties and various levels of support, and you can get as much as a 30 percent discount on the operating system, which comes preinstalled.

If, however, you plan to build your own server, or if you need to upgrade a machine down the road, then by all means buy your own parts and knock together your own server. However, for best motherboard results, try to stick to made-in-America components, or well-known and popular foreign imports. For RAM, there is only a handful of factories left, but you'll be okay buying products from the likes of NEC, Compaq, IBM, TI, and others. For hard disks, IBM, Quantum, and Seagate are the leaders now and may soon be the only players. For CPUs, there's Intel, AMD, and Cyrix. If you are thinking PowerPC and other marginal CPUs, you'll need to talk to the likes of IBM or Motorola. The other peripherals will not interfere with your server.

Motherboards

Motherboards come in a variety of sizes and shapes. The essential components of a server motherboard are as follows:

✦ **Mother form factor:** Motherboards come in several sizes: AT (the form factor of most server boards), ATX, BabyATX, and MicroATX. BabyATX and MicroATX are aimed at the home and have fewer slots than you would want for a server motherboard. Go with AT or ATX.

✦ **Slots:** Slots come in three standards: ISA (the older and slower slots), PCI (which caters to faster data transfer rates), and AGP (Advanced Graphics Port), which is more suited to graphics components (not becoming of a server). Most motherboards include all three of the slot types. Since AGP is for a graphics interface card, there is usually only one AGP slot. Choose a motherboard that gives you about two ISA slots and four to five PCI slots.

✦ **RAM slots:** The RAM slots include SIMMs and DIMMs. SIMM slots are the older 72-pin slots, and the modules have to be mounted in pairs. DIMM memory is much faster. DIMM modules come in 168-pin slots, and the memory can be mounted as single modules. You can put more DIMM RAM in a server than SIMM, which is important for future expansion.

✦ **CPU Sockets:** The CPU sockets include Socket 7, Slot 1, and 370/PPGA. Socket 7 is the older Pentium Pro-type socket, which is inserted like a pancake into the motherboard sockets. Slot 1 CPUs are for the new Pentium II and III CPUs, which are inserted into a single slot and protrude away from the motherboard. Slot 370 CPUs are cheaper than Slot 1 CPUs and are for the Intel Celeron PPGA CPUs.

One of the top motherboards in the United States is SuperMicro, which supplies many leading brands. You can buy SuperMicro boards at Motherboards.com, which sells several other leading brands, including Soyo. Soyo is gaining market share and is becoming very popular with places like Best Buy and CompUSA. Another motherboard maker that has become popular is Tekram (www.tekram.com).

Central Processing Units (CPUs)

The leading CPU maker is still Intel. However, AMD and Cyrix are making their own noises in the *x*86 market. Contact all three manufacturers for Windows 2000 Server compatibility, or check out the HCL under CPUs.

Memory

As mentioned earlier, stick to DIMM slots, which are 168-pin and are much faster than SIMMs; besides, you will not find a newly manufactured motherboard for a server that comes with SIMM slots. DIMM RAM sizes start at 16MB, but it is getting harder to find modules under 64MB. Because Windows 2000 Server requires at least 64MB, there is no need to look around for smaller modules.

Hard Disk Drives

The biggest names in Hard Disk Drives (HDDs) are Seagate, IBM, Fujitsu, Quantum, Western Digital, Maxtor, and Hewlett Packard, in no particular order. For small or bare-bone servers, you can escape with IDE or even Enhanced IDE (EIDE) drives. Anything more — supporting multiple users or high-end applications, Terminal Services, and BackOffice or high-end role servers — demands SCSI hard disk drives. SCSI comes in several flavors: SCSI, SCSI-2, SCSI-3, and Ultra SCSI are the base protocols. Several years ago, it was thought that SCSI would go the way of the dodo, but it continues to surge, and new SCSI standards are emerging all the time.

The advantage of SCSI over IDE or EIDE lies in several factors:

✦ **Speed:** SCSI drives are much faster in access time and transfer rate than IDE drives; however, new IDE drives are being introduced every month that out-perform recent additions to the SCSI lineup.

✦ **Capacity:** SCSI drives are currently available from 9.5GB to 72GB (although this will be out of date by the time you reach the end of the chapter, and IDE technology continues to surprise us).

✦ **Addressing:** Many drives or devices can be chained on a single cable. You can currently address up to 15 SCSI devices with the Ultra SCSI standard.

✦ **Support:** There is more supporting technology available for SCSI that is targeted to server solutions. These include high-end RAID controllers, hot insert hardware, storage silos, and drive array enclosures.

In addition to SCSI, a new standard is beginning to take hold and is showing amazing promise. It is called Fibre Channel Arbitrated Loop or FC-AL. FC-AL drives are connected by coax cable. The drives are incredibly fast, and you can currently address up to 126 of them, as opposed to 15 under SCSI. Table 5-2 lists the differences between FC-AL and SCSI.

Table 5-2
SCSI versus FC-AL

Specification	SCSI	FC-AL
Cable distances	1.5-3 meters	30 meters between devices
Data rates	5MB per second	200MB per second
Addressing	15 devices	126 devices
Array support	Parity	Hot insert support with no special controller, dual porting, CRC for integrity

In addition to the differences listed in Table 5-2, FC-AL is extremely tidy in comparison to SCSI; the devices have a single port for a coaxial connection, and no other configuration is required. SCSI, on the other hand, requires ribbon cable, jumpers, and terminators.

The downside of using FC-AL is that they are a little more expensive than SCSI drives and have not been extensively tested with Windows 2000 (nor have the large SCSI drivers, for that matter). Both standards in large capacity are worth experimenting with; after all, hard disk prices are dropping everyday. At the current rate, a 96GB HDD is expected to cost about $300 by 2002.

Hot insert or hot swap is also an important consideration for server class machines. Your servers should be configured with hot swap drive hardware that will allow you to remove a dead drive while a system is hot and online. This allows you to replace drives without bringing mission-critical servers down.

Hot swap standards come in four levels, as illustrated in Table 5-3.

Table 5-3
Hot Swap Levels

Level	Capability
Level 1	Cold swap. System is offline; no power is applied to the drive.
Level 2	Hot swap reset. System is held in reset state; power is applied.
Level 3	Hot swap on an idle bus. Power is applied.
Level 4	Hot swap on an active bus. Power is applied to the drive.

Mission critical or maximum availability servers should be configured with Level 4 hot swap capability.

HDD Controllers

The standard HDD controllers that are built onto most motherboards suffice for most server and data processing needs. Small business systems configured with IDE or EIDE cards will work well with onboard controllers (that is, on the motherboard) or your vanilla controller that sells for under $50.

SCSI drives need SCSI controllers. These can range from your standard SCSI controllers to faster cards and cards that support mirroring, disk duplexing, disk arrays, and so on. One of the best-known names is Adaptec. Most branded computers that are configured for SCSI usually make their own SCSI controllers or use Adaptec.

A good SCSI controller is of paramount importance, because it makes no sense to install a fast SCSI drive or drive array and then go cheap on controller cards.

Network Interface Cards

Any seasoned network administrator will tell you that you can buy a $10 network interface card (NIC) and spend hundreds of dollars trying to get it to work, or you can spend $75 to $100 and have it installed and bound in less than five minutes.

Stick with the brand name cards like 3Com and Madge. Most of 3Com's products have been tested compatible with Windows 2000. There is zero setup effort with any of the latest 3Com NICs, and as long as you install any of 3Com's 900 series (such as the 3C905), you won't have any hassle.

Plug and Play

Plug and Play (PnP) has arrived on Windows 2000 Server. This technology makes installing devices far less painful than was the case on Windows NT, which did not support PnP. For the most part, the operating system will be able to detect your new components and automatically configure them for operation. You may only have to provide addressing or name configuration. We will look at PnP and the Device Manager in the Post Installation section later in this chapter.

Getting Ready to Install

Before installation, you should prepare a checklist detailing what you are going to install and the items you need to have handy. The following checklists cover several types of installation.

Standalone Servers

Standalone servers do not connect to any domain, but rather to a workgroup. You can create a workgroup from one standalone server or join the server to another workgroup, Windows for Workgroups-style. You can also join a domain post installation. For a standalone server, you need the following items:

✦ Workgroup name

✦ An administrator's password

✦ Network protocols

✦ IP address

✦ DNS IP addresses and host names

✦ NetBIOS name of host

Member Servers

Member servers are members of domains. In order to install a member server into a domain, you'll need several items on your checklist:

✦ Domain name

✦ An administrator's password

✦ Network protocol

✦ IP address

✦ DNS IP addresses and host names

✦ NetBIOS name of host

Role Servers

Role servers do not need to be members of domains. In order to install a role server into a domain, you'll need several items on your checklist:

✦ Domain name

✦ An administrator's password

✦ Network protocol

✦ IP address

✦ DNS IP addresses and host names

✦ NetBIOS name of host

✦ Role service information

Note According to our definition, a member server can be a role server only if you install specific role services onto the server during installation, such as WINS, DNS, DHCP, and so on.

Domain Controller

There are two approaches to installing a domain controller. First, you can raise the machine as a member server and promote it post-installation, and even post-burn-in. Or you can promote it to domain controller status during an automated installation.

We recommend against the latter option, unless you are really confident about your machines and their configuration. If you are an Original Equipment Manufacturer (OEM), you would not need to be concerned about domain controllers and Active Directory because the domain specifics, such as creating a new tree or forest, or joining existing trees and forests, is something that gets done on the customer's network. On the other hand, if you, as a consultant or network engineer, have created an extensive unattended or remote installation regimen that automatically raises the machine as a domain controller, then you know what you are doing. We will look into this a little later.

For now, there are several reasons for not promoting during or just after initial installation. First, promoting a domain controller is a time-intensive operation (Active Directory goes through extensive self-configuration before the installation completes). Second, if there is a problem with the machine, you will have to demote the domain controller, which can be a complicated process. And third, once you have installed and raised a domain controller, you do not want to demote it due to a hardware problem, or risk trashing your domain controller.

 Tip The faster the CPU and the more RAM you have, the quicker you can install and configure Active Directory. On a new server with a 500MHz CPU, 256MB RAM, a super-fast motherboard, and lightning-fast SCSI drives, we were able to install Active Directory, start-to-finish, in under five minutes. On lesser machines, it took as long as 45 minutes.

When Active Directory is demoted, it tears down everything it created and restores the machine to the control of the registry and the local SAM. In fact, it is like watching a movie going backwards. Active Directory asks you for a new Administrator account name and password for the rollback. All configuration changes made to the machine, such as desktop settings, are restored to the default, newly created settings. When you reboot the machine, you are back to where you started. You will not even get earlier changes you made to the registry because the registry is essentially reinstalled when Active Directory comes down (because it is wiped out when you promote the server).

There is a good reason for this. Everything configured on a domain controller is stored in the directory databases, and after the registry is restored, you can re-promote it from scratch. Promoting a domain controller is dealt with in Chapter 9.

Burn in a domain controller machine for several weeks, if possible, before you promote and deploy it. A domain controller running Active Directory for several weeks has already accumulated an extensive configuration, not a good idea for a machine that has to be replaced.

The checklist for a domain controller is as follows:

✦ Domain name. If you are creating a new domain, you will need the name of the parent domain you are installing under, or the existing tree name (or the forest name if you are installing a new domain tree). If you are adding a domain controller to an existing domain, you need to have that name handy as well.

✦ An administrator's password

✦ Network protocols

✦ IP address

✦ NetBIOS name of host

✦ DNS IP addresses and host names

In all of the previous checklists, be certain of the NetBIOS name you are going to use. Once you have supplied this name, it cannot be changed short of reinstalling the machine, if it is still a standalone, member, or role server. If you need to change the NetBIOS name of a domain controller, you will have to reinstall Active Directory. We talk about naming again in the next section.

Installing Windows 2000 Server

We have found, after dozens of installations, that the best practice for installing Windows 2000 Server is to raise a bare-bones operating system and then configure or promote the machine after it has been running and burning in as a standalone or member server for a while. Not only is the installation far quicker, but also this practice allows you to get a minimal server going and then install services and applications into a running system after it has met your specific quality levels.

The only service that should be configured during installation is Terminal Services. Raising a server with this service running in remote administration mode will allow you to connect to a remotely installed server for configuration and promotion. The next few sections will take you through the bare-bones installation.

Partitioning Hard Disk Drives

Give Windows 2000 a hand, and it will take an arm . . . or at least another drive. Installation will assess all the hard drive resources in the system, and if there are two drives (or partitions), the OS will attempt to use both. The first active partition will get snagged for the system files . . . the minimum required to raise the system to a point where you can run recovery tools, or the Recovery Console. Windows 2000 calls this volume — you guessed it — the *system* volume.

 Note   You can control how installation deals with hard disks and partitions by using command-line switches and parameters. Some of these are discussed later in this chapter and as part of unattended installation in the Windows 2000 Resource Kit in Appendix B.

Windows 2000 will then snag a second drive or partition and use it for the boot files . . . the files needed to boot the rest of the operating system all the way to the desktop where you can log in. Windows 2000 calls this volume the *Boot* volume. (This is a reversal of the old naming convention for boot and system partitions.)

There are two reasons for the dual disk consumption. First, Windows 2000 is optimized to use more than one hard disk drive. Second, a minimum boot disk can be configured to hold just the boot files and be formatted as FAT or FAT 32, instead of NTFS. The theory is this: If you lose the base operating system — that is, if you are unable to boot to the desktop — you can at least boot to a DOS diskette and then from DOS copy new base files over the corrupt ones (or replace a defective drive). Many NT and NetWare systems have been configured this way. But a well-designed and managed system need not retain a FAT boot disk, which, due to its poor security, is a risk to the entire system because it does not support file-level security.

However, Windows 2000 Server will allow you to boot to the Boot Options console (when it detects a disaster). Here you have several options, such as Safe Mode with Networking, and from there you can attempt to boot without certain services and debug the problem once you have the OS up and running. You can also boot the Recovery Mode Console, which takes you to a command line that you can use to access NTFS partitions (see Chapter 17 and Appendix B) and the Boot Disks. So, the idea of leaving boot or system files on FAT volumes is old fashioned, the result of bad memories from Windows NT days. We recommend the following partition arrangement options.

Option 1: One HDD

The following arrangement uses one hard disk drive, which forces Windows 2000 to put both boot files and system files onto the same drive and partition.

1. Configure the system with one hard disk drive of about 2GB in size (Microsoft's official recommendation is to supply at least a 1GB partition, but with service packs and new features coming down the road, you need to leave room for expansion).

2. Format the partition during the install as NTFS (see Chapter 21).

3. Let Windows 2000 choose the partition name, the default.

The pros of this partitioning option are as follows: First, you save on hard disk drives. The system files take up no more than 20MB. Second, you can mirror this disk for fault tolerance. (Unfortunately, you can only mirror the disk under hardware disk mirroring because Windows 2000 will not let you mirror a disk that was installed as a basic partition . . . even if you make the disk a dynamic disk.)

The negatives of this partitioning option are that if you have to format the system or boot volumes as FAT, you'll end up with a disk consisting of numerous partitions. This is not necessary on a server and can later lead to problems, such as the inability to mirror or diminishing hard disk space, and the advanced features of dynamic disks (further discussed in Chapter 16). You will also have trouble providing dual boot capability, but dual boot is not recommended, and besides, there is no need to provide dual boot on a production server.

> **Note**   You can dual boot a server to either NT 4.0 or Windows 2000, but only if the NT operating system has been upgraded to Service Pack 4 or later. Service Pack 4 and later upgrade the NT NTFS to read Windows 2000 volumes. NT 4.0 with SP 3 and less will not run on the new NTFS volume, and if you install Windows 2000 before adding at least SP 4 to the Windows NT side, you will lose NT, period. Dual booting to any other operating system (non-NTFS) is not possible on an NTFS-formatted disk.

Option 2: Two HDDs

The following arrangement uses two hard disk drives: Windows 2000 will put boot files on one disk and system files on the second disk.

1. Configure the system with two hard disk drives of about 2GB each in size.

2. Format the drives as NTFS during the install (see Chapter 21).

3. Let Windows 2000 choose the partition names and the default, and put the files where it needs to.

The positive aspect of this partitioning option, as far as we can tell, is that you have the option of leaving the Boot volume formatted as FAT (or FAT32) and formatting the rest of the partitions and drives as NTFS, as discussed earlier.

The negatives of this partitioning option are that you use up a second drive, for a small amount of hard disk space. But if you are bent on dual or multi-boots, the second drive can hold the additional OS.

While there is a performance incentive to use a second hard disk, the increased performance is not worth the effort and the second drive, with the speed and response of modern hard disks. We are also talking about the base operating system here and not Active Directory, SQL Server, or Exchange, which are built to take advantage of additional drives. You would be better off using a second drive as a mirror of the first to gain a fault tolerance feature.

Basic Install

The CD install consists of four stages that take you through running Setup, the Setup Wizard, Networking, and Final Installation Setup.

Initial Setup: Using the boot disks

Insert Disk 1 into your drive A: and then reboot your machine. Alternately, you can run Setup from the DOS command line by typing **A:\winnt**. If your installation kit did not come with boot disks, you can create them from the boot disk folder on the CD (see Appendix B).

1. Executing Setup from the command line or from reboot loads a minimal footprint of Windows 2000 into memory. The code in memory contains the functions that start the Setup program.

2. The machine is rebooted, and the text-based version of Setup starts. The usual licensing information appears on the screen, and you are required to agree to the terms and conditions.

3. The next step is disk partition. Setup will ask you to choose the partition on which to install the operating system. You can select existing partitions or choose to create a new partition.

4. Your next choice is the file system (FAT16, FAT-32, or NTFS). After you have selected the file system, Setup will format the chosen partition. After the format, Setup will immediately begin installing files to the partition. If you have more than one disk in the system and want to install to one disk, then do not format or partition any other media at this time.

5. Setup then saves the initial configuration and restarts the machine.

6. Upon bootup, the first screen you see is the Windows 2000 Setup Wizard. The Windows 2000 operating system files are installed in the C:\Winnt folder.

Tip　If you do not have a local CD, you can run Windows 95, 98, or DOS boot disks with SmartDrive and network drivers installed. These boot disks will put you on the network and allow you to connect to remote CD share-points. From the share, you can execute winnt32.exe (non-DOS mode) and launch the GUI-based initial setup screens.

Initial Setup: Installing from the CD

You can either make your CD bootable (if it is not so already) or execute the winnt.exe file from the local CD drive or from across the network. If you are already in Windows NT or Windows 2000 (a release candidate or beta), you can run winnt32.exe from the I386 directory on the CD. This method of install brings you to the graphical Windows-based installation dialog box, which will prompt you to upgrade an existing installation or install a parallel operating system. Click the first option to install Windows 2000, as illustrated in Figure 5-1. The next screen is the Setup Wizard. You are prompted to either upgrade or install a new copy of Windows 2000 Server. For this exercise, choose the latter.

Figure 5-1: The Windows 2000 welcome and installation dialog box

If you are making CD copies of a Windows 2000 Server installation, products like EasyCD from Adaptec can take Windows 2000 boot files and use them to make a bootable Windows 2000 CD. You will first have to make an exact copy of the original installation image before the utility can make the copy bootable. Generally, the Windows 2000 distribution CD is bootable.

Running the Setup Wizard

The wizard now takes you through the second stage of the installation process. You will be asked for information about yourself, the organization or company licensing the software, and the computer.

Windows 2000 takes this information and begins a non-interactive installation in which it copies software to support machine configuration, installed devices, and so on. After this phase, Windows 2000 will prompt you for the following:

1. **Language Options:** You will be asked to customize language, locale, and keyboard settings. If you are installing in the United States, you can, for the most part, leave these at the default settings. You can also configure the server to use multiple languages and regional settings.

Choosing multiple languages forces Windows to install the character sets from multiple languages.

2. **Name and Organization:** Here, you provide the name of the person responsible for the software and the name of the organization that owns the license.

3. **Licensing Mode:** Here, you can choose to select licensing on a per-server or per-seat basis. If you choose to license per seat, you will have to enter the number of client access licenses (CALs) purchased. If you are going to provide application services using the Terminal Services in Application Mode, then choose the CAL option.

4. **Computer Name:** This is where you get to add the NetBIOS name we told you to prepare for earlier. Windows 2000 will choose a default name for you, which you should change because it won't make very much sense. It is far better to come up with a convenient naming convention that your users will recognize. In the examples given throughout this book, we use MC for Millennium City, followed by an acronym for the role the server plays, and the role number. For example, if the machine is destined to become a domain controller, we will name it MCDC, followed by the server number: MCDC00 or MCDC06. An example of a DNS server would be MCDNS01.

   Windows pretty much leaves you to your own devices when you name your computers. The best rule to follow is to name the machine according to any convention you dream up that works for your situation . . . just be consistent. Resist cute names for several reasons: The names may be hard for your users to relate to, and some may find them annoying (not everyone loves Disney). Server names are also the prefixes for the new Dynamic DNS names assigned to the server. A simple machine name for the genesis.mcity.org domain name would be MCDNS06.GENESIS.MCITY.ORG, which is far better than BULLWINKLE.GENESIS.MCITY.ORG. However, also be careful using names that attract security problems. We once used the name *Checkpointcharlie*, which was subsequently hacked the following week.

5. **Password for the Administrator Account:** This account is installed into the local domain's Administrator account.

6. **Windows 2000 Components:** The next step is to add the optional components and services. Ignore most of these services in trial installations and go directly to the Networking Options. Here, you will have to provide DHCP information, the DNS server address, and others. Some of the services are selected for you by default, such as Transaction Server and IIS. If you are not going to use a service such as transaction server, then uncheck it. The Windows 2000 Components dialog box is illustrated in Figure 5-2.

7. **Terminal Services:** You will also be asked to choose the operating mode of Terminal Services. Choose Administration mode. There is no point in choosing Application Server mode until you are ready, and the mode can be changed any time. (See also Chapter 25.)

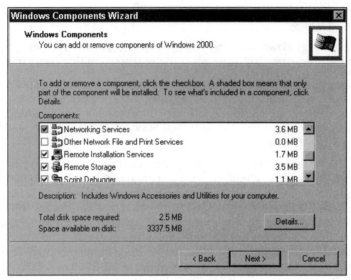

Figure 5-2: The Windows 2000 Components dialog box

8. **Display Settings:** These settings allow you to configure the screen resolution, number of display colors, and video-related information such as refresh rate. You can leave many of these settings to the default. However, change your screen resolution to at least 800×600. Many Windows 2000 folders and menus are jam-packed with icons and information. And 640×480 just does not work. In many cases, you should go with 1024×768 resolution.

9. **Time and Date:** These settings allow you to set time zones and daylight savings information, and to adjust the current date and time. After this information has been applied, Windows 2000 will start phase three of the installation process, the network install.

Windows network install

This phase installs the networking components. Windows 2000 will attempt to detect the network interface cards (NICs). If you use standard well-known brands like 3Com, you'll have no problems getting through the installation. The following list describes the steps, both automatic and interactive.

1. **Network card detection:** After detecting and installing the drivers for the NICs, Windows 2000 will attempt to locate a DHCP server on the network. It does this by broadcasting on DHCP Port 75 and then listening for a response from a DHCP server. If Windows 2000 is not able to obtain an IP address, it will use the auto-configuration protocol and assign itself an IP address. You can then continue with the installation, installing to a new workgroup, and make the necessary network connections later.

2. **Networking components:** Next, you are asked to choose the networking components. The basic options to choose are the client for Microsoft Networks, File and Print Sharing for Microsoft Networks, and TCP/IP. You can install other services and components at any time after installation. If you are installing into an existing NT domain, which does not have DNS or WINS servers in place, then install NetBIOS as well. You can also install IPX/SPX if you are going to integrate with Gateway Services for NetWare (GSNW).

3. **Workgroup or domain:** If you are installing into a domain, you will need the name of the administration account and password that has the authority to create new accounts in the domain. If you have problems installing into the domain, install into a workgroup. If you do not have a workgroup, create any workgroup name on the fly, such as *awshucks,* because you can always change it after installation or change to a domain when you are ready, post installation.

Final installation Setup

This is the fourth phase of the installation, which involves final file copy, configuration, and removal of temporary files. The Setup program copies all remaining files to the hard disk. These include bitmap files, accessories, and services or component files that will either be installed into service or left dormant until activated. Setup will then apply configuration settings specified during earlier interaction.

The new configuration will be saved in the registry databases and on disk to be used for the configuration when the computer starts anew. At this time, all temporary files are removed from the computer. After this activity, the machine is rebooted.

Installing from the Network

You can also install servers from network share-points, which are called distribution drives or servers. Network installs should obviously be limited to local area network installation because anything less than the standard 10Mbit/sec network speed will make installation an excruciatingly slow experience.

If you have not created a distribution share, simply copy the I386 folder on the Windows 2000 Server CD to a drive and share it. Apply the necessary access control to prevent unauthorized users from accessing the distribution files. The process, once you have a distribution point in place, is as follows:

1. Create a FAT partition on the target machine. This partition should be within the earlier recommended parameters. You can use the old faithful DOS FDISK command to create the partition, but if you are using a very large disk (more than 2GB), only Windows 98's FDISK for FAT32 will enable you to configure all the space as one huge drive.

2. Boot to a network client. You can use Windows 95/98 boot disks, but a simple DOS might be all you need. Your DOS client contains the following software:

   - TCP/IP protocol files
   - DOS operating system files for minimum machine life
   - Network interface card drivers (another reason to use good cards that require no configuration)

3. You will also need to create configuration files that log the target machine onto the network and allow it to use the source distribution share-point.

The Network Client folder on the CD in the back of this book includes a network client disk that you can modify, courtesy of the *Windows 2000 Server Bible* lab team.

Once you have connected to the network share-point, you start the installation by executing `winnt.exe` from the distribution server. The following now takes place:

1. `Winnt.exe` creates the four Windows 2000 Setup boot disks using your local drive A: as the target. Have four formatted disks available.

2. `Winnt.exe` creates the `$Win_nt$` temporary folder on your target machine.

3. `Winnt.exe` copies certain installation files to the temporary folder on the target server.

The process that now takes place is identical to installing from the boot disks as described earlier.

Streamlining Setup from the Command Line with Winnt and Winnt32

`Winnt.exe` and `winnt32.exe` can take a number of parameters that help you streamline the install process. Use the network client to get the target server to the distribution folder as discussed earlier. Then run `winnt` with the optional parameters. The syntax is as follows:

```
[pathtowinnt]\winnt.exe [parameter]
```

Winnt

`Winnt` starts the install process from a command line, while `winnt32` starts the installation from within another Win32 operating system. Table 5-4 provides the parameters for the `winnt.exe` command.

Table 5-4
Winnt.exe Optional Parameters

Parameter	Purpose
/a	Turns on the Accessibility feature during the Setup process.
/e:[command]	Executes the command specified in [command] when installation completes.
/I:[inf file]	Specifies the file name of the information file (.inf). This file is used for Setup and replaces the default DOSNET.INF. You do not need to include the path to this file.
/r:[folder]	Name of an additional folder to be created in the folder in which you install Windows 2000. This folder remains after Setup and can be used for custom installations or additional software. This is often used in OEM installations. You can create multiple folders using this parameter.
/rx:[folder]	This parameter provides the same function as /r:[folder], but the folder is deleted when installation is completed.
/s:[sourcepath]	This parameter specifies the location of the Windows 2000 Setup files. You need to provide a full path to the Setup files, either specifying a driver letter or using universal naming convention (UNC) paths. You can also use multiple /s parameters.
/t:[drive letter]	This parameter specifies the drive to which you want Setup to copy its temporary files. Setup will look for a partition that has the most free space.
/u:[answer file]	The answer file is used in unattended mode. You also need to specify the location of the answer file with the /s: switch.
/udf:[id, UDF File]	The UDF parameter specifies a UDF file, which is a file that contains variable parameters to be used in unattended Setup. In other words, parameters specified in the answer file get replaced with parameters specified in the UDF file. Example: /udf:DomainName,NewDomain.udf. Be aware that if you do not specify a UDF file, the unattended Setup will suddenly require human intervention to insert a disk containing the $Unique$.udf file.

Winnt32

To run winnt32 from within a Win32 application, simply open to the command line and execute the winnt32.exe file. To execute winnt32.exe with parameters, simply tack the parameter onto the end of the command thus:

```
[pathtowinnt32]\winnt32.exe [parameter]
```

The winnt32 parameters are listed in Table 5-5.

Table 5-5
WINNT32.EXE Optional Parameters

Parameter	Purpose
/checkupgradeonly	This parameter runs the compatibility test on the existing operating system to determine upgrade potential. A report is saved to a winnt32.log file, which is placed into the installation folder for the upgrades (Windows NT) or to a file called upgrade.txt in the Windows 95/98 upgrade folders.
/cmd:[command]	Runs the command [command] that follows /cmd: after the Setup Wizard completes.
/cmdcons	This is the option that runs the Recovery Mode Console at boot for a failed installation. This can only be run after the installation has failed and terminated.
/copydir:[folder]	This option lets you copy an additional folder into the Winnt installation folder. The folder remains after the setup is completed. You can reuse the parameter.
/copysource:[folder]	Same as above, but the folder is deleted after the installation.
/debug[level:filename]	This option creates a debug log file name with the specified level. The default is a log file named c:\winnt32.log with debug level set to 2 for Warning.
/m:[folder name]	This parameter specifies the location of the folder and its name containing the system file replacements. Setup will first check this folder for files to copy and then checks the installation folder.
/makelocalsource	This parameter tells Setup to copy all installation files to the local hard disk so that if the CD or network drive becomes inaccessible, a local source exists.
/noreboot	This parameter tells Setup not to reboot after the first phase. This will allow you to run additional commands before commencing with the reboot.
/s:[sourcepath]	This parameter specifies the location of the Windows 2000 Setup files. This must be a full path using the drive map letter or the UNC format. You can use multiple /s parameters.

Parameter	Purpose
/syspart:[drive letter]	This option specifies a hard disk to which to copy Setup's startup files. This is a disk, and the partition is then made active and you can use the disk in another machine. When the new machine boots, the second phase of Setup will start automatically.
/tempdrive:[drive letter]	This option lets you specify a drive for the Windows 2000 temporary files. The drive becomes the Windows 2000 installation drive. Setup will use the partition on this drive that has the most space.
/unattend	This switch will allow you to perform upgrades in unattended mode. Run on an older operating system, Setup will attempt to retain all the older settings. You cannot use this switch if you are an OEM because the acceptance of the end user license agreement (EULA) is implicit.
/unattend:[num:answer file]	This switch loads Setup in unattended mode and uses an answer file that you provide. The *num* value is a specification for the number of seconds Setup will wait after copying the files and restarting the computer. This also is only valid if you are running Setup from Windows 2000. You also need to specify the /s switch to specify the location of the answer file.
/udf:[id, UDF File]	The UDF parameter specifies a UDF file, which is a file that contains variable parameters to be used in unattended Setup. In other words, parameters specified in the answer file get replaced with parameters specified in the UDF file. Example: /udf:DomainName,NewDomain.udf. Be aware that if you do not specify a UDF file, the unattended Setup will suddenly require human intervention to insert a disk containing the $Unique$.udf file.

The parameters in these tables are extensive, and many of them have long and difficult strings. It would obviously make more sense to put all the parameters into a single DOS batch file and execute that.

We have included an extensive section on advanced server installation in Appendix B, which deals with remote operating system installation, customizing the Setup file, and performing fully automated unattended installs. These topics require the services of the Windows 2000 Resource Kit, which is covered in detail in Appendix B. We also discuss cloning servers using resource kit tools.

Troubleshooting the Troubled Installation

Although Windows 2000 installs smoothly most of the time, we do not live in a perfect world, and there may be times when an installation fails. The following provides some pointers to determine why an installation failed and what to do about it.

Tip   When Windows 2000 performs an upgrade, it will first gather information relating to installed hardware and software and report this to you before installation begins. If some components will preclude Windows 2000 from installing, you will be given an option to remove those components or circumvent attempts by the installation process to support them in the new environment. Once you have removed or dealt with the offending components, Windows 2000 will let the installation proceed.

There is a possibility that Setup will suddenly stop midway through the installation process. If this happens, you will either get no information (the screen will freeze up) or you'll get a stop error message. You can look up this error message if you have other functioning Windows 2000 systems, or you can look it up on the Microsoft Web site.

After dozens of flawless installations on a myriad of hardware and software platforms, we had become complacent. However, one large server, a Windows NT Primary Domain Controller (PDC) running on a Compaq 6000 with a full house of hardware (array controllers and RAID-5 configuration), failed. Only after several blue screens and after we had debugged all stop error messages and attempted various boot options were we able to get the machine up. Unfortunately, we were never able to promote it to a domain controller. The entire SAM had been corrupted in the upgrading process.

If you have a non-responding system on hand and the three-fingered salute (Ctrl + Alt + Del) does not work, then either hit the Reset button or switch the machine off. Wait for about 10 seconds and then restart the machine.

Several things might now happen. The worst case is that nothing will happen and the machine will hang at a flashing cursor or something. If this happens, start the Setup process again and attempt to watch for what might be responsible for the problem. If the system freezes again, you need to look at the hardware you have installed in the machine and consider replacing parts until you get past the lockup. Specifically, look into the CPU, the system cache (which can be disabled), RAM (which should not be mixed), the system BIOS, network and hard disk controllers, and, especially, the video card. In fact, try replacing your video card before taking out any other device.

We know that this sounds a little longwinded, but a process of elimination might be the only way. After removing and replacing several items and if the installation still freezes, you might have a problem on the installation CD. This is, however, a rare situation and can obviously be confirmed if the same CD fails on another machine.

On the other hand, Setup may recover and return to a point that allows it to continue installation. In the event that you have to reinstall, Setup will detect the earlier attempt and prompt you to repair that attempt. At this point, you can either have faith that Windows 2000 will be able to repair the damage, or you can go with your gut and Windows NT experience and reinstall from scratch, whacking the partition and all.

A word of caution: If at any time you suspect you might have a hardware problem, do not try and force the install by inching forward with repetitive installation attempts. If the server is going into production, it should pass a QC install first, which means flawless installation the first time around.

Cross-Reference We discuss boot options and recovery further in Chapters 16, 17, and Appendix B.

Post Installation

After installing the operating system and logging in as an administrator, Windows 2000 will automatically present you with the *"Configure Your Server"* tool. This tool allows you to configure services such as Active Directory, DHCP, DNS, IIS, and so on. You do not need to use the tool because all the shortcuts to the various consoles can be accessed from the menu items in Administrative Tools, from the Control Panel, and from the command line. So if you wish to close it as soon as you log on, Windows 2000 will not stop you. However, the OS will present this tool to whoever logs onto a server interactively in the capacity of an administrator.

Introduction to the Boot File

The boot file (BOOT.INI) is not a complicated element, but it is very important for many reasons. The file loads a menu onto the screen at startup and allows you to select pre-boot options. It also contains certain parameters that will affect startup. In Chapter 16, we will go over some advanced troubleshooting options that involve the boot.ini file, such as recovering a system disk and booting to working mirrors in a failed mirror.

Table 5-6 looks at the variables of the boot.ini file and how they affect the startup of your server.

Table 5-6
Boot File Variables

Variable	Usage
Timeout	This is the number of seconds to display the loader. It is usually set to 25 seconds.
Default	This is the location of the default operating system that gets loaded on timeout.
Multi	This specifies the hard disk controller number and the type used. You use the SCSI parameter for drives that are connected to a SCSI parameter.
Disk	This is the disk number on which the operating system resides. This value will be 0 for IDE drives. For SCSI drives, you can specify the SCSI ID number.
rdisk	This is also the disk number on which the operating system resides.
Partition	This value represents the partition number of the disk on which the OS resides.
\WINNT=	Name of the OS between quotes. This value can be anything.

The following code is a sample boot.ini file.

```
[Boot Loader]
Timeout=25
Default=multi(0)disk(0) rdisk(0)partition(1)\WINNT
[Operating Systems]
multi(0)disk(0) rdisk(0)partition(1)\WINNT="Windows 2000 Server" /fastdetect
multi(0)disk(0) rdisk(0)partition(1)\WINNT="Windows 2000 Professional" /fastdetect
```

If your OS loses its boot.ini file, you can create one and make sure it points to the correct hard disk and partition. You will notice that partition numbers are not zero-based like the hard drive numbers. The first and primary partition on each disk is labeled partition 1.

The boot variable switches in Table 5-7 are also worth knowing in the event you have problems loading. These switches are used in the operating system section of the boot.ini file.

Further troubleshooting information is covered in Chapter 20.

Table 5-7
Boot File Variables

Switch	Usage
/basevideo	Boots the OS using the standard VGA driver. This is useful if you have problems with a certain VGA card or driver.
/crashdebug	This turns on the Automatic System Recover agent and Restart.
/maxmem:n	This limits the amount of memory to use. This option is useful for debugging possible RAM-related errors.
/scsiordinal:n	This switch assigns 0 to the first SCSI controller and 1 to the second.
/sos	Displays onscreen each driver loading during kernel load. From this, you will be able to determine which drivers may be causing problems.
/soserialmouse	Turns off the detection of the serial mouse. You can also use this switch with the =COMX if you wish to prevent detection on a specific port.

Summary

This chapter took you through the basic install procedure. We recommended that you install only what you need to get the system raised and running. Later, you can begin adding advanced components to the server and establish its role on the network or promote it to be an Active Directory domain controller.

We also took you through an exhaustive discussion of hardware. Unless you plan to install complex adapter or interface cards for specialized purposes, such as modems, telephony cards, sound cards, and the like, you will not have problems as long as you stick to tried-and-tested components.

The next chapter provides the information you will now need to configure and deploy your running server.

✦   ✦   ✦

Configuring Windows 2000 Server

This chapter explores the many tools for configuring and
managing the system, managing users, and controlling
other aspects of Windows 2000.

The Microsoft Management Console

In Windows NT, most management functions are scattered
through various utilities, some of which appear in the Control
Panel. Others are located in the Administrative Tools folder on
the Start menu. Still others are hidden in the deep recesses of
the file system, accessible only by Administrators with the time
to hunt them down. Each typically provides a unique UI and no
means of integrating tools together under a single interface.

One of the many changes in the Windows 2000 interface and
administrative structure over Windows NT is the switch to a
more homogenous approach to administrative utilities. While
many system and operating properties are still controlled
through the Control Panel, most administrative functions have
moved to the Microsoft Management Console, or MMC. The
MMC runs under Windows 2000, Windows NT, and Windows
9x. This section of the chapter examines the MMC and its
component tools.

Tip You'll find additional information about the MMC as well
as additional snap-ins at http://www.microsoft.com/
management/mmc.

Understanding the Function of the MMC

The MMC itself serves as a framework. Within that framework are various administrative tools called *consoles.* In particular, the MMC provides a unified interface for administrative tools. This means that once you learn the structure of one tool, the rest are going to follow suit (within limitations imposed by the differences in function of the various tools). Figure 6-1 shows the MMC with the Computer Management snap-in loaded (more on snap-ins shortly). As you'll learn later in this chapter, you use the Computer Management snap-in to configure most aspects of a system's hardware and software configuration.

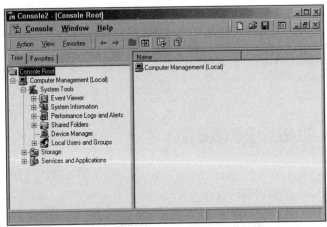

Figure 6-1: The MMC serves as a framework for a wide variety of administrative tools.

Perhaps more important than a unified interface is the fact that the MMC lets you combine administrative tools to build your own console configuration, which you can store by name on disk. The next time you need to work with it, you run the MMC console from the Start menu or double-click its icon or shortcut. For example, let's say you want to put together a custom console for managing a Windows 2000 Internet server. You can integrate the tools for managing DNS, DHCP, and IIS all under one interface. This custom console gives you quick access to most of the settings you need to configure on a regular basis for the server.

The MMC window consists of two panes. The left pane can contain two tabs: Tree and Favorites. The Tree tab generally shows a hierarchical structure for the object(s) being managed. When you use the Active Directory Users and Computers console, for example, the tree shows the containers in the Active Directory (AD) that pertain to users, groups, and computers. The Favorites tab lets you create a list of frequently used items in the tree. The right pane is the details pane. The details pane changes depending on the item you select in the tree. When you select Services in the tree, for example, the details pane shows the list of installed services.

MMC provides two different modes: *user mode* and *author mode.* In user mode, you work with existing consoles. Author mode lets you create new consoles or modify existing ones. Figure 6-2 shows the Services console opened in user mode. Figure 6-3 shows the Services console opened in author mode. As indicated in the figures, author mode offers access to commands and functions not available in user mode.

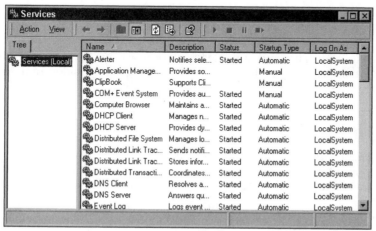

Figure 6-2: User mode restricts the actions a user can perform within a console.

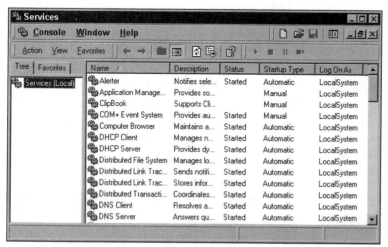

Figure 6-3: Author mode provides the ability to change console options and add new snap-ins.

User mode actually offers three different options: full access, limited access with multiple windows, and limited access with a single window. With full access, an MMC user can access all the window management commands in MMC but can't add or remove snap-ins or change console properties. The limited access options limit changes to the window configuration of the console and use either a single window or multiple windows depending on the mode. A console's mode is stored in the console and applies when you open the console. Console modes can be change via the Options property sheet (click Console ➪ Options). Setting console options is discussed later in the chapter.

Note   The default mode in Windows 2000 is user mode — limited access, single window.

As mentioned earlier, you use author mode to author new consoles or modify existing ones. In author mode, you can add and remove snap-ins, change window options, and set options for the console.

Opening the MMC

You can open MMC consoles simply by selecting them from the Administrative Tools folder in the Start menu or by double-clicking their icons in Explorer. You also can start consoles using a command prompt. The format of the MMC command is:

```
MMC path\file.msc /a /s
```

The following list explains the options for MMC:

✦ Path\file.msc: Replace path with the path to the console file specified by file.msc. You can use an absolute path or use the %systemroot% variable to reference the local computer's path to the Windows 2000 folder. Using %systemroot% is useful when you're creating shortcuts to consoles for use on different systems (where the system root folder might be different).

✦ /a: Use the /a switch to enter author mode and enable changes to the console. Opening an existing console with the /a switch overrides its stored mode for the current session.

✦ /s: Use this switch to prevent display of the splash screen that normally appears when the MMC starts on Windows NT or Windows 9x systems. This switch isn't needed when running the MMC under Windows 2000.

For example, let's say you want to open the DNS console in author mode to add the DHCP snap-in to it. Use this command to open the DNS console in author mode:

```
MMC %systemroot%\System32\dnsmgmt.msc /a
```

 Tip   You can right-click an .msc file and choose Author from the context menu to open the file in author mode.

After opening the DNS console, you add the DHCP console using the Add/Remove Snap-In command in the Console menu. Snap-ins are covered in the next section.

Tip   If you prefer, you can simply open the MMC in author mode, then add both snap-ins using the Add/Remove Snap-In command in the Console menu.

Windows 2000 provides several pre-configured consoles for performing various administrative tasks. Most of these console files are stored in \systemroot\ System32 and have .msc file extensions (for Microsoft Console). Windows 2000 places several of these consoles in the Administrative Tools folder, which you access by clicking Start ⇨ Programs ⇨ Administrative Tools. In essence, each of the pre-configured consoles contains one or more snap-ins geared toward a specific administrative task.

In an apparent effort to simplify the Start menu, Microsoft only includes some of these consoles in the Administrative Tools folder. However, you can open any console by double-clicking its file. When you do so, the MMC loads first and then opens the console. You also can open the MMC and add snap-ins to your own consoles. This gives you the ability to create a custom console containing whichever group(s) of snap-ins you use most often or that are targeted for specific administrative tasks.

Using Snap-Ins

While the MMC forms the framework for integrated administrative tools in Windows 2000, the tools themselves are called *snap-ins*. Each MMC snap-in enables you to perform a specific administrative function or group of functions. For example, you use the DHCP snap-in to administer DHCP servers and scopes. The various MMC snap-ins serve the same function as individual administrative tools did in Windows NT. For example, the Event Viewer snap-in takes the place of the standalone Event Viewer tool (Figure 6-4). The Disk Management branch of the Computer Management snap-in replaces Disk Administrator. The Active Directory Users and Computers snap-in takes the place of User Manager for Domains, and so on.

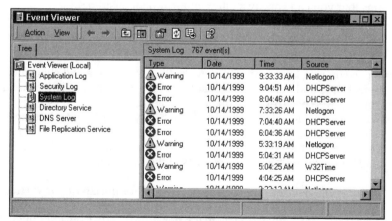

Figure 6-4: Snap-ins perform specific administrative functions and replace standalone tools such as Event Viewer.

Snap-ins come in two flavors: *standalone* and *extension*. Standalone snap-ins are usually called simply *snap-ins*. Extension snap-ins are usually called simply *extensions*. Snap-ins function by themselves and can be added individually to a console. Extensions are associated with a snap-in and are added to a standalone snap-in or other extension on the console tree. Extensions function within the framework of the standalone snap-in and operate on the objects targeted by the snap-in. For example, the Services snap-in incorporates three extensions: Send Console Message, Service Dependencies, and SNMP Snap-in Extension.

You can add snap-ins and extensions when you open a console in author mode. By default, all extensions associated with a snap-in are added when you add the snap-in, but you can selectively disable extensions for a snap-in.

To add a snap-in, open the MMC in author mode and choose Console ➪ Add/ Remove Snap-In. The Standalone page of the Add/Remove Snap-In property sheet shows the snap-ins currently loaded. The Extensions tab lists extensions for the currently selected snap-in and allows you to add all extensions or selectively enable/disable specific extensions.

In the Standalone page, click Add to add a new snap-in. The Add Standalone Snap-In dialog box lists the available snap-ins. Click the snap-in you want to add and click Add. Depending on the snap-in, you might be prompted to select the focus for the snap-in. For example, when you add the Device Manager snap-in, you can select between managing the local computer or managing another computer on the network. Adding the IP Security Policy Management snap-in lets you choose between the local computer, domain policy for the computer's domain, domain policy for another domain, or another computer.

After you configure snap-ins and extensions the way you want them, save the console so you can quickly open the same configuration later. To do so, choose Console, Save, or Save As, and specify a name for the console. Windows 2000 by default will place the new console in the Administrative Tools folder, which appears on the Start menu under Programs, but you can specify a different location if desired.

Taskpads

A taskpad is a page on which you can add views of the details pane and shortcuts to various functions inside and outside of a console. These shortcuts can run commands, open folders, open a Web page, execute menu commands, and so on. In essence, taskpads let you create a page of organized tasks to help you perform tasks quickly rather than using the existing menu provided by the snap-in. You can create multiple taskpads in a console, but the console must contain at least one snap-in. Figure 6-5 shows a taskpad for performing a variety of tasks in the DNS snap-in.

A taskpad can contain a list from the details pane in either horizontal or vertical format. Horizontal works well for multiple column lists (many fields per item), and vertical works well for long lists (few fields per item). You also can configure a taskpad to show no lists. In addition to the list, the taskpad includes an icon for each task with either a pop-up description or text description of the task. You simply click a task's icon to execute the task.

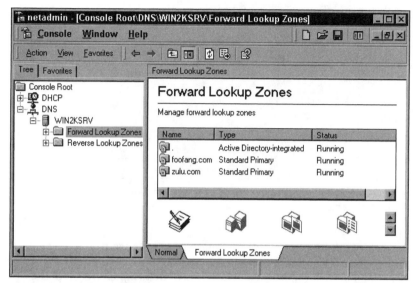

Figure 6-5: Taskpads let you create tasks for performing specific actions, such as these DNS-related tasks.

Creating a taskpad

To create a taskpad, right-click the object in the tree that you want to be the focus of the taskpad, then choose New Taskpad View. MMC starts a wizard to help you create the taskpad. In the first page of the wizard (Figure 6-6), you define the appearance of the taskpad. As you make selections, the wizard shows the results to help you determine the effect of your choices.

In the second page of the wizard, you specify the items to which the taskpad applies. The following list summarizes the options:

✦ **Selected tree item:** This option applies the taskpad only to the selected item in the tree. Using the DNS snap-in as an example, creating a taskpad for Forward Lookup Zones and using this option will cause the taskpad to appear only when you click Forward Lookup Zones. It will not appear if you click Reverse Lookup Zones.

✦ **All tree items that are the same type as the selected tree item:** This option applies the taskpad to all objects in the tree that are the same type as the selected object. Using the previous DNS example, choosing this option will cause the taskpad to display when you click either Forward Lookup Zones or Reverse Lookup Zones.

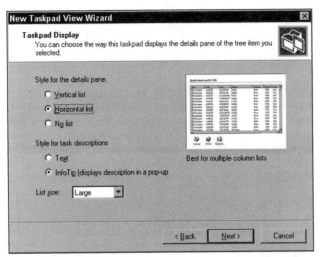

Figure 6-6: The first wizard page helps you configure the way the taskpad appears.

✦ **Change default display to this taskpad view for these tree items:** Select this option to have the MMC automatically switch to taskpad view when the user clicks the object in the tree associated with the taskpad. Deselect the option to have the MMC default to the normal view instead.

The third page of the wizard prompts you for a taskpad view name and description. The name appears at the top of the taskpad and on the tab at the bottom of the taskpad. The description appears at the top of the taskpad under the taskpad name.

On the final page of the wizard, you can click Finish to create the taskpad. The Start New Task wizard option, if selected, causes the Start New Task wizard to execute when you click Finish. This wizard, described in the next section, helps you create tasks for the taskpad.

Creating tasks

After you create a taskpad, you'll naturally want to create tasks to go on it. Select the Start New Task wizard option if you are in the process of creating the taskpad. Or, right-click the node in the tree that is associated with the taskpad, choose Edit Taskpad View, click the Tasks tab, then click New.

The first functional page of the wizard prompts you to select the type of task to add. These include the following:

✦ **Menu command:** Choose this option to execute a menu command. In the subsequent wizard page, you specify the source for the command and the command itself. The available commands fall within the context of the selected source. Select an object, then select the desired command.

✦ **Shell command:** Choose this option to start a program, execute a script, open a Web object, execute a shortcut, or perform any other task you can execute from a command line. The wizard prompts you for the command, optional command-line parameters or switches, startup folder, and window state (minimized, normal, maximized).

✦ **Navigation:** Choose this option to add an icon for an existing item listed in Favorites. See the section, "Favorites," later in this chapter to learn how to add to the Favorites list.

The wizard also prompts you for a task name, description, and icon to associate with each task, and gives you the option at completion of running the wizard again to create another task.

Modifying a taskpad

You can modify an existing taskpad to add or remove tasks or change taskpad view options. Right-click (in the tree) the object associated with the taskpad, then choose Edit Taskpad View. MMC displays a property sheet for the taskpad. The General page shows the same properties you specified when you created the taskpad, such as list type, list size, and so on. Change options as desired.

The Tasks page (Figure 6-7) lists existing tasks and lets you create new ones. New starts the New Task wizard. Remove deletes the selected task. Modify lets you change the task name, description, and icon for the task, but not modify the task itself. To modify the task, remove the task and recreate it. You also can use the up and down arrows to change the order of tasks in the list, which changes their order of appearance on the taskpad.

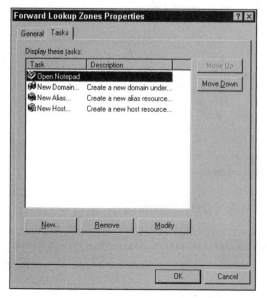

Figure 6-7: Use the Tasks page to add, remove, and modify tasks.

Favorites

The Favorites list in the left pane of the MMC lets you access often-used objects in a console with a single click. The Favorites list appears when you open a console in author mode or if the Favorites list contains any items. The tab doesn't show up in the left pane when the console is opened in user mode or if the Favorites list is blank. It is useful for quickly accessing objects that are buried deep in the tree. You also can use Favorites to simplify the view of the tree for inexperienced users.

To add an item to Favorites, click the object in the tree to which you want to create the shortcut, then choose Favorites ➪ Add to Favorites. Specify a name for the shortcut and the folder in which you want it created. Click New Folder to create a new folder for the shortcut.

You can use the Organize Favorites dialog box to create folders, move items from one folder to another, and rename or delete items. Choose Favorites ➪ Organize Favorites to open the Organize Favorites dialog box.

Other Add-In Tools

Snap-ins are just one of the objects you can add to an MMC console. Other objects include ActiveX controls, links to Web pages, folders, taskpad views, and tasks. The previous section explained taskpad views and tasks. The following list summarizes the additional items:

✦ **ActiveX controls:** You can add ActiveX controls to a console as the details/results view (right pane) for the selected node of the tree. The System Monitor Control that displays system performance status in Performance Monitor is an example of an ActiveX control. Choose Console ➪ Add/Remove Snap-In, select ActiveX Control from the list, and then click Add. The MMC provides a wizard to help you embed ActiveX controls, prompting you for additional information when necessary.

✦ **Links to Web pages:** You can add links to URLs in a console, which can be any URL viewable within a browser (Web site, ftp site, and so on).

✦ **Folders:** Insert folders as containers in the console to contain other objects. You can use folders as a means of organizing tools in a console.

Tip   Would you like to add a local or network folder to a console? Just use the Link to Web page object and point it to the folder instead of an Internet URL.

Customizing MMC to Suit Your Needs

Like most applications, you can customize the MMC to suit your needs or preferences. First, you can configure the settings for a console when you author it to determine the way it displays in subsequent sessions. For example, you might want to configure a console for user mode—limited access, single window, to limit the actions the users can perform with the console. To configure a console, first open the console in author mode. Choose Console, Options to open the Options dialog box for the console (Figure 6-8). Specify settings and then save the console. The changes will take effect the next time the console is opened.

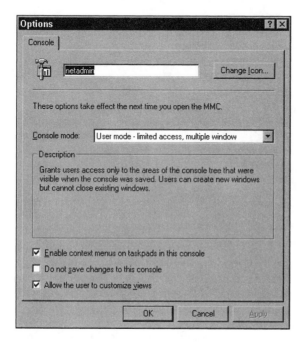

Figure 6-8: Use the Options dialog box to configure the console for future sessions.

The following list explains the available options:

✦ **Change Icon:** Click to change the icon associated with the .msc file. You'll find several icons in systemroot\system32\Shell32.dll.

✦ **Console mode:** Choose the mode in which you want the console to open for the next session. Choose between author mode and one of the three user modes discussed previously.

✦ **Enable context menus on taskpads in this console:** Select this option to enable context menus in taskpads. If deselected, right-clicking a taskpad object will have no effect (no context menu is displayed).

✦ **Do not save changes to the console:** Select this option to prevent the user from saving changes to the console, in effect, write-protecting it.

✦ **Allow the user to customize views:** Select this option to allow users to add windows focused on items in the console. Deselect to prevent users from adding windows.

You also can control view options within the MMC. To do so, choose View ➪ Customize to access the Customize View dialog box (Figure 6-9). The options in the Customize View dialog box are self-explanatory.

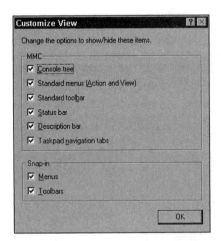

Figure 6-9: Use Customize View to set view properties in the MMC.

Control Panel versus MMC

Even though the MMC now serves as the focal point for many of the administration tasks you'll perform on a regular basis, the Control Panel hasn't gone away. The Control Panel is alive and well and contains several objects for configuring the system's hardware and operating configuration. The tools provided for the MMC do not take the place of the Control Panel objects or vice-versa. However, you will find some of the MMC tools in the Administrative Tools folder in the Control Panel.

The Control Panel in Windows 2000 works much like the Control Panels in Windows NT and Windows 9x. In fact, many of the objects are the same or similar. Latter sections of this chapter explore the Control Panel objects. The following section examines the core set of MMC tools for managing a Windows 2000 system.

MMC Tools

As explained previously, Windows 2000 contains several pre-defined consoles for managing a variety of tasks both on local computers and across the network. The following sections provide an overview of these tools.

Component Services

The primary function of the Component Services console (Figure 6-10) is to provide management tools for COM+ applications. COM+ provides a structure for developing distributed applications (client/server applications). The Component Services console lets you configure a system for Component Services, configure initial service settings, install and configure COM+ applications, and monitor and tune components.

Note Configuring COM+ applications goes hand-in-hand with COM+ application development. For that reason, this book doesn't provide detailed coverage of COM+ configuration.

The three primary branches of the Component Services node under each computer are as follows:

✦ **COM+ Applications:** Use this branch to configure Component and Role properties and settings for the COM+ IMDB Proxy Connection Manager, IMDB Utilities, QC Dead Letter Queue Listener, Utilities, and System Application.

✦ **Distributed Transaction Coordinator:** Use this branch to view the DTC transaction list and monitor transaction statistics.

✦ **IMDB Data Sources:** Use this branch to add or delete IMDB data sources and set properties of existing data sources.

Note You'll notice that the Component Services console that is provided with Windows 2000 includes nodes for the Event Viewer and Services. These are also available as separate consoles. See the sections, "Event Viewer," and, "Services," later in this chapter for more details.

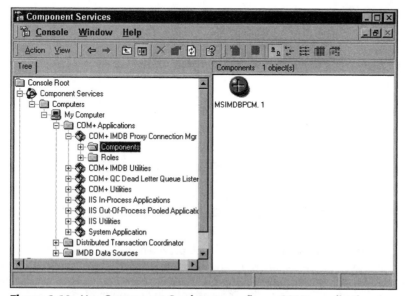

Figure 6-10: Use Component Services to configure COM+ applications as well as general Windows 2000 services.

Computer Management

The Computer Management console (Figure 6-11) provides tools for managing several aspects of a system. Right-click My Computer and choose Manage, or click Start ➪ Programs ➪ Administrative Tools ➪ Computer Management to open the Computer Management console. Computer Management is composed of three primary branches: System Tools, Storage, and Services and Applications. System Tools provides extensions for viewing information about the system, configuring devices, viewing event logs, and so on. Storage provides tools for managing physical and logical drives and removable storage. Services and Applications lets you configure telephony, Windows Management Instrumentation (WMI), services, and the Indexing Service. Other applications can appear under this branch as well, depending on the system's configuration.

You can use Computer Management to manage either the local computer or a remote computer. Right-click the Computer Management node and choose Connect to another computer to manage a remote system. The tasks you can perform are usually the same whether locally or remotely, but some tasks can only be performed within the context of the local system. This chapter assumes you're using Computer Management to manage the local system.

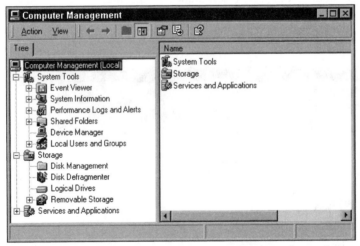

Figure 6-11: Computer Management integrates several snap-ins to help you manage a system, its storage devices, and services.

Tip   This section covers the snap-in extensions provided in the Computer Management console. However, many of these extensions can be used individually within their own consoles. For example, you can open Services.msc to configure services rather than using the Services node in Computer Management. Look in systemroot\System32 for available snap-ins (.msc file extension).

Event Viewer

The Event Viewer snap-in takes the place of the standalone Event Viewer application in Windows NT. Use Event Viewer to view events in the Application, Security, and System logs, as well as to configure log behavior (size, rollover, and so on). See the section, "Event Viewer," later in this chapter for more information.

System Information

System Information provides a place for you to browse information about the system's configuration. Note that System Information only displays information about the system—it doesn't let you configure settings.

The following list summarizes the branches in System Information:

✦ **System Summary:** This branch shows general information about the system including OS name and version, system name, BIOS version, physical and virtual memory, and so on.

✦ **Hardware Resources:** This branch provides information about resource allocation for DMA, IRQ, I/O base addresses, memory, and so on.

✦ **Components:** This branch lists resources for individual components such as the display, modem, network, USB, and so on.

✦ **Software Environment:** Use this branch to view information about driver status, environment variables, network connections, scheduled tasks, and so on.

✦ **Internet Explorer 5:** This branch displays information about Internet Explorer 5 including general information, file versions, cache contents and statistics, certificates, and so on.

Perhaps the most useful aspect of the System Information branch is that you can extract the information to a text file or system information file. The text file can be opened in any text editor, incorporated into a report document, embedded in an e-mail message, and so on. The system information file (.nfo file) uses a proprietary file format that can be read and displayed by the System Information snap-in extension. Saving a system's configuration to disk in .nfo format lets you take a "snapshot" of the system to use as a baseline for comparing later changes or simply as a record of the system's settings. The benefit of saving the configuration to a .nfo file rather than a text file is that you can view it in a hierarchical structure within the snap-in. The benefit of using a text file is that you can incorporate the data in other documents.

To save a .nfo file, right-click any node of the System Information branch and choose Save As System Information File. Specify a file name and click OK. System Information saves the entire branch regardless of where you clicked it (it could take a while for the file to be generated). To view a .nfo file, simply double-click the file (Figure 6-12).

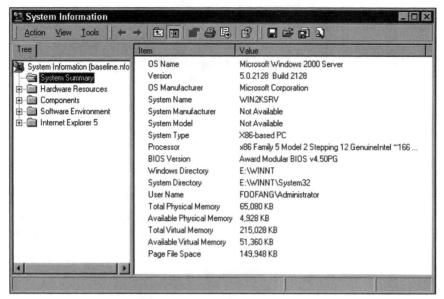

Figure 6-12: You can view a saved `.nfo` file within the System Information snap-in extension by double-clicking the `.nfo` file.

When you save data to a text file instead of a `.nfo` file, you can save only a particular sub-branch, if desired. You can save an individual System Information branch to a text file using one of two methods. First, you can right-click the branch and choose Save As Text File. After you specify a file name, System Information saves the contents of the branch as a tab-delimited file. The node from which you save the file determines the amount of data in it. For example, right-click System Information and choose Save As Text File to save the entire System Information branch to a tab-delimited file. As with the `.nfo` file, saving the entire branch can take a while depending on the speed of your system.

The second method of saving the information to a text file offers one other benefit: You can choose the file delimiting method. Right-click the level from which you want to generate the report file and choose Export List. Specify a file name and from the Save as type drop-down list choose between tab-delimited and comma-delimited, then click Save. To save a single item from the details list, select the option Save Only Selected Rows in the Save As dialog box.

> **Note** Unfortunately, System Information lets you select only a single item, so there is no way to select and save a range of information. You'll have to save the whole branch and then edit the file to eliminate the unwanted data.

You also can print a report of a given branch. To do so, right-click the branch and choose Print.

System Information provides a search feature that you can use to locate specific information about hardware or settings in the System Information branch. This is particularly useful since System Information contains a lot of information.

Follow these steps to perform a search in System Information:

1. Click the level at which you want to search.

2. Choose Action ⇨ Find and enter your search text in Find What.

3. Choose between the following options:

   • Check Restrict Search to Selected Category to search only the currently selected category. Uncheck this to search all categories.

   • Check Search Categories Only to search only the console (left) pane and not the results (right) pane for the specified text. Uncheck this to search the results pane as well.

4. Click Find Next to begin the search.

Performance Logs and Alerts

The Performance Logs and Alerts branch of the Computer Management snap-in provides a tool for setting up performance monitoring. You can configure counter logs, trace logs, and alerts. This branch is useful only for viewing or modifying settings — it doesn't enable you to actually execute any performance monitoring. Instead, you need to use the Performance MMC snap-in. See Chapter 20 for detailed information on configuring performance logs and alerts, and monitoring system performance.

Shared Folders

The Shared Folders branch of the Computer Management snap-in lets you view and manage shared folders, connections, and open files. It takes the place of features formerly found in the Windows NT Server Manager. The Shares node lets you view shares on the selected computer. In addition, you can double-click a share to view and modify its properties and share permissions. See Chapter 20 for information on publishing folders in the Active Directory.

Tip　You can create and manage shared folders through the Explorer interface. The advantage to using Shared Folders instead is that you can see all shares on the system at a glance.

You'll notice that a system includes a handful of shares by default, most of which are hidden shares (suffixed with a $ sign). These shares include the following:

✦ `drive$`: Windows 2000 shares the root of each drive as a hidden share for administrative purposes. You can connect to the share using the UNC path `\\server\drive$`, where *server* is the computer name and *drive* is the drive letter, such as `\\appsrv\d$`. Members of the Administrators and Backup Operators groups can connect to administrative shares on Windows 2000 Professional systems. Members of the Server Operators group can connect to administrative shares on Windows 2000 Server systems, as well as Administrators and Backup Operators.

✦ `ADMIN$`: This administrative share points to the `systemroot` folder on the system (typically, `\WINNT`) and is used by the system during remote administration.

✦ `IPC$`: The `IPC$` share is used to share named pipes and is used during remote administration and when viewing a computer's shares.

✦ `PRINT$`: This share enables remote printer administration and points by default to `systemroot\System32\spool\drivers`.

✦ `NETLOGON`: This share is used to support user logon, typically for storing user logon scripts and profiles. There is no pre-defined `NETLOGON` share for Windows 2000 Professional computers, but such a system will look by default in the `systemroot\System32\Repl\Import\Scripts` folder of the local computer when the user logs on locally in a workgroup for profiles and scripts. In Windows 2000 domains, the `NETLOGON` share points to `sysvol\domain\Scripts` on the domain controller(s).

✦ `FAX$`: This share is present when the fax service is installed and shared. It serves to cache files and cover pages.

Cross-Reference   For a complete discussion of sharing and security, offline folder access, and related topics, see Chapter 22.

The Sessions node lets you view a list of users currently connected to the system. You can disconnect a user by right-clicking the user and choosing Close Session. Disconnecting a user could result in lost data for the user, so you might want to broadcast a console message to the user first. To do so, right-click any branch of Shared Folders and choose All Tasks, Send Console Message.

Tip   When you are viewing sessions for a remote computer, your connection appears as an open-named pipe and can't be closed.

The Open Files branch lets you view files opened by remote users. Right-click an individual file and choose Close Open File to close the file. Or, right-click the Open Files node and choose Disconnect All Open Files to close all files. As when disconnecting users, closing files could result in a loss of data, so try to broadcast a console message to the user first.

Device Manager

The Device Manager is a new feature in Windows 2000, its closest Windows NT cousin being the Devices object in the Windows NT Control Panel. Windows 9*x* users and administrators will find the Device Manager a familiar and welcome sight.

Device Manager provides a unified interface for viewing and managing devices and their resources (DMA, memory, IRQ, and so on). Device Manager displays devices using a branch structure. Expand a device branch to view the devices in the branch. No special icon beside a device indicates the device is functioning properly. A yellow exclamation icon indicates a potential problem with the device, such as a resource conflict. A red X indicates the device is disconnected, disabled, or not in use in the current hardware profile.

Device Manager is the primary tool you use for configuring a system's hardware. To view or manage a device, locate it in the details pane and double-click the device (or right-click and choose Properties) to display the device's property sheet. The contents of the property vary according to the device type. Figure 6-13 shows a typical property sheet for a network adapter.

Figure 6-13: Use a device's property sheet to view and configure settings such as resource usage.

The General page, shown in Figure 6-13, provides general information about a device, such as device type, manufacturer, and so on. Use the Device usage drop-down list to enable or disable the device. Click Troubleshooter if you're having problems with the device and want to use a wizard to help troubleshoot the connection.

Note It isn't practical to cover all the settings for all possible types of devices in this chapter. The following sections explain tasks common to most devices: changing drivers and modifying resource assignments.

Driver changes

The Driver property page lets you view details about, uninstall, and update a device's driver. Click Driver Details to view a list of the files that comprise the device's driver. This list is useful for checking file or driver version to make sure you're using a specific version of the driver. Use Uninstall if you want to remove the selected device's driver.

The Update Driver button opens the Upgrade Device Driver wizard. Use the wizard to install an updated driver for the device. The wizard gives you the option of searching your system's floppy and CD-ROM drives, other specific location (local or remote share), or the Microsoft Windows Update Web site. Just follow the prompts to complete the update. In some cases, changing drivers requires a system restart.

Resource assignment

Because it supports Plug-and-Play (PnP), Windows 2000 can assign device resources such as DMA, IRQ, I/O base address, and UMA memory allocation automatically. In some cases, particularly with legacy devices (those not supporting PnP), you'll have to configure resource allocation manually. To do so, open a device's property sheet and click the Resources tab. If the Resources page doesn't provide any resources to change, click Set Configuration Manually to switch the page to manual property configuration (Figure 6-14).

In most cases, Windows 2000 provides multiple, pre-defined configurations for devices, such as a combination of a specific IRQ and I/O range. Deselect the Use automatic settings option, then select a different configuration set from the Setting based on the drop-down list. To modify individual settings, first click in the Resource settings list the resource you want to change, then click Change Setting. Specify the desired setting in the resulting dialog box and click OK.

Local Users and Groups

The Local Users and Groups branch of the Computer Management snap-in lets you create and manage local user accounts and groups on Windows 2000 Professional computers and member servers. This branch is disabled on a domain controller, since you use the Active Directory Users and Computers snap-in to create user accounts and groups in the Active Directory.

Cross-Reference Users and groups are covered in detail in Chapter 10.

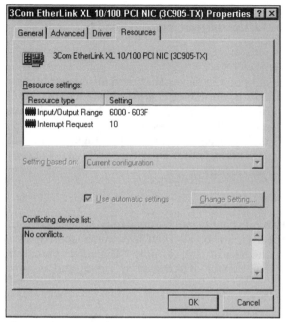

Figure 6-14: Set a device's resource utilization through its Resources property page.

If you're familiar with creating user accounts and groups under Windows NT, you'll have no problem using Local Users and Groups to create accounts. If not, see Chapter 10 for a detailed description of how to create accounts and groups. The primary difference between creating local accounts and groups and the same objects in the Active Directory is that the Active Directory provides for additional account and group properties. In addition, creating accounts and groups requires an understanding of permissions, rights, group policy, and user profiles, all of which are explained in Chapter 10.

Disk Management

The Disk Management node is the place to go to manage physical disks and volumes. Disk Management takes the place of the Windows NT Disk Administrator, and an important distinction is that unlike the Disk Administrator, Disk Management performs most tasks immediately. In Disk Administrator, you must commit changes for most tasks (such as creating or deleting a partition). If you're an experienced Windows NT administrator, keep this important point in mind when making storage changes with Disk Management.

Some of the tasks you can perform with Disk Management include managing partitions, converting basic disks to dynamic disks, creating volumes (basic, spanned, striped, mirrored, RAID-5), creating and deleting physical volumes, formatting disks, and so on. For a complete discussion of storage devices and management (including the Disk Management node), see Chapter 16.

Disk Defragmenter

As a disk is used over time, the data on the disk is scattered into noncontiguous clusters, becoming *fragmented*. Disk performance is greatest when data is not fragmented, as it takes less time to read the data (since the drive heads don't have to move as much to reassemble the data). The Disk Defragmenter node in Computer Management lets you analyze a disk for fragmentation and defragment the disk. See Chapter 21 for a discussion of Disk Defragmenter and other options for improving disk performance.

Logical Drives

The Logical Drives node displays information such as capacity, space used, and free space about logical drives in the system. You also can set volume label for a volume. For NTFS volumes, you can use the Security tab to apply NTFS object permissions to the volume. See Chapter 22 for a discussion of permissions, rights, and assigning object permissions.

Removable Storage

The Removable Storage node provides a tool for configuring and managing removable storage devices and media. You use Removable Storage to track media such as tapes and optical disks and their hardware devices (jukeboxes, tape changers, and so on). Removable storage is a technology subset of Hierarchical Storage Management (HSM) and Remote Storage Services (RSS). These new technologies provide a means for automatic data archival and retrieval of archived data.

The Removable Storage node lets you create and manage media pools, insert and eject media, mount and dismount media, view media and library status, inventory libraries, and assign permissions for security on media and libraries.

Telephony

The Telephony node provides a centralized tool for managing telephony properties for the selected computer, including configuring telephony providers and assigning user permission for various providers.

WMI Control

The WMI Control node in Computer Management provides tools for configuring and managing Windows Management Instrumentation (WMI) on a computer. WMI works in conjunction with the Web-Based Enterprise Management initiative to provide a means of collecting data about computers and their component devices both locally and remotely. WMI functions at the device-driver level, providing event notification from drivers and enabling WMI to collect data for analysis and management purposes. WMI is a key component in enterprise management. The WMI Control node provides a means for configuring general settings, logging, backup and restore of the WMI repository, and security to control WMI access.

Services

In Windows 2000, *services* are applications that perform specific functions such as networking, logon, print spooling, remote access, and so on within the operating system. You can think of services as operating system-oriented applications that function by themselves or in concert with other services or user applications to perform specific tasks or provide certain features within the OS. Device drivers, for example, function as services. Both Windows 2000 Professional and Server include several standard services by default, and many third-party applications function as or include their own services. A background virus scrubber is a good example of a possible third-party service.

Windows NT administrators will remember the Services object in the Control Panel that enables you to configure, start, stop, and pause services. In Windows 2000, the Services node in the Computer Management snap-in takes over that function (Figure 6-15). Services lists the installed services on the target system, and when Detail view is selected, displays description, status, startup type, and account the service uses to log on.

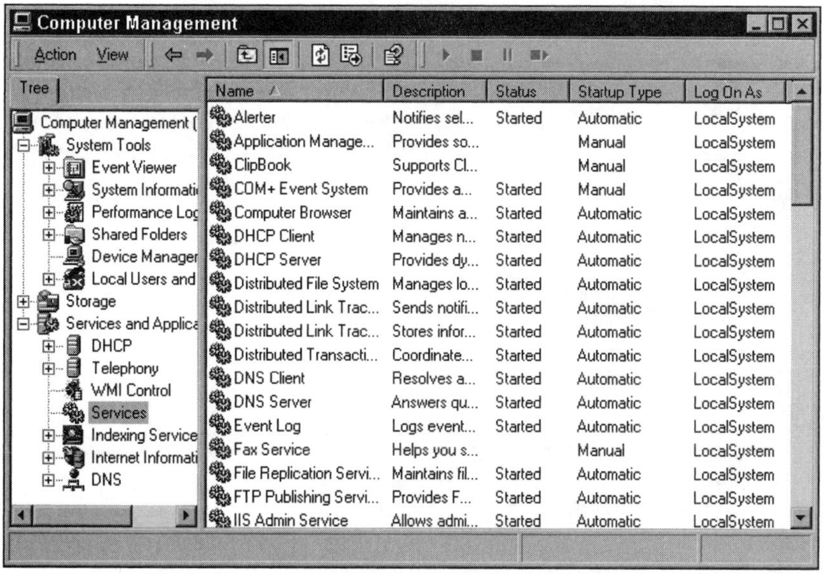

Figure 6-15: Use Services to configure, start, stop, and pause services, as well as view service dependencies.

Starting and stopping services

A running service processes requests and generally performs the task it was designed to accomplish. Stopping a service terminates the service and removes it from memory. Starting a service initializes and activates the service so it can perform its task or function. For example, the DNS Client, when running functions as a DNS resolver, processes requests for name to address mapping in the DNS namespace. If you stop the DNS Client service, it is no longer available to process DNS queries.

Like Windows NT, Windows 2000 supports three startup modes for services:

✦ **Automatic:** The service starts automatically at system startup.

✦ **Manual:** The service can be started by a user or a dependent service. The service does not start automatically at system startup unless a dependent service is set for automatic startup (therefore causing the service to start).

✦ **Disabled:** The service cannot be started by the system, a user, or dependent service.

You set a service's startup mode through the General page of the service's properties. Open the Services node in the Computer Management MMC snap-in (or open the Services.msc console in `systemroot\System32`) and double-click the service. Figure 6-16 shows the General property page for a typical service. From the Startup type drop-down list, choose the desired startup mode and click Apply or OK.

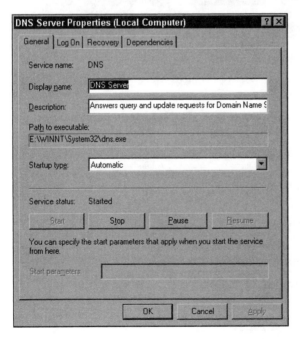

Figure 6-16: Use the General page to configure service startup, control the service (start/stop), and set general properties.

The General tab also lets you start, stop, pause, or resume a service. Starting and stopping were explained previously. Pausing a service causes it to suspend operation but doesn't remove the service from memory. Resume a paused service to have it continue functioning. Open a service's General property page, then click Start, Stop, Pause, or Resume, as appropriate.

You also can start and stop services from a console prompt using the NET START and NET STOP commands along with the service's name, which you'll find on its General property page in the Service name field. For example, use the command NET START ALERTER to start the Alerter service. Use NET STOP ALERTER to stop it.

> **Tip**
>
> NET START and NET STOP are very useful for controlling services remotely. If the telnet service is running on the remote computer, you can telnet to the computer and use NET START and NET STOP to start and stop services on the remote system.

Setting General service properties

Other settings on a service's General property page control how the service is listed in the details pane and how it starts up. Use the Display name field to specify the name that will appear under the Name field for the service in the details pane. Specify the service's description in the Description field. Use the Start parameters field to specify optional switches or parameters to determine how the service starts. These are just like command-line switches for a console command.

Configuring service logon

The Log On property page for a service controls how the service logs on and the hardware profiles in which the service is used. Most services log on using the System account, although in some cases you'll want to specify a different account for a service to use. Some types of administrative services often use their own accounts because they require administrative privileges. So, you'd create an account specifically for the service and either make it a member of the Administrators group or give it the equivalent permissions, subject to its specific needs.

> **Tip**
>
> Avoid using the Administrator account itself for a service to log on. When you change the Administrator password (which you should do often if you use this account), you will also have to reconfigure each service that used the Administrator account to change the password in the service's properties. Using a special account for those services instead lets you change the Administrator account password without affecting any services. Check out Chapters 10 and 11 where we spend a lot of effort to hide the Administrator account and discontinue its use.

The Log On property page contains the following controls:

✦ **Local System account:** Select to have the service log on using the local System account.

✦ **Allow service to interact with desktop:** Select to allow the service to provide a UI for the currently logged-on user to interact with the service. This setting has no effect if the service isn't designed to provide a UI.

✦ **This account:** Select and specify an account in the associated text box (or browse through the account list) to have the service log on with an account other than the local System account.

✦ **Password/Confirm Password:** Enter and confirm the password for the account specified in This account.

✦ **Enable/Disable:** Select a hardware profile from the list of profiles and click Enable to enable the service in that profile or Disable to disable the service in the profile.

Configuring service recovery

Another behavior you can configure for services is what happens when the service fails. You can configure the service to restart, execute a file, or reboot the computer. In addition, you can configure a fail counter to track how many times the service has failed. You set a service's recover options through its Recovery property page (Figure 6-17).

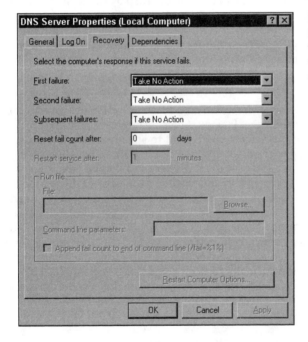

Figure 6-17: Configure service recovery option to specify what actions the service should take when it fails.

The Recovery page contains the following options:

✦ **First failure/Second failure/Subsequent failures:** With these three drop-down lists, select the action (or no action) to take on the specified failure. You can choose to take no action, restart the service, execute a file, or reboot the computer.

✦ **Reset fail count after:** Specify the number of days after which to reset the fail counter to zero.

✦ **Restart service after:** Specify the number of minutes that will pass between service failure and restart. Increase from the default of one minute if the system needs more time to stabilize after the service fails.

✦ **Run file:** Use this group of commands to identify a program or script that will execute when the service fails. For example, you might create a script that broadcasts a message with the fail count and other information to the Administrators group. Use the Append fail count option to append the current fail count to the end of the command line (passing the fail count to the command for internal processing).

✦ **Restart Computer Options:** Click this button to specify the number of minutes to wait before restarting the computer and an optional message to broadcast on the network prior to restart (such as a reboot warning to your users).

Viewing dependencies

You can use the Dependencies page to view other services on which the selected service depends as well as services that are dependent on the selected service. This property page displays information only and doesn't allow you to configure or modify dependencies. The page is self-explanatory.

Indexing Service

The Indexing Service uses *document filters* to read and create a catalog of documents on a system, and enables a quick text-based search through the catalog for documents that meet the search criteria. The document filter extracts information from the document and passes it to the Indexing Service for inclusion in the catalog. You can search using the Search command in the Start menu, the Query the Catalog node of Indexing Service in Computer Management, or a Web page. You can search based on a variety of criteria including document name, author, contents, and so on. You might, for example, use the Indexing Service to build a catalog of internal documents or catalog your organization's Web site(s). The Indexing Service will index the following document types:

✦ HTML

✦ Text

✦ Microsoft Office 95 or later

✦ Internet Mail and News

✦ Other documents supported by an appropriate document filter (such as a third-party filter)

Tip   Indexing Service is useful even on a workstation to index user documents and speed up searching for specific documents or groups of documents.

Use the Indexing Service branch of the Computer Management console to configure the Indexing Service and query the index for a list of documents matching your query criteria. The Indexing Service branch appears in Computer Management even if the Indexing Service is not yet installed. To install the Indexing Service, open the Control Panel and run Add/Remove Programs. Click Add/Remove Windows Components in the left toolbar, select Indexing Service in the Components list, and then click Next and follow the prompts to install the service.

Planning for the Indexing Service

When planning for the Indexing Service, understand that the system configuration determines the service's performance. Indexing Service has the same minimum hardware requirements as Windows 2000 Server, but increasing the number of documents to be indexed increases the memory requirements. See the Help file for Indexing Service (press F1 with Indexing Service selected in Computer Management) for specific recommendations.

You also need to plan the file system to accommodate Indexing Service. Placing the catalog on a FAT volume will enable users to see the catalog even if they have no permission to view individual documents in the catalog. Placing the catalog on an NTFS volume offers the best security as Indexing Service maintains all NTFS security ACLs (Access Control Lists). Users will not see documents in the results list of a query if they don't have the permissions necessary to view the documents. In addition, the Indexing Service uses the System account to log on. If you deny the System account access to a given folder or file, Indexing Service will not be able to access the folder or file and won't index it. Also, encrypted documents are never indexed.

Where you store the index catalog(s) is also important. You should not store catalogs within a Web site (in the Web site's folder) because Internet Information Services (IIS) can lock the catalog and prevent it from being updated. Also, avoid running antivirus or backup software that locks the catalog files, which would cause Indexing Service to time out while attempting to update the catalogs. The best practice is to create a folder on an NTFS volume specifically for your catalog files, and place each catalog in its own subfolder of that primary folder.

Tip   You can change the location of the default System catalog created automatically when you install Indexing Service. First, create the folder to contain the catalog. Then right-click Indexing Service and choose Stop to stop the service. Open the Registry Editor and modify the value of HKEY_LOCAL_MACHINE\CurrentControl Set\Control\ContentIndex\Catalogs\System\Location to point to the desired location. Close the Registry Editor and restart the Indexing Service.

Creating and configuring a catalog

You can create multiple index catalogs to suit your needs. To create a new catalog, open the Computer Management snap-in and right-click the Indexing Service branch. Choose New ➪ Catalog. Specify a name for the catalog and its location, then click OK. The catalog remains offline until you restart the Indexing Service.

Next, expand the newly created catalog in the Indexing Service branch in Computer Management. Right-click Directories under the catalog's branch and choose New ⇨ Directory to display the Add Directory dialog box (Figure 6-18). Specify options according to the following list:

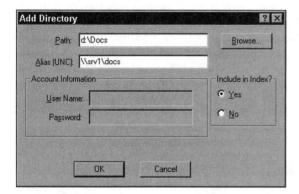

Figure 6-18: Add directories to a catalog to include their contents in the index.

✦ **Path:** Specify the path to the folder you want to add in the catalog or click Browse to the folder.

✦ **Alias (UNC):** If you're specifying a folder on a non-local computer, type the UNC path to the share in the form \\computer\share, where *computer* is the remote computer's name and *share* is the share where the folder is located.

✦ **Account Information:** For a directory on a remote computer, specify the domain\account and password to be used to access the computer.

✦ **Include in Index:** Select Yes to include the folder or No to exclude it from the catalog. This option enables you to exclude a subfolder of a folder that is included in the catalog. Add the parent folder and set it to Yes, then add the subfolder separately and set it to No to exclude it.

After you define the directories for the catalog, stop and restart the Indexing Service to populate the catalog. The Properties branch will be empty until you stop and restart the service.

Querying the catalog

As mentioned previously, you can query a catalog through a computer's Search command in the Start menu, a Web page, or the Computer Management snap-in. To perform a query using the snap-in, open the Indexing Service branch and click Query the Catalog under the desired catalog entry. Windows 2000 provides a query form in which you can specify the query criteria and options, and view the results of the query.

Tuning performance

On a system with a large number of documents, you might want to fine-tune Indexing Service for best performance. Right-click Indexing Service in the Computer Management snap-in and choose Stop to stop the service. Right-click Indexing Service again and choose Tune Performance to display the Indexing Service Usage dialog box (Figure 6-19). The options on the dialog box let you specify how often Indexing Service is used on the computer, and Windows 2000 automatically configures the service based on your selection. Choose the Customize option, then click the Customize button to specify custom settings for indexing and querying. For indexing, you can set a slider control between Lazy and Instant. Lazy causes indexing to function more as a background task, and Instant grants it maximum system resources (which takes resources from other running tasks). For querying, you can set a slider between low load and high load, depending on how many queries the computer receives.

Figure 6-19: Use the Indexing Service Usage dialog box to optimize Indexing Service's performance.

Event Viewer

Microsoft defines an *event* in Windows 2000 as any significant occurrence in the operating system or an application that requires users (particularly administrators) to be notified. Events are recorded in *event logs*. Events and the event log are important administrative tools because they're indispensable for identifying and troubleshooting problems, tracking security access (logon, logoff, resource auditing, and so on), and tracking status of the system and its applications.

Events fall into three general categories:

✦ **System:** These include system-related events such as service startup and shutdown, driver initialization, system-wide warning messages, network events, and other events that apply to the system in general.

✦ **Security:** These include events related to security such as logon/logoff and resource access (auditing).

✦ **Application:** These events are associated with specific applications. For example, a virus scrubber might log events related to a virus scan, cleaning operation, and so on, to the application log.

Note In addition to the three default event logs, other Windows 2000 services create their own logs. The Directory Service, DNS Service, and File Replication Service are some examples of services that create their own event logs. You view these logs with the Event Viewer, just as you do the three standard logs.

Events range in severity from informational messages to serious events such as service or application failures. The primary event categories include informational, warning, error, success audit, and failure audit. The severity of an event is identified by an icon beside the event in the log. Each event has common properties associated with it:

✦ **Date and Time:** This is the date and time the event occurred.

✦ **Source:** This identifies the source of the event, such as a service, device driver, application, resource, and so on. The source property is useful for determining what caused the event (cause and event source are not synonymous).

✦ **Category:** The source determines the category for an event. For example, security categories include logon, logoff, policy change, and object access, among others.

✦ **Event:** Each event includes an event ID, an integer generated by the source to identify the event uniquely.

✦ **User:** This property identifies the user that caused the event to be generated (if applicable).

✦ **Computer:** This property identifies the computer that caused the event to be generated (if applicable).

The Event Viewer MMC snap-in is the tool you use to view and manage the event logs. The Event Viewer presents the logs in the tree pane as individual branches. When you click on a log, its events appear in the contents pane (Figure 6-20).

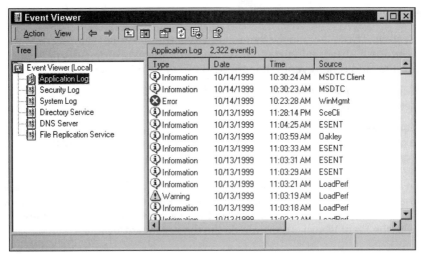

Figure 6-20: Use the Event Viewer to browse the event logs and configure log operation.

Viewing and filtering events

Viewing an event is easy — just open Event Viewer, locate the event, and double-click it (or select it and press Enter). Event Viewer opens a dialog box showing the event's properties (Figure 6-21). The top of the dialog box includes general information about the event such as time and date, event ID, and so on. The Description field provides a detailed description of the event, which most of the time (but not always) offers a decipherable explanation of the event. The bottom portion of the dialog box displays additional data included with the event, if any. You can choose between viewing the data in byte (hexadecimal) or DWORD format. In most cases, it takes a software engineer to interpret the data because doing so requires an understanding of the code generating the data.

Use the up and down arrows in the upper half of the dialog box to view previous and following events, respectively. Click the document button to copy the selected event to the Clipboard.

By default, the Event Viewer shows all events for a selected log. In many cases, it is helpful to be able to filter the view so that Event Viewer shows only events that meet specific criteria. To apply a filter, click a log and choose View ➪ Filter to access the Filter property sheet for the log (Figure 6-22).

You can choose to view events based on their type, source, category, ID, user, computer, or date range. For example, you might want to filter based on source if you're trying to troubleshoot a problem with a specific application, service, or driver. To create the filter, select your criteria in the dialog box and click OK. Choose View ➪ All Records to remove the filter and view all events in the log.

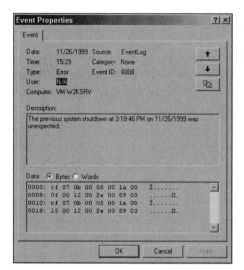

Figure 6-21: An event's property sheet provides detailed information about the event.

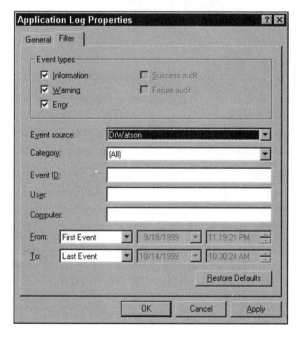

Figure 6-22: Use the Filter page to determine which events are displayed for the selected log in the Event Viewer.

Setting log properties

Each log includes general properties that define the way the log appears in Event Viewer, the size of the log, how it reacts when the maximum size is reached, and so on. Select a log and choose Action ➪ Properties or right-click a log and choose Properties to display its General property page (Figure 6-23).

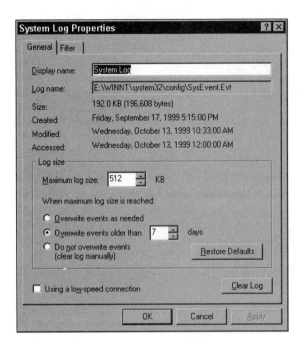

Figure 6-23: Configure a log's appearance and size through its General property page.

Some of the information displayed in the General page is read-only, such as the location of the log file. You can change the Display name property to change the name by which the log is listed in the tree pane in the Event Viewer.

The Log size group of controls specifies the maximum log size and the action Windows 2000 takes when the maximum size is reached. The options are generally self-explanatory. Keep in mind, however, that if you select Do not overwrite events, Windows 2000 will stop logging events to the log when it fills up. Although Windows 2000 will notify you when the log is full, you'll need to monitor the event log and clear it periodically to make sure you don't lose events.

Tip   Using a low-speed connection prevents Event Viewer from downloading all of the event data before you specifically request it and is useful when the logs are located on another computer accessible through a slow network connection (such as dial-up).

Saving and clearing logs

Occasionally you'll want to save an event log and/or clear the log. Saving a log copies it to another event file of a name you specify. Clearing a log removes all the events in the log. You might want to create a benchmark, for example, prior to beginning troubleshooting a problem. Or you might simply want to periodically archive your event logs. In any case, you save the log and then clear it.

To save a log, select the log and choose Action ⇨ Save Log File As or right-click the log and choose Save Log File As. Specify a name and location for the log file and click OK. After you save a log file, you can open the log again in Event Viewer to view its contents. Keep in mind that a saved log is static and doesn't gather a dditional events.

When it's time to clear a log, open the log's General property page and click Clear Log. Windows 2000 will prompt you to confirm the action.

Viewing logs on another computer

You can use Event Viewer to view the log file of other computers in your network (or across the Internet via a VPN connection). To open another computer's event logs, open Event Viewer, right-click the Event Viewer branch, and choose Connect to another computer. Specify the computer's name or browse the network for the computer, then click OK. Select the Local computer option to reconnect to the local computer's event logs.

Arranging the log view

You can arrange the Event Viewer results pane to specify which columns appear and their display order. If you seldom need to see the User or Computer columns, for example, you can turn them off.

To control column display, click any node in the Event Viewer and choose View ⇨ Choose Columns to open the Modify Columns dialog. Add and remove columns as desired and use Move Up and Move Down to change the display order. Click OK to apply the changes.

Tip   You can drag columns in Event Viewer to change their display order.

Performance

Monitoring and tuning system performance is an important administrative function in almost all situations. The Performance MMC snap-in lets you monitor a wide variety of system parameters regarding memory, processor, disk, I/O, and many other objects. The Performance snap-in takes the place of the Windows NT Performance Monitor.

Monitoring a system for optimum performance and fine-tuning the system is a fairly complex task requiring an understanding of the types of objects you can monitor and their relationships to one another. You'll find a discussion of performance tuning and the Performance snap-in in Chapter 20.

Server Extensions

In addition to the MMC snap-ins described in previous sections, Windows 2000 Server incorporates several other snap-ins for managing specific services. For example, the DNS, DHCP, and IIS services all have their own snap-ins. Since these snap-ins are the primary means by which you control these services, they are best discussed in the context of the service. You'll find these snap-ins discussed throughout this book where appropriate.

Data Sources (ODBC)

ODBC, which stands for Open DataBase Connectivity, provides a framework for database engines to communicate with client applications. An example of such a client-server tool is WebBase, a tool from Expertelligence (`http://www.expertelligence.com`) that lets you integrate database queries in Web pages. WebBase makes SQL (Structured Query Language) queries through ODBC drivers to create a Web page based on the results of the query. So, ODBC drivers serve as a middleman between a database and a client application, coordinating trans-actions and translating between the client and the database. In some cases, they can take the place of the database engine. For example, a server doesn't need Microsoft Access installed to enable clients to query an Access database file stored on the server, which is a typical practice of report engines such as Seagate Crystal Reports.

In order for client applications to communicate with a data source stored on a com-puter, you must configure the appropriate ODBC driver and connection on the target server. For example, if the client application needs to access an Access database, you need to first configure the Access ODBC driver on the computer where the database is located. The Data Sources administrative tool lets you configure and manage ODBC drivers and their associated data sources. This section of the chapter explains how to configure ODBC drivers.

 Note   The Data Sources tool is one of the few administrative tools that functions as a standalone utility rather than as an MMC snap-in.

Defining DSNs

You make data sources available to clients by creating a Data Source Name (DSN). There are three types of DSNs:

✦ **User:** A user DSN is visible only to the user who is logged on when the DSN is created.

✦ **System:** A system DSN is visible to all local services on a computer and all users who log on locally to the computer.

✦ **File:** A file DSN can be shared by all users who have the same drivers installed and who have the necessary permissions to access the DSN.

The DSN identifies the data source, the driver associated with a data source, and other properties that define the interaction between the client and the data source, such as timeout, read-only mode, and so on. You use the same process to create a DSN for most data types. The exception is SQL Server, which provides a wizard for setting up a data source.

Defining a data source

To create a data source, you first open the ODBC Data Source Administrator. To do so, click Start ➪ Programs ➪ Administrative Tools ➪ Data Sources. In the ODBC Data Source Administrator, click the tab for the DSN type you want to create, then click Add. Select the desired data source type and click Finish. Except in the case of the SQL Server driver, ODBC prompts you for information, which varies according to the driver selected. Define settings as desired and click OK to create the DSN.

Setting up an SQL Server data source

The Microsoft SQL Server ODBC driver provides a wizard to configure a SQL data source. This section explains the options you find when setting up a SQL Server ODBC driver. The first wizard page contains the following options:

✦ **Name:** This name appears in the Data Sources list on the DSN page for the data source.

✦ **Description:** This optional description appears with the DSN name on the DSN page for the data source.

✦ **Server:** Here, you specify the IP address or host name of the SQL server computer.

The second page of the wizard (Figure 6-24) prompts for connection and authentication options for the data source. The following list summarizes the options:

✦ **With Windows NT authentication using the network login ID:** Select this option to have the SQL Server ODBC driver request a trusted connection to the server. The driver uses the current client logon user name and password to authenticate the request on the server. The specified user name and password must have an association to a SQL Server login ID on the SQL Server computer.

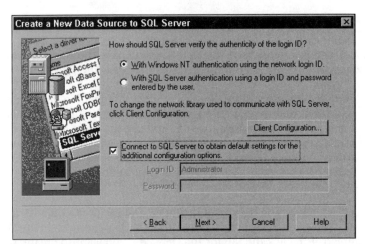

Figure 6-24: Specify connection and authentication options.

✦ **With SQL Server authentication using a login ID and password entered by the user:** Select this option to require the user to specify a SQL Server login ID and password for all connection requests.

✦ **Connect to SQL Server to obtain default settings for the additional configuration options:** Select this option to have the SQL Server ODBC driver connect to the SQL Server identified on the first page of the wizard to obtain the correct settings for options in remaining configuration wizard pages. When you click Next with this option selected, the driver connects to the SQL Server and obtains the data. Deselect this option to use default settings rather than connect to the SQL server to obtain the information.

✦ **Login ID:** Specify the user name to connect to the specified SQL server to retrieve the settings for subsequent wizard pages (see preceding bullet). This user name and the associated Password field are not used for actual data connections after the data source is created, but are only used to retrieve information from the SQL Server for the remaining configuration pages.

✦ **Password:** Specify the password to use with the user name specified in the Login ID field.

✦ **Client Configuration:** Click to use the Network Library Configuration dialog box. Usually you do not have to configure the network client configuration for the data source. Occasionally, however, you might need to specify the network connection mechanism and other options that define how the client connects to the data source. The options in Connection parameters are specific to the network connection type you select from the Network Libraries list of options.

In the next page of the wizard, you specify the database name and other options for the data source. Figure 6-25 shows the page. The following list describes its options:

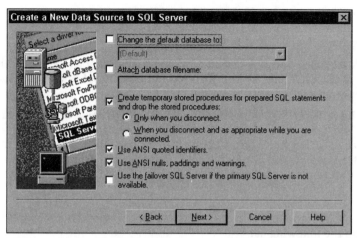

Figure 6-25: Specify the database name and other database options.

✦ **Change the default database to:** Choose a database from the drop-down list to define the default database for the data source, overriding the default database for the specified login ID. Deselect this option to use the default database defined for the login ID on the server.

✦ **Attach database filename:** Specify the full name and path of the primary file for an attachable database. The specified database is used as the default database for the data source.

✦ **Create temporary stored procedures for prepared SQL statements and drop the stored procedures:** Select this option to have the driver create temporary stored procedures to support the SQLPrepare ODBC function, then choose one of the associated options (see the following bullets). Deselect if you don't want the driver to store these procedures.

  • **Only when you disconnect:** Have the stored procedures created for the SQLPrepare function dropped only when the SQLDisconnect function is called. This improves performance by reducing the overhead involved in dropping the stored procedures while the application is running, but it can lead to a buildup of temporary stored procedures. This particularly applies to applications that issue numerous SQLPrepare calls or that run for a long time without disconnecting.

  • **When you disconnect and as appropriate while you are connected:** Have the stored procedures dropped when SQLDisconnect is called, DQLFreeHandle is called for the statement handle, SLPrepare or SQLExecDirect is called to process a new SQL statement on the same handle, or when a catalog function is called. Using this option entails more overhead while the application is running, but it helps prevent a build-up of temporary stored procedures.

✦ **Use ANSI quoted identifiers:** Enforce ANSI rules for quote marks so that they can only be used for identifiers such as table and column names. Character strings must be enclosed in single quotes.

✦ **Use ANSI nulls, paddings and warnings:** Specify that the ANSI_NULLS, ANSI_WARNINGS, and ANSI_PADDINGS options are set to on when the driver connects to the data source.

✦ **Use the failover SQL Server if the primary SQL Server is not available:** Have the connection attempt to use the failover server if supported by the primary SQL Server. When a connection is lost, the driver cleans up the current transaction and attempts to reconnect to the primary SQL Server. The driver attempts to connect to the failover server if the driver determines that the primary server is unavailable.

The final page of the wizard (Figure 6-26) prompts for miscellaneous options as described in the following list:

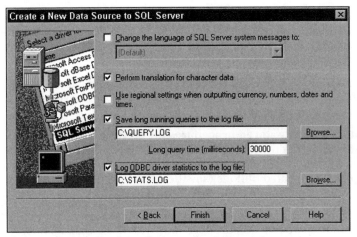

Figure 6-26: Specify miscellaneous database options.

✦ **Change the language of SQL Server system messages to:** Specify the language used to generate SQL Server system messages. The server can contain multiple sets of system messages, each in a different language. This option is dimmed if the server has only one language installed.

✦ **Perform translation for character data:** Select this option to convert ANSI strings using Unicode. Deselect the option to disable translation of extended ANSI codes.

✦ **Use regional settings when outputting currency, numbers, dates and times:** Select this option to have the regional settings of the client computer used to display currency, numbers, dates, and other region-specific elements.

✦ **Save long running queries to the log file:** Log any query that takes longer than the time specified in the Long query time field.

✦ **Long query time (milliseconds):** Specifies the maximum threshold value for logging long-running queries.

✦ **Log ODBC driver statistics to the log file:** Log driver statistics to a tab-delimited log file.

Drivers

The Drivers page of the ODBC Data Sources Administrator lets you view information about installed ODBC drivers. The Drivers page is useful for verifying driver version but doesn't provide any options you can change.

Tracing

Use the Tracing page of the ODBC Data Sources Administrator to configure tracing options to help you troubleshoot problems with a client connection. With tracing turned on, ODBC actions are logged to the specified file. You can view the log using any text editor.

Connection Pooling

Use the Connection Pooling page to specify whether or not ODBC drivers can reuse open connection handles to the database server. You can improve performance by eliminating the need for applications to establish new connections to a server, because the time and overhead involved in establishing the connection is reduced. Oracle and SQL connections are pooled by default, but others are not.

Control Panel Applets

As in Windows NT and Windows 9*x*, the Windows 2000 Control Panel serves as a control center for configuring hardware and operating system settings. Some Control Panel objects control fairly simple sets of options, while others are relatively complex. The following sections explain the more complex Control Panel objects and their functions. Objects that require no explanation (such as configuring the mouse, game controllers, and so on) are not included. Also, note that not all objects appear in the Control Panel by default. The Wireless Link object, for example, only appears on systems with infrared ports or similar wireless hardware.

Tip   You can configure the Start Menu to display the Control Panel objects in the menu. This means you can access individual Control Panel objects through the Start menu without having to open the Control Panel folder. To display the Control Panel objects on the Start menu, right-click the taskbar and choose Properties. Click the Advanced tab, select Expand Control Panel in the Start Menu Settings group, and then click OK.

To open the Control Panel, click Start ⇨ Settings ⇨ Control Panel. If you've configured the Start menu to expand the Control Panel and want to open the Control Panel folder, click Start ⇨ Settings, then right-click Control Panel and click Open. You also can open the Control Panel from My Computer.

Add/Remove Hardware

The Add/Remove Hardware object, when selected, runs the Add/Remove Hardware wizard, which helps you add new hardware, remove hardware, unplug a device, and troubleshoot problems with devices. The wizard scans the system for changes and helps automate the process of installing drivers to support new devices.

If you choose to add or troubleshoot a device, Windows 2000 automatically performs a search for Plug-and-Play (PnP) hardware. If it finds and recognizes a new device, it takes you step-by-step through the process of installing support for the device. If it finds but can't recognize the device, the wizard prompts you to select the device from a list and manually specify the device's driver(s).

To troubleshoot a device, allow Windows 2000 to perform the hardware detection, then locate the device in the Choose a Hardware Device list and click Next. The wizard will help you perform steps to troubleshoot the device. To add a new device, choose Add a new device from the list, then click Next. Follow the prompts to insert the Windows 2000 CD or provide a path to the appropriate driver files when prompted.

If you choose to uninstall a device, Windows 2000 presents a list of all devices. Select the device you want to remove, click Next, and follow the prompts to complete the process. If you're unplugging a device, Windows 2000 presents a list of devices that can be unplugged. Select the device, click Next, and follow the prompts (if any) to complete the process.

Add/Remove Programs

The Add/Remove Programs object (Figure 6-27) serves three functions. It enables you to change the installation of or remove existing programs, install new programs, or add/remove Windows 2000 components. The first two options are geared typically toward user-oriented applications. You use the latter to add or remove components such as Indexing Service, Certificate Services, IIS, additional tools, and so on, to or from Windows 2000. You also can use Add/Remove Programs to add and remove common Windows 2000 components such as the accessory applications (Notepad, wallpaper, games, and so on).

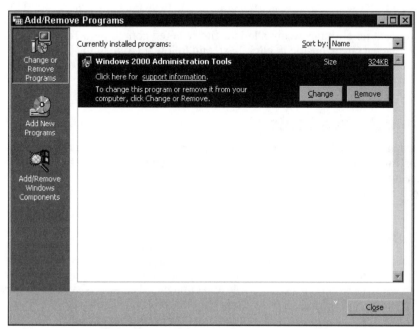

Figure 6-27: Use Add/Remove Programs to install, reconfigure, and remove applications and Windows 2000 components.

The left toolbar in Add/Remove Programs contains three buttons. The Change or Remove Programs button presents a list of installed applications. Select the application you want to modify or remove. Each application will include two buttons, Change and Remove, which will launch the application's Setup program to change the configuration or remove the application, respectively.

Add New Programs offers two functions: seeking the floppy drive or CD for a Setup program, or performing an update from the Windows Update Web site for new Windows 2000 components, device drivers, and system updates. In most cases, an application on CD will autoplay its Setup file, so all you have to do is insert the CD to start installation. Or, you can open the floppy or CD and execute Setup.exe (in rare cases, Install.exe) to install the application. So, though the Add/Remove Programs object isn't all that useful for an experienced administrator in terms of installing new programs, it does give you a portal through which to access the Windows Update Web site (http://windowsupdate.microsoft.com). However, you could simply add a link to the site in your Favorites folder.

The Add/Remove Windows Components object is your primary method for adding and removing Windows 2000 components. When you click Add/Remove Windows Components, Windows scans the system for installed components and displays a component list. Items with a check on white background are installed with all options (such as all accessory programs, for example). A check on a gray background indicates that some of the options for the selected component are installed. No check indicates that no options are installed for the selected component. To install a component, place a check beside it, click Next, and follow the remaining prompts to install the component. Select a component and click Details to view or select individual components.

Administrative Tools

The Administrative Tools object in the Control Panel serves as a container for various administrative tools, including the Computer Management MMC snap-in, the Services snap-in, and others. Each of these tools is covered where appropriate in this chapter or in other chapters.

Display

The Display object in the Control Panel lets you configure desktop settings such as wallpaper, background, color scheme, color depth, and desktop size (resolution). You also can configure a screen saver, enable and configure Web effects, and set general desktop effects and settings. If the system contains multiple display adapters, you can configure settings for each as well as configure how each adapter fits into the desktop.

Folder Options

The Folder Options object in the Control Panel lets you configure how Explorer folder windows appear and function. You can use it to enable/disable the active desktop, specify the type of window use for displaying folders (Web content or classic), specify whether new folders open in the same window or in a new window, and so on. You also can configure other options such as file associations and offline files.

Internet Options

The Internet Options object offers several property pages that let you configure settings for Internet Explorer and related programs such as Outlook Express and NetMeeting:

✦ **General:** Set the default home page, delete cached files, clear the URL history, and set general properties such as fonts, colors, languages, and accessibility features.

✦ **Security:** Use the Security page to configure security level for various *zones.* A zone is a group of Web sites that share a common security level. Click one of the predefined zones and click Sites to add or remove Web sites from the zone. Then use the slider on the Security page to set the security level for the zone, or click Custom Level to specify individual settings for the way Internet Explorer handles cookies, ActiveX controls and plug-ins, scripts, file downloads, and so on.

✦ **Content:** The Content page lets you enable and configure Content Advisor, which helps guard against access to restricted sites (such as sites with adult content). You also use the Content page to configure certificates for use on secure Web sites and for e-mail. Use the Personal Information group on the Content page to create a profile with your name, address, phone, and other information. Bear in mind that this information is visible to Web sites you visit unless you configure the security zones to prevent it.

✦ **Connections:** Use the Connections page to configure your Internet connection(s) and specify how and when Internet Explorer uses auto-connect to connect to the Internet. Click Setup to run the Internet Connection Wizard to create a new Internet connection. Click LAN Settings to configure proxy server settings.

✦ **Programs:** This page lets you associate specific programs with tasks such as e-mail, newsgroups, and so on.

✦ **Advanced:** This page contains several individual options that determine how Internet Explorer handles HTTP versions, multimedia, printing, security, and a variety of other properties.

Licensing

Use the Licensing object (Figure 6-28) to add licenses for Windows 2000 and applications. There are two types of licenses: server and client access. A server license gives you the right to run the product on a particular computer but doesn't give you the right to connect clients to the server. For that you need client access licenses, or CALs. If you have 300 concurrent connections to a server, you need to have 300 CALs to be legal.

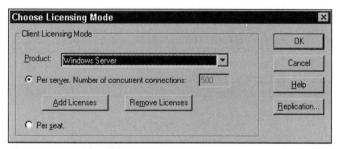

Figure 6-28: Choose between per server and per seat licensing for servers and applications.

You can choose between two licensing modes: per seat or per server. With the *per server* option, you specify the number of concurrent connections for the server or application. When that number of concurrent connections is reached, additional connections are refused. You then can use the Licensing object to add licenses for the product (assuming you've purchased the licenses in question).

You can also choose *per seat* mode, which does not track concurrent connections. Instead, per seat mode assumes you've purchased a CAL for each computer that will access the server or application.

You'll find additional information regarding licensing in Chapter 1 and Chapter 25.

Network and Dial-up Connections

The Network and Dial-Up Connections object in the Control Panel opens the Network and Dial-Up Connections folder. This folder contains icons for each of your network connections including LAN and dial-up connections. Right-click a connection and choose Properties to configure the connection's protocols, bindings, clients, services, sharing, and other properties. For more in-depth coverage of network configuration, refer to Chapter 12.

You can take a shortcut to Network and Dial-up Connections by right-clicking My Network Places on the Desktop and selecting Properties.

Power Options

The Power Options object in the Control Panel controls power-saving features on the computer, such as turning off system peripherals after a specified idle time and setting up hibernation (suspend to disk). You can configure power settings and save the configuration as a power scheme, making it easy to switch between different groups of settings.

The UPS page of the Power Options property sheet controls the UPS service. If a UPS is connected to the computer via one of the computer's ports, the UPS page shows UPS status such as estimated runtime and battery condition. You can configure the UPS through the UPS page or select a different UPS.

Printers

The Printers Control Panel object opens the Printers folder, which contains an icon for each installed printer, as well as a wizard for adding local or remote printers. For detailed information on the Printers folder and printing services, see Chapter 23.

Scheduled Tasks

This object opens the Scheduled Tasks folder, which contains tasks that are scheduled for execution on the system along with a wizard for creating a new scheduled task. The wizard helps you select the application to run, the frequency at which the task runs, user name and password under which the task runs, and other properties. You can use scheduled tasks to automate a variety of tasks including file backup, executing scripts, and so on.

System

The System object provides access to general system properties. You also can open the System object by right-clicking My Computer and choosing Properties. The General page of the System property sheet provides basic information about your system, including OS version, installed memory, CPU type, and registration information.

Network Identification

The Network Identification page is the place to go to change the workgroup or domain to which the computer is assigned, as well as to change its computer name. You also can change the primary DNS suffix for the computer, as well as its NetBIOS name. For more information on network settings and configuration, refer to Chapter 11.

Hardware

The Hardware page offers a handful of features for controlling the system's hardware and resource settings (Figure 6-29). The Hardware Wizard was covered earlier in this chapter in the section, "Add/Remove Hardware." The Device Manager was covered earlier in the section, "Device Manager."

In Windows 2000, drivers can be digitally signed by Microsoft to certify that the driver has been tested and meets certain compatibility criteria defined by Microsoft. Clicking Driver Signing opens a dialog box you can use to configure driver file signature verification. You can choose between the following:

✦ **Ignore:** Windows 2000 installs all driver files whether they have a valid driver signature or not.

✦ **Warn:** Windows 2000 displays a warning when you attempt to install a driver that isn't signed.

✦ **Block:** Windows 2000 prevents unsigned drivers from being installed.

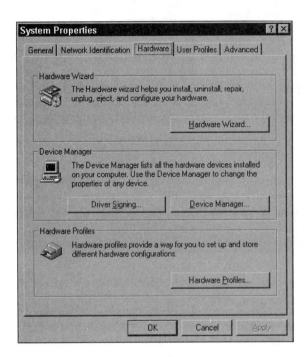

Figure 6-29: Use the Hardware page to add, remove, and configure hardware and hardware profiles.

A *hardware profile* stores information about a specific hardware configuration, including which devices are enabled for a given profile and which ones are disabled. Each hardware profile has a name. When the system boots, it can automatically select a hardware profile based on the hardware it detects at startup. If the system can't determine the correct hardware profile, it prompts you to specify the hardware profile to use.

Hardware profiles are handy for working with different hardware configurations on the same computer. They are most applicable to portable computers, where in a docked configuration you might have a different network adapter, CD-ROM drive, monitor, or other peripherals that are not present when the computer is undocked, and vice versa. By disabling devices when they aren't in use, you can avoid hardware conflicts and make resources (IRQ, I/O base address, and so on) available that would otherwise be allocated to the disabled devices. For this reason, hardware profiles can be useful in a desktop system as well. You might have a piece of hardware you use infrequently that conflicts with another device. When you need to use the device, you can boot the hardware profile in which the device is enabled, then reboot with the other profile when you're through.

Windows 2000 creates a hardware profile automatically named Docked Profile on a portable and named Profile 1 on a non-portable system. You can work with this single profile, disabling devices as needed, or you can create a new profile. To work with hardware profiles, right-click My Computer, choose Properties, click the Hardware tab, then click Hardware Profiles to display the Hardware Profiles dialog box (Figure 6-30). You create a new hardware profile by copying an existing one. So, select a profile and click Copy. Windows 2000 prompts you for a name for the new profile.

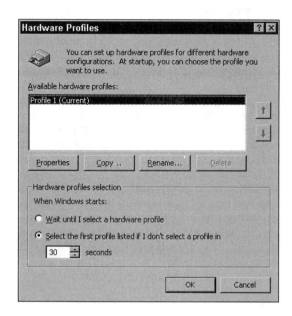

Figure 6-30: Use the Hardware Profiles dialog box to create, remove, and manage hardware profiles.

You can set general hardware profile properties in the dialog box, including specifying how Windows 2000 handles profile selection at boot. Click on a profile and click Properties to set properties for the profile. Within the profile's properties, you can specify whether the computer is a portable and direct Windows 2000 to always include the profile as an option when starting the system.

The Hardware Profiles dialog box gives you a means for managing hardware profiles globally. You use the Device Manager to enable/disable devices in a given hardware profile. On the Hardware page, click Device Manager, then open the property sheet for the device you want to manage. On the device's General page, select an option from the Device Usage drop-down list to specify if you want the device enabled, disabled in the current profile, or disabled in all profiles.

See the section, "Device Manager," earlier in this chapter for more information about the Device Manager.

User Profiles

User Profiles store a given working environment, including desktop configuration, mapped drives and printers, and other properties. When a user logs on, the user profile applies the desktop configuration and other properties. User profiles are most useful for providing a consistent user interface for each user even when other users share the same computer. They're also useful for providing a consistent UI for users who log in from a variety of computers (roaming users).

User profiles are a Windows NT structure that is carried over into Windows 2000. Group policy settings can override settings in a user profile, so user profiles are not necessary per se on Windows 2000 systems. However, they are still useful in mixed environments where Windows NT systems exist, and provide an easy means of configuring the user interface even in homogenous Windows 2000 environments.

A user profile comprises a registry file and a set of folders. The registry file applies settings to the UI such as mapped drives, restrictions, desktop contents, screen colors and fonts, and so on, and is a cached copy of the HKEY_CURRENT_USER portion of the registry. The folders include the user's My Documents, My Pictures, and other folders stored under the Documents and Settings folder for the user.

There are three types of profiles: *personal*, *mandatory*, and *default*. Personal profiles allow users to modify their working environments and retain those changes from one logon session to the next. Mandatory profiles allow certain configuration changes (subject to restrictions in the profile itself), but those changes are not saved for future logon sessions. The only difference between a personal profile and a mandatory profile is the profile's file extension. Personal profiles use a .dat extension for the registry file portion of the profile, and mandatory profiles use a .man extension.

A default profile is pre-configured by Windows 2000 and is applied for new users that log on with no pre-existing profile. The profile is then stored as the user's profile for later logon sessions.

You specify a user's profile through the user's account properties when you create or modify the account. You use the Local Users and Groups MMC console to create and modify local accounts, and use the Active Directory Users and Computers console to create and modify domain accounts in the Active Directory. The Profile page of the user's account properties (Figure 6-31) defines the path to the user's profile, logon script, and other properties. When the user logs on, Windows 2000 applies the profile located on the specified path.

Cross-Reference   Chapter 11 has more information about Group Policy objects and how they're integrated with Active Directory.

Creating a profile

Windows 2000 provides no utility specifically for creating user profiles. Instead, you first log on as the target user to a system with similar video hardware as the user's target workstation (because video settings are stored in the profile and you need to ensure compatibility). You configure the working environment as needed, mapping drives and printers, setting desktop schemes, and so on. When you log off, the profile is stored locally along with the user's folder structure.

Copying profiles

In order to copy a user profile from one location to another, you use the User Profiles page of the System object in the Control Panel. Open the User Profiles page on the system from which you're copying the profile. Select the profile from the list of profiles stored on the computer and click Copy To. Select the local folder or network share where you want the profile copied and click OK.

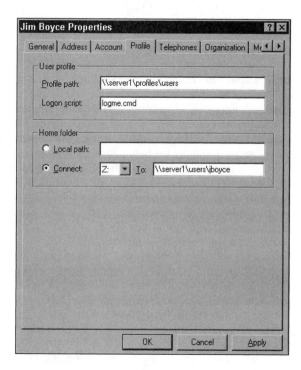

Figure 6-31: The Profile page defines the path to the user's profile.

Supporting roaming users

A roaming profile is the same as a local personal profile except the profile is stored on a network share accessible to the user at logon. You specify the UNC path to the user's profile in his account properties so that when the user logs on, the profile can be applied regardless of his logon location. If a profile exists on the specified path, Windows 2000 applies that profile at logon. If no profile exists on the specified path, Windows 2000 creates a new profile automatically, stores it on that path, and uses the profile for future logon sessions.

Creating a mandatory profile

You create a mandatory profile in the same way you create a personal profile, but with one additional step. After you create the profile and copy it to the target location (such as the user's local computer or a network share for a roaming profile), change the name of the profile's registry file from `Ntuser.dat` to `Ntuser.man`.

Advanced

You can use the Advanced page of the System properties object in the Control Panel to configure performance options for the computer, view and set environment variables, and configure system startup and recovery options.

Performance

Click Performance Options on the Advanced page to display the Performance Options dialog. Here, you can select options to optimize the system for applications or background services. In most cases, you'll select Applications for a Windows 2000 workstation or Background services for a server.

The Performance Options dialog box also lets you change the system's virtual memory allocation (size of the system's swap file) and space allocated to the registry files. Why change swap file size or location? The swap file is used to emulate memory (thus the term *virtual memory*), making the system appear as if it has more physical memory than it really does. As memory fills up, Windows 2000 moves memory pages to the swap file to create space in physical memory for new pages, or it swaps pages between physical and virtual memory when an existing page stored in the swap file is needed. Windows 2000 automatically selects a swap file size based on physical memory size, but in some cases, you might want to increase the swap file size to improve performance. You also might want to move the swap file from the default location to a different disk with greater capacity or better performance (such as moving from an IDE drive to a SCSI drive).

Click Change on the Performance Options dialog box to access the Virtual Memory dialog box, shown in Figure 6-32. Select a drive for the swap file, specify the initial and maximum sizes (Windows 2000 will resize as needed within the range), and click Set. Specify the maximum registry size in the field provided and click OK to apply the changes.

Tip   Changing the maximum registry size doesn't change the size of the registry. It simply imposes a maximum size that when reached, causes Windows 2000 to generate a warning message that the maximum registry size has been reached.

Environment Variables

Use the Environment Variables page to view, delete, and add environment variables. The variables you define in the upper half of the page apply to the user who is currently logged on. Variables defined in the bottom half apply to all users.

Startup/Shutdown options

The Startup and Recovery page (Figure 6-33) lets you configure boot options, how the system handles a system failure, and how debugging information is handled. The options in the System startup group let you specify which boot option is selected by default and how long the boot menu is displayed. These settings are stored in the Boot.ini file, located in the root folder of the drive where the boot loader is located. You can edit the file manually with a text editor to change values, if you prefer.

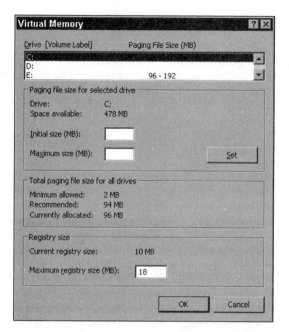

Figure 6-32: Use the Virtual Memory dialog box to control swap file size and registry size.

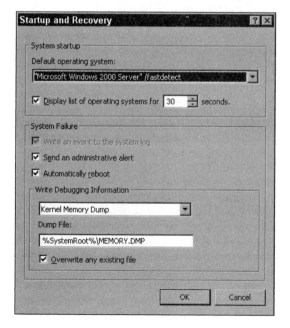

Figure 6-33: Configure startup, recovery, and debugging options.

The System Failure group of controls determines how Windows 2000 reacts when a system failure occurs. The system always attempts to write an event to the system log, if possible. If you need to see the blue screen of death after a system failure to gather information for troubleshooting, deselect Automatically reboot.

Use the Write Debugging Information group of controls to specify the action Windows 2000 takes in creating a memory dump file when a system failure occurs. Microsoft support engineers can use the debugging information to determine the cause of the failure and recommend or develop a fix for the problem.

Summary

Windows 2000 provides several tools for administering system hardware, operating environment properties, users, and other objects. While most of the administrative functions are incorporated into Microsoft Management Console (MMC) snap-ins or extensions, a few — like the ODBC Data Source Administrator — still exist as standalone utilities. The Control Panel, as in Windows NT, still serves as a control center for configuring hardware and OS settings and properties.

Understanding the administrative tools available to you is an important step in configuring and monitoring a system. This chapter examined the majority of the administrative tools you'll work with on a regular basis. Other chapters cover additional administrative tools or cover in more detail some of the tools mentioned here.

✦　　✦　　✦

Active Directory Services

T his part is devoted to directory services. The chapters that follow describe the various strategies that we have found to work (and fail) in all our installations. These chapters follow a sequence or road to understanding that we found best sets the scene for the arduous journey before you.

We have installed Active Directory in a number of companies, and the suggestions we offer in these chapters are the fruit of many lessons learned the hard way . . . by "crash or carry." Many of our earlier sites were reconfigured repeatedly (before they went live) and all now gracefully support their owners' complex business processes. If you follow our steps and add your own logic to the process, you too will be able to sit down with a legal pad and plan a killer AD domain you can be proud of.

Chapter 7 looks at the logical design of the AD deployment, from every corner of the domain forest. Perhaps one of the hardest aspects to grasp in the logical design phase is how the AD can be modeled to mirror the enterprise model. And, because no two companies are alike, every AD deployment is different. This can be very strange territory if you are used to the rigidity of Windows NT networks. We take you into the deep waters (for NT administrators) of enterprise analysis and enterprise resource planning.

Chapter 8 looks at the physical design, how sites interoperate, and how the AD domain controllers replicate their critical data around the enterprise. Chapter 9 covers the installation of the Active Directory, creating domains, and other deployment matters.

Chapters 10 and 11 take you into the critical and extremely complex world of managing user and computer accounts, and setting up organizational units and domain structure. Chapter 11 introduces you to the world of change management, also known as Group Policy, in Windows 2000. Group Policy is perhaps one of the most complex parts of the Active Directory services to master. It is not for the faint of heart, or those with high blood pressure or a tendency to lose hair during frustrating moments. But as this chapter demonstrates, once you master the Group Policy Object, you are on your way to becoming indispensable to any organization.

Logical Domain Structure

This chapter takes you into the realm of enterprise analysis, which is new ground for most system administrators.

Sanity Check

By now, you are probably pretty psyched about Active Directory. And you probably thought we were nuts in the opening chapters when we urged you not to install Active Directory and to deploy standalone servers until you are at home with the new operating system. Now we are going to go overboard. We are going to tell you not to build your new domain until you have a) read this chapter, b) done psychoanalysis of your company, and c) designed your domain on a whiteboard or a math pad and come up with a blueprint. Why? Does Microsoft recommend this? The answer is: Well, sort of.

Microsoft, in both official documentation and in training, is not firm enough in stressing that the root of a namespace cannot be renamed, changed, or deleted without first hacking down the forest and completely reinstalling the domain controller. And this will remain the situation until Microsoft or third parties ship some series Active Directory manipulation and administration tools.

So, before you start, know this: When you delete the root domain, or the last domain on a domain tree, from the server (demotion), you uninstall the namespace. If you screw up the namespace and decide, after many hours of hard work, that you started wrong, you could end up losing those hours spent creating user and computer accounts and configuring domain controllers. And if you go into production, you also take down several colleagues. We thus offer you a mini-guide to enterprise analysis in this chapter in the hope that when you get ready to break ground, you don't slice your toes off in the process.

Keepers of the New Order

These are exciting times for network administrators. We spoke at length in Chapter 1 about the paradigm shift underway in corporate communications, networking, and administration. As a Windows 2000 administrator, you now find yourself at the center of the paradigm shift. You are also a pivotal component in the change that is underway on the planet, in all forms of enterprise and institutional management.

Windows 2000 is a great facilitator in that paradigm shift. Companies are changing; a new order is emerging. The way businesses communicate with their customers is changing. Very little is regarded from a flat or uni-dimensional perspective. Today, corporate workers, owners, and administrators need a multifaceted view of their environment. Managers and executives need to look at everything from a 360-degree panorama of the business — its external environment and its internal environment.

You, the network administrator, specifically the Windows 2000 network administrator, now have a lot more on your shoulders. Everyone is looking at you — what you're worth, what you know, how you conduct yourself — from the boardroom members to the mailroom members, you are the person to take the company beyond the perimeter of the old order. Why?

The tools to facilitate the shift can be found, for one reason or another, in Microsoft Windows 2000. You learned a lot about the Windows 2000 architecture in Chapter 1, so we won't repeat it here, except to say that Windows 2000 Directory, Security, Availability, Networking, and Application services are in your hands, and those of your peer server administrators. The tools you will use to manage all the information pertaining to these services and objects are the Active Directory and the Windows 2000 network.

As mentioned in earlier chapters, Windows 2000 domains are very different from legacy Windows domains. They are also very different from the network management philosophies of other operating systems such as UNIX, NetWare, OS/2, and the mid-range platforms such as AS400, VMS, and so on.

Before you begin to design your enterprise's logical domain structure (LDS), there are a number of important preparations to make. Besides items such as meditating, education, lots of exercise, and a good diet, there are some network administration specifics to consider. We discuss these items in the following sections.

Planning for the LDS

Back in Chapter 4, we discussed the steps to installation and conversion. One of those steps was designing the logical domain structure. If you have been tasked with the installation of or conversion to Windows 2000, the first item on your list should be to understand the steps to achieving the LDS and then implementing it.

Unless you can create an LDS blueprint, the myriad of other management functions, such as creating and managing user accounts, groups, policies, shares and more, will be difficult to implement and cost you a lot in time and material. The following list represents the steps we will take in this chapter to arrive at the point when we can begin the conversion process or even install in a clean or new environment.

1. Prepare yourself mentally.

2. Assemble an LDS team.

3. Survey the enterprise.

4. Design the Logical Domain Structure (LDS).

5. Produce the blueprint.

Preparing Yourself Mentally

Long gone are the days when installing a Windows-based network could be handled with a sprinkling of administration experience gleaned from a few books or an education based on crammed MCSE courses.

Running a successful Windows 2000 domain (no matter what the size) is going to require more than a magazine education in networking, telecommunications, security, and administration. If you have been managing or working with Windows NT server, you have a headstart on the new administrators and administrators from the other technologies who have chosen to defect. Nevertheless, the conversion and installation process is arduous and mentally taxing. And how much time you spend on fixing problems in the future will depend on how well you lay your foundations now. Here is some advice that will help stem the migraine tide from the get-go.

Forget about Windows NT

Trying to create the LDS of Windows 2000 while thinking about Windows NT, and even managing Windows NT, is like trying to meditate at a heavy metal concert. In other words, it is very distracting. We would say that if you are involved in the day-to-day management of Windows NT domains, you should take a break from being an NT administrator while involved in the Windows 2000 LDS planning efforts, at least in the initial phases. You will find it very frustrating to work in both environments at the same time.

This is sobering advice if you have to manage an NT domain while you plan a Windows 2000 domain. You will need to make a special effort to separate the old from the new, the legacy from the up-and-coming.

Forget about Conversion

Trying to think about retrofitting, upgrading, or converting your legacy Windows domains, and even your NetWare or UNIX environments, will only get you into a lot of trouble. Forget about what everyone, including Microsoft, says about this, at least until you have the new domain structure in place and are fully versed in the techniques described in this chapter and the others described in this book. Only when you fully understand the possibilities and the limitations of Windows 2000 domains should you begin to plan your conversion process.

If you try to convert before the Windows 2000 LDS is in place, as we discussed in more detail in Chapter 4, you risk an IT disaster, and losing money and opportunity in many respects. Set up a lab as we discussed in Chapter 4. We can't tell you everything you need to know or beware of in this book, nor can Microsoft. Only you will discover how Windows 2000 accommodates your needs, and how you accommodate its needs. No two organizations are alike.

Stay Out of Active Directory

Before you break out into a cold sweat, this advice applies only to this chapter. The Windows 2000 LDS is just that, logical. Until you have your blueprint in place, your plans approved, the budget in the bank, you don't need to do a thing in the Active Directory.

Yes, Active Directory is the technology that makes the new LDS a reality, and yes, we would not be discussing LDS in such direct terms as we do here if Active Directory were not a reality, but trying to do LDS while tinkering around in Active Directory is counter-productive. Don't think you can stumble your way to a design or blueprint.

We're not saying you shouldn't try to learn about Active Directory hands-on. Learn as much about it as you can. If you know nothing about Active Directory, then you should not be in this chapter just yet, because you should already be au fait with directory service terms and concepts.

If you are not yet up to speed with Active Directory, study Chapter 2, read the wealth of information in the help system, download as much information as you can from Microsoft, and get stuck into books about Active Directory and LDAP. Chapter 2 is the chapter in which you can test examples and concepts in Active Directory. In this chapter, you should be working with design tools and a whiteboard, a very large one.

Note   For information on LDAP, you can download RFC 2254, 2255, 2307 from the Internet. These can usually be located at the Internet Engineering Task Force Web site (www.ietf.org), but you can find these and many other LDAP references at any main search engine.

Assembling the Team

Before you begin, it is vital to assemble a design team. No matter if you are a consultant or administrator for a small company and are attacking this single-handedly, or if you are a leader or part of a team working in a mega-enterprise, designing the domain requires the input of a number of people. In very small companies adopting Windows 2000, the team might consist of you and the owner or CEO.

The Domain Planning Committee

Your domain planning committee will include a number of people, especially if the task is huge, who will assist you in the enterprise analysis you need to undertake. Your team might be made up of the following members.

✦ **Assistant analysts and consultants** to help you quickly survey a large enterprise. The Millennium City example in this book, which is an Active Directory domain structure that spans an entire city, replete with departments and divisions, might need to employ about a hundred analysts to get the survey job done as quickly as possible. It depends on how quickly you need to move, or want to move. If you plan to use your IT department as a test case (going from development to production), then you could probably get away with one or two analysts.

✦ **Documentation experts** to assist you to get information down and in an accessible form as soon as possible. These people should as far as possible be trained in desktop publishing and documentation software, illustration and chart-making software, group-ware, and so on. The documents should be stored in a network share-point.

✦ **Administrators** to be involved in preparing the installation and conversion process. These might include technicians and engineers currently involved in the day-to-day administration of domains, technical support, special projects, and so on.

Domain Management

As the LDS plan progresses from enterprise analysis to approval and implementation and conversion, you will need to appoint people who initially will be involved in the day–to-day administration and management of the new domains.

If you have the resources at your disposal, it will make sense to appoint newly trained staff or hire and train administrators from the legacy pool. These people will help you to build the new Windows 2000 domain and will need to communicate with the administrators of the old domains, and so on. If you are doing everything yourself, then you have your work cut out for you.

Change Control

Appoint a person responsible for change management and control (see Chapter 11). As the development domain begins to roll out phases into production, the conversion team change control process will need to communicate with the MIS/Operations' change control team, discussed in Chapter 4. All proposed changes need to be fully discussed, and all teammates need to have the opportunity to assess the impact and prepare for it . . . or argue against it. Trust us, you don't want to roll out anything without it being signed off at the appropriate levels.

Domain Security

You will need to appoint people or yourself to manage all the security aspects of the new domains. Their role will be to test security in the development domain and to apply the appropriate security mechanisms in the production domains. In addition, they will help you to determine domain policy, Group Policy, delegation, workspace management, and so on.

Cross-Reference   See Chapter 3 for information on Windows 2000 security, and Chapter 11 for information on security policies.

Intra-Domain Communication

A very important component is intra-domain communication, or the communications between Windows 2000 domain users and legacy domain users. You'll need to appoint an Exchange administrator if you plan on integrating Exchange, or else Lotus Notes administrators, Send Mail people, and so on.

A vital component of the LDS is that information is able to flow freely through the enterprise information network and between the operational environments in which the company will find itself when a Windows 2000 domain greets the world.

Education and Information

You will need to generate information to keep management abreast of the development with respect to the conversion process and the emergence of the LDS. Once a plan has been approved, this information will need to be extended to educate people throughout the enterprise.

Surveying the Enterprise

Before you can begin to plan the LDS, you need to survey your enterprise. Consider the job of the land surveyor. He or she sets up the theodolite — an instrument that measures horizontal and vertical angles — and charts the hills and valleys, the lay of the land, the contours, and more. These scientists and engineers determine where it is safe to build a house or skyscraper, where to bring a new road or a bridge, where to place a town or a city. You need to do the same, not to determine where the company is going (which is what enterprise analysts do), but how to plan an LDS with what is already in place and what might be around the corner.

In surveying the corporate structure, you are not going to take on the role of offering management advice about its business, nor will you suggest that new departments or units should be added, moved, or removed to suit the new domain structure. Not only would that be impossible, but also it would likely get you fired or promoted out of networking.

On the other hand, the Windows 2000 LDS needs to be filtered up to the highest levels of management. In fact, the LDS blueprint is what the CIO or CTO is going to drop on the boardroom table, and the IT department is expected to implement the changes desired by management to affect the DNA, e-commerce, the paradigm shift, and more. The Windows 2000 LDS, because of what it may expose, may indeed result in enterprise or organizational change, just don't say it too loud.

Windows 2000 domains reflect the enterprise structure more than any other technology, and the domain structure will be representative of the layout and the landscape of your company, from an administrative and a functional point of view.

Windows NT domain administrators, network administrators, and IT/IS managers have never before contemplated that their careers would take them into enterprise analysis. Large organizations will no doubt hire expensive enterprise analysts, but for the most part it will be an unnecessary expense, unless some serious first aid is needed before a conversion to Windows 2000 can be considered.

In many cases, you already have the resources at hand. They exist in you, and in your peers. You do not have to go overboard studying enterprise analysis, enterprise resource planning (ERP), and customer relationship management (CRM). Of course, having the knowledge will help and may even get you the job you're after. This chapter serves as a guide if you are not sure where to start. The following sections discuss the key concepts of enterprise analysis.

Enterprise Analysis

Enterprise analysis is enterprise land surveying and enterprise engineering come together for the future and good of the company. Enterprise analysts examine where the company is today, what business it is in (many don't know), and where it wants to go (or where the board or shareholders want it to go), and make suggestions on how it should go about achieving its objectives. Enterprise analysts help suggest changes at all levels of the enterprise, in particular in information systems and technology. They provide management with critical actionable information . . . blueprints that start the wheels of change turning.

Without technology, very few of the desires of the corporation will become a reality. You do not need to look far to see how misguided efforts in IT/IS have wrecked some companies, while making others more competitive and profitable. In your new role as enterprise analyst, you are surveying the corporate landscape to best determine how to implement a new Windows 2000-based logical domain structure.

You have two responsibilities. First, you have to study the enterprise with the objective of implementing the new LDS as quickly and painlessly as possible. You may have a lot of money to work with, or you may not have much of a budget. In either case, you are going to need facts fast.

Second, you have to study the enterprise and forecast or project where it might be heading. Is the business getting ready for IPO, to merge, to file Chapter 11, or to be acquired? Is it changing focus? All these items and more will affect the LDS of not only a company, but also the LDS of a city, a hospital, a school, and a government.

You might consider that you are doing the enterprise analysis for the good of the company, but you are doing it for your own good. You will be expected to cater to any change that may happen between sunrise and sunset. And not having the wherewithal to implement or accommodate the sudden business direction that management may throw at you is not good IT administration.

So where do you start? As mentioned before, you can't plan the LDS by just looking up all the groups you created in Windows NT and figuring that just importing them all will do the trick. That would be the worst place to start, and the worst advice anyone can take. Microsoft, we believe, makes too much noise about upgrading Windows NT; we believe that countermands *strategic* LDS planning.

Note   The new Group Policy technology is so sophisticated that it makes upgrading an NT domain and inheriting its groups and user accounts a tricky business. Make sure you fully understand Group Policy before you upgrade an NT domain. It is discussed in detail in Chapter 11.

Here is a short list of starting points. The items may be better in another order for you, and you may add to the list as you deem fit:

✦ **Get management on your side:** This may not be difficult if you are the CIO, or if the LDS directives come from the CIO or CTO. But in order to do the job well, you need to have access to more than would be expected of network or domain administrators. This means that management and HR are going to have to trust you with sensitive information. We would like to add to this point: Get the CEO on board. You are going to need to set up appointments with the most senior staff in the enterprise. They need to know that your research is sanctioned at the very top. You will probably encounter resistance at the departmental head level, where change may be deemed a threat. Advise them in writing that if you do not get cooperation their departments will be left out of the domain conversion or "new order." People tend to go crazy if their e-mail gets cut off, so you can use this as a foot in the door.

✦ **Get hold of organizational charts:** Most enterprises and organizations have these. Hopefully, they are up to date. If they are not, or they do not exist, you are going to have to invest in a software tool that can make organizational charts.

✦ **Tell people what you are doing:** It is important to be frank and open about the process, without exposing the team to security risks.

Enterprise Environments

Before you begin an exhaustive enterprise analysis project, you should take some time to understand the environments in which the enterprise or organization operates. Enterprise analysts often refer to these environments as operational environments. We have been teaching companies about their respective operational environments for several years, long before the advent of Windows 2000. The elements in these environments will feature heavily on both the LDS and physical domain structure (PDS).

There were once only two environments in which an enterprise operated. They were the external and internal environments. The advent of the Internet and wide area networks have resulted in a third environment: the extra environment or the environment "in-between." An analysis of these environments is essential in the formulation of both the LDS and PDS.

To fully investigate the environments, you need to build lists of items to look for, otherwise you will not know where to start and when to finish.

The external environment

The external environment is made up of several components: customers, suppliers, distributors, cleaning staff, and so on. At the physical level, the corporation or enterprise has to deal with the elements of the external environment directly. Examples are: providing access to cleaning staff, dealing with customers, delivery pick up, and more.

The external environment of a city, for example, includes voters, tourists and visitors, businesses, foreign nationals, embassies, consulates, divisions of the United Nations, organized crime, private hospitals, schools and universities, government-sponsored bodies, such as the FBI, INS, and DEA, religious congregations, religious boards, and so on.

The most important technological factor in the external environment is the Internet. Like all enterprises and organizations, the Internet provides resources with which to deal with the elements in the external environment electronically and a means of interconnecting partitions of the internal environment. Any modern city is as present in cyberspace as it is in the physical realm.

Today, the neural network in the external environment is the Internet. The telephone system still plays an important and indispensable part, but it is becoming less pervasive as people find the Internet more convenient in many respects.

The enterprise depends on several components on the Internet that are vital to its existence in general. These include DNS, the locator service for the entity on the Internet, and the Internet registration authorities that provide the entity the right (for a fee) to participate in a global Internet infrastructure. These rights include the registration of your domain names and the assignment of IP addresses, without which you are unreachable.

Here is a short list of items you should pay attention to when you examine the external environment:

✦ How is the company connected to the Internet?

✦ How does the company use the Internet's DNS system?

✦ What are the public domains used by the enterprise?

✦ Who keeps the domains, and makes sure the fees are paid on time?

✦ Are the domains you need to register available?

The internal environment

The internal environment comprises all the departments, divisions, organizational units, and key management entities (KMEs) that work together for the benefit of the enterprise. This environment includes employees, contractors, executives and management, subsidiaries, divisions, acquisitions, equipment, intelligence, information, data, and more.

The internal environment's neural network is the private intranet and its relative KMEs and administrative functions. The intranet is a private network, which is the medium for the Internet protocols, TCP/IP. The local area network is fast becoming a passe term, associated with outmoded and confining protocols such as NetBEUI, Pathworks, IPX, and more. Windows 2000 *is,* for all intents and purposes, an intranet operating system that still knows how to function on a LAN for backward compatibility.

Very important to consider in the internal environment are all the legacy systems and mid-range systems that are going to need facilities in the new realm.

Here is a short list of items you should pay attention to when you examine the internal environment:

✦ How many employees work for the company?

✦ How many remote divisions or branches does the company have?

✦ What functions do the remote divisions perform?

✦ How are the sites interconnected?

✦ Who is responsible for the management of the network that connects each of the sites?

✦ What is the bandwidth of the links between the sites?

✦ How is the company prepared for disaster recovery?

The extra environment

The extra environment is the interface—and the environment in the immediate vicinity of the interface—between the external environment and the internal environment. In some cases, the division may be obvious and thus easy to manage (such as a computer terminal in the public library or a voice mail system). In other cases, the interface is harder to encapsulate or define and thus more difficult to manage (such as how people hear about your product).

Examples in the extra environment are e-mail, communications between the internal and external environments that may need to be monitored, controlled, and rerouted, corporate Web sites that let customers access portions of the internal environment, and so on.

The network environment supporting this environment and its technology is known as an *extranet*. A good example of such an extranet is FedEx, which lets customers tap into the tracking databases to monitor their shipments.

Here is a short list of items you should pay attention to when you examine the internal environment:

✦ What Web sites does the company use? Who manages them? Where are they located?

✦ What call center or help desk functions are in place?

✦ How do contractors and consultants gain access to the enterprise to perform their work without risking exposure to sensitive data?

Working with Organizational Charts

With the organizational chart in hand, you can zero in on the *logical* units of the enterprise and begin enterprise analysis in a "logical" fashion. Figure 7-1 represents a portion of the organizational chart of Millennium City (the entire chart is on the CD in the Millennium City Domain Structure Blueprint PDF). The chart has been adopted from the organizational chart of a major U.S. city, and we will use it throughout the book to see examples of both logical domain structure and physical domain structure, as well as configuration.

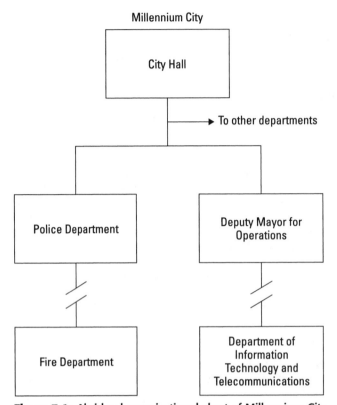

Figure 7-1: Abridged organizational chart of Millennium City

The full chart in Figure 7-1 is huge (more than 50 divisions and hundreds of boards and councils), but you must realize that the LDS you are going to create may need to accommodate such an environment. Obviously, it is going to take many years to fully convert such an organization, and you'll likely be working with Windows 2005 before achieving 100 percent penetration with an organization of this size.

In fact, in organizations of this size, you'll likely never achieve a 100 percent pure Windows 2000 domain structure, and you wouldn't want to. Just a cursory glance at such a chart tells you that you are going to be up to your neck in integration with legacy and mid-range systems, UNIX and Mac platforms, and more.

You need to start somewhere, however. You'll need to start conversion and installation with select departments, starting perhaps with your own department, where you can learn a lot about the conversion process, the fabric of Windows 2000, and the place to set up the labs and development environments that we discussed in Chapter 4.

We have selected three entities out of the chart to use as examples. We are going to convert the Mayor's office (City Hall), the Department of Information Technology and Telecommunications (DITT), and the Police Department (MCPD).

Identifying the Key Management Entities

Key Management Entities (KMEs) are the management, administrative, or service components of a business or organization that, taken as a whole, describe what the entity does. These KMEs are not on the organizational chart and often span multiple departments. For example, payroll processing is a KME that spans the enterprise. While the KME for payroll is concentrated in the Office of Payroll Administration, the KME spans Millennium City because it requires the participation of more than one logical or organizational unit. Every department processes payroll by processing time sheets, data input (time/entry databases), sick leave, raises, check issues, check printing, bank reconciliation, direct deposits, and so on. The KMEs need not be physical groups; they can be logically dispersed between several departments and across several domain boundaries, remote sites, and so on.

All KMEs, once identified, are best represented on a matrix of the enterprise. Each KME represents an area of responsibility that must be measured and evaluated. Once you have identified the KMEs, you will be able to learn about the IT/IS systems and technologies that have been implemented to assist them, and ultimately how both LDS and PDS will emerge to accommodate them. Figure 7-2 illustrates the KME matrix for MIS.

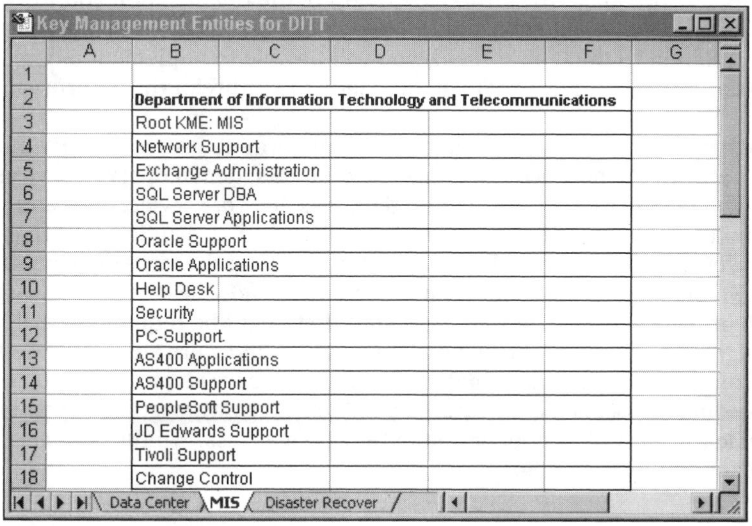

Figure 7-2: KME matrix spreadsheets prepared in Microsoft Excel

MIS people seldom research KMEs or even update previous reports and plans. An important benefit or payoff of such research is that MIS learns how it can improve efficiency in the KME.

It is also important to break the KMEs down further and extract the components that require the services of IT/IS. You will need this information later when you identify where to delegate administration and control in various organizational units and domains.

Strategic Drivers

In the movie *Wall Street,* Michael Douglas' character identifies greed as the strategic driver in his effort to raid companies and make huge profits. Greed certainly is a strategic driver in many companies and organizations, but there are many others, and you could argue that they are subordinate to greed and profit. The Internet is a strategic driver; the ambitions of the CEO and major shareholders are strategic drivers; mergers and takeovers are others; as well as investment in new technology and more.

Strategic drivers are also new laws, new discoveries, new technology, lawsuits, labor disputes, and so on. Knowing what makes the company work and what will keep it working is important in domain planning and structure. You need to have as much information as you can about the enterprise, and where it is headed, so that you are able to give 100 percent where and when needed.

We contend that if you know the strategic drivers of the organization you work for, you will be in a position to cater to any IT/IS demands placed on you. More importantly and in relation to the task at hand, you will be able to implement a domain structure to cater to the drivers that will influence the future of the enterprise.

Use your sixth sense, common sense, and logic in determining strategic drivers. Remember that with the new domain comes new threats, denial of service, viruses, information and intellectual property theft, data loss, loss of service level, and more. A good example: In the weeks prior to New Year's Eve, Y2K, we anticipated that heightened security concerns would come from the CEO of the large distributor we support. So we preempted the request and investigated how best to lock down their RAS and still provide access to key support staff that might be required to dial in during the night. We effectively locked down all access and were able to create a secure zone on the RAS machine, which authenticated users locally before providing access to the domain. Being a good system administrator means going beyond the theories you learn at MCSE school or computer science class. Windows 2000 is the wake-up call for stodgy sysadmins.

Identifying the Logical Units

Look at the organizational chart of Millennium City, and the logical units jump out at you. Every department or organizational unit within each department will impact the LDS in some form or another.

The Mayor's office looks simple enough. There is the mayor and the people who work for him or her, such as public relations people, advisors, and administrative staff. The Mayor's office is probably one of the simplest of the logical units to represent or quantify in the LDS plan. For all intents and purposes, it can be represented as a single organizational unit on the LDS.

In corporations, the offices of the CEO and executive staff can range from being extremely complex to being very simple. But the Department of Information Technology and Telecommunications is very different. What are the logical units within this department? Let's identify some of them in the following list (we cannot deal with every OU within this department because the list would run into too many pages).

1. **Operations:** This unit is responsible for disaster recovery and maintenance of critical systems. The people in this unit make sure systems are online, they watch systems and applications for failures, they monitor production, they print reports, and so on.

   If Operations detects errors or problems, they try to fix them within certain guidelines or parameters. They may be required to restore servers in the middle of the night, or call the on-call staff as needed. Operations staff are trusted employees with heavy responsibilities. They probably need high levels of access to certain systems; they may need to have authority to shut down servers, reboot machines, perform backup, and so on.

2. **Help Desk:** This unit may be part of Operations or a separate unit. Help Desk is responsible for getting staff out of jams with technology, teaching them how to use new applications, and more. They also need special access to systems. Help Desk often needs to troubleshoot applications and systems in the context or stead of the users they need to help. For example, they may need to log in to mailboxes, troubleshoot print queues, and escalate calls to second- and third-level support.

3. **PC Support:** PC Support is a separate organizational or logical unit within the Department of Information Technology. The people who work in this unit troubleshoot desktop PCs, and upgrade, maintain, and ensure that all employees within the entire company, often across physical organizational divides, have the resources they need to do their work.

4. **Security:** The Security staff are responsible for catering to requests for user and machine accounts, changing passwords, access to resources, and more. The security staff work closely with network support in determining group memberships, rights and permissions, access to shares and files, and so on.

5. **Network Support:** That's where you (and we) come in. Network Support deals with the upkeep of the intranet, servers, and WAN resources, dealing with network providers, routers, circuits and more. You also deal with the location of domain controllers, upgrading servers, interconnecting protocols, establishing services, storage, backup and disaster recovery, and more.

Identifying the Physical Units

Between the various departments in an organization, there are numerous physical units to consider. First, departments may be located in separate buildings and in other cities. In Millennium City, for example, the Mayor's office or City Hall is remote from the Department of Information Technology and Telecommunications. The Police Department, for example, is spread over numerous buildings all across town.

We have intranets to deal with, WANs and dedicated connections between departments that cooperate closely. The Police Department of a city of this size employs its own technical team that manages network resources and systems at both the office of the Police Commissioner and at the individual precincts. The Police Department is also hooked into the systems at the Department of Transportation, the District Attorneys Office, the Department of Corrections, and so on. (We will get to more detail about physical units in Chapter 8, but for now understand that your LDS needs to take into account the physical makeup of your organization.)

Documentation

Once you have thoroughly surveyed the enterprise and are familiar with its layout and organization, it is time to document your findings. Be aware that at this point in the LDS design process, the documentation is far from complete, but it nevertheless forms the basis or departure point from which the conversion or management team can begin planning and creating a blueprint. Remember too that the initial conversion project should be open-ended enough to permit you to slide into continuous domain administration and that the documentation should continue to evolve. It will become the "bible" for the present and future administrative teams. The following short list is a suggestion of steps to take to complete documentation and move forward with your LDS and conversion plan:

1. Update the organizational chart and then circulate it to department heads for additions, accuracy, and comment.

2. List the KMEs throughout the enterprise and describe the extent of the administrative function in each KME. You will be noting the size of the KME and complexity. Make a note of where the KME extends beyond departmental or divisional boundaries of the enterprise. There are many formats that the documentation of KMEs might take. We suggest you create a matrix on a spreadsheet, listing departments and divisions in the column headers and the KMEs you have discovered as rows, like the one started in Figure 7-2.

3. Forward the KME matrix to department heads and invite feedback. The KME list is likely to grow, and you'll probably be informed of more KMEs you did not uncover.

4. Divide the organizational chart into sections or make a listing of the divisions or departments you believe or have decided will be the best prospects with which to begin conversion. Note the reasons and mark them for debate at the next conversion team meeting.

The next phase of the LDS plan is the investigation of the administrative models in place over IT throughout the enterprise. What we present here will not get you through Harvard, but it will be enough to give you something to think about.

Administrative Modeling

Administrative modeling deals with management and administrative styles and practices. The following list illustrates several core management styles that may be in place in a company for one reason or another:

✦ The box-oriented company

✦ The human assets-oriented company

✦ The change-oriented company

✦ The expertise-oriented company

✦ The culture-oriented company

It is worthwhile to understand the definition of the term *box* because it will influence the ultimate layout of your LDS. Box refers to the way management controls a company. Enterprise analysts and corporate executives talk about soft-box companies and hard-box companies.

The soft-box driven company management team does not rule with an iron fist and trusts its managers to act in the best interests of the enterprise. It goes without saying that these companies have a lot of faith in their people, and have achieved a system that is comfortable for everyone. The soft-box company is likely to have a small, employee handbook and provides little direct control at certain levels, giving regional managers a wide berth.

The hard-box driven company is very rigid. The employee handbook at this company is likely to be about two bricks thick, and there are probably rules for everything from dress code to eating in your office.

There are good and bad companies in both models. The best exist somewhere between both extremes. However, a hard-box company is more likely to employ a rigid centralized administrative approach at all levels in general and with respect to IT in particular. "Softer" companies are likely to be more decentralized.

Centralized administration and decentralized administration models do not only apply to general administration, they apply also to IT, MIS, or network administration.

Centralized administration

The centralized approach dictates that all management takes place from a single or central department. In a small company, there is really no alternative. The smallest of companies that cannot afford nor need dedicated IT/IS administration usually outsource all their technical and IT/IS support, and the core executive team and the owners make all decisions.

Bigger companies that operate from a single location, or a clinic or a school, may employ the services of small technical teams and still outsource. The really big companies that still operate from single locations will use a centralized administration model, supported by their own teams.

Decentralized administration

The decentralized approach dictates that management or administration is dispersed to geographically remote locations. This is usually a practice among the largest of enterprises. Departments, locations, and divisions, some of them on opposite sides of the world, are large enough to warrant their own MIS or IT departments.

Most multinationals today employ varying degrees of both approaches, and their operations will dictate to what extent administration is both centralized and decentralized. This is probably the most sensible of the management models and varies from corporation to corporation.

Companies determine how much and what makes sense to delegate to the remote locations or seemingly autonomous divisions. For example, they might dictate that remote administrators take care of responsibilities like backup and printer management out at remote centers or depots.

Other systems, even ones located at the remote sites, might make more sense managed from a central location. For example, if you have ten sites and need to install an e-mail server at each site, it does not make sense to hire or train people at the remote sites when a single e-mail administrator, and possibly an assistant, can manage all e-mail servers from a single location. Windows 2000 and a dedicated reliable network make it entirely possible to manage a highly sophisticated IT infrastructure from a remote location with no technical staffing on-site whatsoever. And it would make sense and go a long way to reducing TCO to invest in products like Exchange or Lotus Notes that are designed to function in clusters and are managed from a single location regardless of where the physical equipment is actually located. The advent of such admin-centralized technologies is making the decentralized approach more feasible to adopt. From 1998 to the present, we have managed servers in more than 20 cities throughout the United States, and we have never been physically on-site.

The good, the bad, and the unwise

Each model has its pros and cons. The centralized model is often the most used from an IT point of view, and part of the reason is that legacy systems — both mid-range and Windows NT — do not lend themselves to any meaningful decentralized administration or controlled delegated responsibility. The Windows NT SAM, for example, can only be written to at the primary domain controllers (PDC). Copies of the SAM on the backup domain controllers (BDC) can be read for service requests, but not written to. If at any time the PDC became unavailable to remote locations (loss of link, maintenance, and so on), delegated administration at remote locations becomes impossible.

On the other hand, many companies go overboard and delegate willy-nilly to all departments and divisions. Some companies have carried the decentralized model to the extreme, forcing the remote or otherwise separated units to request their own budgets and acquire and support their own systems. These companies are often impossible to deal with because they have no central buying authority and integration of systems is a nightmare.

Often, newly acquired companies in mergers and takeovers end up looking after themselves as management absorbs them at an agonizingly slow pace. What you end up with is a hodgepodge of systems that are incompatible and impossible to integrate. For example, one side might support Compaq, and the other IBM. Amicable mergers or acquisitions often turn sour because IT and MIS cannot get the two or more technology departments to speak the same language.

Windows 2000 allows you to delegate to various levels of granularity, all the way down to the organizational unit, in tandem with a highly distributed and redundant directory service. As such, Windows 2000 provides the pluses of the centralized model, such as buying of like systems and technology, with the undeniable benefits of decentralized administration, allowed controlled delegation of administrative function, and partial or substantial relief of the administrative burden at HQ.

At Millennium City, you have strong decentralized administration in place. All budget and organization-wide IT planning, however, is done at the Department of Information Technology and Telecommunication. All technical hiring, firing, and requests from Human Resources for staff takes place at the DITT. New systems, maintenance, technical support, help desk, and more is also done here.

However, the Police Department (MCPD) is autonomous and distinct from the main offices of the City. MCPD is a separate administrative authority that will rely on the DITT for investment decisions, choice of technology, and more, but local administrators will keep it going and keep it secure.

DITT thus remains as the command center, ensuring that systems at MCPD can talk to systems at the DA's office or that crime units have familiar access to the Department of Transportation without having to physically go and sit at the department's computers. DITT also ensures that an administrator at the DA's office can apply for an opening at MCPD without having to be retrained on systems at MCPD that are different to systems at the DA. In short, one of the chief functions of the DITT is to strive for homogenous systems as far as possible throughout the city, and that the heterogeneous systems are interoperable and can be integrated.

Logical Domain Structure: The Blueprint

The logical container for domains in Windows 2000 is a forest. Forests contain trees, which have roots, and domain trees make up a Windows 2000 network. It is not necessary to understand forests to design a namespace, and forests are discussed in various contexts in Chapters 2, 3, and 8.

As stressed at the beginning of this chapter, once a domain root has been created, you are for the most part stuck with it, and you don't have many easy change options if the namespace no longer suits you down the road. In the same breath, you must remember that the deeper the namespace, the more flexible it is, and objects can be moved around domains and between domain trees if you later get stuck. However, you don't want to be tearing down domains that are already heavily populated. So use the information culled in the enterprise analysis wisely and plan properly. As we emphasized in Chapter 4, test everything.

The Top-Level Domain

You cannot start or create a Windows 2000 network without first creating a root or top-level domain. What the root should be named and what role it should play perplexes a lot of people. If you are confused, you are not alone, because there are no clear-cut rules that work for every company.

When we refer to the role played by the root, we mean whether the domain should be populated with objects or should just serve as a directory entry point, in a similar fashion to the root domains on the Internet.

Naming the root

One of the first things you have to decide is what to name the top-level or root domain of your Windows 2000 domain. There is more to this name than identity. It is the foundation for your corporate Active Directory namespace. Your enterprise most likely already has a domain name registered with an Internet authority, in which case you already have a namespace in existence, even if you never thought much about it as a *namespace* . . . probably more like a parking space. You're probably thinking, "What the heck does the domain we registered have to do with our corporate network?"

In our example, Millennium City is registered with the InterNIC (Network Solutions, Inc.) as `mcity.org`. But how *your* two namespaces coexist on your intranet and the Internet is not the issue. How you *integrate* the two namespaces is.

You have two options:

1. You can leave your public domain name applicable only in the external environment, resolved by an ISP's DNS server.

2. You can use your public domain name also as the root domain in the directory and on your intranet.

We have pondered over this extensively. Let's examine the two options a little closely:

If your domain name is listed in the .com or .org levels of the DNS, it becomes published on the public Internet and is available as a point from which to resolve your public Internet resources, such as Web servers and mail servers. For example, a query to the root (.org) for mcity.org will refer the client to the DNS server addresses that will be able to resolve MCITY host names authoritatively to servers on the public Internet. DNS servers around the world that regularly service "hits" for the mcity.org will be able to draw on cached records to resolve IP addresses for their clients.

In your case, would you then want to use the public domain name as the domain root in your LDS? In the MCITY example, we saw no reason not to. The results of your enterprise analysis may indicate otherwise, for a number of reasons. We discuss some of them here, as pros and cons:

Reasons to have identical external and internal DNS namespaces are as follows:

✦ The domain suffix is identical in both environments and is less confusing for users.

✦ There is only one namespace to protect on the Internet.

✦ There is one namespace to administer.

Reasons not to have identical external and internal DNS namespaces are as follows:

✦ Domains remain separate, and there is a clear distinction between resources on the outside and resources on the inside. This means that the corporate intranet is more protected, but you will still need a good firewall.

✦ The company may change direction and also change the name.

✦ Proxy configurations for separate namespaces are easier to manage. Exception lists can be created to filter the internal names from the external names.

✦ TCP/IP-based applications such as Web browsers and FTP clients are easier to configure. You would not have to make sure that clients that are connected to both the intranet and the Internet at the same time resolve the correct resources.

Several items in the previous lists demand more discussion.

First, we have a way around the domain suffix problem, a late feature addition. Windows 2000 clients are able to store more than one UPN name to an account, as illustrated in Figure 7-3. This is achieved by allocating additional domain suffixes to the domain, which has to be carefully managed so as not to create conflicts with users in other domains. Down-level clients are stuck with the NetBIOS name assigned to the domain. To add more domain suffixes, open the Active Directory, open Users and Computers, open the account of the user, and select the Account tab. The drop-down list to the right of the User logon name is where you will find the additional suffixes. By the way, any suffix will suffice to log the user on. Later, we show you how to add them.

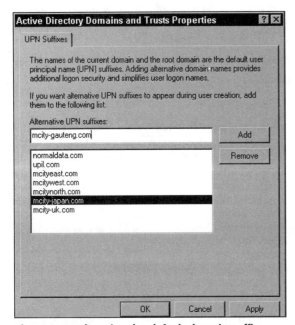

Figure 7-3: Changing the default domain suffix

We do not believe the intranet is any more exposed when you have a single namespace because whatever name you choose as an Active Directory root domain, the domain controller will be hidden behind a firewall. It will be assigned an IP address that a) belongs to your private network, and b) is not locatable from the public Internet — hidden by the magic of network address translation, and so on (see Chapter 12). Nor will any of your other resources be locatable.

You will probably implement firewalls and network address translation to protect your resources. And you will probably be under attack and threats regardless of whether your external DNS domain name is identical to your internal DNS domain name. Most companies already deploy mirrored sites on both sides of a firewall.

The second reason not to use your public domain name is that the identity of the company may change. You could get acquired or broken up, and it would be almost impossible to change the existing root domain to reflect the name of the new company. This may, in fact, be a problem if you anticipate a merger or a name change soon (not usually something that server admins are privy to). This is why we devote such a lot of time and space to enterprise analysis.

You probably got excited about the advantages of the User Principal Name (UPN) we discussed in Chapter 2. You should be aware that the UPN suffix is not locked into the root domain name by any means, or any other domain name for that matter. You can change the UPN suffix at any time for your users if the name of the company changes or the public domain name changes. The underlying GUIDs never change, even if you relocate the objects to other regions of the domain tree, or try and clone them with various resource kit tools.

Note   You cannot make up any UPN. Before you choose a domain suffix, make sure it is registered. If it can't be registered, you need to come up with an alternative.

If you need to plan for a merger or acquisition down the road, or if you have to deal with the outright sale of a certain division, you might be better off not naming your root domain after your public domain name at all.

Another discovery you will make in the external environment is that the public domain name and the enterprise name are different. It is hard to register a domain name that is identical to the enterprise name these days. It would be nice, but it is not always possible. Take the company name Rainbow, for example. There must be an infinite number of companies in the world called Rainbow something or another. But only one will be lucky enough to score the name `rainbow.com`. In this case, you will have no choice but to name the root domain whatever is the next best name.

For the sake of example and because the name was available on the Internet, we went with `mcity.org` (and then a week later someone wanted to buy it from us). But it is unlikely that a city will change its name or be acquired, so if you are setting up a public institution, name changes will not be a major concern.

Getting back to the subject of the supplementary UPN, however, this should definitely reflect your public domain name so that e-mail addresses are the same internally and externally. If the public domain name changes and thus e-mail address suffixes change, you can apply the new domain suffix to the UPNs of all user accounts, as illustrated in Figure 7-4.

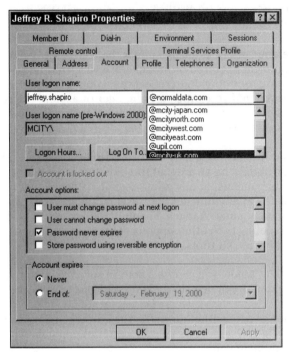

Figure 7-4: Adding multiple UPN suffixes to the domain

The function of the root

The root domain of the first domain tree is the entry point to a forest. Forests are not part of any namespace and are located by attaching or connecting to the root domain in each forest. You can leave the domain root practically empty, with built-in accounts, or you can choose to populate it with OUs, security principals, and other objects. Most small companies will never need a deep domain hierarchy, and even the root domain will suffice in a company of several hundred employees. However, you should seriously consider the following issues about the root domain.

1. If the root domain is "sparse," it will replicate faster and provide an additional measure of fault tolerance. By ensuring that you always replicate the root, you serve to protect your domain "brainstem" in the event that a disaster takes out the lower levels. You can always create a domain and attach it to the root.

2. The administrator in the root domain can reign supreme over the fiefdom like a shogun. A small group of forest-wide "samurai" administrators, serving the shogun, can be located in the root domain, which allows you tighter control over domain administrators in the lower-level domains.

The only drawback is the additional hardware for domain controllers, but the root, being more ceremonial than functional, need not sit on an expensive server. Our first Active Directory was on a Compaq Pentium 133Mhz, with 64MB of RAM.

Again, enterprise analysis will point the way to justifying the reasons to add additional levels to the domain hierarchy, additional domain trees, and separate forests. Figure 7-5, however, illustrates the hierarchy that works for the `mcity` namespace. This is called an *extended* namespace, because it goes beyond what was envisioned by the DNS pioneers.

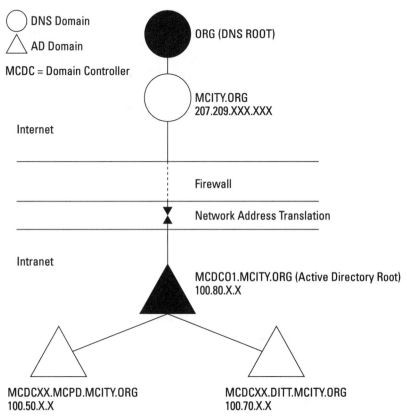

Figure 7-5: The MCITY DNS-Active Directory hierarchy in an extended namespace

Here, we have chosen to stick to one namespace on the Internet, `mcity.org`. This allows the name servers, Web sites, FTP servers, mail servers, and more to be properly resolved by the Internet DNS. The first domain controller in the city (MCDC01), however, becomes the second-level domain that serves as the domain root in the Active Directory forest. As Figure 7-5 shows, this server is located behind the firewall and is further protected with network address translation (see Chapter 12).

We can thus expose the directory to the Internet as `LDAP.mcity.org`, and it can serve as an LDAP directory global catalog server in the so-called extranet, allowing users to look up e-mail addresses, phone numbers, locations, and more.

Under this root domain, we created second-level domains, such as `cityhall.mcdc10.mcity.org`, `mcpd.mcdc10.mcity.org`, and `ditt.mcdc15.mcity.org`. These second-level domains (third level from the Internet roots) are as safe as houses on the intranet, because they cannot be resolved and they exist on private subnets behind a firewall. The intruders would have to break into the network through other backdoors, such as an unguarded modem, the PBX, the RAS servers, or stolen passwords.

This root structure also allows subsidiaries operating under the same Internet root to similarly extend the hierarchy. For example: `mcnippon.mcity.org` is a perfectly legitimate scenario for a domain controller in Japan. So, an enterprise-wide namespace/domain controller policy might be to make all first-layer domains under the root represent geographical, geopolitical, or departmental divisions. The second and third layers would then extend down into the division. This is illustrated in Figure 7-6.

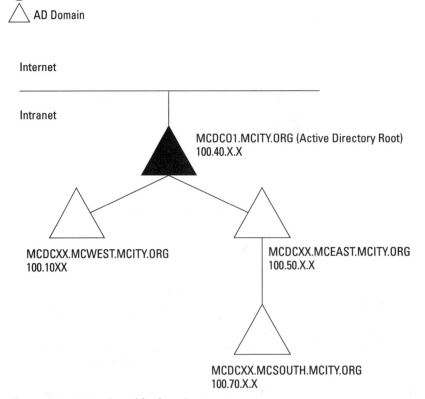

Figure 7-6: Enterprise-wide domain structure

There is only one caveat. Our shogun in the root domain might come under attack. But if anyone can take him out behind our secure server room, firewalls, NAT, Kerberos security, a highly sophisticated encrypted password scheme on a smart card, and a myriad of other protection schemes we don't need to mention, then we can all pack our bags and go home.

Your solution may be different. Here are the alternatives:

✦ **Split namespace.** This namespace, as illustrated in Figure 7-7, is not connected. The root Active Directory domain cannot be resolved from the Internet by any means, yet it *is* a logical extension of the public DNS namespace. In other words, the Active Directory root appears to be an extension of the DNS root, yet it is in its own right an implicit name space. The Active Directory side of the split namespace can become an extension of the DNS root at any time. Internet servers, such as DNS, mail, and FTP can be installed on the Internet, on the intranet (protected behind firewalls and NAT), or in both places.

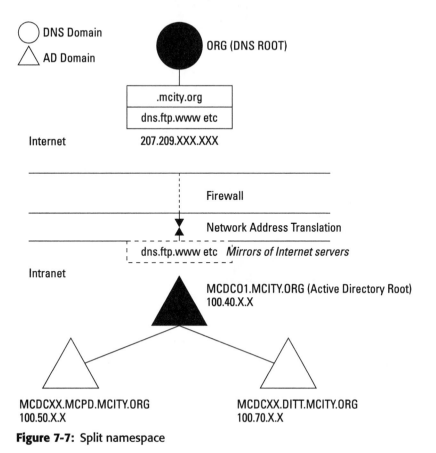

Figure 7-7: Split namespace

✦ **Separate namespaces.** Both namespaces, as illustrated in Figure 7-8, are registered. They cannot be joined and both represent DNS roots. And one is an Active Directory root as well.

✦ **Illegal namespace.** The illegal namespace will not get you brought up on charges of Internet conspiracy (*illegal network* is a network term for an IP address range that cannot be used on the public Internet, because it is already used by a registered owner). If the name conforms to DNS standards and you have not registered it, it is in a sense *illegal,* especially if someone else owns the name. If the name cannot be registered on the Internet, as the example in Figure 7-9 indicates (possibly due to non-standard characters or DNS root domains), then it is also considered illegal. Illegal addresses are used all the time on private networks.

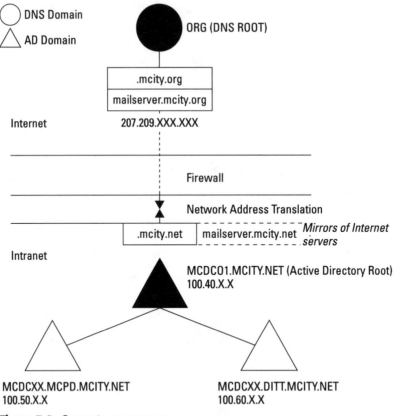

Figure 7-8: Separate namespaces

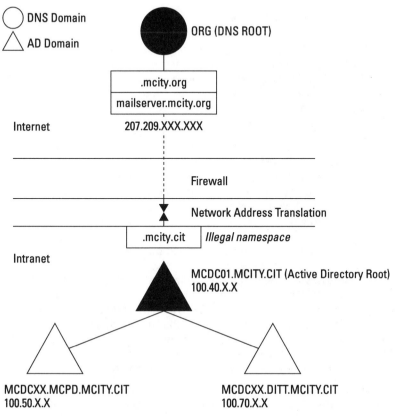

○ DNS Domain
△ AD Domain

ORG (DNS ROOT)

.mcity.org
mailserver.mcity.org

Internet
207.209.XXX.XXX

Firewall

Network Address Translation

.mcity.cit   *Illegal namespace*

Intranet

MCDC01.MCITY.CIT (Active Directory Root)
100.40.X.X

MCDCXX.MCPD.MCITY.CIT
100.50.X.X

MCDCXX.DITT.MCITY.CIT
100.70.X.X

Figure 7-9: Illegal namespace

DNS Naming Practice

We mentioned this earlier; it is good to assign names wisely and protect them as you would a trademark or a copyright. Also, make sure they are registered with the Internet authorities. You should also start getting used to using good DNS language in the blueprint and LDS plan.

Use Internet DNS names

Use internationally recognized standard-approved DNS names for your Active Directory domains. See RFC 1123, which specifies that you can use A-Z, a-z, 0-9, and the hyphen (-). You will notice in Chapter 14 that Windows 2000 supports non-standard naming, and you can put almost any Unicode character in the name. However, resist the temptation, even if you do not *yet* have a persistent connection to the Internet.

Make sure namespaces are unique

You cannot throw an exception on a whiteboard or a legal pad, so duplicate names will go unnoticed and "cloned" namespaces might make it to networks in the enterprise that are not yet connected. For example, if your Active Directory conversion or rollout team is divided between offices and regions, you might unwittingly be creating two or more domain trees in your forest that are identical, but serving different divisions. When you connect them and go live, the whole kaboodle will explode like an egg in a microwave.

Keep legacy clients in mind

The deepest level in the DNS name for a newly created domain becomes the NetBIOS name for NetBIOS clients. This name need not bear any resemblance to the DNS name and can be changed. You get the opportunity to change this name only once, when you install the domain.

Pay particular attention to this name and keep in mind the following suggestions:

✦ **Make the NetBIOS name "palatable" to legacy clients:** Remember, they will see the NetBIOS name of the domain in the domain list when looking for a resource or trying to log on. While Windows 2000 clients can log on as `someone@mcity.org`, NetBIOS clients, using the previous example, will only be able to log on to the default NetBIOS name—such as `genesis` or `cityhall`. This is not too bad, but what if their domain is `eggonyourface.landofoz.mcity.org`. The example seems extreme, but then you never know.

Using an alias, the NetBIOS name can easily be changed to OZ. But you must remember to do it when the domain is created, because you cannot change it short of trashing the domain controller after the installation. Check your plan and make sure the assigned NetBIOS name is marked in red for the conversion team.

It might not be possible, but making the NetBIOS name the same as the last partition name in the DNS (from the top down or reading from right to left in English) will provide a consistency your users will appreciate. For example, if `genesis.mcity.org` is your DNS name, then `genesis` is your NetBIOS name.

✦ **Make sure NetBIOS names do not get duplicated:** If you are raising a second domain in another region, be sure the plan indicates unique NetBIOS names. The two DNS domains will be different, but identical NetBIOS names will not work.

The Second-Level Domains

To add second- and third-level domains under the root, you need good reasons. Each new domain adds administrative burden, additional expenses, and increased total cost of ownership (TCO). The following list, however, provides some valid reasons for creating additional domains levels:

1. Managing separated departments

2. Managing replication overhead and network latency

3. Managing the decentralized administration models

4. Managing autonomous divisions

5. Managing a diversity of domain policy

6. Managing international partitions

7. Managing NT domains

8. Managing security requirements

9. Managing information hiding and resource publishing (divergent view of the directory)

10. Constructive partitioning of the directory

Managing separated departments

If you examine the organizational chart of Millennium City, you can easily see how some divisions or departments are remote from the Mayor's office or City Hall, and from the other departments. In fact, MCITY is so large that few departments share buildings and physical locations. The chasm between the departments is so vast that it might be impractical to extend the root domain out to each site for many reasons.

This may be the case in your enterprise. Perhaps you have several departments spread around the city. Often a company will grow out of its present building and lease additional space across the road. And you will have to span the network backbone, or collapse it between the two locations.

Key to your decision to create second-level domains is that users and network resources need to locate a domain controller nearest to them to authenticate. If you decide to extend the domain across several city blocks, or between the suburbs and downtown, users in the remote department will likely require a partner domain controller on their segment, or suffer bottlenecks when trying to locate the domain controller and other network resources in the main building. Be aware that replication and authentication traffic is also hitting the pipe along with the general network traffic. The domain controller for a new domain will not have to deal with the replication traffic generated between partner controllers in the same domain. There are two factors to consider:

1. Size of the separate location

2. Distance from the existing domain

First, the number of people in the separate location should be your guide, and this information will be in your enterprise analysis documentation. If the separate location is only staffed by a handful of people, the small amount of network traffic they generate and the additional administrative burden they cause will cancel out any perceived benefits of creating a separate domain and locating a domain controller in their offices. (Think equipment costs, installation, and administration.)

Second, the distance from the parent domain is an important consideration. If the site is across the road, extending the backbone is easily handled with the appropriate permissions from the city planning department. However, if the parent domain is in the suburbs and the department is located uptown, it will be difficult, if not very expensive and impractical, to extend the backbone even several blocks. You will likely have to span a full or fractional T1 circuit, or frame relay circuit to connect the two locations. Still, if the department is small and does not generate a lot of network traffic, you could still get away without creating a child domain.

When the population of the separate location increases, you can first locate a collateral domain controller from the parent domain on its network segment, which will allow the users and resources to authenticate faster without having to touch the link. Just remember that you have to watch replication bandwidth and the size of your pipe.

Later, other reasons besides being across the road or downtown will determine the creation of a new domain. Here are a few alternatives to creating a child domain for a separately located department that does not have valid reasons to be its own domain.

✦ Consider Terminal Services (see Chapter 25). Location of domain controllers and issues like replication do not apply in a terminal services implementation. Even a dedicated Internet connection might be enough, depending on the type of work your users are doing. Plus, there are a myriad of other factors that make terminal services feasible, which we discuss in Chapter 25.

✦ Upgrade the link (your intranet connection) and increase bandwidth between the locations to relieve bottlenecks.

✦ Install a partner domain controller. However, first compare the costs and TCO of installing additional bandwidth with the costs of installing a partner domain controller. This is further reviewed in Chapter 8, covering physical domain structure.

The added benefit of a replication partner is fault tolerance, and if you don't have one in the main location, installing one in the separate location provides this payoff.

Managing replication overhead and network latency

Replication overhead and bandwidth are causes for concern when extending the domain to remote locations that are further away than the uptown-downtown example described previously. Again, there are many factors to consider before you create separate domains. Here are four important ones:

1. Size and nature of the remote location
2. Distance from the existing domain
3. Number of remote locations
4. Resources required by the remote locations

Bandwidth is your primary area of focus. The larger the pipe, the less latency in connecting to a remote domain controller. But dedicated networks are expensive to maintain; costs recur. A domain controller is a one-time purchase, virtually management-free if it is a partner. On the other hand, creating a separate domain substantially reduces replication traffic because only a small percentage of domain data is exchanged at the global catalog (GC) level (that is, in comparison to full-blown domain objects). If you have to outfit many remote locations in any event, and they are large, the cost of a dozen or more T1 or bigger circuits will outweigh the cost of creating new domains, one for each remote location.

Another factor, related to the next section, is the resources required by the remote locations. They may need local DHCP services, local WINS services, and local e-mail services. If the remote location is small enough and not too critical an operation, you might get away with installing all these services and the Active Directory on one powerful server. So, the cost of the domain controller is spread over the needs of the location.

Managing the decentralized administration models

These models dictate that you must transfer administrative authority—some call it power—to local or remote facilities. Such administration need not be in IT areas; it may be pervasive throughout the child entity. In this situation, you are not dealing with technological limitations as a reason to create child domains; rather, management has given you a valid reason to create child domains . . . autonomy.

The decision to create the child domain depends on the extent of the transference and the autonomy of the division. If delegation of administrative authority is minimal, you can achieve the decentralization or delegation initiative without having to create a separate domain. Just delegate administrative power wisely, at the OU level or along well-defined KME-OU lines (more about KMEs and OUs later in this chapter).

Managing autonomous divisions

A good example of an autonomous division is the Millennium City Police Department (MCPD). This is also a very good reason to create a separate domain. While MCPD functions under the administration and control of the city and reports directly to the mayor—its CEO, the Commissioner, is a publicly elected official—its internal affairs and operations are very different from the other departments. In fact, the city pays the bills and salaries of MCPD, but just about all other management decisions and administrative functions are handled by the department.

From the point of view of IT administration, MCPD has its own administrators, people who not only know IT but criminal science as well. They know how to leverage technology from the crime-fighting perspective, and their ideas of fault-tolerance, availability, and technological advantage are very different from those of the administrators in, for example, the Taxi and Limousine Commission.

A separate domain gives the MCPD the security and independence of its own domain, while still having the benefit of being attached to the extensive systems at the Department of Information Technology and Telecommunications and City Hall. You may argue, and in your case you may be right, that an autonomous body like a police department requires its own domain, in its own forest, and appropriate trust relationships between the forests. In our example, we feel that one forest suffices.

Managing a diversity of domain policy

When you create a domain, you need to apply domain policy to the domain. Domain policy governs many domain-wide properties, such as password expiration, account lockout, UPN style, and so on. Policy and the attributes of domain objects are generally restricted to domains. (Domains and their contents can also inherit policy from higher-level domains and from the site in which they are placed.)

So if your situation calls for such diversity, it can be achieved by creating separate domains. You need to be really sure that the reasons are valid and that the diversity cannot be simply achieved with OU and groups. It seems insane to create a domain with unusually stringent security policy just to house the accounts of the network administrators. Yet, we have seen this happening . . . incurring the cost of a new domain controller, Windows 2000 server license and all, just to hold the accounts of ten people. Bottom line is: Analyze, evaluate, plan, and test before you come up with weak reasons to partition your directory into numerous domains.

Managing international partitions

International offices and locations provide many good reasons to partition to second- and third-level domains. Here are a few reasons, and you can probably come up with dozens of others:

1. Language barriers.
2. Network limitations. We might get away with extending the domain across the inter-coastal waterway, but not across the Atlantic.
3. Cultural barriers.

4. Geographical and national remoteness. We once had to install an IBM OS/2 telephony system into one of Microsoft's foreign offices because the NT-based equivalent was not approved in that country (a true story). Redmond was a little upset about the "infiltration."

5. Political and security regulations. In some countries, you may distrust the subsidiary enough to put it into a separate forest.

6. U.S. export regulations. This sentence is encrypted.

Managing NT domains

We believe that upgrading or converting your Windows NT domains before you fully understand Windows 2000, and especially Active Directory and the new domain structure, is a bad idea. We said a lot about this in Chapters 1, 4, and 5, but it is worth repeating here. Don't convert until you have completed testing, development, evaluation, and your LDS plan. In fact, our plan calls for phased implementation as opposed to upgrading.

The conversion of a Windows NT domain must be controlled by a phased implementation plan that dictates having your NT domains around for a while. In some cases, we do not even recommend converting NT 4.0 domain controllers to Active Directory domain controllers (see Chapters 4, 5, and 10).

NT 4.0 domains cannot be attached to your domain tree, so you are just going to have to treat them as domains that belong in another forest, and this is going to mean setting up explicit trust relationships between the forests.

Managing security requirements

Windows 2000 is far and away the most secure network operating system in existence, even though out of the box it's riddled with holes. You can lock down Windows 2000 so tight that not even helium can get in. However, lockdown is a relative thing; no system is flawless, and what matters is that it knows how to heal itself and that you pay attention to the necessary security details, discussed in Chapters 3 and 11.

If your plan calls for more severe security restrictions in a segment of the namespace, restrictions that are likely to be intolerable for the majority of your users, you will be left with no alternative but to create a new domain, and possibly a new forest.

A domain is a security boundary for a collection of objects. And this security boundary cannot extend past the domain boundary to other domains without predefined trust protocol. Domain objects require the authentication of users and computers to access them. These so-called users requiring authentication are known as security principals. In other words, you can force all the users of one domain to log on with smart-cards — say in the MCPD domain — that have long encrypted passwords, while requiring short simple passwords in other domains.

Domains thus provide this benefit, and varying levels of security can be established throughout the enterprise. Specifically:

1. Domain password policy, your ultimate security resource, dictates the password usage rules in each domain.

2. Account lockout policy dictates the circumstances for intrusion detection and account closure.

3. Kerberos ticket policy, per domain, dictates the life and renewal of a Kerberos ticket.

Cross-Reference   See Chapter 3 for more information on Kerberos tickets. Policy is discussed extensively in Chapter 11.

Managing information hiding and resource publishing

Separate domains partition the directory and can assist you in selectively publishing and hiding resources. There is a lot of benefit in allowing users to see and know about only what they are allowed to see and know about. Active Directory allows you to publish resources and provide users with divergent views of the directory service (discussed in Chapter 9). This publishing and hiding of information is more critically achieved by using separate domains than by publishing in the domain itself. How objects are exposed is determined first at the domain level, then the OU.

Constructive partitioning of the directory

The beauty of Active Directory is that it lends itself to partitioning and it is distributed. This means that it can be scaled to support billions of objects (accounts, OUs, and custom objects). We don't suggest that you try to stuff a billion objects in a single domain. If you are analyzing an enterprise that supports tens of thousands of users, not partitioning into a deeper domain structure will be counterproductive. The more objects that you have to create, the deeper or wider the structure is likely to be.

Partitioning the Domain

As discussed in Chapter 2, Windows 2000 domains are organized at two levels: the *organizational unit* (OU) and the *group*. Both are containers, but the difference between the two is that groups are *security principals* and OUs are not. Groups *contain* user and computer accounts and must be authenticated to allow their contents to access secured resources in a domain. OUs are not authenticated by the security subsystem and serve rather to structure and partition the domain, and to apply Group Policy.

Many people have commented that OUs should have been endowed with security attributes and that Microsoft should have made them security principals. After all,

Novell Directory Services (NDS) OUs are security principals, and NDS does not offer groups. But Active Directory OUs are not NDS OUs or even X.500 OUs.

Groups are also inherited from NT 4.0 and are not derived from any austere and otherwise bloated specification, like the X.500 directory services. And some hardened NT administrators have ridiculed Microsoft for "porting" groups to Active Directory. But groups, for whatever is deemed good or bad about them, are built into the operating system and were around before the emergence of the directory service. If Microsoft had removed groups from the NT security system, it would have been the operating system's undoing.

In this chapter, we have dispensed advice concerning the strategic analysis of the enterprise in order to build a directory service and a domain structure. Our style and suggestions are derived from years of enterprise analysis of many companies, from the Thai fast food down the road to the likes of KLM Airlines and even Microsoft's own foreign subsidiaries. And we find that our own Key Management Entities (KMEs) discussed earlier in this chapter fit in well with the OU-group relationship and help clearly define the difference that we have between groups and OUs.

Organizational Units

Organizational Units are, on Windows 2000 anyway, the *administrative principals* of the domain. They serve as an organization tool and as a keeper of Group Policy Objects (GPO), administrative control, and as an object filing system. (See Chapter 2 for a more general discussion of OUs.)

Note   The term *administrative principal* is not a Microsoft term (yet). The authors coined it, and you won't find it in the Windows 2000 documentation.

You will learn from your enterprise analysis that how a company is run and how it is organized is not the same thing. At first glance, you would think that the OU would be used to reflect the departmental organization of the company. Companies, small and large, are split into divisions, and divisions are split into departments or business units. Thus, it may seem appropriate to structure your domain using the OU to reflect or mirror the organizational structure of the company.

This may work in many situations, but enterprise organization (departments) should not be your exclusive guide. You will find that you need to be flexible and creative in your approach, and not create any shallow rules for creating OUs. For example, it might make sense to create an OU to contain all the resources of a sales department in a small company. If the company employs ten people, you could easily create one OU for the Sales Department and then add groups to the OU that controls access to the resources in Sales. Delegate an administrator to the OU (if you have one), install policy to manage the workspace of the occupants of the OU, and be done.

But what if Sales employs several hundred people? One huge department would easily call for several OUs, many groups, and various levels of policy and administration.

We thought about this and came up with the following suggestions for the creation of OUs, illustrated in Figure 7-10.

1. Create OUs, not along departmental lines, but for the most part along KME lines.

2. Nest OUs only when the KMEs are large and contain child or already physically nested KMEs.

3. Group KMEs that overlap into a single OU.

4. Populate OUs with groups, as opposed to individual accounts.

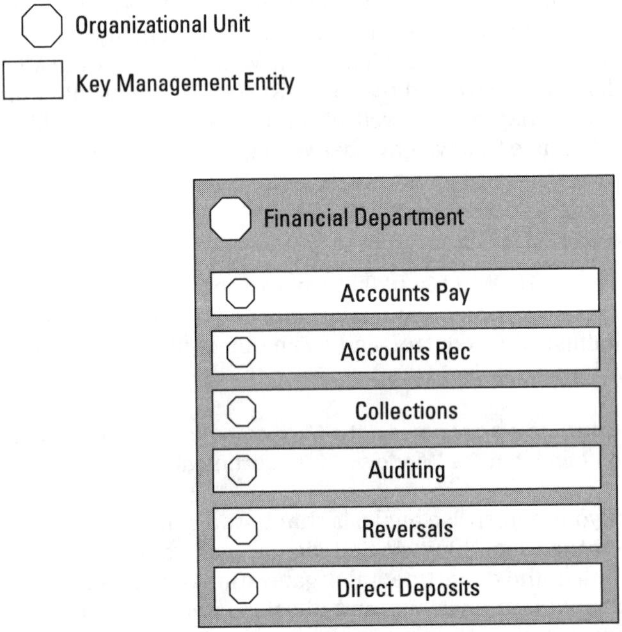

⬡ Organizational Unit

▭ Key Management Entity

⬡ Financial Department

	⬡ Accounts Pay
	⬡ Accounts Rec
	⬡ Collections
	⬡ Auditing
	⬡ Reversals
	⬡ Direct Deposits

Figure 7-10: OU creation according to KMEs of the organization

You will then decide, with the OU leaders, the level of hardness desired in the Group Policy, access to applications, workspace control, security, and so on. From the OU level looking outwards to the domain and inwards to the groups, we begin to see a "social order" developing. This is not unlike the domain system that ruled Japan from the 1600s to the 1800s, where domains were also organized into units, trusted each other at the domain level, and all reported to the shogun. Management was decidedly decentralized.

Now we also see a structure taking shape, a box, and it might even influence business planners outside IT, where the shogun is the CEO sitting in HQ, and inside the forest, the shogun is the administrator sitting in the root domain.

In the first suggestion, look at your KME matrix and create OUs along the lines of the most significant entities. Creating an OU along the boundaries of the Sales Department would be a bad idea if the Sales Department were huge, divided up along product lines or regions. The matrix will identify several KMEs that make up the Sales Department, and it would make sense to create OUs along those lines. Note that we said "for the most part" in the first suggestion because there will always be a gray area where you will create an OU along something other than KME or administration lines or department lines, such as a line of business.

In the second suggestion, we advise to nest OUs only when the parent OU (which may turn out to be created along department lines) is large and contains child OUs. For example, within the Financial Department OU, you can create OUs for Accounts Payable, Accounts Receivable, Collections, and so on. If these KMEs are big or contain specialized KMEs within them, you can then create additional OUs and further nest the structure.

 Tip Avoid excessively deep OU nests, which are not only harder to manage but also require more computer resources. LDAP clients that do not understand the global catalog will search long and deep, and stretch the patience of your clients.

In the third suggestion, we advise you to collect all KMEs that overlap into a single OU. You could group niche KMEs in one parent OU, as long as you do not nest them just to create a hierarchy for "perspective." In some cases, you'll have a KME that has a wide embrace, like Accounts Payable, and within that KME of, say, ten people, is one person who has a very different function or management mandate (such as a comptroller). In such a case, the smaller KME should not be defined by a nested OU, but rather should be included in the parent OU along with its sibling.

So Where Do Groups Go?

Once the OU has been created along the KME lines, the administrators of the OU can decide, with the leaders or all members of the OU, what the OU requires in terms of resources (in other words, which objects do the groups need to see or not see). We suggest populating your hierarchy of OUs with groups and not individual accounts.

Create groups and make the users who work in the KMEs members of the groups as needed. This practice, or policy, also serves to instill a discipline into the practice of assigning groups. NT 4.0 groups tend to show up everywhere at some lazy MIS departments. This way, unless a group is implicitly part of an OU, it should not be there.

What about users who work in KME *X*, are in OU *X*, but need access to the group in OU *Y*? Just "second" the user to the group in the other OU. You don't have to move the user account around. And for all intents and purposes, the user may be a resident in another domain.

User and computer accounts cannot be in more than one place in the directory. But in fact, users often have more than one responsibility, and, needing access to many things, will appear in many groups. For example, we may be working on applications during the week and be on call for the computer room over the weekends.

This approach, call it a philosophy, implies that all users be grouped into a single OU, possibly called HR. That concerned us, so we investigated the idea further. If you look at the attributes of user accounts, they are not variables that get managed often. Many will be set once and then never changed. You can then locate your user accounts in your root OU, in one OU (such as HR), or several root OUs, at least at the top level of your enterprise, reflecting organizational policy. In fact, as long as you ensure that your user or computer accounts are linked to required Group Policy objects (see Chapter 11), you can put the accounts in any folder.

Figure 7-11 now provides a more complete logical domain structure framework from which to expand. It shows user accounts in root OUs along department lines and OUs within the root along KME lines. The child OUs contain groups needed to serve the KMEs. When you achieve an LDS, you will be in a position to decide how and where and when to delegate administration of the OUs and apply policy.

We have made the LDS blueprint for the test phase of MCITY available in this book. But rather than chewing up another acre of trees, you will find it on the CD, under the `mcity` folder.

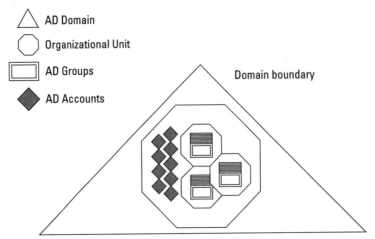

Figure 7-11: Logical domain structure

Summary

Creating a Windows 2000 domain, especially for large and complex entities, is a daunting task. You are strongly advised not to begin upgrade or conversion from an NT domain until you have, firstly, performed a mission critical enterprise analysis of your organization and, secondly, completed a blueprint of the logical domain structure, which has been approved by the entire team and management. Additionally, you cannot start "rollout" until you have done due diligence in the labs and have fully signed off on the physical domain structure . . . and this is what we tackle in the next chapter.

✦   ✦   ✦

Active Directory Physical Structure

This chapter reviews the physical structures of Active Directory. This chapter also introduces you to the relationships between domain controllers, the various roles of domain controllers, global catalogs, and sites.

Past, Present, and Future

Past operating systems had no awareness of the underlying physical network structure on which they were deployed. For small companies, even reasonably sized ones, the network layout, interconnection points and subnets, remote offices, and so on were either laid out long before Windows NT became pervasive or were installed independently of the network operating systems that depended on it.

We typically build networks on which the servers reside on 100Mbps media, the backbone. There is 100Mbps media between floors, and then this network is extended into a 10Mbps network down to the users. Windows NT does not care if the network is 10Mbps or 10,000Mbps . . . it has no built-in means of catering to the available resources.

But this is no longer sufficient, because Windows 2000's physical structure and its multi-master replication technology, global catalog services, public key infrastructure, directory synchronization, Kerberos authentication, and more do need to be sensibly and carefully built according to the physical network resources. Fortunately, the OS also allows you to build a logical network and map it to a present or future physical network. With Active Directory services, you can tailor your Windows 2000 deployment to the available network and merge the two structures into a unified cooperative. The reason for this is Active Directory and its host domain controller server.

Windows NT and Windows 2000 network requirements are very different. Windows NT depends on a single primary domain controller, the PDC, which holds the master database of the domain configuration, accounts, security, and so on. This PDC is a single master domain controller, meaning that only the database on the PDC machine can be written to. If this machine begins to shake or freak out, the network is frozen, in terms of its ability to make changes to the domain. Clearly, this is not a pleasant idea.

Backup domain controllers, or BDCs, back up the PDC. The BDCs can service the domain, in terms of logon authentication, security, and the like. But its registry databases cannot be edited. In order to do that, you must promote the BDC to the role of PDC. Thus, the PDC and BDC exist in a single-master or master-slave arrangement. No matter where you are on a Windows NT network, changes you make to the domain are saved to the PDC, and the PDC then replicates this information out to the BDCs wherever they are. The PDC does this automatically, or you can force the BDC and the PDC to synchronize their databases. Other than this forced synchronization, there is little else you can do to manage or customize this synchronization.

In Windows NT, there is typically one BDC for every remote location and one or two on the local segment, and all reside on the same network. In other words, if the PDC is in Miami and the BDC is in Portland, Windows NT does not know that. The PDC functions independently of the BDC on the other side of the country. Naturally, if the BDC in Portland went down, the Portland users would have a hard time getting authenticated or using network resources, and if their segment lost connectivity to the office in Miami, they would be in trouble. This Windows NT single-master physical domain structure is illustrated in Figure 8-1.

Windows 2000 is very different. While the concept of domain controllers and backup domain controllers remains the same, these services operate as masters, or in a multi-master peer arrangement. There is no PDC; all domain controllers can be edited and updated. Active Directory makes sure that any changes or additions made to one domain controller directory are distributed to the other domain controllers. This is known as multi-master replication technology (and you could call it a philosophy as well). The multi-master arrangement is illustrated in Figure 8-2.

To deploy an ongoing administrative approach in Windows 2000, you must first design the logical structures based on the enterprise's present and future needs, as discussed in Chapter 7. Then map that model to the physical network and ensure that you have the necessary structures to support it, in terms of bandwidth, subnet design, network routes, and so on. It is also possible, as you will see, to cater to areas of your network that do not ideally fit into any logical structures you have.

Windows 2000 and Active Directory allow you to map your logical network model to the physical network with domain controllers (DC), global catalogs (GC), and sites. And Windows 2000 ties everything together between the DCs, the GCs, and the sites with links, bridges, and connection objects to comprise a highly sophisticated directory, directory replication, and directory synchronization service. Before we get down to the railroad work, we should talk about DCs, GCs, and sites in less abstract terms than we have in the previous chapters.

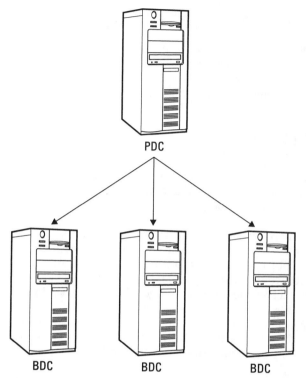

Figure 8-1: The network single-master domain structure of the Windows NT domain

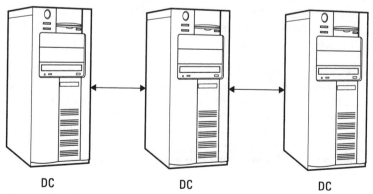

Figure 8-2: The network multi-master domain structure of the Windows 2000 domain

Domain Controllers and Global Catalogs

The three components of Windows 2000 and Active Directory networks are domain controllers (the directory hosts), global catalogs, and sites. They are all interrelated, so a discussion of each individually and then collectively is warranted. Let's kick off with the DCs you have been reading so much about.

Domain Controllers

A domain controller (DC) houses the Active Directory (AD); it is the Active Directory's host. And as you have learned in the previous chapters, Active Directory is the brain or control center of the central nervous system that authenticates users and manages security and access control, communications, printing, information access, and so on.

Active Directory is also a lot more than just domain information. It is also a storehouse of enterprise information, a place where you can place "signposts" that point or redirect users to information and objects of functionality anywhere on the local or wide area network. It is also a place where you can go to find people, places, and things. In the future, Active Directory will become the local "hangout" for all applications.

In addition, Active Directory also stores information about the physical structure of your network. To use the brain analogy again, Active Directory knows how your network is structured and what is required to keep it in good health and service it correctly.

But the one thing we cannot do with our brains is replicate the information in them. If we could, life would be very different. Also, imagine blowing out your brains and then just replacing them with a "hot" standby, a la Plug and Play. Fortunately for us, our brains, left alone, look after themselves pretty well for a period of 70 to 100 years. Active Directory brains are not as fortunate; they can be carried off, fused, trashed, and corrupted.

Imagine that the only DC running a Windows 2000 domain gets fried. Knowing what you do now, the network will be frozen until the DC can be restored. This is not a fortunate position to be in. For starters, your backups (usually taken the night before) are only able to restore you to the state you were in 8 to 12 hours ago. Second, what will now authenticate the restore service writing to the new machine? While we explain how to restore a single Active Directory in Chapter 17, losing the domain controller is not a pleasant event, akin to a human going into a coma and not returning for a few weeks or years, if ever.

So, having another "equal partner" domain controller is essential, even for a small office. It need not cost an arm and a leg, as we discuss in Chapter 9, but you should have one all the same.

The number one rule about Active Directory availability on a Windows 2000 network is to place the DC as close as possible to users. In larger companies, it makes sense to place domain controllers on remote sites, segments, separated offices, or large offices, because the nearer your clients are to the DCs, the quicker they will be able to authenticate and gain access to resources, printers, and communications. Having more than one DC also spreads the load around, a practice called *load balancing*. An office of more than a thousand people all hitting one lonely DC does not make sense.

All the DCs in an enterprise coexist as a "cluster" of sorts, each one backing up the others. They are all responsible for maintaining the identical information about a certain domain, as well as any information that that directory has concerning the other elements and domains in the forest. The DCs keep each other abreast of changes and additions through an extensive, complex, and complicated replication topology. It is certainly far too complicated to grasp at its DNA level. And it is both with tongue in cheek and a design style we will soon discuss that we refer to a Windows 2000 network as a matrix.

The matrix, however, becomes a growing consumer of network bandwidth the larger and more complex the enterprise becomes, or the more it begins to depend on directory services. So, one of the first tasks you or your administrators will have in the management of the domains and directories is the replication provisioning that must take place. The global catalog service (GC) also uses bandwidth and Active Directory and DC resources, as we will soon discuss.

As discussed earlier, this intra-cooperation between all DCs on the matrix is what we call a multi-master arrangement. And if the packets are routed over limited bandwidth, you will see that the router or gateway is a lot more vulnerable to bottlenecks than in the Windows NT domain philosophy of single-master operations.

Let's look at some core facts about DCs that cannot be ignored; we'll be summarizing as we go:

✦ Each domain must have a DC (or one copy of the Active Directory). Like the brain, if the last DC goes into a coma, the network comes to a dead stop.

✦ DCs provide users with the means to function in a workplace, to communicate, and to keep the enterprise alive. Take that away and you have a lot of unhappy people.

✦ You need more than one DC in a domain (or a very good backup/restore plan, or even RAID in a small office).

✦ The various parts of the DC that must get replicated to the other domain controllers, in the same domain, are *schema* changes, *configuration* changes, and the *naming contexts*. The naming contexts are essentially the tree namespaces, the names of the actual objects on the tree, and so on.

Note By now, you have probably realized that your domain controller can only service one domain. How much more sensible and easier would it be if a good machine with tons of resources could be used to host multiple domains? We hope to see this emerge in future generations of Active Directory.

While the Active Directory replicates everything to the other domain controllers, it has some built-in features that facilitate replication. Before we discuss them, look at the illustration in Figure 8-3. Imagine if you poured water in either side of the tube. Your knowledge of science tells you that gravity and other forces in the cosmos act to balance the two sides. It does not matter which side you pour the water into, nature still acts to create equilibrium. This is how Active Directory works; it has automatic built-in mechanisms that ensure that if there is more than one DC on the matrix, it receives the share of information it needs or deserves.

However, if you limit the width of the U-piece, or the tunnel, it will take longer to create the balance. And, naturally, if you block the U-piece, the balance will not occur.

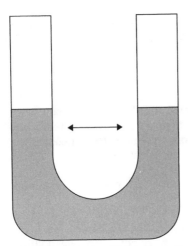

Figure 8-3: Active Directory replication is automatic and for the most part transparent.

Specifically, the Active Directory acts in the following manner to make sure that the replication occurs and that it occurs as painlessly as possible. First, only the changes to objects or new objects get replicated to the other DCs. Second, you can specify how the replication is handled. For example, you can schedule how often and when replication occurs.

By using these features, you can control the bandwidth usage between domain controllers. And if you have remote sites, sensible use of replication services and bandwidth might obviate the need for a separate domain, especially if you are catering to a small office and you do not have a lot of network traffic hitting that U-piece on your network.

Global Catalogs

The global catalog (GC) is not something that Shop-Till-You-Drop, Inc. sends you every month. But if that's what you thought, we will not hold it against you, especially if you thought for a minute we were talking about mail order, because the GC is a totally new concept on Windows networks.

The main purposes of the GC are as follows:

✦ It provides the point of contact and interface for authentication of users into Active Directory domains, which means it holds a full replica of all user accounts in its custodian domain.

✦ It provides fast intra- and inter-domain searches of the Active Directory without actually iterating the trees, or performing what is known in directory service language as "deep searches."

For all intents and purposes, the GC is a subset of the domain that for search purposes holds only the attributes or property information necessary to find an object belonging in a domain other than the one it directly serves. That may sound confusing, because philosophically the GC sits above the domain hierarchy. In fact, the GC is not a hierarchy at all and is not part of the Active Directory domain namespace.

When you search the Active Directory, you either know what you are looking for or you have a vague idea. And by *you,* we also mean any application that needs to look up an object for some reason. As we discussed in Chapter 2, a user object is a leaf or end node on the Active Directory domain tree that is read from right to left (or bottom to top). The user object `jeffreyshapiro.genesis.mcity.org` tells you that if you start at the top of the namespace and from `org` you work your way down three domain levels, you will find `jeffreyshapiro`. You will, of course, also find other objects at the end of this namespace, but at least you have limited your search to a contiguous namespace.

But what if you do not have any information about the root domains? What if you or the application has no entry point (a LDAP shallow search needs at least a root from which to start a search) from which to begin? You would have to commit to a deep search of the forest to find the object. By *deep search,* we mean that you or your application has to traverse every tree in the forest to find the object you are looking for, and this is done through a system of referrals.

A directory service with the potential of MCITY and all its departments would be very long and tiresome to search. That's where the GC comes in. We know this seems like a *deep* explanation, but many have found it confusing at first why there is a catalog when you can, theoretically, search the domain trees. The illustration in Figure 8-4 demonstrates how easy it is to search the GC from an application like Outlook.

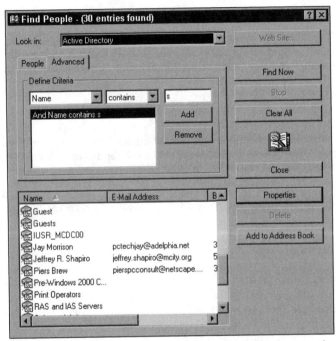

Figure 8-4: Searching for a user in Active Directory from Outlook

The GC contains a partial replica of every domain in the forest and a copy of the schema and configuration-naming contexts used in each forest. In other words, the GC holds a copy of every object in the forest. However, it only holds the key attributes of each object that will be useful for searching. You can thus easily find an object or a collection of objects just by specifying an attribute of an object. In Figure 8-4, we provided a letter and the search returned several objects. In this manner, a user or application can locate an object without having to know in which domain the object resides.

The GC is built in such a way that it is optimized for queries. The query mechanism is built on the LDAP system but uses basic queries that do not return referrals. LDAP referrals pass the search flow from tree to tree, but the GC is not hierarchical. It is a flat database. The following attributes are important considerations:

✦ A GC is located using DNS.

✦ A GC is created in a domain tree; it is housed on a domain controller.

✦ You should install at least one GC per DC site.

✦ The members of universal groups are stored in the GC; however, local and global groups are stored in the GC, but their members are not. Universal groups are only available to native-mode domains. Mixed-mode domains do not need a GC for authentication.

By the way, the GC also holds the access control information of the objects so that security is not compromised in any way.

The GC network carries an overhead separate from the DC network. Remember that they are not integrated; they are separate resources. The GC, in fact, has no understanding of how a domain works, nor does it care. Here are some specifics to keep in mind:

✦ The GC generates replication and query traffic within a site and between sites. So, keep in mind that your network is now going to be hit with both DC and GC traffic. Also, a GC is required for logging onto a native-mode domain. If there is no GC on the local segment, a GC on a remote segment will be used for authentication.

✦ Users may need to be shown how to query the GC, which is an administrative overhead. Or, you will have to make sure your objects are populated with relevant information. For example, if you only store the e-mail address of a person in his or her respective object, and someone looking up this person's e-mail address submits only what he or she knows, such as a last name or first name, there is a chance, albeit remote, that the search will return NULL.

✦ You need at least one GC in a domain, but if that domain is spread far and wide, which is possible, you can add the GC to other domain controllers (we discuss doing exactly that in Chapter 9). Get used to the idea of managing or working with more than one GC, because down the road many applications will begin taking advantage of a permanent catalog service on the network, and we are not talking only BackOffice stuff like Exchange and SQL Server.

GCs are built by the Active Directory replication service, and we will talk about that shortly.

The DC and GC Locator Services

You may have been wondering, with all this superficial discussion of DCs and GCs, how a user locates the correct domain controller to log on to and how the user locates a GC to search. After all, you would imagine that you at least need an IP address or some means of locating the domain, because NetBEUI or other NetBIOS services are no longer a requirement on a Windows 2000 network. The answer is simple, but the architecture is a little arcane and thus may appear difficult to understand. On a very small network, you might be forgiven if you opt out, for now, of trying to understand the locator services; but on a reasonably sized network that extends beyond more than a handful of offices and network segments, understanding this is very important.

Network clients deploy a special set of algorithms called a *locator service* that performs the function of locating DCs and GCs. The latest version of the Windows locator service services both Windows 2000 clients and legacy Windows clients. Thus, both clients are able to use DNS and NetBIOS APIs to locate the DC and GC servers. How do they do this?

If the client can resolve DCs in DNS, which is what all Windows 2000 clients are empowered to do, the client's locator service will search for the DC that is positioned closest to it. In other words, if the client is located on network segment 100.50.*xxx.xxx*, it will check a DNS server provided to it for a DC on the same network segment, regardless of whether the DC it gets is its "home" domain.

If the domain the client is searching for is an NT 4.0 domain, the client will log on to the first DC it finds, which will either be a PDC or any of the BDCs. The upshot of all this locating is that the client first logs onto a site-specific DC and not a domain-specific DC. The next steps that the client takes are worth paying attention to.

If the DC closest to the client (on the same subnet) is the home DC of the client, then well and good, and no further referral or buck-passing is required. But what if the client is located in another network segment, far away from the home DC? A good example is a busy executive who spends every week in a different location, and therefore attaches to a different network each time. The notebook computer the executive is carrying around will receive an IP address of a new network segment that could be many "hops" away from the last segment containing the executive's original domain.

In this case, the client contacts the nearest DC (A). The DC will look up the client's home site and then compare the client's current IP address with the IP address of the closest site containing a domain controller that hosts the client's domain. With that information, the client is then referred (B) to the DC in that nearest domain and obtains service. This is illustrated in Figure 8-5.

This entire matrix of DCs and GCs, replication, and referral services for logon is accomplished by a sophisticated built-in mechanism in Windows 2000, known as *sites*.

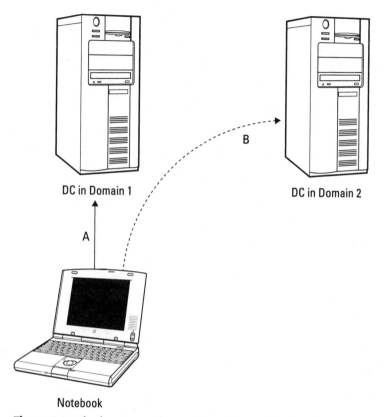

DC in Domain 1   DC in Domain 2

A

B

Notebook

Figure 8-5: The locator service used by clients to look up their domain controllers

Sites

A *site* is a representation of a network location or a group of network locations abstracted as an Active Directory object above one or more TCP/IP network segments. It is managed as a logical unit within the Windows 2000 domain controller matrix.

A site is identified or addressed in Active Directory according to the TCP/IP subnet on which it resides, and it is resolved to that segment via DNS. A site is directly related to a domain as far as intra- and inter-site replication is concerned. But a site is also indirectly related to the other elements in the forest, with respect to the other naming contexts such as the global catalog, the schema, and so on. A site is also a logical container that is totally independent of the domain namespace.

Active Directory requires that a site be "well connected." That term may be relative and somewhat obscure in that a well-connected site, for example, in Swaziland, may be a disaster in the United States. Nevertheless, the definition, according to Microsoft, is that the site should also be accessible via a reliable connection, which would thus preclude the term *site* being used to refer to a machine hanging off the end of a 28.8Kbps modem. You will find that in the real world, you might have to deal with sites of 56 Kbps and 64 Kbps, which is not a lot of bandwidth.

Windows 2000 also requires that the site be fast enough to obtain domain replication in a timely and reliable manner. By defining a site according to a TCP/IP subnet, you can quickly structure an Active Directory network and map it to the physical structure of the underlying network.

Most important, however, is that a site is used for determining replication requirements between networks that contain domain controllers, and for that matter all other replication services, such as WINS, DNS, Exchange, NDS, and more. All computers and networks that are connected and addressed to the same IP subnet are, in fact, part of this site.

A site is used to control several things:

✦ **Authentication:** A site is used to assist clients in locating the DC and GC that are situated closest to them. As discussed earlier, the DC maintains a list of sites and determines which one is closest to the client based on the IP address information it has on hand.

✦ **Replication:** When changes occur in directories, the site configuration decides when the change will be made to other DCs and GCs.

✦ **Collateral Active Directory Services and Applications:** Services such as Dfs can be made site-aware and can be configured according to the site information they obtain from the Active Directory. Applications may also in the future look up specific site information.

Cross-Reference   A site is also a conveyor of group policy, as discussed in Chapter 11.

Replication within Sites

Windows 2000 supports a process known as the *Knowledge Consistency Checker (KCC)*. This technology has been adapted from Exchange Server, which uses it to replicate between Exchange servers. In this case, KCC is used for the replication services between domain controllers within a site.

The KCC essentially sets up replication paths between the DCs in a site in such a way that at least two replication paths exist from one DC to another and a DC is never more than three hops away from the origination of the replication. This topology ensures that even if one DC is down, the replication will continue to flow to the other DCs.

The KCC also sets up additional paths to DCs, but in such a way that there are no more than three connections to any DC. The additional connections only swing into action when the number of DCs in a site reaches seven, thus ensuring that the replication three-hop rule is enforced. This is illustrated in Figure 8-6. The site on the left contains six domain controllers, and each DC supports two replication or KCC connections. The site on the right contains more than six DCs, and so the KCC makes additional direct connections to the DCs to ensure the three-hop rule.

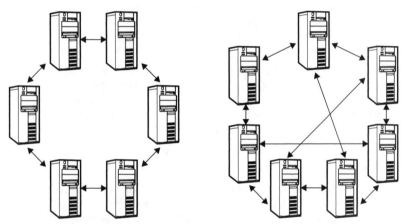

Figure 8-6: KCC connections enforcing the three-hop rule

Active Directory also allows you to define *connection objects.* These are essentially manually configured points of replication between domain controllers. The KCC sets up connection objects automatically; however, these objects have been made available for administrator access so that you can create a specialized replication topology of your own if you need to. For the most part, you can leave the KCC to its own devices and have it set up the connection and replication environment for you.

Site Links

Site links connect two or more sites together. Site links are similar to Exchange connectors and are configured similarly. The links are unidirectional and, like Exchange and WINS, are used to set up the replication network topology.

There is very little work you need to do to create site links because Active Directory automatically creates them when you create sites and add DCs to them. You can, however, manually configure sites, and it may become necessary as you set up links to deal with special circumstances, redundancy, and the like.

Since site links are unidirectional, you will need to establish them in two directions. There are a number of options you can set, which means that site links are managed according to the existing infrastructure of a wide area network. The configuration options are as follows:

1. **Transport provisioning:** This option governs which technology you use to transfer the actual data between the DCs. Active Directory offers you the choice of RPC or SMTP. SMTP is a mail protocol and not a reliable logon authentication data transfer protocol, but it does not require very much CPU bandwidth. RPC, on the other hand, compresses data and is thus more efficient, especially over narrow pipes. You can, however, use SMTP for replication of the GC information, schema and file replication services (FRS), because there is no support for compression in these technologies.

2. **Cost routing:** You can set a cost value to a site to determine which route to the site is the cheapest. You do not want to route over links that cost per transmission as opposed to the total monthly or annual service. You should configure cost for site links wherever you can so that Active Directory can use the route of the least cost.

3. **Frequency:** The frequency value of site link is used to determine in minutes how often the site link should be checked for replication.

4. **Schedule:** The schedule governs when replication *can* occur on the link. If the site is very busy during the day, and the network requires all available resources for mission critical applications, you should prevent replication during these busy periods.

The default settings for site links are 100 minutes for the frequency and every three hours (180 minutes) for the replication schedule. More about links later when we get into the actual configuration.

Site links are simple tools to ensure that replication flows from one domain to another and vice versa. However, for complex structures, they can get a bit tedious. Site links are not transitive. In other words, in a situation where Site A replicates to Site B, and Site B replicates to Site C, no replication between A and C takes place if B goes down.

The way around this is another feature in sites known as *site link bridges.*

Site Link Bridges

You can connect all sites to a site link bridge so that all the sites connected to the bridge know about each other. The site link bridge is like a conference call that all sites listen in on. Site link bridges are easier to manage because you do not have to explicitly link all the sites to each other and create links for every possible path.

We mentioned link cost earlier, and site link bridge costs are the sum of all the links included in the bridge. Your service provider will be able to reconcile link costs with you.

Connection Objects between Sites

As discussed earlier, connection objects can be manually created and managed for replication topology design. We discussed the connection objects in terms of tools used to manage replication topology between DCs on the same site. But you can also use them to manually configure replication between DCs in different sites.

In other words, the replication topology of Active Directory is very flexible (which is why we recommend you explore other uses for it, such as DNS replication). First, you can manage your replication manually, which means you can create all the connection objects yourself. Second, you can leave the replication to Active Directory to fully automate it, and join all sites to the site link bridges. Or, third, you can configure some links automatically and others manually.

If you have special needs or you have a special link that can only be configured manually, then use the manual options. Otherwise, leave KCC and automatic configuration to its own devices.

Understanding Replication

If you manage a wide area network or intranet of any particular size, from a connection between two small sites to a worldwide service, replication in the Active Directory infrastructure is something you would do well to understand.

What Replication Is

Let's recap. As soon as you have more than one DC controller on a network, you will have network replication because of the multi-master replication activity that takes places between DCs of one domain and DCs and GCs of many domains. Replication takes place between DCs servicing the same domain or between DCs in the same forest. Replication is a service that allows changes made at any remote corner of the enterprise to be automatically propagated to other DCs servicing the enterprise. Replication occurs within a site and between sites.

A good example of this replication is changing policy related to certain accounts or organizational units in the Los Angeles domain (say a lockout) and having those changes reflected in the London domain. A locked-out user may be able to gain access to the network if his or her account is disabled by logging on very far away from the DC where the account lockout was made. However, it is very unlikely he or she will beat the replication, and, even if the remote DC did not receive the change in time, access to resources will be barred.

All DCs can be updated, and their databases can be written to, which is why we call this a *multi-master* situation. However, there are certain special situations in which you do not want any DC to be able to make changes to Active Directory.

The first domain controller in the forest is also, by default, appointed certain exclusive forest management responsibilities. These responsibilities have to do with changes that affect the forest on the whole. In this role, the DC is known as the *single-master DC.* The following roles of the "root" DC are as follows:

✦ **The Schema Master (SM):** This DC is the only one in the forest that is allowed to make changes to the schema. Any DC can actually be the schema master. However, you need to promote a DC to the position of schema master before it can play this role. This promotion will lead the new SM, asking the old SM to transfer over the role of the SM.

✦ **Domain Naming Master:** This DC is the only one that can make changes to the domain namespace. This DC can, for example, add or delete domains or reference external directory services.

✦ **PDC Emulator:** Only one DC can be the PDC emulator. This role allows a DC to provide so-called *down-level* services to the NT 4.0 clients and servers. It also fools the down-level Windows NT 4.0 Backup Domain Controllers (BDCs). Also, as long as a PDC emulator or advertiser exists on a mixed-mode domain, it will receive preferential replication of password changes.

✦ **RID Master:** This role DC manages the resource identifiers (RID) pool. RIDs are used to create the security principals, groups, and accounts for users and computers (which are identified according to security identifiers or SIDs). RIDs form part of the SID and are allocated to each DC in blocks of 512 RIDs. Every time that a DC uses up the 512 RIDs, it contacts the RID master for an additional allocation. The RID master is also used to move an object from one domain to another.

✦ **Infrastructure Master:** This role DC maintains references to objects in other domains.

If you are deploying a small network, then the above roles are likely to all be the responsibility of one DC. In larger, multi-domain environments, you may allocate these roles to several DCs in the domain. It is important to be aware of these roles in the event a server in charge of say, RIDs, falls over and leaves you RID-free. For the most part, these DC roles are self-healing between the different DCs, and you are unlikely to encounter any errors relating to the operations.

How Replication Works

Replication has been well designed, because it is so important to an Active Directory infrastructure, and Microsoft has gone to great lengths to ensure that the most up-to-date changes are distributed as efficiently and effectively as possible, without placing undue stress on already overloaded networks. In this regard, there are three crucial duties performed by the replication algorithms:

1. Identifying which changes must be replicated

2. Preventing unnecessary replication

3. Resolving conflicts

The DC replication algorithms are self-learning and self-healing. DCs are able to keep track of the changes that have been made to their data and can also discover the changes that have been made to other DCs. If the DC deduces that it is missing crucial changes made at another DC, it is able to request that those changes be transferred so that it can update its databases accordingly.

How does this extensive replication network remain in sync? Remember the fairy-tale of Snow White and the Seven Dwarfs? The wicked witch constantly strives to stay one step ahead of Snow White by looking in the mirror and requesting updates on who is the better-looking female. The Active Directory replication algorithms behave in a similar fashion, but they have fortunately not been endowed with ego or one-upmanship, lest a DC decide to send a poison apple to another DC.

Romantic tales aside, every DC uses a numerical sequence algorithm, or *USN*, to track the changes made to its databases. Active Directory does not use timestamps to compare changes, as similar replication services do. Active Directory, in fact, only uses timestamps to settle replication collision disputes and in the timestamp field of Kerberos tickets, which checks for replay attacks.

The USN is a 64-bit number that is held by each DC and is important only to that DC. Each object or attribute in the Active Directory has two USNs assigned to it. Each object has a *USNcreated* value and the *USNchanged* value assigned to it.

Whenever an object or property is successfully changed, the "changeUSNs" are advanced and the new value is stored with the object. Each DC maintains a table known as the *high-watermark-vector* that states the highest changeUSN received from a DC's replication partners. Whenever a DC changes an object or a property, it sends the new USNs to the other DCs. In turn, the other DCs check their USN tables, and if the value of the changeUSN they have just received is higher than earlier ones received, or new, the DC will request a copy of the new information, which will be saved to its databases. Each DC is constantly trying to stay current with the other DCs.

This replication strategy is also extremely fault-resistant. If replication fails for some reason (let's say that the DC receiving the update is restarted), the replication attempt starts again exactly from where it left off because the receiving DC will not have incremented its USNs in its high-watermark vector table. If the change does not complete, the DC that was interrupted simply requests the information again.

Obviously, and because we live in a world of friction and gravity, the DCs cannot always be totally in sync. And, in fact, the replication model used is termed *loose consistency* because at any given time that a change may be updated or propagated, another change may already be on its way.

The only time that a DC network is 100 percent current is when there is only one DC or when no changes are made to any of the DCs for a certain period of time. During quiet times or designated periods where changes are forbidden, DC states will converge and become current. This is known in distributed systems lingo as *convergence*. It is thus recommended on large networks that a change "blackout" be enforced at certain times to facilitate convergence.

Active Directory also employs some nifty algorithms that prevent an endless cycle of updates from roaming around the network and DCs from endlessly firing off update requests and USNs. This technology is known as *propagation dampening*. Without it, a DC network will simply grind to a halt because DCs trying to update each other will use up all the available bandwidth. The exact processes that are taking place in propagation dampening are fascinating, but beyond the scope of this book. If you need the torture, you can check the replication white papers at Microsoft for the excruciating details.

The same goes for collision detection. Using version numbers and the timestamp and other binary operations, Active Directory is able to resist the highly remote (but possible) chance that two administrators make a change to the same object in the Active Directory infrastructure at exactly the same time. In fact, only an application designed to do that will succeed, which is what Microsoft did to test collision resistance and assure us all that two DCs will not bump heads and blow up.

Directory Synchronization

No replication topology would be complete without synchronization traffic in the picture. At first glance, you would think that synchronization and replication are one and the same thing. They are not. Replication is information exchange between heterogeneous directories, while synchronization is information exchange between the same or homogenous directories for the purpose of keeping each replica current.

Note Directory synchronization is no small matter. We recommend that you tread carefully here until the tools and techniques mature before you burn up time synchronizing or converting.

For example: If you wish to exchange information between Novell Directory Services and Active Directory, the technology to enable this is a *directory synchronization tool*. There are three ways to consider the interoperation of different directories:

1. **Convert existing directories to Active Directory:** In case you decide to convert your existing directories to Active Directory, you will need to obtain a directory conversion tool. One such tool for NetWare is the Microsoft Directory Migration snap-in. The result of this course of action is that the Novell directory meets the end of its life after the conversion. In this case, you replicate or transfer the information from one directory to the other. And yet other examples are in Microsoft's own backyard. All current BackOffice directories, such as MS Exchange and SQL Server, will be converted to Active Directory.

2. **Integrate directories:** If you choose rather to integrate directories, the tools you will need to deploy are known as directory synchronization tools. These tools will allow you to deploy two directories, each for its own good. The information between them is shared through the synchronization tool. A good example of such integration is an enterprise that is running both Exchange and Lotus Notes.

   Directories can be integrated with third-party tools, or you can make your own using the likes of ADSI, or LDIFDE tools. (LDIF stands for LDAP Data Interchange Format, and LDIFDE stands for LDAP Directory Exchange.) It is worth noting that you can write SQL code against the LDAP directory and move information between LDAP directories.

3. **Deploy more than one directory:** This option is worth considering if you are a while away from deploying Active Directory, you have a huge investment in your current directory services, or your existing systems depend far too much on your current directory infrastructure. You may consider just deploying more than one directory, each one serving a special need, until you are ready to convert or synchronize.

Whatever your decision, if you already deploy a directory service other than Active Directory or a BackOffice tool, you will need to take into account the synchronization and replication traffic that will also be added to your new Active Directory traffic.

Active Directory Site Design and Configuration

The first thing you will find out when you start Active Directory inter- and intra-site design is how well or how poorly your TCP/IP network has been designed. But before you start configuring anything in Active Directory, you first have to make sure the physical network is optimized, in terms of addressing, subnetting, and topology.

Check that the computers on the network that will be attaching to Active Directory are obtaining the correct IP addresses. They should not be sitting on a different subnet from the one you are installing or getting the wrong dynamic IP addresses from a DHCP server. If the IP design is not sensible, location services are not going to resolve DCs as quick as they should, and the logon experience will be disappointingly slow for the user.

Topology

A good place to start when designing the physical structure is network topology. Begin by drawing a topology diagram of each site and then diagrams showing the links between each site.

Once you have the site topology sketched out, you can create a network diagram showing the links between the different sites and how everything feeds back to corporate or enterprise HQ. Show the speed between the links and the different IP subnets that are in place. Also list the names of the routers on the links, which is useful information, the quality and transports being used, and so on. For example, in the WAN network in Figure 8-7, we indicate the IP addresses of the routers, the DHCP scope being used on that segment, the brand and model of the router, whether the site is Token Ring or Ethernet, and so on.

Also indicate on the diagram or in supporting documentation the following:

1. Indicate the speed of the link and the traffic. Your service provider will be able to give you a breakdown of the bandwidth you are using, spike in traffic, and your busiest times.

2. Describe the cost of each link in as much detail as possible. Especially important to note is if a link is pay-by-usage. This will allow you to determine replication strategy to such a site.

3. Describe the quality and reliability of the link.

4. Define your site links using the actual network topology that is already in place as a starting point. After all, if you have a network that is already down, no matter how bad it is, you have to start somewhere. If the links between the sites are reliable, you should map your Active Directory structure to this network as a foundation. Changes can be made later.

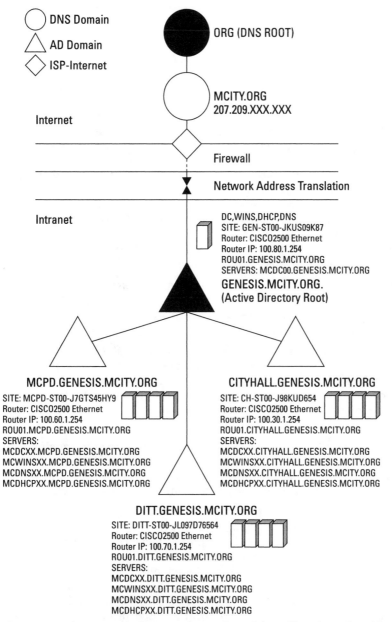

DNS Domain

AD Domain

ISP-Internet

ORG (DNS ROOT)

MCITY.ORG
207.209.XXX.XXX

Internet

Firewall

Network Address Translation

Intranet

DC,WINS,DHCP,DNS
SITE: GEN-ST00-JKUS09K87
Router: CISCO2500 Ethernet
Router IP: 100.80.1.254
ROU01.GENESIS.MCITY.ORG
SERVERS: MCDC00.GENESIS.MCITY.ORG

GENESIS.MCITY.ORG.
(Active Directory Root)

MCPD.GENESIS.MCITY.ORG

SITE: MCPD-ST00-J7GTS45HY9
Router: CISCO2500 Ethernet
Router IP: 100.60.1.254
ROU01.MCPD.GENESIS.MCITY.ORG
SERVERS:
MCDCXX.MCPD.GENESIS.MCITY.ORG
MCWINSXX.MCPD.GENESIS.MCITY.ORG
MCDNSXX.MCPD.GENESIS.MCITY.ORG
MCDHCPXX.MCPD.GENESIS.MCITY.ORG

CITYHALL.GENESIS.MCITY.ORG

SITE: CH-ST00-J98KUD654
Router: CISCO2500 Ethernet
Router IP: 100.30.1.254
ROU01.CITYHALL.GENESIS.MCITY.ORG
SERVERS:
MCDCXX.CITYHALL.GENESIS.MCITY.ORG
MCWINSXX.CITYHALL.GENESIS.MCITY.ORG
MCDNSXX.CITYHALL.GENESIS.MCITY.ORG
MCDHCPXX.CITYHALL.GENESIS.MCITY.ORG

DITT.GENESIS.MCITY.ORG

SITE: DITT-ST00-JL097D76564
Router: CISCO2500 Ethernet
Router IP: 100.70.1.254
ROU01.DITT.GENESIS.MCITY.ORG
SERVERS:
MCDCXX.DITT.GENESIS.MCITY.ORG
MCWINSXX.DITT.GENESIS.MCITY.ORG
MCDNSXX.DITT.GENESIS.MCITY.ORG
MCDHCPXX.DITT.GENESIS.MCITY.ORG

Figure 8-7: The network diagram of a portion of the Millennium City wide area network

Creating DC Sites

To begin creating DC sites, take your list of segments and locations and the topological plan, and start as follows:

1. Create a DC site for each network segment, location, or collections of locations that are part of your so-called reliable WAN or intranet, and assign each location a DC site name. In our case, our first DC site name is zero-based and called GEN00-R. Formulate a naming convention for your sites and for your servers and resources (see Chapter 5). The R in our name means reliable. You will notice that we have used only letters, numbers, and the hyphen. This is because the DC sites are going to be used in the DNS. It is a good idea to stick to the standard RFC DNS names and resist underscores and letters that make your DNS names not only incompatible with RFC DNS but also looking like alphabet soup as well. Another reason for keeping the names simple is that most seasoned administrators will go directly to the command line when debugging DNS. If you ask an admin to type **nslookup somethingcrazy**, you will likely get some nasty remarks sent your way.

2. Create a DC site for each segment that is only accessible via SMTP mail. An SMTP site name on our plan would be named something like GEN05-S, the S standing for SMTP. You can also add information that tells a network engineer more about the site than just protocols.

3. Take network segments that are not self-contained DC sites and merge them with other sites, as long as the bandwidth between the sites is fast and reliable enough for the two segments to operate as a single combined DC site. Remember that site configuration in Active Directory has to do with replicating, so while the site may actually be a physical site, it is not a domain controller site, so to speak.

4. Make a list or a database of the sites that are added to your topology chart and record all the subnet address schemes. It is worthwhile to record all the sites, not only the ones that have a DC in them. You can make the site in the database a DC site. This will help you identify the site as an Active Directory site.

5. Your next step is to mark on your topology diagrams where you are going to place DCs. In other words, mark the sites as being DC sites. Chapter 7 assists you in determining how to partition your forest and plan domains. Now is the time to put that planning and logical design into place.

Note   Microsoft made such a big deal about sites that at first we tended to focus too much on segments. However, if you own a cluster of networks joined by the Mississippi of backbones, you could consider the whole soup one DC site.

Deploying Domain Controllers

Using the information you assembled in the logical design plan discussed in Chapter 7, place your domain controllers in the sites selected in the following manner:

1. Place the root Active Directory DC in the so-called home site. In the example in this book, this site is GENESIS, and if you choose such a domain hierarchy, this site need only consist of a privately addressed subnet that uses network address translation to maintain the segment in such a way that it does not conflict with live networks. A root domain protected in this way is a worthwhile investment. Ignore the replication issue right now.

2. Place a DC in the "home" or head-office site. Your typical first-home DC will be HQ. If you have followed a pilot project or you have performed lab work on Active Directory, you might also consider positioning the next site in the MIS Department. Depending on your network and topology, MIS might be on the same subnet as HQ. In the case of Millennium City, we placed the CITYHALL domain above DITT in the namespace hierarchy, but, in fact, it was the second DC that was raised.

3. Using the logical plan and the site or network topology link information, place your next domain controllers according to the following criteria:

   • There are enough users in the site to warrant a DC on their network segment.

   • The link is unreliable. If the link goes down a lot, users will have a problem authenticating. If a DC is placed into that site, users will be able to continue working. In the same breath, if the link is an on-demand service, you will want to drop a DC in there so that users have authentication round the clock.

   • The site can only receive e-mail or is only open to SMTP mail. In such a case, users must have a local DC because they cannot request logon authentication over SMTP.

While you are placing your DCs, keep in mind the need for GCs. Remember that GCs will add to replication traffic. But they are also essential in the grand scheme of logon things. To refresh, GCs contain a complete copy of their parent domains and a partial replica of all other domains in the forest.

Tip　Try not to get confused between sites and domains. Site links, while configured in Active Directory, are not related to domains or domain hierarchy. A site can contain any number of domains (by virtue of the presence of domain controllers).

Securing Domain Controllers

As you have discovered in the previous chapters, DCs are packed with highly sensitive information. In fact, if a DC in a large enterprise is stolen or accessed while online, anyone with malicious intent or thoughts of enrichment can do a lot of damage.

Domain controllers need to be locked in secure rooms or cabinets with limited and controlled access. You may consider using the Syskey Tool, which is discussed in Appendix B.

Deploying GC Servers

As we warned earlier, it is imperative you place GC servers into your DC sites. If the DC in the site is the root DC, it will automatically be a DC. We find it necessary to keep reminding ourselves that the GC handles the logon authority for its "custody" domain and is essential for native-mode domains — and the application of Universal groups.

It is also worthwhile noting that you should place a backup GC in a sensitive or mission-critical domain, or have an online backup that can scream to the rescue. Losing the DC means losing the GC as well, and if that happens, your users will have to log on with their imaginations.

Understand that the GC holds the membership of the Universal Groups and, as such, when a logon request is made of a native-mode DC, the DC will request the GC to calculate the complete group membership access level of a particular user. With that level of security, if the GC has taken leave, your user will be denied logon.

The only time that you can be lax on the GC availability scene is when you are dealing with a single domain. If this is the case, the GC is used mainly for search and seek.

Deploying DNS Servers

Without DNS, you are in the dark. You can deploy a million DCs and GCs out there, but they will run deep and silent without the locator service provided by DNS. Not only do the clients need to use DNS to locate network services and DCs, but DCs also need to use DNS to locate other DCs and other servers. We have dedicated an entire chapter to DNS; see Chapter 14.

You should place at least one DNS on a DC site and designate secondary DNS servers on other segments and DC sites. The local DNS servers should be authoritative for the locator records of the domains in the DC site. This will obviate the need of clients to query offsite servers for local resources.

You can also install a DNS server on the actual DC and have it integrated with Active Directory. The advantages are that the DNS and the DC are "co-located," which saves the cost of additional equipment; Active Directory will automatically keep DNS well fed, and the DC's replication service will be ideal for DNS replication.

Cross-Reference DNS-Active Directory specific configuration information is included in Chapter 14.

Deploying WINS and DHCP Servers

If you are supporting down-level clients or you need to continue supporting the ancient art of resolving NetBIOS names to IP addresses across the matrix of segments, you will need to remember to deploy your WINS services. Oy, you almost forgot, did you? Just so you remember, we added a section on WINS to Chapter 14.

For the most part, WINS (at least the new WINS) is more self-healing that its ancestor on Windows NT networks. But it should be deployed in any location in which you find it necessary to drop a DC.

DHCP is, of course, critical to all clients: down-level, up-level, and penthouse. The only places on a DC site that will take static IP addresses are the servers.

The chapter that follows will take you through actual deployment and installation of the GENESIS, MCITY, MCPD, and DITT domains, their interconnection and replication matrix, and so on. Before you embark on this, consider the following:

Do a sanity check on the site concept

It is one thing hitting a graph pad or Visio and knocking out the Windows 2000 network of the millennium; it is another trying to map it to the physical reality. In cases where there already is an installed network, you will for the most part have to work with what you already have, which may mean taking the location and making it a separate domain or taking care of replication as if you had the last network in the world.

Make network logon and access to resources your primary focus

This should be your first consideration when it comes to the actual deployment plan. Get an idea of what slow logon or access to network resources entails and feels like over low bandwidth connections, and make that your point of departure. If it is impractical to have a new domain at the location, then you have to either open the pipe for better replication or be very creative with your replication scheduling.

Make network replication traffic your secondary focus

As soon as you have laid the necessary foundations that ensure your users have fast logon authentication and access to all the resources to which they are entitled, you should then work in your replication plans. You will need to make sure that you can pick up propagation from the other domains and that you can get all your necessary updates from the root domain controllers, other domains in the forest, and the updates intended for the global catalog, the other naming contexts, and so on.

Now enough with the theory, let's get down to deployment business in Chapter 9.

Summary

In this chapter, we introduced you to the physical structure of Active Directory. We looked at the three concepts in this physical world that make up Active Directory's physical structures. These are domain controller servers, global catalog servers, and sites. We also discussed how essential it is, even for a small company, to either back up the Active Directory regularly or maintain a redundant (hot) DC.

By maintaining a redundant DC, you ensure the domain has a hot fail-over should one of the DCs stop working. However, you learned that domain controllers and catalogs replicate information to one another to keep the network of controllers current. The degree of currency depends on the situation. For example, domain controllers supporting the same domain will eventually become 100 percent replicas of each other, while domain controllers belonging to different domains will only partially replicate to each other.

We discussed how replication is achieved by a complex collection of heuristic algorithms and how replication consumes bandwidth. On fast Ethernet networks where there is a thick backbone, the replication traffic is tolerable. However, between locations connected with slow links, replication traffic may be too slow to maintain a single domain. An additional domain might be needed to lessen the replication load.

You learned how you can calculate replication traffic using information derived from the Active Directory technical specifications, such as the size of attributes. You discovered that the attribute size remains fairly constant and that replication traffic is predictable and can easily be catered to.

Another management item on your checklist is directory synchronization. Directory synchronization differs from replication because it is an information exchange mechanism that takes place between unlike directories.

The next chapter takes the theory of the past several chapters and puts what you have learned into practice, starting with the installation of domain controllers and the deployment of the Active Directory.

✦   ✦   ✦

Active Directory Installation and Deployment

This chapter deploys an Active Directory infrastructure. Working from the deployment plan blueprint described in this chapter, you will be able to identify and modify the elements of the deployment plan that will suite your configuration. You can make changes as you need, be it a solution for a small network or a WAN connecting multiple domain controllers and an extensive Active Directory tree.

Getting Ready to Deploy

This chapter takes you through the actual installation of the domain controllers for an Active Directory domain. We will be using our fictitious city, Millennium City (MCITY), as the demo. So far, we have put several structures into place according to the blueprint we will discuss next. You may take this blueprint and deployment plan and use it as a template for your own project, expanding or cutting and pasting to and from it as you need, or just use the examples to establish your own strategy. The text in this chapter is abridged, and a more detailed plan is available in PDF format on the accompanying CD. If the plan appears to be a real-life example, that's because it is. This Windows 2000 network and namespace have actually been deployed.

What we espouse here is not the gospel on Active Directory deployment by any means. It works for our environment, situation, and the diversity of our demo organization. Smaller companies may find it too expensive to implement some of our suggestions; others may garner some deep insight. Our purpose is to show a rich implementation.

Note   While Millennium City is a fictitious city (modeled on the organizational chart of a real U.S. city), the following deployment plan was executed and actual domain controllers were set up across a simulated WAN in a test environment. We also upgraded a large Windows NT Primary Domain Controller (PDC) containing several hundred accounts from a live domain, and joined it to the MCITY namespace and the GENESIS forest as part of a live pilot project involving actual users.

Millennium City Active Directory Deployment Plan

The MCITY deployment plan consists of several phases. These phases are described in the plan according to the following contents:

A. Executive Summary

B. Deployment Phases

Phase I: Install and Test Root Active Directory Domain.

Phase II: Install and Test Child Active Directory Domains.

Phase III: Create Organizational Units.

Phase IV: Create Groups and Users (Chapter 10).

Phase V: Establish and Implement Security Policy (Chapter 11).

Phase VI: Establish Trusts with Windows NT Domains or Domains in Other Forests (Chapter 11).

Phase VII: Establish Workplace Management Policy (Chapter 11).

Phases IV, V, VI and VII are not included in the actual plan components discussed in this chapter; they relate to chapters 10 and 11. After consulting these chapters, and with practice, you can extend this plan with these latter phases according to your specific needs.

Executive Summary

The following summary describes the deployment specifics for the GENESIS forest on the MCITY.ORG and GENESIS.MCITY.ORG namespaces (see the MCITY logical structure in Chapter 7).

MCITY Network

The MCITY network (MCITYNET) is managed in the Department of Technology and Telecommunications (DITT). The backbone at DITT connects to a bank of Cisco 4000 series routers that connect MCITYNET to an ATM backbone. The routers and physical network are provided by and managed by a major long-distance provider that offers managed network services (MNS). MCITYNET comprises both the Internet services required by the city and the private wide area network (WAN) and intranet, known as the GENESIS network.

DITT connects to the CITYHALL and MCPD over a dedicated IP network, and to smaller departments over an MNS T1 network. Several locations are connected on smaller pipes from 64 Kbps to 250 Kbps, and so on. The configuration of the GENESIS segment of MCITYNET is outlined in Table 9-1, and also illustrated in Figure 8-7 in the Chapter 8.

Table 9-1 Genesis Network Configuration				
Location	*Genesis*	*Cityhall*	*DITT*	*MCPD*
Subnets	100.10.0.0	100.45.0.0	100.50.0.0	100.70.0.0
DHCP scope	100.10.2.1 to 100.10.2.254	100.45.2.1 to 100.45.5.254	100.50.2.1 to 100.50.5.254	100.70.2.1 to 100.70.254.254
Domain Controllers Reserved Names	MCDC00 to MCDC09	MCDC10 to MCDC49	MCDC50 to MCDC69	MCDC70 to MCDC129
Sites	GEN-ST00 – ST09 JKIJS09K87	CH-ST00 – ST09 J98KIJD654	DITT-ST00 – ST09 JKP09KLJ	MCPD-ST00 – ST40 JKDOP843D

The GENESIS Domain

The root Active Directory (AD) domain and the forest for Millennium City will be called GENESIS. The forest is also called GENESIS because Active Directory forces the forest to take its name from the root domain. After several months of extensive research and testing of Microsoft's Active Directory services on Windows 2000 Server, the Millennium City Windows 2000 testing team have come to a decision on how to best deploy Active Directory services.

It has been decided that for an organization the size of Millennium City, the root domain of the organization's Active Directory namespace needs to be a secure domain accessible only by a small group of senior administrators. These administrators will have the organization's highest security clearance. There will be no user accounts in the domain outside of the core administrators, and no active workplace management — other than what is needed for security, domain controller (DC) lockdown, and to protect and administer in this domain — will be put into place. There are several reasons for the need to establish such a domain.

First, the root domain in any large organization is a target for e-terrorists. If the root domain contains many user and computer accounts and a lot of information, the organization could suffer extensive damages if this domain is destroyed either physically (removal or destruction of the DC servers) or by a concerted network attack, or if its data is accessed by unauthorized personnel. Naturally, a small concern might not need such a "bastion" root domain, but any large enterprise should seriously consider it.

Second, all MCITY first-, second-, and third-level domains are extensively populated by user and computer accounts (security principals) and many groups (see Figure 8-7 in the previous chapter, which identifies the levels on the GENESIS domain tree). There are also numerous OUs in these domains and thus many administrators at various levels of the domain's OU hierarchy. We thus deemed it necessary to establish a root domain with no more than a handful (preferably no more than five) administrators who by virtue of having accounts in the root domain would have the widest authority over the city's namespace, starting from GENESIS down. (This security policy is discussed in Chapter 11.)

Third, the root domain is critical to the city. It might be feasible — if Microsoft makes it possible — in the future to disconnect the root domain from the rest of the domain tree, and graft the tree to another root. However, at present it is not, and losing the domain root would result in the loss of the entire domain tree, taking with it all levels subordinate to the root, in fact everything on the tree. To thus protect the root domain, we will establish partner DCs of the root domain at several remote locations, primarily for redundancy and to locate the root domain over a wide area. These locations will initially be as follows (see Figure 8-7 in Chapter 8):

✦ Location 1: DITT's Network Operations Center (NOC)

✦ Location 2: City Hall's Network Operations Center

✦ Location 3: MCPD (Police Department) Network Operations Center

The lightweight (user accounts) nature of the root domain, which in addition to the built-in accounts only contains a handful of users, makes it easier to replicate its databases around the enterprise. (See Chapter 8 for more detailed discussion of replication topology.)

Finally, the root domain controller is also our *Schema Operations Master* and *Domain Naming Operations Master* for the forest and holds the master schema and other naming contexts that affect the enterprise as a whole, such as the global catalog (GC), that can only be changed on the operations master.

The Schema Operations Master is where all schema updates will be performed, and the Domain Naming Operations Master is where we can make changes to the domain namespace on an enterprise-wide basis.

Physical location of GENESIS

The GENESIS domain's first and second DCs will be secured in the main server room of DITT's network operations center (NOC). These DCs will not be attended to by DITT's operators, but instead will be administered to by the GENESIS administrators. As stated earlier, GENESIS DCs will also be placed in MCPD and CITYHALL, supported by reliable, high-bandwidth pipes.

Although it is important to locate the GENESIS root DC in a secure location, it is also important to make the services of the GENESIS DCs and GC easily available in as many GENESIS locations as possible. This will allow users to be able to obtain the following services without having to contact the DC over many hops on the WAN:

✦ Users should not have to look up the network address of any GENESIS DC, or any DC for that matter.

✦ High availability. The GENESIS DCs need to be in as many places as possible in the city so that the most up-to-date replicas of the GC and other information are nearby.

✦ Reliable query results. Strong and closely located GCs should facilitate rich queries, and users must be able to rely on the currency of the data. They must be able to obtain information on users, groups, and other network services without any interruption in services or lack of data.

Network specifics of GENESIS

The GENESIS domain will be established on a segment of the physical network on which the Department of Technology and Telecommunications (DITT) currently runs. This network currently is supported on a 100Mbps backbone on which the DITT supports its AS/400, UNIX, and Windows NT systems. GENESIS will be established on the same network, but on its own IP subnet. This IP address space is a network supported by Windows 2000 routing services. It can also be supported behind network address translation services (NAT) running on a Windows 2000 role server.

Note   See Chapter 15 for a discussion of Routing and Remote Access (RRAS) and Chapter 12 for a discussion of Network Address Translation.

GENESIS site object specifics

In order to support replication to and from other MCITY domains (inter-site) and between domain controllers belonging to the same domain (intra-site), an Active Directory site will support GENESIS. This site will be named GEN-ST00-JKIJS09K87, as illustrated in Figure 8-7 and Table 9-1. The following DC names have been reserved for this site: MCDC00.GENESIS.MCITY.ORG to MCDC09.GENESIS.MCITY.ORG MCDC50. The NetBIOS name range of these DCs is MCDC00 to MCDC09.

GENESIS subnet object specifics

The subnet address 100.10.0.0 will be assigned to a subnet object. This subnet object will be associated with the GENESIS site object described previously.

Domain health and security

Two partner DCs will support the domain in the main DC site. The main DC site will also house a copy of the GC for the entire MCITY Active Directory namespace.

The administrators in the GENESIS domain will have administrative authority over the resources in the GENESIS domain. The GENESIS domain also has administrative and security authority over the subordinate domains.

The CITYHALL Domain

The CITYHALL domain is the first of the Windows 2000 populated domains. There will be several hundred user and computer accounts in this domain. This domain will support the accounts and network resources for the Mayor's office and the various departments that fall directly under the Mayor.

Physical location of CITYHALL

The CITYHALL domain controllers will be located at City Hall and will fall under the authority of the City Hall network administrators who work directly for the Mayor. We will supply at least two DCs to support the initial deployment of Windows 2000 into City Hall.

Network specifics of CITYHALL

The CITYHALL domain is to be established on the actual network segment assigned to CITYHALL by DITT. This segment is the 100.45.0.0 network. CITYHALL currently is supported on a 100Mbps backbone between the ten floors, and the network is collapsed into a 10Mbps network that services the workstations, printers, and other network devices.

City Hall's IT department also supports AS/400 systems, CICS on IBM S390, and several technologies supported on UNIX systems, such as Oracle and Informix database management systems.

CITYHALL site object specifics

In order to support replication to and from other MCITY domains and several remote locations that will belong to the CITYHALL domain, an Active Directory site will support CITYHALL. The main site will be named CH-ST00-J98KIJD654. The following DC names have been reserved for this site: MCDC10.CITYHALL.GENESIS.MCITY.ORG to MCDC50.CITYHALL.GENESIS.MCITY.ORG. The NetBIOS name range of these DCs is MCDC10 to MCDC50.

CITYHALL subnet object specifics

The subnet address 100.45.0.0 will be assigned to a subnet object. This subnet object will be associated with the CITYHALL site (CH-ST00- J98KIJD654) object described previously.

Domain health and security

At least three partner or peer DCs will support the CITYHALL domain in the main DC site. We have decided to locate one DC in the secure server room of the floor on which the Mayor's office is located. The remaining two DCs will be located in the main server room in City Hall's network operations center (NOC). The DCs will also house copies of the GCs for the entire MCITY Active Directory namespace.

The administrators in the CITYHALL domain will have administrative authority over the resources only in the CITYHALL domain. Some administrators in CITY-HALL are also administrators of the GENESIS domain.

The DITT Domain

The DITT domain contains the resources for the Department of Information Technology and Telecommunications. There will be several hundred user and computer accounts in this domain. This domain will support the accounts and network resources for the IT staff and consultants, and the various departments, that fall directly under DITT.

Network specifics of DITT

The DITT domain is to be established on the network segment 100.50.0.0. See Table 9-1 for the configuration specifics of DITT.

The MCPD Domain

The MCPD domain contains the resources for the Millennium City Police Department. According to the configuration, a large number of IP addresses are required for this network. The IP address range in the DHCP scope will support hundreds of workstations, terminals, and other network devices. This domain is the most complex of the four domains, because numerous domain controllers and sites will have to be configured to cover an extensive network connecting the precincts to the commissioner's offices, the DA's office, and various law enforcement agencies.

Network specifics of DITT

The MCPD domain is to be established on the network segment 100.70.0.0. See Table 9-1 for the configuration specifics of MCPD.

Install and Test the Active Directory Domain Controllers

There are several deployment phases outlined in this plan. Phase I covers the installation and deployment of the GENESIS, CITYHALL, MCPD, and DITT domains.

Note

Instead of repeating the full installation and deployment of each domain, we will first briefly install the root domain. We will then fully demonstrate the promotion of the CITYHALL domain controller and how it joins the GENESIS domain tree and forest. The other domains will join GENESIS in the same fashion. Each domain will then be administered as a separate entity, while still being covered by any policy that might derive from the root. The root administrators have the highest power of administration over all the domains in the forest.

The following sequence of events describes the creation of all the domain controllers. These activities will take you through machine preparation to final deployment:

1. Install the DC machine
2. Promote the server to domain controller
3. Make the server the root DC or join forest and trees
4. Establish the DC in DNS/WINS
5. Establish the DC in Active Directory site
6. Build initial OUs
7. Delegate OU administration
8. Secure DC further and follow disaster recovery protocol

Install the DC Machine

Follow the procedures described in Chapter 5 or Appendix B for installing Windows 2000 Server. Ensure the machine is stable. The best way to do this is to keep it running for about two weeks. You can use Backup/Restore as discussed in Chapter 5 to "burn in" the machine. After several DCs are all built or acquired on the same hardware configuration, you might consider reducing the burn-in period to several days instead of two weeks. If your machine is still running under load after several weeks, consecutive machines configured on identical hardware will likely run without problems. But a few days of tests are required to be certain.

Note You do not need to go to the additional expense of using Advanced Server for a domain controller. All Windows 2000 Servers can be promoted to a domain controller. Providing a fail-over service or a cluster for Active Directory is also a waste of resources and money. A fully redundant server will not only be cheaper, it will make for a more secure Active Directory deployment.

Server name

Pick a name for your machine from the list provided in the deployment plan. This is the NetBIOS name you will use to construct your DNS name. This name is going to be used again when you promote your server to a domain controller. We used the name MCDC00 for the standalone machine that became the root DC for GENESIS. When we promoted this machine, we reassigned this name and DNS resolved this machine as MCDC00.GENESIS.MCITY.ORG. In the case of CITYHALL, the server name reserved for the first DC in this domain is MCDC10. Its DNS name will thus be MCDC10.CITYHALL.GENESIS.MCITY.ORG. Remember, in the case of CITYHALL, it is the first level down from the root GENESIS domain, and also two levels down from MCITY and ORG, which are both Internet domain names. This information is illustrated in Figure 8-7 in the properties for the GENESIS domain. To check this information, open the Active Directory Domains and Trusts and select the domain in the tree, on the left-hand pane. Right-click the domain name and select Properties.

Server IP address

Give your machine a static IP address. You do not need to concern yourself about the subnet address you use now because you will change it later in the next phase of the deployment. However, make sure the IP address you choose is not used on any other machine on the network or as part of any DHCP scope listed in Table 9-1. Create a pool of static IP addresses, or reserve a segment of your scope, that you can use in the lab specifically for the purpose of installation and testing.

Choose a workgroup

During the installation of the server, you will be asked to join it to a domain or a workgroup. You are also given the option of skipping the name and returning to it later. We prefer that you put in a workgroup and that you name the workgroup after the server's name. It cannot be the same name as the server — the installation will not allow that — so just add "wg" after the server name to keep it simple. For example, MCDC00 is the name we gave the server that was destined to become the first DC for GENESIS. The workgroup name is thus MCDCWG00. Joining a domain is not a good idea because that will force you to create a computer account for the server in the domain, which you have to remove later anyway when you install the server into its new domain. Not only is this inconvenient, but you also have to then make sure you can "see" the network and that the server will be able to find the DC of the domain it wants to join.

Services

Leave as many services out of the installation as possible. It is worth repeating here that it is better to first get a bare-bones machine running before adding additional services. However, there is one exception, as described next.

Choose a Terminal Services mode

There is one service that we deem to be the most important, and that is Terminal Services (TS). You will have to select TS from the Windows Components dialog box. You do *not* have to select licensing as well; that is only for application server servers. While choosing services, you will also be asked to choose the mode for TS, so select Remote Administration mode. This will allow you to attach to the machine remotely when it is installed in the new location. The machine can be promoted from the remote location or in the lab, but you should also provide a means to administer it remotely. This is demonstrated shortly. Remote Administration mode, as discussed in Chapter 25, allows up to two concurrent sessions to be used for remote administration without licensing.

Promote to Domain Controller

The steps we take you through in this section demonstrate installing a root domain and a child domain into an existing domain tree. You would perform these same steps to install Active Directory for any new domain controller. The only difference is that you need to choose to create a domain controller according to the choices outlined in Table 9-2. If you are not sure what you need to be installing, you need to do some more preparation and planning. Read the fine print on the dialog boxes until you are sure about your actions, but do not overly concern yourself until the last step because you can always go backwards and forwards in these dialog boxes until you are sure.

Table 9-2 Domain Controller Promotion Choices				
Action	*GENESIS*	*CITYHALL*	*DITT*	*MCPD*
DC for a new domain	Yes	Yes	Yes	Yes
Additional DC for an existing domain	Yes, at any time you need more DCs	Yes, at any time you need more DCs	Yes, at any time you need more DCs	Yes, at any time you need more DCs
Create a new tree	Yes	No	No	No
Create a new domain in an existing tree	No	Yes	Yes	Yes

Action	GENESIS	CITYHALL	DITT	MCPD
Create a new forest	Yes	No	No	No
Place domain tree in an existing forest	No	N/A	N/A	N/A

The creation of the root DC is the easiest. You just need to follow the instructions to create a new domain and a new domain tree in a new forest. This will essentially be the first Active Directory domain you will create for your enterprise, and it is known as the root domain. We recommend a root domain structure similar to the one created here. Your own "Genesis" domain need not be on an expensive server. In fact, our first GENESIS server was a Pentium 133Mhz with 64MB RAM. The replica we show in this chapter is a Pentium PRO 200Mhz. We plan to add a super-server DC for GENESIS capable of holding a huge database and taking many thousands of concurrent queries and logon requests.

Before you begin promotion, make sure your server can talk to the network. The server does not necessarily have to send packets out to other machines. Unlike new Windows NT 4.0 Backup Domain Controllers, there is no need to immediately begin synchronization with the primary domain controller (PDC). However, Windows 2000 will not let you promote the server and install Active Directory if it cannot detect that it is attached to a network. Connecting the server to a hub is good enough, even if it is the only server in the hub.

If the server cannot be contacted from the network, you will obviously not be able to promote it remotely, nor will it be able to join the domain tree. We will now begin the promotion of the DCs and the creation of child domains. You will need to take the following steps to complete the promotion:

1. Promote the server using the command DCPROMO or using the Configure Your Server utility. You can use the DCPROMO command from the command prompt, which is quicker and easier if you plan to promote many servers. The Configure utility is illustrated in Figure 9-1. To open the utility, click Start ⇨ Programs ⇨ Administrative Tools ⇨ Configure Your Server.

2. In the Configure Your Server utility, select the Active Directory item in the menu on the left of the dialog box to switch to the Active Directory page. Scroll down and click the hyperlink "Start the Active Directory Wizard." When the Wizard loads, continue by clicking the Next button.

3. The Domain Controller Type dialog box loads, as shown in Figure 9-2. Make sure to check the option "Domain controller for a new domain." This is the first DC for the domain GENESIS or CITYHALL or any other new domain. The creation of the root domain from here on is a no-brainer. Without an existing forest or domain tree, you cannot install anything else. So, we will now proceed to install a child domain . . . CITYHALL. Click Next.

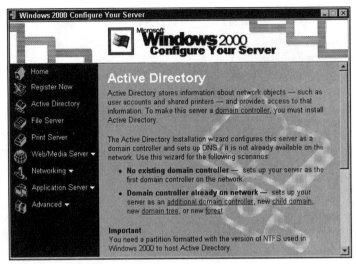

Figure 9-1: The Configure Your Server utility

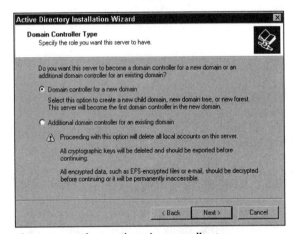

Figure 9-2: Choose domain controller type

4. The Create Tree or Child Domain dialog box loads. Select the option "Create a new child domain in an existing domain tree." Click Next.

5. The Network Credentials dialog box now loads. Here, you are asked to enter the name of a user account in a domain in the existing forest that has the authority to create the domain and join it to the domain tree. Enter the name and password and click Next. In our case, we entered the name of an administrator with such authority in the GENESIS domain.

6. The Child Domain Installation dialog box now loads. Here, you are asked to enter the parent domain. In the example for MCITY, we will add GENESIS for the parent and CITYHALL for the child domain. The DNS name is automatically constructed, as illustrated in Figure 9-3. You can also browse for the correct domain if more than one already exists. Upon browsing, we find that only one other domain exists: the root GENESIS.MCITY.ORG (so far, so good). Only enter the name of the domain itself and not the entire DNS name, which will be automatically built for you. As illustrated in the example, this can be used as the NetBIOS name for a domain as well. Click Next when you are sure you have entered the right information. If you are unsure, go back and check the deployment plan, which is why you create such things.

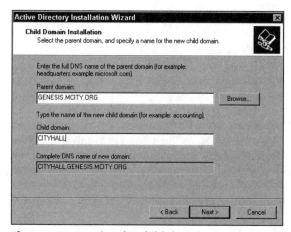

Figure 9-3: Naming the child domain

7. The next dialog box to load is the NetBIOS name we just touched on, and the title of the dialog box is "NetBIOS Domain Name." Choose the default. Check back over previous chapters concerning the choice of names. Domain names should be simple. They need to be accessible to humans, not computers. In this example, we chose the NetBIOS name CITYHALL. Be sure you choose the right name, because you cannot change it after you promote the server. Click Next.

8. The Database and Log Locations dialog box now loads. If you have separate disks, then choose a separate drive letter for the logs, as illustrated in Figure 9-4. This technique is inherited from Microsoft Exchange, which is the foundation for the Active Directory database and replication engines. You will get better performance if you choose two disks. If you are using RAID and only have one drive letter, then configure both locations to point to the same drive letter. Click Next.

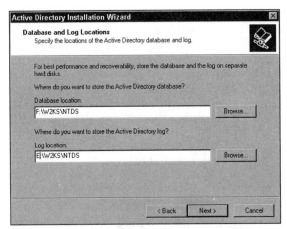

Figure 9-4: Choosing the database and log files hard disk resources

9. The Shared System Volume dialog box loads. You can usually leave this to the default chosen by the server. Click Next.

10. The Permissions dialog box loads, as illustrated in Figure 9-5. If you have Windows NT servers that need to access information on this server, then choose the first option. For security reasons, we have chosen to upgrade all our NT servers in CITYHALL and deploy only Windows 2000 (we have ways and means of spending our taxpayer's money). CITYHALL will then be a native mode domain. For more information on the modes and permissions levels, consult Chapter 10. Click Next.

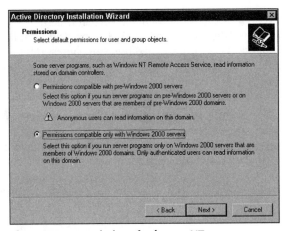

Figure 9-5: Permissions for legacy NT server access

11. The Directory Services Restore Mode Administrator Password dialog box loads. This parameter is the password of the user account that is authorized to start a domain controller in Restore mode for the purpose of restoring system state. Enter the password twice and click Next.

12. The Summary dialog box loads. This means that you are almost done. Check over the details carefully to make sure that you have made the right choices. At this point, you can always go back and change a value or parameter. Once you click Next, however, there is no undoing any mistakes. You can only demote the server and start the whole process all over again. Click Next to begin the promotion, the installation of Active Directory, and the joining of the domain to the tree. If you see the dialog boxes illustrated in the following figures, you are doing fine.

The wizard then starts the installation of Active Directory on the local server. This process can take several minutes. At this point, you can leave the DC to finish; there is no further human intervention needed.

Figure 9-6 illustrates that the new DC has been able to contact the parent DC on the network. In this case, CITYHALL has been able to contact GENESIS. Replication is then started between the two domains. You will notice processor activity related to the replication on the parent domain.

Figure 9-6: CITYHALL is installing into the GENESIS tree.

Next, the wizard sets up a trust relationship between the new domain CITYHALL and its parent GENESIS. Because the domains are part of the same domain tree in the same forest, they can exchange security credentials, which allows trusts between the domains to be transitive and bi-directional.

If all went well, and if the installation took place on the same network segment as the parent, you will notice that the new child domain was placed into the same site as the parent domain. We can leave this as is for now and move it to another site later. Also notice that the Back button has been disabled. There is no going back; the server has now been promoted to a domain controller running Active Directory services. You will now have to restart the server.

Tip   The entire promotion and installation process should take no longer than an hour on a well burned-in machine and on the local area network. On a very powerful machine with very fast hard disks, it can take as little as five minutes. If the process takes longer, or if Windows 2000 seems to be taking hours or even the whole day to write information to the disks, then you have a problem and need to terminate the effort (just be sure the bottleneck is not due to replication that is taking place over a slow link to a remote site). Powering down the machine is the only way to terminate the effort. This, by the way, happened to us only once in more than 30 promotions. After restarting the machine, we started the effort again, and it ran all the way in about an hour.

Towards the end of the promotion period and before restarting, there is usually no way of accessing any former shares or resources on the new DC.

Establish in DNS/WINS

Several important items needed to be taken care of when we first created the root domain GENESIS, or more correctly, GENESIS.MCITY.ORG. You will encounter the same when you install your root domain controller, the first domain in your forest. During the installation, you will be asked for the address of a Domain Name System server, or DNS, or you can choose to install DNS on the server if this was not done before you began the DNS promotion. The Active Directory installation procedure will look for a DNS server into which it must install a new zone and new domain information. This has been fully discussed in Chapter 14, which covers DNS and WINS.

It is a good idea to choose to install and integrate DNS and WINS on the root domain controller. It will make installation a lot smoother. For example, if the new Active Directory cannot locate a DNS server, it will be unable to register any domain, host, or site-specific information into the DNS databases.

During the installation of child domains, however, you will not be prompted for DNS information, even if you installed DNS on the server when you originally set it up as a standalone server. This may change with subsequent releases and service packs. Unless you manually install the new domain into DNS, there will be no way of authenticating to the child domain or managing it from another domain controller. You will get the error message that Active Directory Domains and Trusts is unable to find the domain, or that the server was not started. If your new DC is, in fact, started, then the problem is DNS.

So, let's manually install the new domain into DNS.

1. Open the primary DNS snap-in by clicking Start ➪ Administrative Tools ➪ DNS, or run the snap-in from the command line as described in Chapter 6. The DNS snap-in will load. In this example, the DNS server is hosted on our root DC, MCDC00.

2. Drill down to your root Active Directory domain. Notice that we have the higher-level Internet domains of MCITY and ORG on this DNS as well. Select the root Active Directory domain and right-click. The menu options load, as illustrated in Figure 9-7.

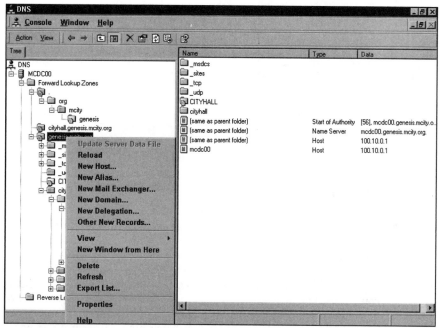

Figure 9-7: Installing the new domain

3. Go down to the menu option New Domain... and select it. The New Domain dialog box will load. In this example, we are going to add the new domain MCPD to GENESIS namespace, so we type **MCPD** in the dialog box.

4. If the domain exists, DNS will immediately pull all the records it needs into its databases. This is illustrated in Figure 9-8, which shows CITYHALL expanded down to the point where we can resolve both the Kerberos and LDAP services on the CITYHALL domain.

5. Close the DNS snap-in.

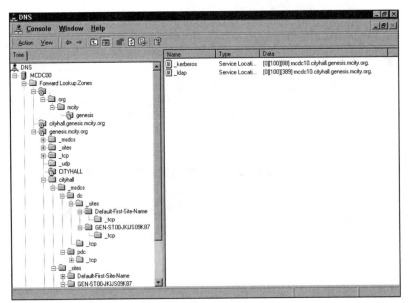

Figure 9-8: The complete domain configuration in DNS

Test DNS and WINS

If your domain controllers have been established in DNS and WINS correctly, you will be able to resolve them. The following tests provide the proof.

1. Check your DNS records: Open the command console and type **NSLOOKUP** and the domain name, as illustrated in Figure 9-9. If the domains have been correctly installed in DNS, you will be able to resolve them. In the illustration, we can correctly resolve CITYHALL and GENESIS to their respective domain controllers. Notice that you cannot yet resolve MCPD to its domain controller. There is a very good reason for this: The domain does not yet exist. Consult Chapter 14 for a more in-depth discussion of DNS.

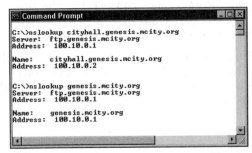

Figure 9-9: Resolving your domain and host names from the command line

2. Check your WINS records: Open the command console and ping the host of the domains from any workstation, as illustrated in Figure 9-10. If you just ping the NetBIOS name, you will be able to resolve it to an IP address as illustrated. You should also be able to ping the entire DNS name, which gets resolved in DNS, not WINS. Remember that clients will need DHCP-assigned IP addresses, which automatically give them DNS and WINS IP addresses. DHCP thus needs to be up and running before clients will be able to resolve anything on the network.

```
C:\WINNT\System32\cmd.exe                                    _ □ X
C:\>ping mcdc10

Pinging mcdc10 [100.10.0.2] with 32 bytes of data:

Reply from 100.10.0.2: bytes=32 time<10ms TTL=128
Reply from 100.10.0.2: bytes=32 time<10ms TTL=128
Reply from 100.10.0.2: bytes=32 time<10ms TTL=128
Reply from 100.10.0.2: bytes=32 time<10ms TTL=128

Ping statistics for 100.10.0.2:
     Packets: Sent = 4, Received = 4, Lost = 0 (0% loss),
Approximate round trip times in milli-seconds:
     Minimum = 0ms, Maximum = 0ms, Average = 0ms
C:\>ping mcdc10.cityhall.genesis.mcity.org

Pinging mcdc10.cityhall.genesis.mcity.org [100.10.0.2] with 32 bytes of data:

Reply from 100.10.0.2: bytes=32 time<10ms TTL=128
Reply from 100.10.0.2: bytes=32 time<10ms TTL=128
Reply from 100.10.0.2: bytes=32 time<10ms TTL=128
Reply from 100.10.0.2: bytes=32 time<10ms TTL=128

Ping statistics for 100.10.0.2:
     Packets: Sent = 4, Received = 4, Lost = 0 (0% loss),
Approximate round trip times in milli-seconds:
     Minimum = 0ms, Maximum = 0ms, Average = 0ms

C:\>
```

Figure 9-10: Resolving the NetBIOS name

If DNS and WINS check out, you are on your way to happy administration. Check that you can open the child domain from its parent DC. This is demonstrated in the next section.

Test Active Directory domains and trusts

If your domain controllers have been established in DNS and WINS correctly, you should be able to log on to the remote domain and administer it. Open Active Directory Domains and Trusts by clicking Start ➪ Administrative Tools ➪ Active Directory Domains and Trusts. The snap-in will load, as illustrated in Figure 9-11. Notice that a domain tree is now apparent. Right-click the child domain and select Manage. If trusts and authentication are all working, you will be able to enter the domain for management, as illustrated in Figure 9-11.

One last exercise before we look at sites and subnets again: Check the trust relationships between the newly created domains. To do this, go to the Domains and Trusts snap-in as illustrated earlier. Select a domain and right-click. Choose Properties and click the Trusts tab. You will see the child domain information in this dialog box. The Trusts tab also tells you that the trust is transitive and working. Notice that we have a non-transitive trust between GENESIS and an NT network. If your trusts are working right, you will be able to drill down into the directory and access a domain.

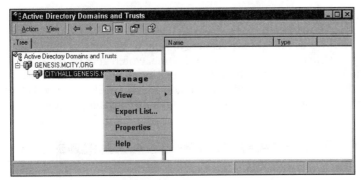

Figure 9-11: Active Directory Domains and Trusts showing the beginnings of the GENESIS tree

Creating Sites

When you promote the first domain controller, Active Directory creates a default site named *Default-First-Site-Name* and places the domain controller server into that site. You can change the name of the default site to reflect the conventions in your deployment plan, or you can create a new site after the promotion and move the server into that domain. We chose the latter for demonstration purposes. The moved server object is illustrated in Figure 9-12. This is further demonstrated when we create the CITYHALL domain.

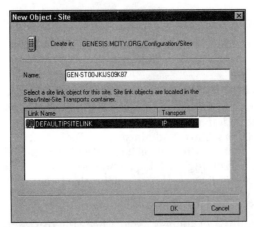

Figure 9-12: Creating the site object and relocating a server to it

Note   It is not necessary to create subnet objects for replication between servers. In the GENESIS setup, Active Directory would be able to replicate to each server in the site.

Active Directory sees the root DC server in the site we created in Chapter 8 and puts the root DC of the child domain in that site. Remember that an Active Directory site is associated with an IP subnet. The Active Directory replication topology is built via the site and subnet topology, between the domain controllers, or both. This technology is derived from the Exchange replication mechanisms, and it works on the principal of joining an Exchange server to a site.

When you have two domain controllers on the same site, which is what we have done in the earlier example for expediency, the replication that takes place between the controllers happens very quickly, or at the speed of your local area network to be more precise. This could be anything from 10 to 100Mbps.

Cross-Reference
Calculating and monitoring replication load and throughput is described in Chapter 20.

With subnets, Active Directory gets the information it needs to build the replication topology. In the previous example, it automatically added the second domain controller to the site we created for GENESIS because they shared an IP subnet. But we are going to take the CITYHALL DC and ship it to its new location, which is the 100.45.0.0 subnet, and this means that we have to manually move the DC object from the site in which it was initially installed to the correct site. Before we do that, we need to make a new site for the DC. This is done as follows:

1. Load the MMC snap-in Active Directory Site and Services. To find the snap-in, go to Start ➪ Administrative Tools ➪ Active Directory Sites and Services, or load it from the command line as explained in Chapter 6. The snap-in loads, as illustrated in Figure 9-13.

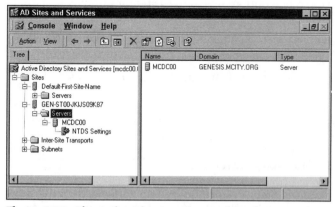

Figure 9-13: The Active Directory Sites and Services snap-in

2. Select the site item in the tree and right-click it. Choose New Site from the Context Menu. The New Site dialog box appears and allows you to create the new site. Enter the appropriate site information and choose the transport (IP or SMTP). Click OK to add the site.

Let's now look at the site object more closely.

The site object

You will notice that each site has a *servers* container. This container holds the DCs that have been placed into this site. There is also an attribute named *Licensing Site Settings* and an attribute named *NTDS Settings*.

The Licensing Site Settings property is used to specify the computer and domain that licenses the site. In the NTDS Settings object, you can disable the Knowledge Consistency Checker (KCC) (see Chapter 8) settings that determine the automatic generation of the replication topology within the site or between this site and other sites. These settings allow you to create additional settings to augment the replication topology of the KCC, but this depends on your situation.

Creating server objects

There is no difference between the server objects you create manually or the server objects created automatically by the AD, save that you have to remove manually what you create manually. The KCC does not know about these objects nor does it care about what happens to them. To create such objects, you need to perform the following steps:

1. Select the server's NTDS Settings property in the console tree and right-click it. Choose the menu option New Active Directory Connection from the context menu. The Find Domain Controllers dialog box loads.

2. Select the DC to create a connection and click OK. This will then open the New Object - Connection dialog box.

3. Supply a name for the new connection object and click OK.

You change the configuration of your connection object easily after creating it by simply opening the connection object's Properties dialog box. Note that you can also set the security levels and access control on the object. But most interesting is the Change Schedule button on the first tab. This allows you to change the replication schedule to suit your environment.

You can, for example, schedule replication to run at night when there is no traffic on the network. But remember that the schedule for a connection object is only one way. To schedule the full replication load, you have to configure the connection object on the other domain controllers as well.

Creating the subnet objects

The Subnets folder holds the IP subnets that are associated with specific site objects. To create a subnet object, you need to perform the following steps:

1. Drill down to the Subnets container in the console tree in the Sites and Services MMC snap-in. Right-click the container and choose New Subnet from the shortcut menu. The New Object - Subnet dialog box loads, as shown in Figure 9-14.

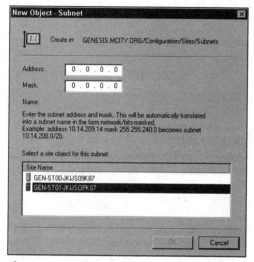

Figure 9-14: The New Object - Subnet dialog box

2. Type the new subnet's network address and mask. This is automatically translated into a properly bit-masked subnet (see Chapter 12).

3. Now select the site in the list to which the subnet is to be associated and click OK.

Now, all servers that reside on this subnet that become DCs will automatically be added to the site associated with this subnet.

Creating the site link objects

Create the site link objects according to the criteria we outlined in Chapter 8. create the object, you will need to perform the following steps:

1. Drill down to the IP or SMTP transport listed in the console tree of the Site and Services snap-in and right-click the transport. Select New Site Link from the Context menu. The New Object - Site Link dialog box loads.

2. Specify a name for the new object and then choose the sites that the link connects. This is demonstrated in Figure 9-15.

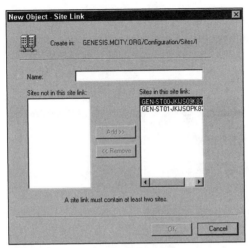

Figure 9-15: New site link object

3. Click OK, and the site link object is created.

Note   When you choose site links, you need to know what you are choosing, and this should be in your deployment plan. For example, if you are going to connect sites to a T1 network, there will typically be only two sites to be linked, one at each end. Adding a third site to the link would be worthless. If you are working with a network cloud, you can also configure a site link bridge, which ensures that all sites get replication due to the transitive link structure that is created with site link bridges.

To configure the site link, right-click the new object and choose Properties from the context menu. The site link properties for the specific site load, as illustrated in Figure 9-16. Add a description for the site link and add the sites to the link by moving them from the pane on the left (Sites not in this Site link) to the pane on the right (Sites in this Site link).

You can then configure the cost of the site links, as discussed in Chapter 8, and any special replication schedule.

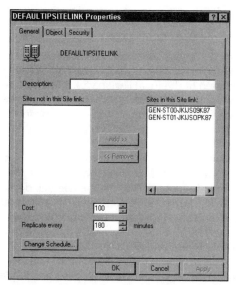

Figure 9-16: Site link properties

Creating the site link bridge object

The process involved in creating the site link bridge object is identical to the process for creating site link objects. The only difference is that you select two or more site links instead of sites.

Now, let's create some facilities for our administrators in GENESIS.

Creating Organizational Units

We have talked extensively about OUs in the previous chapters, and a full discussion about them can be found in Chapters 2 and 7. To recap, OU stands for organizational unit. In Active Directory, the OU represents a partitioning of the domain, yes; but it is more than that. An OU holds security policy, and it is the location for delegating administrative authority (also known as delegation of control).

Now and in the future, the Active Directory OU is going to be compared to the OUs of other directories, such as Novell Directory Services (NDS). Since the publishing of the Active Directory Services Interface (ADSI), the OU has already been slammed for not being a security principal. What is a spade in the hands of one gardener may be something else in the hands of another. Seasoned NT administrators may find it difficult to think in terms of another security principal to replace groups.

Had OUs replaced groups completely, it might have made upgrading very difficult.

OUs are different from groups, as discussed in Chapters 2 and 10. Groups are security principals and can be given access or denied access to any network, computer, or domain resource—in fact, any object defined in the local registry or in the Active Directory. We like OUs because it is possible to model the OU to Key Management Entities (or KMEs); so, they play a role in enterprise administration as opposed to being gatekeepers (see Chapters 2 and 7).

To extend security policy over groups and users, you place them into OUs. OUs are themselves "locked down" with security policy and access control. The policy governs how the users and the groups are allowed to conduct themselves domain- and forest-wide. Most important for security, however, is that the OU is also your computer lockup. This is essentially how you should understand and plan the enterprise group policy. This is covered extensively in Chapters 10 and 11. For now, we will take you through the steps of creating an OU.

Before you create an OU or an OU structure, you should first complete an OU plan as discussed in Chapter 7.

To create an OU, you need to perform the following. Open the Active Directory Users and Computers MMC snap-in.

1. Drill down to the domain in the console tree and right-click it. Choose New and then choose Organization Unit from the ensuing menu.

2. Enter the name of the OU according to the naming conventions you are using and click OK.

Do not try to create an OU hierarchy for the benefit of your users. It's a waste of your resources. In fact, you should do your best as an administrator to hide the OU structure from your users and the network. The user base has a network folder hierarchy to navigate and folders that you may publish in the directory. The OU structure is there for the benefit of change control and management, security policy, and workplace administration.

You can nest an OU inside another OU hierarchy; but you should avoid deep OU nests because they are harder to manage.

Delegate OU Administration

At this point in the creation of your Active Directory DC, you may decide to create additional OUs, or you may come back to the task of OU creation later. One of your most important chores will be to delegate administrative control and management over the OU to an administrator or responsible party. And you might find it useful to assign the task of creating OUs to another individual, preferably a person trained in domain security.

There are two reasons to begin delegation at this point:

1. Delegation can help you manage a complex directory structure by delegating the work as early in the directory-building process as possible.

2. Delegation is an important security consideration. By delegating, you essentially block others from interfering with the workings of a particular OU. Delegation also obviates the need to create special OU security groups or OU administra-tors, which, if given power by group membership to administer an OU, essentially have the power to administer all OUs.

Start the Delegate Control Wizard to perform delegation. This is done by first selecting the OU to which you wish to delegate control and then right-clicking the selection. The OU context menu loads. Select Delegate Control, which is the first option in the menu. The Delegation of Control Wizard launches. Select Next and then click Add to load the list of domain security principals. Choose a user or group account from the list and then click the list of Active Directory users and groups. Click Add to add the user or group and then click Next.

The next screen allows you to select the task to delegate to the user or group. You can select from a predetermined list of tasks, or choose to build a custom list of tasks. If you choose the latter, you will be able to apply a finer control over the task to delegate. The customer list gives you two options: an extensive list of individual objects that can be manipulated by the intended administrator or group, or a short-cut that specifies the OU, all objects in the OU, and any new objects that are created.

If you do not want the delegated party to be able to create new objects, choose the list of objects and uncheck the specific objects that grant control.

When you are done, click Next and the summary page will appear. Check the delegation summary and then click Finish.

Secure the DC and Follow Disaster Recovery Protocol

To properly secure a DC, you should make sure that all objects are properly protected by Access Control Lists or ACLs (see Chapters 3 and 10). ACLs on Active Directory objects contain Access Control Entries that apply to the object as a whole and to the individual properties of the object. This means that you can control not only the administrators or users that you want to see the object in its entirety, but also which properties should be exposed to certain groups or individuals.

Securing the directory is a complex task and time consuming, but it is essential. Each object, just like all other operating system objects, can display a Properties page. You launch the Properties page by right-clicking the object and selecting Properties. The object's Properties page loads.

Click the Security tab. You can now add or remove security accounts from any trusted domain and select the property pages (tabs) that can be read.

In addition to protecting the directory and its contents, it is also important to lock down the server . . . the domain controller. You should first make sure that the Administrator account or any other omnipotent security principal is not logged onto the console, and you should strive to ensure that such omnipotent accounts are not allowed to be disseminated. In Chapter 10, we provide some pointers to preventing this. Meanwhile, lock down the server and only allow accounts to access regions of the directory to which they have been delegated.

By locking down the server, you are not only protecting the directory service but also other critical components of a vital server, such as the registry, storage facilities, and so on.

Be sure to schedule a backup of the directory as soon as the current tasks have been completed.

Summary

In this chapter, we successfully demonstrated the promotion of several servers to domain controllers, which hold the Active Directory namespace and all the functionality that goes with it from (A)ctive to (Z)one.

We also took you through the paces of creating and configuring your replication topology. Finally, we reviewed the creation of OUs. We did not dwell too much on the subject of OUs because they are discussed in detail in other places in the book, particularly Chapter 2.

Now that we have the Active Directory domain structure in place, it is time to add resources to the domains. Users, groups and computers . . . here we go.

✦　　✦　　✦

Managing Users and Groups

If you are passionate about being a network or domain
administrator, then managing users and groups will give
you a lot of satisfaction . . . it can be a very powerful position
in a company. On the other hand, unless you understand the
fundamentals, manage the processes sensibly, and learn the
tools and resources, it can become an extremely frustrating
responsibility. Our administration mantra is: Use your common
sense and learn to do it right before you take up the task. This
chapter helps you to get the best out of the Windows 2000 user
and group management philosophy and tools.

Despite Microsoft's Zero Administration Windows (ZAW)
initiative, user and group management has become a lot more
complex in Windows 2000. The complexity has a lot to do with
the improved User and Group objects and the new support in
Active Directory, such as Group Policy. Combined with the
burden of integrating Windows NT 4.0 and earlier networks,
the administrative task will not be easy in the short-term.

This might improve over the years because many companies
and, especially, administrators are certain to develop tools
for the Active Directory that automate the repetitive stuff
and enhance the experience of working with Active Directory
(and we touch on that in here). In that the directory is open
and supports a widely available API (ADSI) and access protocol (LDAP), we have to give credit where credit is due. For
example, you can extend the User and Group objects to suit
your enterprise requirements or custom applications. What
you will learn in this chapter will put you on the road to such
advanced administration.

In this chapter, we will study User and Group objects and
understand their function. We will entertain user management
practice and policy with respect to user, groups, and computers.
We will also discuss the process of integrating legacy Windows
NT accounts with Windows 2000 domains and how to sensibly
manage users and groups on Windows 2000 mixed and native
mode networks.

This chapter does not discuss management of the user workspace. Advanced items such as Group Policy, user profiles and logon scripts, workspace management, and so on, are discussed in Chapter 11.

The Windows 2000 Account: A User's Resource

No one can work in a company, use any computer, or attach to any network without access to a user account. A user account is like the key to your car. Without the key, you cannot drive anywhere.

What Is a User?

This question may seem patronizing at first, but in a Windows network domain (and also the local computer), the definition of user relates to autonomous processes, network objects (devices and computers), and humans. Human users exploit the networks or machines to get work done, meet deadlines, and get paid. But any process, machine, or technology that needs to exploit another object on the network or machine is treated as a user by the Windows operating systems. In a nutshell, the Windows 2000 security subsystem does not differentiate between a human and a device using its resources. All users are viewed as "security principals," which at first are trusted.

Note   When you install Windows 2000 (not upgrade) or create a new Active Directory domain, the operating system and its elements are completely exposed. The governing policy on a new domain is that everyone can access everything. This makes sense: Keep the doors open until the jewels have been delivered. As soon as you begin adding users to the system, and they begin adding resources that need protection, you should begin using the tools described in this chapter and in several others to lock down the elements and secure the network.

User objects are derived from a single user class in Active Directory, which in turn derives from several parents. Machine accounts are thus derived from the User object. To obtain access to the User object, you need to reference its distinguished name (DN) in program or script code. This is handled automatically by the various GUI objects, but if you plan to write scripts that access the object, you should be referencing the object's GUID.

What Are Contacts?

Contacts are new objects in Windows 2000 networks. They are derived from the same class hierarchy as the User object; however, the Contact object does not inherit security attributes from its parent. A contact is thus only used for communication purposes: for e-mail, faxing, phoning, and so on. Windows 2000 distribution lists are made up of contacts.

You can access active directory contacts from the likes of Outlook and Outlook Express and any other LDAP-compliant client software. The Contact object is almost identical to the object in the Windows Address Book (WAB). Later, we show you how to force Outlook and Outlook Express to default to Active Directory as its contact repository.

Local Users and "Local Users"

The term *local user* is often used to describe two types of users: users local to machines that log on locally to the workstation service, and users that are local to a network or domain. Using the term interchangeably can cause confusion among your technical staff . . . and you have enough confusing things to deal with.

We believe it makes sense to refer to local users as users who log on locally to a workstation or PC or a server. In other words, the local user can log on to the machine he or she is actually sitting at, where accounts have been created, or into a remote machine that has granted the user the "right" to log on locally, such as an application server that is accessed by a terminal session on a remote client.

When referring to generic users on the domain or users collectively, it makes more sense to refer to these users as *domain users* or *domain members.* However, as we will discuss later, a user can also be a member of a local domain, and such an account is often referred to as a local user. On legacy NT domains, this was further confused by the ability to create a "local account," which was meant for users from non-trusted domains. This is no longer the case with Windows 2000 domains. Whether you agree or not, we suggest you decide what the term *local user* means to your environment and then stick to that definition.

Note   Domain controllers (DCs) are not supposed to provide local logon services other than to administrators, and it is documented that there is no way to log on locally (also known as interactive logon) to a DC from another machine. However, we have found that not to be true because Group Policy can be changed to allow local logon. See Chapter 25 for information on how to log on locally to a domain controller.

What Is a Group?

Groups are collections of users, contacts, computers, and other groups (a process known as *nesting*). Groups are supported in Active Directory (much to the horror of directory purists) and in the local computer's security subsystem. How Windows 2000 works with groups is discussed later in this chapter. Figure 10-1 illustrates the group container philosophy.

You would be right to wonder why Microsoft gives us both groups and organizational units (OUs) to manage. Groups, however, are a throwback to the Windows NT era. Remember, Windows 2000 is built on NT, and groups were thus inherited from the earlier technology and enhanced for Windows 2000. Although groups may appear to be a redundant object next to OUs, they are a fact of Windows 2000 and are here to stay. They are also extremely powerful management objects.

Figure 10-1: Groups are collections or concentrations of users, computers, and other groups.

> **Cross-Reference**
>
> The difference between groups and OUs is explained in Chapters 2 and 7, and later in this chapter.

Specifically, we create and use groups to contain the access rights of User objects and other groups within a security boundary. We also use groups to contain User objects that share the same access rights to network objects, such as shares, folders, files, printers, and so on. Groups thus provide a security filter against which users and other groups are given access to resources. This critical role of the groups is illustrated in Figure 10-2.

> **Note**
>
> It is not good practice to stick user accounts into every nook and cranny of a Windows domain. If you start that practice, you will soon have a domain that resembles a bowl of rice noodles at your local dim sum. It is a wonder that Microsoft engineers still allow us to stick a user account anywhere, because that practice is very rare on a well-run network. We believe the only place you should put a user is into a group . . . even if the group never sees more than one member. Make this your number one user management rule: "Users live in groups. Period."

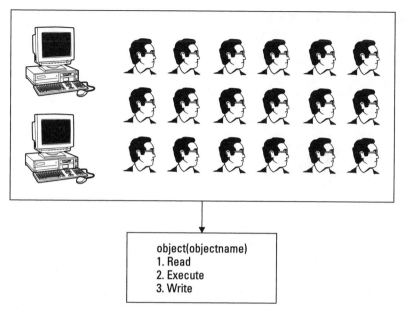

Figure 10-2: Groups provide a security "filter" against which users and other groups are given access to resources.

We can also use groups to create distribution lists (a new type of group). For example, we can create a group, and every user in the group will receive any e-mail sent to it. This is a boon for e-mail administrators.

Groups versus organizational units

Many now feel that the Group object has been rendered redundant by the OU. That might be the case if OUs were recognized by the security subsystem and the access control mechanisms; that is, if they were security principals. But the Group object is a sophisticated management container that is able to bestow all manner of control over the user accounts and other groups it contains.

What we believe is good about the group is that it can be used to contain a membership across organizational and multiple domain boundaries. An organizational unit, on the other hand, belongs to a domain. Complex mergers and acquisitions, and companies that are so dispersed that their only "geographical" boundary is between the earth and the moon, are excellent candidates that could use groups to contain memberships from the organizational units of their acquisitions or member companies and departments. Figure 10-3 illustrates how one group called *Accounting* can contain the department heads and key people from several Accounting departments throughout the enterprise.

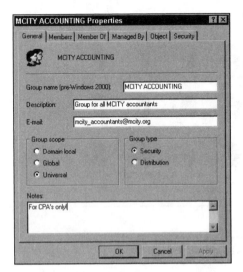

Figure 10-3: The Accounting group is a universal container that allows its members to access resources in the departments of several corporate domains in a forest.

Microsoft could have given the same power to the OU, but it did not, at least in the first version of Windows 2000. Instead, it is hoping we will see how groups and OUs fit into the overall management philosophy. Our guess is that it would have caused a serious delay in the release of Windows 2000 had Microsoft made OU security principals behave like groups. We look at the differences a little later; suffice it to say now that the Group object is certainly not redundant; it is a very powerful management tool.

What is a network from the viewpoint of users and groups?

There are several definitions of a network. From the perspective of users and containers of users, a network is a collection of resources (collection of network objects as opposed to device) that can be accessed for services. Users exploit network objects to assist them with their work. Network resources include messaging, printers, telecommunications, information retrieval, collaboration services, and more.

Administrators new to Windows 2000 should get familiar with the meaning of network object, for it is used to reference or "obtain a handle" on any network component, both hard and soft.

Exploring the Users and Computers Management Tools

Windows 2000 ships with tools to manage local logon accounts and Active Directory accounts. These tools are *Users and Passwords, Local Users and Groups* on standalone machines (including workstations running Windows 2000 Professional) and member servers, and *Active Directory Users and Computers* on domain controllers.

The *Active Directory Users and Computers* MMC snap-in is the primary tool used to create and manage users in network domains. It is launched from the Administrative Tools menu. Figure 10-4 illustrates the Users and Computers snap-in. This snap-in will almost certainly become more sophisticated as the use of Active Directory increases.

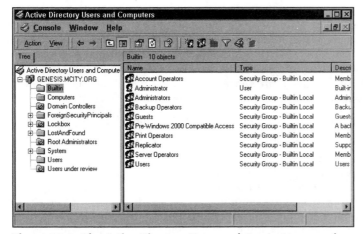

Figure 10-4: The Active Directory Users and Computers snap-in

Run the snap-in. First, let's put the snap-in into advanced mode so that we can see all the menu options in the Users and Computers MMC library. Select any node in the tree and right-click. Select View ➪ Advanced Features from the pop-up list that appears. A check mark will appear, meaning the entire snap-in is in advanced mode and you can access all menu options.

You will notice that you can also check the item above Advanced Features, the "Users, Groups, and Computers as Containers" menu item. But this may give you too much information to deal with in the learning phase. Select this feature when you know your way around this snap-in.

In the left pane, the snap-in loads the tree that represents the domain you are managing. Note that you can select a number of built-in folders:

✦ The **Built-in** folder contains the built-in or default groups created when you install the Active Directory and promote the server to a domain controller.

✦ The **Computer** folder contains any computers that are added to the domain you are managing. It will be empty if you have not added any computers to the domain at this stage.

✦ The **Domain Controllers** folder will always contain at least one computer . . . the domain controller you are currently working on.

✦ The **ForeignSecurityPrincipals** folder is the default container for security identifiers (SIDs) associated with objects from other trusted domains.

✦ The **Users** folder contains built-in user and group accounts. When you upgrade Windows NT to Windows 2000, all the user accounts from the old NT domain are placed into this folder. This folder is not an OU, and no OU group policy can be linked to it. For all intents and purposes, this folder should be blank or at least should not contain any accounts when you first do a clean install of Windows 2000 and promote it to Active Directory. Instead, the built-in accounts should have been placed in the built-in folder, period. We guess it is one of those things that Microsoft did without very much forethought. But they did give us the ability to move items from folder to folder, and it may make more sense for you to move all the built-in objects to the built-in folder . . . especially since you cannot delete them.

✦ The **LostAndFound** folder contains objects that have been orphaned.

✦ The **System** folder contains built-in system settings.

Now, before we proceed, know that there are two levels to understanding how user accounts work. You can cover the basics of user accounts by poking around in the Active Directory User and Computers snap-in MMC panels, or you can make an effort to learn about the most important attributes (compulsory and optional) of user accounts at a lower level. If you are a serious network and Windows administrator, then we suggest the latter. Why?

Firstly, as an administrator, knowing the stuff of which user accounts are made will take your management knowledge and skills to a higher level. You will be able to contribute much more to the overall management of your enterprise network if you know how to perform advanced searches for users, scientifically manage passwords, better protect resources, troubleshoot, and so forth. If you think administrators do not need to know how to program, then think again; it could make a $20K difference, positively, on your salary package.

Secondly, senior administrators and corporate developers may need to circumvent the basic MMC panels and code directly to the Active Directory Service Interfaces (ADSI). On Windows NT 4.0, senior administrators often created scripts that would block manipulate the accounts in the SAM, or security accounts database. User Manager for Domains was often too dumb to be of use in major domain operations. Top Windows 2000 administrators will need to know how to code to the Active Directory, and write scripts (which will require basic programming knowledge) that make life easier and lessen the administrative burden. Knowing everything about User objects will make your services that much more in demand. We suggest you first read Chapters 2 and 7 before you tackle the following text.

Windows 2000 User Accounts

A Windows 2000 user account can be a *domain account* or a *local account*. When you first install any version of Windows 2000 or promote a server to a domain controller, a number of domain and local accounts are automatically created. When you install Active Directory on a server, that is, when you promote it to a domain controller, the local accounts are disabled.

Domain accounts

Domain accounts or network accounts are User account objects that are stored in Active Directory and that are exposed to the distributed Windows networking and security environment. Domain accounts are enterprise-wide. Humans, machines, and processes use domain accounts to log on to a network and gain access to its resources. Each logon attempt goes through a "security clearance" whereby the system compares the password provided by the user against the password stored in the password attribute field in the Active Directory. (Refer to Chapters 2 and 7 for conceptual discussions on attributes.) If the password matches the record, then the user is cleared to proceed and use network resources, perform activities on computers, and communicate.

Note

Remember, Active Directory is a "multi-master" directory service. This means that changes to users and groups are replicated to other member DCs (but not to a local account database). You can manage users on any DC on the network and not worry about locating a primary DC, as was the case with Windows NT 4.0 and earlier. User objects also contain certain attributes that are not replicated to other DCs. These attributes can be considered of interest only to the local domain controller. For example, the attribute LastLogon is of interest only to the local network's domain controller; it is of no importance to the other domain controllers in the domain or the forest.

You can also create a user account in any part of the AD . . . as long as you have rights to create or manage that User object. While container objects such as OUs and groups serve to assist in the management of collections of users, there is no mechanism other than having admin rights to prevent a user account from being created anywhere in a forest.

Local accounts

Local accounts (users) are identical to network accounts in every way, but they are not stored in Active Directory. Local accounts are machine-specific objects. In other words, a local user account can only be validated against a local security database—the SAM or Security Account Manager. Secondly, local accounts only provide access to resources within the "boundaries" of the machine "domain" and no further. An analogy might be that the key to your house only lets you enter your house. All other houses in your neighborhood are off limits.

If you are new to Windows networking, you may be wondering why machines on a Windows 2000 network would have local accounts. As you know, you can create a network of machines and not manage it with Active Directory at all, which would certainly send your cost of ownership soaring. But there are also good reasons why these accounts are better off on the local machine rather than sitting in Active Directory; you will discover these reasons in this chapter. Active Directory users can "connect" to local machines from remote services (such as to the local FTP account), which is achieved by virtue of having the "right" to log on locally at the target machine. Local user accounts can also exist on machines that are part of Active Directory domains, and which are not the domain controllers. You can also make a domain controller an application server for a small business, and allow a number or users to log on locally to the DC by way of terminal sessions. This is discussed in detail in Chapter 25.

Local user accounts are restricted to the Access Control List of the local computer. The local domain itself does not replicate this information off the local machine because it only matters to the local account system, which is not distributed.

 Note   The tools to manage the local, machine native domains can be accessed through the Users and Passwords and Administrative Tools applications in Control Panel.

Predefined accounts

When you install Windows 2000, either as a standalone or member server, or as a domain controller supporting Active Directory, the operating system establishes default accounts. On a standalone machine (server or workstation), the default accounts are local to the machine native domain and established in the SAM. On a domain controller — in Active Directory — the default accounts are network accounts. Built-in accounts cannot be deleted, but they can be renamed or moved from one container to another.

The default accounts include administration accounts that enable you to log on and manage the network or the local machine. Windows 2000 also installs built-in machine or Guest accounts and anonymous Internet user accounts. You will notice that these so-called accounts are disabled by default and must be implicitly enabled.

It is a good idea as soon as feasible to rename the Administrator account to hide its purpose and thus its access and security level (hiding was not possible on Windows NT). If you have security fears, you can audit the activity of the Administrator to determine who or what is using the account and when.

When you demote a domain controller (DC) to a standalone server, and especially if it is the last DC on the network, the OS prompts you for the password you will use for the local Administrator account. In the process of stripping away AD and its administrator accounts, the OS ensures that you will be able to log on locally and gain access to the machine after the conversion. When AD departs from the server, it hands control of the machine back to the machine-specific domain and Security Account Manager (SAM).

Administrator account

The Administrator account is the first user account created when you install Windows 2000, regardless of which of the four versions of Windows 2000 you are installing. The Administrator account is created in both the local SAM and in Active Directory.

The Administrator is the CEO on Windows 2000 and all earlier versions. By logging on as the Administrator, you get total access to the entire system and network. Without the power of this built-in user, it would be impossible to set up the first objects.

The Administrator account is dangerous, however. Over time, the password to this account gets handed around, and your network goes to hell. We have even seen situations where the Administrator's account password finds its way around the world in large corporations, even allowing users in foreign domains to mess things up without the key MIS people at HQ finding out. In one situation, it ended up in the hands of a subcontractor who managed to bring an office to a standstill for a week.

So how do you protect this account from abuse? For starters, you cannot delete or disable the account because then it would be too easy to get locked out of the system or fall victim to a denial-of-service (DoS) attack.

But you can rename this account, which presents an opportunity to conceal the Administrator's true identity and lock down access to it. It then makes common sense, before new (flesh and blood) administrators are added to the domain, to record the Administrator password in a document and then lock it away in a secure place.

1. Rename the Administrator account. Remember to provide a UPN and rename the down-level or NETBIOS name as well, because renaming merely changes the "hidden" attribute and label.

2. Create a new user as a decoy Administrator and endow it with administrator power by assigning the account to the Administrators group. Or leave the account with no powers of administration.

3. Appoint the Administrator (which can be under the new name) account as the manager of this account. This is done on the Organization tab, in the Manager field.

4. Cease using the real Administrator and lock away the password.

You would now be correct in saying, "But that still does not stop someone from getting hold of one of the other administrator accounts and abusing them." But now you have accounts than can be monitored, audited, disabled, and deleted if they become a security risk. And it might pay in certain circumstances to delete and recreate administrators at certain intervals.

Tip   To rename the Administrator account, you need to first give an Administrator account the "right to rename the Administrator account." This right is granted by Group Policy, which is discussed in the next chapter. Once you have renamed the real Administrator, you can create a decoy Administrator account.

It is also a wise move to move the Administrator and administrator type accounts out of the Users folder. There are several reasons for this advice:

✦ Anyone looking for the Administrator will go here first, and denying access to this folder may be impractical.

✦ The security policy governing the Users folder is inherited from the root domain. This means that if for any reason the default or root domain policy changes, it may affect the account without you being aware of the event.

✦ The Administrator accounts are better grouped in the main IS OU where access is controlled by specific OU policy, focused management, and delegated responsibility.

Here's how to move the Administrator account:

1. Open Active Directory Users and Computers. Double-click the Users folder.

2. Select the Administrator account in the right-hand pane and right-click your mouse. Now select the move option. The list of folders and OUs appears.

3. Drill down to a different OU of your choice. Select that OU and click OK. The Administrator account is now moved to the new OU.

 Cross-Reference Another means of protecting the network and the Administrator account, and a sophisticated means of management and troubleshooting, is to use the *RunAs* service. Also known as the secondary login, it allows a user who is logged on with their regular user account to perform functions with the privileges of another account, typically an administrator's. RunAs is demonstrated later in this chapter in the configuration of user accounts (see also Chapter 25).

Guest account

The Guest account is the second of the default accounts that are pre-built when you install Windows 2000 the first time, and when you create a domain controller and install Active Directory. The account is useful for guests and visitors who either do not have accounts on any domain in the forest, or whose accounts may be disabled.

The Guest account does not require a password, and you can grant it certain access and rights to resources on the computer (see Rights and Permissions discussed later in this chapter). We believe the Guest account on any domain should be relocated to an OU whose security and account policy is appropriate to manage security risks. You can leave the Guest account in the Users folder (which is a domain folder and not an OU), but the security policy governing that account in the Users folder is inherited from the root domain. This means that if for any reason the default or root domain policy changes, it will affect the Guest account without you being conscious of the event. The Guest account is also automatically placed into the Guest group, which you may wish to also place in the Visitors OU. You can move the Guest account with Active Directory Users and Computers, just as in the previous example. In our Millennium City network, we've moved the Guest account to the City Hall-Visitors OU.

In the User folder, the Guest account is granted the right to log on locally to a local computer or member server. In the City Hall-Visitors OU, you can grant specific access to the domain resources, such as e-mail, access to printers and devices, and so on. You can also create several Visitor accounts for accounting and auditing purposes and to keep track of the objects each visitor accesses.

Using logon scripts and profiles, you can track activity between each logon and logoff period and use that to generate reports. From these reports, you can run invoices, statements, bills, and so on. If you run a service bureau, then this is the direction you should be considering.

Some organizations do not believe in Guest or Visitor accounts and keep these disabled from the get-go. If you disable the Guest account, you are denying anyone who does not have an account from logging on. In highly secure environments, this policy may be valid. And this was, and still is, the case in many Windows NT domains that do not provide for the additional protection of the OU security policy. But these accounts can be handy even in sensitive environments. Consider the following before taking the easy way out and disabling the account:

✦ With a Guest account, a new user awaiting a user account can get some work done on a computer. They can, for example, begin reading company policy or the employee handbook, and they can fill in employee forms, and so on.

✦ With a Guest account, a user who has been locked out for whatever reason can at least log on to the domain and gain access to the company intranet and local resources. Let's say you have an intranet Web site that allows the user to access the help-desk and open a ticket; then a user who cannot log onto the domain can still generate a ticket for an account lockout problem. Lockouts can and will happen often.

✦ An employee suspected of a misdeed can be asked to log on to a Guest account while the reason for an account lockout is being investigated. This may help diffuse a situation that has the potential of becoming tense. The user's account can also be transferred out of his or her usual OU to the Visitors OU or a holding OU. This gives the user the impression that he or she is still able to log on to the domain, but certain access rights have been removed.

The Internet user account

Windows 2000 also provides default or built-in accounts for anonymous access to IIS and for generic access to Terminal Services. See Chapters 23 and 25.

Account Policy

Before you go creating users, you must first take the time to fully understand how account policy on Windows 2000 affects account creation and management on an account-by-account basis.

The Windows Group Policy technology (which also includes account and security policy) governs how all accounts can be configured on both standalone servers and in the Active Directory. If you create users from the get-go, the accounts will be set up with the default account policy attributes. They will remain this way until Active Directory site, domain, or OU policies override this (when a domain controller and Active Directory is installed and sites, domains, and OUs are created).

On Windows NT 4.0 and earlier, the account policy setup on a workstation or member server survived domain policy, but this is not so any more. You have to specifically force the local policy to take precedence over the domain policy. We explain this in more detail in Chapter 11.

What you should be aware of here, especially if you have been given certain responsibility to create an account and set up a computer, is the order of precedence for security and account policies. The order of precedence, from the highest to the lowest, is as follows:

1. Site Policy

2. Domain Policy

3. OU Policy

4. Local Policy

The local policy governs the local accounts you set up on the computer itself, in its native or machine-specific domain. But the local policy is overridden by the policies of higher precedence, unless you take the steps to avert that behavior.

Security Principals and the Logon Authentication Process

The onus of "good behavior" rests on the shoulders of User and Group objects in Windows 2000. As mentioned earlier, these objects have the total trust of the OS when first installed. They are often referred to as *security principals* and *trustees*. Every other object that is not a security principal or that does not exist in AD within a security context is rejected by the security subsystem, and thus cannot present for rights and access. The Contact object is a good example of an object that is not a security principal. You may create other non-security objects and register them in the Active Directory.

Several security principals are defined to the security subsystem by default. These include groups such as Domain Users, Domain Admins, and so on.

When a user attempts to log on to Windows 2000, by way of the AD or the local security authority (LSA), the security system checks to see if the user exists and if the password provided matches the password stored in the relevant database. If the user is authenticated, Windows 2000 creates an *access token* for the user (see Chapters 1 and 3).

If the domain controller does not receive the correct password or the user account is unknown, the user is gracefully returned to the logon dialog box. But once a user is authenticated, Windows then proceeds to activate whatever rights and permissions the user has on the network.

The process that Windows 2000 uses to "follow" the user through the domain is known as *access token assignment*. In other words, the access token is assigned to the user for the duration of the logon and acts as a security tag a user wears when "roaming" from computer to computer and from resource to resource. User account information is replicated to all domain controllers in the enterprise, even across slow WAN links.

 Cross-Reference To more fully understand the authentication process at the lower levels of Windows 2000 and the security subsystem, refer to Chapters 1 and 3.

Security Identifiers

The *security identifier* (SID) is a unique value of variable length that is used to identify an account (known as a *trustee* to the kernel) to the security subsystem. Windows refers to the SID rather than the user or group name when referencing these objects for security purposes. The SID is not the same thing as the object identifier or OID. OIDs are explained in Chapter 7. SIDs guarantee that the account and all its associated rights and permissions are unique. If you delete an account and then recreate it under the same name, you will find that all rights and permissions of the deceased account are gone. This is because the old SID was deleted with the original account.

When you create an account, the system also creates the SID and stores it in the security structures of AD or the SAM. The first part of the SID identifies the domain in which the SID was created. The second part is called the *relative ID* (RID), and that refers to the actual object created (which is thus relative to the domain).

When a user logs onto the computer or domain, the SID is retrieved from the database and placed in the user's access token. From the moment of logon, the SID is used in the access token to identify the user in all security-related actions and interactions.

Both Windows NT and Windows 2000 also use the SID for the following purposes:

✦ To identify the object's owner

✦ To identify the object owner's group

✦ To identify the account user in access related activity (see Access Control Entries in Chapter 3)

Special well-known SIDs are also created by the system during installation to identify the built-in users and groups. When a user logs on to the system as Guest, the access token for that user will include the well-known SID for the Guest group, which will restrict the user from doing damage or accessing objects they are not entitled to.

SAM and LSA Authentication

The Windows 2000 SAM is inherited from NT 4.0 SAM and works the same. However, it no longer plays a part in network domain management. Standalone and member servers use the Windows 2000 SAM to authenticate or validate users that have local accounts, including autonomous processes. The SAM is still buried in the registry and plays an important role in Windows 2000, and it is an integral part of the Local Security Authority (LSA). LSA authentication exists for several reasons:

✦ To process local logon requests.

✦ To allow ISVs and customers with special requirements to use the LSA to gain local authentication services. An access control application might use the LSA to validate holders of magnetic access control cards and the like.

✦ To provide special local access to devices. In order for a device to be installed and gain access to system resources, it might have to be authenticated by the LSA. Such an example is a tape-backup device driver, which might need to gain access to a local database management system or to machine-protected processes that require it to be logged on locally.

✦ To provide heterogeneous local authentication. Not everyone will be able to take advantage of the Active Directory authentication and logon process, and not everyone will want to. The LSA thus provides these "users" (processes) with a local logon facility they were accustomed to, or built for, on Windows NT 4.0 and earlier.

As discussed earlier in Chapter 4, when you set up a standalone server, Windows creates default or *built-in* accounts. These are actually created in a local Windows 4.0-type domain stored in the local SAM. The two local domains created are Account and Builtin.

When you first install Windows 2000, these local domain systems are named after the NETBIOS-type name of the machine. If you change the machine's name, the domain name will be changed to the new machine name the next time you restart the server. In other words, if you set up a standalone server named LONELY1, a local domain named LONELY1 will be created in the local SAM. The OS will then create the built-in accounts for this domain. Later, you'll be able to create any local user in the local legacy domain. Services will also use the local domain for system accounts.

Note   The Active Directory includes a SAM service provider that allows Windows 2000 domain controllers to interoperate with NT 4.0 domain controllers. Such service providers also exist for other directory services, such as Novell NDS.

User Accounts in Action

A user account is like a bank account. Without a bank account, there is no way you can access the services of a bank, store money, pay bills, take out loans, and manage your financial affairs. When a user comes to work and cannot log on, the scene that ensues is like a bank account that has been closed unexpectedly.

Getting Familiar with RunAs

Before you proceed with account creation and management, you should take some time to understand the *RunAs* application and service. It will be invaluable to you in your administration endeavors, especially for troubleshooting account problems.

 Note   RunAs is also known as *secondary* or *alternate logon.*

RunAs allows you to execute applications, access resources, or load an environment or profile, and so on, using the credentials of another user account, without having to log off from the account you initially logged onto your computer with. RunAs is a non-graphical executable that resides in the %System%\System32 folder of your server or workstation. It is also a service that can be accessed from various locations in the operating system. You can link to it from the desktop, or create scripts and applications that make use of its services. You can also create a shortcut to an application and allow it to be executed using the credentials of any another user account (provided you have the password to the other account).

In this chapter, we will not explain all the available parameters and switches that can be used with RunAs from the command line because that has been provided in Appendix A, and you can execute RunAs from the command line with the /? switch and obtain a list of RunAs options and their usage.

RunAs essentially allows you to operate an environment or application in the security context of another user account, while remaining in your current security context or in your current logged-on state. The simplest, but very useful, feature of RunAs lets you test a logon name and account password without having to log off from your workstation. Perhaps the best way to describe RunAs usage is to provide a simple example.

Create a shortcut to the Command Console on the desktop and allow it to be used to test a User ID and password as follows:

1. Create a shortcut to the command prompt on your desktop. This is explained at the beginning of Appendix A.

2. Right-click the shortcut and select Properties. On the Shortcut tab, check the "Run as different user" option.

3. Click OK.

You will now notice that when you right-click the shortcut the Run as. . . line has been added into the Context menu in bold type. But you can just double-click the shortcut icon and the Run As Other User dialog box will appear. Now you can enter your user's account, domain, and password.

If you investigate RunAs further, you will discover that you can test alternate logons and troubleshoot problems such as access to shares, printers, and so on. You can log on and switch to the environment provided by the alternate account, and you can allow users to run an application in the context of another account.

Naming User Accounts

You can make your life as a user administrator more enjoyable if you follow the recommended convention for naming user accounts. You can and should plan your user namespace carefully, publish the rules and policy surrounding the chosen convention, and stick to it. There is nothing worse than inheriting a directory of accounts where no naming convention exists.

In order to set up your naming convention checklist, consider the following:

1. User account names must be unique in the domain the accounts are created. For example, you cannot have two names set up as `mcity\john samuels` or `johns@mcity.org`. One must become `johns1@mcity.org`. You can, however, create an account with the same UPN prefix in another domain. For example: `johns@mcity.mcpd.org` or `mcpd\johns`.

2. The user account prefix can contain a maximum of 20 characters in any case. The logon process is not sensitive to the case. The field, however, preserves the case, allowing you to assist in naming convention, such as `JohnS` as opposed to `johns`.

3. The following characters are not permissible in the account name:
   `" < > ? * / \ | ; : = , + [ ]`

4. You can use letters and dashes or underscores in the name to assist with convention, but remember, account names may be used as e-mail addresses. Follow the suggestions in UPN naming convention described later.

Passwords

Accounts do not always have to have passwords. As discussed earlier, this is controlled by Group Policy. Many administrators use the method of combining initials and numbers for passwords, and we keep them consistent throughout the enterprise.

In order to set up your password convention checklist, consider the following:

1. The passwords can be up to 128 characters in length. That does not mean Microsoft expects you to saddle your users with a password that takes all day to input. But smart cards and non-interactive logon devices can use a field of that length.

2. Do not create passwords that are less than five characters; a minimum of eight is recommended.

3. The following characters are not permissible in the password:
   " < > ? * / \ | ; : = , + [ ]

Password management is a nightmare for everyone. Most administrators we know keep lists of passwords in various database files and helpdesks because users often find themselves locked out of domains and resources for "no apparent reason." To troubleshoot and assist the user, we often need to log on to his or her account and "experience" what might be going wrong. Many administrators troubleshoot this way; it helps to be in the user's context when troubleshooting. The new RunAs service we describe in this chapter is a useful tool for managing user accounts and troubleshooting passwords.

The password issuance and management-style questions are similar from platform to platform, especially from NetWare to Windows NT and Windows 2000. In giving users passwords, you have three choices that can be adapted and become policy:

✦ Assign the passwords.

✦ Let the user choose the password.

✦ Assign passwords to certain users; allow others to set their own.

All three choices have their pros and cons, and every company will have a reason for going with one option or the other.

If you go with the first option, you will either have to adopt a password-naming scheme that lends itself to easy recollection by administrators (as secure as an open field) or enter the user's passwords in a secure database.

The former is not really secure because it would not take much to figure out the scheme the administrators are using. A popular password-forming approach is to join the users' initials and parts of their social security numbers, driver's licenses, or some other form of number society issues us. For example: *jrs0934*. This scheme has been in place at several companies we worked. In that several thousand accounts were set up under the scheme, it has been a nightmare to change it.

The second approach, letting users select their own passwords, is more secure but fraught with danger. Firstly, users who have lots of sensitive stuff on their machines and in their folders often assign weak passwords that can easily be cracked. We have found users choosing *12345678* and giving us the excuse they were going to change it later . . . three months later.

Secondly, having users choose their own passwords can be nightmarish on corporate networks. When troubleshooting problems, administrators often have to ask for the passwords over the telephone (for all to hear) and in e-mail. And then there are the occasions when we have to reset the password anyway because the owner is either not present or Windows 2000 rejects the password. We have not seen "correct password rejection" on Windows 2000 yet, but we have seen it happen many times on Windows NT, even seconds after resetting it in the NT User Manager. It is just one of those quirky things we learned to live with.

We believe the best policy is to go with the third choice: Assign a password for most corporate users and allow selected users (who demand the security and who can justify it) to set their own passwords. The latter users fall into groups that have access to company financial information, bank account numbers, credit card numbers, personnel records, and so on. Paranoid executives fall into the latter group as well.

Generate secure passwords (as opposed to obvious acronyms). Record the password in a secure place: either a database management system that is hard to crack, like an encrypted Microsoft Access database file, or in an SQL server table. The one weakness of this option is giving new users their passwords. Often, the password ends up going through several hands before ending up at the user. You could create a temporary password assignment scheme.

You might also try your hand at adding a field to the Active Directory User object that displays the password in plain text (the schema is there to be extended, see Chapter 6). You can secure the objects in the AD so that only certain administrators have access to the field. You would also have to create a GUI to read the field because the Account tab on the User Properties dialog box is off limits to such wild ideas.

Protecting passwords is more important under Windows 2000 than under Windows NT, or any other OS for that matter. The reason is the Single Sign-on Initiative (SSO) and the Kerberos ticket-granting service discussed in Chapter 3. On older OSs, you need new user IDs and passwords for just about any service, such as voice mail, fax mail, SQL Server, Internet access, and so on. As more applications support the SSO, one password will eventually suffice for all. But this is a double-edged sword. If the password or access falls into mischievous hands, the culprit will have access to everything authenticated in the SSO process.

Logon

We have discussed the concept of local logon in various places, but this is a right and not an automatic privilege. In order for a user to connect to the machine standing next to him or her or to a remote machine across the network, he or she would need authority in two places:

1. The domain the user is a member of must allow the user to request logon permission from a machine. The default is to allow the user to request logon from any machine, which means the target machine's SAM gets to say yes or no and not the domain.

2. The target machine must give the account the right to log on locally.

Unless the target machine has special software on it that requires local logon and authentication, it makes more sense to provide access to resources on remote machines via domain groups.

Granting Remote Access

Remote access privileges are the most sought after rights in any organization. By being given access to RAS, users may be allowed to telecommute, work from home, or access the network and servers from the road. Road warriors also give you the most headaches because remote policy is by its very nature governed by more stringent security requirements.

When setting up groups, it may pay to also create remote user groups in specific OUs. You will certainly run into problems putting every remote user into an enterprise-wide remote user group. Users who are restricted at certain levels when they work on the premises will find life more open and accessible when connecting from home. And users who have a wide berth in the office will find life claustrophobic on the outside.

Remote Access Service is discussed in detail in Chapter 15.

Creating a User Account

In this example, we're creating user accounts for the Driver Compensation Program (DCP) in Millennium City. They exist in the DCP OU, which resides in the CITYHALL domain.

Select the domain, right-click the DCP OU created earlier, and select New ⇨ User. The Create New Object dialog box loads, as shown in Figure 10-5. The most important information you will need here is the old SAM account name of the user that is connecting or a new NetBIOS name. This is the name the user used or still uses to log on to the legacy NT domain. It is not the name of the machine that is connecting. Remember that this is a NetBIOS name; it must be less than 20 characters, and you need to watch for the illegal characters discussed earlier.

Note   You can create a new user account anywhere in the domain and later move it as needed.

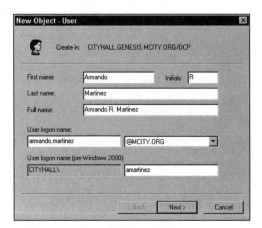

Figure 10-5: Create New Object - User dialog box

The User Principal Name

In the beginning, on legacy NT, we had little flexibility with logon names. We would typically use contractions of first and last names, such as *jshapiro* or *jeffreys,* or names typically assigned to people serving 25 years to life, such as *psjrs08676.*

Now, everything is different. The user's logon name and e-mail addresses are the same. There are good reasons to do this. First, this change supports the SSO initiative, better known as Single Sign-On. As long as the resources the user needs access to support TCP/IP, RFC 822 naming, and Kerberos authentication, the user ID or the resulting authentication certificates can be relayed to these technologies. Second, the UPN allows you to use an e-mail address to log on to the domain from anywhere on the Internet. As long as the domain controller is exposed to the Internet, or the packets find the DC through a firewall, it is possible to log on and access resources.

As discussed earlier, if you can resolve CITYHALL.GENESIS.MCITY.ORG on the Internet, you'll be able to log in. The prefix part of the UPN provides the so-called user ID, while the suffix identifies the domain.

So, given that life would be easier if your users' logon IDs and e-mail addresses were the same, you have some serious restructuring to do. Perhaps the best place to start is at your e-mail server. Here, all the accounts are set up with UPNs already. And if you have been running an Exchange server, then all the better. Simply dump all the names into a comma separated file (.csv) and use these as the basis for your UPNs.

Using first and last names as a UPN is a good idea. RFC 822 requires that you separate the elements of the UPN with acceptable characters. Obviously, the @ sign is not acceptable, nor is the & (ampersand). Simple dot notation works the best: `user.name@adomain.com` or `jeffrey.shapiro@mcity.org`.

Figure 10-5 shows you the two logon types that can be used, the UPN (armando. martinez) and the down-level NetBIOS name (amartinez). In the first one, the user enters the prefix part of the UPN as the User ID and the suffix as the domain name. This may be less comfortable for people accustomed to logging into Windows NT domains or NetWare.

If you are not yet ready to move users to Windows 2000 but plan to in the near future, now is the time to start preparing for UPNs. For example, if your e-mail server accounts do not make attractive UPNs (such as `zp-badboy5.shapiroj@ wierdestofcorps.com`), now is the time to change them. You seldom if ever need to type your e-mail address every time you send a message, but you do need to type at least the prefix every time you log in to Windows 2000. Try keeping the UPNs as short as possible without turning everyone's name into an acronym. For example `jshapiro` works better than `jeffrey.shapiro`, which is better than `js`. Anyone who ends up with a UPN of more than, say, eight letters may never want to log in again.

Before you add the name, you will need to check that the UPN you entered when you created the account conforms to the standards you have set for your network. This double-checking exercise is worthwhile here because there will be many times when the UPN has to be entered after the account has been created. If you copy an account, the UPN field will have to be updated. Remember, the UPN conforms to the Internet standard e-mail address governed by RFC 822, such as `jeffrey. shapiro@mcity.org` or `jeffreys@mcity.org`.

Click Next to fill in the password in the next dialog box, shown in Figure 10-6. Click Finish when you're done. That's all there is to creating a user. Next, you need to set the properties for the user.

Figure 10-6: Adding the password to the New Object - User dialog box

Setting properties

After the account has been created, you need to set the Properties to define the user's rights and privileges, access to resources, contact information, and so on. To access the property sheets of the user account object, simply double-click the account in Active Directory, or right-click it and select the Properties option in the Context menu. In this example, you double-click Armando R. Martinez, and Armando's Properties dialog box loads, as illustrated in Figure 10-7.

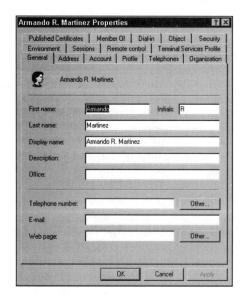

Figure 10-7: The User Properties dialog box

The User Properties dialog box has a lot of tabs that you can use to configure the User object and populate it with information. Many of the tabs are self-explanatory, so the following sections do not describe them all, just the ones that you need to set when creating a new user account.

Account tab properties

The options on the Account tab are security options, and they need to be managed carefully. If you've used the NT 4.0 User Manager application, you will recognize many of these.

✦ **Account expires:** Set this to Never to indicate that the account never expires. Set one of the other options, X and Y, if you want the account to exist for only a certain period of time. Locking a person out at some future date is valuable for applications services and for temps and subcontractors who will be classified a security risk at some future date.

✦ **Home folder:** This should be a directory on a file server somewhere. When the user logs in, his or her home directory will be immediately accessible. You can set this path to a folder on the user's local machine. In this case, we want to set the path to a share on the SQL Server 2000 machine so that the user has immediate access to data entry tools on that server.

✦ **First, Last and Initial:** When you enter the First, Last, and Initials, the display name is formed automatically. You can also change the display name to suit a company standard or policy. We want to leave the display name as is — that way, wherever users of CITYHALL are logged on, we will be able to spot them immediately in open file lists, connection lists, owners, and so on.

✦ **Description:** This information can describe the purpose of the account, or it can be information that better identifies it. The bigger the network, the more important it is to fill in this field. In this case, we'll insert "DCP Entry Team Leader" to describe the purpose of the account.

✦ **Office:** Enter the user's physical office address.

✦ **Telephone number:** Enter the user's telephone number and extension, if any.

✦ **E-mail:** Enter the user's e-mail address. It might be intuitive for this field to default to the UPN, but it doesn't. However, the field is also not e-mail format-sensitive, so if an SMTP format is out, you can enter a cc:Mail address, an X:400 address, or something else. It is important to keep the entries here consistent because access to this field is open via the ADSI and the field will no doubt be a key repository of information for many people-tracking tools, ERP apps, communications applications, and more. At the time of this writing, we don't know what e-mail applications will be using this field, but it is available to access.

✦ **Web page:** Enter the user's home page, if applicable. The idea of this field may be foggy at first, because why would you have all your users worry about home pages? However, these fields can be used for other applications, such as an ISP whose user accounts "rent" homepages. If you are an ISP, you can set up user accounts in the directory to manage access and accounting from the directory. The field is a string data type, so an IP address is feasible here too.

✦ **Address:** On the Address tab, enter the user's address.

✦ **Logon to:** This is the path of the workstation or server to which the users can log in. For an administrator, leave this at the default. If the employee were new or questionable, we would restrict him or her to the department's machine and lock the person out of the other MIS machines. For the sake of demonstration, Figure 10-8 shows the restriction in force. This restriction applies to all member machines, not just workstations, as it might suggest. By not setting any values in this dialog box, you give the user access to all machines on the network.

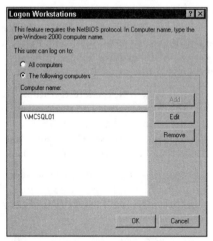

Figure 10-8: Logon restrictions

By forcing the users to log on to their own workstations, we are by omission barring them from logging on locally to any other machines. Of course, you can restrict the local logon at the target machine.

✦ **Account Options:** This is where you set password policies, which were discussed earlier in this chapter. To comply with the Millennium City password policy, we'll check the options "User cannot change password" and "Password never expires." Choose a secure password for the user.

More account options

The Account options section on the Account tab determines how users and computers are authenticated on the network. The following options are self-explanatory:

✦ User must change password at next logon.

✦ User cannot change password.

✦ Password never expires.

✦ Store password using reversible encryption. Use this option if the user is authenticating from an Apple computer.

✦ Account is disabled. Select this option to prevent the user from authenticating.

✦ Smart card is required for interactive logon. This option requires that the user have a card reader attached to his or her machine before he or she can log on.

✦ Account is trusted for delegation. This will allow the user of this account to delegate administrative function in the domain tree to others.

✦ Account is sensitive and cannot be delegated. This negates the option of allowing the user to delegate.

✦ Use DES encryption types for this account. DES supports multiple levels of encryption, including MPPE Standard (40-bit), MPPE Standard (56-bit), MPPE Strong (128-bit), IPSec DES (40-bit), IPSec 56-bit DES, and IPSec Triple DES (3DES). See Chapter 3 for further information on DES and security.

✦ Do not require Kerberos pre-authentication. Refer to Chapter 34 for more information on Kerberos.

Logon hours

The Logon Hours controls, shown in Figure 10-9, are available from the Account tab. By default, logon time is set to always, meaning that users can log in whenever they want, but you may wish to restrict this for several reasons. MCITY is set up to deny access to the domain controllers every Saturday night for about 12 hours. This is the time, once a week, when we power down the servers and perform maintenance. You may have a tighter security arrangement, for example, that only allows logon during working hours.

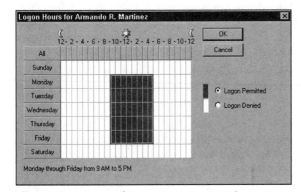

Figure 10-9: Logon hours

To set logon hours, do the following:

1. On the Properties dialog box, select the Account tab and click the Logon Hours button. The Logon Hours dialog box loads.

2. To allow a user to log on at certain hours, click the rectangle on the days and hours for which you wish to deny or allow a user logon time. The blue boxes denote logon times allowed, while the white boxes denote logon times disallowed. By default, the entire box is blue, indicating that logon is allowed all the time.

3. When you click OK and close the dialog box, the logon hours are saved.

Profile tab properties

The Profile tab contains a "User profile" group box and a "Home folder" group box. The User profile fields let you enter information that determines the resources a user connects to as soon as he or she authenticates to the domain. You can also enter logon script information, if applicable. The Home folder fields let you enter the path to the user's personal folder, which can be a folder used by a group as well. This folder can also be redirected according to Group Policy, as discussed in Chapter 11.

✦ **Profile path:** Enter the user's profile path here. In our case, it's \\mcdc01\profiles\amartinez.

✦ **Logon Script:** If you're using logon scripts for your users, enter the appropriate file name here. For our example, we'll enter \\mcdc01\profiles\eredmond\eredmond.scr.

✦ **Local Path:** Enter the path to the folder on a network server or workstation. It can be a local folder as well, and you can just leave this field blank to default to the default local folder on the user's local hard disk. (Get used to entering information here, especially if you are going to set up resources for terminal users. Remember that terminal users' local paths are the servers they sign onto by default, and if you redirect users to any of a number of servers, you need to define Home folders.)

✦ **Connect:** This information allows you to map a drive letter to the Home folder path.

Organization tab properties

This tab lets you provide information about the user's organization, his or her title, and superiors. Remember that this account information is being entered into a directory, which will be used by people researching information related to users.

✦ **Title:** This is the user's title: for example, VP or CEO.

✦ **Department:** This is where the user works.

✦ **Company:** This is the name of the company.

✦ **Manager:** This is the user account of the individual who manages this user or account.

✦ **Direct Reports:** This is a list of users who directly report to this user account (information supplied in the Manager field in other accounts will show up in this list).

Member Of tab properties

This tab lets you add the user to a group on this domain or in groups in other domains in the forest.

✦ **Member of:** Enter the names of groups the user is required to be a member of. This is done by clicking the Add button and selecting the groups from a domain that appears in the Select Groups list.

Dial-in tab properties

This tab lets you give the user dial-in (RAS) privileges, authentication options, and IP addressing options. See Chapter 5 for a detailed discussion on RAS.

Renaming User Accounts

Windows 2000 lets you rename user accounts because the SID remains the same. All you are doing is changing the values of certain attributes in the object. To rename a user account, you can right-click the account in Active Directory Users and Computers and select Rename or click the entry once. The entry can now be renamed in the same fashion as renaming any other object name in Windows 2000, such as a file or a folder name.

Note When you rename the account, you are only changing the name property as you see it in the AD list. This is very different behavior from legacy NT account management where the username and account name were one and the same thing. Changing the account name does not change the logon name (UPN) or the legacy NetBIOS name.

Deleting and Disabling User Accounts

It is common sense not to willy-nilly delete accounts. Once the account is deleted, you can never get it back. The SID can be tracked, but it can never be resurrected. There is no undelete feature, and the account and SID are lost forever as active objects. If you wish to render an account unusable, disable it. If you are an experienced administrator of Windows NT, then this practice is not new to you, and it is easy to disable an account in Active Directory. Just select the account in Active Directory Users and Computers and right-click. Select Disable Account from the menu items.

You can consider policy to delete any disabled account within a certain time frame, say six months. However, unless you have a very good reason to delete the account, leave it disabled indefinitely. Deleted accounts are like zombies. They will return from their graves to haunt you. Often, temps leave the company only to return six months later to perform similar duties, and having to recreate the same account all over again, with the same access rights and permissions, group memberships, and so on, is a exercise in futility.

Copying Accounts

Copying accounts is a no-brainer. Simply right-click the account you want to copy and select Copy. Copying accounts may not save you a lot of time if you have a lot of accounts to create. You may be better off with a script or special program, especially if many of the account attributes for each user will be different.

Consider having new employees fill in a form in a database or on the intranet. Then parse the form and use the values to create the user account in a script.

Computer Accounts

A *computer account* is also a security principal, a direct descendant of the User object. In order for a computer to participate in a Windows network, whether Windows 2000 or NT 4.0, it must be able to log on securely to a domain in some fashion. Windows 2000 adds additional security and control over the computer by requiring it to have an account — just like a user.

When you join a computer to a domain, you create an account for the computer, and Windows generates a SID. The procedure is identical to that of creating human user accounts.

The first computers you add to a Windows 2000 domain are the domain controllers. These servers are the domain security outposts. You cannot create a Windows 2000 domain without first "raising" a domain controller. The act of promoting a machine to domain controller service demotes any authority the local SAM had. Directory services are created, and full domain security is located in the Active Directory.

When you add the first member server, standalone server, or Windows 2000 Professional workstation to the domain, Windows establishes two new groups to assist with machine management: the Domain Admins Group and the Domain Users Group.

Creating a computer account is simpler than creating the User account. You need only select the OU in which you wish to place the computer and select New ⇨ Computer from the snap-in menu option. Obviously, you need authority to create the account. By placing the computer into an OU, you place it under the influence of Group Policy, which is discussed in Chapter 11.

Group Accounts

Group management in Windows 2000 is a vast improvement over legacy NT group management. The group's role as an administrator-appointed mustering or container tool has been replaced by the OU, which means administrators can create and use groups more scientifically, now that its only purpose as a security principal is to provide and control access to computer and network resources.

A group is nothing more than a container for managing user accounts. However, the most important role of a group is that you can assign permissions to it rather than having to grant permissions to individual users. It is not very often that you have to create a user who is so peculiar to an organization that he or she has rights and access to resources no one else has. Even the Administrator account, of which there is only one, is placed into several groups to gain access to sensitive resources and information.

Windows 2000 groups come in two flavors: *security groups* and *distribution groups*.

✦ **Security group:** This is the standard Windows 2000 security principal stored as an entry in the ACL. Security groups, however, can now be mailed to. In other words, all the members in the security group that have an e-mail address stored in their User account objects can receive e-mail.

✦ **Distribution group:** This group is not a security principal and is used only as a distribution list. You can store contacts and user accounts in the distribution group. Because contacts do not contain the overhead of user accounts, it makes more sense to include only contacts in large groups. This group is also compatible with Microsoft Exchange and can play a large part in your telephony and messaging applications as well. When you upgrade Exchange to support Active Directory, you can eliminate the Exchange distribution lists and reduce the administrative burden on the e-mail administrators.

The Scope of Groups

Both group types have three scope types. Scopes determine the ability to contain members and nest groups from other domains and forests across the enterprise and even on an intra-enterprise relationship basis. The three scope types are: *Universal, Global,* and *Domain Local.* Windows NT supported only Global and Local group types.

✦ **Universal groups:** These groups can include members from any Windows NT or Windows 2000 domain in a forest. The members can be groups of any of the three scope types, and they can come from any domain in the forest. This scope was created for users who need access to resources in other domains. A good example of a universal group is a user who works mainly in USA-Domain but who frequently travels to London where he or she logs onto UK-Domain. This user would be able to log on to UK-Domain and still gain access to his or her USA-Domain resources. Members of universal groups can be given access and permissions for any resource in any domain in the forest.

✦ **Global groups:** These groups can include members only from the originating domain. These members can be other global groups and contact groups. Global groups can be given access to resources in any domain in the forest, and the members can be members of any of the groups in the forest. You can nest global, local, and universal groups in a global group.

✦ **Domain local groups:** These groups can include members from any domain in the forest. Its members can be any user or group from anywhere in the forest. However, you can only nest other domain local groups from the same domain. The members of this group scope cannot be members of groups set with the global and universal group scope types.

Note   Group scopes can be elevated only if they do not belong to other groups in the lower level, and only on native-mode networks. In other words, you can move a global group to a universal group only if the global group does not belong to another global group. You will also notice that you cannot change the scope of a universal group, because Universal scope objects are the weakest security principals of all the groups.

Let's recap common group use and management on Windows NT, which will serve to help you understand Windows 2000 groups. On legacy NT domains, we create and work with two types of groups, *domain local* and *global* groups. Domain local, or just local, groups are restricted to the domains in which they are created; they cannot be given entry into other legacy NT domains. Global groups, on the other hand, can be given entry into other legacy domains, and even Windows 2000 domains for that matter.

Local groups can contain global groups from the local domain and any trusted domain, but a local group cannot contain, or nest, any other local group.

It is considered good management practice on legacy NT domains to create local groups as resource groups that access the domains as the primary security principals, almost as bastions, to borrow a UNIX term. In other words, local groups are the front-line containers holding the access and permissions control that users require to get to their resources. (This practice continues in Windows 2000 domains.)

When a collective of local users, or even one user, requires access to the resources in their "home" domain, we give them access or membership to the local group. If a foreign group of users — that is, users from another domain — requires access, we give that global group membership to the local group. This allows us to restrict user access permissions to the local resource groups while retaining global groups for intra-domain access and organizational grouping.

However, the global group is also a security principal and is used to control access in the same way as the local group. This ability has led many companies, especially those that have only one local LAN, to abolish the use of the local group (except in the case of built-in groups) and make every group *global*. Why worry about local groups when global groups serve both as security principals and as organizational "departments" into which members who do similar work and need the same resources can be assembled? Table 9-1 provides a list of scopes and their limitations.

It is not uncommon to find global groups like *Accounts Payable, Shipping,* and *Logistics* in many NT domains. Although you cannot do much harm in such management practice, Microsoft did not intend groups to function as tools of business administration. Enter the organizational unit (OU). OUs have been covered extensively in Chapters 7 and 8, but let's discuss them here briefly in the context of managing groups and users. Organizational units are created to provide hierarchical administrative delegation, organizational structuring, and for setting Group Policy (which we will discuss in Chapter 10). Groups are used for granting and denying users access to computer and network resources. Global groups also traverse domain boundaries. A group can contain users and global groups from other domains, both on a single domain tree and across a forest of domains. OUs are only valid on a contiguous domain space, in the domain they were created in.

Table 9-1 **Group Scopes and Their Limitations**			
Group Scope	*Members*	*Permissions*	*Nesting*
Universal Group	Can come from any domain in the forest. The members can be other universal groups, global groups, and users and contacts from any domain in the forest. Cannot host local groups.	Can be granted on any domain in the forest	Can be a member of any local and universal group in the forest
Global Group	Can only come from the owner domain. Can host other global groups and users from the owner domain. Cannot host universal groups.	Can be granted on any domain in the forest	Can be a member of any group in the forest
Local Group	Can come from any domain in the forest. Can host global groups and users and contacts from any domain in the forest. Can also host other local groups from the owner domain.	Can only be granted by the domain owning the group	Can only be a member of other local groups in the owner domain

So now that we have abolished the group role as an organizational tool, let's be sure of its purpose in life. Instead of granting individuals access rights in every corner of the domain, we should instead grant them membership to certain access groups.

It is far easier to first create a group with a predetermined purpose, such as "access to the very large label printer." You would then assign security and management definitions to this group, and assign any necessary permissions to the group. Once the group is set up, you need to merely add a user to the group, and the group's restrictions and access permissions will be cumulative to the permissions that the user may have already applied elsewhere in other groups or individually, and would override any weaker values assigned elsewhere. The first trait of a group is the permissions that have been assigned to it. Permissions allow the users of a group to gain access to resources and information to which the group as a unit has been given access. In other words, the group permissions define the mode or level of access that members of the group gain.

Think of this in terms of classes on a plane. Business people may join the First or Business Class to gain access to better meals, more room, and seating arrangements that can accommodate in-flight board meetings, room to work with files and documents, and so on. If a flyer does not have a First or Business Class ticket, he or she does not have access or privileges to any services paid for by the First and Business Class flyers.

To summarize:

✦ Groups are mostly collections of user accounts.

✦ Users or members of groups inherit the blanket permissions assigned to a group.

✦ Users can be members of more than one group.

✦ Groups can be members of organizational units, which can be members of other OUs. And groups can also be members of other groups.

This flexibility offered by OUs and groups is somewhat dangerous, however, because it can result in an over-nested organizational mess if taken to the extreme. You should plan this carefully, before you are unable to see the forest for the trees.

The Elements of Groups

Like User objects, Group objects exist in two places in Windows 2000: in Active Directory and in the local registry. Groups are used for the following:

1. To manage user and computer access to network objects, local objects, shares, printer queues, devices, and so on

2. To create distribution lists

3. To filter Group Policy

In Windows 2000, you specify the purpose of the group when you create it. If the group is meant to contain security principals, then you set it up as a security group. Otherwise, you specify the group as a distribution list containing contacts.

Windows 2000 groups operate identically to Windows NT groups, but with more functionality. In fact, the underlying group technology has merely been elevated to the Active Directory level. Instead of adding individual users to resources (such as shares and device access), the best management policy is to add them to a group that needs the necessary access. Even if you only have one user that needs access to a share-point, create a group for that user. Do not fall into the habit of adding individuals to shares, because before long you'll have these lonesome access cases spread all over the place, which is a security risk.

Predefined Groups

Like legacy NT, Windows 2000 will install predefined groups when you install certain components or features of the operating system. You do not automatically get all the groups installed at the same time just by installing every service that ships with the OS. For example, you will not see *Domain Admins* listed in the Users and Computers Snap-in until you create the first computer account. The following list defines the base built-in groups installed when you install the first domain controller and create a computer account.

Take some time out to study this list and understand what each group bestows on its members. The groups are created for your convenience and serve broad purposes. But they represent a quick start to setting up a domain. Later, when your planning is underway (it is never complete), you can create new groups that serve security needs as tight as clams. These lists are not exhaustive, and you'll find many more groups listed in the Users and Computers snap-in. Also, many third-party applications will create additional groups that are specific to their applications. A good example is groupware applications like helpdesk, CRM, and ERP applications. The predefined groups are illustrated in Figure 10-10.

✦ **Administrators:** The only user account placed into this group at installation is the Administrator. You can add any user account to this group to immediately bestow wide access and power to the user.

Administrators do not get access to everyone's files and folders by virtue of the wide power they are given in this group. If a file or folder's permissions do not give access, then Administrator is also locked out. This ensures protection and allows owners or managers of sensitive shares, files, and folders to lock-down their resources securely.

✦ **Users:** The local Users group is the default group for any user account created in Windows 2000. Do not confuse this with the Users folder into which the Anonymous and Guest accounts are placed.

✦ **Account Operators:** This group gives wide administrative power to its members. Operators can create users and groups and can edit and delete most users and groups from the domain (permissions permitting). Account operators can also log on to servers, shut down servers, and add computers to the domain.

Account operators cannot delete Administrators, Domain Admins, Backup Operators, Print Operators, Server Operators, or any global or universal groups that belong to these local groups. They also cannot modify the accounts of any members of the superior groups.

✦ **Backup Operators:** Members can back up and restore systems. But they can only use a backup program to back up files and folders. They can also log on to domain controllers and backup servers and shut them down.

✦ **Print Operators:** Members can create, delete, and manage the print share-points on print servers. They can also shut down print servers.

✦ **Server Operators:** Members can manage member servers.

✦ **Replicators:** This is not a group that contains human users. It only contains the user account used to log on to the replicator service to perform replication functions.

✦ **Guests:** This is the built-in group that contains accounts for casual users or users that do not have accounts on the domain. Users in this group can usually log on without passwords and make very limited or controlled use of the system. It is ideal for service-based systems. We earlier recommended moving the accounts from this group into a visitor's OU, which can be further secured with Group Policy.

The following list presents the important global groups. These automatically have membership in local groups.

✦ **Domain Admins:** Use this group to provide administrative powers to administer the domain, domain controllers, and member servers and workstations. You can prevent anyone from accessing a member server by simply removing this group from the member's Administrators group. This group, by virtue of being a global group, can be added to the local groups in other domains and can be added to universal groups.

✦ **Domain Users:** The Domain Users group is a global group, and it thus makes sense to include every user in your domain in this group, regardless of the other groups they are in. You can then add this group to the Users local group, and whenever you need to grant access to "all," simply admit the group to the object granting permission. There is a good reason we put "all" in quotes and did not use the term *everyone:* The *Everyone* group that Windows admits to shares and folders by default means exactly that — everyone. If you create a user account from the command line using the `net user` command and do not specify group destination or domain, the user is automatically sent to the Domain User group. However, the account is also physically located in the root of the domain and not in any folder or OU. You can move it to a folder or OU after you create it.

The following list includes several "special" groups that are also created. These groups cannot be edited, disabled, or deleted, and do not have the ability to add members to these groups. They can be removed from shares, folders, and permission lists, but are not apparent in the Active Directory Users and Computers snap-in. Windows 2000 stores objects into these groups that need to be presented to the security subsystem.

✦ **Everyone:** This "group" means everyone that uses the computer and the network. By admitting this object to a share, you implicitly open all doors to the object, even if the user is an account on an alien OS, on a far-away planet. If they exist, they can access your object. We believe it is better to remove the *Everyone* group from your resource and use the Users group (containing Domain Users). At any time you get a call to get someone out of an open share, you can simply knock them out of the Domain Users or Users group.

✦ **Interactive:** All local users using the computer.

✦ **Network:** All users connected to the computer over the network. The Network group and the Interactive group are combined to form the Everyone group.

✦ **System:** This group contains specialized groups, accounts, and resources dependent on by the operating system.

✦ **Creator Owner:** This group contains the owner and/or creator of folders, files, and print jobs.

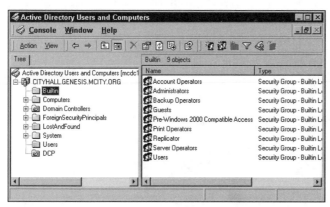

Figure 10-10: Windows 2000 default built-in groups are created automatically upon installation.

Groups on Member Servers

There is another good reason why the Domain Admins group is a global group: It can be admitted to the local group on a member server (and even a workstation for that matter). As discussed earlier, the domains created in the local machine environment are, for all intents and purposes, full-blown "domains" used to manage these computers.

The users and groups in the "local" domains work the same way as in the network domains. When you attach a non-domain-controller machine to Windows 2000 domains, the Domain Admins group is automatically added to the member computer's Users group.

Another group worth mentioning on the local machine is the Power Users group. This group has a similar role to the domain's Domain Admins group, except that members of this group do not have total control. This allows the managers of these computers to keep tight control over the local users.

Nesting Groups

Nesting groups is an efficient way of delegating the management of group membership. In native mode, you can create a universal group and delegate the control over membership to an enterprise or senior administrator whose job it is to manage the membership of the global groups. Global group administrators are the ones responsible for managing the membership of the global groups . . . granting membership to users or local groups.

Nesting is useful in enterprises that are dispersed across geographical boundaries or that have built multiple domains. At MCITY, we have created a universal group called GENESIS DCP that contains the senior users from GENESIS.MCITY.ORG\DCP. In the example in Figure 10-11, the universal group DCP.GENESIS.MCITY.ORG has been nested into the CITYHALL local DCP group.

 Note Domains must be in native mode to nest security groups. The universal group is not available in mixed mode. See the section "Mixed Mode versus Native Modes" later in this chapter.

Figure 10-11: Nesting in action: The local group DCP contains the universal group GENESIS DCP from the GENESIS.MCITY.ORG domain.

Group Creation

This section describes an example of how to create a new group.

Run the MMC Users and Groups snap-in and double-click an organizational unit we created earlier. Navigate to the OU where you want to create the group. Select Action ⇨ New ⇨ Group. This action opens the Create New Object (Group) dialog box, as illustrated in Figure 10-12. The options are as follows:

✦ **Name of new group:** This is the unique name you give the new group.

✦ **Down-level name of the new group:** This is added for you automatically and is based on the name you provided the new group (you may have to provide a down-level name that differs from the Windows 2000 name).

✦ **Group scope:** The options here are Domain Local, Global, and Universal.

✦ **Group type:** Security and Distribution. Keep in mind that if you choose a group of type Security, the weak Universal group is not an option in a mixed-mode domain.

Enter the information into the fields illustrated in Figure 10-12 and click OK.

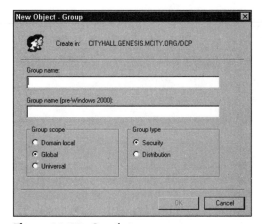

Figure 10-12: Creating a new group

Setting Up the Group

Once the group is created, navigate to the newly created group; right-click it and select Properties, or double-click it in the list. With the Properties page, illustrated in Figure 10-13, you can specify the settings you need to set up the group.

General tab

This page contains fields for the general information you need to add to the Group object. You can also change some of the information you added when you created the group, as discussed in the following list:

+ **Group name (Pre Windows 2000):** Enter the legacy Windows group name here. If the name you provide when you set up the group later causes problems, you can edit it at any time.

+ **Description:** Enter a brief description of the group. What you enter here appears in the Users and Computers snap-in Description column.

+ **E-mail:** Enter an e-mail address for the group. Any e-mail sent to the group will be distributed to its members.

+ **Group scope:** These radio buttons let you change the group scope. If the group is in a mixed-mode domain, the Universal scope option will remain disabled. You also cannot change a group's scope from Global to Domain Local, and vice versa.

+ **Group type:** These radio buttons allow you to change the group type.

+ **Comments:** Enter text in this field to assist in the documentation of your domain objects.

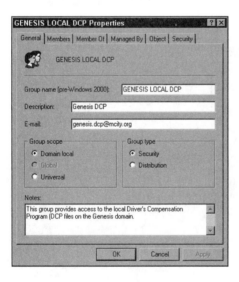

Figure 10-13: The General tab lets you enter or edit the base properties of the group.

Members tab

The Members tab allows you to add members to the group. You can add computers, users, groups, and contacts to the Members list.

✦ **Add:** Click Add. The complete list of all objects that can be given membership of this group appears. Double-click a user, and his or her name is added to the list. Click OK.

Member Of tab

The Member Of tab provides a view of membership from the membership lists of other groups. It also lets you join other groups.

✦ **Add:** Click Add. The complete list of all container objects to which this object can be given membership appears. Double-click the Users group and click OK.

Managed By tab

The Managed By tab provides a host of fields that identify the name, address, and contact information of the person who manages the group.

✦ **Change:** This is the only item you can add or change on this tab. The other properties are inherited from the manager's User object. You can protect the object at the permissions level later.

Security tab

The Security tab, shown in Figure 10-14, can control access permission to the object and protect it from being changed by unauthorized entities.

✦ **Add:** Click Add to configure the security of this object. This is where you get to add groups that have specific permissions to manage this object.

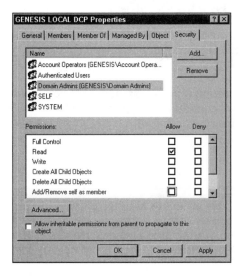

Figure 10-14: The Security tab lets you apply security measures to this object.

More about adding users to groups

You can add many objects to a group. These objects, all called *group members,* can be users, other groups, contacts, or computers. Adding computers to groups has some interesting consequences for management, as you will discover in Chapter 11. For now, however, we want only to add a single user account to a group of choice. To add members requires only a few steps. Simply select the group in Active Directory Management and right-click the selection, as described earlier. Then click Properties. The Properties dialog box appears and is labeled YOUR DOMAIN'S GROUP Properties. Select the members tab and click the Add button on the left bottom corner of the dialog box.

A second-level dialog box appears, named Select Users, Contacts, or Computers. Now select the user (notice that you can "look in" several places or domains for the user account, and you can search the entire directory). When you have located the user account, click Add. Your user is now added into the currently selected group, as indicated in the Members list. You can select more than one user in the top list by holding down the Ctrl key. You can also hold down the Shift key and drag the cursor over the list to select multiple users. In this case, however, we were only interested in one user. Also, notice that when you click Add, the accounts are listed serially (this should have been a drop-down list) in the name field for confirmation. Clicking OK puts them into the object list at the bottom of the dialog box.

Managing Groups

In Windows 2000, an individual or group can be delegated the task of managing users, or members, of specific organizational units. In our case, we will likely assign the management of the GENESIS DCP group to the DCP manager who also maintains the GENESIS DCP organization unit. In addition, Group Policy is used to control the work environments of the users in these groups and OUs. The DCP group we created might be refused access to the RAS, while another group that works remotely is granted access to RAS via the Group Policy.

You will need to fully understand how Group Policy works, and what you learn here will be insufficient to perform the task without making mistakes and having to redo things. Only practice and a lot of experience, working with many, many users over a few years, will prepare you for the job.

Rights and Permissions

The Windows 2000 security system controls access to network objects and protects network and machine-specific resources in two ways: rights and permissions. *Rights* are granted to users and groups (and don't forget, that includes processes, threads of execution, and so on that operate in the context of a security principal). Many rights would not normally be exploited by a human user, such as the right to lock a file in memory, which prevents it from being paged out to disk. But a thread of execution, requiring the ability to do so, would.

Permissions belong to the objects that are the essence of the operating system. With that bit of information in hand, you'll be pleased to know that objects are given rights to perform certain things, but as objects in Active Directory, you need permission to manage them. The difference between rights and permissions has confused administrators for years. When Windows 2000 lets you do something on a machine or on the network, that is a right, making rights something granted to users. Rights, for example, include the right to *log on locally,* the right to *log on as a service,* and the right to *act as part of the operating system.* But when you need to access an object in a defined way, you need to obtain permission. Permissions include permission to change objects, read them, execute them, delete them, and so on. A printer is a good example of an object you need permission to use. Another way of looking at the difference is that rights involve the ability to function, while permissions control access.

Permissions are granted by both the file system (over its objects) and by the Active Directory over its respective objects.

Rights come in two flavors: Privileges and Logon Rights. They can be bestowed on individuals by enabling rights in a Group Policy object (User Rights Assignment and Logon Rights Assignment) and linking the object to the user account. Association does this . . . and it takes place when you place a user account into an OU. The user account can also inherit any privilege defined in the GPO of a domain or site (see Chapter 11).

It is best to bestow privileges and rights through group membership, as discussed earlier, rather than on an individual basis. When you need to remove a privilege or logon right, you need only remove the user account from the group.

 Permissions are fully discussed in Chapters 8, 14, and 21.

Privileges

The rights bestowed to users and groups to provide them with the ability to perform certain functions in the computing environment are known as privileges. Privileges often override permissions, where necessary. A good example is the Right to Backup Files and Directories, which overrides any permission that denies access to a user. The Backup Operators group needs to be able to read and change (reset the archive bit, or overwrite during a restore) the files it is backing up, no matter what permissions the owner of the objects has. Table 10-2 explains the privileges, their purpose, and to whom they are assigned by default.

Table 10-2
Privileges and Predefined Groups

Right	What It Allows	Default Groups Assigned To
Act as part of the operating system	Allows a process to operate as in the context of a secure or trusted part of the OS	Everyone, Authenticated Users, Power Users, Administrators
Add workstations to domain	Allows a user to add workstations (computer accounts) to a domain	Not assigned to a default group
Back up files and directories	Allows users to back up files and folders	Administrators, Backup Operators
Bypass traverse checking	Moves between folders to access files	Everyone
Change the system time	Sets the internal clock of the computer	Administrators, Power Users
Create a pagefile	Allows the user to create a pagefile	Not assigned to a default group
Create a token object	Allows a process to create an access token via the LSA	Not assigned to a default group
Create permanent shared objects	Allows a user to create permanent objects	Not assigned to a default group
Debug programs	Debugs low-level processes and threads	Administrators
Enable computer and user accounts to be trusted for delegation	Delegates responsibility	Administrators
Force shutdown from a remote system	Shuts down a remote computer	Administrators
Generate security audits	Generates security audit entries	Administrators
Increase quotas	Allows a user to increase the disk quotas	Administrators
Increase scheduling priority	Increases the execution priority of a process	Administrators
Load and unload device drivers	Installs and removes device drivers	Administrators

Right	What It Allows	Default Groups Assigned To
Lock pages in memory	Allows a user to prevent pages from being paged out to `pagefile.sys`	Not assigned to a default group
Manage auditing and security log	Specifies which objects can be audited	Administrators
Modify firmware environment values	Modifies system environment variables	Administrators
Profile single process	Performs profiling on a process	Administrators
Profile system performance	Performs profiling on a computer	Administrators
Remove computer from docking station	Unlocks a computer from the docking station	Administrators
Replace a process level token	Allows a user to modify a security access token	Not assigned to a default group
Restore files and directories	Allows users to restore files and folders	Administrators, Backup Operators
Shut down the system	Shuts down Windows 2000	Administrators, Backup Operators, Everyone, Power Users, and Users
Synchronize directory service data	Allows a user to synchronize directory service data	Not assigned to a default group
Take ownership of files or other objects	Allows the user to take ownership of all objects attached to the computer. This right overrides permissions.	Administrators

Logon rights

Logon rights dictate how a user can log on to a computer or a domain. Logon rights are also bestowed in Group Policy. They are defined in the GPO and specifically linked to groups and users (preferably via group membership) through association with a site, domain, or OU. Table 10-3 explains the logon rights.

Table 10-3
Logon Rights and Predefined Groups

Right	What It Allows	Groups Assigned To
Access this computer from the network	Allows a user to connect to the computer over the network	Everyone, Authenticated Users, Power Users, Administrators
Deny access to this computer from the network	Revokes this right	Not assigned to a default group
Deny logon as a batch job	Revokes this right	Not assigned to a default group
Deny logon as a service	Revokes this right	Not assigned to a default group
Deny logon locally	Revokes this right	Not assigned to a default group
Log on as a batch job	Allows a user to log on using a batch-queue facility	Administrators
Log on as a service	Allows a security principal to log on as a service, which allows the process to operate in a security context	Not assigned to a default group
Log on locally	Allows a user to log on to a local machine, at the keyboard	Print Operators, Authenticated Users, Server Operators, Backup Operators, Administrators, Power Users, Account Operators

Mixed Mode versus Native Mode

Your domains must be in *native mode* to use the advanced group features in Windows 2000. Specifically, you cannot create a universal security group in mixed mode (you can only create a universal distribution list, which is not a security principal). You also cannot nest security groups in mixed mode, nor convert groups from one scope to another. This is a severe limitation, and you may wish to consider promoting the scope as soon as it is feasible. Mixed mode domains support Windows NT 4.0 domain controllers (the legacy Backup Domain Controllers or BDCs).

Note   Before committing to new Windows 2000 applications, check with the ISV to see what groups are required by the application and the features it needs to use. Some applications may require you to promote the domain to native mode when it is not practical for you to do so.

The Zen of Managing Users and Groups

Managing users is demanding and requires an assertive personality in an administrator. Managing a small group of, say, 25 people may not be such a big deal (you think), but as the number of users grows, so the task becomes more and more complex. Users depend on the network to get their jobs done. And thus the life of the administrator or user manager is a never-ending exercise in tolerance, assertiveness, concentration, and understanding. The less savvy your administration skills, the more you have your work cut out for you.

It is a good idea for any serious administrator to take a course in enterprise resource planning (ERP), human resources, customer relationship management (CRM), business management, and administration in general. Understanding how the various departments function autonomously and in concert with the rest of the company will go a long way to effective user management.

User management is not simply the task of allowing users to log on to a network. You need to provide access, protect resources, track utilization, audit activity, and much more. Setting up users and groups is often easier than managing them in the long term. Just moving a group from one domain to another can be a complex process. And if your company happens to absorb or acquire the IT department of another company, you could be saying goodbye to 40-hour weeks for a long time, especially if nobody knows who owns what shares, folders, files, and so on.

So where do you start? The preceding material in this chapter gave you a thorough understanding of Windows 2000 user and group architecture, and how user and group accounts are created and deployed. With that information, you now need to plan the best way to use this information to manage the network. Every company is different and, thus, you will best determine your needs. You do, however, need to plan ahead and use common sense. We might suggest task lists as the best way to begin user and group management projects. Before you begin, establish the following protocols:

1. Create an IT-HR/Windows 2000 physical workgroup to oversee new policy or changes in policy and change control with respect to user management and access to resources. The ability to create objects and delegate their management and control (down to the finest grain) to individuals, groups, teams, and project leaders can prove very beneficial, but also very dangerous.

2. Your team needs to consider new policy and the ramifications of delegated responsibility with respect to managing user accounts and the collateral services such as security, access to shares, devices, information, and other information-based resources.

3. You will need to set up new policy with respect to the delegation of control and management of objects. It would have to be decided at what level IT and MIS would be prepared to give control to the department heads and group leaders, and the people they delegate.

4. This team might be called the Directory Administrator's Team, with a leading figure like the CIO or MIS in charge.

5. Appoint a person (employee or consultant) to work with HR and analysts to establish or improve corporate structure. Many organizations do not get remodeled or restructured for some time because few really care. But now it is possible to involve IT directly in the corporate structure, especially since the Active Directory makes it possible for several teammates to collaborate on setting the corporate structure and model in the directory, as opposed to on paper or in flow charts and diagrams. The task ahead would be to create organizational units based on the layout and scope of the entire organization.

6. A term often used in business or corporate analysis is *Key Management Entity.* Key Management Entities are all the key aspects of a business that need to be managed. Accounts Receivable, Accounts Payable, Materials Management, Shipping, QC, and QA are examples of KMEs. These KMEs can now also be modeled in AD, inheriting directly from the models and structures typically associated with corporate analysis software and ERP technology (such as the likes of products from SAP and Baan).

7. Appoint teammates who would be responsible for migrating users to the new OUs and groups on a per-OU basis. If you are relocating users from Windows NT, these members would need to be members of the old Domain Admins group. The problem many companies face is that shares and permissions are just dished out with no record of what groups, shares, user policies, profiles, file permissions, and so on, are in place. This would have to be properly documented. It is almost impossible to properly extract information that documents the NT domain.

8. Invite the people responsible for customer relationship management (CRM) to join the directory administrator's forum with a view to incorporating helpdesk and the external environment into the directory. For example, what if the group decided it might be worthwhile to set up OUs for user groups (customers)?

Delegating Responsibility

The best means of putting policy and change control under management would be to involve the department heads and team leaders across the board. Several items in this regard need to be considered when you delegate:

✦ Do the respective department heads want the new responsibility? Do they carry sufficient weight to shirk the idea of managing their own groups? And do they carry sufficient weight to manage their peers?

✦ If policy dictates that they must participate, is management behind the new initiative to enforce the policy?

✦ Once the department heads have agreed to participate in the management of their own groups, will they need to delegate the function to a member who will require some training in managing?

Change management for users and groups is even more important under Windows 2000 because with the devolution of administrative power comes decentralization, even in a central location. It is thus worthwhile to set up a permissions request or user access request committee consisting of members of HR, MIS-Security, and the network administrators.

The teams or individuals responsible for new users (employees) should receive user and group account requests from HR once new employees are cleared. An e-mail or form is sent to the MIS-Security person who is responsible for setting in motion the steps to set up the user with his or her basic needs, inside the organizational unit to which they are assigned. Such a person is equipped with sensitive information about all various resources in operation at the company. For example, this person is aware of what shares represent what on the Payroll server, or how access is provided to the AS400, the Remote Access Server, and so on.

Employees and team leaders can also motivate or request changes to the profiles and rights of the workers under them: for example, if a user gets promoted or assigned new administrative functions. He or she may now need certain read-only rights changed to full control, or rights to delete, copy, and move files. The requestors do not need to know what groups they are in. The HR manager's job is to help the department requesting a new employee clear the employee to work for the company and set the new employee up with all the resources he or she needs to do his or her job as efficiently as possible.

The MIS-Security checklist or account request and setup form might contain the following:

✦ **User ID (logon):** `jeffrey.shapiro@mcity.org`

✦ **Password:** Made up according to a system or policy

✦ **Devices:** Printers, drives, scanner, modems, and so on

✦ **Share-points:** Folder or directory shares

✦ **Applications:** For the discussion of policies and profiles, see Chapter 12

✦ **Facility:** Help, training, setting up workstations, and so on

✦ **Logon hours:** Regular hours and overtime

✦ **Messaging:** E-mail, voice mail, fax mail

✦ **Organizational Unit:** Assigned by HR

✦ Describe the user's needs and any special circumstances

Once this list (which may be longer or shorter) is complete, it can be given to the network administrator or engineer responsible for user account creation, in the respective organizational unit. This person does not question how or why the account is set up or what is assigned; he or she just creates the account.

Under the Windows 2000 domain, the above practice will now take place on a department or OU basis as opposed to being enterprise-wide or centralized, under the control of a handful of techies. Requests from users and organizational units or departments should be directed to the helpdesk. A good idea is to use e-mail forms or an HTML form on the company's intranet Web site.

Of course, you can still appoint a single administrator to manage user accounts. But it makes sense on Windows 2000 to encourage decentralized management (to a point, of course).

User and Group Management Strategies

The objective behind this section is to discuss strategies that lessen the burden on the administrator. Starting with the management of groups and users, there is now so much power in the hands of the Windows 2000 Server and domain administrators that it is possible, without care and forethought, to become bogged down in a quagmire of administrative spaghetti. Like many other management systems and technologies, it is possible to abuse the power (such as Group Policy, coming up in Chapter 11) and end up with a situation that is counter to the intention of order and sanity.

Keep Your Eye on TCO

What is TCO? It stands for Total Cost of Ownership. In a nutshell, it means that the total cost of a computer, a network, an application, or a whole IT department for that matter, greatly exceeds the cost of its acquisition. Once the asset is acquired, it has to be managed and kept up, and all the functions that keep the system going contribute towards TOC.

Many habits of administrators can send TCO to the doghouse. A seemingly simple oversight can cause hours of downtime, and can cost the company thousands in consulting fees and technical support from Microsoft. At $195 a pop, getting Microsoft on the line to help identify your mistakes is a sure way of making certain you are not around by the next service pack release.

Almost all of the items we will discuss here affect TCO. The two basic considerations are: Don't manage users, manage groups; and refuse new group requests.

Don't manage users, manage groups

Illogical user management contributes to the TCO bottom line, so where at all possible, you do not want to manage the access and security needs and privileges of users on an individual basis. We have discussed this aspect of user management earlier, but there may come times when you have no choice but to provide a user with "direct" access to a resource, without first putting that person into a group. If you do this, make sure you keep that situation as temporary as possible. Then, as soon as you can, add the user to a group and get rid of the solitary assignment.

Refuse new group requests

The first rule you need to learn is to be as stubborn and assertive as possible when it comes to new group requests. Every time you create a new group, you add to TCO in several ways:

✦ You add traffic to your network and systems. New groups require permission to access resources, they need storage space in the Active Directory, and they need to be replicated to domain controllers and global catalogs, and so on.

✦ Creating groups for every little need is a waste of time. If two groups need access to the same resource, such as a printer, why admit two groups to the resource? Keep one group and either add all users that need the same level of access to the group, or nest.

✦ You give yourself more work in documenting and maintaining the groups.

To lessen your load, first do the following before creating new groups:

1. Check if a built-in group can satisfy the needs. It makes no sense to create a group for every little device. For example, if a printer object admits everyone, then there is no need to create another group for it (unless you have specialized auditing or security needs . . . discussed in just a moment).

2. Check if a group you or someone else earlier created will suffice to meet the user's needs. Nine times out of ten you can easily find several dozens of groups that have become redundant, because people create new ones without checking if others exist that serve their purpose.

Determine the Access and Privileges Needed

From the request form, you should be able to determine the needs of the users or the group in determining what group creation or management action you need to take. If you find you have to keep going back to people for more information, the forms are not working properly, or people are not complying with the protocols. In determining the needs, you need information concerning the following:

✦ **Access to applications and libraries:** If the applications are on the servers, or users are Terminal Services clients, they will need access to the shares and folders containing the applications. They will also need access to policy and script folders, home directory, specialized paths, attachments (such as to SQL Server), and so on.

✦ **Access to Data:** Applications and users need access to data: database tables, freestanding data files, spreadsheets, FTP sites, storage, and so on. Determine what data is needed and how best to access it.

✦ **Access to Devices:** Users and applications need access to printers; communications devices, such as fax servers and modem pools; scanners; CD changers; and so on. All network devices are considered objects, and their access is also governed by permissions.

✦ **Communications:** Users need accounts on mail servers, voice messages boxes, and in groupware applications.

✦ **Privileges and Logon Rights:** Users need certain rights and power to perform their duties efficiently and in the shortest possible time.

Most of the time, requests are easily fulfilled: User X requires an account, and he or she needs to be placed in the B group for access to the C share. X needs e-mail and must be able to dial in to the RAS at any time of day or night, and so on. This is not a difficult request, but when you get complicated requests, you need as much information as possible.

Determine the Security Level

The request form should be clear on the security needed over the user and the resources he or she is accessing. If the data is extremely valuable or very sensitive, you may need to consider auditing objects, tracking file and folder access, and so on. See Chapter 19 on security. The levels or lengths you go to protect the resources depends on the needs of each organization. For example, you might consider short-term passwords, restricting logon hours, restricting logon location, and so on.

Protect Resources and Lessen the Load with Local Groups

The best practice in group management has been inherited from our experience with Windows NT: First create "gatekeeper" groups, which are local groups that control the access to resources, and expose what needs to be exposed for broad and even tightly controlled purposes. Then nest global and universal (if in native mode) groups in the local groups, providing a second level of access control and permissions.

The practice of creating gatekeeper groups also encourages a delegation of responsibility and a form of decentralized management that is still safe and not out of touch. Assign people, who only have to admit global or universal groups when requested, the responsibility of managing local groups. Then assign the membership of the global groups to the department or organizational unit administrators.

Delegate with Care

In line with the previous item, it is important to delegate with care. Over time, we expect that administrative power will become decentralized, but you still need to maintain a watchful eye over the "higher level" administrators. You may have to create admin groups for each OU where you have delegated responsibility or create one OU admin group and manage the individuals via OU Group Policy, and so on.

Keep Changes to a Minimum

If you do a good job managing users and groups, there is no need to keep changing things around. The fewer changes you have to make, the better. Remember, too, every time you change something in the domain, the change needs to be propagated around the network to all the domain controllers. If you have a wide area network and your domain traverses geographical divides, constant changes can cause latency and costly delays while remote domain controllers lag behind in updates and replication.

Summary

In this chapter, we discussed how the new User and Group objects in the Active Directory allow us to more cohesively manage users and groups on Windows 2000-based networks. We also discussed the creation of users and groups and how to best administer them.

Most importantly, we stressed using common sense when creating and managing users and groups and delegating responsibility. Now, on to a more complex subject . . . managing the workspace.

✦   ✦   ✦

Change Control and Policy and Workspace Management

This chapter discusses workplace management and change control services.

What Is Change Control?

During the writing of this chapter, one of our clients almost lost a small fortune in business due to the lack of change control. Our client is a small (only five people) insurance broker. One of the brokers, Dave, writes marine insurance, and on a fine cool January day in Florida, he got the break the company was waiting for . . . an order for a policy to insure a $10 million yacht . . . the premium would be a killer.

He returned from the marina shaking and shivering, realizing that he was about to write the policy of his career. The commission would be staggering, and from this many more deals would flow. You get a name for writing big policies like this. Nothing would stand in his way . . . nothing but his faithful workstation.

Dave likes to fiddle with his computer. When he is not looking for insurance business, he likes playing around with his desktop settings, fonts, resolution, and more. Dave lives in Control Panel more than his apartment. We had maintained a "loose" change management policy in this company. In other words, we maintained minimal desktop control because Dave was the only wild card and was considered an advanced user. The company had been our client for several years, and we had never had an issue with users changing anything that could cause a problem.

On the day that Dave needed to write up his policy, his desktop went berserk. He logged into his workstation as usual, but when he opened the insurance application, the application began to tremble and then the session froze. If you know insurance, you know that if you cannot write the policy, the client will make another call. Dave was getting ready to jump off the jetty with an anchor around his neck.

We jumped in and disabled Dave's account. And because we were deploying the Windows Desktop and agency software applications through terminal services, we were able to get Dave back to his policy writing in record time. He admitted that he had changed his font again and some other "things" that he could not remember.

The client learned a lesson and advised that no employee (all four of them) was allowed to tamper with the applications or desktop sessions. But we learned a bigger lesson. Change control is as important for our small clients as it is for the big ones. It cannot be ignored anywhere.

Change control on Windows NT and other server environments has been lacking since the invention of client/server. Policy and profile maintenance is possible on Windows NT and Windows 9x desktops, but it is not secure, and users can override settings with little effort. A Windows NT workstation/server environment is more secure. But change control empowerment is still lacking.

Windows 2000 and Active Directory change all this with the introduction of Group Policy. Group Policy governs change control policy on many facets of the operating system. These include the following:

✦ Hardware configuration and administration

✦ Client administration and configuration (desktop settings, logon, connection, and more)

✦ Operating system options and policy, such as IntelliMirror and remote OS installation

✦ Application options and policy (such as regional settings, language and accessibility, deployment, and more)

✦ Security options and policy

✦ Network access

We are not going to take you through every detail of creating and managing Group Policy objects because the Windows 2000 Help system adequately handles that. But we will show you how to take control of the change control issue, apply security policy, and more. But before we get to that, let's discuss the science and philosophy of change control and management.

Understanding Change Management

In our highly complex worlds of information technology and information systems, the only constant is change. The more complex and integrated our IS systems become, the more important it is to have change control. Managing change has thus become one of the most important MIS functions in many organizations. If you do not manage change, the unexpected results of an unmanaged change could render you extinct.

Processes, routines, functions, algorithms, and the like do not exist in vacuums or some form of digital isolation from the rest of the universe. Just as in life, all processes depend on or are depended on by other routines or processes. When you change the way a process behaves, you alter its "event course." In other words, you alter its destiny. Altering the event course of a process is in itself not the problem. Problems arise when processes dependent on a particular course of events are no longer afforded the opportunities they were expecting.

Think about how you feel and are inconvenienced when a person you were going to meet does not turn up or cancels the engagement unexpectedly. In software and computer systems, such events can have catastrophic results. They in turn fail, and their event courses are also altered. When processes begin to crash, an unstoppable domino effect takes place, leading to systems failure and disaster from one end of the system to the other.

Besides the first example when Dave's job was almost toasted, here are other examples:

✦ The FTP service on a server is turned off. AS/400 connections expecting to find the connection up are not able to transfer route information to a network share. A process that was expecting the information to be in the FTP folder cannot calculate the daily routes for orders that need to go out. The trucks do not arrive, and the orders do not get established. The orders are not shipped. Clients place more than $10 million in business elsewhere.

✦ A software engineer makes a change in source code that reintroduces the Millennium bug into the process pool. Programs begin to collapse because the receiving data function does not know how to deal with data that appears to be more than a hundred years old.

✦ A user downloads new software from the Internet onto his company's notebook computer. The new software contains a backdoor virus that silently attacks the notebook's anti-virus suite. It inserts a replacement file into the anti-virus software and causes the software to reload the old inoculation data file, which is akin to taking an antibiotic that has expired. When the user connects back to the corporate network, the hostile code moves to the network servers and does the same thing. Once on the servers, the virus shuts down the company systems, and the company almost goes insolvent as a result.

These examples sound far-fetched, but they are not. We have seen all three of them on our networks. Such is the need for change control. In fact, the unit of time in which no change takes place is too small to be studied by humans.

So, we have to control change; we have to manage it in such a way that the effects of change are planned for and that all dependencies are informed and allowed to compensate when change comes. In a nutshell, no change can be allowed to take place without a) the proposed change being put to a board of change management for consideration; b) the consequences of the change are fully investigated, and the change is deemed necessary. Because change is always inevitable, another factor comes into change control — contingency planning, of which disaster recovery is a part.

In the past, problems caused by unmanaged change affected standalone systems. Because computers were once islands and isolated, the effects of the change were local and confined. When we started to network, change control problems began to affect the global corporate or organizational environment. But the effect was, and still is to a large extent, confined to the corporate or enterprise information network.

However, in the world of e-commerce, change control has become critical because any change that causes an unplanned-for new course of events will affect the external environment where systems crashes can have catastrophic results and cause untold damages and liability. In the world of Internet banking, for example, a change control disaster can affect many people who have no relationship with the bank . . . besides its innocent account holders.

In various parts of this book, we have also discussed service level and quality of support. As you know, more and more people are signing service level agreements that guarantee availability of systems all the time. These agreements have to be covered with effective change control management.

The change control or change management board reviews all changes and, based on the board's research, consultation, and findings, a change request is either approved or denied. (In the companies we consult for, all change management approvals have to be signed off by the officer in charge.)

But the problems arise when you have a fully functional board and compliant team leaders, but no means of enforcing change control policy at all levels of the enterprise. To figure out how this all comes together, let's look at change control conceptually. The respective parts of change control or change management systems resemble the justice system, or at least the enforcement parts of it. They include the items listed in Table 11-1.

Table 11-1 Change Control	
Description	**Purpose**
Change Control Board	A group of people in an organization responsible for reviewing change requests, determining validity, deciding change of course or procedure, and so forth. This board also determines regulation and enforcement protocol and deploys change management resources.
Change Management	Functions to manage signed-off or approved change or contingency. Change management may include lab tests, sandpit projects, pilot projects, phased implementation, incremental change, performance monitoring, disaster recovery, backup/restore, and so on.
Change Control Policy	Rules, and the formulation thereof, governing change control and management.
Change Control Rules and Enforcement	The enforcement of policy and the methods or techniques of such enforcement.
Change Control Tools	On Windows 2000 networks, this includes local security policy to protect machines, Group Policy to enforce change policy throughout the forest, security policy throughout, auditing, and so on.
Change Control Stack	The change control "stack," which comprises the various layers that are covered by change control.

To better understand where in the information systems environment change control needs to be enforced, consider the change control stack in Figure 11-1.

At the bottom of the change control stack (CCS) is the hardware (physical) area. Objects in this layer that you place under change control enforcement are all hardware, computer components, and hardware requirements. The following list provides an idea of what is covered by change control at the hardware or physical layer:

✦ Hardware compliance with the existing infrastructure

✦ Hardware acquisition and determination of hardware needs

✦ Technology deemed necessary or not

✦ Protection and security of storage, and access to media (such as FDDs and CD-ROMs)

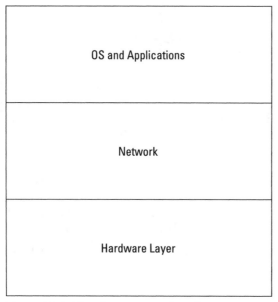

| OS and Applications |
| Network |
| Hardware Layer |

Figure 11-1: The change control stack

✦ Protection of network interface cards

✦ Access to memory and system components

✦ Availability and stability of hardware device drivers

✦ Hardware problem abandonment point (when do you give up trying to fix a part or computer and buy a new one)

✦ Parts replacement (such as procedure for replacing media, and so on)

✦ Hardware availability (such as RAID, clustering, load balancing, and so on)

Next up is the network layer, which encompasses change control on the data link, network, transport, and session layers of the OSI model.

Note   According to Newton's Telecom Dictionary, The Open Systems Interconnect (OSI) model of the International Standards Organization (www.iso.ch) is the only accepted framework of standards for interconnection for communication between different systems made by different vendors. The OSI model organizes the communications process into a system of layers. OSI has become the foundation model for many frameworks in both software and computer hardware engineering. The OSI model is also referred to as the OSI stack.

The following list includes areas that are targets of change control at the network layer of the CCS:

✦ Security needs (encryption, IPSec, access to routers, circuits, hubs, and so on)

✦ Quality of service

✦ Network bandwidth

✦ Topology

✦ Transport technology (Ethernet, SNA, Token Ring)

✦ Routing, bridging, switching

As we get higher up the CCS, the number of variables begins to increase (there are more opportunities for change and thus change control, because we are getting into the area where the user lives). The following list includes areas that are targets of change control at the operating systems and applications layer of the CCS:

✦ Logon/user authentication

✦ Network services

✦ File systems and storage

✦ Network protocols

✦ Device driver installation and version control

✦ Device operation

✦ Application services

✦ Disaster recovery services

✦ Internet/intranet services

✦ Media services and telephony

✦ File transfer

✦ Sharing and access control

✦ Virus protection

✦ Directory services

✦ User levels/access to resources

✦ Communications

✦ Desktop configuration (menus, shortcuts, icons, access to folders, and so on)

✦ Access to information (such as access to the Internet)

✦ Cultural and regional options

✦ Accessibility

✦ Access to software/applications

✦ Access to data

Not only are there more factors or "opportunities" for change control in this top layer, but also it is the most vulnerable of the layers. While certain parts of the operating system and the lower layers provide a barrier to entry due to their complexity, this does not mean that change control should be any more lax or less important. The more obscure the service, regardless of the layer it resides in, the higher the risk of a skilled attacker doing undetectable and lasting damage. However, it goes without saying that the biggest threat to the stability or health of IT/IS systems comes from users. Most of the time, it is just a case of "curiosity killed his computer" (remember Dave). But users also generate security threats, introduce viruses, download hostile applications (most of the time unwittingly), and so on.

The User

First, the term *user* rarely refers to a single biological unit. This is why we have security groups, as discussed in Chapter 10. As soon as you define or categorize the levels of user groups that you need to support in your organization, you will be able to apply change management procedures that can be enforced on those groups.

If you are involved in client management, you should make an effort to become a member of the change control team. You should also get to know your users, the type of software and applications they need, and how they work with their computers, treat their computers, and interact with their computers.

There are two main types of user or worker, as discussed in the following list:

✦ **Knowledge workers:** Your knowledge workers are usually the workers who are applying a particular skill set or knowledge base in their job. These people are your engineers, technical support people, accountants, lawyers, designers, and so on. Knowledge workers usually have a permanent office. These people use their computers for most of the day. Their machines are constantly in use, and losing them would be costly for the company. They can be considered advanced users.

✦ **Task-oriented workers:** These workers are data entry personnel, receptionists, office assistants (to varying degrees), order takers, and so on. Most of these users would not need more than a terminal and a terminal service account to perform their duties. These users can be considered your basic users.

The two main types of user are further broken down into the following categories (by computer resource used):

✦ **Stationary (office) workstation user:** This user (usually a knowledge worker) does not need a notebook computer because he or she only needs the machine at work. This machine is usually a small-footprint workstation running Windows 9*x*, Windows NT Workstation, or Windows 2000 Professional.

✦ **Remote workstation user:** This worker connects to the network from home or a remote office, over a WAN connection or modem. The user still uses a fixed desktop computer because he or she does not move around.

✦ **Notebook/docking station user:** This user uses his or her computer at work *and* at home. The user is usually accommodated with a docking station at home and at the office, which makes it easier to connect and disconnect from the network.

✦ **Multi-user workstation:** This computer does not belong to any specific user. Users making use of this resource are usually guests, users that move around from location to location, temp staff, shift staff (such as call center or customer service representatives), and so on.

✦ **Mobile computer:** This is usually a notebook or laptop computer, sans docking station, that spends most of its life in a carrying case stuffed inside the cubby of a jetliner. Mobile users can either connect to the office from the road (such as a hotel or conference center) or from branch locations where they will be able to connect to the corporate network.

In each of these cases, you will need to establish workstation and user management policy with respect to each user and computer. Also note that it often makes more sense to further tag your user as being advanced or basic in the literacy level of computer usage. We have had knowledge workers who cause endless problems for the administrators, and basic workers who should be writing software instead of using it.

Create a list or database of these categories and in each category list a computer name and a user name (pay close attention to these lists because we will return to them later). For example:

Mobile Computers

✦ Mobile Computer Accounts

1. MCPD98

2. MCPD99

3. MCPD100

4. MCPD101

✦ Mobile Computer Users

1. Henry R. James

2. Catherine H. Anderson

3. Jill J. Smith

4. Michael F. Wolf

User Applications

You now need to create another list underneath each user that determines what each requires in terms of software and hardware to perform his or her functions. You will create two lists. The first is for basic users who need no more than the standard applications adopted by the enterprise. For example, if your company has adopted Microsoft Exchange 2000, then Outlook 2000 will be on that list, as will MS Word, Excel, and other applications . . . if the company has standardized on Microsoft Office components, which is very common.

A second list next to the first one will be an advanced user choice list. The user (if policy allows) will be able to choose a specialized list of software for which he or she must justify deployment. This justification, by the way, is presented to change control or management for review. A good example is a software engineer who is hired to create a certain application. He or she will then request that a development tool or component be installed or made available to complete the task.

Managing software is a daunting task for anyone. In a small organization, one person can typically be saddled with the job of managing anywhere in the region of 10 to 20 applications. In large companies, the number of software components can run into the thousands. Defining and enforcing policy regarding installation and configuration of applications is thus critical. Why do you have to do this? Consider the following if you allow users to install their own applications:

✦ The application may be unstable and could damage existing systems. For example: During the early beta testing of Windows 2000 Professional, a technical support engineer at one of our clients installed the Release Candidate 3 code on his workstation to check it out. The code corrupted the databases belonging to help desk and shut down the call center for three days.

✦ Applications may not be legally obtained. If you do not enforce change control policy, your enterprise may be risking lawsuits and criminal charges. You cannot claim ignorance of users using illegal or pirated software. Your boss goes away for 20 years or more if your users steal software.

✦ The act of installing the software can introduce viruses and security risks to the network. If the user installs from a source on the Internet, there is the risk that the download may bring with it hostile applications. We have seen backdoor viruses pop out of downloaded zip files and kill a machine in under a minute.

✦ Increased cost of support. Users are likely to run into problems and will come to you for help with an application you likely know nothing about. It is amazing how the network or server administrator is expected to know everything about every application that has ever been invented.

Application Management

Another category in addition to applications is application management and configuration. This involves determining and managing the deployment process, local and remote installation, configuring the software, user education, user support, and so on. Windows 2000 provides nifty services to manage deployment and configuration.

Information for Workstation Lockdown

You now have a lot of information with which to determine how best to lock down workstations. Let's recap what you know, or should know, before you learn about Group Policy:

1. You should know what type of user you support.

2. You should know the category of workstation the user uses.

3. You should also know what applications are required and how they are used (usage level). For example: Is the user advanced or basic?

4. You should know the list of applications your classes of users need.

In addition to this list, it is imperative to understand the following information before you can begin to determine how best to lock down a workstation.

1. Have users logged onto their computers as the local administrator? This is common practice on NT workstations because it is not possible to log on as a domain user in an offline state, or if a domain controller cannot be found. If users have access to the local account and registry, they may circumvent change management policy. Decide which users fall into this category and which may be candidates to obtain a Windows 2000 desktop or session.

2. Do your users install their own unauthorized software on their computers? If you do not have policy to control this malady in an enterprise, you need to formulate this policy as soon as possible.

3. Do your users store data on their own workstations? If they do, you need to plan or devise a strategy to have them move the data to network share points or folder resources published in Active Directory folders. Understand that the data is at risk in such practice, because workstations do not typically get backed up, which means data can be lost when a computer crashes or is stolen. In Windows 2000, we talk about folder redirection, which is a way of making sure that a user's documents or data folders reside on the server where the data is backed up. More about this later.

4. How often do users call with "broken" workstations or desktop configurations? A broken configuration is usually the outcome of a user trying to install his or her software or hardware on the machine. Another form of broken configuration results from users tampering with the operating systems, fiddling with registry settings, Control Panel applets, and so on. The problem stems from users who have a false sense of security because they have a home computer they have mastered. They then eschew policy that strips them of that power at work. However, only your administrators, and only a few at that, or power users who are testing software as part of change management board activity, should have such rights over the enterprise or corporate computer property. The risk of a change causing damage to the workstation or network services is just too high to be up for discussion with users who consider themselves king of computers.

Windows 2000 Group Policy

The change control tool on Windows 2000 is the Group Policy Editor (GPE). As illustrated in Figure 11-2, this application is an MMC snap-in from which policy can be applied to the security principals — computer, users, and groups — of a Windows 2000 network. And as discussed earlier, Group Policy can be applied to items such as security management and hardware configuration as well.

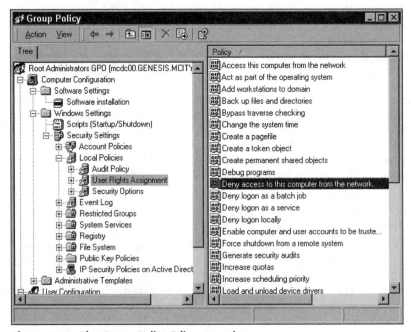

Figure 11-2: The Group Policy Editor snap-in

Group Policy is applied by creating an object that contains the properties that extend control of the computer and user's access to network and machine resources. This object is known as the Group Policy Object or GPO. When a security principal is a member of a container that is associated (linked) to the GPO, that security principal falls under the influence of that GPO. When a container is linked to multiple GPOs, the result is that the effects of all GPOs on the linked container are merged. This is illustrated in Figure 11-3.

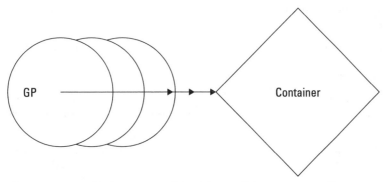

Figure 11-3: Multiple Group Policy Object policies merge to affect the container.

Note Sophisticated object-oriented engineering is at work in the GPO application process. The Group Policy architecture is complex, spans hundreds of pages, and is beyond the scope of this book. It is, however, well worth studying if you are an engineer at heart, because such advanced knowledge can only make you a better server or network administrator. You can search for the GPO architecture papers on the Microsoft Web site.

Group Policy is not applied directly to an individual security principal (although you can attain such granular control by creating specific OUs), but rather it is applied to collections of security principals. As you are aware, there are three places where security principals gather under one roof on a Windows 2000 Network: the *site,* the *domain,* and the *organization unit.* As GP applies to all three types of containers, you can refer to this as a *GP hierarchy.*

Windows 2000 Group Policy is vast and extremely powerful. It will take some getting used to, and you will need to spend a lot of time trying different things, as you will later see. In large companies, the role of managing GP should be assigned to individuals, possibly members of the Change Management Board. Managing GP can easily become a full-time occupation for an administrator. GP will become your main technology with which to manage change, user configuration and desktop settings, workstation lockdown security, software installation, and so on.

GPOs have more than 100 security-related settings and more than 450 registry-based settings, and the GP technology can also be extended or enhanced with certain APIs. Specifically, GP technology provides you with the following functionality:

✦ The GPO is configured and stored in Active Directory, or it can be defined as a local policy object. Standalone computers are secured or locked down with local GPOs. GP, however, depends on Active Directory.

✦ You apply GPOs to users and computers in AD containers (domains, sites, and OUs).

✦ The GPO is secure. You can lock down a GPO just like any other object in Windows 2000 (by now, you should be familiar with the Security tab on the property page of any object).

✦ The GPO can be filtered or controlled by membership in security groups. This, in fact, speeds up application of policy on the membership of the security group.

✦ The GPO is where the concentration of security power is located on Windows 2000 networks.

✦ The GPO is used to maintain Microsoft Internet Explorer.

✦ The GPO is used to apply logon, logoff, and startup scripts.

✦ The GPO is used to maintain software and software installation.

✦ The GPO is used to redirect folders (such as My Documents).

✦ The GPO does not expose the user profile to tampering when policy is changed, as was the case with Windows NT 4.0.

Types of Group Policy

Group Policy has influence over just about every process, application, or service on a Windows 2000 network. Both servers and workstations are influenced by GP, and therefore, unless you deploy Windows 2000 Professional, GP will *not* be pervasive throughout the enterprise. Windows 9*x* and NT 4.0 Workstations are not influenced to the same extent as Windows 2000 clients because client-side extensions are not present in these legacy desktop operating systems.

This means that a network consisting of many different versions of Windows (in some cases, as many as five versions) is also going to be less secure, or at least not as manageable. Obviously, a hard-to-manage or control network is going to be a lot more expensive to maintain in the long run. The initial cost of upgrading to Windows 2000 throughout the enterprise will pay off in the long run. In terms of security, such as being able to stave off a hacker thanks to encryption or being able to save critical data thanks to folder redirection — and there are many more examples — you can not only save a bundle going "native," you may even save the company. The more versions you eliminate, the more secure and more manageable life is going to be for you.

There are many different types of Group Policy "collections." The following list describes the "intent" of these collections (the term "policy collection" is not a Microsoft term as far as we know, but it is useful for describing the policy types).

✦ **Application deployment:** These policies are used to govern user access to applications. Application deployment or installation is controlled or managed in the following ways:

- **Assignment:** GP installs or upgrades applications and software on the client computers. The assignment can also be used to publish an icon or shortcut to an application and to ensure that the user cannot delete the icon.

- **Application publication:** Applications can be published in Active Directory. These applications are then "advertised" in the list of components that appears when a user clicks the Add/Remove icon in Control Panel.

✦ **File deployment:** These policies let you place files in certain folders on your user's computer. You can, for example, take aim at the user's My Documents folder and provide him or her with files that he or she needs to complete a project.

✦ **Scripting:** These policies allow you to select scripts to run at predetermined times. They are especially useful for ensuring that scripts get processed during startup and shutdown, or when a user logs off a machine and a new user logs onto the same machine (refer to the earlier discussion in this chapter on the different types of users). Windows 2000 is able to process VB scripts, Jscripts, and scripts written to the Windows scripting host.

✦ **Software:** These policies allow you to configure software on user workstations on a global or targeted scale. This is achieved by configuring settings in user profiles, such as the desktop settings, Start menu structure, and the other application menus.

✦ **Security:** Perhaps no other collection in Windows 2000 is as important as the security policies, given that in current times, the next hacker who wipes out the assets could be the kid next door.

Besides being able to *eventually* reduce the total cost of ownership (through lowering the cost of administration), there is a piece of advice you should consider with respect to Group Policy. It exists not to create problems for users and administrators, but to secure the environment and enhance the work and user environment. You thus need to be sure that you have the wherewithal to balance the two needs, or you could end up with cold pizza instead of rare sirloin for dinner.

In your endeavors to secure the environment, you will no doubt come across conflicts that violate the tenet to maintain a "user friendly" environment. Going wild on pass-word length is a good example. If you set password length too long to increase security, users will not only get peeved, they will also start sticking the passwords on their monitors because they are hard to remember. That is not security. If you must have tight security, your choice in such a matter might be to take the security need to management and suggest smart cards or biometrics. Remember that locking down an environment should not lock out the user at the same time.

The environment can be enhanced in many different ways. When users need access to new software, which of the following three methods of delivery is more pleasing or enhancing to the user, from the user's perspective?

1. Waiting hours or days for the administrator to show up at your desk with the new software.

2. Being asked to log on to a network distribution point and install the software yourself.

3. Taking a break while the software mysteriously installs itself onto your machine with seemingly no human intervention.

Enhancing the users' environment also means helping them easily locate applications, intelligently redirecting folders or mapping their folders to resources, and automating processes during the twilight times of the workstation, logoff and logon.

Before you study how Group Policy works, you should at least take some time to get familiar with the technology.

The Elements of Group Policy

A programmatic discussion of the elements is beyond the scope of this book. However, it helps to understand the various elements with which you interact. Several components make up GP from the administrator's perspective. These components include the following:

✦ The Group Policy Object

✦ Active Directory containers

✦ Group Policy links

✦ The Policy or Group Policy

✦ Explain text

✦ The Group Policy Editor

✦ Computer Configuration and User Configuration nodes

✦ GP Containers and GP Templates

✦ The `gpt.ini` file

The Group Policy Object

The Group Policy Object or GPO is the object that contains Group Policy properties. The GPO is really a container, at the highest level, into which properties or attributes are stored. Policy is conveyed by association with a GPO . . . that is, its properties "rub off" on a user or computer object contained inside a GP target. GPOs have to be created and named for a particular container before their policies can be used.

Active Directory containers

Active Directory containers are the targets of the GPO. By establishing a link with a GPO, a container falls under the influence of the GPO and its policies. The containers that can be linked to GPOs are *sites, domains,* and *organization units.* But GP can also be associated with a standalone or computer; and all computers can be linked to their local GPO.

Group Policy links

GP links are the means by which containers are associated with GPOs. You can research links for a particular domain, as discussed later in this chapter. By "discovering" the links, you can establish which GPO is influencing a particular container and therefore its members (see the section "How Group Policy Works," later in this chapter).

The Policy

The Policy or Group Policy (GP) is the property of the GPO. The policy is the actual setting that is applied through the association discussed earlier. All GPOs have the same policies. You do not add or remove a policy from a GPO. But policy is activated in several ways. The policy first has to be *defined* and then possibly *enabled* or *disabled* or otherwise activated in the particular GPO. Once it has been enabled or defined, you can then manipulate the settings that comprise the policy.

Figure 11-4 illustrates a policy that needs to be defined before it can be made useful. In the figure, we have chosen to define a policy for the DNS Server. Once the policy has been defined, you can set its startup criteria. In this case, we have defined the DNS Server and set its startup parameter to *Automatic.* Other policies require you to simply enable or disable the policy, while others require definition, enabling, and then further configuration or setup.

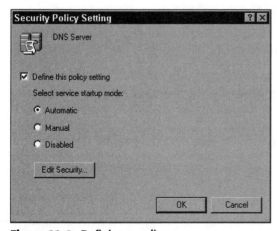

Figure 11-4: Defining a policy

Explain text

The explain text is accessed on the Explain tab of a policy. Not all policies have an explain text tab. Explain text essentially describes what the policy achieves and any instructions as to how to apply the policy, and even circumstances where you shouldn't apply the policy.

The Group Policy Editor

The Group Policy Editor (GPE) is the MMC snap-in that provides access to the configuration of a GPO. To edit or create a GPO for a container, you first have to load a used or new GPO into the GPE. The GPE is illustrated in Figure 11-5.

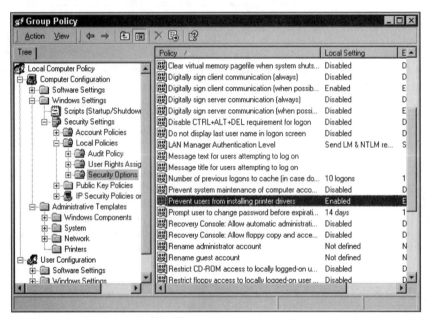

Figure 11-5: The Group Policy Editor

Computer Configuration and User Configuration

A GPO is divided into two nodes. These nodes are known as the Computer Configuration and User Configuration. Each node contains the policies for the respective security principal. You can apply policy to either of the nodes for any GPO.

Where GPOs Live

All GPOs store their information in two locations: the GP Container (GPC) and a GP Template (GPT). These objects are identified by a globally unique identifier (GUID), which keeps the objects in the two locations synchronized. When a GPO is born, information associated with it is transferred to the two locations.

For the GPT, the OS creates a folder for its use in the `Sysvol` structure in the `systemroot`. The actual folder name of the GPT is its GUID. A typical GPT folder looks like this:

```
systemroot\SYSVOL\sysvol\genesis.mcity.org\Policies\
{31B2F340-016D-11D2-945F-00C04FB984F9}
```

The GPC lives in the Active Directory. It builds itself a hierarchy of containers in the space it is given in the directory in which to store computer and user configuration information.

The GPC deals with the version (used for synchronization), status (enabled/disabled), and settings (of extensions) and any policy settings defined by extensions. The SYSVOL side of the GPO holds a list of client-side extensions, User Configuration state, Computer Configuration state (`registry.pol`), and registry settings that derive from administrative templates.

As a general rule, policy data that is small and seldom changes is stored in the GPC, while data that is large and changes often is stored in the GPT.

GPT structure

The default contents of the GPT structure are security related, but as you configure the user and machine environment, the GPT structure will begin to fill up with folders and information related to a broad range of GP and change management information.

Table 11-2 lists some of the folders and information that find their way into the GPT structure.

Table 11-2
The GPT Structure

Folder	Purpose
\ADM	This holds the ADM files that are associated with a GPT.
\MACHINE	This holds the REGISTRY.POL file that relates to machine registry settings.
\MACHINE\APPLICATIONS	This holds the AAS files used by the Microsoft Windows Installer.

Continued

Table 11-2 *(continued)*	
Folder	**Purpose**
\MACHINE\DOCUMENTS & SETTINGS	This holds files that are used to configure a user's desktop when he/she logs on to this computer.
\MACHINE\MICROSOFT\WINDOWSNT\SECEDIT	This holds the GPTTMPL.INI Security Editor file.
\MACHINE\SCRIPTS	This contains the startup and shutdown folders.
\MACHINE\SCRIPTS\STARTUP	This holds scripts and other files related to startup scripting.
\MACHINE\SCRIPTS\SHUTDOWN	This holds scripts and other files related to shutdown scripting.
\USER	This holds the REGISTRY.POL file that relates to user registry settings.
\USER\APPLICATIONS	This holds the AAS files used by the Microsoft Windows Installer.
\USER\DOCUMENTS & SETTINGS	This holds files that are used to configure a user's desktop.
\USER\SCRIPTS	This holds logon and logoff scripts.
\USER\SCRIPTS\LOGON	This holds scripts and other files related to logon scripting.
\USER\SCRIPTS\LOGOFF	This holds scripts and other files related to logoff scripting.

The GPT.INI file

In the root folder of each GPT, you will also find a file called the `gpt.ini`. There are two important entries in this file that are related to local GPOs:

1. `Version=x` This entry is the version number of the GPO, and x is the placeholder for a number placed by a version counter function. Typically, the version number is zero-based, and each time that you modify the GPO this counter is incremented by 1.

2. `Disabled=y` This entry refers to the local GPO and tells the dependant functions if the local GPO is disabled or not. If you disable the GPO, the value placed here is 0, and when you enable it, the value is changed to 1.

How Group Policy Works

The Windows 2000 Group Policy (GP) application hierarchy is typically site first, then domain, and then OU. In other words, if GP is set for a site, all objects in that site feel the effects of the GP, including the domain and all its members. If you then apply GP to a domain, the merged GP for all objects in the domain is inherited from the site and the domain. If you further apply GP to an OU, if GP is set for the domain and the site, then the GP on any object in the OU is a combination of all three.

So, the combined control in the OU may be derived from the domain policy and the site policy as well, unless the inherited policy is expressly blocked by a built-in override mechanism that can be enabled or disabled (discussed later in this chapter) and the access control mechanisms on groups and users discussed in Chapter 10.

You can also force policy directly on an object by linking the GPO to the object and then setting the link to forbid overriding.

Local or Non-Local GPOs

GPOs also come in two flavors — local GPOs and non-local GPOs — and since the local GPO is applied to a computer before the non-local GPO, the actual inheritance hierarchy for a computer is first local GPO, then non-local site, then domain, and finally OU. Also, local GPO is first applied to the computer, and then any policy that is to be applied from the DC takes place after the user logs in.

Each Windows computer has one local GPO that governs it. You can open the local GPO by running `gpedit.msc` from the command line on any Windows 2000 computer, or you can pull up the MMC snap-in from installed menu items (to customize the MMC, refer to Chapter 6). But it is important to remember that a non-local GPO can override the local GPO. The reason is coming up next.

GP Application

The architecture of Active Directory dictates that policy applied later to an object overrides policy that is applied earlier. In other words, if you remove the rights that allow a person to log on to a computer locally in the local GPO, and then later restore that right in a site or domain GPO, the restored setting becomes the effective control because it was applied later. The exception is that anything not defined does not change the existing control, and any control specifically enabled or disabled earlier is allowed to persist.

Tip Any GPO control state that is disabled or enabled in an earlier container persists. This is useful for controlling access and certain security mechanisms on individual computers, where specifically disabling an option prevents an administrator from enabling it unintentionally or on purpose at the non-local (domain) level.

It is also important to note that you can create multiple GPOs for a container. The order of control application is that policy applied later overwrites policy applied earlier. In other words, if you have two GPOs to an OU, any settings that say "yea" in the first GPO in the list are then overwritten by GPOs that say "nay" later in the list. This is called *administrative order,* and the order can be rearranged by using the Up and Down buttons, as illustrated in Figure 11-6.

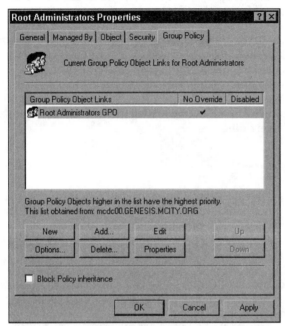

Figure 11-6: Applying the GPO link

When you set a No Override on a GPO by checking this option on the Group Policy tab, GPOs that are linked at the lower levels cannot override the higher GPO's effective settings. The use of No Override also prevents GPOs that are linked at the same level from overriding. When you have several links at the same level in the AD that are set to No Override, you need to arrange them according to a priority you determine. Links that are higher in the list have the priority.

It is important that you understand this when applying GP to a domain or even to a site. There are numerous settings that you will want to remain in force, and a local administrator might attempt to override you. As long as you set the No Override on the higher GPO, the setting you enabled will be enforced at the lower levels of the directory.

Note   The No Override setting is applied to a link, rather than to the actual GPO. The Block Policy inheritance setting is applied to the domain or OU, and it thus applies to all GPOs linked at that level or higher. Sites do not have a higher authority.

Conversely, you can also block inheritance of GP from higher GPOs. This is done by checking Block Policy inheritance on the GP tab of the Properties sheet of the domain or OU. This option does not apply to sites, because in terms of GP, they are the highest in the hierarchy. There is a catch (just when you thought you found a security flaw); the No Override option — if enabled — takes precedence.

To investigate the links maintained by a GPO, do this:

1. Open the Group Policy console in MMC by selecting the Group Policy tab on the container's property sheet. The path is Container ➪ Properties ➪ Group Policy tab ➪ Edit button.

2. Right-click the node (Site, Domain, or OU) in the GP console and select the Links tab. Then, select the domain in the drop-down menu, as illustrated in Figure 11-7, and click the Find Now button.

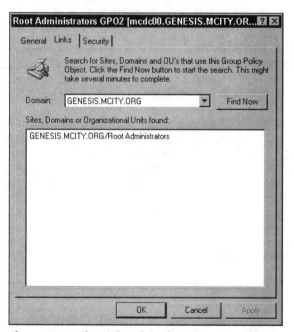

Figure 11-7: The Links tab in the GPO properties

When you edit a GPO, any settings you change are not immediately applied to the container's possessions, but the change in policy is immediate. The GPO settings are then applied to the object by default every 90 minutes. However, this can be changed, and we will discuss how shortly.

There is a possibility that conflicts can arise due to the application of GP. For example, an account lockout can occur when you set the number of attempts at a logon password too low. If a user gets the password wrong several times in succession, which can easily happen if the user has the caps lock on, you will need to reset the lockout post haste.

An account lockout could be the result of several security policies doing what they were supposed to do, but the results not being the original intention. To unlock an account in such a case, open the Active Directory Users and Computers snap-in and drill down to the user account. Go to the Action menu and select Properties. On the property page, select the Account tab. You will see that the Account Lock Out checkbox has been checked. The OS did this in compliance with GP. Uncheck the box, and the user will now be able to log in (as long as the caps lock is off).

Tip   While the GP of a parent container can override a child's GP, if the child's GP contradicts the parent, the child will prevail. Rather than creating a tug of war between the override, inheritance, and access control associations, you should strive to keep things simple and fully document all GP, group memberships, and any peculiar associations.

Filtering Policy

GP can also be filtered out of the range of security principals residing in security groups. In other words, you can narrowly define which security group of users or computers is influenced by GP. This is achieved by setting the discretionary access control list (DACL) permissions on the group. Not only does the GPO take effect on the security principals much faster, but you can also restrict a specific security policy from being able to create AD links to GPOs.

The DACL is a list of permissions on an object (in this case, a GPO). You use the DACL to allow or deny access to the GPO according to the membership in the group. There are two ways to apply the filter:

1. Right-click on the root node of a Group Policy console, click Properties, and then select Security.

2. A longer way around, which may or may not be appropriate, is to open to the container in Active Directory (site, domain, or OU), right-click, and select the Properties page option from the Context menu. Then click the Group Policy tab on the Properties page and select the GPO in the GPO list on this tab. Right-click the GPO, select Properties, and then select the Security tab.

Now you can specify which groups are influenced or not in the container by checking or unchecking the Apply Group Policy access control entry (ACE). You should also know that by default authenticated users have both the Apply Group Policy and Read permissions checked, but not Write or Full Control. What this means is that the users cannot modify the GPO. And you can thus also apply more stringent access to the GPO.

These techniques also allow you to use the Security tab on the GPO to determine which administration group can modify GP. We will be using such techniques to tighten the security of our domain, as demonstrated later in this chapter.

Delegating Control of GP

GP can be delegated as follows:

- ✦ Delegate GP link assignment for a site, domain, or OU.
- ✦ Delegate the creation of GPOs.
- ✦ Delegate the management of GPOs.

Delegation is performed through the delegation of rights to use MMC consoles and particular management snap-ins related to GP. These are themselves controlled through GPOs. To delegate access to GPO duties, you essentially control who has access to the Group Policy MMC snap-ins. The path to this is as follows: Drill down to the container in AD and right-click the item. Select Properties and then select Group Policy. Select a GPO, or if one is not created, then make one. Click Edit and you will load the Group Policy console. Drill down to User Configuration ⇨ Administrative Templates ⇨ Windows Components ⇨ Microsoft Management Console ⇨ Group Policy. Under the Group Policy node, you will find 12 policies related to Group Policy snap-ins.

Administrators can administer Group Policy by being a member of a domain administrator group or the built-in administrators group. Non-administrators have to be given *log on locally permission* before they can administer GP, and this is done under Computer Configuration ⇨ Windows Settings ⇨ Security Settings ⇨ Local Policies ⇨ User Rights Assignment ⇨ Log on locally.

Local GPOs

The local GPOs that exist on every Windows 2000 machine only have security settings configured (and most of them are disabled). The local GPO is stored in the %SYSTEMROOT%SYSTEM32\GROUPPOLICY directory. The following permissions are set through the DACLs:

- ✦ Administrators (Full)
- ✦ Operating System (Full)
- ✦ User (Read)

How GP is Processed

GP is almost entirely processed from the client side. The only service using GP that processes entirely from the server is the Remote Installation Service, and that's because a client-side OS does not yet exist to process policy.

A group of DLLs called client-side GP extensions performs client-side processing after first making a call to a DC for a GPO list. The processing order is obtained from the GPO list. The rule of precedence in processing is that Computer Configuration gets preference over User Configuration. However, what if a user is placed in one OU and his or her computer is placed in another OU? Which GPO becomes the effective GP conveyor? In Chapter 7, we suggested putting all your users into a small collection of OUs and then placing their computers into other OUs that could be associated with key management entities (KMEs).

The following GP behavior transpires to keep a sanity check on things. A feature known as the *Group Policy loopback* allows you to bestow GP based or dependent on the computer used. The loopback feature allows you to choose two modes by which you can govern choice of User or Computer Configuration.

Merge mode

When a user logs onto a computer and the loopback feature is in merge mode, the GP objects are read according to the User Configuration and then again according the Computer Configuration. By reading in the Computer Configuration last, the Computer Configuration is given priority. This means that the computer-related GP has a higher precedence than the user's GP. If the user's specific GP is not affected by the computer's configuration, then the User Configuration policy is applied.

Replace mode

This mode forces GP to ignore the user's GP configuration. In other words, only the GP in the Computer Configuration applies.

GP processing streams

GP processing can be performed asynchronously or synchronously. Asynchronous processing can occur on other threads, and thus the processing happens much quicker. Synchronous processing threads wait for one process to complete before they start. You can customize the processing behavior of GP processing, but you would only consider this for specialized applications in which you need to apply the GP as quickly as possible. The rule is that for speed, use asynchronous processing and for reliability, use synchronous processing.

GP refresh rate

The default refresh rate is every 90 minutes. Thus, any changes made to the GP that apply to a particular user or computer will only become effective in this default time. You can change the default using the GP setting in Administrative Templates. A setting of zero forces the refresh to kick off every seven seconds. You would configure a narrower refresh interval for tighter security application, or a specialized processing situation. The default refresh rate seems long and could be shortened to at least 60 minutes.

Note   Setting shorter refresh intervals causes increased network traffic, and very tight intervals on user computers can interfere with the work environment. Very long refresh intervals are easier on the network, but make for a less secure environment. The longest time is 45 days, and if you need to make a security policy change, such a time would be useless.

To change the setting, you need to edit the Default Domain Controllers GPO. This is linked to the DC's OU. Open the GPO and drill down to the Computer Configuration ⇨ Administrative Templates ⇨ System ⇨ Group Policy ⇨ Group Policy Refresh Interval for Computers node.

Tip   On several domain controllers we installed, the refresh policy was disabled. You may want to check that this is not the case on your DCs. The documented DC refresh rate is five minutes.

Administrative GP settings, such as Folder Redirection and Software Installation, only take place during or after the computer starts up or when the user logs on, and not during the periodic refresh period described earlier. There is an obvious reason for this. If software was targeted for removal, you would have a hard time explaining why the application began to remove itself while your user was using it.

Optional GP processing

Every client-side extension has a policy parameter for controlling the processing of GP. By default, the client-side extension only updates the GP when it determines at the refresh interval that the GP has changed. This is done for performance optimization. But for security purposes, you can make sure that at every refresh interval, GP will be refreshed even if the policy has not changed.

You should be very selective in applying this because you will see increased network bandwidth and slower GP refresh.

GP processing over low bandwidth

GP will set a flag on the client-side extension when low bandwidth networks are detected. When the flag is raised, the following GP processing takes place:

✦ Security policy is always processed.

✦ Policy in Administrative Templates is always processed.

✦ Software installation is skipped.

✦ Scripts are turned off.

✦ Folder redirection is skipped.

✦ Internet Explorer maintenance is turned off.

How does GP detect low bandwidth? The client-side extensions simply ping the DC and analyze the response data. But low bandwidth is relative. What's low to you and me in Miami could be as fast as blazes in the Land of Oz.

Using a built-in algorithm, GP works out the response rate based on data and time parameters and the connections being used. If the result of the calculation is equal to the 500Kbps default, then GP considers that a slow link and makes the necessary adjustments in GP processing. But you can change the default as you deem fit in the Computer Configuration/Administrative Templates/System/Group Policy node of the GPO. The exact policy is "Group Policy slow link detection." Remember to set this for users as well in the User Configuration node. The target policy in User Configuration is identical.

User Profiles also have a time-out policy over slow links. This is located in the Computer Configuration node, and the target policy is the Administrative Templates/System/Logon node of the GPE. If the extension cannot ping the server, it defaults to measuring file system performance, which is how NT measures performance. The policy can be configured for connection speed threshold in Kbps and a threshold transit time in milliseconds.

Specifying domain controllers for GP

When setting up your Active Directory infrastructure, it is important to be sure that GP settings are properly propagated and disseminated throughout the enterprise, and that replication is not a course for corrupted GP information.

You have several considerations. If you support a small enterprise that usually contains one DC on the same network as everyone else, you should not have to concern yourself where GP is edited. But in a large enterprise, you may want to studiously control the target DCs for GP changes, and who has the ability to make such changes.

We have discussed how you can delegate (or restrict) power to edit GP, and you can also determine which DC is the target to receive the changes. Problems can occur if you have more than one DC receiving GP edits and more than one administrator applying changes. Your GP edit may become overwritten during replication, and you could suffer GP editing collisions. And depending on the location of the DC, it might not always be accessible for GPO editing and creation.

There are two routes to setting domain controller options for GP. One way is via the GP Editor snap-in. The other way is via GP settings that allow you to set DC options by editing policy in the Administrative Templates node.

To access the setting in the former option, you need to open the Default Domain Policy and then select the root. In the View menu, you will now see a DC Options menu item. Select that item. The dialog box illustrated in Figure 11-8 loads.

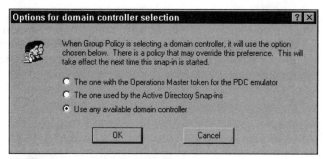

Figure 11-8: Domain controller options

The dialog box has three options. Choose the option that best applies to your network environment as follows:

✦ **The one with the Operations Master token for the PDC emulator:** This is the default option according to Microsoft documentation, but we have found that to not always be the case, especially when you have more than one DC on the same network segment. However, this option ensures that only one DC is the target for GPO creation and editing, and that the other DCs receive GP updates from one source. This option will force the console to use the same DC every time you or someone else uses it, which is why the option is part of the console and not the snap-in in the first place. In addition, you should limit the number of people that can apply GP in a certain domain, or you should schedule the GP tasks as part of change management. (The DC with the Operations Master token is usually the first DC created for a forest, but it can abdicate this honor if forced to.)

✦ **The one used by Active Directory Snap-ins:** Snap-ins include an option that allows you to change the DC that is the focus of the snap-in (all MMC consoles allow you to choose a computer). As long you are sure you are "aimed" at the right DC, this option will work. But if you don't pay attention to detail, this could be a problem down the road.

✦ **Use any available domain controller:** This option is the least desirable but would suffice, such as when working with a close-knit group or cluster of DCs on a fast network.

The option that we prefer overrides all the above by setting the option in GP. The GPO makes sure that all snap-ins select the primary domain controller emulator for a domain when editing a GPO.

You can also use the policy to specify how GP chooses the domain controller. In other words, you can specify exactly which DC should be used by setting the option as policy.

Drilling to the following policy can access these settings: Open the default domain GPO and drill down to User Configuration ⇨ Administrative Templates ⇨ System ⇨ Group Policy. The options in the policy are the same as the ones demonstrated in the DC options dialog box in Figure 11-8 and discussed earlier. The exact policy is called "Group Policy domain controller selection."

Putting GP to Work

As discussed earlier in this chapter, two key areas of GP and change management are software change control and security. These represent two key areas in change control and change management, which are serviced by the GP technology of Windows 2000.

The Software Policies

The software policies include policy to manage applications and Windows 2000 and its respective components. In the following examples, we demonstrate modification and manipulation of the settings and environment using the GPE snap-in.

To edit software GPOs, do the following:

1. Open the Active Directory Users and Computers snap-in and drill down to the site, domain, or OU in which you wish to locate your GPO. (These are often referred to as the SDOU containers, which stands for Site, Domain, or Organization Unit container.)

2. Right-click the container, select Properties, and then select the Group Policy tab.

3. Select the GPO link to edit or create a new GPO. Click the Edit button.

4. Expand the User Configuration node from its root through the following path: User Configuration ⇨ Administrative Templates ⇨ Control Panel ⇨ Display. In this example, we are going to set a policy, by disabling the Background tab, that does not allow the user to change the pattern and wallpaper on the desktop. This is illustrated in Figure 11-9.

5. Right-click the policy to modify it and then select Properties from the Context menu.

6. First check if the policy is implemented, defined, or enabled. If not, define or enable the item by checking it. Then choose the setting for the policy, as illustrated in Figure 11-9. Click Apply and OK to get back to the console.

That's all there is to making a simple software or Windows 2000 policy change. You will notice as you browse the software-related policies that some of these require you to add more details, such as path name and the like. Also, as your Windows 2000 software asset base grows, so will the number of policies.

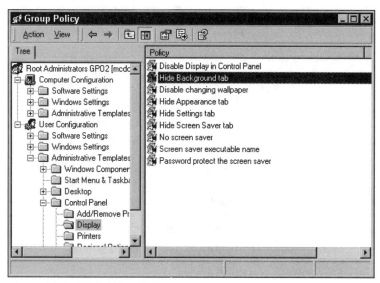

Figure 11-9: Editing the GPO

The Security Policies

These policies govern the extent of the security configuration of Windows 2000 networks. Security GP is available for deployment at every port that poses a security risk to the system as a whole, such as logon/logoff, communications, file systems, hardware and media, and so on.

Table 11-3 lists the GP related to security areas:

Table 11-3 Security GP	
GP	**Purpose**
Account Policy	These policies configure passwords, account lockout, authentication, Kerberos, and so on.
Local Policies	These policies configure auditing, user rights definitions, and so on.
Restricted Group	These policies group membership for security sensitive groups. The built-in Administrator group is an example of a restricted group.

Continued

Table 11-3 *(continued)*	
GP	**Purpose**
System Services	These policies configure security and the default startup behavior for services running on the computer (see Figure 11-4, which provides an example of applying policy on a service).
Registry	These policies configure security on the registry keys.
File System	These polices configure security on the file system.
Active Directory	These polices configure security on directory objects in each domain.
Public Key	These policies configure the encrypted data recovery agents, trusted certificate authorities, and other parameters related to your public key infrastructure or PKI.
IP Security	These policies configure policies related to IPSec.

Group Policy and Change Management: Putting It All Together

The number one rule of change control policy engagement is this: *Change control policy is enforced over the user by way of the computer.* In other words, the target of change control is the user's computer, and there are ways to enforce this, as you have already found out.

If you are able to enforce change policy over the computer, you are effectively enforcing the policy over the user. If the user has no control over the computer, the user is no longer in a position or in power to circumvent policy. While the GPO is divided into two configuration "lobes," User and Computer, the Computer Configuration takes precedence.

Caution With the power that GP yields, all the elements of Windows 2000 — access control, GP inheritance, GP override blocking, GP refreshing, GPO links, OU nesting, domain nesting, and more — it is possible to cook up a GP soup that no one can fathom, so take care in the planning stage.

But it becomes impractical to restrict a user to any particular computer. Terminal sessions would be impossible to manage, and you would have a hard time managing computers for roaming users and task-oriented staff. So, the user's identification to the network, or logon ID *and* the workstation's identification on the network, are merged or combined under Windows 2000 to provide the change control "blanket" that filters rights and privileges, and thus control, to the user *and* on the computers he or she uses.

This power is not only a boon with security and change control, it is also the main player in the functionality of IntelliMirror . . . having the user's desktop follow him or her to any PC, local or remote. Now that you have determined that you need change management and control, you also need enforcement. In other words, you create the change control body, provide policy to carry out the whims of the change control board, and enforce change control at all levels of the enterprise through GP (and other mechanisms you will find and customize to suit your environment).

Don't Accept the Default Policy

When it comes to dealing with GP on a Windows 2000 network, an unsafe attitude would be to assume that whatever Microsoft has installed as default Group Policy is adequate. It would be foolish to believe that the default settings are adequate for several reasons. First, every enterprise is different, so what you set in GP may work for you but not the company around the corner. Second, the criteria Microsoft has used to set the default GP is not widely known and is not appropriate for the majority of Windows 2000 users (and we don't think that Microsoft intended that either). And third, what Microsoft documented as being default was, in many cases, found not to be so when we installed and tested the services and components.

Where then do you start with GP? You could follow the cowboys who have stated that planning is for politicians and that the best way to tackle Windows 2000 is to just install it and to heck with all this ramp-up, pilot project, testing, lab tripe. Or you could take the more conservative approach and test. There might be a place for yahoo-type antics. If you need to get a server up and running just to use a particular Windows 2000 service as soon as possible . . . then you could get away with the install-and-run approach.

What we recommend is that you go back to the lab and browse GP. This is probably the best method of getting to know GP, and at the same time you will find out how the server is configured from the time you reboot it, after Active Directory promotion.

Without worrying about desirable change management policy for now, open the GPE of your new domain controller and start at the top of the directory. Starting with the site, work your way down through each container in the SDOU hierarchy and investigate the GPO links that are in place. You do this as discussed earlier by opening up the Properties page of the container and selecting the Group Policy tab. Edit each link you see in the container and then investigate the settings defined or enabled in each object, in both User and Computer Configurations.

It is unlikely at the birth of a new domain that any settings will be blocked or overridden in any way. So you can safely assume that the policy that has been set up for the site into which you have placed your root DC filters down to the "bottom" of the directory. In other words, any OU you now create will inherit from higher up. The domain, of course, is in the middle of this hierarchy, so you need to then investigate GP applied at the domain level to see what effects that may have on your desired control at the OU level. Each domain created gets a default domain GPO. Study the information and document it on your help desk or change management system. If you do not have a change management system, even a database or word processing document will do—it may get unwieldy, but for now it will do.

Establishing a GP Attack Plan

We discussed OU strategy and groups and users extensively in the earlier chapters. But before you go there, first sit down with the policy required by change management and security, and separate out policy required from one end of the forest to another from policy that is required from one end of a domain to another. If there is only one domain in the tree, this should not take long. This research does not have to be exhaustive because the list is going to change and is going to get very much longer.

With that Global Policy wish list, you edit the GPO first for the site in which you have located your root DC, the one that sits at the very top of the namespace in the twilight world between the Active Directory domain and the Internet domain or namespace. In that site, establish the policies you would like to see defaulted throughout the enterprise. A good example is password length. If there is no GPO linked to the site, then create one and open it up for editing. This is illustrated in Figure 11-10.

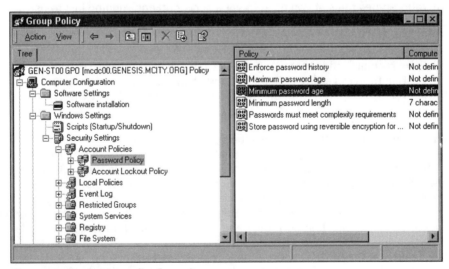

Figure 11-10: Setting policy for a site

Whatever policies you set at this level will then filter down to the various domains and OUs that you create. Notice that when you first went into the policy, the setting for password length was not even set. Then, if you open the domain GPO, you will find that the default length is 0 characters. That level of security is about as secure as a ripe apple in a tree. That's like asking the burglar to mind the store while you go out for five minutes.

Go through all the policies in the site and define what satisfies your change management and security plans for now. You first objective no doubt is to lockdown the network and install some form of security. Later, and before you deploy, you can batten down the hatches further as your needs dictate.

Dealing with Computer Accounts

Look at the logical plan we discussed in Chapter 7. It is feasible, most of the time (and we say most of the time because every company has its own requirements), to concentrate your computer accounts into the OUs that represent your KMEs. With that in mind, you can create OUs along KME lines or functions and collect your computers for the KME into the respective OU.

You can also, and it makes more sense to do so, add a bunch of computers to a security group and then locate that security group in the respective OU. Now, wherever that computer group is added, and it may be feasible that the group will appear in other OUs through association, the computers will be influenced in the order they received policy. For a group of computers, that order is first the OU in which they reside alone or in a group, and then later any other structure that is affected by GP that the group is admitted to. Remember that the last GP applied overrides the previous unless you expressly forbid it or block inheritance.

Getting Started

To discuss all the possible ways and means of enabling change control and management would require more than the scope of this book allows. However, the best place to start is to ensure that you fully understand the concepts. For starters, understand that the change control and management or configuration technologies deployed in Windows 2000 fall under an umbrella philosophy called IntelliMirror, which all started with the Zero Administration Windows (ZAW) initiative some years ago.

You could literally start anywhere in your enterprise implementing the IntelliMirror technologies. You might start with installation and rollout of the operating system, or with software installation and configuration, or with user settings, and so on. Every segment of the change management matrix is extremely complex.

The following suggestions provide a starting point for change configuration using GP- and IntelliMirror-related technologies. We prefer to start with configuring the logon/logoff scenario, locking down desktops, customizing and locking down the Start menu, redirecting folders, and so on. These areas represent, for us, the most urgent needs for clients already in business for some years and well entrenched in their business processes and resources. We can't go over everything here because there are over 500 settings to consider in Group Policy alone, so after you digest this short review, you will need to review all related technologies and stack them up against the change management you have begun to implement or are planning.

Customizing Logon/Logoff

There is a void time (where the user stares at the screen) between the computer starting up and the presentation of the login screen (where the user is asked to press Ctrl-Alt-Del). There is also a void time just after the user logs off.

In this void time, you can use policy to run various options. For example, you can run an anti-virus checker, pull or push something to the network, synchronize offline files and folders, run diagnostics, or gather intelligence into a data file that represents the user's activities while logged on at the machine. Depending on the applications, you can have a million reasons to run something in void time during logon/logoff. Figure 11-11 illustrates some of the policies that can be used to customize logon/logoff.

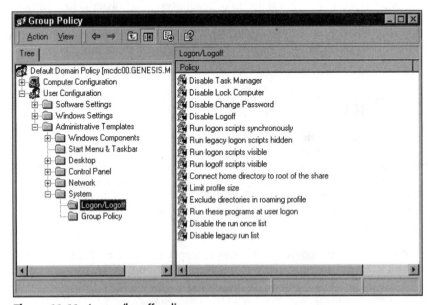

Figure 11-11: Logon/logoff policy

Locking Down the Desktop

Locking down the desktop is an important component in change control and takes us back to the first anecdote of the chapter. But GP can not only prevent users from causing problems by making unauthorized changes on their computers, GP can also enhance the scope and flow of users' work.

You can also create custom configurations for Internet Explorer to enforce download and browsing policy, and so on. Other policies that are extremely useful can achieve the following:

✦ Prevent users from changing the path to their My Documents folders. This will be often used if you need to ensure that users' documents and other work-related files are redirected to a server folder where they are certain to be backed up.

✦ Disabling the Control Panel prevents users from fiddling with the settings that govern their displays, network connections, communications, and so on. You can also hide specific Control Panel programs if your users need access to certain items.

✦ Hide access to the CD-ROM and the floppy disk drive. By taking away these ports, you prevent users from introducing viruses or rogue software to the network, and you ensure that the enterprise is able to control software piracy. (Remember that you have to lock down access to the Internet and e-mail as well to be 100 percent sure no viruses are being introduced to the systems.) You can also hide the hard disk drives from the users.

✦ You can disable the Command Console so that users cannot execute commands from the command line. For hackers, the command line on a computer is like making it to the first floor.

✦ You can also disable access to the registry editing tools like Regedt32 and Regedit.

Controlling the Start Menu

GP lets you disable portions of the Start menu so that they are not visible to the user. You can also customize the Start menu to reflect the needs of change management. For example:

✦ You can remove the Run menu item from the Start menu. This option also locks down the keyboard shortcut that opens the Run menu.

✦ You can add the Logoff item to the Start menu, which you want to do for terminal session users.

✦ You can also disable the drag and drop shortcut menus on the Start menu. This serves to prevent users from reordering or removing items and the sequence of items from the Start menus.

Folder Redirection

Each user is given access to a number of personal folders on a domain and on a workstation. These include My Documents, My Pictures, and Application Data. To protect a user's files, the intellectual property of the enterprise, and application data, a valuable feature of Group Policy enables you to redirect every user's collection of personal folders and application data to a network server.

There are three important benefits this bestows on the enterprise. First, by forcing data to be stored on the network server, both personal and application data can be regularly backed up.

Second, the data and files can be regularly frisked for viruses. Data that is stored on local machines in an enterprise is usually never backed up, and forcing antiviral technology onto every workstation is not a 100 percent surefire solution to the virus malady. Despite installing virus checkers onto every workstation, you can never ensure that everyone has the latest data file on the thousands of new viruses that are being launched every month. Protecting one server is easier than setting up processes to make sure every computer is adequately protected.

Third, you can ensure that no matter where users log on, even as terminals on an application server, they will always have access to their same folders and their application data will always be saved and accessible from the same place.

Redirecting folders is easy and can be done from any special folders you place into service. You can also redirect everyone to a share-point, and folder redirection can be enabled by group membership as well.

To enable folder redirection, drill down to User Configuration ➪ Windows Settings ➪ Folder Redirection in the SDOU of choice, as explained in the earlier section in this chapter, "Putting GP to Work."

To redirect a folder, do the following:

1. Right-click the folder, such as My Documents, and select Properties from the shortcut menu. The "My Documents Properties" dialog box will load.

2. Select the option "Basic - Redirect everyone's folder to the same location" in the drop-down list. Or to redirect according to group membership, you can choose the "Advanced - Specific locations for various user groups" option.

3. Then enter a target folder in the Target folder location field. You need to enter a UNC name here and use the %username% variable if you need to. You can also select the path via the Browse option. If you selected Advanced, you need to select the group this applies to.

4. Click the Settings tab on the dialog box to further configure the redirection criteria, such as rights, removal policy (which kicks in when policy is removed), and so on. Click Apply and then OK when you are done.

Now, after all that work, you need to make sure your backup and virus checkers "sweep" the new redirected resources.

Older Versions of Windows

As mentioned earlier, a mixed environment is problematic. No user or computer logging into earlier versions of Windows can be influenced by Windows 2000 GP. To protect your environment, you will need to continue to work with the older technologies, such as the System Policy Editor on Windows NT 4.0 (`poledit.exe`). Consider moving the older environments to Windows 2000 as soon as possible, either via upgrading to Windows 2000 Professional or via terminal services discussed in Chapter 25.

You have enough power in GP to go very far in achieving total control of your environment. Final words come in the form of a reminder. Often, we tend to forget about disabled users with special needs. You should take care to record the needs of these users because you can go a long way in making sure they do not have to suffer with what we take for granted.

Summary

This chapter discussed the importance of change control and change management and the ability to use Windows 2000 Group Policy to satisfy, as far as possible, the needs of the enterprise with respect to change and security.

We looked at how unmanaged change can lead to disaster. We also assessed our user and security environment to better understand the elements that need to fall under change management in the enterprise.

Our study of Group Policy was hardly a dent in this vast and critical component of Windows 2000. We looked at the elements of Group Policy Objects, how they are created and applied, and how the policy they embody is linked to objects that are deemed to require association with such policy.

We discussed how GP is inherited from sites to domains, and then to organization units, and how GP can be filtered via security groups that are placed into various containers. We finally stressed the importance of coming to grips with GP and understanding the effect it has on the health of the enterprise.

This chapter caps our sojourn into Active Directory services that spanned five chapters. But there is still plenty more to tackle. The Windows 2000 Help files cover more specific elements of Active Directory and its management realm.

✦   ✦   ✦

Networking and Communications Services

◆ ◆ ◆ ◆

◆ ◆ ◆ ◆

Without the network there is no Windows 2000. These chapters explore the networking standards and how Windows 2000 supports — and is supported by — the various protocols and internetworking technologies. We should stress that you need a thorough and complete understanding of TCP/IP to succeed with Windows 2000.

You will no doubt find much familiar ground in these chapters if you have NT experience. However, you are also introduced to new features in services such as DHCP, DNS, and Remote Access and Routing.

Windows 2000 Networking

This chapter provides a detailed discussion of Windows 2000 networking, including an explanation of TCP/IP, routing, network address translation (NAT), legacy protocols, and other topics related to Windows 2000 network configuration.

TCP/IP on Windows 2000

A little more than a decade ago, TCP/IP was used only by a relatively small number of computers connected to the Internet. As the number of networks connected to the Internet grew explosively, and as companies expanded to include more and more networks within the enterprise, TCP/IP has come to be the protocol of choice for most organizations. The reasons are many but commonly include standardization, ability to route, and of course, need for Internet connectivity.

Windows 2000 offers strong support for TCP/IP. It can be considered its primary protocol for and the foundation of Active Directory, which is the keystone of Windows 2000 networks. On the client side, the TCP/IP protocol enables full support for connecting to both peer and server computers running TCP/IP, the Internet, and TCP/IP-based services such as networked printers. On the server side, Windows 2000 offers all the configuration and management tools you would expect, including support for dynamic address allocation through DHCP, name resolution through DNS, NetBIOS name resolution through WINS, and a full range of configuration and troubleshooting tools.

Windows 2000 offers a few new features to support TCP/IP clients. Windows 2000 DHCP clients, for example, can request updates for their host records with a Windows 2000 DNS server, enabling DHCP clients to have up-to-date host entries in their domains. Windows 2000 DHCP servers can also initiate updates on behalf of TCP/IP clients, including non-Windows 2000 clients. Windows 2000 DHCP servers can request an update of the client's pointer record in DNS as well.

Tip   Windows 2000 includes other new features related to TCP/IP, such as Internet Connection Sharing (ICS), which enables a single Internet connection to be shared by other users on the local network. For more information on ICS and other remote access related topics, see Chapter 15.

On both the client and server sides, Windows 2000 provides easy TCP/IP configuration. As in other areas of Windows, you configure TCP/IP through various dialog boxes. But, Windows 2000 also includes command line utilities such as Ipconfig to help you view and manage a system's TCP/IP configuration. A very useful feature is the ability to change IP addresses and other settings without requiring the system to reboot.

Before you begin configuring and using TCP/IP in Windows 2000, you need to have a basic understanding of how TCP/IP works, which is provided in the following section. If you're already familiar with TCP/IP and are ready to configure it in Windows 2000, refer to the section "Configuring TCP/IP" later in this chapter.

TCP/IP Basics

TCP/IP stands for Transmission Control Protocol/Internet Protocol. The IP portion of TCP/IP provides the transport protocol. TCP provides the mechanism through which IP packets are received and recombined, ensuring that IP traffic arrives in a useable state. TCP/IP arose from the ARPANET, which was the precursor to today's Internet. TCP/IP is standards-based and supported by nearly every operating system, including all Microsoft operating systems, UNIX, Linux, Macintosh, NetWare, OS/2, Open VMS, and others. This wide compatibility and ability to interconnect dissimilar systems are the primary reasons TCP/IP has become so popular.

While TCP/IP is most often used to provide wide-area networking (such as on the Internet), it is an excellent choice as a local network transport protocol, particularly where organizations wish to serve network resources to local clients through an intranet. You can use TCP/IP as your only network protocol or use it in conjunction with other protocols such as NetBEUI. For example, you might use TCP/IP for Internet connectivity and use NetBEUI for sharing local resources. One main advantage to this option is that NetBEUI is non-routable and therefore relatively secure from unauthorized access from the Internet. As long as you don't bind the file and printer sharing client to your TCP/IP protocol, your local resources can be fairly safe from outside access.

IP Addressing

Any device that uses TCP/IP to communicate is called a *host*. This includes computers, printers, routers, and any other device that uses TCP/IP. As smart devices begin to pervade our daily existence, it's conceivable that even your washing machine or microwave oven will be a host, if not on the Internet, then at least on your home intranet.

Each host must have a unique *IP address* that identifies the host on the network so that IP data packets can be routed to and from the host. IP data packets are simply data encapsulated in IP format for transmission using TCP. Each address must be unique. Identical addresses on two or more hosts will conflict and prevent those computers from communicating properly. In fact, Windows 2000 shuts down the TCP/IP protocol on a computer if it detects an address conflict at TCP/IP initialization.

IP addresses are 32-bit values usually expressed in dotted decimal notation, with four octets separated by decimals, such as 192.168.0.221. Each IP address contains two separate pieces of information: the network address and the host address. How these two items of information are defined in the address depends on the address' *class*.

There are five classes of IP addresses: Class A to Class E. But there are only three classes you should concern yourself with for Windows 2000 networking: A, B, and C, which accommodate networks of various sizes. Class A networks yield the highest number of host addresses, and class C networks yield the lowest number. Table 12-1 lists information about each class. The designation w.x.y.z indicates the portion of the IP address that defines network and host ID portions of the address.

<table>
<tr><td colspan="5" align="center">Table 12-1
IP Address Classes</td></tr>
<tr><td>*Class*</td><td>*Network ID*</td><td>*Network Host ID*</td><td>*Number of Available Networks*</td><td>*Number of Hosts per Network*</td></tr>
<tr><td>A 1-126</td><td>w</td><td>x.y.z</td><td>126</td><td>16,777,214</td></tr>
<tr><td>B 128-191</td><td>w.x</td><td>y.z</td><td>16,384</td><td>65,534</td></tr>
<tr><td>C 192-223</td><td>w.x.y</td><td>z</td><td>2,097,151</td><td>254</td></tr>
</table>

As Table 12-1 indicates, the address range 127.x.y.z is missing. 127.x.y.z is reserved on the local computer for loopback testing and can't be used as a valid network address. Addresses 224 and higher are reserved for special protocols such as IP multicast and are not available as host addresses. In addition, host addresses 0 and 255 are used as broadcast addresses and can't be used as valid host addresses. For example, 192.168.120.0 and 192.168.120.255 are both broadcast addresses that are not available for use as host addresses.

The number of addresses in a given address class is fixed. Class A networks are quite large with over 16 million hosts, and class C networks are relatively small with just 254 hosts. The class you choose depends on how many hosts you need to accommodate, but most important, whether you are using a public address range or a private one. The address ranges listed here are reserved by convention for private networks:

✦ 10.0.0.0, subnet mask 255.0.0.0

✦ 169.254.0.0, subnet mask 255.255.0.0

✦ 172.16.0.0, subnet mask 255.240.0.0

✦ 192.168.0.0, subnet mask 255.255.0.0

However, if you're not connecting your systems to the Internet, you can use any IP address class, except the loopback addresses, for your needs. For example, a Class A addressing scheme can provide a large number of host addresses for your enterprise. But, if you're connecting the network to the Internet, at least some of the addresses need to be valid, public addresses that fall in the range described in Table 12-1 (excluding the private ranges mentioned previously).

If all your systems connect to the Internet directly rather than through a proxy server or other device that performs network address translation (NAT), each host must have a unique, valid public IP address. If you use NAT, only those hosts on the public side of the Internet connection need valid, public addresses. Those hosts on the private side can use one of the private address ranges described previously, but only NAT and proxy services will allow the public addresses to translate to the private ones. This means you can accommodate a large, class A network internally if needed. Figure 12-1 illustrates a network that uses private IP ranges but connects to the Internet through a proxy server and router with public addresses.

Subnetting

Each host in addition to an IP address needs a *subnet mask*. The subnet mask, like an IP address, is a 32-bit value typically expressed as four octets separated by periods. The subnet mask serves to strip the IP address into its two components, network ID and host ID, which enables traffic to be routed to the appropriate network and then to the destination host. Table 12-2 shows the subnet masks for the three standard network classes.

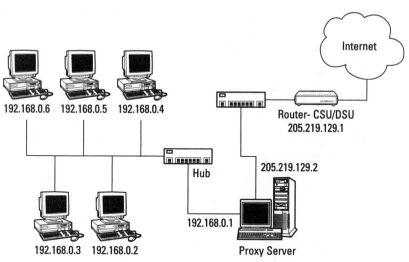

Figure 12-1: This network uses private IP addresses internally and a proxy server to connect to the Internet.

<table>
<tr><td colspan="3">Table 12-2
Standard Subnet Masks</td></tr>
<tr><td>*Class*</td><td>*Binary Value*</td><td>*Subnet Mask*</td></tr>
<tr><td>A</td><td>11111111 00000000 00000000 00000000</td><td>255.0.0.0</td></tr>
<tr><td>B</td><td>11111111 11111111 00000000 00000000</td><td>255.255.0.0</td></tr>
<tr><td>C</td><td>11111111 11111111 11111111 00000000</td><td>255.255.255.0</td></tr>
</table>

In addition to masking the host ID from the network ID, a subnet mask also can serve to segment a single network into multiple logical networks. For example, assume that your small company obtains Internet access from a local ISP. The ISP uses a class C address space to accommodate a group of clients, of which your company is one. The ISP uses a subnet mask of 255.255.255.224 to divide the network into eight subnets with 30 hosts each. Table 12-3 lists the host ranges for each subnet.

Table 12-3 Sample Subnet	
Subnet	**Host Range**
0	205.219.128.1 – 205.219.128.30
1	205.219.128.33 – 205.219.128.62
2	205.219.128.65 – 205.219.128.94
3	205.219.128.97 – 205.219.128.126
4	205.219.128.129 – 205.219.128.158
5	205.219.128.161 – 205.219.128.190
6	205.219.128.193 – 205.219.128.222
7	205.219.128.225 – 205.219.128.254

In this example, the ISP uses the first address range (subnet 0) for a routing cloud (a network subnet that functions solely for the purpose of routing) and the remaining seven subnets to accommodate the customers. You're the first customer and you get subnet 1, with addresses from 33 through 62. Figure 12-2 illustrates the network.

Tip   You can calculate subnet masks manually, but it's a real chore. Instead, download a copy of Net3 Group's IP Subnet Calculator from your favorite shareware/freeware site, such as www.tucows.com.

As you're designing your network and assigning IP addresses and subnet masks, keep in mind that all nodes on the same logical segment need to have the same subnet mask. This places them in the same logical network for routing purposes.

Note   A full understanding of subnetting is essential for the deployment of Active Directory across multiple sites in an enterprise, or even the Internet. See Chapters 8 and 9 in Part III.

Obtaining IP Addresses

There are two scenarios for assigning IP addresses: Your systems are connected to the public Internet, or they're not. Systems that are connected to the Internet directly rather than through a proxy server or other device doing network address translation must have unique, valid IP addresses, often termed "legal" addresses. This means you can't arbitrarily choose an address range for these systems. Instead, you need to obtain an address range from your ISP to ensure that you are using unique addresses (and that proper routing takes place). The number of addresses you need to obtain depends on how many hosts you will have on the public side of your proxy server or other NAT device, if any. For example, assume you configure your network so that a proxy server sits between the router and all other hosts. You therefore only really need three public addresses: one for each side of the router and one for the public side of the proxy server. The hosts on the private side of the proxy server can use private addresses.

If your network is not connected to the Internet, you could theoretically choose any network address range, including a public range in use by someone else, but you will not be able to connect your network to the Internet without Network Address Translation (NAT). You should, however, follow the convention of using one of the reserved address ranges for your private network (discussed previously in this chapter) because it will make life easier for you when and if you install NAT services, as discussed later in this chapter. You won't have to re-address all of your hosts later if you decide to connect the network to the Internet — you simply need to provide some means of network address translation through a router (such as RRAS discussed later) or a proxy server.

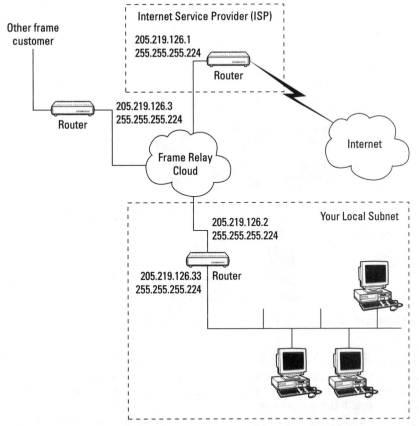

Figure 12-2: This ISP serves seven customers with a class C address space and a subnet mask of 255.255.255.224.

Gateways and Routing

TCP/IP subnets use *gateways* to route data between networks. Usually, a gateway is a dedicated router, but it could be any device running routing services, such as a Windows 2000 Server running the Routing and Remote Access Service (RRAS). The router maintains IP address information about remote networks so it can route traffic accordingly. Traffic coming from the local network with a public address gets routed out through the appropriate port on the router. Figure 12-3 shows a simple network with two connections to the Internet. The second connection provides redundancy in the event the primary connection fails.

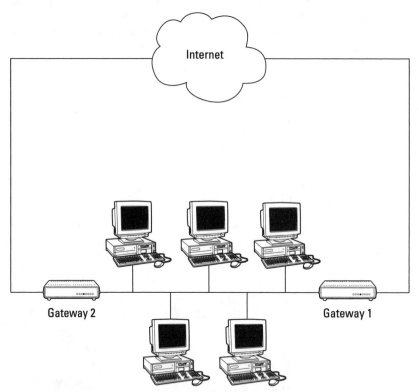

Figure 12-3: A simple network with two gateways to the Internet

On the host, IP inserts the originating and destination addresses into each packet. The host then checks (using its subnet mask) the destination address to determine if the packet is destined for another host on the same local network or for a host on another network. If the packet is for a local host, it is sent directly to the local host on the same subnet. If the destination host is on a remote network, IP sends the packet to the local host's *default gateway,* which routes the traffic to the remote network. You can configure multiple gateways if more than one is present on the network, and the local host attempts to connect through them in turn. If the default gateway is down, the host attempts to reach the next gateway in the list. The packet then travels through (possibly) several other routers until it reaches its destination.

Standalone subnets do not require gateways, since there is nowhere for the traffic to go—all traffic is local. Subnets connected to other subnets or to the Internet require at least one gateway.

Dynamic Host Configuration Protocol

Since every host must have a unique IP address, how you allocate and manage addresses is an important consideration when setting up an IP network. You can allocate addresses in one of two ways: *static addressing* or *dynamic addressing.* With static addressing, you simply assign a specific IP address to each host. The address doesn't change unless you manually reconfigure the host's TCP/IP properties (thus the term *static*). Static addressing is fine for small networks where you don't need to add or remove nodes or change addresses very often. As the number of nodes increases, however, static addressing can become an administrative nightmare. It's easy to accidentally assign conflicting IP addresses, and when subnet properties change (such as default gateway address), you have to manually reconfigure those properties.

Dynamic addressing through the Dynamic Host Configuration Protocol (DHCP) is a much better solution than static addressing, particularly for large networks or dynamic networks in which IP properties change. DHCP enables a DHCP server to automatically allocate IP addresses and related properties (gateway, DNS servers, and so on) to clients as the clients boot. A dynamically assigned address and associated properties is called a *lease.* Depending on the configuration at the DHCP server, a lease can have an infinite duration or can expire after a certain period. If a lease expires, the client can *renew* the lease to obtain a new IP address (which could be the same as the one provided by the previous lease).

DHCP in Windows 2000 offers some additional benefits in its interaction with Windows 2000-based DNS servers. A Windows 2000 DHCP client can request that the Windows 2000 DNS server update its host address in the DNS namespace for its domain. This means that even if the client receives a new IP address each time it boots, its host record in DNS will remain accurate. Windows 2000 DHCP servers can also request host record updates on behalf of clients, including non-Windows 2000 clients that don't support dynamic DNS updates.

Note See Chapter 13 for detailed information on DHCP and how to configure Windows 2000 DHCP clients and servers.

Domains and Name Resolution

IP hosts communicate using IP addresses, but humans would have trouble remembering more than a few IP addresses. How would you like to try to remember the addresses of all the Web sites you visit in a week's time? *Domain names, host names,* and *name resolution* help simplify internetworking for the user.

Domain names identify networks using a dotted format similar to IP addresses, except that domain names use letters (usually words) rather than numbers. For example, the domain mcity.org identifies a specific network in the .org domain. Each host in the mcity.org domain has a *host name* that identifies the host uniquely on the network. The host name and domain name combine to create a Fully Qualified Domain Name, or FQDN, that uniquely identifies the host. For example, a host in the mcity.org domain might have the host name server1. The FQDN for the host would be server1.mcity.org. If the domain contains delegated subnets, those figure into the FQDN, as well. For example, assume mcity.org includes a subdomain called support. The host named fred in support.mcity.org would have the FQDN fred.support.mcity.org.

Note   There is not necessarily a correlation between a computer's FQDN and e-mail address. While the user in the previous example might have the e-mail address fred@support.mcity.org, there is no correlation with his computer's FQDN. The host name and e-mail account have nothing in common.

There isn't any direct connection between FQDNs or IP addresses, so some method is required to *map* host names to IP addresses. When you type http://www.mcity.org in your Web browser, for example, some translation needs to occur to map www.mcity.org to its IP address so your browser can connect to the site. That's where DNS comes in.

DNS

DNS stands for Domain Name System, and DNS provides a distributed database to enable host names to be mapped to their corresponding IP addresses. DNS name servers maintain records for domains they host and respond to queries for a given host name with the IP address stored in the DNS database for that host. For example, when you attempt to connect to www.mcity.org, your computer submits a DNS request to the DNS server configured in your computer's TCP/IP properties to resolve the host name www.mcity.org into an IP address. The DNS server looks up the data, passes the address back to your computer, which connects to the site using the IP address. The only interaction you provide in the process is to enter http://www.mcity.org in your browser. Everything else happens behind the scenes.

Note   The name resolution process described here is simplified for the purpose of this discussion. See Chapter 14 for a detailed explanation of how DNS works.

WINS

Another name resolution service provided by Windows 2000 is Windows Internet Name Service, or WINS. WINS provides much the same service for NetBIOS names that DNS provides for TCP/IP host names. NetBIOS stands for Network Basic Input Output System. NetBIOS is an application programming interface (API) that programs can use to perform basic network operations such as sending data to specific computers on the network. NetBIOS is used by earlier Microsoft operating systems such as Windows 95 and 98 and Windows NT to identify and locate computers on the network. Just as DNS provides a means for mapping host names to IP addresses, WINS provides a means of mapping NetBIOS names to IP addresses for systems running NetBIOS over TCP/IP.

Note NetBIOS is not required in Windows 2000, as Windows 2000 uses host names and DNS to locate hosts on the local network. See Chapter 14 for a complete discussion on how to configure WINS.

Unless you are using applications that use NetBIOS over TCP/IP, you don't need to configure WINS on your computer.

Obtaining a domain name

You should obtain a domain name if your network will be connected to the Internet and to protect a root Active Directory domain name, discussed in Chapters 2 and 7. The domain will identify your computers on the Internet. Domain management was until recently managed by a single organization called InterNIC (now Network Solutions). You can register a domain through any authorized domain registration organization or connect to http://www.networksolutions.com to register your domain. See Chapter 14 for additional information on domain names and domain registration.

Preparing for Installation

You now have enough information to begin configuring TCP/IP. Before you jump in with both feet, however, do a little planning. Make sure you have the following information:

✦ **Network address and domain:** Obtain valid public addresses from your ISP for computers connected directly to the Internet. Decide which reserved address space (192.168.y.z or 169.254.y.z) you'll use for computers on private network segments. Register your domain with Network Solutions or another domain registration authority. This step is only required if you intend to use DNS to enable users on the Internet to connect to your network and its resources.

✦ **Identify an IP address for the computer:** Obtain the IP address(es) you will be assigning to the computer if you are allocating them statically. If you're using DHCP, you don't need to obtain a specific IP, nor do you need the IP address of a DHCP server on your network. Windows 2000 TCP/IP locates the DHCP server automatically at startup.

✦ **Subnet mask:** Determine the subnet mask you'll need for the computer based on the way your network is configured.

✦ **Default gateway(s):** Determine the IP addresses of the router(s) that will function as the computer's gateway(s).

✦ **DNS servers:** Determine the IP addresses of the computers that will serve as the client's DNS servers.

✦ **WINS servers**: Determine the IP addresses of the computers that will serve as the client's WINS servers (if any).

✦ **Bindings**: Decide which clients and services you'll bind to TCP/IP. For example, you'll probably not want to bind TCP/IP to the File and Printer Sharing service to prevent users on the Internet from potentially gaining access to your computer's shared resources.

Configuring TCP/IP

Windows 2000 installs TCP/IP by default unless you override the installation during setup. However, you can add the protocol later if it was not installed by Setup or was deleted after installation. The following sections explain how to install and configure TCP/IP.

Installing TCP/IP

To install TCP/IP, right-click My Network Places and choose Properties, or click Start ➪ Settings ➪ Network and Dial-Up Connections to open the Network and Dial-Up Connections folder. Right-click the network interface on which you want to install and configure TCP/IP, then click Properties to display the connection's property sheet. Make sure that TCP/IP isn't listed in the list of installed components, then click Install. Click Protocol ➪ Add. Select TCP/IP in the list of available components and click OK to add the protocol.

Configuring TCP/IP

Open the Network and Dial-Up Connections folder to configure TCP/IP. Right-click the network interface whose TCP/IP properties you want to change and click Properties to open its property sheet. Double-click TCP/IP or select TCP/IP and click Properties to display the General property page. Use the following list as a guide to configure options:

✦ **Obtain an IP address automatically:** Select this option to use DHCP to automatically obtain an IP address and other configuration properties.

✦ **Use the following IP address:** Select this option if you need to assign a static IP address.

✦ **IP address:** Specify a static IP address in dotted octet format.

✦ **Subnet mask:** Specify the subnet mask for the interface in dotted octet format.

✦ **Default gateway:** Specify the default gateway your computer should use to route non-local IP traffic.

✦ **Obtain DNS server addresses automatically:** Select this option to automatically retrieve the list of DNS servers from a DHCP server. This option is only available if you obtain the IP address automatically.

✦ **Use the following DNS server addresses:** Select this option to statically assign DNS server IP addresses.

✦ **Preferred DNS server:** Specify the IP address of the DNS server you want to use by default for resolving host names to IP addresses.

✦ **Alternate DNS server:** Specify the IP address of the DNS server you want to use for resolving host names if the preferred DNS server is unavailable.

These properties are sufficient for computers connected in a small private network, but in most cases, you'll need to configure additional properties. Click Advanced on the General tab to access the Advanced IP Settings property sheet. The following sections explain the options on each property page.

IP settings

Use the IP Settings tab to configure additional IP addresses for the computer and additional gateways. The Add, Edit, and Remove buttons in the IP addresses section lets you add, modify, and remove IP addresses and associated subnet masks on the computer. You might add multiple IP addresses to a server to host multiple Web sites, for example, with each site at its own IP address. Click Add to display a simple dialog box in which you type the new IP address and subnet mask to add. Select an existing address and click Edit or Remove to modify or remove the address.

Use the Add, Edit, and Remove buttons in the Default Gateways section to add, modify, or remove gateways. In small networks, there is often only one gateway, but in larger networks, multiple gateways are often used to provide fault tolerance and redundancy, enabling users to continue to connect outside their local network should one gateway become unavailable. Click Add to specify the IP address of another gateway, or select an existing address and click Edit or Remove to modify or remove the selected gateway, respectively. The metric value of a gateway specifies the relative cost of connecting through the selected gateway. When routing is possible through more than one gateway, the one with the lowest metric is used by default.

Tip   Here's an example of when the metric value comes into play. Assume your network has two connections to the Internet. Connection A is the one you want to use most because you pay a flat, monthly fee for it. Connection B is charged by bandwidth usage, and you only want to use B when A is unavailable. So, you'd assign a metric of 1 to A and a higher value to B to ensure that traffic always goes through A if it's available.

The Interface metric value on the IP Settings page specifies the relative cost of using the selected network interface. The default value is 1. This setting performs the same function for multi-homed systems (those with multiple network interfaces) as the metric value assigned to the default gateway(s). However, this value determines which interface is used to route traffic when multiple interfaces can be used to route the traffic. The interface with the lowest metric is used by default.

DNS

Use the DNS tab (Figure 12-4) to configure DNS settings for the connection. In addition to specifying DNS servers, you can configure other options that control the way the client performs name resolution and enable dynamic DNS updates. The following list explains the available options:

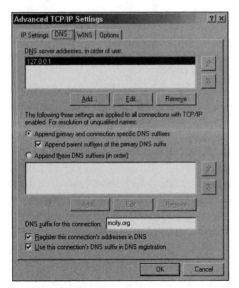

Figure 12-4: The DNS tab controls how the client interacts with DNS servers.

✦ **Append primary and connection specific DNS suffixes:** Select this option to append the primary DNS suffix and connection-specific DNS suffix to unqualified host names for resolution. You define the primary DNS suffix for the computer through the computer's Network Identification property page (right-click My Computer, choose Properties, click Network Identification). The primary DNS suffix applies globally to the system unless overridden by the connection-specific DNS suffix, which you set in the property "DNS suffix for this connection" (described later). For example, assume your primary suffix is mcity.org and your connection-specific DNS suffix is support. mcity.org. You query for the unqualified host name fred. This option then causes Windows 2000 to attempt to resolve fred.mcity.org and fred.support.mcity.org. If you have no connection-specific DNS suffix specified, Windows 2000 will only attempt to resolve fred.mcity.org.

✦ **Append parent suffixes of the primary DNS suffix:** This option determines whether or not the resolver attempts resolution of unqualified names up to the parent-level domain for your computer. For example, assume your computer's primary DNS suffix is `support.mcity.org` and you attempt to resolve the unqualified host name `jane`. The resolver would attempt to resolve `jane.support.mcity.org` and `jane.mcity.org` (attempting to resolve at the parent level as well as the computer's domain level).

✦ **Append these DNS suffixes (in order):** Use this option to only append the specified DNS suffixes for resolving unqualified names.

✦ **DNS suffix for this connection:** Use this option to specify a DNS suffix for the connection that is different from the primary DNS suffix defined in the computer's Network Identification property page.

✦ **Register this connection's addresses in DNS:** Select this option to have the client submit a request to the DNS server to update its host (A) record when its host name changes or IP address changes. The client submits the full computer name specified in the Network Identification tab of the System Properties sheet along with its IP address to the DNS server. You can view the System properties through the System object in the Control Panel, or right-click My Computer and choose Properties.

✦ **Use this connection's DNS suffix in DNS registration:** Select this option to have the client submit a request to the DNS server to update its host record when the host name changes or IP address changes. The difference from the previous option is that this option registers the client using the first part of the computer name specified in the System properties along with the DNS suffix specified by the option "DNS suffix for this connection" on the DNS page. You can use this option along with the previous option to register two different FQDNs for the host.

Tip Use the DNS tab when you need to add more than two DNS servers.

WINS

Use the WINS tab of the connection's TCP/IP properties to configure WINS services. You can use the Add, Edit, and Remove buttons in the WINS addresses group to add, modify, and remove WINS servers by IP address. The following list explains the other options on the page:

✦ **Enable LMHOSTS lookup:** Select this option to enable the computer to use a local LMHOSTS file to resolve NetBIOS names to IP addresses. LMHOSTS provides a way to supplement or even replace the use of WINS servers to resolve NetBIOS names. See Chapter 14 for more information on using LMHOSTS.

✦ **Import LMHOSTS:** Click to import an LMHOSTS file into your local LMHOSTS file.

✦ **Enable NetBIOS over TCP/IP:** Select this option to use NetBIOS over TCP/IP (NetBT) and WINS. This option is required if the computer communicates by name with other computers running earlier versions of Windows 9*x* or NT. NetBT is not required in a homogenous Windows 2000 environment or when connecting to computers on the Internet through DNS.

✦ **Disable NetBIOS over TCP/IP:** Select this option to disable NetBT in those situations where it is not needed (see previous item).

✦ **Use NetBIOS setting from the DHCP server:** Use this option to have the DHCP server automatically assign WINS settings.

Options

The Options tab of the TCP/IP properties lets you configure IP Security (IPSec) and IP Filtering options. IPSec provides a means for you to selectively permit and deny IP traffic based on policy settings and offers a way to very tightly control IP traffic coming to and from your computer. To enable and configure IPSec, select IP Security and click Properties. In the IP Security dialog box, select "Use this IP security policy," then select the desired policy from the list of available policies and click OK.

Note IPSec and configuring IPSec policies are discussed in Chapter 3 and Chapter 11 respectively.

TCP/IP filtering provides a less refined way than IPSec of controlling IP traffic to and from your computer, and is useful when you need to restrict traffic on a global scale and don't need the level of control offered by IPSec. Select TCP/IP Filtering and click Properties to configure filtering. Figure 12-5 shows the TCP/IP Filtering dialog box. As the illustration indicates, you can configure traffic for TCP ports, UDP ports, and IP protocols to permit all or permit only those ports or protocols specifically listed.

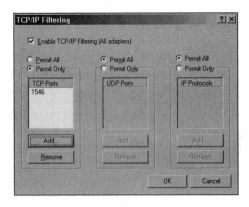

Figure 12-5: Use the TCP/IP Filtering dialog box to control traffic based on TCP ports, UDP ports, and IP protocols.

IP Routing

Except in self-contained private networks, routing plays an important role in TCP/IP. Routing enables packets destined for external subnets to reach their destinations and for traffic from remote networks to your own to be delivered to your network. Windows 2000 includes a service called Routing and Remote Access (RRAS) that enables a Windows 2000 server to function as a dedicated or demand-dial router (establishing connections only as needed). This section of the chapter discusses IP routing and the routing elements of RRAS in particular.

IP Routing Overview

A *router* works in concert with other network hardware to direct network traffic to its intended destination. For example, when you open your Web browser at the office and connect to `http://www.cnn.com` to check the current news, your network router directs the traffic out to the Internet, where other routers take care of getting the traffic to the site, then back again with the responses. Another example is when you dial into your ISP from home. The ISP's router(s) connects its network to the Internet and processes traffic going to and from your computer, and to and from the other connected customers' computers.

A typical router essentially sits on the fence between two or more subnets. This fence is typically known as a *hop,* and each time a packet traverses a router, its *hop count* is incremented. The router exists on all subnets to which it is connected, and therefore has connectivity to each subnet. When traffic comes into the router from a particular interface, the router directs the traffic to the appropriate interface. Figure 12-6 illustrates a typical routing situation. If the number of hops a packet takes to reach a destination is determined to be excessive by a router, the packet will be terminated and a message will be sent back to the sender indicating that the packet expired in transit. This is a safeguard that prevents data that cannot be routed to an interface from eternally moving around the Internet. The typical hop limit is 30 for most routers.

A router examines each packet that comes in to determine the destination network for the packet. It does this by examining the destination address stored in the packet's header. The router then decides which of its interfaces to use to route the traffic and sends it on its way. For example, assume that a router has three interfaces: one for the local network, one for another local network, and a third that connects to the Internet. Assume that the first local network (A) is on subnet 208.141.235.33 – 208.141.235.62 and the second local network (B) uses 208.141.235.129 – 208.141.235.158. A packet comes into the router from subnet A with the destination address 208.147.235.137. The router routes the packet out through the interface connected to subnet B. Another packet comes in with the destination address 205.135.201.130, so the router sends that packet out through the interface connected to the Internet because it doesn't belong in either of the local subnets.

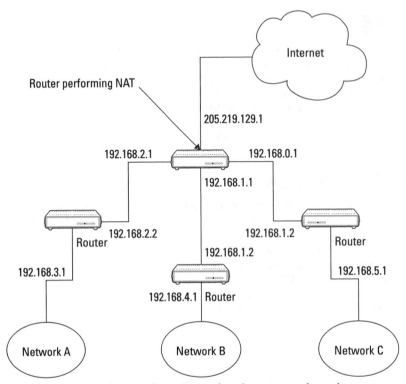

Figure 12-6: Several networks connected to the Internet through routers

Routers use *routing tables* containing *routes* to determine where to send packets. Routes help the router know where different networks are located relative to its interfaces so it can send packets out on the appropriate interface and have them delivered to the proper destination. Each route in the routing table falls into one of the following types:

✦ **Network route:** These provide a route to a specific network ID, and therefore to all host addresses within that network.

✦ **Host route:** These provide a route to a specific host, defining not only the network but also the address of the host.

✦ **Default route:** The default route is used to route all traffic for which there is no specific network route or host route. For example, a router connecting a local network to the Internet would have a default route pointing all traffic to the Internet interface.

Each route in the routing table has certain general properties:

✦ **Network ID/host address/subnet mask:** These properties identify the destination network ID or host address and the destination subnet. The router checks destination addresses in packets against these entries to determine a match. If the packet address matches the criteria, the router uses the forwarding address and interface data associated with the route to process the packet.

✦ **Forwarding address:** The router forwards matching packets to this address. The address could be that of another router or the address of a network interface on the local router (directing the traffic out a specific port on the router).

✦ **Interface:** This is a port number or other logical identifier of the port through which the traffic is routed for the given route.

✦ **Metric:** The metric specifies the relative cost of the route based on cost, available bandwidth, and so on. Where multiple routes exist to a given network or host, the route with the lowest metric is used.

So, when a packet comes in to the router, the router checks the destination address in the packet's header against the routing table to determine which route applies to the packet. If the router matches the destination address with a route, it forwards the packet using the forwarding address associated with the route. If the router finds no matching route, it forwards the packet using the default route (if one is configured on the router). The default route is used to handle any traffic for which there is not a specific route.

How do routers learn their routes? One method is for routers to learn routes dynamically from other routers and propagate them to other routers. Routers communicate with one another using routing protocols, with the two most common protocols for IP routing being Routing Information Protocol (RIP) and Open Shortest Path First (OSPF). Windows 2000 supports both (and can support additional protocols). RIP and OSPF are explained shortly.

A second method is for routers to use static routes. When you configure the router, you create the static route, which creates the static route entry in the routing table. A router can use static routes to handle all its traffic, a common situation for small to mid-sized organizations. For example, if you only connect a few local subnets to the Internet, you can use static routes to handle all traffic, with a default route handling traffic to the Internet. You'll read more about static routes later in the section "Configuring Static Routes."

RIP

RIP for IP, one of the two routing protocols included with Windows 2000 for routing IP traffic, offers the advantage of being relatively easy to configure. RIP is appropriate mainly for small to mid-sized businesses because it is limited to a maximum hop count of 15. RIP considers any address more than 15 hops away to be unreachable.

When a router using RIP first boots, its routing table contains only the routes for physically connected networks. RIP periodically broadcasts announcements with its routing table entries so adjacent routers can configure their routes accordingly. So, after a router starts up, it uses RIP announcements from adjacent routers to rebuild its route table.

RIP also uses triggered updates to update routing tables. Triggered updates occur when the router detects a network change, such as an interface coming up or going down. The triggered updates are broadcast immediately. Routers that receive the update modify their route tables and propagate the changes to adjacent routers.

 Note   Windows 2000 supports RIP v1 and v2. RIP v2 adds additional features such as peer security and route filtering.

OSPF

OSPF offers an efficient means of handling routing for very large networks such as the Internet. OSPF uses an algorithm to calculate the shortest path between the router and adjacent networks. OSPF routers maintain a *link state database* that maps the inter-network. The link state database changes as each network topology change occurs. Adjacent OSPF routers synchronize their link state databases and recalculate their routing tables accordingly.

Because of its scalability, OSPF is geared toward large networks. It's also more complex to configure. If yours is a very large network, OSPF could well be a good choice for your routing needs. For smaller networks, consider using RIP. In situations where you're only connecting a few networks together, static routes could be the best and easiest solution of all.

Microsoft Routing and Remote Access Service

In addition to providing remote access services to enable a Windows 2000 server to act as both a dial-up server and client, RRAS enables a Windows 2000 server to function as a router for persistent connections and as a demand-dial router, connecting only when requested by a client to do so. For example, you might have two divisions of a company that need to transfer data between networks only occasionally. Maintaining a leased line or a direct Internet connection between the two isn't feasible because of the cost involved, so you set up a demand-dial router that will call the other router (over a dial-up connection, for example) when any traffic needs to be routed to the other network.

Configuring RRAS for routing

Although Setup installs RRAS by default when you install Windows 2000 Server, you still need to enable the service to begin configuring and using it. To do so, choose Start ➪ Programs ➪ Administrative Tools ➪ Routing and Remote Access to open the RRAS console. Right-click the server in the left pane and choose Configure and Enable Routing and Remote Access to start the RRAS Setup Wizard. You can use the wizard to automatically configure RRAS for specific applications or configure the service manually. This section explains the options offered by the wizard if you choose the Network Router option. See Chapter 15 for detailed information on configuring RRAS as an Internet gateway, remote access server, or VPN server.

If you enable RRAS and choose to configure it manually, then later decide you'd like to run the wizard, you can do so, but you will lose the current configuration settings. To reconfigure the service through the wizard, open the RRAS console, right-click the server, and choose Disable Routing and Remote Access. After the service stops, right-click the server again and choose Configuring and Enable Routing and Remote Access.

The wizard prompts for the following information if you choose the Network Router option:

✦ **Protocols:** Specify the protocols to be supported, which must already be installed on the RRAS server. All installed protocols are enabled for RRAS by default. You can, however, disable specific protocols after the wizard finishes.

✦ **Use demand-dial connections:** Select Yes if you want to enable demand-dial connections or No to disable them. You can change the configuration easily afterwards to enable or disable demand-dial connections if you're not sure at this point.

✦ **IP address assignment:** You can choose to assign addresses through DHCP (see previous option) or from a static address pool. If you choose to use a static pool, the wizard prompts you for the range of addresses to use.

You also can allow remote clients to request a pre-assigned IP address configured at the client side. See the section "Configuring Protocols" later in this chapter for a detailed explanation.

Configuring a Basic Router

As mentioned previously, RRAS can use static routes, dynamic routes, or a combination thereof to provide routing services. This section of the chapter explains how to set up a simple router that uses static routes rather than dynamic routing. Most of the steps in this section are also applicable to a dynamic router, so you should read this section before moving on to "Dynamic Routing," later in this chapter, even if you won't be using static routes.

Configuring the router address

By default, the router uses the first IP address bound to an interface to process routing tasks on that interface. An interface that has only one address assigned therefore doesn't require configuration of its address. You might, however, have multiple addresses assigned to each interface for other purposes. In such a case, you need to configure the address the router interface will use.

To do so, open the RRAS console by choosing Start ➪ Programs ➪ Administrative Tools ➪ Routing and Remote Access. In the console, expand the IP Routing branch and then click General. In the right pane, right-click the interface you want to configure and choose Properties to display its property sheet. Set the IP address, subnet mask, and gateway (if required) for the interface on the Configuration page. Click Advanced if you need to specify a metric for the interface.

Configuring static routes

After you set up RRAS for routing, you need to either add static routes or configure the router to use RIP or OSPF. The exception is when you have only two networks connected by a router. In this situation, the router can route the traffic without a specific route.

To add a static route, open the RRAS console and expand the IP Routing branch. Click Static Routes, then right-click the right pane (or on Static Routes) and choose New Static Route to display the Static Route dialog box (Figure 12-7). The following list explains the options:

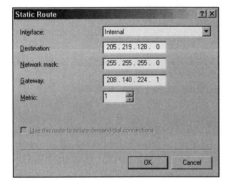

Figure 12-7: Use the Static Route dialog box to add a static route.

✦ **Interface:** Select the network interface to be used to forward packets that fit the criteria for the route. For example, to route traffic destined for the Internet, select the network interface on the server that is connected to the Internet.

✦ **Destination:** Specify the address criteria for matching packets. RRAS will check the destination address in the packet header against this address to determine if the route applies to the packet. You can specify a network address, host address, or a default route or 0.0.0.0. For a network address, use the low broadcast address for the network. For example, for the class C network 205.219.128.*x*, use 205.219.128.0. For a host, specify the actual IP address of the host.

Note Creating a default route using 0.0.0.0 causes all traffic for which there is no other applicable route to be forwarded through the interface defined by the default route entry.

✦ **Network mask:** Specify the network mask for the destination network or host. For a default route, enter 0.0.0.0.

✦ **Gateway:** This is the address to which the packets will be forwarded for this route and must be an address directly reachable on the router's external network segment (interface for the route). For example, you might specify the address of the router port on the same subnet for the next adjacent router.

✦ **Metric:** Specify a value to define the relative cost for the route. A lower metric indicates a lower cost. In many cases, administrators use the number of hops to the destination as the metric. When multiple routes apply to a given packet, the route with the lowest metric is used unless it is unavailable.

✦ **Use this route to initiate demand-dial connections:** Select this option to have the router initiate a demand-dial connection when it receives packets applicable for the selected route. This option is available only if at least one demand-dial interface is configured for the router.

Create static routes to accommodate each specific network segment in your network. Create a default route to handle all other traffic.

Adding and configuring a demand-dial interface

You need to add a demand-dial interface if you're installing RRAS to include the ability to function as a demand-dial router as well as a LAN router. A demand-dial router automatically dials a connection to a remote network when traffic from the local network needs to be routed to the remote network reachable through the demand-dial connection as defined by the route for that network.

To install a demand-dial interface, open the RRAS console and expand the server where you want to install the interface. Right-click Routing Interfaces in the left pane and choose New Demand-Dial Interface to start the Demand Dial Interface Wizard. The wizard prompts for the following information:

✦ **Interface name:** Specify a friendly name for the interface. RRAS by default suggests the name Remote Router. Keep in mind that if you configure the demand-dial interface to allow remote users (routers) to connect to this interface, the interface name is automatically used as the local account name. Using the suggested name Remote Router, for example, causes Windows 2000 to create a user account named Remote Router.

✦ **Connection type:** You can select between physical devices such as modems, ISDN, network adapters, and so on, or specify that the connection will use a virtual private networking (VPN) connection. Selecting the VPN option will cause the wizard to also prompt you for the tunneling protocol to use (PPTP or L2TP). See Chapter 15 for detailed information about VPN and tunneling protocols.

✦ **Phone number or address/alternates:** For a dial-up device, specify the phone number of the remote interface. Specify the IP address of the remote interface if connecting through a non-dial-up device (such as a physical network connection).

✦ **Route IP packets on this interface:** Select this option to enable IP routing on this demand-dial connection. TCP/IP must already be installed on the server.

✦ **Route IPX packets on this interface:** Select this option to enable IPX routing on this demand-dial interface. IPX must already be installed on the server.

✦ **Add a user account so a remote router can dial in:** Select this option if you want to create a user account remote routers can use to dial in to this demand-dial connection. When the remote router receives a packet that needs to be forwarded to the local demand-dial interface, the remote router uses the account and password stored in its dial-out credentials to connect to the local router. The credentials at the remote router must match the account and password you create through the wizard. See "Dial-out credentials" later in this list to configure the local account and password that the local router will use when connecting to remote routers.

✦ **Send a plain-text password if that is the only way to connect:** Select this option to allow RRAS to transmit its credentials using plain text rather than encryption if the remote router doesn't support encryption or doesn't support the types of encryption supported by the local router.

✦ **Use scripting to complete the connection with the remote router:** Use this option to specify a script RRAS will use when connecting to the remote router. Scripts can be used to automate the logon process and other connection tasks. Scripts are most applicable to dial-up connections that require menu-based selections to authenticate and log on (such as SLIP servers). SLIP stands for Serial Line Interface Protocol and is a connection protocol typically found on older, UNIX-based servers.

✦ **Dial-out credentials:** Specify the user name and password the local router will use to authenticate its access to the remote router. On a remote Windows 2000 router, you would use the option "Add a user account so a remote router can dial in" discussed previously to configure the associated account on the remote router.

Setting demand-dial filters

By default, RRAS allows all IP traffic through the demand-dial interface. However, you can create filters to restrict the type of traffic allowed. For example, you might want to restrict TCP port 80 to block Web browser traffic through the interface. You can create filters to restrict traffic going to or from specific networks, or you can create a filter that blocks specific packets to or from all addresses. The demand-dial interface will establish a connection to the remote router only if the packet is not blocked by the configured filters.

To configure filters, open the RRAS console and open the server on which you want to configure filters. Open the Routing Interfaces branch. In the right pane, right-click the interface where you want to configure filters and choose Set IP Demand-dial Filters to display the Set Demand-dial Filters dialog box, shown in Figure 12-8.

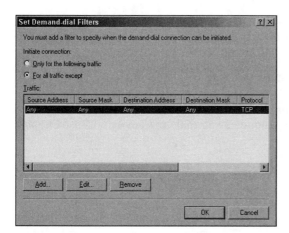

Figure 12-8: Use filters to restrict traffic through the demand-dial interface.

Configure the filter using the following list as a guide, then click OK and repeat the process to add any other required filters:

✦ **Source network:** Select this option to base the filter on the network from which the packet was sent. Specify an IP address and subnet mask to define the source network or host.

✦ **Destination network:** Select this option to base the filter on the destination address in the packet's header (where the packet is going). Specify the address and subnet mask of the destination network or host.

✦ **Protocol:** Specify the protocol type to filter. Select Any to filter all traffic or select a given protocol type and specify the accompanying information, such as source and destination ports.

Setting permitted dial-out hours

You might want to restrict a demand-dial connection to specific hours to limit the times at which the router will forward traffic on the interface. For example, you might want to disable the demand-dial interface during the weekend. To configure dial-out hours, open the RRAS console and then open the server you want to configure. Click the Routing Interfaces branch, then right-click the demand-dial interface and choose Dial-out Hours. Use the Dial-out Hours dialog box to specify the hours at which the interface can be used. The options in the dialog box are self-explanatory.

Changing dial-out credentials

You can modify the credentials the router uses to connect to the remote router when it initiates a demand-dial connection. You might have entered it incorrectly when you set up the router, the remote administrator may have changed the account at the other end, or you might need to change the account and password for other reasons. Open the RRAS console and the server you want to modify. In the RRAS console, right-click the demand-dial interface you want to change and click Set Credentials. Specify the new user name, domain, and password as needed.

Setting dialing properties

In some situations, such as when you're using a modem connection, you'll want to configure dialing properties such as redial attempts, redial interval, idle time before disconnect, and so on. To configure dialing properties, open the RRAS console, open the Routing Interfaces branch, right-click the demand-dial interface, and choose Properties. Use the controls on the General and Options property pages to configure the dialing properties. The options are self-explanatory. For more information on configuring modems and dial-up connections, see Chapters 6 and 15.

Configuring security methods

RRAS gives you the ability to configure the security/authentication methods that RRAS uses for authenticating with the remote router for a demand-dial connection. To configure authentication methods, open the properties for the demand-dial connection and click the Security tab. The settings you can configure here for authentication methods are the same as those you can configure for incoming RAS connections. For a detailed description of authentication methods, encryption, and protocols, see Chapter 15.

Modifying network settings

RRAS uses the protocols and other network properties configured for an interface when you add the interface. You might need to remove or add a protocol or make other network property changes for a routing interface. For example, you might want to add the ability to route IPX as well as IP, requiring that you install IPX on the interface. You can do so through the RRAS console. Open the property sheet for the routing interface, choose Properties, and click the Network tab. You can configure dial-up server settings, network protocols and bindings, and other network properties. See Chapter 6 if you need more detailed information on how to configure network settings in Windows 2000.

Enabling or disabling routing

On occasion, you might need to enable or disable a router, such as taking the router down for maintenance. You can stop or pause the RRAS service to stop routing on all interfaces, or you can take down a specific interface. To stop, pause, or restart RRAS, open the RRAS console, right-click the server you want to manage, and choose the task you want to perform (stop, start, and so on) from the All Tasks menu.

To take down a specific interface, open the RRAS console and then open the IP Routing branch. Click General to display the routing interfaces, then right-click the interface to bring down, and choose Properties. Deselect the option "Enable IP router manager" to take down the interface. Select the option to bring it back up.

Dynamic Routing

If yours is a more complex network than the one described in this section, you might want to use a routing protocol such as RIP or OSPF to provide dynamic route table creation and management. The following sections explain how to add and configure RIP and OSPF. This chapter assumes you have some knowledge of RIP or OSPF and primarily need to know where to go to add and configure routing protocols in Windows 2000 RRAS.

Adding and Configuring RIP

Before you can configure RIP on an interface, you need to add RIP. In the RRAS console, open the server you want to manage, then expand the IP Routing branch. Right-click General and choose New Routing Protocol. Select RIP Version 2 for Internet Protocol from the list and choose OK. A new node labeled RIP appears under the IP Routing branch.

Next, you need to specify the interface on which RIP will run, as by default no interfaces are configured when you add RIP. Right-click RIP and choose New Interface. RRAS displays the available interfaces. Select the one on which you want to run RIP and click OK.

The third step is to configure RIP. RRAS presents a property sheet for RIP when you add the interface. You can also display the RIP properties by double-clicking the interface in the right pane with RIP selected in the left pane. The following sections describe the options you can configure for RIP.

General

Use the General page to configure how RIP handles updates, enable or disable authentication, and other general properties, as explained in the following list:

✦ **Operation mode:** Choose the method RIP uses to update routes. You can choose auto-static update mode or periodic update mode. With auto-static mode, RRAS sends out RIP announcements only when other routers request updates. Any routes learned through RIP when in auto-static mode are treated as static routes and remain in the routing table until manually deleted, even if RRAS is restarted or you disable RIP. This is the default mode for demand-dial interfaces. Periodic update mode generates RIP announcements automatically at the interval defined by "Periodic announcement interval" on the Advanced property page. Routes learned through RIP with this mode are treated as RIP routes and are discarded if the router is restarted. This is the default mode for LAN interfaces.

✦ **Outgoing packet protocol:** Select the protocol RIP should use for outgoing RIP announcements. Select RIP version 1 broadcast if no other adjacent routers support RIP version 2. Select RIP v2 broadcast in a mixed environment with adjacent routers using RIP v1 and RIP v2. Select RIP v2 multicast to send RIP announcements as multicasts, but only when all adjacent routers are configured to use RIP v2 (RIP v1 doesn't support RIP v2 multicast announcements). Select Silent RIP to prevent the router from sending RIP announcements and to function in listen-only mode, listening for announcements from other routers and updating its routing table accordingly, but not announcing its own routes.

✦ **Incoming packet protocol:** Specify how you want the router to handle incoming RIP announcements. Select Ignore incoming packets to have the router function in announce-only mode and not listen to announcements from other routers. Otherwise, select the required mode depending on the mix of adjacent routers and their support for RIP v1 and/or v2.

✦ **Added cost for routes:** This number is added to the hop count for a route to increase the relative cost. Increase the number to help limit the traffic on the route if you have other, less costly routes that can be used if they are available. The default is 1, and the maximum number of hops for IP and RIP can't exceed 15.

✦ **Tag for announced routes:** You can use this value to assign a tag number to be included with all RIP v2 announcements.

✦ **Activate authentication/Password:** Select this option to enable the inclusion of a plain text password for incoming and outgoing RIP v2 announcements, and then specify a corresponding password in the Password field. If this option is enabled, all routers connected to this interface must be configured for the same password. This option serves only as a means of identifying routers and doesn't provide security or encryption of RIP traffic.

Security

The Security tab lets you specify which routes to accept or reject that come in via RIP announcements from other routers. You can accept all routes, accept only routes that fall within a specified network range, or ignore all routes in a specified range. For outgoing RIP announcements, you can configure RRAS to announce all routes, announce only those routes that fit a specified network range, or exclude routes that fit a specified range.

Neighbors

The Neighbors tab lets you define how the router interacts with neighboring routers. The options are as follows:

✦ **Use broadcast or multicast only:** Select this option to issue RIP announcements only using the outgoing packet protocol specified on the interface's General property page.

✦ **Use neighbors in addition to broadcast or multicast:** Select this option to define specific routers to which RRAS sends unicast RIP announcements as well as to issue RIP announcements using the outgoing packet protocol specified on the General page.

✦ **Use neighbors instead of broadcast or multicast:** Select this option to define specific routers to which RRAS sends unicast RIP announcements and not issue RIP announcements through the broadcast or multicast protocol specified on the General page. Use this option in networks that don't support RIP broadcasts.

Advanced

You can use the Advanced tab to set several advanced options for RIP on the selected interface including the interval between RIP announcements, route expiration period, and other settings. The following list summarizes the settings:

✦ **Periodic announcement interval:** Specify the interval in seconds at which RIP announcements are issued from the local router. You can specify a value between 15 seconds and 24 hours (86,400 seconds), and this setting is only applicable if you've selected periodic update mode on the General tab.

✦ **Time before routes expire:** This value defines the time-to-live of routes learned through RIP. Routes that do not update in the specified time are marked as invalid. You can specify a value between 15 seconds and 72 hours (259,200 seconds). The setting only applies if the interface uses periodic update mode.

✦ **Time before route is removed:** Specify the number of seconds a route learned through RIP remains in the routing table before it expires and is removed. Valid values range from 15 seconds to 72 hours. This setting applies only if the interface uses periodic update mode.

✦ **Enable split-horizon processing:** Select this option to prevent routes learned on a network from being announced on the same network. Deselect the option to allow those routes to be announced.

✦ **Enable poison-reverse processing:** Select this option to assign a metric of 16 (marking them as unreachable) to those routes learned on a network that are announced on the same network.

✦ **Enable triggered updates:** Select this option to allow the router to generate triggered updates when the routing table changes. Set the maximum time between triggered updates through the option "Maximum seconds between triggered updates" on the General page of the global RIP property sheet. To view this property sheet, right-click the RIP node in the IP Routing branch of the RRAS console and choose Properties.

✦ **Send clean-up updates when stopping:** Select this option to have RIP announce all routes with a metric of 15 to adjacent routers when the local router is going down, indicating to the other routers that the routes are no longer available. When the router comes back up, RIP will announce the routes again with their appropriate metrics, making those routes available again.

✦ **Process host routes in received announcements:** Host routes in RIP announcements are ignored by default. Select this option to include them in received announcements.

✦ **Include host routes in sent announcements:** Host routes are not included by default in outgoing RIP announcements. Select this option to include host routes in outgoing announcements.

✦ **Process default routes in received announcements:** Default routes received in RIP announcements are ignored by default. Select this option to add them to the local routing table. Note that this could have the consequence of disabling routing if the default route is not applicable to the local router.

✦ **Include default routes in sent announcements:** Default routes are not included by default in outgoing RIP announcements. Select this option to include them. In most situations, you should not include default routes unless those default routes are applicable to all other networks on the selected interface.

✦ **Disable subnet summarization:** Select this option to have subnet routes summarized by class-based network ID for outgoing announcements on networks that are not part of the class-based network. Subnet summarization is disabled by default and requires RIP v2 broadcast of RIP v2 multicast support on all applicable routers.

General RIP properties

There are a handful of general properties you can set for RIP in addition to those discussed in the previous sections. To set these properties, open the IP Routing branch in the RRAS console, right-click RIP, and choose Properties. Use the General tab to configure logging and the Security tab to define the routers from which the local router will process RIP announcements.

Adding and Configuring OSPF

You add and configure OSPF in much the same way as RIP, although the configuration properties are considerably different. To add OSPF, open the RRAS console and open the IP Routing branch for the server you want to manage. Right-click General and choose New Routing Protocol. Select Open Shortest Path First (OSPF) from the list and click OK. RRAS adds an OSPF branch to the IP Routing branch.

Next, specify the interface on which OSPF will operate. Right-click OSPF and choose New Interface. Select the network interface from the list and click OK. RRAS displays the property sheet shown in Figure 12-9. The following sections explain the properties for the connection. You can also modify these properties later by double-clicking the interface in the right pane with the OSPF branch opened.

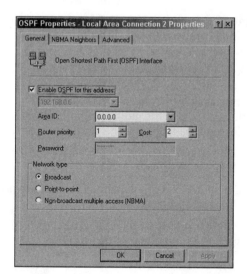

Figure 12-9: The OSPF Properties sheet

Setting interface properties

The interface properties for OSPF define the way OSPF operates on the selected interface. If you have more than one router interface using OSPF, you need to configure each according to your network's needs and the neighboring routers. The following sections explain these interface properties. See the section "Setting Global OSPF Properties" later in this chapter to configure general OSPF properties.

General

Use the General tab shown in Figure 12-9 to specify the address on which the router interface responds, area ID, and related properties. The following list explains the options:

✦ **Enable OSPF for this address:** Select to enable OSPF on the listed IP address for the selected interface. If you have more than one IP address bound to the selected interface, you must enable or disable and configure options for each IP address. The Area ID, Router priority, Cost, and Password apply to the IP address and can be configured differently for each address on the same interface if needed.

✦ **Area ID:** Select one area ID to associate with the address set above. Each address can have a different area ID. By default, only the backbone area ID of 0.0.0.0 exists. Create other area IDs through the Areas tab of the general OSPF properties for the router. See the section "Setting Global OSPF Properties" later in this section for more information on creating area IDs.

✦ **Router priority:** The router with the highest priority number becomes the designated router when multiple routers exist on the network, and takes precedence. If the priority numbers are the same (causing a tie), the router with the highest router ID value takes precedence. Specify a value to set the router's priority as needed within the context of the other routers in the network.

✦ **Cost:** Use this option to set the interface's metric, or relative cost. When two or more interfaces can be used for a given route, the one with the lowest metric is used by default unless it is unavailable.

✦ **Password:** Specify the clear text string used for identification purposes to other routers in the area. The default password is 12345678, and all routers in the same area must use the same password. This option is dimmed if plain text passwords are disabled for the area. Open the global properties for OSPF and edit the properties for the selected area to enable the plain text password.

✦ **Broadcast:** Select this option if the interface is connected to a broadcast-type network such as Ethernet, Token Ring, or FDDI.

✦ **Point-to-point:** Select this option if the interface is connected to a point-to-point network such as T1/E1, T3/E3, ISDN, or other dial-up network.

✦ **Non-broadcast multiple access (NBMA):** Select this option if the interface is connected to an NBMA network such as Frame Relay, X.25, or ATM.

NBMA Neighbors

The NBMA Neighbors tab of the interface's OSPF properties enables you to define the neighboring routers when you select NBMA as the network type on the General page. Select an IP address for the interface (if the interface has multiple addresses bound to it), then specify the IP address of neighboring routers.

Advanced

The Advanced tab lets you configure various intervals, transit delay, and MTU values for each address on the selected interface. These values are explained in the following list:

✦ **IP address:** Select the IP address for which you want to change the settings.

✦ **Transit delay:** Specify the estimated number of seconds required to transmit a link state update packet over the selected interface. The default is 1 second.

✦ **Retransmit interval:** Specify the number of seconds between retransmission of link state advertisements for adjacencies. The value should be greater than the total expected round-trip time between any two routers on the attached network.

✦ **Hello interval:** Specify the interval at which the router broadcasts *hello packets*. Hello packet transmission is a means of discovering network structure (neighboring routers). Routing metrics are configured based on the length of time it takes a packet to make the trip between the source and the destination. The hello interval value must be the same for all routers on the common network. A shorter interval enables network topology changes to be detected more quickly but has the effect of generating more OSPF traffic in a given timeframe. Suggested value for X.25 is 30 seconds; for a LAN, the suggested value is 10 seconds.

✦ **Dead interval:** Specify the period after which adjacent routers will consider this router down. The other routers decide that the router is down if they haven't received a response to hello packets within the specified amount of time. The value must be the same for all routers on the common network segment and should be set as a multiple of the hello interval. A common practice is to set the dead interval to four times the hello interval.

✦ **Poll interval:** Specify the period of time for network polls on NBMA interfaces. Network polls enable routers to determine if a dead neighbor has come back up or the connection has been restored. The poll interval should be at least twice as long as the dead interval.

✦ **Maximum transmission unit (MTU) size (bytes):** Specify the maximum size that IP datagrams can be transmitted without fragmentation. The default size for Ethernet networks is 1,500.

Setting global OSPF properties

RRAS provides several options that control OSPF globally. To configure these global properties, open the IP Routing branch in the RRAS console, then right-click OSPF and choose Properties. The following sections explain the global options in the OSPF property sheet.

General

The General tab configures the address identity of the OSPF router and logging options:

✦ **Router identification:** Specify the IP address on the server used to uniquely identify the OSPF router.

✦ **Enable autonomous system boundary router:** Select this option to configure the router to advertise routing information from other sources such as static addresses and RIP.

✦ **Event logging:** Select the desired logging level (self-explanatory).

Areas

You use the Areas tab to add and configure OSPF areas. Double-click an existing area or click Add to create a new entry. The following list summarizes the options for an area:

✦ **Area ID:** Specify a 32-bit number in dotted decimal format to identify the OSPF area. 0.0.0.0 is reserved for the backbone. While you can use the IP network number for a subnet, the number does not have to correlate to an IP address or IP network ID.

✦ **Enable plaintext password:** Select to require a plain text password for the area. All OSPF routers in the area on the same network segment must use the same password. Routers on different segments can use different passwords.

✦ **Stub area:** A stub area is an OSPF area that doesn't enumerate external routes but does accept external route data from other OSPF routers. Select this option to configure the area as a stub area.

✦ **Stub metric:** Specify the metric of the summary default route advertised into the stub area.

✦ **Import summary advertisements:** Select this option to import inter-area routes into this stub area. Deselect to base all non-intra-area routes on a single default route.

Use the Ranges page to define ranges of IP addresses that belong to the selected area. The ranges are used to summarize the routes within the selected OSPF area.

Virtual Interfaces

Use the Virtual Interfaces tab to create virtual links between a backbone area router and an area border router that can't be physically connected to the backbone area. The virtual link is used to transmit routing data between the two. You can specify the transit delay, retransmit interval, hello interval, dead interval, and plain text password for each virtual link.

External Routing

If you select the option "Enable autonomous system boundary router" on the General tab of the global OSPF properties, you can use the External Routing page to define the route sources from which the router will accept routes. Select Accept or Ignore, then select the route sources from the list that you want to either accept or ignore. Click Route Filters to build a list of routes to be accepted or ignored based on their destination addresses or network masks.

DHCP Relay Agent

A DHCP relay agent (BOOTP relay agent) functions as a sort of DHCP proxy, enabling DHCP clients on a given IP subnet to acquire IP leases from DHCP servers on other subnets. The DHCP relay agent relays messages between DHCP clients and DHCP servers. The DHCP relay agent component provided with Windows 2000 RRAS serves that function. Figure 12-10 illustrates a Windows 2000 server functioning as a DHCP relay agent.

 Note   The DHCP relay agent can't run on a Windows 2000 server that also is running the DHCP Server service or Network Address Translation (NAT) with automatic addressing enabled.

Setting up a DHCP relay agent is fairly simple. In the RRAS console, select the server you want to function as a DHCP relay agent. Open the IP Routing branch, right-click General, and choose New Routing Protocol. Select DHCP Relay Agent from the list and click OK to add it to the IP Routing branch.

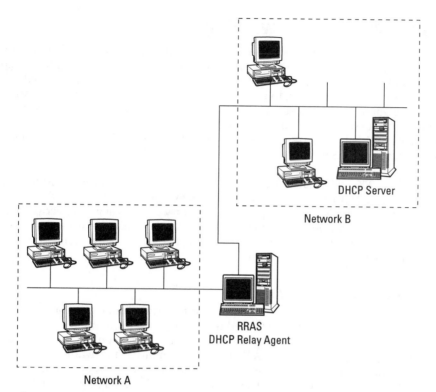

Figure 12-10: A Windows 2000 server operating as a DHCP relay agent

Next, add the interface(s) on which the DHCP relay agent will function. Right-click in the right pane or on DHCP Relay Agent and choose New Interface. Select the appropriate network interface and click OK. RRAS displays a property sheet for DHCP Relay that includes the following options:

✦ **Relay DHCP packets:** Select to enable DHCP relay or deselect to disable DHCP relay.

✦ **Hop-count threshold:** Specify the maximum number of DHCP relay agents to handle DHCP relayed traffic. The default is 4; the maximum is 16.

✦ **Boot threshold:** Specify the interval the server waits before forwarding DHCP messages. Use this option to enable a local DHCP server to have a chance to respond to requests before forwarding the message to a remote DHCP server.

The final step is to define the list of DHCP servers to which the local relay agent relays messages. In the RRAS console, right-click DHCP Relay Agent under the IP Routing branch and choose Properties. RRAS displays a dialog box you can use to specify the IP addresses of the remote DHCP servers.

IGMP – Multicast Forwarding

Most IP traffic is *unicast*, or directed to a single destination. A Windows 2000 server running RRAS can function as a *multicast* router, broadcasting IGMP (Internet Group Management Protocol) traffic to multiple hosts. Multicasting is most often used for audio or video conferencing to enable multiple hosts to receive the same data. Clients configured for multicast listen for the multicast traffic, and all others ignore it. Chapter 13 discusses how to configure multicast scopes for a DHCP server, enabling it to assign multicast addresses to clients that request them. This chapter explains how to configure RRAS to function as a multicast forwarder.

Note   Windows 2000 does not include any multicast routing protocols. Multicast routers exchange group membership information with one another to help determine how multicast traffic is routed. Windows 2000 only provides limited multicast routing, but does function as a multicast forwarder, forwarding multicast traffic to listening clients. Windows 2000 can be configured as a multicast router through the addition of third-party protocols.

Overview of multicast forwarding

A Windows 2000 multicast forwarder listens for multicast traffic on all attached networks and forwards the traffic (based on its multicast destination address) to attached networks where listening clients reside or to other routers for networks where participating clients reside. A Windows 2000 multicast forwarder also listens for IGMP Membership Report packets and updates its multicast forwarding table accordingly, enabling it to forward traffic to those destinations requesting it.

The IGMP routing protocol included with Windows 2000 is not an IGMP routing protocol per se, but enables a Windows 2000 server to function as a forwarder. After you add the protocol to Windows 2000, you configure one or more interfaces to handle IGMP. You can configure the interface to function in either *IGMP router mode* or *IGMP proxy mode*, as explained in the following sections.

IGMP router mode

An IGMP interface running in router mode sets the network adapter for the interface in *multicast-promiscuous mode*, which passes all multicast packets received on the interface to the higher networking layers for processing.

Note   Not all network adapters support multicast-promiscuous mode. If you're setting up a multicast forwarder, verify with the NIC manufacturer that the adapter supports this mode.

The interface also tracks multicast group membership, querying periodically for IGMP Membership Report messages and updating its forwarding table accordingly. Each entry in the table specifies the network ID where multicast clients are listening and the multicast address on which those clients are listening. The table does not reference individual hosts, but rather the interface forwards traffic to any networks where there is at least one client listening for multicast traffic.

Tip   When multiple routers in a network function as IGMP routers, one is automatically elected to be the querier and performs all membership queries.

IGMP proxy mode

IGMP proxy mode enables a local intranet router to pass IGMP traffic to and from multicast-capable clients and routers on the Internet (referred to as *multicast backbone,* or MBone).

An interface running in IGMP proxy mode functions as a proxy for IGMP Membership Report packets. RRAS listens on the selected interface for IGMP Membership Report packets and retransmits them on all other interfaces running in IGMP router mode. This enables IGMP multicast groups connected to the proxy mode router to have upstream routers update their multicast tables

The interface running IGMP proxy mode also serves as a gateway of sorts for IGMP traffic coming to the local network from the upstream multicast router, forwarding that traffic to the appropriate clients. Traffic from local clients to the Internet also passes through the interface. For both incoming and outgoing traffic, TCP/IP itself handles the forwarding.

Setting up a multicast forwarder

The first step in configuring a multicast forwarder is to add the IGMP protocol to the router. In the RRAS console, open the IP Routing branch of the designated server, right-click General, and choose New Routing Protocol. Select IGMP from the list and click OK to add it to the IP Routing branch.

Next, add at least one interface for IGMP. Right-click IGMP in the left pane and choose New Interface. Or, select IGMP in the left pane and right-click anywhere in the right pane, then choose New Interface. Select the interface on which you want to run IGMP and click OK. RRAS displays the IGMP Properties sheet. The General tab lets you choose between router mode and proxy mode for the interface. Select the protocol version using the IGMP protocol version drop-down list if you select router mode.

The Router tab contains several options that control how IGMP functions on the interface:

✦ **Robustness variable:** This variable indicates the relative robustness of the subnet to which the interface is attached.

✦ **Query interval:** Specify the interval at which IGMP queries are broadcast on the interface.

✦ **Query response interval:** Specify the maximum amount of time the router should wait for response for General Query messages.

✦ **Last member query interval:** Specify the time, in milliseconds, the router waits for a response to a Group-Specific Query message, and the time between successive Group-Specific Query messages.

✦ **Startup query interval:** Specify the time, in seconds, between successive General Query messages sent by the router during startup. The default value is ¼ of the query interval.

✦ **Startup query count:** Specify the number of General Query messages to send at startup.

✦ **Last member query count:** Specify the number of Group-Specific Query messages sent with no response before the router assumes there are no more members of the host group on the interface being queried.

✦ **Automatically recalculate defaults:** Select to have RRAS automatically recalculate values for Startup query interval, Startup query count, and Last member query count at startup. The default for Startup query interval is ¼ the query interval. The default for Startup query count and Last member query count is the same as the Robustness variable.

✦ **Group membership interval:** This read-only property displays the calculated group membership interval, which is the period of time that must pass before the router decides that there are no more members of a multicast group on a given subnet. The value is calculated as (Robustness variable) × (Query interval) + (Query response interval).

✦ **Other querier present interval:** This read-only property displays the calculated querier present interval, which is the period of time that must pass before the router decides that there are no other multicast routers that should be the querier. The value is calculated as (Robustness variable) × (Query interval) + (Query response interval) ÷ 2.

Network Address Translation

Windows 2000 Server's RRAS provides full-featured network address translation (NAT) services. Network Address Translation is not new, and was born out of the high demand for IP addresses. With the Internet growing the way it is, it is virtually impossible to obtain a large range of IP addresses, especially for a small company. The most an ISP will assign to a small company is less than one-sixteenth of a class C subnet, and you have to be spending a lot of money on dedicated Internet services to get that many addresses.

Most small businesses are deploying ADSLs (asymmetric digital subscriber lines), which are cheaper and often faster than dedicated Internet access connections, such as Frame Relay or dedicated ISDN. But an ISP will only assign you a single IP address. If you plan to install a number of hosts on your internal network, such as DNS, mail, Active Directory, Web, and FTP services, and need to route Internet traffic to these hosts, you will need a NAT.

Note   NAT services in Windows 2000 Server are typically aimed at small or home businesses. A larger company would most likely use a firewall, which has NAT built into its packet inspection technology. Most routers, even for small offices, now come with NAT support.

NAT alleviates the demand for a larger number of IP addresses by mapping externally assigned IP addresses to internally or privately assigned private addresses (translating from one IP address to another). This means that one IP address can typically be used to target a whole range of IP addresses on the concealed network.

Windows 2000 NAT and the RRAS service takes NAT further. NAT can inspect inbound packets to host names and query the internal IP address of the host from an Internal DNS. It will then route the packets that have arrived at the public address to the internal hosts, and route the packets to the correct service via the ports it has been configured to use.

Configuring NAT

As we discussed at the beginning of this chapter, you typically assign the Class B network of 192.168.0.0 to an internal network in a small company. Armed with the IP addresses of your Internal hosts and the IP addresses assigned to you by your ISP, open Routing and Remote Access as described earlier in this chapter and perform the following steps:

1. You need to first add Network Address Translation as a routing protocol, which you do by right-clicking the General node and selecting New Routing Protocol. Next, select the server in the console tree and expand its node down to NAT. The interfaces (NICs) appear in the details pane on the right.

2. Add the interface to the protocol. Right-click NAT and select New Interface. You will have the option to configure the interface for the internal network or the external network (Internet). Select the interface to configure and right-click. Select Properties. The Local Area Connection Properties dialog box will appear.

3. Make sure to check the option Translate TCP-UDP headers, which is essential if you only have one address from an ISP.

4. On the Address Pool tab, enter the IP address assignment provided by your ISP. In many cases with ADSL, you will be given a dynamically assigned address, which should remain persistent, which means the same IP address gets renewed every time the DHCP lease expires. But you can ask an ISP to reserve the number for you as well.

5. On the Special Ports tab, in the Protocol drop-down list, select either UDP or TCP. Then click ADD. The Add Special Port dialog box will load.

6. In the incoming port field, type the Well-Known port number typically assigned to the IP service in question: for example, port 21 for FTP or port 25 for SMTP.

7. In the outgoing port field, type the private port you wish to assign to the same service. It could be a Well-Known port of the outgoing IP service or any port used by your internal resources. (Using high port numbers, such as 5000, provides additional security; this makes it more difficult for hackers to focus on unknown ports.)

8. In the Private address field, type the private address of the TCP/IP service (typically the host).

9. Enter the public IP address to be translated (as opposed to the interface) in the field On this address pool entry.

That's all there is to configuring NAT; however, you should plan the deployment carefully. To point clients to the Internet for browsing and other services, you would configure the private outgoing IP address on the NAT as your gateway to the Internet. NAT will translate this address to the correct public address.

 Cross-Reference   See the section on Internet Connection Sharing (ICS) in Chapter 15.

Troubleshooting TCP/IP

When TCP/IP works well, life is good. Occasionally, however, TCP/IP connections will fail and you will need to determine the cause of the problem. Windows 2000 includes a handful of TCP/IP utilities you can use to test connectivity and troubleshoot connections. This section of the chapter examines TCP/IP troubleshooting in general and the tools included with Windows 2000 for that purpose.

Common Troubleshooting Concepts

As is the case when troubleshooting any problem, the first thing to consider when troubleshooting TCP/IP connections is whether anything has changed in the system's configuration. Problems with a newly installed computer typically point to an invalid IP address, wrong subnet mask, or incorrect default gateway. If TCP/IP has never worked on the system, open the TCP/IP properties for the connection and verify that they are correct.

For systems that have been working but have stopped, you need to more narrowly define the problem. For example, if you've been able to connect to a specific Web site but can't anymore, see if you can connect to other sites. If the problem lies with one site, it's almost surely a problem on the server side and not something you can correct on your end. However, if a range of Web sites work but others do not, you probably have a DNS or routing problem. The same holds true for FTP sites and for local resources such as other computers on your local segment.

A methodical, logical approach will help you identify the point of failure, if not the cause. While you could work from the problem backwards, we prefer to troubleshoot from the local computer outward until we find the point of failure. For example, you should first ping the loopback address (type **ping 127.0.0.1** or **ping localhost** from a command prompt) to verify that TCP/IP is functioning on your computer. Then, you can begin moving farther out into the network and Internet until you find the point at which communication breaks down. Ping a computer on the local segment, and if successful, ping the internal side of the router. If that works, ping the external side of the router, then a system past the router. If the ping fails at any point, it typically indicates that the packets generated by the ping command are not being returned, either because the remote node is configured to discard ping traffic or a problem with the routing table is preventing the packets from being returned. If **ping localhost** fails, you probably have a problem with your network interface card or a corrupt TCP/IP protocol stack.

The following list describes common problems and potential solutions:

✦ **TCP/IP won't initialize on the host or a service fails to start:** These problems typically point to a configuration error. Open the properties for the interface and check the settings for TCP/IP closely to make sure they are correct, particularly that you haven't specified a conflicting static IP address. For multi-homed systems, check the priority order of the interfaces. To do so, open the Network and Dial-Up Connections folder and choose Advanced ⇨ Advanced Settings. On the Adapters and Bindings tab, use the Up and Down arrows for the Connections list to move the primary adapter to the top of the list. Also, verify in the same property page that TCP/IP is bound to the selected adapter.

✦ **Communication to other hosts fails, or other hosts don't respond:** This often results from an IP address conflict, network hardware failure, or possibly an incorrect DHCP lease. Use the `ipconfig /all` command to check your IP address, subnet mask, and default gateway settings.

✦ **Pinging localhost works but you can't communicate with local or remote hosts:** Verify that you have the correct subnet specified. The ability to ping local hosts but not remote hosts can be caused by incorrect default gateway setting or router problems.

✦ **You can ping the local computer by name, but you cannot ping remote computers by name:** You're having a problem with DNS. Verify that you are specifying valid DNS servers in the system's TCP/IP configuration and that those servers are available.

✦ **You can ping a non-Windows 2000 workstation but can't connect to it using a NET console command:** You might be experiencing a problem with NetBIOS name resolution. Check WINS settings and verify that you haven't disabled NetBIOS over TCP/IP on the WINS page of the computer's TCP/IP settings. You might also have a problem with the workstation service on the local computer or the computer you are trying to connect to. This is not a TCP/IP problem, but you would not be alone thinking it is. If the workstation service is stopped, try restarting it. If you can restart it and still have the problem, then name-IP address resolving is the likely cause. If you cannot restart the workstation service, you will likely have to reboot the culprit machine. A dead workstation service points to an installation that went bad.

✦ **You can connect to a host or Web site by IP address but not by host name:** This is clearly a DNS issue. Verify that your system is configured for valid DNS servers and that the servers are available. (See Chapter 14 for troubleshooting DNS entries.)

Windows 2000 includes several utilities you can use to troubleshoot TCP/IP connectivity. The following sections explain these tools, starting with the most basic and sometimes most useful tool: `ping`.

Ping

Ping stands for Packet InterNet Groper, and it works like a submarine's sonar: It bounces a packet off a remote host and listens for the return packet. If the packet comes back, you have basic TCP/IP connectivity between the two hosts. No response can indicate routing problems, a configuration problem with TCP/IP on the local host, unavailability of the remote host, or increasingly, that the remote host is configured to ignore ping traffic.

The `ping` command generates Internet Control Message Protocol (ICMP) packets and transmits them to the designated host, then waits for a response. The version of ping included with Windows 2000 sends four packets by default and waits for a period of one second for the response from each. You can specify the number of packets to transmit and the timeout period to override the defaults, if desired. For example, you might send a larger number of packets to test response time over a more realistic sample period. Following is a sample output from ping:

```
C:\>ping 192.168.0.6

Pinging 192.168.0.6 with 32 bytes of data:

Reply from 192.168.0.6: bytes=32 time=16ms TTL=128
Reply from 192.168.0.6: bytes=32 time<10ms TTL=128
Reply from 192.168.0.6: bytes=32 time=16ms TTL=128
Reply from 192.168.0.6: bytes=32 time<10ms TTL=128

Ping statistics for 192.168.0.6:
    Packets: Sent = 4, Received = 4, Lost = 0 (0% loss),
Approximate round trip times in milli-seconds:
    Minimum = 0ms, Maximum =  16ms, Average =  8ms
```

Ping is also useful in identifying name resolution problems. If you can ping a host by IP address but not by host name, one of the following could be the cause:

✦ There is no valid host record in the remote host's domain. Add an entry to the DNS zone or add an entry in your local Hosts file for the remote host.

✦ You have an incorrect entry in your local Hosts file for the host. Remove or correct the entry in the Hosts file.

✦ Your DNS configuration is incorrect (pointed to wrong or unavailable DNS servers). Correct the configuration and try again.

Before you begin testing any connectivity problem, you should verify that you can ping your own workstation. You use ping to perform an internal loopback test that verifies whether or not TCP/IP is functioning on your computer. Use one of the following commands to ping your own computer:

```
ping 127.0.0.1
ping localhost
ping YourIPAddress
```

Following is the syntax for the ping command:

```
ping [-t] [-a] [-n count] [-l size] [-f] [-i ttl] [-v tos]
[-r count][-s count] [[-j HostList] | [-k HostList]]
[-w timeout] DestinationList
```

Table 12-4 describes the switches you can use with ping.

Table 12-4

Ping Command Switches

Switch	Function	Use
-t	Ping continuously until terminated by Ctrl+C. Press Ctrl+Break to view statistics	Perform extended testing or check for intermittent problems
-a	Resolve address to host name	Test name resolution and troubleshoot Hosts file
-n count	Number of packets to send	Perform extended testing
-l size	Specify packet size in bytes; the default is 64, the maximum is 8,192	Check for packet fragmentation and response time
-f	Set Don't Fragment flag in packet	Prevent routers from fragmenting packet
-i ttl	Set packet time-to-live	Increase to timeout on slow connections
-v tos	Set Type of Service field	Specify type of action remote router should perform on the packet
-r count	Record packet route; specify from 1 to 9	Determine route of outgoing and incoming packets
-s count	Set time stamp for number of hops specified by count	Set current hop count for the packet

Continued

	Table 12-4 *(continued)*	
Switch	**Function**	**Use**
-j HostList	Route packets using host list; specify maximum of 9 hosts	Direct traffic through specific route; hosts can be separated by intermediate gateways (loose source route)
-k HostList	Route packets using host list	Similar to -j but hosts can't be separated by intermediate gateways (strict source route)
-w timeout	Set packet timeout in milliseconds	Increase to overcome timeout on slow connections
DestinationList	Remote host(s) to ping	Specify destination to ping

Ipconfig

Use ipconfig to display configured TCP/IP properties for all adapters, set certain properties, renew or release address leases, and update host records through dynamic DNS. Ipconfig is useful for determining TCP/IP settings on any system, but is most helpful for determining settings on systems that obtain settings through DHCP. Knowing your address and related settings is the first step in troubleshooting any connectivity problem. In addition, you can use ipconfig to release and renew a lease, set a class ID, manage the DNS cache, and request an update of the host record in DNS.

Note   The equivalent tool for IPCONFIG in Windows 9x is WINIPCFG.EXE.

The following is the syntax for ipconfig:

```
Ipconfig [/all | /renew [adapter] | /release [adapter] |
/flushdns | /registerdns /showclassid [adapter] | /setclassid
adapter [classid]
```

Table 12-5 lists the switches and their uses.

Table 12-5
Ipconfig Command Switches

Switch	Function	Use
/all	Show all TCP/IP properties including MAC address, and so on	Obtain complete information; omit to view only address, subnet mask, and gateway
/renew [adapter]	Renew DHCP properties on adapter	Omit adapter to renew DHCP properties on all adapters
/release [adapter]	Release current DHCP lease on adapter	Release address, disabling TCP/IP for adapter; omit adapter to release all leases
/flushdns	Purge local DNS resolver cache	Overcome problems with bad cache entries
/registerdns	Refresh all leases and register host name with DNS	Ensure up-to-date host records in DNS; dynamic updates require a Windows 2000 DNS server
/displaydns	Display contents of local resolver cache	Check cache for potential bad entries
/showclassid	Display all class IDs allowed for adapter	Class IDs allow DHCP to assign properties on a client-by-client basis, using the class ID as the client identifier
/setclassid	Set the current class ID for adapter	See above

Netstat

The netstat command provides three primary functions: monitoring connections to remote hosts, viewing protocol statistics for a connection, and extracting the IP address of a host to which you've connected using domain names (or determining domain name if connected by address). The syntax for netstat is as follows:

```
netstat [-a] [-ens] [-p protocol] [-r] [interval]
```

Table 12-6 describes the options you can use with netstat.

Table 12-6
Netstat Command Switches

Switch	Function	Use
-a	Display all connections	Show all connections, including server connections
-e	Show Ethernet statistics	Use with -s
-n	Show addresses and port numbers in numerical format	Use numerical rather than host.domain format
-s	Show statistics on per-protocol basis	netstat by default shows TCP, UDP, ICMP, and IP
-p protocol	Show connections for protocol	View connections for a specific protocol
-r	Show contents of routing table	Troubleshoot routing problems
interval	Specify interval for update; terminate with Ctrl+C	Omit interval to display information a single time

As mentioned previously, you can use netstat to determine the IP address of a remote host. To do so, issue the command netstat -n. The following examples first issue netstat with no parameters, then use -n to derive IP addresses:

```
C:\>netstat

Active Connections

  Proto  Local Address          Foreign Address          State
  TCP    bart:netbios-ssn       NOTE2KSRV:1117           ESTABLISHED
  TCP    bart:3454              ftp.BayNetworks.COM:ftp  ESTABLISHED

C:\>netstat -n

Active Connections

  Proto  Local Address          Foreign Address          State
  TCP    192.168.0.1:139        192.168.0.2:1117         ESTABLISHED
  TCP    209.105.38.181:3454    134.177.3.22:21          ESTABLISHED
```

This example shows two connections: a local connection to a server named NOTE2KSRV and another to ftp.baynetworks.com. Note that the second example displays the IP address rather than the host name.

Hostname

Use the `hostname` command to derive the host name of the local computer. If no host name is set through the DNS properties for the computer, the computer name set in the Network Identification tab of the computer's properties is used as the host name. Using the `hostname` command is often easier than opening the properties for the connection to hunt for the host name. There are no options for the `hostname` command.

Tracert

Being able to determine the route used to connect to a given host is extremely useful in troubleshooting routing problems. Use `tracert` to trace the route used to connect to another host and determine where, if at all, a connection is failing. For example, if you're having problems reaching sites on the Internet, you can use `tracert` to locate the problem and identify the router where the traffic is dying.

Like `ping`, `tracert` generates ICMP packets, but the `tracert` command sends a series of ICMP packets to the destination host using steadily incrementing time-to-live (TTL) values. Each gateway decrements the TTL value by one. The first packet has a TTL of 1, so it gets decremented to 0 by the first gateway, which then sends a ICMP Time Exceeded packet back to the originating host (your computer) along with the transit time in milliseconds. The local host then transmits the next packet with a TTL of 2. The first gateway decrements it to 1, and the second gateway decrements it to 0. The second gateway then sends back the ICMP Time Exceeded packet. Subsequent packets make it one gateway, or *hop,* further than the previous one before being expired. The result is a table showing the data for each packet. When the packets stop coming back, you've identified the problem router.

The following is a sample output from `tracert`:

```
C:\>tracert ftp.happypuppy.com

Tracing route to ftp.happypuppy.com [199.105.102.130]
over a maximum of 30 hops:

  1    110 ms   109 ms    125 ms  USR1RRT-TS1.DialUp.rrt.net [209.105.38.198]
  2    109 ms    94 ms    125 ms  CISCO1RRTGW-TS.DialUp.rrt.net [209.105.38.50]
  3    281 ms   110 ms     94 ms  border1-h4-0.ply.mr.net [207.229.192.1]
  4    109 ms    94 ms    110 ms  core1-A0-0-0-722.PLY.MR.Net [137.192.7.141]
  5    125 ms   109 ms    109 ms  Serial5-1-0.GW2.MSP1.ALTER.NET [157.130.98.189]
  6    109 ms   109 ms    125 ms  152.ATM3-0.XR2.CHI4.ALTER.NET [146.188.209.134]
  7    141 ms   125 ms    125 ms  194.ATM3-0.TR2.CHI4.ALTER.NET [146.188.208.230]
  8    140 ms   141 ms    125 ms  106.ATM7-0.TR2.EWR1.ALTER.NET [146.188.136.126]
  9    141 ms   125 ms    140 ms  196.ATM6-0.XR2.EWR1.ALTER.NET [146.188.176.81]
 10    172 ms   141 ms    140 ms  192.ATM9-0-0.GW3.EWR1.ALTER.NET [146.188.177.169]
 11    907 ms   953 ms    891 ms  ftp.happypuppy.com [199.105.102.130]

Trace complete.
```

The following is the syntax for `tracert`:

```
Tracert [-d] [-h max_hops] [-w timeout] hostname
```

Table 12-7 describes the switches for tracert.

Table 12-7
Tracert Command Switches

Switch	Function	Use
-d	Suppress display of resolved names of interim systems	Simplify output
-h max_hops	Specify maximum hops to trace	Limit testing to specified number of hops
-w timeout	Set time in milliseconds to wait for reply	Overcome slow connections
hostname	FQDN or IP address of destination host	Specify destination

Arp

The `arp` command, which stands for Address Resolution Protocol, lets you view the arp table on your local computer, which associates physical MAC addresses of other computers on the local network with their IP addresses. The arp table speeds up connections by eliminating the need to look up MAC addresses for subsequent connections. Viewing the contents of the arp table can be useful for troubleshooting connections to specific computers on the network.

The following is the syntax for the `arp` command:

```
arp [-a] [-d ipaddress] [-s ipaddress macaddress] [hostaddress]
```

Table 12-8 describes the options for `arp`.

Table 12-8
arp Command Switches

Switch	Function	Use
-a	Show arp table data for all hosts	Provide detailed view
-d IPAddress	Remove entry for *IPAddress* from arp cache	Clear up connection problem due to bad arp cache entry

Switch	Function	Use
`-s IPAddress MACAddress`	Add new `arp` cache entry for *IPAddress* pointing to *MACAddress*	Add entry for specified host
`HostAddress`	IP address of host interface to be viewed or modified	Applicable in multi-homed systems

Route

You can use the `route` command to view or modify entries in the local computer's static routing table. Static routes are used in place of implicit routes determined by the default gateway for the computer. For example, you can add a static route to direct traffic destined for a specific host through a gateway other than the default to improve response time, reduce costs, and so on. The `route` command is also useful for troubleshooting, either for identifying incorrect static routes or for adding temporary routes to bypass a problem gateway.

The syntax for `route` is as follows:

```
Route [-f] [print|add|delete|change] [destination] [MASK netmask]
[gateway] [METRIC metric]
```

Table 12-9 explains the options for `route`.

Table 12-9
Route Command Switches

Switch	Function	Use
`-f`	Clear all gateway entries from table	
`-p`	Use with `add` to create persistent route	Non-persistent routes are lost at each boot
`print`	Print a route	
`add`	Add a route to the table	Use `-p` to make the route persistent for subsequent sessions
`delete`	Delete a route from the table	
`change`	Modify an existing route	
`destination`	Specify host address	

Continued

	Table 12-9 *(continued)*	
Switch	**Function**	**Use**
MASK *netmask*	Use subnet mask specified by *netmask*	If MASK isn't used, defaults to 255.255.255.255
gateway	Specify address of gateway for route	
METRIC *metric*	Specify the metric, or cost, for the route using the value *metric*	
IF *interface*	Specify the interface for routing table to modify	

You can use the wildcards * and ? with the print and delete switches. As with file names, a * matches any number of characters, and a ? matches one character.

Nbtstat

Use the nbtstat command to display statistics for NetBIOS-over-TCP/IP (NetBT) connections. You also can use nbtstat to purge the name cache and reload the Hosts file, which offers the benefit of reloading the LMHOSTS file without rebooting.

The following is the syntax for nbtstat:

```
Nbtstat [-a RemoteName] [-A RemoteAddress] [-c] [-n] [-R] [-RR]
[-r] [-S] [-s] interval
```

Table 12-10 describes the switches for nbtstat.

	Table 12-10 **Nbtstat Command Switches**
Switch	**Function**
-a *RemoteName*	Show NetBIOS name table for computer *RemoteName*
-A *RemoteAddress*	Show NetBIOS name table for computer at the IP address *RemoteAddress*
-c	Show contents of the NetBIOS name cache
-n	Show NetBIOS names for the local computer
-R	Purge the NetBIOS name cache and reload LMHOSTS

Switch	Function
-RR	Submit Name Release packets to WINS, then refresh
-r	Show NetBIOS name resolution statistics
-S	Show current NetBIOS workstation and server sessions by IP address
-s	Show current NetBIOS workstation and server sessions by name
Interval	Number of seconds between subsequent display of protocol statistics

Legacy Protocols

While the previous sections of this chapter have been devoted to TCP/IP, Windows 2000 supports additional network protocols as well. The following sections explain these protocols and their properties, but do not provide a detailed explanation of how these protocols are structured or function.

NetBEUI

NetBEUI stands for NetBIOS Enhanced User Interface. NetBEUI is one of two protocols that support NetBIOS, the name resolution method used by previous Microsoft operating systems including DOS, Windows 3.*x*, Windows for Workgroups, Windows 9*x*, and Windows NT.

NetBEUI is useful on small networks because it is easy to install and configure. As the number of nodes on the network increases, however, NetBEUI becomes less practical because of the amount of network traffic it generates. Also, NetBEUI is not routable, which limits it to local segments only.

 Tip
NetBEUI can be routed if encapsulated in PPTP or L2TP for a VPN connection. This enables you to use NetBEUI for accessing resources on remote networks, but it also requires a TCP/IP link between the two networks.

There are no configurable properties for NetBEUI. Simply install the NetBEUI protocol on the selected interface and ensure that all nodes using NetBEUI on the network have unique names.

IPX/SPX

Like TCP/IP, IPX/SPX is actually two protocols: Internetwork Packet eXchange and Sequenced Packet eXchange. IPX/SPX provides connectivity for Novell NetWare servers and clients, but it can also serve as a primary network protocol when no NetWare servers are present.

With IPX/SPX, two types of numbers are used to route traffic: the *external network number* and the *internal network number*. The external network number is associated with the physical network adapter and network. All nodes on the network that use the same frame type (explained shortly) must use the same external network number. You can specify an external network number manually or allow Windows 2000 to detect it automatically. The external network number is a hexadecimal value from one to eight digits.

The internal network number identifies a virtual network in the computer, and programs identify themselves as being located on this virtual network rather than the physical network identified by the external network number. Each virtual network appears as a separate network to the user. By default, Windows 2000 assigns the value 00000000 as the internal network number. The internal network number helps improve routing in multi-homed systems or in a system where more than one frame type is used on a single adapter.

The following are the configuration properties for the IPX/SPX protocol:

✦ **Internal network number:** This property defines the internal network number associated with the interface.

✦ **Auto frame type detection:** Select this option to allow Windows 2000 to automatically detect the frame type. If multiple frame types are detected in addition to 802.2, NWLink defaults to 802.2.

✦ **Manual frame type detection:** Select this option to manually configure frame type or configure multiple frame types. You specify the internal network number for each. Choose 802.2 for NetWare 3.3 or later on Ethernet. Choose 802.3 for other Ethernet configurations. Choose 802.5 for Token Ring adapters.

DLC

DLC stands for Data Link Control. All network adapters have a DLC address or DLC identifier (called a DLCI, or *del-see*). Some protocols, including Ethernet and Token Ring, use DLC exclusively to identify nodes on the network. Other protocols use logical addresses to identify nodes. TCP/IP, for example, uses the IP address to identify a node. However, at the lower layers of the network, some translation still needs to take place to convert the logical address to the DLC address. Address Resolution Protocol (ARP) performs this translation for TCP/IP.

DLC is required as a protocol only for those situations where DLC is used rather than a logical address. For example, DLC enables Windows 2000 computers to connect to IBM mainframe systems and use DLC-enabled network printers.

There are no user-configurable properties for DLC.

SNMP

SNMP stands for Simple Network Management Protocol and provides a standardized means for managing hosts on TCP/IP (and IPX) networks. SNMP provides a standardized means for hosts to communicate with one another and is commonly used for remote monitoring and configuration. For example, you might use an SNMP management tool to manage routers or other devices in your network, gather information about workstations on the network, detect unauthorized attempts to reconfigure certain network devices, and so on.

Understanding How SNMP Works

SNMP functions through *SNMP management systems* and *SNMP agents.* A management system is an application that requests information from SNMP agents and directs agents to perform certain tasks, such as setting options on the remote device, returning configuration data, and so on. For example, you might have a non-Windows 2000 router on the network that contains firmware to enable it to function as an SNMP agent. You use a management system (SNMP-aware application) on your local workstation to manage the router, by viewing and changing the router's configuration and monitoring its status.

SNMP management systems send SNMP *messages* to agents, which respond to those messages. In most cases, the management system requests information from a *management information base,* or MIB, managed by the agent. The MIB is a set of objects that function as a database of information about the managed host. The only message an SNMP agent generates on its own is a *trap,* which is an alarm-triggered event on the agent host. A system reboot on the agent host is an example of a trap.

SNMP uses *communities* to provide a limited amount of security for SNMP and a means of grouping SNMP management systems with agents. Agents respond only to management systems in their list of communities to which they belong. The community name serves as a password for access by the management system to the agent. Agents can belong to multiple communities.

The SNMP service included with Windows 2000 enables a Windows 2000 computer to function as an SNMP agent to allow remote administration of the following:

✦ Windows 2000 Server

✦ Windows 2000 Professional

✦ Windows 2000-based DHCP

✦ Windows 2000-based WINS

✦ Internet Information Services (IIS)

✦ LAN Manager

✦ Exchange 2000

✦ SQL Server 2000

Windows 2000 does not include any management system software, and the SNMP service functions only as an SNMP agent. However, there are third-party SNMP management tools for Windows 2000 and related services.

Installing and Configuring SNMP

You add the SNMP service through the Add/Remove Programs object in the Control Panel. After you open Add/Remove Programs, click Add/Remove Windows Components. Open the Management and Monitoring Tools item and select SNMP Service, then click OK. Click Next to install the software.

The following sections explain how to configure the SNMP service (set community names and other tasks). You manage the SNMP service through the Computer Management console. Right-click My Computer and choose Manage, or double-click the Computer Management icon in Control Panel/Administrative Tools. After the console opens, expand the Services and Applications branch and select the Services node. You'll find the SNMP service included in the list of installed services.

Configure agent properties

After installing the SNMP service, you need to configure agent properties, which includes general information such as who is responsible for managing the agent host and the types of services with which the agent will interact on the computer.

Open the Services node of the Computer Management console and double-click the SNMP Service or select the service and choose Action ⇨ Properties to display the service's property sheet. The General, Log On, Recovery, and Dependencies pages are the same as for other services. Click the Agent tab to configure the following agent properties:

✦ **Contact:** Specify the name of the person responsible for managing the host computer.

✦ **Location:** Specify the physical location of the computer or the contact's location or other information (phone number, extension, and so on).

✦ **Physical:** Select this option if the agent host manages physical hardware such as hard disk partitions.

✦ **Applications:** Select this option if the agent uses any applications that transmit data using the TCP/IP protocol.

✦ **Datalink and subnetwork:** Select this option if the agent host manages a bridge.

✦ **Internet:** Select this option if the agent host is an Internet gateway.

✦ **End-to-end:** Select this option if the host uses IP. This option should always be selected.

Configure traps

Use the Traps tab of the SNMP service to configure computers to which the SNMP service sends traps. From the Community name drop-down list, select the community for which you want to assign a trap destination. If you have no communities set yet, type the community name in the combo box and click Add to List. Then, click Add to display a simple dialog box in which you specify the host name, IP address, or IPX address of the remote computer to receive the trap notification. Repeat the process to add other trap destinations as needed.

Configure security

Use the Security tab of the SNMP Service's properties to configure the communities in which the agent participates and optionally a list of hosts from which the agent accepts SNMP packets. By default, the agent accepts packets from all hosts. The Security page contains the following options:

✦ **Send authentication trap:** Select this option to have the agent send a message to all trap destinations if the agent receives an SNMP request from a host or community not listed in the "Accepted community names" list or "Accept SNMP packets from these hosts" list. The message is sent to all hosts in the trap destination list on the Traps property page to indicate that a remote management system failed authentication (potentially indicating an unauthorized access attempt).

✦ **Accepted community names:** Use this list and the associated buttons to modify the list of communities in which the agent participates and the community rights for each. You can select from the following rights:

- **None:** Prevent the agent host from processing any SNMP requests from the specified community. For example, you might configure None for the Public community for enhanced security.

- **Notify:** Select this option to allow the agent host to only send traps to the selected community.

- **Read Only:** Use this option to allow remote consoles to view data in the local MIB but not change it. This option prevents the agent from processing SNMP SET requests.

- **Read Write:** Use this option to allow remote consoles to make changes on the managed system. This option allows the agent to process SNMP SET requests.

- **Read Create:** Use this option to allow the agent to create new entries in the SNMP tables.

✦ **Accept SNMP packets from any host:** Select this option to allow the agent to process requests from all hosts in the "Accepted community names" list.

✦ **Accept SNMP packets from these hosts:** Select this option to define a specific list of hosts from which the agent will process SNMP requests.

Translating events to traps

In order to trap events and enable the agent to transmit the traps to the management systems defined in its Traps properties, you need to first translate the event to an SNMP trap. For example, to trap a system shutdown, you need to convert the system event 513 to an SNMP trap.

Windows 2000 provides two utilities you can use to translate local events to SNMP traps. The first, Evntcmd.exe, is a command-line utility you can integrate in batch files or use dynamically from a command console. For a description of command switches for Evntcmd, issue the **evntcmd /?** command at a console prompt. The other tool, Evntwin.exe, provides a graphical user interface for translating events to traps. Click Start ➪ Run and enter **evntwin** to run the Event to Trap Translator.

To translate a trap, select the Custom option and click Edit to expand the dialog box to include the Event Sources and Events lists (Figure 12-11). Search through the Event Sources list to find the source of the event you want to trap (such as Security for system shutdown, startup, logon, and so on). In the Events list, locate and select the event you want to trap, then click Add. Windows 2000 displays the Properties dialog box, which lets you specify the following two options:

✦ **If event count reaches:** Specify how many times the event can occur before a trap is generated.

✦ **Within the time interval:** Specify an optional time interval in which the number of events specified by the previous option must occur to generate a trap.

After you specify the properties for the trap, click OK to add it to the list. Repeat the process for any other events you need to trap.

Setting general properties

You can configure a handful of settings in the Event to Trap Translator to limit trap length and throttle the number of traps transmitted by the agent. With the Event to Trap Translator program open, click Settings to display the Settings dialog box. Configure the following options as needed:

✦ **Limit trap length:** Select this option to limit the length of data sent with the trap to the number of bytes specified by the following option.

✦ **Trap length *n* bytes:** Set the size in bytes for the trap. Any additional data is truncated if the trap exceeds the specified length.

✦ **Trim insertion strings first:** Trim insertion strings from the trap data before truncating the data when the trap exceeds the specified length.

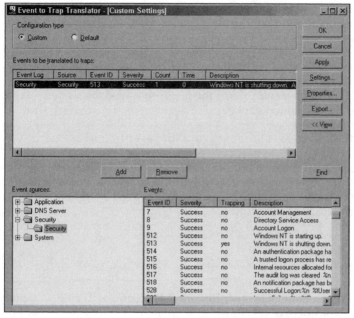

Figure 12-11: The Event to Trap Translator expanded to show event sources

✦ **Trim formatted message first:** Trim formatted message text from the trap data before truncating the data when the trap exceeds the specified length.

✦ **Apply throttle:** Select to limit the number of traps that can be sent in a given period of time.

✦ **Don't apply throttle:** Select to allow an unlimited number of traps to be transmitted.

✦ **Number of traps:** Set the maximum number of traps allowed in the given time frame when throttling is turned on.

✦ **Interval of time (seconds):** Set the interval in seconds that the specified number of traps can be transmitted before throttling takes effect.

Exporting the trap list

After you've taken the time to weed through the event list and create traps for a number of events, you probably will want to archive the data in case you experience a problem with the Event to Trap Translator or the system and need to reconfigure the traps. You might also want to configure the same traps on several other systems without having to reconfigure them manually. The solution in both situations is to export the trap list. After you have the traps configured as needed, click Export in the Event to Trap Translator. Windows 2000 prompts you for a file name. Save the file in an appropriate archive location or where you can access it from the other workstations. The file automatically receives a .cnf file extension.

Use the `Evntcmd` command to load the event list into the system. For example, the following command will load the file `events.cnf` from a network share into the local computer:

```
Evntcmd \\srv2\config\events.cnf
```

Use the following command to load the file from a local file named `netevents.cnf` to a remote system named `work23`:

```
Evntcmd -s work23 c:\snmp-stuff\netevents.cnf
```

When configuring traps on a remote computer, the SNMP service need not be running on the local computer. You will, however, have to copy the `evntcmd.exe` application to the local computer, as it is not installed by default (but rather, installs with the SNMP service).

Summary

The Transmission Control Protocol/Internet Protocol, or TCP/IP, is rapidly becoming the protocol of choice for many networks, partly because of the proliferation of the Internet, but also for the flexibility the protocol offers. TCP/IP is a complex protocol, however, so there are several issues to address when you configure a network for TCP/IP. Once you understand addressing and subnet issues, you need to decide how systems will receive their IP addresses (statically or dynamically) and assignments for name servers, gateways, and so on. You can use DHCP to automatically configure TCP/IP settings for clients on the network, which simplifies administration and helps protect against address conflicts from statically assigned addresses. You can have local clients retrieve IP address leases from an external network through a DHCP relay agent. A Windows 2000 server running Routing and Remote Access Service (RRAS) can function as a DHCP relay agent.

Routing is another important aspect of TCP/IP. Windows 2000 RRAS can function as a router, supporting dedicated and demand-dial connections. RRAS supports RIP and OSPF, and can function as a DHCP relay agent. RRAS also supports IGMP, enabling you to configure a Windows 2000 server running RRAS to perform multi-cast forwarding and limited routing. Through Network Address Translation (NAT), you can use RRAS as a proxy and Internet gateway, helping to secure your local network from outside intrusion.

You'll find several tools included with Windows 2000 to help you troubleshoot TCP/IP connections. The `ping` command, for example, is one of the most useful tools for checking basic TCP/IP connectivity. Other tools enable you to trace network routes, view IP configurations, view routing tables, and perform other troubleshooting tasks.

In addition to TCP/IP, Windows 2000 includes support for additional legacy protocols including NetBEUI, IPX/SPX, and DLC. NetBEUI is a good choice for small networks and supports older Microsoft client platforms such as Windows 3.*x*, Windows 9*x*, and Windows NT. IPX/SPX provides connectivity to NetWare servers, but also can be used as the primary protocol when no NetWare servers are present on the network. DLC is used primarily for connecting to IBM mainframes and network-connected printers.

One final topic covered in this chapter is SNMP, or Simple Network Management Protocol. Windows 2000 includes an SNMP agent that enables the computer to respond to SNMP requests from local and remote management services. You can configure a Windows 2000 server to generate traps for specific events and have those traps transmitted to specific management services for monitoring and administration purposes.

✦ ✦ ✦

DHCP

This chapter covers configuring and managing a Windows 2000 Server-based Dynamic Host Configuration Protocol (DHCP) server and DHCP clients.

Overview of DHCP

The TCP/IP protocol, which is required for Internet connectivity and is rapidly becoming a protocol of choice for many intranets, requires that each node on the network have a unique IP address. This includes any individual network object such as a server, workstation, printer, router, and so on. You can assign IP addresses to network nodes either *statically* or *dynamically*. With a statically assigned address, you specify a fixed address for a given node, and that address never changes unless you manually change it. Static assignment is the option to use when the network node must have the same IP address all the time. Web and FTP servers or devices such as printers that don't support anything other than static assignments are prime examples of such situations.

You also can assign IP addresses dynamically through the Dynamic Host Configuration Protocol. DHCP enables network nodes to take IP address assignments from a DHCP server automatically at startup. Although dynamic assignment means that IP addresses for network nodes can and do typically change each time the node is restarted, that poses a problem only in those situations in which a computer needs the same IP address for every session. In all other situations, including for most workstations and many servers, dynamic assignment enables you to manage a pool of IP addresses more effectively to prevent address conflicts. DHCP also lets you allocate a smaller number of IP addresses than the number of computers using them, provided the maximum number of live nodes at any given time doesn't exceed the number of available addresses. An example of such a situation is when you're using a server to provide dial-up access for multiple users. You might allocate 20 IP addresses to accommodate 50 dial-in users. Each user would receive a unique IP address assignment from the DHCP server at connection time, to a maximum of 20 concurrent connections.

Perhaps the most important benefit to DHCP is in the area of administration. DHCP makes it much easier to manage the IP address configuration of clients, since you can affect all changes from a central server, rather than requiring changes on individual clients. The more computers on the network, the greater the advantage DHCP brings to address management. Rather than manually reconfiguring network settings at several hundred (or more) workstations when a network change occurs, you can simply change the settings at the server and either push the changes transparently to the user or allow the changes to take place when the clients restart.

The Windows 2000 DHCP Server

Windows 2000 Server includes a built-in DHCP service that offers excellent functionality for allocating and managing addresses. The DHCP Server service is built on industry standards (Request for Comments or RFCs) defined by the Internet Engineering Task Force (IETF). This adherence to standards ensures that the DHCP service will accommodate not only Windows 2000 clients but other clients as well, including UNIX, Macintosh, and so on.

As with other Windows 2000 services, you manage DHCP on a Windows 2000 server through the Microsoft Management Console (MMC). The DHCP service console snap-in enables you to create DHCP scopes (a range of addresses and corresponding properties), assign global properties, view current assignments, and perform all other DHCP administration tasks.

In addition to supporting the IETF standards, the Windows 2000 DHCP service extends the functionality of DHCP to include logging, monitoring, and other features that integrate DHCP with the Windows 2000 operating system. In addition, several new features were added in Windows 2000 to improve DHCP's usefulness, administration, and integration with other services such as DNS. These features are discussed in the following sections.

Support for Dynamic DNS

DHCP provides for dynamic address assignment and therefore can make it difficult to maintain accurate name-to-address mapping in DNS servers. As soon as a node changes its address, records in the DNS database become invalid. Windows 2000 DHCP integrates with DNS by enabling the DHCP server and clients to request updates to the DNS database when address or host names change. This capability enables the DNS database to remain up-to-date even for clients with dynamically assigned IP addresses.

Dynamic DNS (DDNS) functions through a client-server mechanism. Windows 2000 DHCP clients support DDNS and can directly request that a Windows 2000 DNS server update their host resource records (also called A records) when the clients' IP addresses or host names change. Windows 2000 DHCP servers can also submit requests on behalf of clients, although a DHCP server can request an update to both the clients' host and pointer (PTR) records. Host records are used for host-to-address mapping, and pointer records are used for reverse lookup.

A Windows 2000 DHCP server also can act as a proxy for non-Windows 2000 DHCP clients to perform dynamic DNS updates. For example, a Windows 2000 DHCP server can perform updates for Windows 95/98 and Windows NT clients, which do not natively support dynamic DNS and are therefore unable to submit requests to either the DHCP server or DNS server to update their resource records. Figure 13-1 illustrates how DHCP and DNS interact.

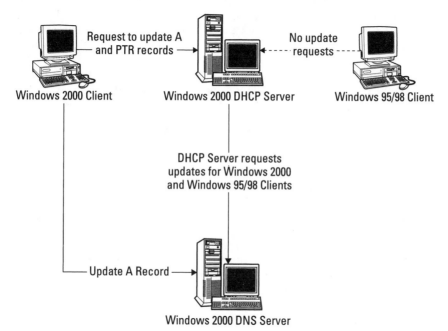

Figure 13-1: DHCP supports automatic updates to DNS when host name or IP address changes occur.

 See the section "Configuring Windows 2000 DHCP Clients" later in this chapter for an explanation of how to configure clients to use DDNS.

Vendor and User Classes

Vendor classes enable you to define a set of DHCP settings for a specific equipment vendor and apply those settings to any node falling into that class. User classes enable you to do much the same thing, defining DHCP settings to apply to a specific group of nodes. Vendor and user classes offer enhanced flexibility in assigning custom settings to individual nodes or groups of nodes without affecting others on the same network.

Through a vendor or user class, a node can request a custom set of DHCP settings to suit its configuration. For example, you might assign shorter lease durations to notebook PCs because they leave the network frequently. You define a user class called Notebook and assign to it a shorter lease period. The client, which presents the user class to the server, receives the shorter lease based on that user class.

Multicast Address Allocation

Multicast addresses enable IP traffic to be broadcast to a group of nodes and is most commonly used in audio or video conferencing. A standard IP address is also known as a *unicast address* because traffic is broadcast to a single address. A multicast address, however, enables a group of computers to receive the same data packets with a single broadcast. This is different from a situation in which the same traffic is sent using multiple broadcasts to a group of unicast addresses. The use of multicasting enables a group of computers to receive the same data without duplicating the packets and thereby reducing packet traffic.

Unauthorized DHCP Server Detection

Unauthorized DHCP servers can cause real problems in a network by allocating incorrect or conflicting configuration information to clients. For example, an administrator or power user might install and start a DHCP server, unaware that one or more DHCP servers already exist on the network. There was previously nothing to prevent this "rogue" DHCP server from starting. Windows 2000 addresses that potential problem.

The Active Directory stores a list of authorized DHCP servers. When a Windows 2000 DHCP server in a domain starts, it attempts to determine if it is listed as an authorized server in the AD. If it is unable to connect to the AD or does not find itself listed in the AD as an authorized server, it assumes it is unauthorized and the service does not accept DHCP client requests. If the server does find itself in the AD, it begins processing client requests.

Workgroup DHCP servers (standalone servers not belonging to a domain) behave somewhat differently. When a workgroup DHCP server starts, it broadcasts a DHCPINFORM message. Any domain-based DHCP servers on the network respond with DHCPACK and provide the name of the directory domain of which they are a part. If the workgroup DHCP server receives any DHCPACK messages from domain DHCP servers, the workgroup server assumes it isn't authorized and does not service client requests. If a workgroup DHCP server detects no other servers or detects only other workgroup DHCP servers, it begins processing client requests. Therefore, workgroup DHCP servers will not operate on a network where domain-based DHCP servers are active, but can coexist with other workgroup DHCP servers.

Automatic Client Configuration

Windows 2000 DHCP clients attempt to locate a DHCP server at startup and renew any unexpired leases (a lease is an IP address and the associated data allocated from a DHCP server). If no DHCP server is found, the client pings the default gateway defined by the lease. If the ping succeeds, the client continues to use the lease and automatically attempts to renew the lease when half the lease time expires.

If the client is unable to locate a DHCP server and pinging the default gateway fails, the client assumes that it is on a network without DHCP services, automatically assigns itself an IP address, and continues checking for a DHCP server every five minutes. The client assigns itself an address in the class B subnet 169.254.0.0 (subnet mask 255.255.0.0), but prior to assigning, the address tests to determine that the address is valid and doesn't conflict with other nodes.

Automatic address assignment is a useful feature, particularly for small peer networks in which there is no DHCP server (such as a home network). It enables users to move between networks with relative ease and eliminates the need to reconfigure their systems. For example, a user can move his notebook from the office to home and have a valid address within the current network without having to reconfigure TCP/IP each time.

Improved Monitoring and Reporting

The DHCP service performs its own monitoring and logs events to the System log, which you can view with the Event Viewer console. DHCP has also been enhanced in Windows 2000 to provide additional monitoring and statistical reporting. For example, you can configure DHCP to generate alerts when the percentage of available addresses in a given scope drops below a certain point.

Installing and Configuring the DHCP Server

The process of installing DHCP is relatively simple. Configuring a server and putting it into service is much more complex, however, particularly if you are new to DHCP. The following sections explain how to install the DHCP service and configure global and scope-specific settings.

Installing DHCP

As with other services, you add DHCP through the Add/Remove Programs object in the Control Panel. Open Add/Remove Programs and click Add/Remove Windows Components. Open the Networking Services item and select Dynamic Host Configuration Protocol, click OK, and then click Next. Follow the prompts to complete the software installation. After the software is installed, you can begin configuring and using DHCP without restarting the server.

Using the DHCP Console

Windows 2000 provides an MMC console to enable you to manage DHCP servers both locally and on remote computers (Figure 13-2). You can perform all DHCP administrative functions through the DHCP console. To open the DHCP console, choose Start ⇨ Programs ⇨ Administrative Tools ⇨ DHCP.

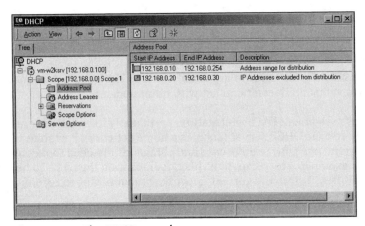

Figure 13-2: The DHCP console

By default, the DHCP console connects to the local DHCP server, showing the server's IP address in the left pane. You can use the console to manage DHCP servers both locally and remotely. To connect to a different server, right-click the DHCP node (the top-most node) in the left pane and choose Add Server. Type the name or IP address of the server you want to manage and click OK. DHCP adds the server to the list.

Like most MMC consoles, DHCP functions as a two-pane console with the tree pane to the left and the contents pane to the right. The following sections explain how to configure DHCP using the console.

Creating Scopes

A DHCP *scope* is a set of properties that define a range of IP addresses and related settings such as DNS servers, default gateway, and other information that the client needs to obtain from the DHCP server. Before you can begin using DHCP to assign addresses, you need to create at least one scope. Scopes can be active or inactive, so you also need to make the scope active before the server can allocate addresses from the scope to clients. This chapter assumes you're going to fully define the scope before activating it.

DHCP provides a wizard to take you through the process of creating a scope. To create a scope, right-click the server in the tree and choose New Scope. Or, select the server and choose Action ➪ New Scope. The wizard prompts for the following information:

✦ **Name:** This is the friendly name that appears in the DHCP console for the scope. An example might be "Houston Office scope."

✦ **Description:** This optional description appears on the scope's General property page (right-click the scope and choose Properties to view). Assign a description to help you recognize the purpose of the scope. For example, you might use the address range in the description.

✦ **Start IP address:** Specify the beginning address of the range of IP addresses you want to assign to the scope using dotted octet format.

✦ **End IP address:** Specify the ending address of the range of IP addresses you want to assign to the scope using dotted octet format.

✦ **Length** or **Subnet mask:** You can specify the subnet mask for the address range using either the address length or subnet mask in dotted octet format.

✦ **Exclusions, Start address and End address:** Use this page to specify one or more ranges of addresses to be excluded from the scope. Addresses in an excluded range are not used by DHCP or allocated to clients. If the addresses you want to exclude fall outside of the address range defined for the scope, you don't have to explicitly define an exclusion. For example, assume you create a scope with the included range 192.168.0.100 through 192.168.0.254. You do not have to create an exclusion for 192.168.0.1 through 192.168.0.99, which are implicitly excluded. However, using this same example, you would need to create an exclusion if you wanted to prevent the address range 192.168.0.150 through 192.168.0.160 from being allocated to clients. If, however, you do choose an exclusion range, it must fall within the scope created on the previous page.

✦ **Lease duration:** This property defines the length of time an IP address assignment is valid and is applicable to all clients unless modified by a user or vendor class assignment (in effect, it is the default lease period). When the lease duration expires, the client must request a renewal of the address, and failing that (because the address might already have been reassigned while the client was offline, for example), request a new address lease. The default is eight hours. See the section, "Defining and Implementing User and Vendor Classes," later in this chapter for additional information.

✦ **Configure other options:** The wizard gives you the option of configuring the default gateway and DNS server properties to assign to the scope. See the section "Setting General Scope Options" later in this chapter for more information.

✦ **Activate the scope:** Although you can activate the scope immediately after creating it, you should make sure you've fully defined all required scope properties prior to activation to ensure that clients receive all necessary DHCP properties. You can activate the scope later after fully defining the scope.

After you create a scope, it shows up in the DHCP console as a branch under the server's node in the tree pane, as shown in Figure 13-2. You'll see multiple scope branches if the server hosts more than one scope. Each scope branch includes the following objects:

✦ **Address Pool:** This branch lists the included address pool for the scope along with any exclusion ranges. Each scope has only one inclusion range, but can contain multiple exclusion ranges.

✦ **Address Leases:** This branch lists current client address leases, including the IP address, name, and lease expiration.

✦ **Reservations:** This branch lists address reservations, which reserve specific IP addresses for specific users based on the user's MAC address (physical network adapter address). See the section "Creating Reservations" later in this chapter for more information.

✦ **Scope Options:** This branch lists additional properties passed to clients when they receive address leases from this scope. Typical properties include default router, DNS name server assignments, time server, and time offset. The following section explains how to configure these settings.

Setting General Scope Options

You can specify a wide range of scope properties in addition to those discussed so far. These properties are given to clients when they receive a lease from the server. For example, the scope's properties can assign the default gateway and DNS servers the client should use, a time server for synchronizing the client's internal clock with the network or server, and many other properties. In most situations, you'll only need to configure the default gateway and DNS servers, although some situations might warrant configuring other properties as well.

To configure general scope options, open the DHCP console and then open the scope you want to modify properties for. Right-click Scope Options and choose Configure Options to display the Scope Options property sheet, shown in Figure 13-3.

The General tab enables you to configure properties that apply to all clients receiving address leases through the scope. As Figure 13-3 shows, you select an item by clicking it, and then you specify the value(s) for the item in the lower half of the property sheet. Enable or disable properties by selecting or deselecting their checkboxes in the list. Set the value for each one and then click OK.

The Advanced tab (Figure 13-4) lets you configure global properties for specific vendor and user classes. The default vendor classes are as follows:

✦ **DHCP standard options:** These are the same options that appear on the General tab by default and apply to all client connections for which no vendor or user class is specified.

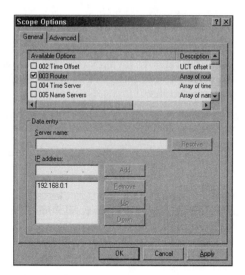

Figure 13-3: The Scope Options property sheet

✦ **Microsoft options:** These options define Microsoft-specific DHCP properties for Microsoft clients.

✦ **Microsoft Windows 2000 options:** These options define Microsoft Windows 2000-specific properties for Windows 2000 clients.

✦ **Microsoft Windows 98 options:** This selection can be used to define Windows 98-specific options, although by default none are defined.

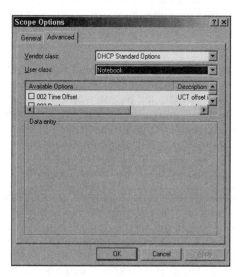

Figure 13-4: The Advanced tab

By default, there are three user classes defined:

✦ **Default BOOTP Class:** These properties apply to clients that receive a lease via BOOTP. BOOTP enables clients to retrieve a valid address along with a boot image that enables the computer to boot. BOOTP is typically used as a mechanism to boot diskless workstations.

✦ **Default Routing and Remote Access Class:** These properties apply to clients that receive a lease through RRAS connections.

✦ **Default User Class:** These properties apply to all clients not handled by a different user class.

Note   See the section "Defining and Implementing Vendor and User Classes" later in this chapter for detailed information on configuring and using vendor and user classes to customize lease properties for specific systems and users.

Default gateway

The Router lease property defines the default gateway assigned to the DHCP client. You can specify an array of addresses, giving the client multiple gateways to use. If the client's primary gateway fails for some reason, traffic will route through the next available gateway, providing fail-over insurance against a loss of connectivity. To assign a gateway to the array, enter the IP address in the IP address box in dotted octet format, then click Add. You can enter a host name in the Server name box and click Resolve if you know the host name of the gateway but not its IP address. Clicking Resolve performs a DNS lookup and returns the IP address in the IP address field if successful. You can specify multiple IP addresses, clicking Add to add each one to the array. Use the Up and Down buttons to change the order of the list. The client then tries the routers in sequence, starting with the top router.

Domain name and DNS servers

In addition to assigning one or more gateways, you will probably also want to assign at least one DNS server. Select 006 DNS Servers in the list and then add the IP addresses of the DNS servers to the list, just as you would when adding a router to the router list. The order of servers in the list defines the order in which the client will attempt to resolve names to addresses. Use the Up and Down buttons to change the order.

Domain name

Another property you should consider setting is the domain name. This property defines the client's domain and is used to create the user's fully qualified domain name (FQDN). The client appends its host name to the domain name to create the FQDN. You can specify the domain name within the client's DNS properties, but setting it through DHCP instead enables the domain name to be changed dynamically when the client is granted a lease. If all the systems on the network use DHCP, this enables you to change your entire organization's domain without changing any client settings — you simply change the domain name property in the DHCP server. Because of potential unseen pitfalls (clients with statically assigned domain names, for example), this isn't the recommended way of changing domain names.

Other scope properties

You can configure a wide range of other properties that are passed to the DHCP client when a lease is granted. Review the list of properties and configure those that apply to your network and client needs.

Configuring Global DHCP Options

Within each scope, you can configure properties such as domain name, gateway, and DNS servers, as explained in the previous section. These properties apply to all leases granted through the selected scope. You also can configure these properties to apply globally to all scopes defined on the server. These global options are used unless overridden by a scope-assigned property.

To configure global DHCP options, open the DHCP console, right-click the Server Options node, and choose Configure Options. The DHCP console displays the same property sheet you use to assign properties for a scope. Select and configure properties as needed.

Creating Reservations

A *reservation* assigns a specific IP address to a specific MAC address. The MAC address is a unique hardware-based address that uniquely identifies a network adapter (NIC) on the network. Reservations enable a specific adapter to receive the same IP address assignment from the DHCP server and prevent the address from being leased to any other adapter. In effect, leases let you enjoy the flexibility offered by DHCP while still enabling you to assign a static IP address. Through reservations, you ensure that the NIC always has the same IP address, but enable other configuration changes to be applied dynamically (such as domain name, router, DNS servers, and so on).

Note   Reservations do not assign the same IP address to a computer per se, because the reservation is associated with the NIC's MAC address, not the computer name. This is only a real distinction in multi-homed systems (those containing multiple NICs).

Before creating a reservation for an NIC, you need to know the NIC's MAC address. On Windows NT and Windows 2000 systems, you can use the ipconfig command at a console prompt to view MAC addresses for NICs in the computer. Open a console prompt on the system and issue the command ipconfig /all. The command lists network configuration data for each NIC, including the MAC address.

When you have the MAC address of the client's NIC, open the DHCP console and then open the scope where you want to create the reservation. Right-click the Reservations node and choose New Reservation to open the New Reservation dialog box (Figure 13-5). Use the following list as a guide to configure the reservation:

✦ **Reservation name:** This name appears in the DHCP console next to the reservation IP address (left pane). You can specify the computer's name, user name, or other information to help you identify the NIC for which the address is reserved.

✦ **IP address:** Specify the IP address within the scope to reserve for the specified NIC.

✦ **MAC address:** Enter the MAC address of the NIC for which the address is reserved.

✦ **Description:** This optional description appears in the contents pane of the DHCP console.

✦ **Supported types:** You can designate the type of client (DHCP, BOOTP, or both) that can use the reservation.

Figure 13-5: Reservations assign an IP address to a specific network adapter.

Setting Global Scope Properties

Before you activate a scope and begin using it, there are a handful of properties you should configure that apply to the scope on a global basis. To set these properties, open the DHCP console, right-click the scope, and choose Properties to display the Scope Properties sheet. The General tab lets you modify the scope-friendly name, IP address range, lease period, and description. These options are self-explanatory.

The DNS tab determines how DHCP integrates with DNS. You'll find an explanation of how to configure DHCP clients to use DDNS in the section "Configuring Windows

2000 DHCP Clients" later in this chapter. For now, you can use the following list as a guide to configuring settings on the DNS page:

✦ **Automatically update DHCP client information in DNS:** Select this option to direct the DHCP server to attempt to update client DNS information in the DNS server. The server will by default attempt to update the client's host and pointer records to associate the client's host name with its IP address.

✦ **Update DNS only if DHCP client requests:** Select this option to have the server update the DNS records only if the client requests the update. Currently, only Windows 2000 clients can request the update.

✦ **Always update DNS:** Select this option to update the DNS records regardless of whether the client requests an update.

✦ **Discard forward (name-to-address) lookups when lease expires:** Select this option to have the DNS server discard the host record for a client when its lease expires.

✦ **Enable updates for DNS clients that do not support dynamic update:** Select this option to enable the DHCP server to update host and pointer records with DNS for clients that don't support dynamic update (such as earlier versions of Windows).

The Advanced property page lets you configure the types of clients the DHCP server will handle with the selected scope. You can support DHCP only, BOOTP only, or both. If you select BOOTP only or both, you can configure the lease duration for BOOTP clients using the lease duration group, specifying a lease duration or configuring the scope to provide unlimited leases to BOOTP clients.

Activating and Deactivating a Scope

At this point, you should have enough data in the scope to activate it, although you might want to further configure your DHCP server by implementing vendor or user classes, using superscopes or multicast scopes, and so on (both are discussed later in this chapter). When you're ready to activate the scope, open the DHCP console. Right-click the scope in question and choose Activate. To deactivate a scope and prevent it from being used to assign leases, right-click the scope and choose Deactivate.

Authorizing the Server

An additional step for domain-based DHCP servers is to *authorize* the server. Authorizing a server lists it in the Active Directory as an authorized DHCP server. As explained earlier, Windows 2000 DHCP servers attempt to determine if they are authorized at startup and prior to processing client lease requests. Domain-based DHCP servers attempt to check the AD to determine if they are listed as an authorized server. If the server is unable to contact the AD or doesn't find itself listed, it does not begin servicing client requests. A workgroup-based DHCP server queries the network for other DHCP servers; if it identifies any domain-based DHCP servers, it assumes it is not authorized and does not service client requests. If no domain-based DHCP servers respond, however, the server starts servicing client requests. This means that multiple workgroup-based DHCP servers can operate on the network concurrently.

When you install the DHCP service on a domain-based server, the server is unauthorized by default. You must authorize the server before it can begin servicing client requests. Authorizing a server simply lists the server in the AD. To authorize a domain-based DHCP server, open the DHCP console, right-click the server in the left pane, and choose Authorize.

Defining and Implementing User and Vendor Classes

Vendor and user classes are new features incorporated into the Windows 2000 DHCP service. Vendor classes enable you to create new, predefined scope options without having to go through the lengthy process of submitting RFCs and getting approval for adding new options. You can use vendor classes to create options specific to a particular device or operating platform, and then assign those options based on user classes.

User classes enable you to assign unique scope options to individual clients. For example, you may apply a specific DHCP configuration to all notebook users that, among other things, sets the lease expiration at one hour rather than the default of eight hours. You can incorporate other special properties to suit that group's requirements as well.

Vendor Classes

In many respects, a vendor class is really just a container object that groups together custom DHCP options. You name the vendor class and assign to it new scope options not otherwise defined by the standard options. To create a vendor class, you specify a display name for the vendor class, description, and ID. The display name and description are primarily for convenience and identification within the DHCP console. The ID uniquely identifies the vendor class.

Creating a vendor class

To create, modify, or remove a vendor class, open the DHCP console. Right-click the server on which you want to work with vendor classes and choose Define Vendor Classes. DHCP displays a DHCP Vendor Classes dialog box that lists all currently defined vendor classes. Click Add to display the New Class dialog box, shown in Figure 13-6.

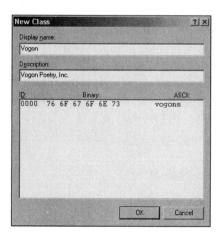

Figure 13-6: The New Class dialog box

The Display name is the friendly name for the vendor class within the DHCP console. You can include an optional description to further identify the vendor class. The ID is the data that clients use to request a specific set of DHCP options based on their vendor class. Click in the ID box under the Binary column if you want to enter the data in hexadecimal, or click under the ASCII column to enter the ID in ASCII characters. Choose a string that uniquely identifies the vendor class but is also easy to remember (and perhaps easy to type). Bear in mind that this is an identifier string only and needs to have no real relationship with the actual vendor name or other product information. However, using the vendor name in the ID will help you recognize the purpose for the vendor class.

Configuring vendor class options

After you create a new vendor class, you need to specify the DHCP options that will be available to that vendor class. To do so, open the DHCP console, right-click the server on which you want to define vendor class options, and choose Set Predefined Options. DHCP displays the Predefined Options and Values dialog box. Select the option class you want to modify values for and then click Add. DHCP displays the Option Type dialog box, shown in Figure 13-7.

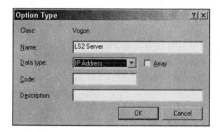

Figure 13-7: Use the Option Type dialog box to add vendor class options.

Provide information in the dialog box using the following list as a guide:

✦ **Name:** This is the name of the option as it appears in the Available Options list of the Scope Options property sheet. Specify a descriptive name such as Name Servers.

✦ **Data type:** Select from this drop-down list the type of data represented by the class option (byte, word, long, IP address, and so on).

✦ **Array:** Select this option if you're creating an array, such as a DNS server list or gateway list.

✦ **Code:** Specify a unique numeric code for the option.

✦ **Description:** Specify an optional description to help describe the function of the option value.

You may have surmised that creating a vendor class and assigning class options to it can be a time-consuming task, particularly if you need to assign many options. Whenever possible, you should use standard DHCP options and only override selected options with vendor class options when needed.

Note Windows 2000 incorporates three predefined vendor classes: Microsoft Options, Microsoft Windows 2000 Options, and Microsoft Windows 98 Options. The Microsoft Options and Microsoft Windows 2000 Options currently define three options: Disable NetBIOS, Release DHCP Lease on Shutdown, and Default Router Metric Base. You can use these options to implement the associated features for Windows 2000 clients. There are no predefined scope options for Windows 98 clients.

User Classes

While vendor classes enable you to define new DHCP scope options, user classes enable you to allocate DHCP scopes (whether standard or vendor class-defined) on a client-by-client basis. Each client can be configured with one or more user class IDs that the client submits to the DHCP server. The server responds with an appropriate lease based on the settings defined for that user class ID. For example, you might create a user class ID called *notebook* and configure its DHCP options to decrease the lease period. Or you might have a group of computers that requires a different set of DNS servers or default gateway. You can use user class IDs in all of these cases to assign DHCP options on a selective basis.

Note User classes must be supported at the client level. Currently, only Windows 2000 clients support user classes. This capability is not currently included with Windows 98 or Windows NT clients.

When a client submits a class ID to a DHCP server, the server provides all the default options defined for the scope not otherwise defined by the class ID. You can allocate DHCP options using the default options for the scope and apply selective options with the user class. This means you don't have to duplicate the default settings for a user class, but instead only have to configure those settings that are unique to clients in that user class.

Creating a user class

You define a user class in much the same way that you define a vendor class. Open the DHCP console, right-click the server at which you want to define the user class, and then choose Define User Classes. Click Add in the DHCP User Classes dialog box. As you do with a vendor class, specify a display name to appear in the DHCP console, an optional description, and the class ID. The class ID is the data you'll configure at the client level to enable it to request a lease based on the class ID. You can enter the class ID in either hexadecimal or ASCII format.

Configuring user class options

After you create a user class, you need to assign to it the DHCP scope options that need to apply to each client having the specified class ID. To do so, open the DHCP console and expand the server in question. Right-click Scope Options, choose Configure Options, and then click Advanced to display the Advanced tab, which is the same as shown in Figure 13-3. You can select options from the DHCP Standard Options vendor class or use any other defined vendor class. Select the desired user class from the User class drop-down list. The scope options that are predefined for the selected vendor class appear in the Available Options list. Browse through the list at configure scope options as you would for the default options.

There is no need to configure options that will otherwise be assigned through the global options for the scope. Instead, you only need to configure those options that are unique to the user class. For example, if all you're doing with the user class is reducing the lease period, then you only need to configure the Lease value within the user class. All other settings can be assigned to the client through the global scope properties. When you've configured all necessary properties, click OK.

Configuring a Client to Use Class IDs

You can assign multiple class IDs to a Windows 2000 client, although only the last one assigned is actually used to retrieve DHCP data. Each client by default assumes the class ID "Default BOOTP Class," which enables Windows 2000 clients that require BOOTP to retrieve settings from the DHCP server. If you assign any other class IDs, however, the class ID assigned last takes precedence and the client takes on all global scope options plus the scope options assigned to that last class ID. The scope options are not cumulative — the client will not take on all options for all class IDs assigned to the adapter in question.

You use the `ipconfig` command to assign a class ID to a Windows 2000 client. You can assign class IDs manually through a command console or through a startup script. The syntax for assigning a class ID is as follows:

```
ipconfig /setclassid [adapter] [ClassIDString]
```

To configure a client with the class ID "portable" on the default network connection (Local Area Connection), use the following command:

```
ipconfig /setclassid "Local Area Connection" portable
```

Tip You might want to rename your network connections using simpler names, if only to make it easier to perform `ipconfig` commands. To rename a network connection, open the Network and Dial-Up Connections folder, right-click the connection, and choose Rename. For example, you might rename "Local Area Connection" simply, "LAN."

Creating and Using Superscopes

Windows 2000 supports a DHCP feature called *superscopes,* which is an administrative feature that enables you to create and manage multiple scopes as a single entity. You can use superscopes to allocate IP addresses to clients on a *multinet,* which is a physical network segment containing multiple logical IP networks (a logical IP network is a cohesive range of IP addresses). For example, you might support three different class C logical IP networks on a physical network segment. Each of the three class C address ranges is defined as one of three individual child scopes under a superscope.

In many cases, you won't plan or set out to use a multinet, since using a single logical IP network is much simpler from an administration standpoint. However, you might need to use a multinet as an interim measure as your network size grows beyond the number of addresses available within the original scope. Or, you might need to migrate the network from one logical IP network to another, such as would be the case if you switched ISPs and therefore had to switch address assignments.

Tip Superscopes are useful on high-speed wide area networks, especially when planning for and managing shallow Active Directory domain trees (trees with multiple Active Directory sites and few domains). This is discussed in Chapters 8 and 9.

You also can use superscopes to support remote DHCP clients located on the far side of a DHCP or BOOTP relay agent. This enables you to support multiple physical subnets with a single DHCP server. Figure 13-8 illustrates a situation in which a single DHCP server supports multiple logical IP networks on the local physical network, as well as logical IP networks on the far side of a relay agent.

Naturally, you'll want to assign certain scope options, such as the default gateway within each scope, to place the option within the context of the scope. You can apply global options that can apply to all scopes in a superscope at the server level. All scopes on the server, whether in a superscope or not, will use the global options when options are not specifically defined within the individual scopes. For example, all clients can probably use the same set of DNS servers, so you'd define the DNS server array at the server level.

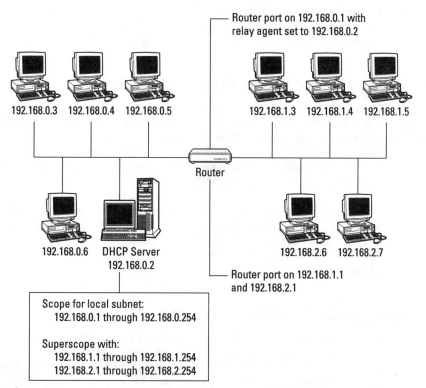

Figure 13-8: A single DHCP server can support multiple local IP networks and remote networks.

 Tip Keep in mind that superscopes are really just an administrative feature that provides a container for managing scopes as groups on the same server. A superscope does not actually allocate options of its own. DHCP options come either from the server (global) or from the properties of the individual scopes within the superscope.

Creating a Superscope

You can create a superscope only after you define at least one scope on the server (this prevents you from creating an empty superscope). Windows 2000 lets you select which existing scopes will be moved to the superscope. You can create additional scopes within the superscope afterwards. You can create multiple superscopes and create scopes both inside and outside of a superscope. So, a given server might have two superscopes with four scopes each, along with three scopes defined at the server level that are not part of either superscope.

To create a superscope, open the DHCP console. Right-click the server you want to create the superscope in and choose New Superscope (the command is not available if no scopes exist on the server). Windows 2000 prompts you to choose a friendly name for the scope and which existing scopes will be added to the superscope. Hold down the Shift key while selecting to choose multiple scopes.

Activating and Deactivating a Superscope

Windows 2000 automatically activates the superscope if one or more scopes in the superscope are active when you create the superscope. If not, you can activate individual scopes in the superscope, then activate the superscope itself. To activate individual scopes, right-click the scope and choose Activate. If the superscope contains only one scope, Windows 2000 activates the superscope as well. Otherwise, right-click the superscope and choose Activate.

You can deactivate an individual scope within a superscope, or you can deactivate the superscope, which deactivates all scopes in the superscope. Deactivating a scope prevents it from servicing additional client requests for address leases. Right-click either a scope or superscope and choose Deactivate to deactivate the scope or superscope.

Removing Scopes from a Superscope

You can remove one or more scopes from a superscope if necessary to restructure the scopes on the server. Removing a scope from a superscope does not delete the scope or deactivate it. Instead, it simply makes it a scope directly under the server branch rather than a child scope of the superscope. This enables you to add it to a different scope or eliminate the superscope without affecting its individual scopes.

To remove a scope from a superscope, open the DHCP console and open the superscope in question. Right-click the scope and choose Remove from Superscope. If the scope being removed is the only scope in the superscope, Windows 2000 removes the superscope (as you can't have an empty superscope).

Deleting Superscopes

Deleting a superscope removes the superscope and places its child scopes directly under the server branch of the DHCP server. The scopes are unaffected and continue to service client requests—they are simply no longer a member of a superscope. Open the DHCP console, right-click the superscope to be deleted, and choose Delete.

Creating Multicast Scopes

A *multicast scope,* as explained earlier, is used to broadcast IP traffic to a group of nodes using a single address, and is traditionally used in audio and video conferencing. Using multicast addresses simplifies administration and reduces network traffic because the data packets are sent once to the multicast address rather than individually to each recipient's unicast address.

A Windows 2000 DHCP server can allocate multicast addresses to a group of computers much like it allocates unicast addresses to individual computers. The protocol for multicast address allocation is Multicast Address Dynamic Client Allocation Protocol, or MADCAP. Windows 2000 can function as both a DHCP server and MADCAP server, independently. For example, one server might use the DHCP service to allocate unicast addresses through the DHCP protocol, and another server might allocate multicast addresses through the MADCAP protocol. In addition, a client can use either or both. A DHCP client doesn't have to use MADCAP, and vice versa, but a client can use both if the situation requires it.

As the use of multicasting is somewhat specialized, this chapter assumes you have a working knowledge of multicast addressing, routing, and so on, and focuses on explaining how to configure a Windows 2000 DHCP server to act as a MADCAP server.

Tip   For additional information on using multicast scopes, open Help in the DHCP console and search for "multicast scope."

You can create multiple multicast scopes on a Windows 2000 DHCP server as long as the scope address ranges don't overlap. Multicast scopes exist directly under the server branch and cannot be assigned to superscopes, which are intended only to manage unicast address scopes. To create a multicast scope, open the DHCP console, right-click the server that you want to create the multicast scope in, and choose New Multicast Scope. Windows 2000 starts a wizard that prompts you for the following information:

   ✦ **Name:** This is the friendly name as it appears for the scope in the DHCP console.

   ✦ **Description:** Specify an optional description to identify the purpose of the multicast scope.

   ✦ **Address range:** You can specify an address range between 224.0.0.0 and 239. 255.255.255, inclusive, which gives you a large range of addresses to use.

   ✦ **Time to Live (TTL):** Specify the number of routers the traffic must pass through on your local network.

   ✦ **Exclusion range:** You can define a range of multicast addresses to exclude from the scope, just as you can exclude unicast addresses from a DHCP scope.

   ✦ **Lease duration:** Specify the duration for the lease. The default is 30 days.

You can choose to activate the scope through the wizard or activate the scope later. Right-click a multicast scope and choose Activate to activate the scope.

Configuring Windows 2000 DHCP Clients

Configuring Windows 2000 clients to use DHCP is a relatively simple process. At the client, right-click My Network Places and choose Properties, or choose Start ➪ Settings ➪ Network and Dial-Up Connections to open the Network and Dial-Up Connections folder. Right-click the connection you want to configure for DHCP and choose Properties. Double-click the TCP/IP protocol in the list of installed components or select it and click Properties to display its property sheet.

You can configure the client to obtain its IP address from the DHCP server, obtain DNS server addresses through DHCP, or both. The controls on the General tab are self-explanatory.

Configuring DNS Options for DHCP

You can configure a Windows 2000 client to use Dynamic DNS (DDNS) to automatically update its host record when its host name changes or its IP address changes (including through DHCP lease renewal). Click Advanced on the General property page for the TCP/IP protocol for the connection to display the Advanced TCP/IP Settings dialog box. Then, click the DNS tab to display the DNS page, as shown in Figure 13-9.

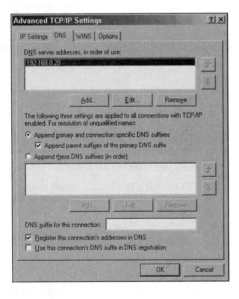

Figure 13-9: The DNS tab of Advanced TCP/IP Settings

Two settings on the DNS page control integration of DHCP and DDNS for the client:

✦ **Register this connection's addresses in DNS:** Select this option to have the client submit a request to the DNS server to update its host (A) record when its host name changes or IP address changes. The client submits the full computer name specified in the Network Identification tab of the System Properties sheet along with its IP address to the DNS server. You can view the System properties through the System object in the Control Panel, or right-click My Computer and choose Properties.

✦ **Use this connection's DNS suffix in DNS registration:** Select this option to have the client submit a request to the DNS server to update its host record when the host name changes or IP address changes. The difference from the previous option is that this option registers the client using the first part of the computer name specified in the System properties along with the DNS suffix specified by the option "DNS suffix for this connection" on the DNS tab.

Summary

DHCP provides a means through which you can allocate IP addresses to clients automatically when the clients start up, making it much easier to manage IP leases and corresponding properties in a network. Rather than modifying clients manually when a required change occurs (such as DNS server change, router change, and so on), you simply modify the properties of the scope on the DHCP server and allow the clients to retrieve the new data when they renew their leases. Through class IDs, you can allocate specific scope properties to clients to satisfy unique requirements of the client, such as gateways, DNS servers, lease duration, and so on.

The DHCP server service provided with Windows 2000 also enables a Windows 2000 server to act as a multicast address provider, allocating multicast addresses to clients that require them. A server can function as a unicast scope server, multicast scope server, or both.

A new management feature provided with the DHCP server service is the ability to create superscopes, which essentially act as containers for scopes. You can use superscopes to manage a set of address scopes as if they were a single scope.

✦   ✦   ✦

DNS and WINS

In Chapter 2 and the chapters in Part III, you learned that Active Directory domains are modeled on Internet domains. You also learned that Windows 2000 networks rely on TCP/IP as the network protocol of choice. In order to resolve Windows 2000 domain controllers and many other hosts running Windows 2000 services, you need to fully understand and be able to configure Domain Name Service (DNS). This chapter explains the services you can use to create DNS. It also covers Windows Internet Name Service (WINS) name servers, and includes coverage of Dynamic DNS (DDNS), client configuration, and related topics.

Overview of Domain Name Services

The Internet comprises many millions of devices including computers, routers, printers, and other devices, and each device is called a *node*. Each node requires a unique IP address to differentiate it from others and allow traffic to be routed to and from the node. Intranets also can employ the TCP/IP protocol and require that each node have a unique address, although in the case of an intranet, these IP addresses can come from a non-public reserved address space such as 192.168.0.*x*. Nodes on the Internet must have a unique, public IP address. IP addresses are difficult for most people to remember, and their sheer number makes it impractical to try to do so. The Domain Name Service (DNS) overcomes this problem by enabling users to work with names rather than addresses. In effect, DNS provides a means of *mapping* names to addresses. Rather than typing 207.25.71.9 to connect to CNN's Web site, for example, you connect with your browser to www.cnn.com. DNS takes care of translating www.cnn.com into the appropriate IP address. Mapping a name to an IP address is called *name resolution*.

The Internet arose from a network called the ARPANET, which comprised a relatively small number of computers in the 1970s (mostly defense and educational systems). With few nodes, it was relatively simple to provide name resolution. The Stanford Research Institute (SRI) maintained a single text file named `Hosts.txt` that contained the host-to-address translations for all the ARPANET's hosts. The operating systems (predominantly UNIX) used the `Hosts.txt` file to resolve names to addresses. System administrators copied the `Hosts.txt` file from SRI to their local systems periodically to provide an updated list.

As the number of hosts grew, the continued use of a `Hosts.txt` file to provide name resolution soon became impractical. In the mid-1980s, the DNS system was developed to provide a dynamic name resolution system that no longer relied on a static name-to-address map. Before you learn about the DNS system, however, you need to understand domain names.

Understanding Domain Names

As mentioned previously, each device on an IP network is a node. Many nodes are also termed *hosts*. Generally, a host is a computer, router, or other "smart" device, but any device can be considered a host and have a host name associated with it. In Windows 2000, a computer's name as it appears on the LAN is typically its host name. Assume for example that your computer's name is fred and that your computer resides in the `mcity.org` domain. The host name is fred, the domain name is `mcity.org`, and the Fully Qualified Domain Name (FQDN) of your computer is `fred.mcity.org`. The FQDN identifies the host's absolute location in the DNS namespace.

Domain names are not limited to a single level, as in this example. Assume that the `mcity.org domain` comprised several sites, each with their own subdomains. For example, assume the domain was divided into three subdomains: east, midwest, and west. The domain names would be `east.mcity.org`, `midwest.mcity.org`, and `west.mcity.org`. These domains could further be divided into subdomains, such as `sales.west.mcity.org`, `support.west.mcity.org`, and so on. Taking this example one step further, consider a host named fred in the `support.west.mcity.org` domain. This host's FQDN would be `fred.support.west.mcity.org`.

Table 14-1 lists the original top-level domains. Note that the root of the domain namespace is a null (""), often represented by a dot. The dot is omitted from Table 14-1.

Table 14-2 lists new top-level domains that at this time are proposed for implementation.

 Tip   See `http://www.gtld.com` for information about the new domain namespace.

Table 14-1
Original Top-Level Domains

Suffix	Purpose	Example
com	Commercial organizations such as businesses	microsoft.com
edu	Educational organizations such as colleges and universities	berkeley.edu
gov	Governmental organizations such as the IRS, SSA, NASA, and so on	nasa.gov
mil	Military organizations such as the army, navy, and so on	army.mil
net	Networking organizations such as ISPs	mci.net
org	Noncommercial organizations such as the IEEE standards body	ieee.org
int	International organizations such as NATO	nato.int

Table 14-2
New, Additional Top-Level Domains

Suffix	Purpose
shop	Online commerce organizations
web	Internet-related organizations
arts	Arts-related organizations
info	Information-related organizations
rec	Recreational organizations
firm	Businesses and professional organizations
nom	Primarily personal domain names

Several other domain types exist in addition to the domain types specified in Tables 14-1 and 14-2. The .us domain, for example, is used by governmental, regional, and educational institutions in the United States. Other countries have their own domains, such as .uk for the United Kingdom, .jp for Japan, and so on.

Tip   The Information Sciences Institute of the University of Southern California manages the `.us` domain, and its Web site provides links to enable you to research, register, and delegate within this domain. Point a Web browser to `http://www.nic.us` for more information on the `.us` domain or to request delegation for `.us` subdomains.

Until recently, an organization called InterNIC was responsible for managing and allocating domain names within the top-level domains. InterNIC became a for-profit business named Network Solutions and therefore had to give up its monopoly on the domain namespace. However, Network Solutions still has the ability to allocate domain names, as do a multitude of other companies on the Internet. To acquire a domain name for your organization, point your Web browser to `http://www.networksolutions.com`. You can use the Network Solutions site to perform a lookup of domain names to determine if the names are in use or are available, register new domains, modify domains, and so on.

Today's DNS System

Today's DNS system functions as a distributed database through a client/server relationship between DNS servers and clients requiring name resolution. The entire namespace of all domains comprises the DNS namespace. By using a distributed database architecture, DNS allows for local control over each domain while still enabling all clients to access the entire database when needed.

The DNS namespace comprises a hierarchical structure of domains, with each domain representing a branch on the tree and subdomains residing underneath. At the topmost level are the *root servers* that maintain the *root domains,* which currently include `.com`, `.net`, `.org`, `.mil`, `.edu`, `.gov`, and `.int`. The root of the domain namespace is a null ("") , often represented by a dot. Figure 14-1 illustrates the DNS namespace.

The root servers maintain only a limited amount of information about a given domain. Typically, the information includes only the name servers identified as *authoritative* for the zone (having authority over the domain's records). Records that map names to addresses within individual domains reside on the name server(s) for the domains in question. These name servers are typically managed by ISPs for the ISP's clients or by companies that manage their own domains. Certain other domains such as the `.us` domain are *delegated* to other organizations (ISPs, state agencies, educational institutions, and so on) that manage the domains for the respective domain holders. Distributing the DNS namespace in this way allows users to control their own domains while still remaining a part of the overall namespace.

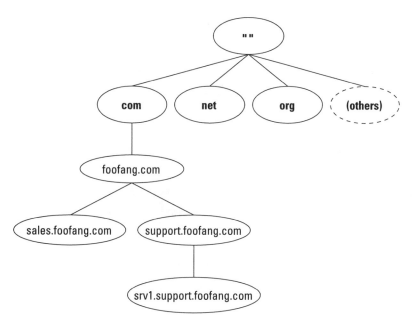

Figure 14-1: The DNS namespace is a hierarchical distributed database.

Name Servers, Resolvers, and Forward Lookup

DNS clients called *resolvers* submit queries to DNS servers to be resolved into IP addresses. For example, assuming that you want to connect to www.mcity.org, www is the host's alias (if the host name is something else) and mcity.org is the domain name (the same host could also be ftp.mcity.org). The resolver on your client computer prepares a DNS query for www.mcity.org and submits it to the DNS server identified in your client computer's TCP/IP settings, which in this case we'll assume is a DNS server on your LAN. The DNS server checks its local cache (which stores results of previous queries) and database and finds that it has no records for www.mcity.org. So, the DNS server submits a query to the root server for the .org domain. The root server looks up the mcity.org domain and responds with the IP address(es) of the name servers for the domain. Your DNS server then submits a query to the specified DNS server for mcity.org, which responds with the IP address of the host aliased to www. Your DNS server in turn provides this information to your resolver, which passes the data to your client application (in this case, a Web browser), and suddenly the www.mcity.org site pops up on your browser. Mapping a host name or alias to its address in this way is called *forward lookup*. Figure 14-2 illustrates a forward lookup request.

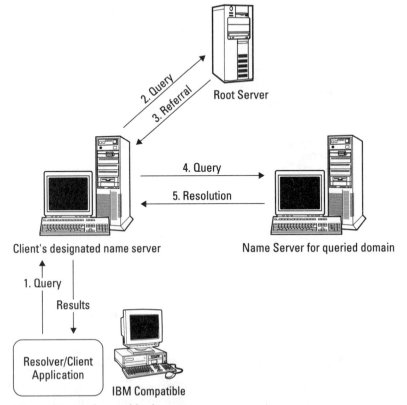

Figure 14-2: A forward lookup query

> **Tip** Keep in mind that domains and IP address ranges have no direct relationship. A single domain can use any number of different subnets, and host records in a domain can point to hosts outside of your local network and even outside of your domain. For example, you might outsource e-mail for your organization, which would mean that your domain would contain mail-related records that would point to a server outside of your subnet and LAN.

Name servers range from the root servers all the way down to the name servers at your department or organizational level. In most cases, a given name server manages all of the records for some portion of the DNS namespace called a *zone*. For the most part, the terms *zone* and *domain* are synonymous, but they are not the same. A zone comprises all of the data for a domain with the exception of parts of the domain delegated to other name servers (see "Configuring Subdomains and Delegation" later in this chapter). A zone is the part of the domain hosted on a particular name server. The domain comprises the whole of the domain wherever its components reside. When the entire domain resides on a single name server, then zone and domain are synonymous.

A name server that has full information about a given zone is said to be *authoritative* or *has authority* for the zone. A given name server can be authoritative for any number of zones, and can be both authoritative for some and non-authoritative for others. In addition, a name server can be either a *primary master* or *secondary master*. A primary master maintains locally the records for those domains for which it is authoritative. The system administrator for a primary master can add new records, modify existing records, and so on, on the primary master. Figure 14-3 illustrates the relationship between zones and domains.

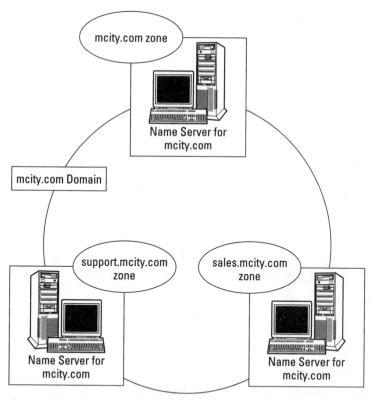

Figure 14-3: Portions of a domain can be delegated to name servers in subdomains.

A secondary master for a zone pulls its records for the zone from a primary master through a process called a *zone transfer*. The secondary master maintains the zone records as a read-only copy and periodically performs zone transfers to refresh the data from the primary master. You control the frequency of the zone transfers according to the requirements of the domain in question, the desired amount of network traffic (reducing network traffic by reducing zone transfers if needed), and any other issues pertinent to your domain(s). A secondary master is essentially a backup DNS server. A server can function as a primary master for some zones and a secondary master for others. The difference is in how the server handles the zones, not the zones themselves.

Domain Records and Zone Files

Each zone contains records that define hosts and other elements of the domain or a portion of the domain contained within the zone. These records are stored collectively in a *zone file* on the DNS server. A zone file is a text file that uses a special format to store DNS records. The default name for a zone file is *domain*.dns, where *domain* is the name of the domain hosted by the zone, such as mcity.org.dns. Windows 2000 stores zone files in %systemroot%\System32\Dns. Windows 2000 provides an MMC console to enable you to manage the contents of the zone files with a graphical interface (more on the console later in this chapter).

Each zone contains a certain number of *resource records* that define the hosts and other data for the zones. There are several different types of records, with each serving a specific purpose. Each record has certain properties associated with it that vary from one record type to the next. Table 14-3 lists the record types and their purposes.

Table 14-3
Windows 2000 DNS Resource Records

Record	Purpose
SOA	Specifies authoritative server for the zone
NS	Specifies address of domain's name server(s)
A	Maps host name to an address
PTR	Maps address to a host name for reverse lookup
CNAME	Creates alias (synonymous) name for specified host
MX	Mail exchange server for domain
SRV	Defines servers for specific purpose such as http, ftp, and so on

Record	Purpose
AAAA	Maps host name to Ipv6 address
AFSDB	Location of AFS cell database server or DCE cell's authenticated server
HINFO	Identifies host's hardware and OS type
ISDN	Maps host name to ISDN address (phone number)
MB	Associates host with specified mailbox; experimental
MG	Associates host name with mail group; experimental
MINFO	Specifies mailbox name responsible for mail group; experimental
MR	Specifies mailbox name that is proper rename of other mailbox; experimental
RP	Identifies responsible person for domain or host
RT	Specifies intermediate host that routes packets to destination host
TXT	Associates textual information with item in the zone
WKS	Describes services provided by specific protocol on specific port
X.25	Maps host name to X.121 address (X.25 networks); used in conjunction with RT records
WINS	Allows lookup of host portion of domain name through WINS server
WINS-R	Reverses lookup through WINS server
ATMA	Maps domain name to ATM address

The primary record is the SOA, or Start of Authority. The SOA record indicates that the server is authoritative for the domain. When you create a new zone, Windows 2000 automatically creates the SOA record for the zone. NS records identify name servers, and a zone should contain NS records for each name server in the domain.

Address, or A records, map host names to IP addresses. Multi-homed hosts — those that have multiple IP addresses — can be represented by multiple A records, each mapping the same host name to the different addresses of the host. A DNS lookup retrieves all matching records when multiple A records reference the same name. The name server sorts the address list so the closest address is at the top of the list to improve performance when the resolver and name server are on the same network. Otherwise, addresses are rotated through subsequent queries to respond in round-robin fashion. One query responds with the address of server A first in the list, for example, and subsequent queries respond with the addresses of servers B and C, respectively, as first.

CNAME (canonical name) records map an alias name to a FQDN, and are therefore called *alias* records. So, A and CNAME records typically work hand-in-hand. You'll create a host (A) record for a host, then use CNAME records to create aliases. For example, you might create a host record for server.mcity.org, then use CNAME records to create aliases for www and ftp that point to that server.

Mail Exchanger, or MX records, are another common resource record type. MX records enable servers to route mail. The MX records in a zone determine how mail is routed for the domain hosted by the zone. An MX record includes the FQDN of the mail server and a preference number from 0 to 65535. The preference number determines the priority of the mail server specified by the MX record. When multiple mail servers exist for a domain, the zone will include multiple MX records. Mail delivery is attempted based on the preference number, with the lowest-numbered server(s) being tried first. If the MX records all have the same preference number, the remote mail server has the option of sending to any of the domain's mail servers with the given preference number.

Service Resource (SRV) records offer the same flexibility for other services that MX records offer for mail routing. You create SRV records for specific services such as HTTP, FTP, LDAP, and so on. Resolvers that are designed to work with SRV records can use the preference number to connect to hosts offering the specified service. As with MX records, servers with lower preference numbers are attempted first.

The Pointer (PTR) record is another common record type. Pointers map addresses to names, the reverse of what host records do, a process called *reverse lookup*. You'll learn more about reverse lookup in the following section. For now, simply understand that when you create or modify resource records for forward lookup, the Windows 2000 DNS service can automatically create or modify the associated PTR record.

Each record has certain properties associated with it, and many properties are common to all records. Each record, for example, has a time-to-live, or TTL property. The TTL value, a 32-bit integer, specifies the number of seconds the resolver should cache the results of a query before it is discarded. When the specified TTL period is reached, the resolver purges the entry from the cache, and the subsequent query for the item is sent to the name server rather than pulled from the cache. Although the TTL value and caching speed performance by caching often-used queries, the dynamism of the Internet requires that records be able to change. Mail servers, Web servers, FTP servers, and other hosts can and do change addresses, and those changes need to be reflected in the DNS namespace. The TTL value enables caching but also allows for query results to grow stale and the resolver to query for fresh results. You'll need to adjust the TTL value for records to suit the type of record and how often you want the record updated across the intranet/Internet. If you're not sure what value to use initially, settle for the default value.

Tip The TTL value is optional for most resource records. The minimum default value specified with the SOA record is used if no TTL is specified for a record. In addition, the Windows 2000 DNS GUI presents some data differently from the way it is stored. The TTL is a 32-bit integer in the data file, for example, but the GUI represents it in the format DD:HH:MM:SS for readability.

Reverse Lookup

Forward lookup maps names to addresses, enabling a resolver to query a name server with a host name and receive an address in response. A *reverse query,* also called *reverse lookup,* does just the opposite—it maps an IP address to a name. The client knows the IP address but needs to know the host name associated with that IP address. Reverse lookup is most commonly used to apply security based on the connecting host name, but it is also useful when you're working with a range of IP addresses and gathering information about them.

Address-to-name mapping through the regular forward lookup mechanism is simply not practical, as it requires an exhaustive search of the entire DNS namespace to locate the appropriate information. Imagine scanning through the New York City phone book trying to match a phone number with a name, then multiply that task by the number of computers on the Internet, and you'll understand that reverse lookup requires a special mechanism to make it practical.

The solution is to create a namespace of IP addresses, or in other words, a domain in the namespace that uses IP addresses rather than names. In the DNS namespace, the `in-addr.arpa` domain serves this purpose. The `in-addr.arpa` domain serves as the root for reverse lookup. To understand how the `in-addr.arpa` domain and reverse lookup work, you need to first examine IP addresses.

Each IP address is a dotted octet, or four sets of numbers ranging from 0 to 255, separated by periods. An example of a valid IP address is 208.141.230.30. The `in-addr.arpa` domain delegates each octet as a subdomain. At the first level is `n.addr.arpa`, where *n* represents a number from 0 to 255 that corresponds to the left-most octet of an IP address. Each of these domains contains 256 subdomains, each representing the second octet. At the third level are subdomains that represent the third octet. Using the IP address given in this example, the reverse lookup zone would be 230.141.208.in-addr.arpa. Figure 14-4 illustrates the reverse lookup domain `in-addr.arpa`.

As the example illustrates, reverse lookup zones are structured in reverse notation from the IP address range they represent. Take a forward lookup as an example, assuming we're querying for the host `bob.support.midwest.mcity.org`. The lookup starts in the `.org` domain, moves to `mcity`, then to `midwest`, then to `support`, then finally locates the `bob` host record. Reverse lookups happen in the same way, moving from least significant to most significant, right to left. Using the address from the previous example, the reverse lookup starts in `in-addr.arpa`, moves to the 208 subdomain, then to 141, then to 230, where it finds the PTR record for the .30 address and maps it to a host name. Using reverse notation to create the reverse lookup zones enables the query to start with the first octet of the address, which in this example is 206.

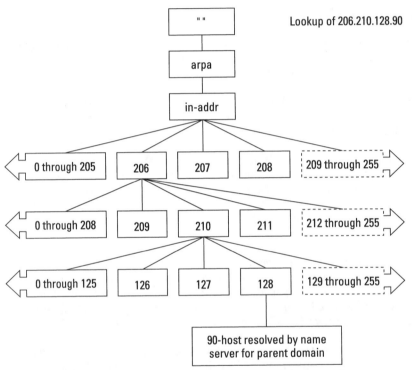

Figure 14-4: The domain in-addr.arpa provides the ability to perform reverse lookup, mapping addresses to host names.

The upper-level reverse lookup domains are hosted primarily by large ISPs such as Cable & Wireless, AT&T, and so on, which delegate the subdomains to individual customers (or handle reverse lookup for them). Your primary concern is probably creating reverse lookup zones for your subnets. Creating a reverse lookup zone is a relatively simple task and is much like creating a forward lookup zone. The only real difference is that rather than manually creating records in the reverse lookup zone, you'll rely on the DNS service to do it for you automatically.

Cross-Reference You'll find detailed steps for creating both forward and reverse lookup zones in the section "Microsoft Domain Name Services" later in this chapter.

Delegation

Previous sections have dealt to a limited extent with the topic of *delegation*, which is the primary mechanism that enables DNS to be a distributed namespace. Delegation enables a name server to delegate some or all of a domain to other name servers. The delegating server in effect becomes a "gateway" of sorts to the delegated domain, with individual domain records residing not on the delegating server but on those servers to which the subdomains are delegated.

The .us domain is a perfect example of subdomain delegation. Among other subdomains, the .us domain is where you'll find the domains for K12 schools. A typical domain for a school would be *school.city.k12.state.us*. For example, Jefferson High School in Pleasant, Minnesota, might use the domain jefferson.pleasant. k12.mn.us. K12 domains in Minnesota are maintained by the state of Minnesota, which delegates subdomains as needed. Using this example, assume that an ISP in Pleasant hosts the domain records for all the schools in the city. The state therefore delegates pleasant.k12.mn.us to the Pleasant ISP, which maintains the zone files for all the school subdomains in Pleasant. Figure 14-5 illustrates the process.

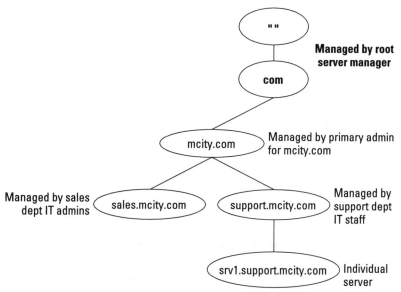

Figure 14-5: Delegation enables local control of subdomains where another organization has control and responsibility for the parent domain.

In this example of delegation, the root server for the .us domain controls the mn.us domain. The k12.mn.us domain is delegated to the state of Minnesota, which further delegates domains to individual K12 districts. Each district might host its own domain files, or an organization such as an ISP might host for them, including the zone files for the individual school subdomains. Or, each school might control its own domain. In such a case, the school's subdomain is delegated to the school.

Delegation provides two primary benefits. First, it reduces the potential load on any given name server in the delegation chain. Imagine that all domains in k12.mn.us were hosted by the state of Minnesota. This would mean that the state would have to host several thousand domains, imposing a significant load on the server, but perhaps more important, a significant load on the poor administrator who would administer the zones. This leads to the second benefit: Delegation allows for decentralized administration, enabling organizations (such as a single school) to administer its own domain and have control over its resource records.

Delegation also plays a role in other domains. Using our mcity.org domain, for example, you might configure DNS to delegate the east.mcity.org subdomain to the East coast office, midwest.mcity.org to the Midwest office, and west.mcity.org to the West coast office. This enables each office to manage its own resource records without creating separate domains for each.

See the section "Configuring Subdomains and Delegation" later in this chapter for detailed steps on creating and delegating subdomains.

Caching, Forwarders, and Slaves

Previous sections have touched briefly on DNS caching. The number of queries that could potentially hit an active and popular domain on the Internet could easily overwhelm a name server. Caching helps reduce that load and reduce network traffic. Each server caches successful and unsuccessful resolution queries for a period of time defined by the server's administrator. When a resolver queries the server for an address, the server checks its cache first for the data, and if the data exists in the cache, submits the cached data to the client rather than looking up the data again.

Caching unsuccessful queries is called *negative caching.* Negative caching speeds response, reduces server load, and reduces network traffic by eliminating repeated queries for names that can't be resolved (such as non-existent domains or hosts). As with positive caching, however, negative cache results age and expire, enabling lookups to succeed when the domain or host record does become available.

Name servers can function as *caching-only servers,* which don't maintain any zone files and are not authoritative for any domain. A caching-only server receives queries from resolvers, performs the queries against other name servers, caches the results, and returns the results to the resolvers. So, a caching-only server essentially acts as lookup agent between the client and other name servers. At first glance, caching-only servers might seem to make little sense. However, they reduce network traffic in two ways. First, caching-only servers reduce zone transfers since the caching-only name server hosts no zones and therefore requires no zone transfers. Second, caching-only servers reduce query traffic past the caching-only server as long as query results for a given query reside in the server's cache. Because the cache is cleared when the server restarts, the most effective caching-only server is one that remains up for extended periods.

A name server typically attempts to resolve queries against its own cache and zone files, and failing that, queries one or more other name servers for the information. In certain situations, you might not want all name servers for an organization to be communicating with the outside world for network security, bandwidth, or cost reasons. Instead, you'd forward all traffic through a given name server that would act as a sort of agent for the other name servers in the organization. For example, assume that you have a few relatively slow or expensive Internet connections to your site and one with higher bandwidth or that is less costly. Servers A, B, and C connect through the former, and server D connects through the latter. Rather than have all servers generating traffic through their respective links, you might want to funnel all traffic through server D. In this case, server D would act as a *forwarder,* which forwards off-site name queries for other name servers on the network. Servers A, B, and C would handle queries against their local caches and zone files, and failing those queries, would pass the query on to server D.

Name servers can interact with forwarders either exclusively or non-exclusively. When interacting non-exclusively, the server attempts to resolve queries against its cache and own zone files first. Failing that, the server forwards the request to the designated forwarder. If the forwarder fails the query, the server attempts to resolve the query on its own through other name servers. In order to prevent a server from doing this, you need to configure it as a *slave,* or function in exclusive mode with the forwarder. When functioning as a slave, a name server first attempts to resolve a query against its cache and local zone files. Failing that, it forwards the query to the designated forwarder. If that fails, the forwarder responds with an unsuccessful query, and the local server fails the request to the client resolver without attempting any further resolution.

You also can configure a slave name server as a *caching-only slave.* In this configuration, the server hosts no zone files. It attempts to resolve queries against its local cache only, and failing that, forwards the query to the designated forwarder and takes no further action to resolve the query. It does not itself fail the request to the resolver.

Recursion, Iteration, and Referrals

Figure 14-6 illustrates a query for resolution of the host name `jane.support. mcity.org`. As the figure shows, the name server directly queried by the client has to perform several queries to find a definitive answer to the query. The other name servers do relatively little work, mostly responding with *referrals,* which simply point the originating server to a different name server further down the namespace hierarchy. In effect, these other servers are saying, "I don't have the answer, but so-and-so does," referring to the name server contained in the referral.

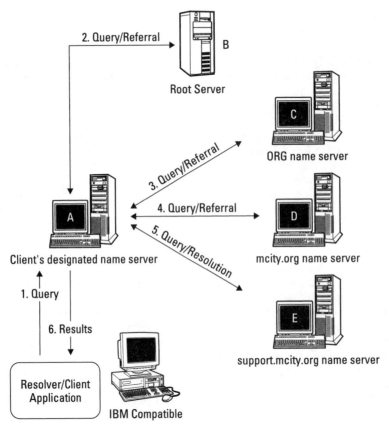

Figure 14-6: Resolution of the host name `jane.support.mcity.org` shows recursion and referrals.

DNS uses two primary means to resolve queries: *recursion* and *iteration* (also referred to as *non-recursive*). A recursive query is the method used by server A in Figure 14-6. In this example, the resolver sends a recursive query to server A, which starts the resolution process by querying the root server B. Server B responds with a referral to server C, which hosts the root of the `.org` domain. Server C responds with a referral to server D, which hosts the `mcity.org` domain. Server D responds with a referral to server E, which hosts the delegated `support.mcity.org` subdomain. Server E contains the appropriate host record and returns the address for `jane.support.mcity.org`. So, in a recursive query, the queried server (in this case A) continues to query other servers until it finds a definitive answer, then it returns that answer to the resolver. A recursive query places the most load on the client's name server.

An iterative query places the majority of the load on the client. In the iterative query shown in Figure 14-7, the client resolver requests resolution of the same host, `jane.support.mcity.org`. In this instance, however, name server A simply responds with the best information it already has for the query. If the resolved query resides in Server A's cache, it responds with that data. Otherwise, it gives the client a referral to a name server that will help the resolver continue the query on its own. In the case of Figure 14-7, Server A provides a referral to server B, which gives the client resolver a referral to C, and so on until server E finally provides the answer to the resolver.

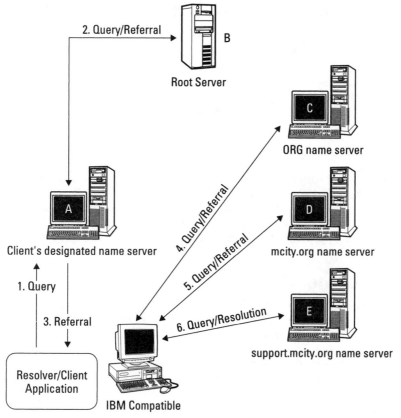

Figure 14-7: An iterative query of `jane.support.mcity.org`

One main difference between recursive and iterative queries is the fact that recursive queries place the majority of the responsibility for resolving the query on the name server, while the iterative query places the responsibility with the client resolver. This means that in order to adequately process iterative queries, a client resolver has to be more complex and "smarter" than one that only relies on recursive queries. It also means that recursive queries tax the client's designated name server(s) much more than iterative queries. Name servers in general and Windows 2000 in particular enable you to disable the server's support for recursive queries, forcing the clients to use iterative queries. You might choose this option in situations where you need to limit the load on the server. Another reason to disable recursion is if you're setting up a name server that services only the LAN or WAN and you don't want it to attempt to resolve queries for domains outside of that general area.

Microsoft Domain Name Services

Windows 2000 Server includes the Microsoft Domain Name Services (DNS) service that you can use to set up and manage a Windows 2000 DNS server. As with other services, Windows 2000 provides an MMC console to enable you to manage DNS servers, zones, and resource records. The previous sections of the chapter explained the concepts behind the DNS service. This section focuses on installing and configuring DNS and setting up zones and domains.

Installing DNS

You can install DNS through the Add/Remove Programs object in the Control Panel. Open the Add/Remove Programs object, and in the Add/Remove Programs window, click Add/Remove Windows Components. Double-click Networking Services or select the item and click Details. Select Domain Name System (DNS) and click OK. Follow the remaining prompts to complete the installation of the software.

Overview of the DNS Console

The DNS console included with the DNS service enables you to set up a DNS server, create and manage zones, create and manage resource records, and so on. In short, the DNS console is a single point of contact for all DNS management. Figure 14-8 shows the DNS console.

By default, the DNS console shows the local server, but you can connect to any Windows 2000 DNS server through the console. To do so, right-click DNS in the left pane and choose Connect to Computer. Select the option "The following computer" and then specify the computer's name or IP address in the corresponding text box. Click OK to connect.

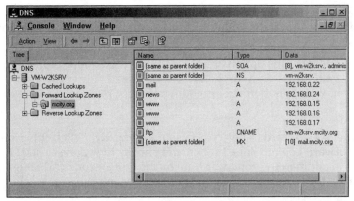

Figure 14-8: Use the DNS console to manage DNS servers locally and remotely.

When you connect to a server, you'll find two primary branches in the left pane: Forward Lookup Zones and Reverse Lookup Zones. Expanding the Forward Lookup Zones branch displays all forward lookup zones, each under its own sub-branch. Expanding the Reverse Lookup Zones branch displays all reverse lookup zones in their own sub-branches.

What the contents of a zone branch look like depends on whether the zone is for a Windows 2000 domain or simply a DNS domain. If it's for a Windows 2000 domain, you'll find additional branches for domain-related services and objects such as Kerberos, LDAP, sites, and so on.

The following sections explain how to use the DNS console to create and manage zones, resource records, and servers.

Creating Forward Lookup Zones

Each domain you host for DNS requires a Forward Lookup Zone, zone file, and associated records. You create the zone with the DNS console using one of three options:

✦ **Active Directory integrated:** This option creates the zone in the Active Directory, or AD, which provides for replication, integrated storage, security, and the other advantages inherent in the AD. The zone file is stored within the AD. You can only create an AD-integrated zone on a domain controller . . . giving the DNS service direct access to the database mechanisms of AD. You can't create AD-integrated zones on member servers that function as DNS servers.

✦ **Standard primary:** This option creates a standard primary zone using a `.dns` file in %systemroot%\System32\Dns (default location). You can add and modify resource records in a primary zone.

✦ **Standard secondary:** This option creates a standard secondary zone using a `.dns` file in %systemroot\System32\Dns. This is a read-only copy of a zone on another server. You cannot create or modify resource records in a secondary zone.

Windows 2000 provides a wizard to help you create a zone. Right-click either on the server or on the Forward Lookup Zone branch and choose New Zone to start the New Zone Wizard. In addition to prompting you for the type of zone (AD integrated, primary, secondary), the wizard prompts for the following information:

✦ **Forward Lookup Zone / Reverse Lookup Zone:** Choose the type of zone you want to create. In this case, choose Forward Lookup Zone.

✦ **Zone name:** Specify the full name of the zone, such as `mcity.org`, `support.mcity.org`, and so on. If you are specifying a second level zone such as `support.mcity.org`, you should make sure you first create the first level zone for `mcity.org` on its designated name server. You'll then delegate `support.mcity.org` on that server to the current server.

✦ **DNS zone file:** Specify a zone file name under which to store the zone's records if you're creating a standard primary or standard secondary zone. Specifying an existing file enables you to migrate existing resource records to the new zone. AD-integrated zones are stored in the AD and don't require an external file.

After you create a forward lookup zone, you can begin populating it with resource records. Before doing so, however, you should first create any required reverse lookup zones. Creating the reverse lookup zone(s) before creating the resource records will enable DNS to automatically create the PTR records in the reverse lookup zones for resource records you create in the forward lookup zones.

Creating Reverse Lookup Zones

You create a reverse lookup zone in much the same way you create a forward lookup zone. The primary difference is that you specify the subnet for the zone and the DNS console converts that to the appropriate reverse zone name. For example, enter 208.141.230 when prompted, and the DNS console creates the reverse lookup zone 230.141.208.in-addr.arpa. You do not have to specify three octets unless you're creating a reverse lookup zone for a domain that uses a class C address space. Specify the appropriate number of octets to define your reverse lookup zone. In addition, you can choose to specify the DNS file name yourself, but remember to enter it in reverse notation.

Creating Resource Records

After you create a zone, you can populate it with resource records. When you create a zone, the Windows 2000 DNS service automatically creates the SOA record and NS record for you. You can modify these records if needed.

To create new records, right-click the zone in the left pane or right-click the right pane and choose New Host, New Alias, or New Mail Exchanger to create A, CNAME, or MX records. Or choose Other New Records to create other types of resource records. The information you provide varies slightly depending on the type of record you're creating.

Host records (A)

Host or A records map a host name to an IP address and are the primary means by which names are resolved. Each host in your network that you want visible through DNS needs to have a host record in its corresponding zone.

When creating a host record, you specify the host name (such as www, ftp, fred, server, and so on) and the IP address to map to that host. Note that you can't add a host name containing periods, as anything after the period will be considered part of the domain name. Select the option Create associated pointer (PTR) record to have DNS automatically create a pointer record in the reverse lookup zone for the domain. DNS chooses the appropriate reverse lookup zone based on the IP address you specify for the host.

Tip   If you need to create a host name that contains a period, first create a parent-level zone for the second half of the name. For example, if you're attempting to create joe.support in the mcity.org domain, you first need to create a support zone as a subdomain of mcity.org. Then, create the host record for joe in the support.mcity.org subdomain.

Alias Records (CNAME)

Alias, or CNAME, records map an alias name to an existing FQDN. For example, assume you're the administrator for mcity.org and you have a server in your network named srv1, with a corresponding A record for srv1 that points to the server's IP address. You want to use the server as a Web server. So, you create an alias for www that points to srv1.mcity.org. Users connect to www.mcity.org, and DNS actually routes them transparently to srv1.mcity.org.

When creating an alias record, you specify the alias name and the FQDN of the host to which the alias points. As with a host record, you can't include a period in the host name for the alias. The FQDN for the alias can and will have periods in it, as by definition a FQDN contains the domain name in which the host resides.

Mail Exchanger Records (MX)

Mail Exchanger or MX records enable mail to be routed through or to a domain. They specify mail exchangers, or servers that process mail for the domain. For MX records, specify the single-part name for the mail exchanger in the Host or domain field. If you leave this field blank, the mail exchanger name is the same as the parent domain name. In the Mail server field, specify the FQDN of the server that will act as the mail exchanger. The FQDN you specify here must resolve to a host (A) record in the zone, so make sure you create the A record for the mail exchanger as well as the MX record. You can click Browse to browse the DNS namespace for the appropriate hostname if you're not sure what it is. Finally, specify the preference number for the mail exchanger in the Mail server priority field.

Service Location Records (SRV)

SRV records are another common resource record type that offers excellent flexibility when a domain contains multiple servers for specific services, such as multiple HTTP servers. SRV records enable you to easily move a service from one host to another and designate certain hosts as primary for a given service and others as secondary for that same service. For example, you might designate a server as the primary Web (HTTP) server and two others as secondary servers to handle HTTP requests when the primary is heavily loaded or offline.

Resolvers that support SRV records submit a request to the DNS server for servers in the subject domain that provide a specific TCP/IP service (such as HTTP). The DNS server responds with a list of all servers in the domain that have a corresponding SRV record for the requested service type.

To create an SRV record, right-click the zone and choose Other New Records. Select Service Location from the list and click Create Record to display the New Resource Record dialog box for SRV records, as shown in Figure 14-9.

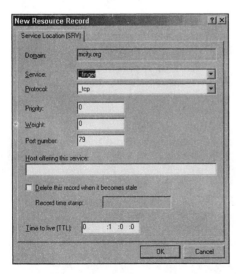

Figure 14-9: Use the Service Location (SRV) tab to create SRV records for specific services offered by specific servers.

Fill in the fields for the SRV record using the following list as a guide:

✦ **Service:** Select the predefined service type offered by the target server (ftp, http, and so on).

✦ **Protocol:** Select either tcp or udp, depending on the requirements of the service.

✦ **Priority:** Specify an integer between 0 and 65535. This value specifies the preference order of the server, just as the preference number for an MX record identifies the priority of the target mail exchanger. A lower value places the server higher in the priority list (0 is highest priority); a higher value gives the server a lower priority. The client tries the server with the highest priority first, and failing that, attempts connections to other servers in decreasing priority. Multiple servers can have the same priority value.

✦ **Weight:** Specify an integer between 0 and 65535 to allocate a weight to the target server for load balancing purposes. When multiple servers have the same priority value, the weight value serves as a secondary priority indicator. Hosts with a higher weight value are returned first to the resolver client. Use a value of 0 to turn off weighting if you don't need load balancing. Using a value of 0 speeds up SRV queries and improves performance.

✦ **Port number:** Specify an integer from 0 to 65535 to indicate the tcp or udp port number used by the target service.

✦ **Host offering this service:** Specify the FQDN of the target server offering the service. The FQDN must resolve to a valid name supported by a host record in the server's domain.

Other record types

You can create other types of resource records by right-clicking the zone and choosing Other New Records. The DNS console displays the Resource Record Type dialog box. Select the type of record you need to create, then click Create Record. DNS displays a dialog box that prompts for the required data, which varies from one record type to the next.

Configuring Zone Properties

A zone's properties determine how the zone performs zone transfers, ages resource records, and other behavior for the zone. The following sections explain the options available for a zone. To set these options, open the DNS console, right-click the zone, and choose Properties.

General zone properties

A zone's General property page lets you configure the following options:

✦ **Status:** Click Pause to pause a zone and stop it from responding to queries. Click Start to start a paused zone. You might pause a zone while making extensive changes to the records in the zone or performing other administrative tasks on the zone.

✦ **Type:** You can change a zone's type through the General page to any of the three supported types (AD-integrated, standard primary, or standard secondary). For example, if a server for a primary standard zone fails, you can change its secondary zone on a different server to a primary zone.

✦ **Zone file name:** Use this property to change the file where the zone records are stored. By default, the zone file name is `zone.dns`, where *zone* is the name of the zone. For example, `support.mcity.org` would be stored by default in `support.mcity.org.dns`.

✦ **Allow dynamic updates:** Use this option to allow/deny dynamic updates by Dynamic Host Configuration Protocol (DHCP) clients and servers to resource records in the zone and corresponding pointer records. See the section "Dynamic DNS" later in this chapter for detailed information.

✦ **Aging:** Click to specify aging properties for records in the zone. See the section "Configuring Scavenging" later in this chapter for a detailed explanation.

Start of Authority properties

The Start of Authority (SOA) property page for a zone enables you to configure the zone's SOA record. The property page contains the following properties:

✦ **Serial number:** DNS uses this value to determine when a zone transfer is required. The DNS service increments the value by 1 each time the zone changes to indicate that the zone is a new version. Other servers performing zone transfers with the server use this value to determine whether or not a zone transfer is needed. If the value is higher than the remote server's records for the zone, the server initiates a zone transfer to update the remote server's zone records. Use the Increment button to increment the serial number and force a zone transfer.

✦ **Primary server:** Specifies the host name of the primary master for the selected zone. If you need to change the value, type the host name of the primary master or click Browse to browse the network for the primary master. Make sure you include a period at the end of the host name.

✦ **Responsible person:** Specifies the e-mail address of the person responsible for managing the zone. The data takes the form of an FQDN. For example, `administrator@mcity.org` should be entered as `administrator.mcity.org`, replacing the @ symbol with a period.

✦ **Refresh interval:** This value specifies how often servers that host secondary copies of the zone should check the currency of their zone data against the primary zone data. The default is 15 minutes.

✦ **Retry interval:** This value specifies the amount of time that must elapse before a server hosting a secondary copy of the zone retries a connection to the primary zone if a previous connection attempt failed. This value should usually be less than the Refresh interval and defaults to 10 minutes.

✦ **Expires after:** Specifies the period of time a server hosting a secondary copy of the zone can wait before discarding its secondary data if its zone data hasn't been refreshed. This prevents the secondary servers from serving potentially stale data to client requests. The default is 24 hours.

✦ **Minimum (default) TTL:** This value specifies the amount of time that querying servers can cache results returned from this zone. When this period expires, the remote server removes the record from its cache. The default is 1 hour.

✦ **TTL for this record:** This value specifies the time-to-live for the SOA record itself. The default is 1 hour.

Name server properties

The Name Servers page lets you modify the NS records for the zone. The advantage to using this method rather than manually changing each record is that you can view all NS records in the zone in a single dialog box. To modify a record, select the record and click Edit. Windows 2000 DNS displays a dialog box you can use to modify the host name, IP address, or time-to-live value for the NS record. If modifying the host name, make sure the name contains a period at the end. You can click Add to add a new NS record.

WINS properties

The WINS page determines if the DNS service attempts to resolve names through WINS that it can't resolve on its own. Use the following properties to configure WINS integration:

✦ **Use WINS forward lookup:** Select this option to allow the DNS service to query WINS for any names it can't resolve on its own through DNS.

✦ **Do not replicate this record:** Select this option to prevent the DNS server from replicating WINS-specific resource data to other DNS servers during zone transfers. You will need to use this option if you are performing zone transfers to servers that don't support WINS (such as non-Microsoft DNS servers).

✦ **IP address:** Specify the IP addresses of the WINS servers to query.

✦ **Time-to-live:** Specify the TTL value for this record.

✦ **Advanced:** Click to set the cache timeout and lookup timeout periods. The cache timeout specifies the amount of time other servers can cache results returned through a WINS lookup. The lookup timeout specifies the amount of time the DNS server can wait for a response from the WINS server(s) before generating a "name not found" error.

Zone transfer properties

The Zone Transfers page of a zone's properties specifies the servers that can request and receive a copy of the zone's data through a zone transfer. You can configure the zone to allow all servers to request a transfer, only servers listed on the zone's Name Servers property page, or only servers included in a list of IP addresses that you define.

Click Notify to specify how other servers are notified of zone updates. You can configure the zone to automatically notify servers listed on the Name Servers property page for the zone or servers included in a list of IP addresses that you define. Deselect the option "Automatically notify" if you don't want the DNS server to notify the other servers when the zone data changes.

Managing DNS Server Options and Behavior

You can use the DNS console to configure various options that determine the way the DNS service functions. The following sections explain the different properties and behavior you can configure, including how to set up a forwarder and perform monitoring and logging.

Configuring Multi-Addresses on a DNS Server

By default, the DNS service responds on all IP addresses bound to the server. Why use multiple addresses for DNS on a single server? One good reason is this: When you register a domain, you must specify two name servers for the domain. But you might have only one DNS server because of the cost of the server or other considerations. You can assign two (or more) IP addresses to the server, assign two NS host names to the server, and use both host names and their corresponding IP addresses to register the domain.

For example, assume that `mcity.org` only has one DNS server. You bind two IP addresses to the server, 192.168.0.2 and 192.168.0.3 (using reserved IP addresses in this example). You then create two host records, ns1 and ns2, that point to the .2 and .3 addresses, respectively. When you register the domain, you specify `ns1.mcity.org` on 192.168.0.2 and `ns2.mcity.org` on 192.168.0.3. To the outside world, it appears you have two physical name servers, but you really only have one that responds on both IP addresses. The server only runs one instance of the DNS service, maintains only one zone file for `mcity.org`, but appears to actually be two different servers.

There is no real performance penalty to allowing the DNS service to respond on all bound IP addresses, but in some situations you might want to reduce the addresses to only those you specifically want associated with the DNS service. You might allocate two addresses that will always be used for DNS but in effect "reserve" the other IP addresses on the server for other uses. For example, assume you have the addresses 192.168.0.2 through .10 bound to the server. If you allow the DNS service to respond on all addresses, it's conceivable that users might start using 192.168.0.10 for DNS if they know it's there. A few months down the road, you remove .10 from the server because you want to use it elsewhere. Suddenly, those users who have been using .10 as a DNS server find themselves unable to resolve. If you start out limiting DNS to a specific set of addresses that will always be used on the server for DNS, you can avoid the problem.

You configure the addresses on which the server responds through the Interfaces tab of the server's property sheet. Open the DNS console, right-click the server, and choose Properties to display the property sheet for the server. On the Interfaces page, choose "All IP addresses" if you want the server to respond to DNS queries on all IP addresses bound to the server. Choose the option "Only the following IP addresses" if you want to limit the server to responding on only the IP addresses listed in the associated box. Use Add and Remove to change the contents of the list.

Using a Forwarder

The section "Caching, Forwarders, and Slaves" earlier in this chapter discussed the use of forwarders and how they enable you to funnel DNS requests through specific servers for purposes of administration, access, or bandwidth control. You configure a Windows 2000 DNS server to use a forwarder through the Forwarders page of the server's property sheet. Open the DNS console, right-click the server, choose Properties to display the property sheet, and then click the Forwarders tab. Use the following controls to configure forwarding:

✦ **Enable forwarders:** Select this option to direct the DNS server to forward initial requests from client resolvers to the DNS servers specified in the following box.

✦ **IP address:** Specify the IP address of a server to which queries should be forwarded. You can specify multiple servers.

✦ **Forward time-out (seconds):** Specify the time in seconds that the DNS server will wait for a response from a listed forwarder. At the end of this timeout period, the local DNS server submits a query to the next server on the list until it receives a response or cycles through the list.

✦ **Do not use recursion:** Select this option to configure the server as a forwarding-only slave, preventing the server from attempting to resolve queries on its own if the forwarder is unable to resolve the query. Leave this option deselected (the default) to allow the local server to attempt resolution if the forwarders are unable to respond to the query.

Configuring Advanced Settings

The Advanced page of a DNS server's property sheet lets you set several advanced options that control the way the server functions. To configure the following settings, open the DNS console, right-click the server, choose Properties, and click the Advanced tab:

✦ **Disable recursion:** Select this option to prevent the server from performing recursive queries. With this option selected, the server replies with referrals instead of recursively querying until a resolution is reached.

✦ **BIND secondaries:** Windows 2000 DNS servers by default use compression and submit multiple resource records in a single TCP message when performing zone transfers to optimize zone transfer speed. This method is compatible with servers running BIND (Berkeley Internet Name Domain) version 4.9.4 and later, but is incompatible with earlier versions of BIND. In order to optimize performance, leave this option deselected if your server will not be performing zone transfers with these earlier systems. Select this option to have the Windows 2000 DNS server perform slower, uncompressed zone transfers for compatibility with these older systems.

✦ **Fail on load if bad zone data:** The Windows 2000 DNS service will by default continue to load a zone even if it detects errors in the zone data, logging the errors but not failing. Select this option if you want the DNS service to stop loading the zone if the zone data contains errors.

✦ **Enable round robin:** The Windows 2000 DNS service will by default rotate and reorder a list of host records when a given host name is associated with multiple IP addresses. This round-robin behavior enables an administrator to perform load balancing, directing traffic to multiple computers with the same host name but different IP addresses (such as multiple servers hosting `www.mcity.org`). With this option selected, the server responds to queries with each address in turn. Deselect this option if you want to disable round robin and have the server return the first match in the zone.

✦ **Enable netmask ordering:** When a given zone contains multiple host records that map the same host name to multiple IP addresses, the Windows 2000 DNS service can order the response list according to the IP address of the client. Windows 2000 DNS checks the IP address of the client against the addresses of the host records, and if a record falls in the client's subnet, the DNS service places that host record first in the list. This directs the client to the requested host that is closest and typically fastest for the client to access, which is very important for Active Directory services, as explained in Chapter 8. This option is selected by default. Deselect this option to prevent the DNS service from reordering responses based on subnet. Netmask ordering supercedes round-robin ordering, although round robin is used for secondary sorting if enabled, and is also useful where subnets are in different geographical locations.

✦ **Secure cache against pollution:** The Windows 2000 DNS service does not add unrelated resource records added in a referral from another DNS server to the Windows 2000 server's cache. However, it will cache referrals that might not match the queried host name, such as caching a referral for `www.sillycity.com` when querying for `www.mcity.org`. Selecting this option prevents the DNS service from caching non-related referrals.

✦ **Name checking:** Internet host names were originally limited to alphanumeric characters and hyphens. Although this limitation was maintained when DNS was developed, it posed a problem in some situations, particularly for supporting international character sets. This option controls how the DNS service performs name checking. Windows 2000 by default uses the UTF8 (Unicode Transformation Format) character set, which provides the broadest and least restrictive character set support. Select Strict if you need to limit names to the standard format.

✦ **Load zone data on startup:** The Windows 2000 DNS service by default loads zone data from the Active Directory (for AD-integrated zones) and from the registry. You can configure the server to load only from the registry or load from a BIND 4 boot file. This latter option enables you to essentially duplicate a BIND server under Windows 2000, importing all of the zone data. Note that the boot file — typically called `Named.boot` — must use the BIND 4 format rather than the newer BIND 8 format.

✦ **Enable automatic scavenging of stale records:** Stale records typically are those that point to hosts no longer on the network. Accumulation of stale records can lead to decreased storage space, degradation of server performance, incorrect name-to-address resolution, and inability for a host to have the DNS service create its resource record (through Dynamic DNS). Scavenging, which is turned off by default, enables the DNS server to use time stamps and other properties to determine when a resource record is stale and automatically remove it from the zone. Records added automatically through DDNS are subject to scavenging, as is any record manually added whose time stamp you have modified from its default of zero. Resource records with a time stamp of zero are not subject to scavenging. Select this option and configure the associated scavenging period. Note that scavenging must be enabled for individual zones in their properties, as well. For additional information on scavenging, see the section "Dynamic DNS" later in this chapter.

✦ **Reset to Default:** Select this option to reconfigure all advanced settings to their defaults.

Setting Root Hints

Root hints direct a name server to the root servers for domains at a higher level or in different subtrees of the DNS namespace and in effect provide a road map for a DNS server to resolve queries for domains outside of its area of authority. For DNS servers connected to the Internet, the root hints should point to the Internet root name servers. For DNS servers that only provide services to a private network, the root hints should point to the root server(s) for your domain or organization. Servers that function as forwarders for local clients requesting resolution of Internet names should have their root hints point to the Internet root servers, while the other name servers in the organization should point to the local root server for the organization's private network.

By default, the Windows 2000 DNS service uses a cache.dns file that contains the list of Internet root servers. You'll find cache.dns located in \%systemroot%\ System32\Dns. Browsing the file in Notepad or WordPad will illustrate that the file contains entries for NS and A records for the Internet root servers. If you're connecting a name server to the Internet, use the cache.dns file to ensure that you have the appropriate root hints. If you're creating a name server for your internal network, however, you should instead use a cache.dns file that contains the NS and A records of the name servers higher in your local namespace rather than the root Internet servers.

You can edit the cache.dns directly using Notepad or WordPad if you need to modify its entries. If you prefer, you also can use the interface provided by the DNS console to modify the cache.dns file. To do so, open the DNS console, right-click the server that you want to modify the cache.dns file of, then choose Properties. Click the Root Hints tab to display the Root Hints page. Use Add, Edit, and Remove to add, modify, and remove entries from the cache.dns file, respectively.

Note   Entries in the cache.dns file consist of an NS record and a corresponding A record for each name server, located on two separate lines. The first line specifies the NS record. This line begins with an @ symbol, followed by a tab, then NS, another tab, then the FQDN of the root server. On the next line, specify the FQDN of the server, a tab, then A to indicate an A record, another tab, and finally the IP address of the server.

If you are running internal name servers that don't need root hints to servers higher in the local area, you should eliminate root hints altogether. The easiest way to do this is to rename or delete the cache.dns file, then stop and restart the DNS server.

Tip   Although the root name servers change infrequently, it is possible for the root servers to change for a variety of reasons. You can acquire a new list of root server records via FTP from Network Solutions by downloading the file ftp.rs. internic.net/domain/named.root. You can use the file directly as your cache.dns file without modifications.

Configuring Logging

The DNS service by default does not perform extensive logging because the number of potential queries in a relatively small amount of time can be quite large, particularly for servers that serve a large portion of the namespace or a large number of clients. You can configure logging for reasons of troubleshooting, security, and so on, through the properties for the DNS server. Open the DNS console, right-click the server, choose Properties, and click the Logging tab. Select the items to be logged and click OK. The DNS service stores log entries in \%systemroot%\System32\Dns\Dns.log. If yours is a busy server, however, understand that logging even a few items can consume a lot of server time and create a potentially very large log file.

Monitoring and Testing

The Monitoring property page for a DNS server enables you to issue test queries against the local server and recursive queries against other name servers. This helps you test the server and its ability to communicate successfully with other name servers. This is an extremely useful tool, as most other methods for this type of testing typically use a cumbersome command-line interface. To display the Monitoring page to perform testing, open the DNS console, right-click the server, choose Properties, and then click the Monitoring tab to display the Monitoring page shown in Figure 14-10.

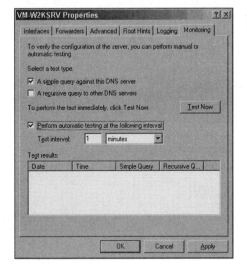

Figure 14-10: Use the Monitoring page to issue test queries.

The following list explains the options on the Monitoring page:

✦ **A simple query against this DNS server:** Choose this option to perform an iterative test against the local server.

✦ **A recursive query to other DNS servers:** Choose this option to perform a recursive query against other DNS servers (which start with the DNS servers defined in the local server's TCP/IP properties).

✦ **Perform automatic testing at the following interval:** Select this option to perform periodic, automatic testing using the testing options specified previously.

✦ **Test interval:** Specify the frequency of automatic tests.

✦ **Test results:** This list shows the results of tests and includes the test date, time, and results.

Applying Security

Windows 2000 provides the ability to restrict access to a DNS server and/or selected zones, enabling you to control who has the ability to modify the server, add records, remove records, and so on. You can configure security for a server overall only if the server is a domain controller participating in the Active Directory. You can't configure security on member servers that host the DNS service or on standalone DNS servers. In addition, you can configure security on individual zones only if the zones are stored in the AD (set up as AD-integrated zones).

To apply security to a server overall, open the DNS console and connect to the server. Right-click the server and choose Properties to display its property sheet. In addition to the property pages discussed in previous sections, you'll find a Security tab. Click the Security tab to display the Security page, which enables you to define the permissions that groups or users have within the DNS server. Security at the server level acts as the first line of defense in protecting the server in general and the zones housed on the server.

You also can configure security for individual zones as a second layer of security, enabling you to designate specific users or groups the ability to manage a given zone. Open the DNS console, right-click the zone in question, and choose Properties. Use the Security page in the zone's property sheet to configure security for the zone.

Managing the Server and Cache

You use the DNS console to manage the DNS server in addition to managing individual zones. The following lists common administrative tasks and explains how to accomplish them with the DNS console:

✦ **Update data files:** The DNS service automatically stores changes to the data files at set intervals and when the service shuts down, writing changes in memory to disk. It's a good practice to update the data files manually when you add a number of records or make other changes to ensure that those changes are written to disk in the event of a problem with the server that would otherwise prevent the updates from occurring. To update the data files within the DNS console, right-click the server and choose Update Server Data Files.

✦ **Stop, start, pause, resume, or restart the DNS service:** You can control the DNS service on the local computer through the Services branch of the Computer Management console (right-click My Computer and choose Manage). You might find it easier to use the DNS console, however, particularly when managing a remote DNS server. In the DNS console, right-click the server, choose All Tasks, and choose the desired action (Start, Stop, and so on).

✦ **Clear the cache:** If a server's cache becomes polluted with bad records or you're having problems correctly resolving queries, clearing the cache can fix the problem if the problem is related to the cached queries. In the DNS console, right-click the server and choose Clear Cache to clear the contents of the cache. Note that this does not affect the root hints defined by the `cache.dns` file.

Configuring Subdomains and Delegation

If yours is a small organization, you'll likely only have a single domain. Larger organizations, however, often segregate services and delegate responsibility and administration for different parts of the organization's namespace. Or, you might simply be hosting the DNS records for another organization. You accomplish these tasks through *subdomains* and *delegation.*

A subdomain is a child of an existing domain. For example, `support.mcity.org` is a subdomain of `mcity.org`. The domain `west.support.mcity.org` is a subdomain of `support.mcity.org`. The `mcity.org` domain serves as the primary domain for all of these. The `mcity.org` name server could host the resource records for all of its subdomains, providing centralized management of the organization's namespace. Queries for hosts in the subdomains would be handled by the `mcity.org` name server(s). However, the `mcity.org` domain could also delegate the subdomains to other name servers, such as name servers hosted at the subdomain location. For example, `mcity.org`—located in Florida—might delegate `support.mcity.org` to the name servers for the support group located on the West coast. In this case, queries would come to the `mcity.org` name server, which would refer the query to the `support.mcity.org` subdomain. The only real difference is that in the former example, all the zones and data reside on the `mcity.org` server, and in the latter, they are parceled out to other servers as required by the domain structure.

Setting Up Subdomains

Whether or not you'll be hosting a subdomain on the primary name server for the organization or delegating it, the first step is to create the subdomain. You accomplish this task through the DNS console. In the console, open the server where you want to create the subdomain, then open the parent domain. For example, to create the subdomain `support.mcity.org`, open the `mcity.org` zone. Right-click the parent zone and choose New Domain. Windows 2000 prompts you for the subdomain name. Enter the single-part name (**support** in this example) and click OK. The subdomain appears as a sub-branch under the parent domain. After you create the subdomain, you can begin adding records to it. Just right-click the subdomain and choose the type of record you want to create. As when creating records for a parent domain, you can only specify the single-part name for the host. For example, if you're creating a host record for `jane.support.mcity.org`, you would create a host record for jane in the `support.mcity.org` subdomain.

Tip   Before creating resource records in a subdomain, verify that you have created the reverse lookup zone for the subdomain. This will enable the DNS service to automatically create pointer records for hosts you define in the subdomain.

Delegating a Subdomain

Rather than host a subdomain's records under the parent domain's name server, you might prefer to delegate the subdomain to another server. For example, assume that the Support group will host its own DNS records on its own servers. In this case, you need to perform the following steps to delegate `support.mcity.org`:

1. On the Support group's name server, create the zone `support.mcity.org` and support reverse lookup zone, then populate the zone with the appropriate resource records for the hosts in `support.mcity.org`.

2. On the parent name server hosting `mcity.org`, open the DNS console and then open the `mcity.org` zone. Right-click the zone and choose New Delegation to start the New Delegation Wizard.

3. In the wizard, specify the delegated domain name (in this example, **support**). The wizard automatically assembles the FQDN for the delegated domain using the parent domain as a postfix. Click Next.

4. On the Name Servers page, click Add to add the FQDN and IP address of the server(s) on which the subdomain's records are hosted. In this example, you'd specify the name and address of the server that hosts `support.mcity.org`.

5. Specify the time-to-live (TTL) value for the resource record that points to the delegated server using the format days, hours, minutes, and seconds. Click OK.

6. Repeat steps 4-5 to add other name servers that host the subdomain's records, click OK, and then click Finish to complete the process.

DNS and Active Directory

The Windows 2000 DNS service provides integration with the AD to provide to the DNS service the advantages inherent in the AD — security, ease-of-management, replication, and so on. In fact, DNS integration with the AD is required for domain controllers (DCs) because the Windows 2000 Netlogon service uses DNS for locating DCs. A DC can run the DNS service itself or rely on other servers in the domain to provide DNS services, but a name server that supports dynamic updates and that is authoritative for the domain must be present.

See the section "Dynamic DNS" later in this chapter for more information on DDNS and dynamic updates.

Integrating DNS in the AD provides a measure of fault tolerance for DNS. Because the DNS data for integrated zones is replicated throughout the DCs for the domain, any DC running the DNS server can service client requests for resolution of names in the hosted domains. This means that there is no single point of failure for a given domain as long as it is hosted in an AD-integrated zone. One server can go offline, and others can continue to process requests for the domain. Also, changes to records in an AD-integrated zone are automatically replicated to other DCs running the DNS service, simplifying administration. When you bring a new DC on line that is running the DNS service, the zone records are automatically replicated to the new DNS server. Synchronization of AD-integrated zones is also potentially more efficient than a standard zone transfer, as data is selectively transferred rather than transferring an entire zone.

Security, which was discussed previously in the section "Applying Security," is another important advantage to AD integration. You can apply access control lists (ACLs) to a server and to individual zones to define which users or groups have the ability to modify the server and records in the secured zones.

Only primary zones are supported for AD-integration. Secondary zones must be stored in standard zone files. By migrating all zones to the AD, however, you effectively eliminate the need for secondary zones because the zones will be replicated to other servers for redundancy and fault tolerance, the main purpose of secondary zones. If you maintain Windows NT-based DNS servers, however, you'll still need to rely on secondary zones.

When you create a zone using the DNS console, the wizard gives you the option of creating three types of zones: AD-integrated, standard primary, and standard secondary. Choose AD-integrated if you want to take advantage of the benefits offered by the AD for DNS.

The AD is a complex topic that requires quite a bit of explanation in its own right. Refer to Part III, "Directory Services," for a detailed explanation of the AD's structure, function, replication, and administration.

Dynamic DNS

Dynamic DNS (DDNS) enables a Windows 2000 DNS server to automatically update resource records for clients when their host names or IP addresses change. Host name changes can occur when the remote computer changes computer name or becomes a member of another domain (which implicitly changes its FQDN). The use of DHCP is another argument for DDNS. As DHCP leases expire, a client computer's address can and will likely change. This makes it difficult to maintain accurate DNS records for hosts on the network that use DHCP for address allocation. DDNS resolves the problem.

DDNS functions through a client-server mechanism. Windows 2000 DHCP clients support DDNS and can directly request that a Windows 2000 DNS server update their host resource (A) records when the clients' IP addresses or host names change. Windows 2000 DHCP servers can also submit requests on behalf of clients, although a DHCP server can request an update to both the clients' host and pointer (PTR) records.

A Windows 2000 DHCP server also can act as a proxy for non-Windows 2000 DHCP clients to perform dynamic DNS updates. For example, a Windows 2000 DHCP server can perform updates for Windows 9x and Windows NT clients, which do not natively support dynamic DNS and are therefore unable to submit requests to either the DHCP server or DNS server to update their resource records. Figure 14-11 illustrates how DHCP and DNS interact.

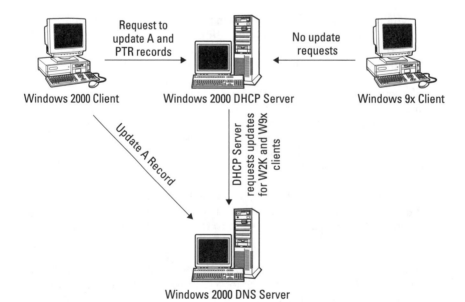

Figure 14-11: DHCP supports automatic update to DNS when host name or IP address changes occur.

For a detailed discussion of configuring a Windows 2000 DHCP server to support DNS, see Chapter 13.

Configuring DDNS

Most of the configuration to support DDNS occurs on the client side. There are, however, some configuration steps to take on the server side to properly implement DDNS. You enable dynamic updates on a zone-by-zone basis, and the types of updates allowed depend on whether or not the zone is stored in the AD. AD-integrated zones give you the additional option of allowing only secured updates, which uses the ACL for the zone to determine who can perform an update. Standard zones not stored in the AD can only be configured for unsecured updates or no updates.

Windows 2000 clients by default attempt to perform an unsecured update and, failing that, attempt a secured update. If you're having problems getting client records to update from servers or clients outside of a domain, make sure you have not configured the zone for secured updates only. Also, for optimum security, you should avoid using a DC as a DHCP server, because updates from the DHCP server will always succeed, even when the zone is configured for secure updates only.

You configure a zone's DDNS behavior through the zone's properties. Open the DNS console, right-click the zone, and choose Properties. The option "Allow dynamic updates" determines whether or not the server will accept dynamic updates for records in the zone. You can choose one of the following three options:

✦ **No:** Select this option to prevent DHCP clients or servers from updating resource records in the zone.

✦ **Yes:** Select this option to allow DHCP clients and servers, including those outside of the domain, to perform unsecured updates to the zone's resource records. DHCP servers can also update pointer records for dynamically updated host records.

✦ **Only secure updates:** Select this option to require the DHCP client or server to authenticate in the domain to be able to perform dynamic updates of host or pointer records.

See the section "Configuring DNS Options for DHCP" in Chapter 13 for information on how to configure a client for DDNS.

Configuring Scavenging

As explained earlier in this chapter, it's possible for records to become stale in a zone. For example, a notebook user's computer might update its host record in its zone, then the user disconnects from the network without shutting down. The computer remains off the network for an extended period, but the computer's host record still remains in the zone. This means the record becomes stale and potentially points to the wrong IP address (or the user might change his computer's host name). You can configure Windows 2000 DNS to *scavenge* records, removing those that are stale.

Windows 2000 uses a time stamp to determine whether or not a record is stale. The server scans the data at an administrator-defined interval, checking the resource records' time stamps to determine if they have exceeded the refresh interval. If so, the server scavenges the record (removes it from the zone). Scavenging by default applies only to dynamically created records and has no effect on records you create manually. However, the DNS server applies a time stamp to resource records you create manually, but sets the time stamp to zero to indicate that the record is not subject to scavenging. You can modify the value to allow the DNS service to scavenge these records, as well.

You configure scavenging in two places: at the server level and at the zone level. At the server level, you enable scavenging globally for the server and set the scavenging frequency, or frequency at which the server performs scavenging. The default value is seven days, and the minimum is one hour. To configure scavenging at the server level, open the DNS console, right-click the server, and choose Properties. Click the Advanced tab to display the Advanced property page. Select the option "Enable automatic scavenging of stale records," then use the Scavenging period control to specify how often the server should perform a scavenging operation. The more dynamic the network, the more frequently you should let the server perform scavenging. Choose a value that fits your network needs.

You also need to configure scavenging on a zone-by-zone basis. Scavenging can only be applied to primary zones. Open the DNS console, right-click the zone for which you want to configure scavenging, then choose Properties. On the zone's General property page, click Aging to display the Zone Aging/Scavenging Properties dialog box (Figure 14-12).

The dialog box contains two controls:

✦ **No-refresh interval:** This property essentially specifies the time stamp's time-to-live. Until this period expires, the record's time stamp can't be refreshed.

✦ **Refresh interval:** This property defines the period of time the time stamp can remain unrefreshed before the server scavenges the record.

As explained previously, scavenging occurs automatically at the interval defined in the server's general scavenging properties. You can, however, manually initiate a scavenge. Open the DNS console, right-click the server, and choose Scavenge Stale Resource Records.

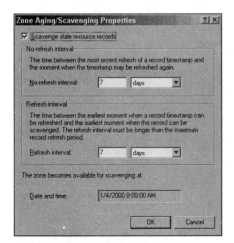

Figure 14-12: Configure the zone's scavenging properties through the Zone Aging/Scavenging Properties dialog box.

Windows Internet Name Service

NetBIOS, which we described in Chapter 12, is a legacy API that has for many years served as the means by which we connect to file systems and network resources on corporate local area networks. But then along came TCP/IP and crashed the NetBIOS party, spiked the punch, and became the protocol of choice everywhere, not asking permission from authority higher up the OSI stack. As a result, many clients on a network cannot see the IP-flavored host names that map to IP addresses; instead, they can only see NetBIOS-flavored names. The solution? Map the NetBIOS names to IP addresses.

WINS, which stands for Windows Internet Name Service, was developed by Microsoft to provide a DNS-like NetBIOS Name Service (NBNS) to map NetBIOS names to IP addresses. The *Internet* in WINS is a little misleading because a NetBIOS name on the Internet is like a goldfish trying to breathe in olive oil. But in essence, it also signifies taking a NetBIOS name and turning it into a *neo-host* name that can be mapped to an IP address. And as long as IP rules supreme, and you take the input/output out of NetBIOS, it is nothing more than a label, even at the functional or application levels of the network.

But WINS is more than just a name-IP address resolver. It enables centralized management of NetBIOS namespace data and eliminates the need to remotely manage multiple LMHOSTS files (which perform the same function for NetBIOS lookup that Hosts files perform for DNS lookup).

WINS also helps reduce NetBIOS broadcasts on the network to maximize bandwidth utilization, since clients can query the WINS server for a name-to-address mapping, letting them communicate directly with remote hosts rather than generating broadcast traffic on the network.

WINS is needed on old Windows networks because the only way the down-level operating systems flag their presence is via NetBIOS, and in many respects, it has been convenient even since the days TCP/IP first showed up. Imagine a Windows network where every server was only listed under its IP address.

WINS is also essential for getting those NetBIOS names resolved over TCP/IP subnets. NetBIOS is not routable and it was never intended to be, nor are the primary protocols that carry NetBIOS names, such as NetBEUI (although they can be encapsulated in TCP/IP communication packets that can be routed, a practice often used to route SNA traffic over TCP/IP). The only way then to allow NetBIOS to coexist in the routable world of IP addresses and IP internetworks is via WINS.

 Note   WINS communications take place in datagrams over the UDP port 137, which is reserved for NBNS.

Microsoft's strategy, in line with all the other Internet builders, is to abolish reliance on NetBIOS and to support TCP/IP and its successors as the only routable protocol on all networks. This strategy will allow network administrators to gradually abolish NetBIOS from their networks as they replace down-level or NetBIOS-named computers and devices and allow them to switch to native mode Windows 2000 deployment, which is more secure and rich.

But for many companies, WINS and NetBIOS will be around for many years. In fact, we predict the last vestiges of NetBIOS, and thus WINS, will only vanish by about 2005. Change is not an overnight phenomenon in large corporate environments, where huge investments in corporate intranets are also underway. In fact, had it not been for Y2K, many companies would have kept Windows NT 3.51 around. The reasons to keep WINS around are patent when you consider two inescapable facts.

1. **Investment in legacy systems:** NetBIOS has been the "driving" force on Windows networks since the advent of the networkable personal computer. In all those years, Windows has become the pervasive desktop operating system, and it is now poised to become the dominant server operating system.

   Our guess is that no one really knows how many copies of Windows are running in the world. And figures range from tens of millions to hundreds of millions. So, a huge investment in legacy or "so-called" down-level Windows operating systems still exists, from simple clients to mega-servers, and will remain as such for many years to come. In so far as these systems, especially the servers, still use NetBIOS names, WINS will be needed to resolve these names into IP addresses. In short . . . the best of both worlds — an entrenched namespace coexisting with an indispensable protocol.

2. **Investment in legacy applications:** Many applications still use NetBIOS names in their code. So NetBIOS will be a fact on these networks until all applications are no longer dependent on NetBIOS, or until they can be removed from your network and information systems.

How WINS Works

All Windows 9*x* and Windows Server operating systems can request services of WINS. In order to request a name-IP address resolution, the client queries any WINS server designated to it on the network. It tries to contact WINS servers in the order assigned in the WINS address list in its TCP/IP configuration. The client will try to connect to the WINS server three times before giving up and moving onto the next WINS server in the list.

When the client boots and authenticates on the network, it registers its name and IP address with the designated WINS server. If for some reason the client does not register automatically, the registration will take place when the client next makes a query or targets a folder on a remote server.

The process to connect to a NetBIOS name using TCP/IP is described in this example, as follows:

1. Computer MCSQL01 logs onto the network and makes a registration request with WINS. The NetBIOS name and IP address are thus recorded to the WINS database.

2. Now you come along and you need to connect workstation SQLCLIENT (at 10.5.4.132) to \\MCSQL01\SHARE1 (at 100.50.2.32), which you see in the browse list. The SQLCLIENT will need to make a request of the WINS server for the IP address of MCSQL01 in order to effect a connection to the server via TCP/IP. In other words, the client needs to turn the target address \\MCSQL01\MYSHARE into \\100.50.2.32\MYSHARE because the only way to connect to the remote server, via several routers, is TCP/IP.

3. If the WINS server is unavailable, SQLCLIENT will try two more times before trying the next WINS server in its list. Assuming that MCSQL01 happened to register with WINS and an IP address exists, the resolve will be successful and the connection can be established.

4. Finally, and we do not mean to be cheeky because we have had to do this on many occasions with the old WINS, if you cannot see or connect to the share, you can phone the owner or admin of the server and ask him or her for the IP address. It is okay for network administrators to do this to troubleshoot connections. It's not okay for users to do this every time they need a file or a printer.

WINS Registration

The WINS architecture is very different to DNS. WINS maintains a database of name-IP address mappings. It is not hierarchical. When a client registers a mapping, the WINS server issues a successful registration message to the client. Encapsulated in that message is a time-to-live (TTL) value, which is like a "lease" on the name, held in trust by WINS for a certain period of time.

But what if the name is already registered with WINS and the client makes a new registration attempt, or another client tries to register with the same NetBIOS name? WINS does not ignore the request; it sends out a "verification" request to the currently registered owner of the mapping. The request goes out three times at 500-millisecond intervals. If there is more than one IP address for the client, which is often the case on NT or Windows 2000 servers, WINS will try each address it has for the registered owner. This verification regimen continues until all IP addresses have been "called" or the owner responds.

If the owner responds, the client requesting the registration gets a polite decline. However, if the owner does not respond, the client requesting registration gets free passage.

Mapping Renewal

WINS mappings are not persistent, and the WINS database is in a constant state of change. Leases on mappings are assigned on a temporary basis to allow other computers to claim the mapping later. The short-term lease method also allows clients with DHCP-assigned IP addresses to register their new addresses with WINS.

If the WINS client remains online, it will need to renew its lease before expiration on the WINS server. The client achieves this by renewing automatically after one-eighth of the TTL has elapsed. If the client does not receive a renewal notification from the server, it will continue to attempt renewal every two minutes until half of the TTL has elapsed. After that, the client will move on to the next WINS in its list and begin the renewal attempt with that server. WINS is a multi-master replication architecture, and it thus doesn't matter which of the WINS servers honors the WINS registration request, as far as the client and the networking-resolving process are concerned. However, if the next WINS in the list fails to honor the request, the client "hits" the leading server again.

Upon a successful registration renewal, the client will attempt to renegotiate the next lease renewal when 50 percent of the TTL has elapsed.

When WINS clients are powered down normally, that is, by issuing the shutdown command, they send a message to WINS requesting release of the mapping. The message includes the entire mapping NetBIOS-IP address. The WINS server will honor the request as long as the records check out. In other words, the mapping must exist or the values for IP address and name must be the same as in the message. If the request checks out, the record is *tombstoned;* otherwise, it remains in the database.

The New WINS

As important as WINS has been for many diverse Windows-based networks, the WINS service on NT 4.0 is not something we look back on fondly, and for many with thousands of users spread over dozens of subnets, it has been more a case of WINS and LOSSES.

While WINS performed with a measure of fault-tolerance on small intranets, it often let us down on large networks, losing connections, missing replication with its peers, and collecting garbage that had to be manually deleted from the database. Often, intra-domain communications between sites would break down because records were not updated and the clients were unable to succeed with connections to critical services in other domains. Many network managers pleaded with Microsoft to rebuild the WINS service, and now a very different animal exists under Windows 2000.

The features will not mean much to new administrators working with WINS 2000, but they will be welcome news for the old and the brave among you. Two important features are worthy of mention in this chapter: persistent connections and manual tombstoning.

Persistent Connections

WINS should never be implemented as a single-server solution, unless a very small collection of users depends on the service and the business can afford the down-time and collapse of service level. On networks serving a lot of users or small offices that need to maintain critical connections over the intranet, WINS should be implemented in groups of two or more servers. Not all servers need to be on the same subnet, however, because should a local WINS fail, the client will be able to hit a secondary on another subnet because they already know the static address (via DHCP) of the secondary WINS server.

WINS servers thus coexist as loose clusters (they interoperate, but do not really function as a single logical unit). When a client registers with WINS, or whenever WINS tombstones a record, the information is replicated out to WINS servers that are configured as replication partners. Often, replication on the old WINS on NT 4.0 would fail because requests to reestablish would not take place. This would result in widely dispersed WINS databases being inconsistent and out of touch with each other.

Users on the intranet depend on the maintenance of connections between clients and servers placed at opposite ends of the intranet. When WINS servers are not able to comply with requests, the user usually gets the "Network Path not Found" error message, and the attempted connection fails. This message may seem like the host is down, but often it is WINS that is at fault, so first try to ping the host by name to confirm a WINS problem before anything else.

Tip   Always keep a database of your static IP addresses handy. If you can ping the host that is not being resolved by WINS and you can manually map to a known share on the host, for example, such as \\192.168.4.8\shares, then you can be almost certain WINS is in trouble.

Windows 2000 WINS can be configured to request a permanent connection across the intranet with any or all replication partners. There are two significant advantages of persistent replication.

Firstly, significant overhead associated with starting and stopping connections is reduced. Legacy WINS would have to reestablish connections with replication partners every time it needed to replicate. There is always a chance on a very large intranet that a connection cannot be established automatically and will require human intervention.

Secondly, the speed of replication has been greatly increased because the updates can be sent directly to the replication partner without having to go through the motions of first establishing connections.

Manual Tombstoning

You can now manually mark records for deletion using the manual "tombstoning" feature in Windows 2000 WINS. This means that manual deleting requests get orderly and consistent propagation to replication partners. On Windows NT WINS, manual deletes on one server was a problematic effort, because there was a chance that a replication partner could reestablish the previously deleted record.

When you manually tombstone a record, the information is propagated to all replication partners (which occurs quickly with the persistent connection option). Tombstoned records are deleted from all servers after the propagation and after all partners have received the tombstoned records.

WINS Installation and Configuration

WINS does not require a dedicated server, or your most powerful CPU. The service can also be installed on a DNS, DHCP, or DC server, even a Remote Access Service (RAS) server.

Installing WINS

To install WINS, the server needs a static IP address, preferably one dedicated to WINS traffic. So, you can either *multi-home* the machine (install more than one NIC) or assign another IP address to a single interface.

If you did not install WINS with the operating system, do the following:

1. Load the Add/Remove Programs applet from the Control Panel.

2. Click the Add/Remove Windows Components option and then click Components. The Windows Components Wizard launches.

3. Go to the Components list box, select Networking Services, and then click the Details button. The Networking Services checklist box loads.

4. Scroll down to the WINS option (do not uncheck anything; this will only remove the other components). Click OK to begin the installation of WINS. After the installation, you will need to configure the service.

5. Go to My Network Places, right-click, and choose Properties. You can also get to this point by going to Start ➪ Settings ➪ Network and Dial-up Connections. Right-click Local Area Network Connection and select Properties. The Local Area Connection Properties dialog box loads.

6. Select TCP/IP from the connections protocols list on the first tab and then select Properties. On the Properties dialog box, click the Advanced button. The Advanced TCP/IP Settings dialog box loads. This dialog box is illustrated in Figure 14-13.

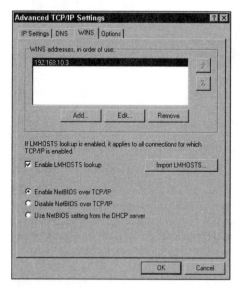

Figure 14-13: Advanced TCP/IP Settings dialog box

7. Select the WINS tab and then click the Add button. Enter the IP address installed on the local NIC you are using. Repeat the process to add a secondary WINS IP address. Close the Network Connections dialog box and click OK all the way out. Installation is complete.

Configuring WINS

WINS, like DNS and many other services in Windows 2000, now uses the Microsoft Management Console for configuration and management. To launch the WINS snap-in, go to Administrative Tools and select the WINS option or (easier) open the Run facility and run the `winsmgmt.msc` shortcut. The WINS snap-in is illustrated in Figure 14-14.

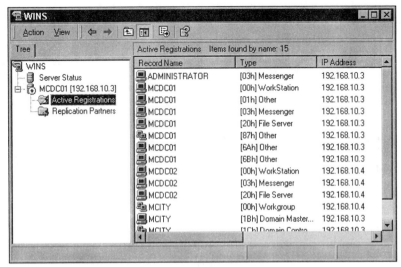

Figure 14-14: The WINS MMC snap-in

One of the perks of WINS is that clients register themselves with the service and for the most part you do not have to manually enter mappings. However, there are exceptions, one of them being non-WINS clients and static entries.

Static entries

By entering static mappings, you ensure that WINS clients can resolve the IP addresses of non-WINS clients. Non-WINS clients include machines running under other operating systems, networks, network devices, domains, and so on. You can even insert a static IP address for another WINS server, if the connection to that WINS server is unreliable and you cannot afford to have the server lose a lease and not be able to renew it.

To create a static mapping:

1. Select the Active Registrations node on the WINS tree and right-click. Choose New Static Mapping from the Context menu. The New Static Mapping option can also be selected from the Action menu.

2. In the Create Static Mapping dialog box, type the name of the target to be resolved in the Computer Name database field.

3. Add a scope name in the optional Scope edit field. This field should not be used because NetBIOS scopes are not recommended. The support is included for advanced NetBIOS solutions and applications.

4. In the Type edit field, enter the type of name to be resolved. The following list explains the static entry types:

   • **Unique:** This is a unique name that can be mapped to a single IP address. Use this type when you need to add a static mapping for a server — usually another WINS server.

   • **Group:** Choose this type for a name that maps to a group. A group is a logical unit on the intranet. Group members, regardless of their nature, usually have their own IP addresses, but these do not need to be stored in WINS.

   • **Domain Name:** Choose this type to map an IP address to a domain name.

   • **Internet Group:** Choose this type to group resources, such as routers, hubs, and printers. You can store up to 25 members in an Internet group.

   • **Multi-homed:** Choose this type for the name of a host that has more than one IP address (multi-home usually refers to a host with more than one network interface card, but Windows 2000 can assign multiple addresses to a single interface.)

5. In the IP Address edit field, enter the IP address of the client and click OK to store the entry.

The proxy agent

The WINS proxy agent extends the WINS services to non-WINS clients by listening for their name registration requests and broadcast resolution requests and then forwarding them to the WINS server. To set up this service, you will need to tinker in the registry.

Drill down to the following subkey:

```
HKEY_LOCAL_MACHINE\SYSTEM\CurrentControlSet\Services\NetBT\
Parameters
```

Under the parameters key, you will find the entry for EnableProxy. Change this value to 1 (enabled). Unfortunately, you will have to restart the server.

Once enabled, the proxy agent will forward the non-WINS client's broadcasts requesting name registration to the WINS server. The name does not get registered; the intention of the proxy is to check that the name has not already been registered.

When the agent detects a name resolution broadcast, it checks its NetBIOS name cache and will attempt to resolve the name to an IP address. If the name is not cached, the agent forwards the broadcast as a resolve request to the WINS server. The WINS server responds to the agent, and the agent then responds to the non-WINS client.

Configuring Windows 2000 Clients for DNS and WINS

Configuring Windows 2000 clients to use DNS and WINS is a relatively simple task. It primarily means configuring the clients with the appropriate DNS and WINS server IP addresses. If you're using DHCP, you can configure the DHCP server to provide the DNS and WINS server data to the DHCP clients automatically.

To learn more about DHCP and how to configure both DHCP servers and clients, see Chapter 13.

If you're not using DHCP, or need to configure the DNS or WINS settings separately from the dynamically assigned IP address on the client, you can configure the client's DNS/WINS settings manually. To do so, log on to the client computer and open the properties for the client's TCP/IP connection. Click Start ➪ Settings ➪ Network and Dial-Up Connections to open the Network and Dial-Up Connections folder. Right-click the connection to be configured and choose Properties. On the General page, locate the TCP/IP protocol in the list of installed components and choose Properties to display the TCP/IP property page shown in Figure 14-15.

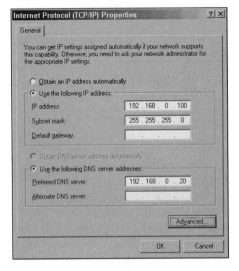

Figure 14-15: Configure DNS and WINS settings through the connection's property page.

If you select the option "Obtain an IP address automatically," you can select the option "Obtain DNS server addresses automatically" to receive the DNS server address list from the DHCP server. If you prefer, you can specify the addresses explicitly by choosing the option "Use the following DNS server addresses," and then filling in the IP addresses of the preferred and alternate server. The client resolver will attempt to resolve through the preferred server first, and if the preferred server fails to respond, the client will try the alternate server.

To configure additional DNS properties, click Advanced, then click the DNS tab to display the DNS property page, as shown in Figure 14-16. As the figure illustrates, you can specify more than two DNS servers if desired and change the order of DNS servers in the list. The resolver tries the DNS servers in order from top to bottom.

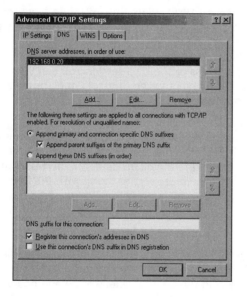

Figure 14-16: Use the DNS page to configure additional DNS options.

The following list explains the options on the DNS page:

✦ **Append primary and connection specific DNS suffixes:** Select this option to append the primary DNS suffix and connection-specific DNS suffix to unqualified host names for resolution. You define the primary DNS suffix for the computer through the computer's Network Identification property page (right-click My Computer, choose Properties, click Network Identification). The primary DNS suffix applies globally to the system unless overridden by the connection-specific DNS suffix, which you set in the property "DNS suffix for this connection" (see following). For example, assume your primary suffix is mcity.org and your connection-specific DNS suffix is support.mcity.org. You query for the unqualified hostname fred. This option then causes Windows 2000 to attempt to resolve fred.mcity.org and fred.support.mcity.org. If you have no connection-specific DNS suffix specified, Windows 2000 will only attempt to resolve fred.mcity.org.

✦ **Append parent suffixes of the primary DNS suffix:** This option determines whether or not the resolver attempts resolution of unqualified names up to the parent level domain for your computer. For example, assume your computer's primary DNS suffix is support.mcity.org and you attempt to resolve the unqualified hostname jane. The resolver would attempt to resolve jane.support.mcity.org and jane.mcity.org (attempting to resolve at the parent level as well as the computer's domain level).

✦ **Append these DNS suffixes in order:** Use this option to only append the specified DNS suffixes for resolving unqualified names.

✦ **DNS suffix for this connection:** Use this option to specify a DNS suffix for the connection that is different from the primary DNS suffix defined in the computer's Network Identification property page.

✦ **Register this connection's addresses in DNS:** Select this option to have the client submit a request to the DNS server to update its host (A) record when its host name changes or IP address changes. The client submits the full computer name specified in the Network Identification tab of the System Properties sheet along with its IP address to the DNS server. You can view the System properties through the System object in the Control Panel, or right-click My Computer and choose Properties.

✦ **Use this connection's DNS suffix in DNS registration:** Select this option to have the client submit a request to the DNS server to update its host record when the host name changes or IP address changes. The difference from the previous option is that this option registers the client using the first part of the computer name specified in the System properties along with the DNS suffix specified by the option "DNS suffix for this connection" on the DNS page. You can use this option along with the previous option to register two different FQDNs for the host.

Tip   Configuring Windows NT and Windows 9x clients for DNS is very similar to configuring Windows 2000 clients. Right-click Network Neighborhood and choose Properties, or open the Network object in the Control Panel. Locate and double-click TCP/IP, then click DNS to set the DNS properties.

Using Hosts and LMHOSTS Files for Name Resolution

As explained previously in this chapter, DNS servers resolve host names to IP addresses, and WINS servers primarily resolve NetBIOS names to IP addresses. In some cases, though, it's helpful to be able to resolve host names to addresses without contacting a DNS or WINS server. For example, you might have several hosts on the local network whose host names and addresses don't change, so there is no real need to put a load on the local name server for resolution if you can avoid it. Or, you might not have a name server available for some reason but still need to enable an application to resolve host names.

Windows 2000 offers two methods for resolving host names to addresses that you can use in conjunction with or in place of name servers to provide name resolution. These two methods rely on ASCII files to store a database of host-to-address entries, just as the original ARPANET relied on the Hosts file for name resolution. You can use a local Hosts file in conjunction with or in place of DNS and a local LMHOSTS file in conjunction with or in place of WINS.

Using a Hosts File for Name Resolution

A Hosts file maintains a host table that maps host names to IP addresses. Windows 2000 can look up entries in the Hosts file to resolve names without having to query a DNS server for resolution. Windows 2000 creates a file named Hosts in the `\%systemroot%\system32\drivers\etc` folder. Hosts is an ASCII file that you can edit with Notepad or other word processor. The file uses the same format as the Hosts file on 4.3 BSD UNIX (stored in /etc/hosts) and by default includes an entry that maps localhost to 127.0.0.1 (used for loopback testing and troubleshooting).

Tip You should make a backup copy of the Hosts file before modifying it in case you experience any problems in modifying the file. Also, do not change or remove the entry for localhost.

Entries in the Hosts file take the format *IP Address* <tab> *host name*. You can specify more than one host name for a given IP address, but you must use multiple entries for hosts in different domains, each entry on its own line. Also, entries in Hosts are case-sensitive, so in the following example, the first two entries would enable proper resolution if the user specified the host name in either uppercase or lowercase:

```
192.160.0.124    joe.mcity.org
192.160.0.124    JOE.MCITY.ORG
192.168.0.203    jane.support.mcity.org
```

You can include a single host name for each entry or specify multiple host names for a single IP address if they fall in the same domain. The following, for example, are valid entries:

```
192.168.0.224    me   tarzan   jim.support.mcity.org
192.168.0.198    you  jane     jane.sales.mcity.org
```

Each of the entries in this example specify three host names for each IP address.

Windows 2000 parses the entries in the Hosts file in sequential order until it finds a match. You can speed up lookup time by placing the most often-used host name entries at the top of the file.

Using the LMHOSTS File for Name Resolution

Windows 2000 automatically resolves NetBIOS names for computers running TCP/IP on a local network. You can use an LMHOSTS file to resolve IP addresses of computers on other networks to which yours is connected by a gateway when a WINS server isn't available.

LMHOSTS is an ASCII file, with the entry format similar to entries in a Hosts file. In addition, LMHOSTS supports special keywords that are explained later in this section. Windows 2000 includes a sample LMHOSTS file in \%*systemroot*%\system32\ drivers\etc. As with the Hosts file, you should make a backup copy of LMHOSTS before modifying it.

Windows 2000 parses each line in LMHOSTS sequentially at startup, which means you should place often-accessed names at the top of the file for best performance. Here are a few rules for structuring an LMHOSTS file:

✦ Each entry must include the IP address in the first column, with the NetBIOS name in the second column. Additional keywords, if any, appear in subsequent columns. Columns are separated by at least one space or tab character. Some LMHOSTS keywords follow entries, while others appear on their own lines (discussed shortly).

✦ Each entry must reside on a separate line.

✦ Comments begin with the pound (#) character, and special LMHOSTS keywords also begin with the # character. Reduce comments to a minimum to improve parsing performance. Place often-accessed entries near the top of the file for best performance.

✦ The LMHOSTS file is static. Like the Hosts file, you must manually update the file to create new entries or modify existing ones.

Windows 2000 TCP/IP reads the LMHOSTS file at system startup, and entries designated as preloaded by the #PRE keyword are read into the name cache at that time. Other entries are read only after broadcast name resolution queries fail. The entire file is parsed at each query so you should place often-used names near the top of the file and reduce comments to a minimum to improve performance.

You can include the following special keywords in an LMHOSTS file:

✦ #PRE. Preload the entry into the name cache at startup. If you want names stored in a remote LMHOSTS file to be added to the name cache at startup, use the #INCLUDE and #PRE statements in combination, as in the following example:

```
#INCLUDE     \\srv1\public\lmhosts     #PRE
```

✦ #DOM: <domain>. Designates remote domain controllers located across one or more routers. Entries that use the #DOM keyword are added to a special Internet workgroup name cache that causes Windows 2000 TCP/IP to forward requests for domain controllers to remote domain controllers as well as local domain controllers. The following example identifies a domain controller named *server1* in the domain support.mcity.org and preloads the entry into the name cache at startup:

```
192.168.0.212   server1   #PRE   #DOM:support.mcity.org
```

✦ #INCLUDE<filename>. Includes entries from separate LMHOSTS file. Use #INCLUDE to include entries from a common, shared LMHOSTS file or your own set of entries stored on your own computer. If you reference a remote LMHOSTS file on a server outside of your network in an #INCLUDE statement, you must also include an entry for the IP address of the remote server in the LMHOSTS file before the #INCLUDE statement that references it. Do not use #INCLUDE to reference an LMHOSTS file on a redirected network drive unless your drive mappings remain the same from one session to another. Otherwise, use the UNC path for the file. The following example includes an LMHOSTS file from a network server:

```
#INCLUDE   \\server1\public\Lmhosts      #Includes shared
Lmhosts file
```

✦ #BEGIN_ALTERNATE. Signals the beginning of a *block inclusion,* which is a block of multiple #INCLUDE statements. The statements within the block designate primary and alternate locations for the included file, and the alternate locations are checked if the primary file is unavailable. Successful loading of any entry in the block causes the block to succeed, and subsequent entries in the block are skipped. You can include multiple block inclusions within an LMHOSTS file. The following is an example of a block inclusion:

```
#BEGIN_ALTERNATE

#INCLUDE      \\server1\public\lmhosts        #Primary source

#INCLUDE      \\server2\public\lmhosts        #Alternate source

#INCLUDE      \\netserv\shared\lmhosts        #Alternate source

#END_ALTERNATE
```

Tip   Addresses of servers specified in a block inclusion must be preloaded through entries earlier in the file. Entries not preloaded are ignored.

✦ #END_ALTERNATE. Signals the end of a block of multiple #INCLUDE statements.

✦ \0xnn. Use this keyword to specify nonprinting characters in NetBIOS names. Enclose the NetBIOS name in quotation marks and use the \0xnn keyword to specify the hexadecimal value of the nonprinting character. The hexadecimal notation applies to only one character in the name. The name must be padded to a total of 16 characters, with the hexadecimal notation as the 16th character. The following is an example:

```
192.168.0.89   "janetrs   \0x14"    #Uses special character
```

Summary

DNS provides the primary means through which Windows 2000 clients resolve host names to IP addresses. The client's computer uses a *resolver* to request resolution of a name from one or more DNS servers. The client can also use a Hosts file to statically map names to addresses and bypass the need to access a DNS server for name resolution.

DNS in Windows 2000 is dynamic and enables clients and DNS servers alike to request that a DNS server that is authoritative for the client's zone update the client's host and pointer records. A client can directly request an update of its host record, and a DNS server can request an update of both the host and associated pointer record on behalf of the client. Zones that are stored in the Active Directory can be secured through ACLs to require authentication before dynamic updates are allowed.

WINS provides the same capabilities for resolving NetBIOS names to addresses that DNS provides for host names. Windows 2000 includes a WINS server service that enables a Windows 2000 server to function as a WINS server, and also integrates DNS and WINS to provide additional capabilities. Although WINS is not always an optimum solution, it nevertheless offers several advantages for name resolution where NetBIOS names are still used.

✦   ✦   ✦

Remote Access

This chapter covers the remote access services provided with Windows 2000 to enable dial-up access (client and server) for remote connectivity, including dial-up connections to the Internet.

Windows 2000 RAS and Telephony Services

RAS stands for Remote Access Services. In Windows 2000, RAS enables Windows 2000 clients to dial other systems for access to remote networks, including the Internet, and enables Windows 2000 computers to act as dial-up servers for remote clients. The Routing and Remote Access Service (RRAS) enables a Windows 2000 Server to function as a router. RAS and RRAS are integrated into a single service in Windows 2000. This chapter examines the features in RRAS for dial-up networking that enable a Windows 2000 computer to function as both a dial-up server and dial-up client.

Cross-Reference You'll find a detailed explanation of the Routing and Remote Access Service and how to use it for routing in Chapter 12.

The following sections provide an overview of these RAS features. Later sections explain protocol, security, and configuration issues.

Overview of Windows 2000 RRAS

Remote access enables a client computer to connect to a remote computer or network and access the resources of the remote computer or network as if they were local. For example, users who are frequently on the road can access the company file server(s), printers, mail system, and other resources from remote locations. Clients also can use remote access services to connect to public networks such as the Internet. Figure 15-1 illustrates one implementation of remote access.

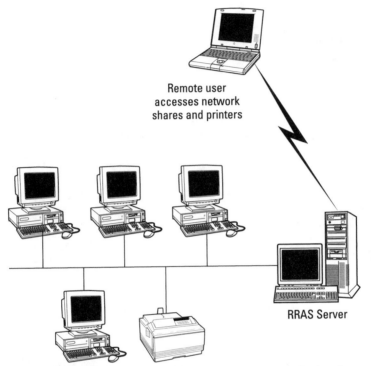

Figure 15-1: RRAS enables remote users to connect to the local computer or network, and also supports dial-out connections from Windows 2000 clients.

The Routing and Remote Access Service in Windows 2000 provides three primary functions:

✦ **Dial-up client:** You can use the RRAS service to create and establish dial-up connections to remote networks, including the Internet, through a variety of media, including modem, ISDN, infrared, parallel ports, serial connection, X.25, and ATM. Windows 2000 dial-up clients support a wide range of authentication protocols and other connectivity options, which are discussed in depth in later sections of this chapter. Support for tunneling protocols enables clients to establish secure connections to remote networks through public networks such as the Internet.

✦ **Dial-up server:** A Windows 2000 server can function as a dial-up server, allowing remote clients to connect to the local server and optionally to the local network through the same types of media support for dial-out connections (see previous). You can also use RAS to support terminal service client sessions because RAS issues an IP address to the connecting clients and binds the necessary protocols to the RAS connection.

Windows 2000 supports several authentication protocols and can authenticate users against local or domain user accounts, or it can use RADIUS (Remote Authentication Dial In User Service), an industry standard authentication mechanism. Once connected, a remote user can browse, print, map drives, and perform essentially all other functions possible from either the local server or local area network.

✦ **Routing services:** The routing components of RRAS enable a Windows 2000 server to function as a unicast and multicast router. Windows 2000 provides for routing, packet filtering, connection sharing, demand-dial routing, and several other features that make it an excellent choice for LAN and WAN routing.

RRAS in Windows 2000 integrates the remote access and routing services that formerly were separate services in Windows NT Server. RRAS in Windows 2000 is an extension and improvement upon Windows NT's Routing and Remote Access Service, which was issued as an add-on for Windows NT Server. Although Windows 2000 RRAS integrates dial-up networking and routing into a single service, they are treated as separate issues in this book because of the different focus for each.

One of the key benefits of Windows 2000 RRAS is its integration with the Windows 2000 operating system. On the client side, integration means that once a remote connection is established, the client can access resources on the server transparently as if they were local resources. The client can map remote shares to local drive letters, map and print to remote printers, and so on. Except in very rare circumstances, applications can use remote resources seamlessly without modification to make them RAS- or network-aware.

On the server side, integration means that Windows 2000 can use a single authentication mechanism to authenticate users both locally and from remote locations. RRAS can authenticate against the local computer's user accounts or accounts in the domain, or it can use an external authentication mechanism such as RADIUS. Through its support for RADIUS, Windows 2000 RRAS enables a Windows 2000 server to function as a gateway of sorts to the network while offloading authentication to another server, which could be any RADIUS platform including a UNIX server.

Note   RADIUS stands for Remote Authentication Dial-In User Service. RADIUS is a standard, cross-platform protocol for authentication commonly used for dial-in authentication.

Windows 2000 RRAS also provides close integration with the Active Directory (AD). This AD integration provides for replication of users' remote access settings, including access permissions, callback options, and security policies, among others. AD integration also means simplified administration with other AD-related services and properties.

As you'll learn later in the section "RAS Connection Types and Protocols," Windows 2000 RRAS supports a wide range of connection protocols, including PPP, SLIP, and Microsoft RAS Protocol. Windows 2000 RRAS supports authentication methods, including MS-CHAP, EAP, CHAP, SPAP, and PAP. Network protocols supported include TCP/IP, IPX/SPX, NetBEUI, and AppleTalk to support Microsoft, UNIX, NetWare, and Macintosh resources and clients.

New Features of Windows 2000 RRAS

If you're familiar with RAS or RRAS in Windows NT, you'll find all of those same features in Windows 2000 RRAS. You'll also find several enhancements to existing features along with many new features, including those discussed in the following sections.

AD integration

As mentioned previously, Windows 2000 RRAS integrates with the Active Directory. AD integration enables client settings to be replicated throughout the organization to provide expanded access by clients and easier administration. Integration with the AD also can simplify administration by enabling you to browse and manage multiple RRAS servers through the AD-aware RRAS management console snap-in, providing a single point of management for RRAS services in an organization.

Bandwidth Allocation Protocol and Bandwidth Allocation Control Protocol

The Bandwidth Allocation Protocol (BAP) and Bandwidth Allocation Control Protocol (BACP) enable Windows 2000 RAS to dynamically add or remove links in a multilink PPP connection as bandwidth requirements for the connection change. When bandwidth utilization becomes heavy, RAS can add links to accommodate the increased load and enhance performance. When bandwidth utilization decreases, RAS can remove links to make the connection more cost efficient. You configure BAP policies through a remote access policy that you can apply to individual users, groups, or an entire organization.

MS-CHAP version 2

Previous versions of RAS supported Microsoft Challenge Handshake Authentication Protocol (MS-CHAP) to authenticate remote clients. MS-CHAP v2 provides stronger security and is designed specifically to support Virtual Private Network (VPN) connections, which enable remote clients to establish secure connections to a private network through a public network such as the Internet. MS-CHAP v2 provides several security enhancements:

✦ LAN Manager coding of responses, formerly supported for backward compatibility with older remote access clients, is no longer supported for improved security. MS-CHAP v2 no longer supports LAN Manager encoding of password changes for the same reason.

✦ MS-CHAP v2 supports *mutual authentication,* which provides bi-directional authentication between the remote client and the RAS server. Previously, MS-CHAP only provided one-way authentication and did not provide a mechanism for the remote client to determine if the remote server actually had access to its authentication password for verification. Version 2 not only enables the server to authenticate the client's request, but also allows the client to verify the server's ability to authenticate its account.

✦ MS-CHAP v2 also provides stronger encryption. The 40-bit encryption used in previous versions operated on the user's password and resulted in the same cryptographic key being generated for each session. Version 2 uses the remote client's password, along with an arbitrary challenge string, to create a unique cryptographic key for each session, even when the client password remains the same.

✦ Version 2 provides better security for data transmission, using separate cryptographic keys for data sent in each direction.

Extensible Authentication Protocol

The Extensible Authentication Protocol (EAP) enables authentication methods to be added to RAS without redesigning the underlying RAS software base, much like new features in NTFS 5.0 enable new functionality to be added to the file system without redesigning the file system (see Chapter 21 for a complete discussion). EAP enables the client and server to negotiate the mechanism to be used to authenticate the client. Currently, EAP in Windows 2000 supports EAP-MD5 CHAP (Challenge Handshake Authentication Protocol), EAP-TLS (Transport Level Security), and redirection to a RADIUS server. Each of these topics is covered in more detail later in this chapter.

RADIUS support

Windows 2000 RRAS can function as a RADIUS client, funneling logon requests to a RADIUS server, which can include the Internet Authentication Service, also included with Windows 2000, running on the same or a different server. The RADIUS server doesn't have to be a Windows 2000 system, however, which enables RRAS to also use UNIX-based RADIUS servers or third-party RADIUS services you might already have in place. One of the advantages to using RADIUS is its capability for accounting, and several third-party utilities have been developed to provide integration with database back-ends such as SQL Server to track and control client access.

See the section "Using RADIUS" later in this chapter for detailed information on configuring and using RADIUS.

Remote access policies

Windows 2000 improves considerably on the flexibility you have as an administrator to control a user's remote access and dial-up settings. Windows NT RAS gave you control only over callback options, and settings were assigned on a user-by-user basis. Although Windows 2000 still lets you assign remote access permissions through a user's account, you also can use a remote access policy to define the remote access settings for one or several users. Remote access policies give you a fine degree of control over users' settings, controlling options such as allowed access time, maximum session time, authentication, security, BAP policies, and more.

See the section "Remote Access Policy" later in this chapter for additional information on configuring and using RAS policies.

Support for Macintosh clients

Windows 2000 adds remote access support for Macintosh clients by supporting AppleTalk over PPP for Macintosh clients. This enables Macintosh clients to connect to a Windows 2000 RAS server using the standard PPP and AppleTalk protocols.

Account lockout

Windows 2000 RAS enhances security by supporting account lockout, which locks a RAS account after a specified number of bad logon attempts. This feature helps guard against dictionary attacks in which a hacker attempts to gain remote access by repeatedly attempting logon using a dictionary of passwords against a valid account. You can configure two settings that control lockout — the number of bad logon attempts before the account is locked out, and how long the account remains locked before the lockout counter is reset.

The Routing and Remote Access Management Console

Microsoft has integrated most administration and management functions into Microsoft Management Console (MMC) snap-ins, and RRAS is no exception. The Routing and Remote Access console snap-in enables you to configure and manage an RRAS server. Figure 15-2 shows the Routing and Remote Access console.

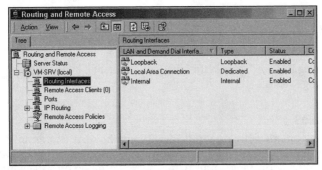

Figure 15-2: The Routing and Remote Access console

The RRAS console serves as a central control center for managing most RRAS properties. In addition to configuring ports and interfaces, you can configure protocols, global options and properties, and RRAS policies through the RRAS console. Later sections of this chapter explain how to use the RRAS console to perform specific configuration and administration tasks. Open the console by choosing Start ⇨ Programs ⇨ Administrative Tools ⇨ Routing and Remote Access.

RAS Connection Types and Protocols

Windows 2000 supports several connection types and network protocols for remote access. The following sections explore these connection types and network protocols.

Serial Line Internet Protocol

The Serial Line Internet Protocol (SLIP) is a connection protocol that originated in the UNIX realm. SLIP offers limited functionality in that it does not support error detection or correction. Windows 2000 clients can use SLIP to connect to UNIX servers (or other servers requiring SLIP), but Windows 2000 Server does not support SLIP for dial-in connections.

Point-to-Point Protocol

The Point-to-Point Protocol (PPP) was developed as a standardized alternative to SLIP that offered better performance and reliability. Unlike SLIP, PPP is designed around industry-designed standards and enables essentially any PPP-compliant client to connect to a PPP server. Windows 2000 supports PPP for both dial-in and dial-out connections. On a Windows 2000 RAS server, PPP enables remote clients to use IPX, TCP/IP, NetBEUI, AppleTalk, or a combination thereof. Windows-based clients including Windows 2000, Windows NT, Windows 9*x*, and Windows 3.*x* can use any combination of IPX, TCP/IP, or NetBEUI, but AppleTalk is not supported for these clients. Macintosh clients can use either TCP/IP or AppleTalk. PPP supports several authentication protocols, including MS-CHAP, EAP, CHAP, SPAP, and PAP.

Microsoft RAS Protocol

The Microsoft RAS Protocol is a proprietary protocol developed by Microsoft to support NetBIOS and is used for Windows NT 3.1, Windows for Workgroups, MS-DOS, and LAN Manager remote access. Clients must use the NetBEUI protocol, and the remote access server acts as a NetBIOS gateway for the client, supporting NetBEUI, NetBIOS over TCP/IP, and NetBIOS over IPX. The Microsoft RAS Protocol is provided for backward compatibility with older Microsoft operating platforms. Unless you are connecting to one of these older systems, choose PPP as your connection protocol.

Point-to-Point Multilink Protocol and BAP

The Point-to-Point Multilink Protocol (PPMP, or simply Multilink) enables multiple PPP lines to be combined to provide an aggregate bandwidth. For example, you might use Multilink to combine two analog 56Kbps modems to give you an aggregate bandwidth roughly equivalent to 112Kbps. Or, you might combine both B channels of an ISDN Basic Rate Interface (BRI) connection to provide double the bandwidth you would otherwise get from a single channel.

The Bandwidth Allocation Protocol (BAP) works in conjunction with Multilink to provide adaptive bandwidth. As bandwidth utilization increases, BAP enables the client to aggregate additional connections to increase bandwidth and improve performance. As bandwidth utilization decreases, BAP enables the client to drop connections from the aggregate link to reduce connection costs (in cases where multiple connections incur their own charges).

Cross-Reference   See the section "Using Multilink and BAP" later in this chapter to configure and use multilink connections.

Point-to-Point Tunneling Protocol

The TCP/IP protocol suite by itself does not provide for encryption or data security, an obvious concern for users who need to transmit data securely across a public network such as the Internet. The Point-to-Point Tunneling Protocol (PPTP) provides a means for encapsulating and encrypting IP and IPX for secure transmission. PPTP is an extension of PPP that enables you to create a Virtual Private Network (VPN) connection between a client and server.

PPP frames in a PPTP session are encrypted using Microsoft Point-to-Point Encryption (MPPE) with encryption keys generated using the MS-CHAP or EAP-TLS authentication process. PPTP by itself does not provide encryption, but rather encapsulates the already encrypted PPP frames. In order to provide a secure connection, the client must use either MS-CHAP or EAP-TLS authentication. Otherwise, the PPP frames are encapsulated unencrypted (plain text). Figure 15-3 illustrates how PPTP encapsulates data. PPTP is installed by default when you install Windows 2000 RRAS.

Tip   PPTP is a good choice for creating secure connections to a private network through a public network such as the Internet when the remote network isn't configured to support IPSec.

Layer Two Tunneling Protocol

Layer Two Tunneling Protocol (L2TP) is a draft protocol that combines the features of PPTP with support for IP Security (IPSec) to provide enhanced security. Unlike

PPTP, which relies on MPPE for encryption, L2TP relies on IPSec to provide encryption. Therefore, the source and destination routers must support both L2TP and IPSec. Figure 15-3 illustrates how L2TP encapsulates data. L2TP is installed by default when you install Windows 2000 RRAS.

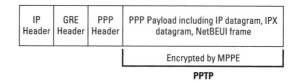

IP Header	GRE Header	PPP Header	PPP Payload including IP datagram, IPX datagram, NetBEUI frame

Encrypted by MPPE

PPTP

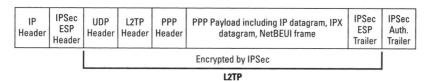

IP Header	IPSec ESP Header	UDP Header	L2TP Header	PPP Header	PPP Payload including IP datagram, IPX datagram, NetBEUI frame	IPSec ESP Trailer	IPSec Auth. Trailer

Encrypted by IPSec

L2TP

Figure 15-3: PPTP and L2TP use different methods for encapsulation and encryption.

Tip

L2TP provides better security than PPTP by supporting IPSec and is a better choice for creating VPN connections than PPTP when the remote network is configured to support IPSec. See Chapter 3 for a discussion of Windows 2000 security and IPSec.

Transport Protocols

As mentioned previously in this chapter, RRAS supports four network protocols: TCP/IP, IPX, NetBEUI, and AppleTalk. A Windows 2000 RAS server supports all four protocols for incoming connections. Windows 2000 RAS clients support all except AppleTalk. When you install RRAS, Windows 2000 enables all currently installed protocols for incoming and outgoing RAS connections. As you'll learn later in the section "Configuring RAS for Incoming Connections," you can configure the supported protocols to enable clients to access only the RAS server or access the LAN. You configure access on a protocol-by-protocol basis.

TCP/IP

As a dial-out protocol, TCP/IP enables you to connect a Windows 2000 client to nearly any TCP/IP-based network including the Internet. You can statically assign the IP address, subnet mask, default gateway, and other settings for the dial-out connection or allow the remote server to assign the connection properties. As a protocol for incoming connections, TCP/IP enables essentially any client that supports TCP/IP and PPP to connect to a Windows 2000 RAS server. As you'll learn later in the section "Configuring RAS for Incoming Connections," you can allocate addresses from a static pool or use DHCP to allocate addresses and other connection properties to remote clients. In addition, clients can request a predefined IP address (defined at the client side through the connection properties).

IPX

The IPX protocol is used primarily in environments where Novell NetWare clients or servers are used. Support for IPX enables a Windows 2000 RAS server to coexist with NetWare servers and enables clients to access NetWare resources through the RAS connection. A Windows 2000 RAS server hosting IPX also serves as an IPX router, handling RIP, SAP, and NetBIOS traffic between the local network and the remote client. In addition to using the IPX protocol, the remote client must run a NetWare redirector. The server must be running the IPX/SPX/NetBIOS-compatible protocol.

Note   The Windows 2000 Professional NetWare redirector is Client Service for NetWare. In Windows 2000 Server, the redirector is Gateway Service for NetWare.

A Windows 2000 RAS server allocates IPX network numbers and node numbers to connecting clients. The server can generate the IPX network number automatically or, as it can for TCP/IP, allocate numbers from a static pool assigned by an administrator. If assigning a number dynamically, the server first verifies that the number is not already in use on the network. The server then allocates that number to all remote access clients. Assigning the same network number to all clients reduces RIP announcements from the RAS server.

NetBEUI

NetBEUI is a good protocol choice for small, non-routed networks (NetBEUI is not a routable protocol). Because it is non-routable, NetBEUI can offer some measure of security for a private network that is connected to the Internet. Internal systems that don't require Internet access can use NetBEUI and be invisible to computers on the Internet. Supporting NetBEUI for Windows 2000 RAS enables NetBEUI clients to dial into the RAS server and gain access to resources shared on the server or on the network by other NetBEUI clients. However, NetBEUI clients will need access to a WINS server on the network where they connect to resolve IP-addressed resources.

AppleTalk

The AppleTalk protocol is used by Macintosh network clients. Windows 2000 RAS supports AppleTalk to enable remote Macintosh clients to connect to the server and access resources shared by the server or other AppleTalk clients on the network. In order to use AppleTalk for RAS dial-in, you must install the AppleTalk protocol on the RAS server.

Configuring RAS for Inbound Connections

RRAS in Windows 2000 really takes three distinct directions: routing, inbound connections (RAS server), and outbound connections (RAS client). This section explains how to configure a Windows 2000 server as a RAS server. When you install Windows 2000, Setup by default installs RRAS, so you don't need to install it separately. You do, however, need to configure it. The following sections explain how to configure modems, ports, protocols, encryption, and other properties to set up and manage a RAS server.

Enabling RRAS

Although Windows 2000 installs RRAS by default, you still need to enable the service to begin configuring and using it. To do so, choose Start ➪ Programs ➪ Administrative Tools ➪ Routing and Remote Access to open the RRAS console. Right-click the server in the left pane and choose Configure and Enable Routing and Remote Access to start the RRAS Setup Wizard. You can use the wizard to automatically configure RRAS for specific applications, or you can configure the service manually. The following sections explain the options offered by the wizard.

Tip   If you enable RRAS and choose to configure it manually, then later decide you'd like to run the wizard, you can do so but will lose the current configuration settings. To reconfigure the service through the wizard, open the RRAS console, right-click the server, and choose Disable Routing and Remote Access. After the service stops, right-click the server again and choose Configuring and Enable Routing and Remote Access.

Internet connection server

Select this option to configure the RRAS server to enable local network clients to connect to the Internet. As such, the RRAS server functions as an Internet gateway. See the section on network address translation in Chapter 12 for detailed information on configuring RRAS to function as an Internet connection gateway. Optionally, you can configure the server to use Internet Connection Sharing (ICS) to allow shared access by local clients to an existing Internet connection on the server. The previously mentioned section of Chapter 12 also covers ICS.

Remote access server

Select this option to configure the RRAS server to enable remote access clients to connect through the server to access resources on the server or on the local network. The wizard prompts for the following:

✦ **Protocols:** Specify the protocols to be supported, which must already be installed on the RRAS server. All installed protocols are enabled for RRAS by default. You can, however, disable specific protocols after the wizard finishes.

✦ **Network interface:** The wizard prompts for the network interface to which to assign remote clients, which determines where the addresses and other access properties come from. In a multi-homed server, select the network interface where the DHCP server is located, if allocating addresses through DHCP.

✦ **IP address assignment:** You can choose to assign addresses through DHCP (see previous option) or from a static address pool. If you choose to use a static pool, the wizard prompts you for the range of addresses to use. See the section "Configuring Protocols" later in this chapter for detailed information regarding address assignment.

Cross-Reference

You can allow remote clients to request a pre-assigned IP address configured at the client side. See the section "Configuring Protocols" later in this chapter for a detailed explanation.

✦ **RADIUS:** You can configure the RRAS server to use RADIUS for authentication and accounting. You specify the IP address or host name for the primary and alternate RADIUS servers, along with the RADIUS shared secret, which essentially is a password the RRAS server uses to authenticate its right to access the RADIUS servers. Windows 2000 includes a RADIUS server called Internet Authentication Service (IAS) that you can use for RRAS and other applications requiring RADIUS authentication, or you can use any RADIUS server. See the section "Using RADIUS" later in this chapter for more information.

Virtual private network server

Select this option to configure RRAS as a VPN server, enabling clients to use PPTP or L2TP to dial in from a public network such as the Internet (or direct dial-up) and establish a secure connection to the local network. By default, RRAS configures five ports each for PPTP and L2TP, but you can add or remove ports as desired. The wizard prompts for the same information described in the previous section and also prompts for the network interface through which the RRAS server connects to the Internet. The VPN server must have a second network interface for the internal LAN.

Network router

Select this option to configure the RRAS server to function as a router. The wizard prompts you to verify that the required protocols are installed (listing them for you), then prompts you to choose whether or not you want to use demand-dial connections to access remote networks. If you choose No, the wizard completes the configuration and terminates. If you answer Yes, the wizard asks if you want to assign IP addresses through DHCP or a static address pool (if IP is installed on the server). Choosing Yes does not cause the wizard to configure any demand-dial connections; you configure those through the RRAS console after the wizard finishes.

Manually configured server

Select this option if you want to manually configure all RRAS server settings. Windows 2000 configures the server as a RAS server and router with default settings. You can run the wizard again if desired to automatically configure the server, although you'll lose the current configuration settings. See the previous section, "Enabling RRAS," to learn how to restart the wizard.

Note The following sections assume you are configuring the server manually rather than using the wizard, or fine-tuning settings after running the wizard.

Configuring Modems and Ports

One of the first steps to take in setting up a Windows 2000 RAS server is to install and configure the hardware and ports that will handle the incoming calls. You configure a standard modem through the Control Panel. If the modem is not already installed, open the Control Panel and double-click the Phone and Modem Options object. Click the Modems tab, then click Add to start the Add/Remove Hardware wizard. You have the option of selecting the modem manually or letting Windows 2000 search for it. Repeat the process for any additional modems you are installing on the system.

Cross-Reference For additional help installing hardware, refer to Chapter 6.

Other types of dial-up equipment require different installation and configuration steps that vary from one item to the next. It isn't practical to cover all types in this chapter, so you might have to refer to the manufacturer's documentation to learn how to properly install the hardware. If you're setting up a server connected to the Internet to act as a VPN server for your local network, install the network hardware, connect the system to the Internet, and verify that the server has connectivity to both the LAN and Internet. You configure ports for incoming access through the RRAS console. If you click on the Ports node, the console displays the installed RAS ports. Windows 2000 by default installs both the PPTP and L2TP protocols for VPN support and adds five ports for each protocol (to support up to five incoming connections of each type.) You can view the status of a given port by double-clicking the port in the list or right-clicking the port and choosing Status. Windows 2000 displays a Port Status dialog box for the port that shows line speed, errors, and protocol-specific data such as IP address, IPX address, and so on.

To configure ports, right-click Ports in the right pane of the RRAS console and choose Properties. Windows 2000 displays a Ports Properties dialog box listing each of the port types. For example, all PPTP ports appear under a single item in the list, as do all L2TP ports and individual modems. Select the port type you want to configure and click Configure. Windows 2000 displays the Configure Device dialog box shown in Figure 15-4.

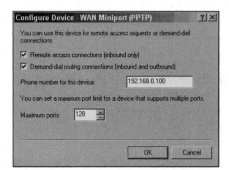

Figure 15-4: The Configure Device dialog box

The following list explains the options in the Configure Device dialog box:

✦ **Remote access connections (inbound only):** Select this option to allow the selected port to handle incoming connections only and not function as a demand-dial router for outgoing connections.

✦ **Demand-dial routing connections (inbound and outbound):** Select this option to allow the port to handle incoming calls and function as a demand-dial router to service local clients for outgoing calls.

✦ **Phone number for this device:** This option is used for Called-Station-ID and BAP-enabled connections and to identify the IP address for PPTP and L2TP ports. Some devices support automatic recognition of the device's phone number for Called-Station-ID, so you only need to add the number manually if the device doesn't support automatic recognition. The number must match the number defined in the Called-Station-ID attribute of the remote access policy that is in effect, or the call is rejected. For BAP, this property is passed to the client when it requests an additional connection so it knows what number to dial for the new connection. For PPTP and L2TP ports, enter the IP address in dotted decimal format to assign to the VPN interface of the server.

✦ **Maximum ports:** Use this control to specify the maximum number of ports enabled on a multiport device or protocol (such as PPTP or L2TP).

Configuring Protocols

In addition to configuring the ports used by the RRAS server, you also need to configure the protocols to be used by remote access clients. You should verify that you have the necessary protocols installed prior to attempting to configure the protocols for RRAS. The following sections explain the options you have for each of the supported RRAS protocols.

TCP/IP

You can assign IP addresses to remote access clients using one of three methods: DHCP, a static address pool, or by allowing the client to request a pre-assigned IP address.

Assigning addresses through DHCP

When the RRAS service starts, it checks for the availability of a DHCP server (if configured to use DHCP for address assignment) and obtains ten leases from the DHCP server. The RRAS server uses the first lease for itself and assigns the remaining addresses to RAS clients as they connect, recovering and reusing addresses as clients disconnect. When the pool of ten addresses is exhausted, the RRAS server obtains ten more, and the process repeats as needed. When the RRAS service stops, it releases all addresses, making them available for other DHCP clients on the network.

The RRAS service will use Automatic Private IP Addressing (APIPA) if it is unable to locate a DHCP server at startup. APIPA enables Windows 2000 to assign addresses in the class B address range 169.254.0.1 through 169.254.0.254 (subnet mask of 255.255.0.0). APIPA is designed to allow automatic IP configuration when no DHCP server is available. Because APIPA is intended for use in internal, single-segment networks, it does not allocate settings for default gateway, DNS servers, or WINS servers.

RRAS by default selects a network interface at random from which to obtain the DHCP leases for RAS clients. You can, however, specify the interface to pull addresses from a specific network segment/server when the RRAS server is multi-homed (multiple network interfaces). You do so through the IP page of the server's properties. In the RRAS console, right-click the server and choose Properties, then click the IP tab (Figure 15-5). Use the Adapter drop-down list at the bottom of the property page to select the adapter, or choose "Allow RAS to select adapter" if you want to allow RRAS to automatically select an adapter.

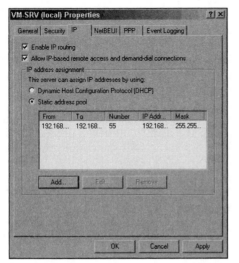

Figure 15-5: The IP tab

Note The Adapter drop-down list only appears on multi-homed systems.

Using a static address pool

You can assign addresses to RAS clients from a static pool if you have no DHCP server on the network or simply prefer not to use DHCP for the RAS server. In previous versions of RRAS (Windows NT), you could configure included and excluded address ranges. In Windows 2000, however, you only create included ranges. You can achieve the same effect as an excluded range by simply creating multiple included ranges that don't include the address range you want to exclude.

You configure the static address pool through the IP property page for the server. In the RRAS console, right-click the server, choose Properties, and then click the IP tab. Select the option "Static address pool" and then click Add to display the New Address Range dialog box. You specify a starting address for the range, then either the ending address or the number of addresses to include in the pool. Windows 2000 determines the ending address for you if you specify the number of addresses, and it also determines the required subnet mask based on the selected address range. Click OK to add the range, then repeat the process if you need to add other ranges.

When defining static address pools for RRAS, make sure you don't use addresses already allocated to other systems or to DHCP servers on the network. If the static address pool is in a different subnet from the local network, you must either enable IP routing on the RRAS server (configured through the IP page of the server's global properties) or add static routes for the subnet.

Allowing clients to use pre-assigned IP addresses

In some situations, it's advantageous for clients to be able to use the same IP address for each remote session. For example, users might work with applications that expect remote users to be at specific IP addresses. Arbitrarily allowing clients to request pre-assigned IP addresses could lead to address havoc and potential routing problems, but Windows 2000 overcomes that problem by allocating the remote client's IP address through his or her account properties. Enabling a client to request a pre-assigned IP address requires two steps. First, you must configure the applicable remote access policy to allow the user to request a pre-assigned IP address. Second, you must specify the address in the user's account properties.

Cross-Reference You configure the remote access policy through the RRAS console. See the section "Remote Access Policy" later in this section for detailed information on configuring and managing remote access policies.

Where you modify the user's account properties depends on the network configuration. On a standalone server (no domain), you modify the user's properties through the Local Users and Groups node of the Computer Management console. Open the account's properties and click the Dial-In tab. Select the option "Assign a Static IP Address" and specify the desired address in the associated text box. For information on other properties on the Dial-Up page, see the section "Remote Access Policy" later in this chapter. You'll find the same properties for users in a domain in the Active Directory Users and Computers console. Configure properties as you would on a standalone server.

Enabling/disabling IP for RRAS

Windows 2000 RRAS by default enables for RRAS all protocols installed on the server. You can selectively disable a protocol if you don't want to allow that protocol to be used for remote connections. To enable or disable IP for RAS, open the RRAS console, right-click the server, and choose Properties. On the IP property page, select or deselect the option "Allow IP-based remote access and demand-dial connections" to enable or disable IP for RAS, respectively.

IP routing and restricting access to the RAS server

By default, the RRAS server allows remote clients access not only to the local server, but also to the network (subject to permissions and policies applied to the remote client or local resources). As such, the RRAS server provides IP routing to the remote clients, routing traffic between the remote client and the LAN. You can prevent remote clients from accessing the LAN by disabling IP routing on the RRAS server. To do so, open the RRAS console, right-click the server, and choose Properties. On the IP page, deselect the option "Enable IP routing" to prevent remote clients from accessing the LAN and to restrict their access only to resources on the RRAS server.

 IP routing must be enabled if you're using the RRAS server to provide LAN or demand-dial routing. See the section "Network Address Translation" in Chapter 12 for a detailed discussion of Windows 2000 routing through RRAS.

NetBEUI

One of the advantages to NetBEUI is that as a simple, non-routable protocol, it is easy to configure. For RRAS, you have three options that control how NetBEUI is used for remote clients. You configure these properties through the server's properties. Open the RRAS console, right-click the server, choose Properties, and click the NetBEUI tab. Use the following options to configure NetBEUI:

✦ **Allow NetBEUI based remote clients to access:** Select this option to allow remote clients to use NetBEUI; deselect to disable NetBEUI for RRAS on the selected server.

✦ **This computer only:** Select this option to allow remote clients to access only resources shared on the RRAS server, but not the network to which the server is attached.

✦ **The entire network:** Select this option to allow remote clients to access resources on the RRAS server as well as resources shared on the LAN to which the server is connected. Access to resources is subject to object permissions and policies just like local users.

IPX

The first step in configuring IPX is to decide how IPX network and node numbers will be assigned to remote clients. You also can enable/disable IPX for RAS connections and control which resources the IPX clients can access. Open the RRAS console, right-click the server, choose Properties, and click the IPX tab to configure the following properties:

✦ **Allow IPX based remote access and demand-dial connections:** Select this option to enable IPX for RRAS; deselect to prevent remote clients from using IPX for remote connections.

✦ **Enable network access for remote clients and demand-dial connections:** Select this option to allow remote IPX clients to access IPX-based resources (NetWare servers, for example) on the LAN to which the RRAS server is connected; deselect to allow remote IPX clients only access to resources on the RRAS server.

✦ **Automatically:** This option allows the RRAS server to automatically allocate IPX network numbers to remote access clients and demand-dial routers that request connections to the RRAS server.

✦ **In the following range:** Use this option to specify a range of IPX network numbers the RRAS server will use to allocate network numbers to remote clients and demand-dial routers.

✦ **Use the same network number for all IPX clients:** Use this option to have the RRAS server assign the same IPX network number to all clients, reducing RIP announcements and corresponding network traffic.

✦ **Allow remote clients to request IPX node number:** Select this option to allow remote access clients and demand-dial routers to request a specific IPX node number when the connection is established.

AppleTalk

There is essentially no configuration necessary for AppleTalk on a RRAS server. Use the AppleTalk page of the server's properties to enable or disable AppleTalk for remote connections.

Configuring Authentication

After you have configured protocols on the RRAS server, you need to turn your attention to authentication and encryption, configuring the server to suit your needs.

Configuring PPP

Windows 2000 offers a few options you can configure that control PPP connections to the server. In the RRAS console, right-click the server, choose Properties, and click the PPP tab. The PPP page offers the following options:

✦ **Multilink connections:** Select this option to allow remote clients to request and use multilink connections. This option enables multilink connections but does not explicitly enable dynamic link management through BAP or BACP, which is controlled by the following option. See the section "Using Multilink and BAP" later in this chapter for additional information.

✦ **Dynamic bandwidth control using BAP or BACP:** This option enables the server and client to use Bandwidth Allocation Protocol and Bandwidth Allocation Control Protocol to dynamically multilink connections, adding links when bandwidth utilization increases and removing links when bandwidth utilization decreases.

✦ **Link control protocol (LCP) extensions:** LCP extensions enable LCP to send Time-Remaining and Identification packets, and to request callback during LCP negotiation. Deselect this option only if the remote clients don't support LCP extensions.

✦ **Software compression:** Select this option to have the RRAS server use Microsoft Point-to-Point Compression protocol (MPPC) to compress data transmitted to remote clients. Deselect this option if the remote clients don't support MPPC.

Configuring authentication

As mentioned earlier in this chapter, Windows 2000 RRAS supports several authentication standards. You can configure RRAS to accept multiple authentication methods, and the server will attempt authentication using the selected protocols in order of decreasing security. For example, RRAS attempts EAP first if EAP is enabled, then MS-CHAP version 2, then MS-CHAP, and so on.

You configure the authentication methods for RRAS through the Security page of the RRAS server's properties (accessed from the RRAS console). Click Authentication Methods on the Security page to access the Authentication Methods dialog box shown in Figure 15-6. Select the authentication methods you want to allow, then click OK. The following sections provide an overview of each method and where applicable, and how to configure and enable them.

Cross-Reference

You can require a specific authentication method for a client through a remote access policy. The following sections don't cover configuring authentication through a remote policy for each authentication protocol, but you will find coverage of that topic in the section "Remote Access Policy" later in this chapter.

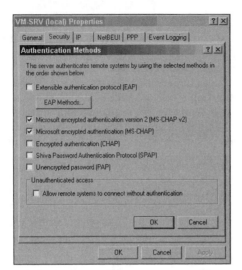

Figure 15-6: You can configure multiple authentication methods through the Authentication Methods dialog box, and RRAS attempts them in decreasing order of security provided.

EAP

EAP stands for Extensible Authentication Protocol. EAP enables the client and server (or IAS, if used for RAS authentication) to negotiate an authentication method from a pool of methods supported by the server. Windows 2000 EAP provides support for two EAP types: EAP-MD5 CHAP and EAP-TLS. Both the client and authentication server must support the same EAP type for authentication through EAP, and you can install additional EAP types from third parties on a Windows 2000 server.

EAP-MD5 CHAP functions much the same as standard CHAP, but challenges and responses are sent as EAP messages. EAP-MD5 CHAP authenticates with user names and passwords. EAP-TLS, on the other hand, uses certificates to authenticate remote clients, using a secured private key exchange between client and server. EAP-TLS provides the most secure authentication of all the methods supported by Windows 2000.

Note   Windows 2000 supports EAP-TLS only in domain environments (either mixed mode or native). RRAS on a standalone server does not support EAP-TLS.

Enabling RRAS to support EAP requires three steps. First, enable EAP as an authentication method in the Authentication Methods dialog box through the RRAS server's properties. Then, if necessary, configure the remote client's remote access policy to allow EAP, as explained later in the section "Remote Access Policy." Finally, configure the client to use the appropriate EAP type. See the section "Configuring Outgoing Dial-Up Networking Connections" in this chapter for a detailed explanation.

Configuring EAP-RADIUS

In addition to supporting the two EAP types described previously, Windows 2000 also enables authentication messages for any EAP type to be relayed to RADIUS servers (such as Windows 2000 systems running IAS). EAP-RADIUS encapsulates and formats the messages going from the RRAS server to the RADIUS server as RADIUS messages. The RADIUS server encapsulates the EAP response as a RADIUS message and passes it to the RRAS server, which relays it to the client. In this way, the RRAS server functions as a relay and doesn't actually perform the authentication, nor does it require the EAP type used to be installed on the RRAS server. Instead, the EAP type must be installed on the RADIUS server.

In addition to configuring the client to use EAP and the appropriate EAP type, you must enable EAP authentication on the RRAS server, configure it to point to the appropriate RADIUS server, and also install the required EAP type on the RADIUS server. You configure the RRAS server to accommodate EAP through the Authentication Methods dialog box for the server, as explained previously. To point the RRAS server to the RADIUS server, open the server's Security property page and select RADIUS Authentication from the Authentication Provider drop-down list. Click Configure ⇨ Add to display the Add RADIUS Server dialog box shown in Figure 15-7.

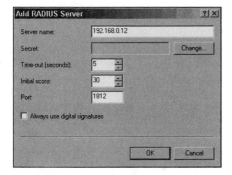

Figure 15-7: The Add RADIUS Server dialog box

Use the following list as a guide to configure RADIUS server options:

✦ **Server name:** Specify the FQDN or IP address of the RADIUS server.

✦ **Secret:** Enter the secret string used by the RADIUS server to authenticate access to the RADIUS server. You can use any alphanumeric characters and special characters in the string, up to 255 characters. The shared secret is case-sensitive.

✦ **Time-out (seconds):** This is the period of time the RRAS server will wait for a response from the RADIUS server before timing out and failing the authentication.

✦ **Initial score:** This value indicates the overall responsiveness of the RADIUS server. This number changes dynamically as the responsiveness of the RADIUS server changes. RRAS queries the servers in order of highest to lowest score (the higher the score, the better the responsiveness). Use this option to specify an estimated initial score.

✦ **Port:** Specify the UDP port used by the RADIUS server for incoming authentication requests. The default is 1812 for newer RADIUS servers and 1645 for older RADIUS servers.

✦ **Always use digital signatures:** Select this option to force the RRAS server to send a digital signature with each RADIUS message. The signature is based on the shared secret. Make sure the RADIUS server supports and is configured for receipt of digital signatures before enabling this option. If you're using IAS and the client for this server is configured to require the RRAS server to always send a digital signature, you must select this option.

See the section "RAS Logging and Accounting" later in this chapter to configure the RRAS server for RADIUS authentication.

Repeat the process described previously to add other RADIUS servers as required.

MS-CHAP version 2

MS-CHAP v2 (Microsoft Challenge Handshake Authentication Protocol) is an improvement on the original MS-CHAP v1 that addresses a handful of security issues. With MS-CHAP v2, the authentication server sends a challenge to the client containing a session ID and arbitrary challenge string. The client returns the user name, an arbitrary peer challenge string, and a one-way encryption of the received challenge string, peer challenge string, session ID, and user password. The server checks the client response and returns a success/failure and an authenticated response that is based on the two challenge strings, the encrypted client response, and the user password. The client verifies the authentication and, if it's valid, accepts the connection. The RAS client terminates the connection if the authentication is not valid.

See the section "New Features of Windows 2000 RRAS" earlier in this chapter for a list of improvements MS-CHAP v2 offers over v1.

MS-CHAP v2 is enabled by default for authentication on Windows 2000 RRAS servers. There are no other configuration steps to take other than to configure the client to use MS-CHAP v2. See the section " Configuring Outgoing Dial-Up Networking Connections" later in this chapter for more information. To disable MS-CHAP v2 on the RRAS server, open the RRAS console and then open the property sheet for the server. On the Security tab, click Authentication Methods and then deselect the MS-CHAP v2 option.

MS-CHAP

MS-CHAP represents version 1 of the Microsoft Challenge Handshake Authentication Protocol. With MS-CHAP, the authentication server sends a challenge to the client containing a session ID and arbitrary challenge string. The remote client responds with the user name and encryption of the challenge string, session ID, and user's password. The server checks the supplied credentials and authenticates access if the credentials are valid.

MS-CHAP is enabled by default for Windows 2000 RRAS servers, and there are no other configuration steps except to verify that the client is configured to use MS-CHAP.

CHAP

This option enables the server to use Message Digest 5 Challenge Handshake Authentication Protocol (MD-5 CHAP, or simply CHAP). CHAP uses a standard mechanism for encrypting the authentication response and is supported by several non-Microsoft remote access clients. As such, CHAP provides a means of supporting remote clients that do not support MS-CHAP or EAP (while still providing some level of encryption and security).

The first step to enable remote clients to authenticate on a Windows 2000 RRAS server with CHAP is to enable CHAP in the Authentication Methods dialog box. In the RRAS console, open the properties for the server and click the Security tab, then click Authentication Methods. Select "Encrypted authentication (CHAP)." Then, if you're using remote access policies to control allowed authentication methods, modify the policy as needed to allow the appropriate clients to use CHAP.

In order to support CHAP, user passwords must be stored using reversible encryption. While you can enable reversibly encrypted passwords for all users in the domain, you might wish to only enable reversible encryption for those clients requiring CHAP authentication. You can selectively enable reversible encryption if the accounts are stored in the Active Directory. To do so, open the Active Directory Users and Computers console, then open the user's property sheet. On the Account tab, select the option "Store password using reversible encryption" in the Account Options group, then click OK or Apply.

You need to modify the default domain policy if you want to apply reversible encryption for all users in the domain. On a domain controller, choose Start ➪ Programs ➪ Administrative Tools ➪ Domain Security Policy. Open the branch Security Settings/Account Policies/Password Policy and enable the option "Store password using reversible encryption for all users in the domain." On a standalone server, choose Start ➪ Programs ➪ Administrative Tools ➪ Local Security Policy to modify the password policy to enable reversible encryption.

Each user for which reversible encryption has been enabled needs to modify his or her password so that the new password will be stored with reversible encryption. Configuring the user's account or the domain or local policy for reversible encryption does not automatically change the way the passwords are stored. You can reset the users' passwords yourself or have the users change passwords during their next logon session. Since the users can't change passwords through CHAP authentication, they must either log on to the LAN to change their passwords or use MS-CHAP through the remote connection to change their passwords, and then switch to CHAP for future remote sessions. The alternative for those users who can't log on to the LAN or use MS-CHAP is for the administrator to reset the password.

Cross-Reference

The final step is to configure the remote client to use CHAP. See the section "Configuring Outgoing Dial-Up Networking Connections" to learn how to configure Windows 2000 remote access clients.

SPAP

SPAP stands for Shiva Password Authentication Protocol. Shiva is a corporation that develops and markets several remote access solutions, including the Shiva LAN Rover. Clients connecting to a Shiva LAN Rover use SPAP for authentication, as do Shiva clients connecting to a Windows 2000 RRAS server. SPAP is disabled by default for a Windows 2000 RRAS server. SPAP offers a lower degree of security than the methods described previously, so you should enable SPAP only if you need to support Shiva clients. You can enable SPAP through the Authentication Methods dialog box in the RRAS server's properties.

PAP

Password Authentication Protocol (PAP) uses plain text to transmit passwords, making it susceptible to compromise. You should therefore only use PAP to support clients that do not support any of the other authentication methods, or in situations where security is not an issue. Enable PAP for the RRAS server through the Authentication Methods dialog box in the RRAS server's properties.

Unauthenticated access

You can configure a Windows 2000 RRAS server to allow unauthenticated remote access, enabling any user to log on whether he or she provides a valid user name and password or not. While unauthenticated access can pose a security risk, it nevertheless has some uses. Because unauthenticated access is applicable in few situations, it is not covered in detail here. To learn more about unauthenticated access, open the RRAS console, open Help, and open the topic Remote Access/Concepts/Remote Access Security/Unauthenticated Access.

Disabling Routing (Remote Access Server Only)

If you're using RRAS to only provide dial-in remote access and don't require routing, you can disable routing and allow the server to function as a remote access server only. This reduces some of the overhead in the RRAS server and can improve performance somewhat. You might also want to disable routing for security reasons that might be applicable to your network.

To disable routing, open the RRAS console and then open the properties for the server on which you want to disable routing. On the General page, deselect the Router option and leave the Remote access server option selected. Click OK and allow Windows 2000 to restart RRAS to make the change take effect.

RRAS Logging and Accounting

Windows 2000 RRAS, like many other services, logs events to the Windows 2000 System log, which you can view and manage with the Event Viewer console. You configure logging options on the Event Logging page of the RRAS server's property sheet. Open the RRAS console, open the property sheet for the server, and click the Event Logging tab. The Event Logging page offers a handful of options that control the amount of information logged to the System event log; the options are self-explanatory. You also can enable logging of PPP events for troubleshooting purposes.

By default, a Windows 2000 RRAS server uses Windows 2000 accounting, which means that certain aspects of remote sessions are logged to the log file designated by the entry in the Remote Access Logging branch of the RRAS console. Windows accounting is applicable when you are using IAS to provide authentication. If you're using a RADIUS server, however, you'll probably want to configure RADIUS to perform the accounting for you. The following sections explain both options.

Using Windows accounting

Windows 2000 RRAS by default does not log remote sessions, but you can enable logging for security and troubleshooting. To use Windows accounting, open the RRAS console, right-click the server, choose Properties, and click the Security tab. Select Windows Accounting from the Accounting Provider drop-down list, then click OK to close the property sheet.

Then in the RRAS console, open the Remote Access Logging branch. You'll find one item in the right pane labeled Local File. Double-click Local File, or right-click it and choose Properties, to display the Local File Properties sheet. The Settings page contains the following options:

✦ **Log accounting requests:** Select this option to log accounting requests from the RRAS server to the accounting server to indicate that it is online and ready to accept connections or going offline, and to start and stop accounting for a user session.

✦ **Log authentication requests:** Select this option to log authentication requests sent by the RRAS server to IAS on behalf of the client, along with responses from IAS to the RRAS server indicating acceptance/rejection of the remote client's authentication request.

✦ **Log periodic status:** This option enables you to log periodic status requests for a session sent by the RRAS server to IAS, although the option is generally not recommended because of the potentially large log file that usually results.

The Local File page of the Local File Properties sheet determines the format for the local log file as well as the log's location, file name, and how often a new log file is created. The options are generally self-explanatory.

Using RADIUS accounting

You configure RADIUS accounting through the Security tab of the RRAS server's properties. Open the RRAS console, right-click the server, choose Properties, and click the Security tab. Select RADIUS Accounting from the Accounting Provider drop-down list, then click Configure. In the RADIUS Accounting dialog box, click Add to add a RADIUS accounting server and configure its properties. The following list explains the options:

✦ **Server name:** Specify the FQDN or IP address of the RADIUS server.

✦ **Secret:** Enter the secret string used by the RADIUS server to authenticate access to the RADIUS server. You can use any alphanumeric characters and special characters in the string, up to 255 characters. The shared secret is case-sensitive.

✦ **Time-out:** This is the period of time the RRAS server will wait for a response from the RADIUS server before timing out and failing the accounting request.

✦ **Initial score:** This value indicates the overall responsiveness of the RADIUS server. This number changes dynamically as the responsiveness of the RADIUS server changes. RRAS queries the servers in order of highest to lowest score (the higher the score, the better the responsiveness). Use this option to specify an estimated initial score.

✦ **Port:** Specify the UDP port used by the RADIUS server for incoming authentication requests. The default is 1813 for newer RADIUS servers and 1646 for older RADIUS servers.

✦ **Send RADIUS accounting on and off messages:** Select this option to have the RRAS server send Accounting-On and Accounting-Off messages to the accounting server when the RRAS service starts and stops.

Configuring a VPN Server

A secure Virtual Private Network (VPN) connection enables remote access clients to establish secure connections to the RRAS server or to the local network to which the RRAS server is connected from a non-secure network such as the Internet. Once connected by a VPN connection, the remote user has the same capabilities and security as he or she would have if connected locally to the network. A common use for VPN is to allow remote users to access files, printers, and other resources on the office LAN when they are on the road or working from other locations.

In a VPN connection, the data packets are encapsulated with additional header data that provides routing data to enable the packet to reach its destination. For example, remote clients connecting to the Internet can use NetBEUI, which is not routable, as the protocol to reach their LAN in a VPN connection because the NetBEUI packets are encapsulated as IP traffic, which is routable. The segment of the connection in which the data is encapsulated is called a *tunnel.*

Data is encrypted before it is encapsulated to make the data secure as it travels through the public network. *Tunneling protocols* manage the traffic flow between the client and server. Windows 2000 by default supports two tunneling protocols: Point-to-Point Tunneling Protocol (PPTP) and Layer 2 Tunneling Protocol (L2TP). These protocols are described earlier in this chapter in the section "RAS Connection Types and Protocols." Windows NT and Windows 9.*x* clients support PPTP, and Windows 2000 clients support both PPTP and L2TP. Non-Microsoft clients that support PPTP or L2TP can also connect to a Windows 2000 VPN server.

When you set up a Windows 2000 RRAS server manually or configure it through the wizard as a remote access server, Windows 2000 automatically installs both PPTP and L2TP and configures five ports for each protocol, meaning you can connect five remote VPN clients with each protocol. If you use the wizard to configure the server as a VPN server, the wizard creates 128 ports each for PPTP and L2TP. In either case, you can change the number of virtual ports available for connections through the Ports branch in the RRAS console (explained later).

Tip   If you use the wizard to configure the server as a router, Windows 2000 configures five ports each for PPTP and L2TP, but enables them for demand-dial router connections only. If you want to also enable remote clients to establish VPN connections through the server, you need to enable the VPN ports for remote access. If you attempt to connect to a VPN server and receive a message that the client attempted to connect to a port reserved only for routers, the server is probably not configured to accept remote access clients on the VPN ports. Open the RRAS console, open the server in question, right-click the Ports node, and choose Properties. Double-click the PPTP or L2TP port entry and select the "Remote access connections" option to enable remote clients to establish VPN connections.

The easiest way to configure a VPN server is to run the configuration wizard and select the VPN option. See the section "Configuring RRAS for Incoming Connections" earlier in this chapter for an explanation of the options offered by the wizard. The following sections explain changes you can make after installation or how to configure the server for VPN manually.

Tip

Don't forget to enable the remote clients' accounts for remote access either through the individual account properties or the remote access policy. This is required for VPN connections just as it is for standard RAS connections.

Configuring VPN Ports

You use the RRAS console to make all changes to the VPN server's configuration. One of the changes you'll surely want to make at some point is the port configuration. Open the RRAS console, open the server to be changed, right-click the Ports branch, and choose Properties. The Ports Properties sheet shows the available ports, port type, and limited other information. Click a port type, then click Configure to display the Configure Device dialog box similar to the one shown in Figure 15-8.

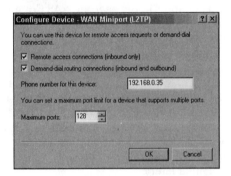

Figure 15-8: The Configure Device dialog box

Use the Configure Device dialog box to configure port properties, which vary somewhat from one type to another.

Use the following list as a guide to configure port options:

✦ **Remote access connections (inbound only):** Select this option to enable the port type for incoming remote access connections. Deselect the option to prevent incoming connections on the selected port type.

✦ **Demand-dial routing connections (inbound and outbound):** Select this option to enable incoming and outgoing demand-dial routing on the port type. Deselect to disable routing for the selected port type.

✦ **Phone number for this device:** For PPTP and L2TP ports, specify the IP address assigned to the VPN interface on the server through which the incoming connections arrive.

✦ **Maximum ports:** Change the number of ports of the selected type with this control.

Enabling L2TP for VPN

Windows 2000 by default configures five L2TP ports when you install RRAS for remote access and 128 ports if you install RRAS for VPN. There are some additional steps other than configuring ports that you need to take to ensure that L2TP provides a secure connection, as explained in the following sections.

Obtaining and installing a certificate

L2TP uses IPSec to provide encryption, which requires that you install a computer certificate on the RRAS server as well as the client to provide encryption/decryption capability for IPSec. You must have a Windows 2000 Server running Certificate Services on your network (or locally on the RRAS server) from which to obtain the certificate. This certificate server is called a Certificate Authority (CA). An enterprise root CA can be configured to allocate computer certificates automatically to computers in the domain. Or, you can use the Certificates console to request a certificate from an enterprise CA. You also can connect to `http://server/cersrv`, where `server` is the address or name of the CA, to request a certificate. Use this last option if your RRAS server is not a member of a domain or if you need to request the certificate from a standalone CA.

Chapter 3 discusses IPSec, certificates, and Certificate Services.

Configuring L2TP over IPSec filters

Unlike PPTP, which uses Microsoft Point-to-Point Encryption (MPPE), L2TP relies on IP Security (IPSec) to provide encryption to secure the VPN connection. You therefore need to configure IPSec filters accordingly on the RRAS server's public interface to restrict all but L2TP traffic. This will ensure that only secure L2TP traffic moves through the RRAS server. To configure the filters, first note the IP address of the RRAS server's public interface (the one connected to the Internet). Then, open the RRAS console, open the IP Routing branch, and click General. Right-click the interface on which you want to set the filters and choose Properties.

On the General page of the interface's property sheet, click Input Filters to display the Input Filters dialog box. Click Add to display the Add IP Filter dialog box (Figure 15-9). Select the option Destination Network, then in the IP Address field, specify the IP address of the server's Internet network interface. In the Subnet Mask field, enter **255.255.255.255**. Select UDP from the Protocol drop-down list, enter **500** in both the Source Port and Destination Port fields, and click OK.

Back on the Input Filters dialog box, click Add again and add another Destination Network entry for the same IP address and subnet mask as the first entry, but add UDP port entries of 1701 for both Source Port and Destination Port fields. Click OK, then in the Input Filters dialog box, select the option "Drop all packets except those that meet the criteria below," and click OK.

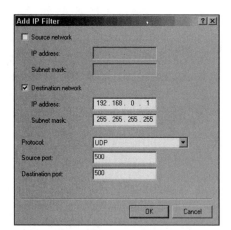

Figure 15-9: The Add IP Filter dialog box

Next, you need to add filters to restrict traffic for outgoing packets to the appropriate ports for L2TP. On the General page of the interface's property sheet, click Output Filters. Just as you did for the input filters, add two output filters for the server's public network interface IP address, subnet mask 255.255.255.255, with the first filter using UDP port 500 for Source Port and Destination Port and a second using UDP port 1701 for Source Port and Destination Port.

Using Multilink and BAP

As mentioned earlier in this chapter, Windows 2000 supports the use of multilink connections, which enables a client to connect to the RRAS server using multiple, aggregated links. Bandwidth Allocation Protocol (BAP) provides a means for the bandwidth utilization to be dynamic. As bandwidth usage increases, the client can request another connection to improve performance. As bandwidth usage decreases, connections can be dropped to make them available to other clients or reduce connection costs. Enabling multilink and BAP requires a few steps: enable multilink, configure remote access policies, configure ports, and configure the clients.

First, open the RRAS console, right-click the server, and choose Properties. On the PPP page, select Multilink connections to allow clients to request multilink connections. Select "Dynamic bandwidth control using BAP or BACP" to enable clients to use BAP/BACP to dynamically manage aggregation. Click OK to close the property sheet.

The second step is to enable multilink in the appropriate remote access policy. The default policy allows all clients to use the settings defined globally for the RRAS server, so enabling multilink and BAP for the server enables it for all remote clients unless modified by a remote access policy. If you want to restrict the use of multi-link and BAP to selected users, you need to modify the remote access policies accordingly. Apply one policy for those requiring multilink support and a different policy for those who do not.

In the RRAS console, open the server's branch and click Remote Access Policies. Double-click the policy you want to modify (or create a new one). Click Edit Profile and select the Multilink tab for the policy (see Figure 15-10). Configure settings based on the following list:

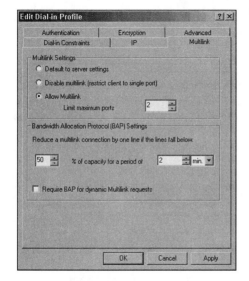

Figure 15-10: The Multilink tab

✦ **Default to server settings:** Select this option to use the global settings defined by the RRAS server.

✦ **Disable multilink (restrict client to single port):** Select to disable multilink for remote clients covered by the policy and limit them to a single connection.

✦ **Allow Multilink:** Select to allow remote clients covered by the policy to use multiple connections.

✦ **Reduce a multilink connection by one line if the lines fall below:** Specify the utilization threshold value and duration the server uses to determine when to drop a link.

✦ **Require BAP for dynamic Multilink requests:** Select to require the client to use BAP to manage multiple links. If the client doesn't use BAP, multilink connections are refused and the client is limited to a single link.

Next, you need to specify the phone number for each port used for multilink connections to enable the server to pass that data to the client when the client requests another link. The client uses the link number to dial the next link. In the RRAS console, open the server, right-click the Ports branch, and choose Properties. Double-click the port for which you need to set the dial-in number, or select the port and click Configure. Specify the phone number in the field "Phone number for this device," then close the dialog box and the Ports property sheet.

See the section "Configuring Outgoing Dial-Up Networking Connections" later in this chapter to learn how to configure Windows 2000 clients to use multilink and BAP.

Remote Access Policy

Although you can rely on global settings on the RRAS server to provide security and enable/disable access, you will find that you have much greater control over remote clients through the use of remote access policies. Like other group policies, remote access policies enable you to configure access on a user, group, or global basis. Windows 2000 RRAS by default creates a single remote access policy. You can modify this policy and/or create additional policies to suit your needs.

You mange remote access policies through the RRAS console. In the console, open the server to be managed and then open the Remote Access Policies branch. The right pane shows the configured remote access policies. The default policy, "Allow access if dial-in permission is enabled," is actually configured to deny access. Double-click the policy and note that the option "Deny remote access permission" is selected. This setting applies unless overridden by per-user settings in each user's account, which effectively disables access for all users unless their accounts are configured to allow access. Selecting the option "Grant remote access permission" for this policy enables all users to gain remote access.

You can use the default remote access policy as-is, add other conditions to it, or create new policies to fit specific users, groups, or situations. For example, assume you want to grant remote access to a sales group but limit the group's members to one link (disable multilink). You want to also enable your Administrators group to gain access but allow them to use multilink. So, you need to create two policies. We'll use this example to illustrate how to create and configure policies. First, create the policy for the Sales group.

Configuring an RRAS server to use RADIUS authentication causes the Remote Access Policy branch to disappear from the RRAS console for the selected RRAS server. This is because the remote access policies on the RADIUS server take precedence. Also, configuring RRAS to use RADIUS accounting causes the Remote Access Logging branch to disappear from the console, as logging is handled by the RADIUS server.

Creating a New Policy

In the RRAS console, open the server, then open the Remote Access Policy branch. Right-click the right pane and choose New Remote Access Policy to start the Remote Access Policy Wizard. The wizard prompts for the following information:

✦ **Policy friendly name:** This is the policy name as it appears in the RRAS console. Specify a name that identifies the purpose of the policy or affected users. In this example, use Sales as the friendly name.

✦ **Conditions:** Use the Conditions page of the wizard to specify the criteria by which the policy grants or denies access. In this example, click Add, select Windows-Groups, and click Add. Select the Sales group ➪ OK ➪ Next.

✦ **Grant/Deny:** Select which action is applied to the selected criteria. In this example, we want the Sales group granted access, so select "Grant remote access permission." If you wanted to explicitly prevent the Sales group from using remote access, you would instead select the "Deny remote access permission" option.

✦ **Edit Profile:** You can click Edit Profile to edit the other properties for the remote access policy or simply click Finish to complete the wizard. The properties you can change by clicking Edit Profile are the same as those made available by double-clicking the policy in the console.

If you click Edit Profile in the wizard or double-click a policy and then click Edit Profile in the policy's Settings page, RRAS displays the Edit Dial-In Profile property sheet shown in Figure 15-11. This sheet contains several tabs, which are described in the following sections. After you configure the Sales group's policy to deny multilink, you run the wizard again to create another policy for the Administrator's group, this time granting multilink permission.

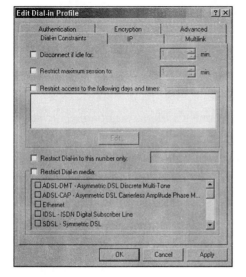

Figure 15-11: The Edit Dial-In Profile property sheet

Dial-In Constraints

The Dial-In Constraints tab determines when the user can connect, for how long, and other properties that define the user's connection in general. The options in the bottom of the page let you specify which dial-in media types are available to users to whom the policy applies. For example, you might select Virtual Private Networking (VPN) to allow the remote users only to connect through a VPN connection. The options on the Dial-In Constraints tab are self-explanatory.

IP

The IP tab of the remote access policy's properties determines how the client IP address is assigned and which input/output filters, if any, apply to the connection. You can force the server to assign an IP, allow the client to request a specific IP, or let the global server settings define how the address is assigned (the default).

Click From Client if you want to apply a filter to incoming packets to limit them to specific protocols or ports. Click To Client to set up filters to control packets going to the remote client. See the section "Configuring L2TP over IPSec Filters" earlier in this chapter for more information on creating filters.

Multilink

The Multilink tab determines whether or not the remote client can use multilink, the maximum number of ports, and criteria that determine when BAP drops a link if bandwidth usage drops. These options are generally self-explanatory. See the section "Using Multilink and BAP" earlier in this chapter for additional information.

For our example, the Sales group needs to be denied the use of multilink. Select the option "Disable multilink (restrict client to single port)" to prevent anyone in the Sales group from using a multilink connection.

Authentication

The Authentication tab determines the authentication method(s) allowed for remote clients covered by the policy. Through this page, you can enable EAP or other authentication methods allowed for the remote clients. You can select multiple methods or select a single method if you need to ensure that the selected group always uses the same authentication method.

The option "Allow remote PPP clients to connect without negotiating any authentication protocol" enables remote clients to establish a connection without authenticating. Although this capability is useful in a limited number of situations, it presents a security risk because you have no control over who can gain remote access. So, use this option sparingly.

For more information on authentication methods, see the section "RAS Connection Types and Protocols" earlier in this chapter.

Encryption

The Encryption tab defines the levels of encryption that can be used by clients covered by the policy:

✦ **No Encryption:** Select this option to enable remote clients to connect without using encryption. If no other encryption options are selected, remote clients are prevented from using encryption.

✦ **Basic:** Select this option to enable remote clients to use IPSec 56-bit DES or MPPE 40-bit encryption.

✦ **Strong:** Select this option to enable remote clients to use IPSec 56-bit DES or MPPE 56-bit encryption.

Advanced

The Advanced tab enables you to configure additional RADIUS connection properties for remote clients covered by the remote access policy. Because there are so many, it isn't practical to cover all of them in this chapter. Click Add on the Advanced page and browse the list to determine which, if any, you require for the selection policy.

Prioritizing Policies

Each remote access policy has a unique order number, and policies are evaluated and applied in the order of priority. You can change the order to define the way policies are applied, which determines the final applied result. To change the order, right-click a policy and choose either Move Up or Move Down to change its position and order number.

Configuring Outgoing Dial-Up Networking Connections

In addition to using RRAS to support dial-in users, you can also configure dial-out connections. For many users, this means creating a dial-up connection to the Internet, although with Windows 2000 Server, it's more likely that you'll be creating demand-dial router or client connections to another server or to a router. Network Address Translation and routing are covered in detail in Chapter 12. This section of the chapter assumes you need to configure Windows 2000 dial-up connections to a RAS server or the Internet.

Creating a Connection

As with nearly every configuration issue, Windows 2000 provides a wizard to automate creation of dial-up connections. Click Start ➪ Settings ➪ Network and Dial-Up Connections to open the Network and Dial-Up Connections folder. Then double-click the Make New Connection icon to start the wizard, which offers the following four options:

✦ **Dial-up to private network:** Select this option if you're dialing a private network such as a RAS server at your office, or other non-Internet connection. The wizard prompts you for the phone number and dialing properties, whether the connection can be used only by you or by all users on the computer, and whether to enable connection sharing for the connection. Connection sharing is most applicable to an Internet connection; see the section "Internet Connection Sharing" later in this chapter for details.

✦ **Dial-up to the Internet:** Select this option to configure a dial-up connection to an Internet Service Provider (ISP) or other RAS server that functions like an Internet access server. This option runs the Internet Connection Wizard, which lets you specify how you connect to the Internet (LAN or modem), configure proxy and automatic configuration settings, and optionally configure e-mail accounts in Outlook Express. The options are generally self-explanatory.

✦ **Connect to a private network through the Internet:** Select this option to create a VPN connection through the Internet to a private network. The wizard prompts for the IP address or FQDN of the VPN server, which users can use the connection (you or all), and whether to enable connection sharing for the connection.

✦ **Accept incoming connections:** Under Windows 2000 Professional, this option lets you configure a connection for incoming calls. Under Windows 2000 Server, however, this option simply informs you that you need to use RRAS to configure a RAS server and gives you the option of opening the RRAS console.

Configuring Connection Properties

After you create a connection, you can modify its properties. Most of the properties are self-explanatory, and you can configure such properties as the server's phone number or, in the case of a VPN server, the IP address or FQDN. Other options configure such properties as redial attempts, idle time before hang-up, and so on. You should have no trouble configuring these settings. Simply right-click a connection in the Network and Dial-Up Connections folder and choose Properties to access its property sheet.

The following sections explain a handful of configuration issues that are perhaps not as intuitive as the others.

Security and authentication

The Security property tab for a connection (Figure 15-12) lets you specify the authentication method used for the connection. By default, Windows 2000 sets up the connection to allow unsecured passwords, which means the client can send the password in plain text, making it susceptible to interception.

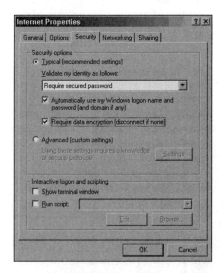

Figure 15-12: The Security tab

You can select Require Secured Password from the "Validate my identity as follows" drop-down list to force the connection to require encryption for the password. The method used for encryption depends on the authentication method negotiated with the remote server. The following two options work in conjunction with the Require Secured Password option:

✦ **Automatically use my Windows logon name and password (and domain if any):** Select this option to have the connection automatically use your current logon name, password, and domain for logon to the remote server.

✦ **Require data encryption (disconnect if none):** Select this option to force data encryption for the connection and disconnect if the server doesn't offer a supported encryption method. You can prevent encryption through the Advanced properties (explained next).

Note   You also can use a smart card for authentication. Select the option "Use smart card" from the Validate drop-down list to use a smart card for authentication. This option must be supported by the remote server for the connection to succeed.

Select Advanced on the Security page and click Settings if you want a finer degree of control over authentication settings (such as configuring EAP or other protocols). Use the Data Encryption drop-down list to specify if encryption can be used or is required for the connection. The options are self-explanatory.

If you choose any protocols other than EAP, you simply need to select which protocol(s) you want the connection to attempt. You can select multiple protocols. If dialing a Windows 2000 RAS server, the server will attempt authentication based on the security offered by each method, choosing the most secure whenever possible.

Configuring EAP

Configuring a client to use EAP takes a little more effort. Select the option "Use Extensible Authentication Protocol (EAP)," then select either MD5-Challenge or Smart Card or Other Certificate from the associated drop-down list. If you select Other Smart Card or Other Certificate, click Properties to display the Smart Card or Other Certificate dialog box. Select options using the following list as a guide:

✦ **Use my smart card:** Select this option if you have a smart card reader attached to your system and a smart card to use for authentication.

✦ **Use a certificate on this computer:** Select this option to use a certificate installed on your computer to provide authentication.

✦ **Validate server certificate:** Select this option to have your computer verify that the certificate provided by the server is still valid (not expired). Deselect the option to have the client accept the server's certificate without checking it.

✦ **Connect only if server name ends with:** Use this option to limit connections to servers that reside in a specified domain. For example, enter `mcity.org` if you only want to connect to servers in the `mcity.org` domain (`server1.mcity.org`, `ras.mcity.org`, and so on).

✦ **Trusted root certificate authority:** Select the trusted root certificate authority for your server.

✦ **Use a different user name for the connection:** Select this option if the user name stored in the smart card or associated with the certificate you're using is not the same as the user name you need to use to log on in the remote domain.

Configuring protocols

Just as you can with a LAN connection, you can configure a dial-up connection for more than one protocol. Or, perhaps you have more than one protocol enabled for a connection and want to turn off the protocol for dial-up but leave it enabled for the LAN. To change your protocol settings, open the Network and Dial-Up Connections folder, right-click the connection, and choose Properties. Click the Networking tab, then select/deselect protocols as desired. You can also remove a protocol, but keep in mind that removing it removes it from the computer altogether, and other connections won't be able to use it.

For more information on configuring network protocols, see Chapter 12.

Using Multilink and BAP

As explained earlier in this chapter, some dial-up servers support multilink connections that enable you to connect to the RAS server with multiple links (two or more modems, for example) to create an aggregate connection with a total bandwidth equal to the sum of all connected links. Windows 2000 dial-up networking supports multilink dial-out connections and can optionally use Bandwidth Allocation Protocol (BAP) to dynamically add and drop links as needed to accommodate changes in bandwidth usage. The remote server you connect to must support multilink and must also support BAP if you use BAP on the client side.

Most ISPs that support multilink also charge you for the ability to use multiple connections. Paying for multiple user accounts won't work for multilink, as Windows 2000 treats the individual connections as a single one and uses a single user name/password pair for establishing all links. Plus, the server needs to support multilink to enable bandwidth to be aggregated on the server side for your connections. Just dialing two separate accounts would give you two non-aggregated connections.

Before configuring multilink for a dial-up connection, you need to first install the multiple devices you'll be using to dial out. If you only have one device installed, the multilink options are not shown. If multiple devices are installed but only one is selected for the connection, the multilink options are dimmed.

After installing all connection devices, open the Network and Dial-Up Connections folder, right-click the connection, and choose Properties. On the General page, select all of the devices you want to use to establish the multilink connection. If you need to configure different numbers for each one, make sure that the option "All devices call the same numbers" is deselected, then select each modem from the drop-down list and specify the number to dial through that modem. If the remote access server uses a single number with a hunt group to distribute calls, select the option "All devices call the same numbers."

Next, click the Options tab to display the Options property page. The drop-down list in the Multiple devices group provides three options:

✦ **Dial only first available device:** Select this option to only dial a single link (use one device only). This option enables you to dial a single link for the connection when other installed devices are busy. For example, you might use two modems to connect to two different remote networks. Selecting this option enables the second connection to automatically use the available device to dial.

✦ **Dial all devices:** Select this option to have Windows 2000 automatically dial all available devices to create a multilink connection to the remote server.

✦ **Dial devices only as needed:** Select this option to use BAP to manage bandwidth usage. Windows 2000 will dial other links for the connection depending on the settings you configure for BAP. Click Configure to display the dialog box shown in Figure 15-13. These four controls enable you to specify criteria BAP uses to determine when to connect or disconnect links.

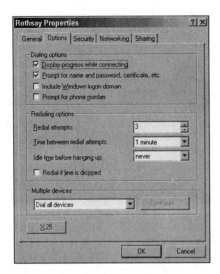

Figure 15-13: The Options tab

 Windows 2000 does not automatically reinitialize dropped multilink links unless you're using BAP. Selecting the option "Dial all devices" might get you an aggregate link, but there is nothing to prevent the connection from suffering attrition as links are dropped and not re-established. You can force links to reinitialize by setting relatively low usage conditions. Select "Dial devices only as needed" from the Options page of the connection's properties and then set automatic dialing to low values such as 1% for 5 seconds.

Configuring Dial-Up Networking to Connect to the Internet

In most cases, you can run the wizard to create a new dial-up connection to the Internet and use it as-is without problems. However, you might want or need to fine-tune some of your settings for cost or performance reasons. The following sections examine common properties you might want to modify.

Controlling disconnects

Most ISPs implement an idle-disconnect period, causing a connection to be dropped if there is no activity for a given amount of time. In most cases, the idle-disconnect works well, but some ISPs don't implement it and others that are configured for idle-disconnect seem to work sporadically. If you're paying for your connection by the hour, idle-disconnect can save you a lot of money if you forget to disconnect or want the system to disconnect after a long, unattended download.

You'll find the option "Idle time before hanging up" on the Options property page for the connection. If your ISP doesn't use idle-disconnect or you want to ensure your connection disconnects even if the ISP doesn't drop you, select the idle time that can occur before your system automatically hangs up the connection.

The other side of the disconnect issue is the fact that you might want your system to stay connected past the ISP's idle-disconnect period. For example, you might be performing a long, unattended download, but the remote server occasionally is idle for too long and the ISP drops your connection. In this situation, you can download and use one of the many connection utilities that keeps minimal traffic on your connection to ensure that it won't be dropped. You'll find several such utilities at `http://www.tucows.com`. Or, simply open your e-mail client and configure it to check your e-mail every few minutes. The traffic going to the mail server will be sufficient to keep your connection live.

Online security

Another potential problem is that in some cases, other users on the Internet can see your local folders and potentially gain access to your files. You can prevent that from occurring by disabling the File and Printer Sharing service from the dial-up connection. Open the Network page of the connection's property sheet and deselect the File and Printer Sharing service. Also, deselect any protocols other than TCP/IP if they are enabled and you don't need them for a specific reason.

Using RADIUS

Windows 2000 Server includes a service called Internet Authentication Service (IAS) that enables a Windows 2000 server to function as a RADIUS (Remote Authentication Dial-In User Server) server. In addition to providing authentication services, RADIUS also performs accounting and keeps track of user logon, session duration, logoff, and so on. You can use IAS to provide authentication for RRAS, IIS, or other services, including providing authentication for non-Microsoft dial-up servers. Any dial-up modem pool that supports RADIUS, for example, can authenticate clients through a Windows 2000 server running IAS.

Installing and Managing IAS

You install IAS through the Add/Remove Programs object in the Control Panel. With the Add/Remove Programs object open, click Add/Remove Windows Components. Open the Networking Services item and select Internet Authentication Service, then click OK ➪ Next. Windows 2000 installs the IAS service without further prompting.

Note   The IAS service does not have to be installed on the same server as RRAS. In fact, the IAS server could actually be located not only on a different server, but also in a different subnet. You specify the IP address or FQDN of the IAS server when you configure the RRAS server to enable RRAS to locate it.

Windows 2000 installs the Internet Authentication Service console to enable you to manage and configure IAS. Choose Start ➪ Programs ➪ Administrative Tools ➪ Internet Authentication Service to start the IAS console. The following sections explain how to use the IAS console to configure and work with IAS.

Configuring IAS to Accept Connections

IAS uses certain security measures to restrict which services can connect to a RADIUS server for authentication. Services that use IAS to authenticate remote users are called *clients*. So, you need to configure IAS to allow specific clients — such as your RRAS server — to connect to a RADIUS server to authenticate users. To enable a client to connect, open the IAS console and then open the Clients folder. Right-click Clients, or right-click in the right pane and choose New Client, to start the Add Client wizard. The wizard prompts for the following information:

✦ **Friendly name:** This is the client name as it appears in the IAS console. Select a name that identifies the client (such as RRAS Server 1).

✦ **Protocol:** This option specifies the protocol the client will use. By default, RADIUS is the only protocol listed and available.

✦ **Client address (IP or DNS):** Specify the client's IP address or FQDN. You can verify an FQDN by clicking Verify, which will attempt to resolve the name to an IP.

✦ **Client-Vendor:** Use this option to specify the client device manufacturer/type. This selection is optional unless you are using remote access policies to restrict access based on vendor type. Select the appropriate type from the list. Select Microsoft for a Windows 2000 RRAS server. Select RADIUS Standard if the client is a RADIUS proxy or if the client type doesn't appear in the list.

✦ **Client must always send the signature attribute in the request:** Select this option to require the client to send a digital signature attribute in access request packets for PAP, CHAP, or MS-CHAP authentication. IAS always requires the client to include the signature if you're using EAP. Authentication attempts that don't include a signature are discarded if this option is selected.

✦ **Shared secret/Confirm shared secret:** A shared secret is a string used as a password to enable the client to gain access to the IAS server. Like any password, the shared secret specified at both the client and server sides must match exactly. You can use any alphanumeric characters and special characters in the string, up to 255 characters. The shared secret is case-sensitive. Use a string containing a combination of letters, numbers, special characters, and different cases to help protect against dictionary attacks. You can use the same shared secret for each client or specify a different one for each (for better security).

Configuring IAS Global Options

There are a handful of global options you need to configure for IAS to control the way IAS functions. Open the IAS console, right-click the IAS server's main branch, and choose Properties.

Configuring service properties

The Service page contains the following options:

✦ **Description:** Specify a friendly name to help differentiate this IAS service from others on the network.

✦ **Log rejected or discarded authentication requests:** Select this option to write an event to the Windows 2000 Application event log each time the network access server (the client) sends a rejected or discarded authentication request. See the section "Configuring Logging" later in this chapter for more information.

✦ **Log successful authentication requests:** Select this option to write an event to the Windows 2000 Application event log each time a remote access client successfully authenticates. See the section "Configuring Logging" later in this chapter for more information.

Configuring ports

The RADIUS property page lets you configure the ports IAS uses for authentication and accounting. By default, IAS uses ports 1812 and 1645 for authentication and 1813 and 1656 for accounting.

Tip Ports 1645 and 1646 are included to support older RADIUS clients, which by default do not use the new ports, 1812 and 1813. The RADIUS client must be configured to use the appropriate port. See the section "Configuring EAP-RADIUS" earlier in this chapter for more information on configuring RRAS for the appropriate RADIUS ports.

Configuring realm translation

Realm names provide a means for RADIUS to route authentication requests to a server that holds the remote user's credentials. In other words, the realm name identifies the RADIUS realm in which the user's credentials reside. The realm name can be a prefix or suffix with a separator character between the user name and realm name, such as *user@somewhere* or *somewhere/user*.

IAS doesn't use realm names, but other RADIUS servers can. You can configure IAS to strip out the realm portion to authenticate against the domain. For example, assume your company contracts Internet access from an ISP for your remote users. For administration purposes, you maintain a RADIUS server against which the accounts are authenticated, and the ISP simply redirects the authentication requests it receives from your users to your RADIUS server. The requests coming from the other server contain the realm name, so you need to strip out the realm name before authenticating the user against the domain.

The Realms page of the IAS service's properties lets you define rules by which the IAS service parses names, enabling you to strip the realm and (if needed) replace it with something else. You can define multiple rules, and IAS processes the name using all rules in order. To add a rule, click Add and specify the text to locate and text for replacement. Leave the Replace field blank if you simply want to delete the Find text from the name.

Note   The Find field can't be an empty string.

IAS supports a pattern-matching syntax you might find useful for complex replacement tasks. Table 15-1 lists the syntax and provides samples.

Table 15-1
Pattern-Matching Characters

Character	Description	Example
\	Marks next character as special.	/n/ matches the character "n" The sequence /\n/ matches a line feed or newline character.
^	Matches beginning of input or line.	
$	Matches end of input or line.	
*	Matches preceding character zero or more times.	/fo*/ matches either "fo" or "foo."
+	Matches preceding character one or more times.	/fo+/ matches "foo" but not "f."

Character	Description	Example
?	Matches preceding character zero or one times.	/a?ve?/ matches the "ve" in "never."
.	Matches any single character except a newline character.	
(pattern)	Matches pattern and remembers the match. Use "\(" or "\)" to match parentheses characters.	
x|y	Matches either x or y.	/g|food?/ matches "good" or "food."
{n}	n is a nonnegative integer. Matches exactly n times.	/e{2}/ does not match the "e" in "Deb," but it matches the first two "e's" in "freeeeak."
{n,}	n is a nonnegative integer. Matches at least n times.	/e{2,}/ does not match the "e" in "Deb," but it matches all the "e's" in "freeeeak." /o{1,}/ is equivalent to /o+/.
{n,m}	m and n are nonnegative integers. Matches at least n and at most m times.	/o{1,3}/ matches the first three "e's" in "freeeeak."
[xyz]	A character set. Matches any one of the enclosed characters.	/[abc]/ matches the "b" in "bravo."
[^xyz]	A negative character set. Matches any character not enclosed.	/[^abc]/ matches the "u" in "quiet."
\b	Matches a word boundary, such as a space.	/mo*e\b/ matches the "me" in "come here."
\B	Matches a nonword boundary.	/he*r\B/ matches the "her" in "come here."
\d	Matches a digit character. Equivalent to [0-9].	
\D	Matches a nondigit character. Equivalent to [^0-9].	
\f	Matches a form-feed character.	
\n	Matches a line feed character.	
\r	Matches a carriage return character.	
\s	Matches any white space, including space, tab, form-feed, and so on. Equivalent to [\f\n\r\t\v].	

Continued

Character	Description	Example
	Table 15-1 (continued)	
\S	Matches any non-white-space character. Equivalent to [^ \f\n\r\t\v].	
\t	Matches a tab character.	
\v	Matches a vertical tab character.	
\w	Matches any word character, including underscore. Equivalent to [A-Za-z0-9_].	
\W	Matches any nonword character, excluding underscore. Equivalent to [^A-Za-z0-9_].	
\num	A reference back to remembered matches, where num is a positive integer. \1 replaces what is stored in the first remembered match. This option can be used only in the Replace field when configuring realms with IAS.	
/n/	?n, where n is an octal, hexadecimal, or decimal escape value. Allows embedding of ASCII codes into regular expressions.	

Note   A realm is to UNIX what a domain is to Windows 2000. It can also be loosely defined as the security boundary of a network. With the wholesale adoption of Kerberos authentication, Windows 2000 domains are, essentially, Kerberos realms. See Chapter 3 for a full discussion on Kerberos and realms.

Configuring Logging

Like RRAS, IAS can perform logging of accounting requests, authentication requests, and periodic status. You can configure IAS to use one of two formats: IAS-compatible or database-compatible. Both options create a delimited text file. The latter is useful for importing the log file into a database such as Access or SQL Server.

You configure logging through the IAS console. In the console, click the Remote Access Logging branch, then double-click the Local File item in the right pane to display its properties. Use the Settings page to configure which events are logged. Use the Local File page to control the size of the log, how often the log is replaced, and its location.

Tip See the branch "Remote Access Logging" in IAS Help for more information on interpreting IAS log files.

Internet Connection Sharing

In many small organizations or departments within larger organizations, users on the LAN need access to the Internet for e-mail or other Web access. Providing individual connections for each user is often impractical and expensive in terms of hardware, dial-up accounts, and administration. Through a feature in Windows 2000 called Internet Connection Sharing (ICS), however, multiple users can share a single Internet connection, thus overcoming the drawbacks to providing individual access.

A Windows 2000 computer sharing a connection through ICS in effect becomes a proxy server, name server, and router for the clients. More than that, however, the computer becomes a DHCP server, allocating addresses to the other computers on the network. ICS uses the class C address space 192.168.0.0 (mask 255.255.255.0) to allocate addresses. When you enable ICS for a dial-up connection, Windows 2000 automatically assigns the address 192.168.0.1 to the network interface through which other users access the shared connection. For example, a server with a single network card and a modem connection to the Internet would have its network card's IP address changed to 192.168.0.1 when the connection was shared. As other computers booted, they would be assigned addresses in the same address range, and 192.168.0.1 would be their default gateway.

ICS is designed to enable small business and home networks to share an Internet connection and does not provide any flexibility of configuration. For example, you can't change the address range assigned by ICS to the LAN clients, disable the DHCP allocation, disable DNS proxy, or make other changes. For these small networks, however, ICS is almost a one-click configuration for setting up a shared Internet connection. If you need finer control over connection sharing, or if your network contains Windows 2000 domain controllers, DHCP servers, or DNS servers, you need to use Network Address Translation (NAT) instead. Chapter 12 covers NAT in detail.

Configuring the Server for ICS

You enable ICS through the properties of the Internet connection in the Network and Dial-Up Connections folder. Once you've configured the Internet connection and tested it from the server to make sure it works, open the Network and Dial-Up Connections folder, right-click the connection, and choose Properties. In the connection's property sheet, click the Sharing tab to display the Sharing page shown in Figure 15-14.

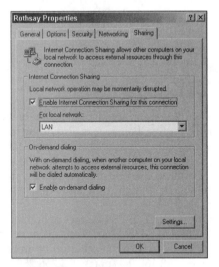

Figure 15-14: The Sharing tab

A computer sharing a connection to the Internet through ICS must have two network connections. One is the connection to the local area network where the other clients reside, and the second is the connection to the Internet. This second connection can be a dial-up connection (modem, cable-modem, ISDN, and so on) or a network adapter for a direct Internet connection.

The first step in sharing a connection is to create the connection and test it. Once the connection works as expected, you can configure it for sharing with other users on the LAN. Follow these steps to configure ICS:

1. Open the Network and Dial-Up Connections folder, then open the properties of the Internet connection you want to share. This is the connection that connects the ICS host computer to the Internet, not the local LAN connection.

2. Click the Sharing tab.

3. Select "Enable Internet Connection Sharing for this connection."

4. Select the connection where the clients are located via the "For local network" drop-down list. If you have only one network connection, it will be selected by default. On multi-homed systems (those with more than one network adapter), it's doubly important to select the correct interface. Selecting the wrong one could cause DHCP problems for other users on the selected network segment.

5. Select "Enable on-demand dialing" if you want the proxy computer to automatically dial the Internet when a client requests a connection.

6. Click Settings if you want to configure applications and services, or click OK to allow all traffic.

Tip To ensure that your dial-up connection isn't connected when not being used, open the Options tab for the Internet connection and configure "Idle time before hanging up" for an appropriate length of time (such as 30 minutes). Many ISPs configure the connection to be dropped at their end when a certain idle time has passed, often 15 to 20 minutes.

Configuring the Clients

The clients that connect through the ICS server don't need any special software or support for ICS, nor do you have to configure applications (such as Internet Explorer) to connect through a proxy server. All you have to do is make sure the clients reside on the same subnet as the ICS host and use it as their default gateway. The easiest way to accomplish this is to configure the clients to obtain their TCP/IP settings automatically (use DHCP).

Note If you prefer, you can configure the client computer settings manually, assigning each a static IP address in the Class C range 192.168.0.2 through 192.168.0.254, with a subnet mask of 255.255.255.0. Assign 192.168.0.1 as the default gateway for the client computers.

Configuring Applications and Services

Windows 2000 enables you to configure remote applications for local clients and local services for remote clients. For example, if you're hosting a Web site on the network, you need to configure ICS to provide that service to remote clients. The following sections explain how to configure remote applications and local services. Click Settings on the Sharing property sheet to configure applications and services.

Configuring remote applications

Use the Applications tab to configure remote applications for access by other users on your LAN. Click Add to define an application. The following list explains the available options:

- ✦ **Name of application:** This is the friendly name for an application as it appears in the Applications tab.

- ✦ **Remote server port number:** Specify the port number on the remote server for the remote application.

- ✦ **TCP:** Select this option if the remote port is for TCP.

- ✦ **UDP:** Select this option if the remote port is for UDP.

- ✦ **Incoming response ports:** Specify the incoming ports for TCP or UDP for the remote application.

Configuring local services

Use the Services tab to define local services that can be accessed by remote clients, such as a Web site you host on your network. Select existing services from the Services list to enable those services to be provided to the remote network. Click Add on the Services tab to add a new service. The following list explains the available options:

✦ **Name of service:** This is the friendly name as it appears in the Services tab.

✦ **Service port number:** Specify the port number used by the local service (such as 80 for HTTP/Web site).

✦ **TCP** or **UDP:** Select the appropriate option depending on which type of port the service uses.

✦ **Name or address of server computer on private network:** Specify the IP address or FQDN of the local computer that hosts the service.

Summary

Windows 2000 RRAS integrates routing with remote access into a single service. Remote users can connect to a Windows 2000 RRAS server to gain access to resources on the server or to resources on the network. The users can authenticate against the server's local accounts, against domain accounts, or against a RADIUS server. Windows 2000 Server includes the Internet Authentication Service that you can use to configure a Windows 2000 computer as a RADIUS server, providing full authentication and accounting services. Windows 2000 supports several authentication methods offering varying degrees of security for both Windows authentication and RADIUS authentication.

Virtual Private Networking support in RRAS enables remote clients to establish a secure connection to a Windows 2000 server or its network through a public network such as the Internet. In addition to supporting PPTP, Windows 2000 RRAS also adds support for L2TP, which provides additional security over PPTP. Demand-dial router connections can also use PPTP and L2TP, making Windows 2000 RRAS a good solution for establishing secure network-to-network connections over the Internet.

Dial-up networking in Windows 2000 enables all versions of the operating system to function as a remote access client. While RAS dial-out is more prevalent on workstations, the same capabilities are available in Windows 2000 Server. You can create dial-up connections to private networks, the Internet, or individual computers. Support for Internet Connection Sharing enables a single dial-up connection to be shared by multiple users. Where flexibility of configuration is needed or when you need to support a large number of users, however, Network Address Translation should be used instead of ICS.

✦   ✦   ✦

Availability Management

Microsoft has gone the extra mile in providing an operating system that meets the most stringent of availability requirements. In these chapters, we explore the new storage technology, remote and removable storage services, and disaster recovery.

We also highlight the support for ensuring service level in any enterprise. The operating system comes equipped with an array of diagnostic, performance, and monitoring tools, which will assist you in ensuring that your servers and their applications continue to be of service. As the demand for high availability increases proportionately with the surge of e-commerce and mission critical systems, so too will the demand for reliability, failover, and redundancy, all of which Windows 2000 addresses.

✦ ✦ ✦ ✦

Storage Management

This chapter introduces Windows 2000 storage. A new addition to the operating system is a dynamic storage management environment that essentially provides "free" fault-tolerance (RAID-1 and RAID-5), enforceable disk quotas, and an MMC plug-in that replaces the clunky disk management environment of Windows NT 4.0.

Windows 2000 Storage

If there are three things that every IT or network administrator can be sure of happening regarding storage, they are the following:

+ No matter how much hard disk storage you plan for, or think you need, you will always need more.

+ A hard disk will crash or falter within the lifetime of its host computer system.

+ A hard disk will crash at the worst possible time (usually for you).

Applications and servers crash, and users get peeved when you run out of storage or you lose storage. When you lose storage that was keeping critical data — data keeping the company alive — your world turns inside out. Data loss costs us billions every year. There are many examples where losing data destroyed a business, and where a good set of backups saved a business from certain disaster. There are four actions you need to take to counter or survive the fallout from the three certainties:

+ You need to evaluate your storage needs.

+ You need to develop policies for sound storage use.

✦ You need to develop and follow a storage implementation plan.

✦ You need to implement a disaster recovery and backup/restore plan.

The file system, storage management, and fault-tolerant capabilities of Windows NT were short on features and manageability, and did not support the 99.9 percent availability initiative (see Chapter 1). Administrators frequently turned to third-party products to keep their data safe. Microsoft has responded to your needs, finally, with three very useful storage services: Disk Management Service, Removable Storage, and Remote Storage. These services depend on the NTFS 5.0 file system for many features.

In this chapter, you will investigate these three services. You will be able to plan your storage needs and decide what components of the Windows 2000 Server storage services meet your objectives and needs.

Storage Management

To evaluate your storage needs, consider first the practice of storage management. Storage management is practiced on three tiers: You need to manage *access to storage* (media), you need to manage *access to data* (availability), and you need to *protect data* (backup/restore). Let us first look at the *access to storage* tier.

Access to Storage

Storage is located in two places on a network: on the host server from the perspective of the server and on a remote volume from the perspective of clients. Computer systems require local storage on which to store system files and boot files to start operating systems and begin services. You do not need large volumes of storage for local operating systems and boot files. The most any server will require is a partition of about 2GB, and that should easily service the OS files and server registry. It should also be sufficient for local services, processes, upgrades, service packs, uninstall folders, and more.

Do the local volumes need to be particularly fast? Not necessarily, because access to boot files is only needed at startup and a fully functional server, in full production, seldom updates the system files or the registry. So, you do not need to create volumes that provide fast I/O, and you do not need to spend a lot of money on very fast disks.

Note   Storage considerations for client workstations may be very different than servers, which is what we are largely concentrating on in this chapter. However, workstations and thin clients do not need large volumes, and the practice of locating most applications and data on network servers (good for licensing, security, and backups) is fast becoming the universal practice again.

The storage access tier goes down yet another level: data access. Within the host computer, you can configure a single disk or an array of disks to hold data. Data disks need to be built according to the needs of your organization and the purpose of the server.

The data volumes will typically hold applications that run on the server, databases that hold systems data, such as Active Directory, WINS, DNS and DHCP databases, and more.

Your data volumes may need to be fast. If your applications or services will make numerous reads and writes to the data volumes, you will need to plan for fast I/O solutions. Depending on your budget, you may be in a position to spend a little more money for fast disks, or you might consider striping volumes instead, or striping volumes on fast disks.

You need to note the type of applications that will be opened from the data volumes, the type of data that will be accessed from the volumes, and the number of users and applications that need to simultaneously read and write to the volumes. You shouldn't need to calculate data-access time, but certain applications may require you to calculate latency, disk performance, access times, transfer rates, and so forth. Good examples of such applications are busy shopping carts on Web sites or database servers on the company intranet.

The server and hard disks may have to service as many as 1,000 concurrent requests for data at any given time. And these requests may come to the hard disk as requests to write data and to read data, in which case you need to establish acceptable levels of performance for data access time and for transfer rate (the time it takes to retrieve and save data to the media).

The three benchmarks of hard disk performance should be understood because they may be important to your applications. When you are dealing with tens of thousands of hits a day on a Web site, or a massive data transformation operation, hard disks can take a knock. A very busy mail server can chew through several disks in its lifetime.

The three benchmarks are as follows:

1. **Access time.** This is the time it takes for a hard disk to register a request and prepare to scan the surface of a disk.

2. **Seek time.** This is the time it takes for a hard disk to find and assemble all the parts of a file.

3. **Transfer rate.** This is the time it takes for a hard disk to transfer data on and off the disk.

Another angle on storage access is space. If your databases are expanding and users are generating new files every day, you will need to watch disk space consumption and plan accordingly. Your policy should be one in which every effort should be made (within budget and the requirements of the business) to continually strive to keep the volumes from filling up more than, for example, 70 percent of the available space reported to applications. Depending on your requirements and the rate of usage, your policy might dictate that you keep disks at less than 50 percent or 60 percent capacity at any given time.

You have several options in managing disk capacity, and how and what you choose to do will vary from server to server, application to application, and business to business. The following list highlights the options you have, made possible with Windows 2000 storage services and technology:

✦ Volumes can be spanned, or extended. This is the process of chaining volumes of unallocated space together. When a disk approaches the capacity threshold that you have set, a new volume can be "bolted on" to extend the capacity. For faster I/O on spanned volumes, you can also add striping support.

✦ Users can be given enforceable disk space quotas, as groups (all users have the same quota) and as individuals. As you will later see, it is possible to assign an across-the-board quota giving all users on a volume the same quota, and thereby create a ceiling no user can violate.

✦ You can mount into the file system name space on a given folder. This topic is introduced in this chapter and given full coverage in Chapter 21.

✦ You can redirect folders to volumes and root shares on other servers. This is a feature of the so-called distributed files system (Dfs), which is fully covered in Chapter 21.

✦ You can compress data on volumes. Compression is covered in Chapter 21.

✦ You can create a Hierarchical Storage Management system (HSM). With Windows 2000 Remote Storage Services (RSS) and Removable Storage Services (RSS), you can automatically move files that are not needed on a local or network volume to removable media, such as tapes and portable disks. The HSM system is introduced in this chapter and dealt with at length in Chapter 21.

✦ Windows 2000 also introduces a highly sophisticated automated data encryption service, which is discussed in Chapter 22.

Important factors to consider with any of these options are the data-transfer rate, the data-access rate, and the latency or delay in getting files from redirected or remote storage to the users. The bar chart in Figure 16-1 provides some insight into the data-transfer and data-access strengths of the various storage solutions. The Distributed File System (Dfs) is at the top of the availability scale, and indicates high scores for number of concurrent users and capacity, but a lower score for response. On the other end of the availability scale are striped volumes, which are not fault-tolerant, but score high on the number of users, capacity, and response. Whatever option works for you, you will still have to do some lab work to get accurate feedback.

Tip

Check your application's documentation or call the vendor's technical support for the recommended storage requirements.

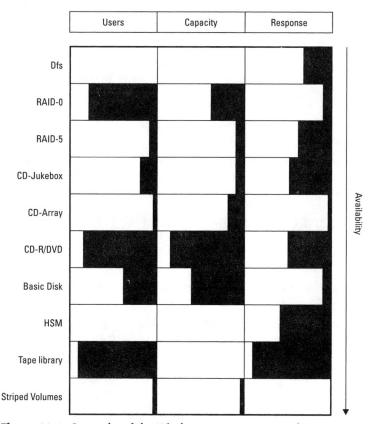

Figure 16-1: Strengths of the Windows 2000 storage options

Access to Data

The second tier of storage management is maintaining availability. If your business and applications call for 99.9 percent availability — applications and users need uninterrupted access to data — you should consider all available hardware and software options. The following services or features of Windows 2000 storage can be employed to meet the 99.9 percent initiative:

✦ **Mirrored volumes:** Windows 2000 dynamic volumes allow you to create RAID-1 compliant mirrored volumes.

✦ **RAID-5 fault tolerance:** RAID-5 or striping with parity is fully supported. You can build, manage, and break a RAID-5 array with three or more disks.

✦ **Fail-over servers:** The above solutions can be cloned onto hot standby servers without automatic fail-over. Automatic fail-over is a feature of the clustering service that is supported in Windows 2000 Advanced Server and Windows 2000 Datacenter Server, which are not covered in this book.

Windows 2000's fault-tolerant dynamic volumes are given comprehensive coverage in this chapter. You can also consider the HMS and Dfs solutions described previously as additional support for the 99.9 percent availability initiative.

Protecting Data

Data protection initiatives need to respond to several threats: file corruption, theft, natural disasters, virus attacks, and lost data (user-deleted files, fried hard disks). The primary services that support the backup and restoration of data are as follows:

✦ **Removable Storage Services:** Discussed later in this chapter and in Chapters 17 and 21, Removable Storage Services work with backup technology, media, and robotics to provide a comprehensive data protection media management system.

✦ **The Backup/Restore Service:** This is fully discussed in Chapter 17, and as part of the HSM system in Chapter 21.

✦ **Remote Storage Services (RSS):** Also discussed in Chapter 21, the RSS is responsible for moving online data to offline backup technology. RSS, the Removable Storage Services, and Backup/Restore work in concert to affect an HSM system.

Support for Legacy Systems

Almost all Windows 2000 disk fault tolerance and disk extension is possible via the Disk Management service, which allows you to create dynamic volumes on which you can configure extended volumes, mirrored volumes, and RAID-5 arrays. You can also easily manage these volumes. However, Windows 2000 dynamic disks are not compatible with older versions of Windows or any other operating system. In other words, Windows 95, 98, and NT cannot read from or write to dynamic volumes installed as local volumes.

Note   Although dynamic volumes can only be locally accessed by Windows 2000, this does not mean you cannot read or write to a share or a publishing folder in Active Directory residing on a dynamic volume.

At the time of this writing, there was no way to upgrade or service pack a legacy 9*x* or NT 4.0 machine to read a dynamic volume. A study of the Windows 2000 architecture suggests that the support for dynamic disks is deep in the new operating system and not something that can be tacked onto NT with a service pack.

Disk Management Services

Windows 2000 provides many built-in features that can assist in making a sound storage plan a reality. The operating system provides sophisticated disk and volume management in the form of two disk-centric services: the fault-tolerant disk manager (FTDISK) and the logical disk manager (LDM). FTDISK and its associated tools, like FTEDIT, are inherited from Windows NT; it is a basic disk utility.

The LDM is a new introduction responsible for the management of dynamic, logical volumes. Dynamic volumes are storage objects, abstracted above disk spanning partitions and infused with dynamic or virtual storage attributes that unfortunately only Windows 2000 understands. The Windows 2000 disk/volume management architecture is illustrated in Figure 16-2.

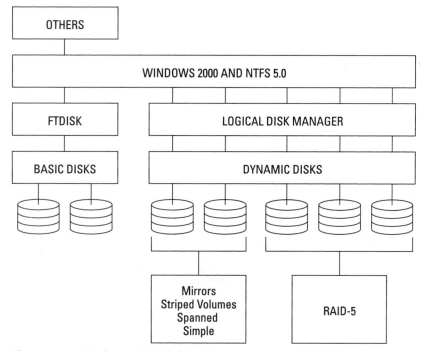

Figure 16-2: Windows 2000 disk/volume management architecture

Employing the services of both FTDISK and the LDM, Windows 2000 storage services can basically be split into two tiers: Basic Storage and Dynamic Storage. Disks can be configured for one of the two systems. The differences and employment of the two systems is explained later in this chapter; however, one major benefit of dynamic storage is the support for mounted volumes.

Mounted Volumes

In terms of dynamic disks and dynamic volume management, mounted volumes provide a means of rapidly adding and removing disk space from a system. Installing or importing a dynamic disk and then mounting the volume anywhere in the file system namespace, such as into a folder, is an elegant solution to the problem of adding or removing disks from a system without shutting down the computer and betraying the 99.9 percent availability initiative.

Mounted volumes can be constructed out of single dynamic volumes or fault-tolerant arrays of dynamic disks. Because a dynamic volume is an object that encapsulates disk space, you can graft dynamic volumes together in various ways to extend and protect the storage space (spanning, mirrors, and so on). Then you can take the entire extent (capacity) of the volume and graft it into the file system namespace. For example, you can mount the volume onto the d:\ disk as d:\data and then extend the d:\data volume as applications, service level, and availability require.

Volumes, and thus the volume mount points, can be extended as needed. The only limitation is the physical hardware architecture (usually SCSI) and the physical storage space for the hard disk.

Mounted volumes consist of dynamic disks created in the Disk Manager, discussed later in this chapter. However, you need to become familiar with the advanced features of NTFS before you can mount volumes into the file system. We cover this important topic, volume mount points, in Chapter 21.

Disk Defragmentation

Another topic worthy of introduction here is disk defragmentation. NTFS is in itself an orderly and efficient file system, and we, and many administrators we know, have never really needed to defragment an NTFS disk. However, disk defragmentation has been introduced into Windows 2000. We discuss it later in the storage housekeeping section of this chapter and in depth in Chapter 21.

Removable Storage

Windows 2000 is the first Microsoft product to introduce a holistic removable storage management system built into the operating system. Removable storage is any media that can be taken out of host equipment and relocated off site. Removable storage typically includes tape drives systems, recordable and rewriteable compact disks and DVD-ROMs, and even removable hard-disk technology such as ZIP disks, portable or external hard drives, and more.

Removable Storage Services allows you to install and configure single tape drive units (like Quarter Inch Cartridge) or highly sophisticated and expensive robotic library and archive systems (such as CD-R changes and DLT systems). You can also gather your removable media resources into collections of removable storage, known as a *media pool*.

 Removable media, such as QIC, DAT, and DLT, are discussed in Chapter 17.

Media pools refer to two concepts in backup administration. First, they refer to collections of media, regardless of the type, from which a backup system can check out and check in media required for any instance of backup or restore processing. Then there are media pools, a la Windows 2000, which are collections of tapes, carts, and disks organized under a single management system.

Media pools are not new to IT, and a stronger definition might be "a collection of like and unlike storage media collected together as a single storage resource." Windows Backup and Remote Storage Services draw on media pools according to the rules and regimens set up to protect data, and they support 99.9 percent availability.

Remote Storage and HSM

Remote storage is the service that makes Windows 2000 look a lot like UNIX. HSM is the widely known (in UNIX and mid-range circles anyway) acronym for Hierarchical Storage Management, which is a major feature of Remote Storage Services, or RSS. Like removable storage services, Windows 2000 is the first Microsoft operating system to introduce HSM capability.

But please do not go running off to your server to dig around in RSS to look for the HSM option, because you will not find it. HSM is really a system (some call it a philosophy) and consists of numerous components and services that unite to form a cascade of continually migrating and translocating data throughout the enterprise information network (technically speaking, RSS *is* an HSM system). HSM supports the 99.9 percent availability mission by moving unused data off local storage when the disks start getting full, or at pre-configured intervals. It can also participate in a generation-rotation backup system, as discussed in the next chapter, but this is not yet a feature of RSS.

The hierarchical system of data storage has several levels. There is a *data retrieval level,* which starts out at the top of the hierarchy. Data at the top of the hierarchy is online and always in a highly available or retrievable storage state. Data at the bottom end of the hierarchy is usually offline and in a latent state of retrieval.

High-availability data resides on local fast hard disks, in fast access network storage silos or storage area networks (SANs), or arrays of hard disks servicing clusters. At the lower end of the hierarchy, data is stored on tape cartridges, compact disc libraries, tape libraries, and even slower hard disk arrays.

How does the data get from the high-availability state to the other end of the hierarchy? This is what you set up in RSS. A file that passes a test — such as time since last accessed — is moved off the fast front-line volumes and down the hierarchy to the slower media. In a well-designed system, the files that are not being accessed eventually end up on tapes checked into a library. The actual file migration can be triggered according to events, such as hard disk space checking, and so on.

The RSS does not move all evidence of the file off the hard disk at the top end, but leaves an empty file name on the volume as a *marker.* All the data is drawn out of the file and sent to remote storage. From the user's perspective, the file still exists on the hard disk. When the user needs to access it again in the future, the file is checked out of the archive system and returned to its original location. In fact, the user need never know the data was actually somewhere else in the system. The only giveaway would be the slower access time when trying to open a large file that is in remote storage.

The *storage level* breaks out into two hardware-specific levels. The lower level is the remote storage level, which is responsible for the storage of data that has been drawn from local storage where it is no longer being accessed. Remote storage monitors file space on the local volume it is managing. When available space drops to a certain level, remote storage will move "stale" files to free up hard disk space. The capabilities of the remote storage system are the following:

✦ You can set up and configure remote storage devices such as tape drives and libraries.

✦ You can configure volumes for RSS management and HSM.

✦ You have more disaster recovery options and more tools to protect the 99.9 percent availability initiative.

✦ You can manage volumes for remote storage and HSM.

When remote storage needs to check data into a library, it interfaces with the removable storage system—via media pools—described earlier to copy the data to online libraries. The combination of the two services (remote and removable storage) provides the following benefits:

✦ You can deploy low-cost local, remote, and removable storage as a means of continually drawing unused or stale data off the local storage, which needs space for applications and data. This means that as long as you have removable storage media, such as carts or compact discs, you can continuously free up space on the local volumes.

✦ You can implement a data backup and archival system that more intelligently stores data in an archival state (where the data is available at any time) than traditional backup software. You can deploy a systematic data access, archival, and backup plan. Backup practice alone is not a perfected science, as you will see in Chapter 17. The data backup process (speaking generally and not specifically about the Backup program) leaves a lot to be desired.

✦ The HSM system allows you to view all storage resources on your network as a contiguous storage space . . . like one huge hard drive, hence the term *storage area network* or *SAN*. Now, your network is not only your computer, it is also your hard disks as well.

Although HSM is not a substitute for traditional regular backup, because there is only one instance of the data, you might consider installing a system that makes regular, rotation-managed backups of the offline media.

Before we get into setting up Remote Storage and an HSM system, we need to become fully competent with local storage services and Disk Management, Removable Storage and backup, and the NTFS. We devote this chapter to local storage, Disk Management, dynamic volumes, and fault tolerance on dynamic volumes. You should then become familiar with media pool configuration, backup strategy, and NTFS 5.0, discussed in Chapters 17 and 21.

The Disk Management Snap-in

This is the perfect time to introduce the Disk Management Snap-in. It is loaded into the Computer Management console, which is located in the Control Panel, under the Administrative Tools folder. You can also load it by executing `compmgmt.msc` at the command prompt or by selecting Start ⇨ Run and entering `compmgmt.msc`.

The Disk Management Snap-in is a leaf or node on the Storage branch of Computer Management. You can configure the view of devices from the View menu. The snap-in is illustrated in Figure 16-3.

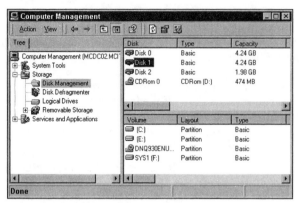

Figure 16-3: The Disk Management Snap-in in Computer Management

The Disk Management Snap-in is the only application you need to manage disks and volumes in a Windows 2000 system . . . intuitively. From it, you can configure basic disks and partitions, create simple volumes, create and work with spanned volumes, create and work with stripe sets, add disks, change storage types, configure removable storage, and manage media disks on any Windows 2000 remote server. The only thing you cannot do is create fault-tolerant or spanned volumes on basic disks. You can only manage such disks if they were created on NT 4.0. Disks can also be managed from the command prompt as discussed in Appendix A and with the services of command line tools like FTEDIT, discussed in Appendix B.

Note You need the appropriate permissions to work with any disk on any computer that can be loaded into the snap-in viewer.

Figure 16-3 illustrates the Disk Management Snap-in attached to remote computer MCDC02.MCITY.ORG. This server started off with one basic local disk (C:). While writing this chapter, we pulled two old Quantum Vikings with 4.5MB SCSI disk drives out of a storage (shoe box storage) and installed them into MCDC02. The pair of disks was impossible to install on Windows NT. The computer would recognize the Adaptec controller card, but always tossed us a Blue Screen of Death (BSOD) upon boot up. It was something about the hardware NT did not like, and the Adaptec-suggested workaround was more expensive than buying two new disks.

On Windows 2000, however, the drives installed with no pain at all. The operating system immediately detected the foreign drives and installed them into the system as if they were Plug and Play. At first, Windows 2000 recognized the drives as basic partitions. The disk list and volume list views are illustrated in Figure 16-3.

Before we proceed, you should understand that you cannot set up a disk to be both a basic and a dynamic disk, but you can set up a Windows 2000 server to support and write to both basic and dynamic disks in the same machine. This is important if you plan to continue running legacy Windows servers and clients, because they cannot directly access the new dynamic volumes.

Basic Storage

Basic storage is the industry standard. Hard disks are divided into a system of partitions. A partition is essentially a part of a physical disk's total storage space that acts as a separate standalone unit. When you install a hard disk, you have to first divide it into partitions. You chop the physical disk space into a primary partition and assign it a hard drive letter such as C:, and a system of extended partitions can be set up as logical drives (assigned any drive letter other than the letter the primary partition is using).

Disks that are set up for basic storage are known as *basic disks*. Basic disks can consist of primary partitions, extended partitions, and logical drives. Basic disks can contain up to four partitions. You can set up the disk to contain four primary partitions, or three primary partitions and one extended partition. Basic disk architecture is illustrated in Figure 16-4.

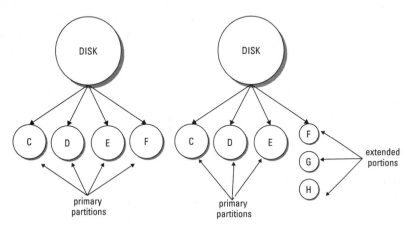

Figure 16-4: Basic disk architecture

Primary partitions cannot be further divided into logical drives, but extended partitions can. Any primary partition can be *active,* which means it can contain a boot sector from which operating systems can be started. Primary partitions can also be tiny, just enough to hold the necessary files to start the OS. For example, on early NetWare servers, the primary needed to be no larger than 30MB, just enough to boot the server. The remaining extended space was then configured as an extension holding the actual operating system, the NetWare system (SYS) volumes.

Basic storage (on Windows NT 4.0 and earlier) provided us with only partition-centric disk management architecture. You could (on the server platform) create mirrored sets, stripe sets, spanned sets, and RAID-5 volumes. On Windows 2000, under basic management and using FTDISK, these sets can be broken up in the same fashion as you did on Windows NT, which also includes having to restart the server after configuration of the sets. But as mentioned earlier, these disks cannot be created by Windows 2000 Disk Management.

Dynamic disks cannot and do not contain partitions or logical drives (these are unmounted when you upgrade a disk to dynamic storage). The LDM sees the entire underlying disk as one whole partition and then encapsulates the storage object on top of that.

Primary Partitions

The active primary partition is the part of a disk on which you start the operating system. In other words, the primary active partition is where you install the boot files that start the operating system. On dual boot or multi-boot systems, you can install several operating systems, and different versions of the same operating system, in the active partition.

You can only boot the operating system if it knows how to work with the underlying file system. In other words, you cannot boot to Windows 95 or Windows 98 on an NTFS file system, but you can boot Windows NT or Windows 2000 from a FAT system. File systems are discussed in depth in Chapter 21.

Extended Partitions

Extended partitions are created out of the free space that exists after all primary partitions have been created. There can only be one extended partition, which will include all the remaining free space left on a disk after you create a primary partition.

Extended partitions are divided into *segments* (one or more), and each segment can be set up as a logical or virtual drive. You do this from within Windows 2000. Using Windows 2000 disk management and storage tools, extended partition segments can be configured to represent logical drives, and they can be assigned drive letters.

System Partitions

As described in Chapter 5, the most common setup for Windows 2000 is to create a partition that can store boot files, and then configure the remaining space as a single extended data partition. We usually create a "system" partition and a "data" partition on Windows NT, but you might not be able to do that if Windows 2000 is allowed carte blanche access to all available storage. Windows 2000 refers to the partition it boots from as the System partition, which is the converse of all other, non-Microsoft operating systems.

When you install Windows 2000, it creates a *bootable partition* (in the system partition) that contains only the necessary hardware- and OS-specific files that are required to start the operating system. You can then install all system files into another disk's primary partition or an extended partition. This makes for some interesting recovery possibilities, which we will discuss later in Appendix B.

When you first install and boot to Windows 2000, all disks are configured as basic, and the fault tolerance is created and managed by FTDISK. However, basic volumes, once configured, remain fixed. They can only be converted or upgraded to dynamic disks, where they become the responsibility of the LDM.

The conversion to dynamic storage takes place from within Windows 2000, using the Computer Management snap-in.

Dynamic Storage

Windows 2000 now supports a standard known as dynamic storage in which a single disk is configured as a single active partition. This configuration is known as a *dynamic disk.* Dynamic disks are not created from the raw drive, but are created by converting a basic disk.

Dynamic disks support volumes, which are storage objects that can consist of portions of a single dynamic disk or several dynamic disks. The cool thing about dynamic disks is that they can be configured into several different types of volumes, from simple volumes to redundant arrays of volumes supporting various levels of fault tolerance and striping. The volume types are simple, spanned, mirrored, striped, and RAID-5 level.

The LDM brings the following features to Windows 2000 volume management:

✦ **Online Management:** RAID configuration can be created, broken, and rebuilt without rebooting the system. This feature allows you to install a working system, meet service level requirements as soon as the system is available, and then continue to work on the running system to meet data protection and storage requirements, while the system is live and servicing users and applications.

✦ **Extendable File Systems:** Volumes can be extended or mounted while the system remains up.

✦ **Self-identification:** LDM disks are self-identifying. In other words, once a disk is configured, it can be removed from one system and added to another system or host while both systems are hot. Differences in the target system, such as SCSI addressing, controllers, and so on, do not compromise the disk (see Importing Volumes, discussed later).

✦ **MMC:** The LDM's GUI is the Disk Management Snap-in. You can delegate the disk administrator task and use Disk Manager to attach to the storage services of remote computers.

As mentioned previously, the wonderful thing about dynamic disks is that they can be managed, even resized and added to, without shutting down, rebooting, or restarting the operating system. The RAID-5 level volumes support the full RAID-5 standard and are thus ideal for storage arrays and mission critical systems.

If your application or server calls for Windows 2000 exclusive use, the server should be set up with dynamic disk volumes to obtain the full benefits of Windows 2000 storage features and the distributed features of both storage and the file system. The various installation options you have are covered in Chapter 5. For the time being, Table 16-1 sheds light on the differences, as they affect you, between basic and dynamic disks.

Table 16-1
Basic Disks

Feature	Basic	Dynamic	NT 4.0	Windows 2000
Create/Delete Partitions	Yes	N/A	Yes	Yes
Create/Delete Logical Drives	Yes	N/A	Yes	Yes
Format/Label/Active	Yes	Yes	Yes	Yes
Delete Basic Volume Set	Yes	N/A	Yes	Yes
Break Basic Mirror	Yes	N/A	Yes	Yes
Create/Repair Basic RAID	Yes	N/A	Yes	No
Repair Basic Stripe Set	Yes	N/A	Yes	No
Repair Basic RAID-5	Yes	N/A	Yes	No
Basic Management	Yes	N/A	Yes	No
Upgrade to Dynamic Disk	Yes	N/A	No	Yes
Create Dynamic Volumes	N/A	Yes	No	Yes

Feature	Basic	Dynamic	NT 4.0	Windows 2000
Span Dynamic Volumes	No	Yes	No	Yes
Full Dynamic RAID-0	No	Yes	No	Yes
Full Dynamic RAID-1	No	Yes	No	Yes
Full Dynamic RAID-5	No	Yes	No	Yes
Dynamic Management	N/A	Yes	No	Yes
Volume Mount Points	Yes	Yes	Yes	Yes

Dynamic Disks

The disks that are managed by the LDM service are called dynamic disks. The LDM does not really touch the physical disk or the drivers, but rather works with logical disk objects that are an abstraction layer above low-level system code that goes down various layers, via drivers, to the physical disk itself. The logical-dynamic disks are similar in concept to the logical printers in Windows 2000. You do not actually manage the disk, but rather you interface with the object, which acts as a service proxy, setting and changing various properties. You do not do this directly; it is done by the Disk Management Snap-in discussed earlier.

Note Microsoft has chosen to offer limited support for fault tolerance on basic disks. You need to upgrade disks to dynamic status to get the full suite of software fault-tolerance functionality. It thus appears that Microsoft is being obtuse with respect to backward compatibility, because Windows NT and Windows 98 and earlier cannot read dynamic volumes installed into the local host either. But we believe the lack of support is more a case of incompatible code. Our guess is that Microsoft is at work on an API that will change that. If you want to get the full functionality of Windows 2000 storage services, upgrade those NT 4.0 servers and 9x clients.

The dynamic disk objects are managed as groups, or as a collection of disk objects. When you set them up for fault tolerance, each disk manages a tiny database on its media that contains information about all the other disks in the host. Thus, any changes to the disk configurations that control the fault-tolerance mechanics of the disks, such as mirror and parity information, are updated to all the disks. Disk configuration is thus no longer maintained in the registry, and the configuration databases are not currently accessible through any formal storage API.

The disk groups can be collections of simple volumes, concatenated or extended volumes, stripe sets, mirror sets (RAID-1), and stripes sets with parity (RAID-5). The logical disk architecture thus allows the volumes to be extended at any time without rebooting the host.

You can convert basic disks to dynamic disks, and you can convert them back again to basic disks. You do not lose any data converting to a dynamic disk, but you do lose your data if you convert back again. You should, therefore, fully understand the differences and benefits, before you convert, because for the most part, it's a one-way street. It is also worth repeating that Windows NT cannot directly comprehend dynamic disk volumes.

Also, in order to understand how dynamic disk configuration and the five volume types apply to your storage plans, you should *first understand each volume type.* It is also important to understand that although you can promote a basic disk to a dynamic disk, any hard partitions created, especially on primary active system and boot partitions, cannot be extended. You first have to delete the partitions and configure the disk as a basic disk, then promote it. But, deleting the partitions will no doubt destroy the data on the disk, so you need to either copy the data to another disk or back it up to remote or removable storage. If you have applications, share-points, and configurations that are particular to the disk you need to convert, you will have to plan this very carefully.

Tip   Installing Windows 2000 with more than one disk in the system may be a problem in certain situations, because you cannot make disks fault-tolerant if a partition existed before you created the dynamic disk. This is highlighted and a workaround is provided in Chapter 5.

The five dynamic volume types

The following list describes the five volume types, from simple to RAID-5:

✦ **Simple volumes:** A simple volume is disk space configured from a single disk. Simple volumes on their own do not provide much benefit, but do provide a starting point to extend storage space on the local system. You need to start with simple volumes if you are aiming to extend volumes, span volumes, or prepare for fault tolerance in the near future. Simple volumes can also be mounted to NTFS folders to increase local storage on the server without shutting down the server or affecting service level and users. (Mounted volumes are discussed in detail in Chapter 21.)

✦ **Spanned volumes:** Take simple volumes and chain them together to extend the hard disk space on a local volume, and you have a spanned volume set. Spanned volumes can consist of between 2 and 32 physical disks in the same system. Spanning is supported by NTFS and the FAT32 file system.

Windows 2000 writes the first disk and when that disk is full, it simply writes to the second disk and so on until it runs out of space on the 32nd disk. Spanned volumes are not fault-tolerant, so if any disk in the span breaks, the data on that disk is lost.

✦ **Striped volumes:** These volumes provide similar service to spanned volumes, but all the disks are configured as a single volume, tantamount to having one drive C: consisting of 32 disks. Striped volumes are used more for efficiency and for extending storage. The operating system writes to any free space on any of the disks in the set. Disk I/O is more efficient.

If one disk in the volume breaks, you lose the data in the entire volume. Striped volume sets are essentially RAID level 0 (Redundant Array of Inexpensive Disks) or *RAID-0,* in that you create an array of disks but you do not provide for any fault tolerance.

Striped volumes seem set to become obsolete because the concept was born in the days when hard disks were more expensive and did not have the capacity and bandwidth they have today, and will have in the future. Today's disks also read and write data much faster than anyone would have believed possible in the last decade (SCSI-2 drive platters, for example, have already reached 10,000 RPM). Also, the risk of having one disk failure take out the entire array is far too ghastly an idea to contemplate. If you use the full array set (32 10GB disks), one disk failure could potentially cause irrecoverable harm. Can you sleep well at night knowing that any one of 32 drives in some absurdly huge array might fail at any time?

✦ **RAID-1 volumes (mirroring):** This is the first level of software fault tolerance provided by Windows 2000. Essentially, a mirrored volume set consists of two identical copies of a simple volume. If one hard disk fails, you can carry on working on the survivor until a new simple volume is added back to the mirror. Mirrored volumes are ideal for providing inexpensive fail-over potential, as described in Chapter 17 on disaster recovery and backup/restore . . . you could call a mirrored volume set "the poor admin's fail-over."

✦ **RAID-5 volumes (fault-tolerant arrays):** These volumes are Windows 2000 software fault-tolerant striped redundant array (RAID) volume sets. The operating system adds a parity-information stripe to each disk partition in the volume. This stripe is used to reconstruct the data when a disk in the array breaks. You need at least three disks of any size to construct a RAID-5 volume. RAID-5 volume sets provide two benefits; they stripe data across the entire logical drive consisting of all the disks, and the data on any lost disk is recoverable because it is rebuilt from data on the remaining drives.

The fault-tolerant volume sets deserve more coverage.

RAID-1: Disk Mirroring

Disk mirroring is the process of creating a 100-percent identical "clone" of a hard disk, hence the term "mirror." The mirroring process is done in real time or concurrently to both disks. When you create a mirrored set, both disks are configured under the same drive letter and appear as a single disk to the OS, so when one disk goes belly up, the other can continue regardless.

Windows 2000 allows any partition to be mirrored to another disk of equal or larger size in the system. But you should be aware that in the actual mirroring process, only half of the total or combined disk space is usable (because the other half is used for the mirror). Still, with hard disk costs falling, configuring a server with a mirrored volume set and then making that volume set the system and boot partition is a very cost-effective means of maintaining 99.9 percent availability. It is certainly better than constantly backing up system files to tape storage as we explain in the next chapter, and the practice is actually cheaper because restoring a system needs to take seconds and not hours.

Remember, too, that Windows 2000 cannot save you from bad hardware, and a mirrored volume set with both drives still working will die if you lose the hard-disk controller. If your systems are catering to service level agreements, high availability requirements, and more, consider hardware duplexing. Duplexing uses two disk controllers in the mirroring process, thereby eliminating another point of failure in your system. You can even consider investing in RAID controllers and hardware-enabled RAID; we will discuss this shortly.

What if you cannot afford to have both disks die at the same time? There are many process control environments that require maximum availability of storage. A mirrored set destroys the 99.9 percent initiative as soon as one of the disks fails. This is when software RAID-5 steps in. The requirement for RAID-5 is that a minimum of three disks needs to be online. If one fails, you do not lose the array or access to storage, and you still have two disks to keep you going until a third can be installed and RAID-5 reestablished.

RAID-5: Fault-Tolerant Striping with Parity

As mentioned earlier, the Windows 2000 software disk striping with parity is RAID-5-compliant. All disks are configured as a redundant array, and the data is striped across all the disks in the array. In order to support RAID level 5, you need a minimum of three disks in the array. The fault tolerance is achieved by striping the parity data needed to recover a disk on *all* the disks. You always need a third disk in the set to maintain the RAID level and keep fault tolerance healthy.

Stripe sets with parity are set up in the same way as non-redundant stripe sets. However, each partition in the stripe set must be on a separate disk. Windows 2000 will also make all the partitions the same size. If you have one disk with 1GB of space and two others with 1.8GB and you create your stripe set *from* the 1GB drive, the effective space to be used for the set is only 3GB. You will be throwing away the other 1.6GB.

It is important to plan fault-tolerant striping and to work out exactly what you need for each system. As explained in capacity planning in Chapter 4, you can't always be too accurate, but it is important to invest in sensible solutions. For example, set up a RAID-5 volume set out of a specialized RAID-5-compliant storage array, and use hot-swappable (also known as "hot-pluggable") components and high-quality and reliable cabinets, power supply units, and cooling systems.

Try also not to mix and match drives and controllers even though it is possible to do that. The best service and performance will come from drives from the same manufacturer, that have been tested with that manufacturer's controller and drivers, and that have identical performance specifications. Remember that the fastest and most expensive disk in an array is only as good as the slowest and cheapest disk in the array.

Software RAID

While the software RAID capabilities of Windows 2000 are impressive, administrators may prefer to stick with hardware RAID, especially levels 5 and higher. There are several reasons for such sentiment. First, applications requiring 99.9 percent availability, in clustered or fail-over environments, will require hardware RAID-5 storage units. These units come with hot-pluggable components and RAID-5 controllers and processors built in. It would not make much sense to set up software RAID-5 with such equipment under the hood of your server.

Second, software RAID-5 eats CPU time. To establish RAID-5 (striping with parity), the processor has to write to the fault-tolerant databases on each disk, concurrently. And no matter how powerful a CPU you have, you will want applications to get almost all the attention of the CPU.

Hardware RAID equipment, called RAID controllers, use their own CPUs, built onto the hard-disk controller, to exclusively handle parity and striping. They will always be faster than software RAID, even on a 1000 MHz quad-CPU system. No matter how big the CPU, or how many you have in the system, applications will always win in the war for CPU time, and so it should be.

Of course, if you are installing Windows 2000 Datacenter Server, with say 16 CPUs on board, you'll probably have a lot of CPU time to spare. But then, we do not know of a single Datacenter Server platform that is *not* shipping with hardware RAID. That would be like buying a Porsche with vinyl-covered seats.

Disk mirroring is another story, however, and it makes sense to install a mirror set in every critical server you have. With two controllers, CPU time is not part of the equation. When a disk fails, you have to install a new volume and reestablish the mirror. And since this can be done without bringing the system down, you have essentially met 100 percent storage availability, although lofty scientists will argue that no system is 100 percent available.

Dynamic Storage Management

Dynamic disk management involves creating simple volumes after they have been added as basic disks into cold or running systems. Once you have your basic system running—with one or two simple dynamic volumes—you will be able to extend and reconfigure your system as your needs or plans dictate.

Note Although you can extend and reconfigure volumes in a running system, you will still require hardware that supports hot insertion and extraction of components.

Creating Simple Volumes

Creating a simple volume only takes a few steps. Although you can create a simple dynamic volume with NTFS, FAT16, or FAT32, you can only extend the volume with NTFS. The following checklist prepares you to upgrade the basic disk for upgrading to a dynamic volume.

Note You should back up all your data on any drives you intend to configure.

✦ Make sure there are no extended partitions or logical drives on the hard disk. If there are such partitions or logical drives, or you are upgrading Windows NT 4.0 or another OS, relocate or back up the data on these partitions, because the upgrading process will dismount them, and formatting to NTFS version 5.0 will destroy any data on the disk.

✦ If the disk will contain your boot files, it need not be very large. A 2GB drive will be sufficient to hold your boot files and the operating system files. You do not need to give the disk the volume label, *System,* because Windows 2000 does that anyway, and sets it apart from *Data* disks or *Applications* disks.

✦ Establish a policy for assigning drive letters. If you are supporting Terminal Services, you should reserve the C: and D: drive letters for clients. For example: Citrix Metaframe environments can map the client's hard disk as drive C:. In other words, drive C: is actually on the workstation or the client, not on the server. The *System* volume is then assigned something higher than C:, anything from D: to Z:. Windows 2000 can assign 26 drive letters, including A: and B:.

To create a simple volume, follow these steps:

1. Click the Disk Management node on the Storage tree to load the Disk Management Snap-in.

2. Put the disk list into List view. This is done by first clicking the Disk Management node and then selecting View ⇨ Top. You can also upgrade to a dynamic disk in graphical view (as illustrated in Figure 16-5).

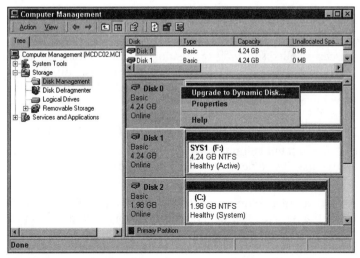

Figure 16-5: Selecting the option to upgrade to a dynamic disk

3. Right-click the disk and select the option "Upgrade to Dynamic Disk. . .". The upgrade list loads to allow you to confirm the action (see Figure 16-6). At this point, any file systems that have been installed to the disk will be dismounted. Windows requires you to confirm this action. You will not lose data on the drive.

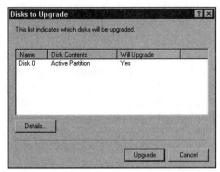

Figure 16-6: Confirming the action to upgrade

4. Click Upgrade to proceed. The upgrade takes a few minutes.

That's all there is to creating a simple volume. You can now work with the simple volume, create spanned RAID volumes, and so on.

Extending Simple Volumes (Spanning)

The process of creating dynamic volumes and then extending them or adding them to existing resources is called *spanning,* or creating spanned volumes. Spanning is the process of combining unallocated space from multiple drives into one logical volume. After you have created a simple volume, as instructed previously, you will now add it to an existing volume. The following checklist applies to extending volumes:

✦ Dynamic system disks, which contain boot information, cannot be extended.

✦ Spanned or extended volume sets cannot be broken without destroying the data on the disk. If you need to break a spanned volume, the data must be backed up.

✦ You cannot extend a volume by using another volume that has already been created, or that was a basic volume that was upgraded to a dynamic volume. You can only use unallocated space. If you wish to use a volume for spanning, you have to first back up any data you need and then delete the volume.

✦ Spanned volumes, as explained earlier, cannot be used for fault tolerance.

To span volumes, follow these steps:

1. Click the Disk Management node on the Storage tree to load the Disk Management Snap-in.

2. Put the disk list into "Graphical" View by selecting View ➪ Bottom.

3. Right-click the disk showing unallocated space and select the option "Create Volume." The Create Volume Wizard launches and takes you through the procedure. You can choose to use all the unallocated space or a portion of it.

4. During the course of creating the extension, you are going to be asked for a drive letter. Have a chosen letter ready; you don't want to be wasting time confirming this when creating the extension. It is important to make sure that applications will not choke on the drive letter you assign to the extension. For example, you may have a database management system (DBMS) already installed on the media that maintains a drive mapping for certain tables to D:. If you come along now and change the drive letter to X:, your DBMS will not work as intended. The drive letter may be changed later, but it may be inconvenient and even impossible if the drive letter you need is already assigned.

To break a spanned volume, follow these steps:

1. Click the Disk Management node on the Storage tree to load the Disk Management Snap-in.

2. Put the disk list into Graphical View by selecting View ➪ Bottom.

3. Right-click any of the disks in the spanned or extended set. (They will be the same color and will have the same drive letter.) Select the option Delete Volume, as illustrated in Figure 16-7. Before you can delete the volume set, you will be warned that the entire span is going to be trashed, along with any data stored on it.

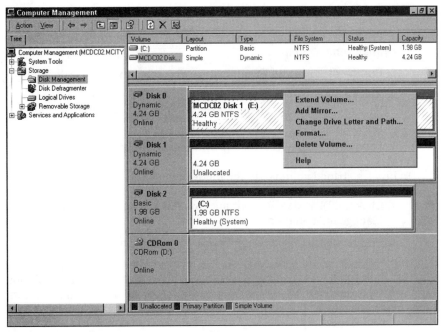

Figure 16-7: Volume management options

After going ahead with the volume delete, the dynamic disks are returned to their Unallocated state. The disks are now ready for export or use in a fault-tolerant configuration.

Creating and Managing RAID-0 Volumes (Striping)

The process of creating striped volumes and then extending them or adding them to existing resources is called striping or creating striped volumes. The following checklist applies to striped volumes:

✦ Dynamic system disks, which contain boot information, cannot be striped.

✦ Striped volumes cannot be broken without destroying the data on the disk. If you need to break a striped volume, the data must be backed up.

✦ You cannot stripe a volume by using another volume that has already been created, or that was a basic volume upgraded to a dynamic volume. You can only use unallocated space. If you wish to use a volume for striping, you have to first back up any data you need and then delete the volume.

✦ Striped volumes, as explained earlier, cannot be used for fault tolerance.

To stripe volumes, follow these steps:

1. Click the Disk Management node on the Storage tree to load the Disk Management Snap-in.

2. Put the disk list into Graphical View by selecting View ⇨ Bottom.

3. Right-click the disk showing unallocated space and select the option Create Volume. The Create Volume Wizard launches and takes you through the procedure.

4. Follow the steps described previously in the Spanning section.

To break a striped volume, do the following:

1. Click the Disk Management node on the Storage tree to load the Disk Management Snap-in.

2. Put the disk list into Graphical View by selecting View ⇨ Bottom.

3. Right-click any of the disks in the striped volume. (They will be the same color and will have the same drive letter.) Select the option Delete Volume. Before you can delete the striped volume, you will be warned that the entire volume is going to be trashed, along with any data stored on it.

After going ahead with the volume delete, the dynamic disks are returned to their Unallocated state. The disks are now ready for export or use in a fault-tolerant configuration.

Creating and Managing RAID-1 Volumes

RAID-1 level sets are fault-tolerant mirrored volumes. You create mirrored sets in a similar fashion to extending volumes as described previously. The following check-list applies to creating mirrors:

✦ Mirrors are created using two dynamic disks. Write down the disk IDs that you are going to mirror and decide on how much hard disk space you are going to allocate to the mirrored volume.

✦ You can use unlike disks, but you must remember that the fault-tolerant storage space is only as large as the smallest disk.

✦ You cannot mirror a volume by using another volume that has already been created, or which was a basic volume that was upgraded to a dynamic volume. You can only use unallocated space. If you wish to use a volume for a mirror, you have to first back up any data you need and then delete the volume.

To mirror volumes, follow these steps:

1. Click the Disk Management node on the Storage tree to load the Disk Management Snap-in.

2. Put the disk list into Graphical View by selecting View ➪ Bottom.

3. Right-click the disk showing unallocated space and select the option Add Mirror. The Create Volume Wizard launches and takes you through the procedure. You can choose to use all the unallocated space or a portion of it, as illustrated in Figure 16-8.

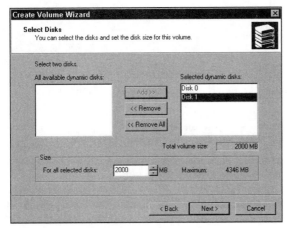

Figure 16-8: Selecting the disks to mirror

4. Click Finish to create the mirror job and continue until the entire process is complete. The mirrored set will begin formatting as soon as it has been created.

Figure 16-9 shows the mirror set created and formatted (volume E:). It also illustrates that the mirror has been established on 2GB of dynamic disk space. The remaining unallocated space can be used for creating simple volumes, striped volumes, or one new spanned volume (which is what we decided to do).

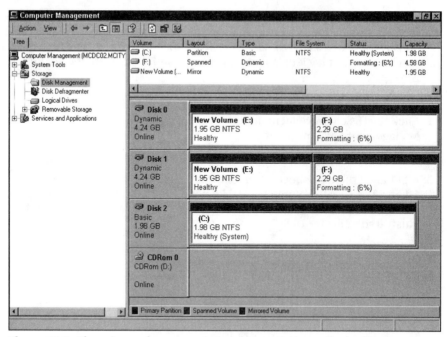

Figure 16-9: The mirror volumes created and formatted as a single drive

Creating and Managing RAID-5 Volumes

You create RAID-5 volumes in a similar fashion to the RAID-1 sets described earlier.
The following checklist applies to creating RAID-5 sets:

✦ RAID-5 volumes are created using three or more dynamic disks. Write down
the disks that you are going to include in the configuration and decide on how
much hard disk space you are going to allocate to the volume.

✦ You can use disks of different sizes, but you must remember that the fault-
tolerant storage space on the smallest disk is what gets configured on the
other disks.

✦ You cannot configure a RAID-5 volume by using volumes that have already
been created, or which were basic volumes that were upgraded to dynamic
volumes. You can only use unallocated space. If you wish to use a volume for
a RAID-5 configuration, you have to first back up any data you need and then
delete the volumes or partitions.

✦ Follow the advice given in the checklists for the previously described volume
configurations.

To install RAID-5 volumes, do the following:

1. Click the Disk Management node on the Storage tree to load the Disk Management Snap-in.

2. Put the disk list into Graphical View by selecting View ⇨ Bottom.

3. Right-click the disk showing unallocated space and select the option Create Volume. The Create Volume Wizard launches and takes you through the procedure, which is not much different from the disk mirroring choice described earlier.

4. Click Finish to create the RAID-5 volume and continue until the entire process is complete. The RAID-5 set will begin formatting as soon as it has been created.

 Note You can gather up any unused space left over from creating mirrors or RAID-5 volumes and use it to span or stripe.

Importing Volumes

Dynamic volumes can be removed from one computer and installed into another Windows 2000 computer without having to reconfigure the hard disk. As we mentioned earlier, dynamic volumes are self-identifying. The attributes of the volume are persistent even after disconnection from the host in which they were configured.

To import a foreign disk, follow these steps:

1. Ensure the disk is in a *healthy* state before removal.

2. After inserting the disk into the new host, open Computer Management and select Disk Management. Select Action ⇨ Rescan Disks.

3. Right-click the disk marked *Foreign* and then click Import Foreign Disks. Proceed with the import.

When the import process is completed, select the Rescan Disks option again to verify that the import worked. You should also do this on the system the disk came from to bring disk information current.

Managing Storage with Disk Quotas

Disk quotas were introduced to Windows NT with Service Pack 4; however, the quotas were not easy to enforce, and few administrators we know tried to work with them. They were also set via user profiles, which often interfered with a user's workflow. Windows 2000's disk quota services, however, allow you to allocate space to users at the volume level . . . and enforce them. The new quota technology is a very different animal.

Note   Disk quotas are only supported on NTFS 5.0 Volumes.

Before we get into the doing part, let's discuss the why part:

Why Do You Need Disk Quotas?

Remember what we said at the beginning of this chapter: No matter how much hard disk space you think you need, it is never enough. It is one thing managing your own hard disk space, the storage requirements of applications and databases, and so on; managing users is a different story.

Keeping track of available storage is a continuous effort, but it is essential. All computer services depend on hard disk space. If the disk runs dry, the IIS services like FTP will fail, databases will crash, backup jobs will collapse, and systems will die.

The disk quota is a means of controlling and enforcing a user's ability to save data to a volume. It is enforced at the user level, but restricted (and limited) to a specific volume. You can set a user's quota and let Windows 2000 monitor the user's disk consumption. Then, when the user attempts to save data to the folder that will use up the quota, Windows will react with a warning at a certain threshold and then deny access to the user until he or she has deleted unused or unnecessary files. Quotas, thus, not only help you protect platter space, they force your users to do their own housekeeping.

In the storage plan hinted at previously, you will determine how much storage you need for a particular server or application. Let's say a server hosts a SQL Server 2000 database environment, and you devote 20GB to it, leaving 10GB for the application and 10GB more free for future growth and users. The wild card is *users*. What if you have a share-point on the same volume as the database and for one reason or another it cannot be relocated to another server? We have such servers in commission, and on Windows NT 4.0, we have to constantly watch them.

With disk quotas, you can set a cap on the hard disk consumption of all your users and enforce the limits. In the SQL Server database example, you could assign 5GB for future application consumption and cap the share-point at 5GB, a total of 10GB (note in the plan what the SQL Server administrator has configured for automatic expansion of the database sizes). How do you do that? Let's now examine the quota service, learn how to apply and enforce quotas, and then explore the results.

How the Quota System Works

The quota service or system is not difficult to set up and manage, but you should understand how it works and any limitations that would affect how you set up volumes and services in the future.

Ownership

Quota calculations are based on ownership. When you create a folder or file, the OS adds the disk overhead of the new objects to your account. This makes for an extremely robust and manageable situation and forces you to account for your actions on a volume. With this system of checks and balances, a user cannot simply "pick up" a file and copy it, because by doing so he or she gains ownership to the copy and the file size is debited against his or her quota account.

Permissions have no bearing on the quota system, and, as you will soon discover, the quota limit is enforced on the whole volume, regardless of your rights and permissions in a particular share, folder, or file.

Be aware, however, that many applications can change ownership of files depending on who accesses a file and when. This means that in share-points where sharing files is the order of the day, quota levels will be in a constant state of flux. A user might end up over the quota limit just by looking at files. To counter this, the quota technology can employ a threshold, and you can decide at what point users get notice from the file system that they are running out of space.

Many applications also function in the OS, in the context of a user account. A good example is your backup program, which may need to do things as a user account in the Backup Administrator's group. You would likely not be restricting administrator or system accounts. However, an application could work in the context of a user account and be given a quota limit, and this would be a very effective means of putting the reins on an application that has a habit of filling up volumes with log entries and the like.

You can also instruct the quota service to write entries into the event log, giving you data on which to set triggers for disk space analysis algorithms. You would need to experiment with your applications, but with threshold reporting and log entries, there is no longer an excuse that the server or application crashed because the computer ran out of disk space.

The quota system gives everyone unlimited disk space "credit" as soon as quotas are enabled on a volume. Until you set limits and thresholds, no restrictions apply.

File compression

The quota service ignores compression and applies the original size of a compressed file to the account. The reason for this is that file compression ratios vary across different file types and versions. For example, graphics files might not compress as readily and uniformly as text files or applications.

Disk space/quota analysis

The quota service or system, once enabled on a volume, gathers disk space usage information about all users who own files and folders on a volume. This information is reported to the Quota Entries for Local Disk (disk), as illustrated in Figure 16-10.

This information is useful for determining who has access to file objects in a volume without having to drill into folders and dig around in user groups. (You could look at sessions, but they are not persistent; ownership survives disconnection from the volume).

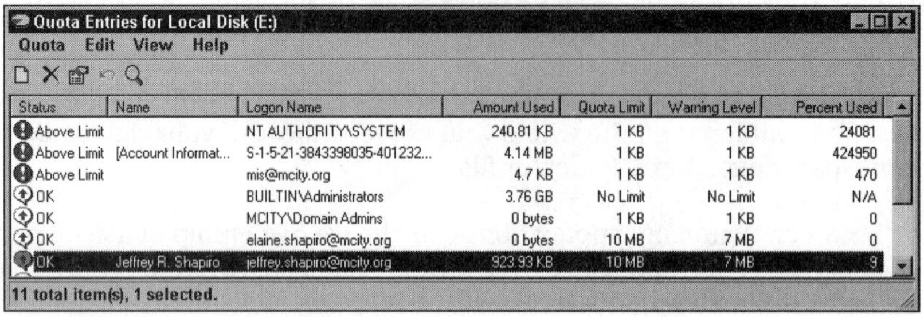

Figure 16-10: The quota entries for a local disk

Setting Disk Quotas

In order to set quotas, you need to gather information about who's using what and where on a volume. User information that is not specifically reported to the Quota Entries application upon startup of the system has to be looked up and added manually.

To set up quotas, do the following:

1. Make sure you are a member of the Administrators group. You need permission to set quotas.

2. Double-click My Computer and right-click the disk on which quotas will be enabled. This action loads the Local Disk Properties dialog box shown in Figure 16-11. This is the quickest way to get to the Disk properties dialog box if you do not have the Computer Management console open.

   Another route to disk Properties is via the Disk Management Snap-in in Computer Management, but this method isn't as efficient. In Disk Management, put the drives into Disk view, right-click, and select Properties. The (physical) Disk Properties loads to reveal the volumes on the media. Right-click the volume to enable the Volume Properties button. Click the Properties button (whew) to launch the Local Disk Properties dialog box.

3. Click the checkbox "Enable quota management." This starts up the service and allows the quota system to begin monitoring user disk space consumption.

4. Click the checkbox "Deny disk space to users exceeding quota limit." This option causes quota services to send an alert to an individual. Checking this option is not sufficient to deny a user disk space. You still need to set limits across the board or in the Quota Entries for Local Disk application.

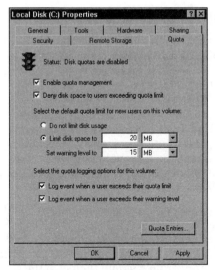

Figure 16-11: The Quota tab

5. Check "Do not limit disk usage" to allow users to use as much hard disk space as they need. Or check "Limit disk space to" and provide a size in KB, MB, or higher in the drop-down lists provided. This value is an "across the volume" disk space limit that affects all users. In other words, when the limit has been reached, no user can save a file or create a new one. This is a quick and highly effective means of putting a ceiling and a threshold on disk space consumption on a volume.

6. Next, set the warning level to an amount you feel appropriate. This is the threshold. After the warning has been issued, the users can continue using hard disk space until they max out and can no longer save to the disk.

7. Finally, you can check the option to have quota services log events when users exceed their limits and when users exceed their warning levels.

Adding disk quota entries

To add quota entries, click the Quota Entries button in the Local Disk Properties dialog box for the disk. You can insert quota entries as follows:

1. Select Quota from the application menu and then select New Quota Entry.

2. The standard Select Users/Add dialog box loads, from which you can select and install users into the Entries list.

Common Sense Disk Quota Management

If there is one thing users (in fact anyone) do not like to be told is that they have "exceeded their limit." That's akin to being told by the bank that "you have no more money and have exceeded overdraft limits." The following suggestions are intended to help you make wise use of this critical service:

✦ Enable thresholds for all users. It is not a good idea to bring a user's workflow to an abrupt end. At least with thresholds, the user can take evasive action, such as deleting files or moving files to other volumes or backups before the quota ceiling kicks in. Also, set a realistic threshold; it makes no sense to warn users that they are about to run out of storage space and then kick in the limit as soon as they try to save their work.

✦ Be careful not to set quotas before users have had a chance to install any *legal* applications or components on the volume they need access to. If this happens and the installation crashes because the quota limit is reached, you could log on to the server as an administrator and reinstall the application. The administrator or Administrators groups would then own the new installation, and this would not affect the quota. Notice that we put *legal* into italics above. The quota system helps prevent illegal installations (Group Policy works for this, too) and can put an end to software piracy taking place under your nose (users just love to copy whole CDs to storage; we've all done it).

✦ Monitor hard disk usage and individuals or problem users on a continuous basis. A flexible quota system works best, but you need to weigh flexibility against cost of administration.

✦ Avoid groups of users who all log on under the same user ID and password. A lot of companies do this, and it makes no sense; it's insecure and risky. It is difficult to keep track of a quota when four-score plus 20 are using the same ID.

✦ Keep track of quotas for users who no longer need to access or store data on a volume. You cannot delete the quota until the user has removed all the files or transferred ownership.

Troubleshooting

Unfortunately, managing disk and storage is not a set-it-and-forget-it task. ZAW and change control initiatives aside, like most other server and administrative tasks, you have to regularly monitor your storage.

Volume States

During the lifetime of a disk or dynamic volume, the integrity of the disk, and thus the data, may become threatened. Disk Administrator posts status information on each disk or volume, reflecting the state it is in. Table 16-2 represents the various states shown in Disk Management, and the problems, if any, to expect with each state.

Table 16-2
Volume States

State	Description
Healthy	The volume checks out for normal operations, and there are no known problems. This status is displayed for both basic and dynamic volumes.
Healthy (At Risk)	The volume is available, but Windows 2000 has detected read and write (I/O) errors on the disk. This state is only reported on dynamic volumes. This status is reported even if only one of the volumes on the disk reports I/O problems.
Initializing	This is reported by the LDM and only applies to dynamic disks. There is no need for user intervention unless the system hangs and the status remains unchanged. The correct sequence of events is that the status returns to healthy.
Resynching	This status applies to basic mirrored sets and dynamic mirrored volumes. Resynching is the process of making sure that both sets of data (one on each mirror) are identical. The resynching process might take a long time if the mirrors are large. Do not attempt to access the volumes while the resynching is in process.
Regenerating	This status applies to RAID-5 sets and dynamic RAID-5 volumes. RAID-5 volumes are accessible during the regeneration process. When the task is complete, the disk status returns to healthy.
Failed Redundancy	This status applies to RAID-5 sets and dynamic RAID-5 volumes. It means that one of the disks in the array is offline and fault-tolerant integrity is at risk. Fault tolerance is hosted when you are down to two disks in the array. You can continue to access the volume, but if you lose the second disk in the array, you lose the volume and the data because the striping and parity goes south. If you have five disks or more in the array, you have more time to replace the disk, but complacency is not a virtue in IT or network administration.
Failed Redundancy (At Risk)	This status applies to dynamic RAID-5 volumes. It means that the array is no longer fault-tolerant and that I/O errors have been detected on the media. This status appears on all the disks in the array. The disk and the fault-tolerant status can be reactivated.
Failed	This status applies to both basic and dynamic disks. It means that the volume cannot be restarted and will require user intervention.

When Good Disks Go Bad

Should a volume report "Failed Redundancy," "Failed Redundancy (At Risk)," or just "Failed," there are several calls you can make to the FTDISK and the LDM.

Step 1: To attempt to reactivate Failed Redundancy, try the following:

1. Click the Disk Management node on the Storage tree to load the Disk Management Snap-in.

2. Put the disk list into Graphical View by selecting View ➪ Bottom.

3. Right-click the disk indicating Failed Redundancy status, and select the Reactivate Disk menu option for dynamic volumes or Repair Volume for basic disks. If the reactivation succeeds, the volume recovers itself and returns to Healthy status.

Step 2: If a Failed Redundancy disk does not recover, try the following:

1. Attempt to reactivate the disk manually. This is done using the Reactivate Volume command for dynamic disks (both Mirrors and RAID-5) and the Resynchronize Mirror command for basic mirrored disks. Both commands should normally execute automatically after executing the commands in Step 1. If a basic RAID-5 disk is still offline, you can try to run the Regenerate Parity command.

2. If the disk is still offline and second attempts to reactivate fail, the disk has to be replaced. To replace a failed mirror, go to Step 1 above, but select Remove Mirror or Failed RAID-5 Disk region. After extracting the bad disks, you should follow the instructions for creating mirrors earlier in this chapter. To repair a RAID-5 volume, you need to use the Repair Volume command, which will take you through replacing the culprit disk.

3. To repair a failed mirror on a basic disk, you can use the Repair Volume command. If the disk does not return to healthy status, you should then try to force the repair using the Resynchronize Mirror command. If a basic RAID-5 disk fails, use the Repair Volume command to return the disk to healthy status. The Repair Volume command attempts to regenerate parity automatically. If the volume still reports the Failed Redundancy status, try using the Regenerate Parity command manually. If the basic disk is still offline, it will have to be replaced.

Step 3: To attempt to reactivate Failed Redundancy (At Risk) disks, try the following:

1. Try to reactivate Failed disks in the same fashion as Step 1 above, then attempt to reactivate the disks manually.

2. If initial attempts to return the Disk to healthy status succeed, the status may report the Failed Redundancy status (minus the At Risk part). This is usually a good sign, and going through the paces in Steps 1 and 2 previously should return the disk to healthy status. The likely scenario is that the disk data is out of sync or parity information needs to be regenerated. Use the Reactivate or Resynchronize commands described previously and then run Chkdsk on the dynamic volumes from the command line (Chkdsk may not work for basic disks). If you are still having no luck, you may need to replace the hardware, in which case if you follow the advice in Chapter 17 and perform regular back-ups, you do not have a problem. If you don't have backups, pray that a third party can recover the data from the dead hardware.

Step 4: To replace disks, do the following:

1. If you can spare disks from other computers, you can import them into the new host using the Foreign Disk import options described earlier in this chapter. This option only works for dynamic disks, however. If you need to replace basic disks and you are not using hardware RAID and hot-swappable components, you will have to power down the server.

2. Install the disks and, using the management options described earlier in this chapter, you can easily re-integrate the disks into the arrays.

Summary

This chapter provided a thorough investigation of Windows 2000 storage services. In particular, we covered the installation and management of local hard disks and the configuration and management of extended dynamic disks and fault-tolerant arrays.

Of particular importance is understanding both the benefits and limitations of dynamic volumes or disks. On the one hand, the dynamic volumes is a great improvement in local storage management on the Windows 2000 platform. On the other hand, dynamic volumes is not a pervasive standard. It is still very much "Microsoft technology," and other operating systems will choke on these volumes if you try to access them directly.

We still have a while to go in covering all of the Windows 2000 storage services. Chapter 17 extends Chapter 16 with a discussion of media pools, backup, restore, and disaster recovery.

✦   ✦   ✦

Disaster Recovery: Backing Up and Restoring

Every MIS or network administrator has a horror story
to tell about backing up and restoring systems or data.
One organization, where we now manage more than a dozen
backup servers, has data processing centers spread all over
the United States, and all are inter-connected via a large private wide area network. In mid-1999, a valuable remote
Microsoft SQL Server machine just dropped dead. The IT
doctor said it had died of exhaustion . . . five years of faithful
service and never a day's vacation. After trying everything
to revive it, we instructed the data center's staff to ship the
server back to HQ for repairs.

The first thing we asked the IT people at the remote office
was: "You've been doing your backups everyday right?" "Sure
thing," they replied. "Every day for the past five years." They
sounded so proud, we were overjoyed. "Good, we will have to
rebuild your server from those tapes, so send them all to us
with the server." To cut a frustrating story short: The five
years' worth of tapes had *nada* on them, not a bit nor a byte.
Zilch. We spent two weeks trying to make sense of what was
on that SQL Server computer and to rebuild it. We refuse to
even guess the cost of that loss.

We have another horror story we will later relate, but this
example should make it clear to you that backup administration, a function of disaster recovery, is one of the most important IT functions you will have the fortune to be charged with.
Backup administrators need to be trained, responsible, and
cool people. They need to be constantly revising and refining
their practice and strategy; their companies depend on them.

This chapter serves as an introduction to disaster recovery/backup-restore procedures on Windows 2000 networks, the Backup-Restore utility that ships with the Windows 2000 operating system, and the Windows 2000 Removable Storage Manager. Before we get into this chapter, we should consider several angles on the backup/restore functions expected of administrators.

Why Back Up Data?

You back up for two reasons, and even Windows 2000, with its fancy tools, rarely highlights the differences:

✦ Record-keeping (such as annual backups performed every month)

✦ Disaster Recovery (DR) or System Recovery

You should make an effort to decide when a file is no longer valuable to the disaster recovery period, and then it should be archived out for record-keeping. Depending on your company's needs, this may vary from a week to a couple of weeks, or from a month to a couple of months, and even years. There is no point buying media for annual backups for a site you know is due to close in six months.

What To Back Up

Often, administrators back up every file on a machine or network and dump the whole pile into a single backup strategy. Instead, they should be splitting up our files into two distinct groups: System and Data.

✦ *System files* comprise files that do not change between versions of the applications and operating systems.

✦ *Data files* comprise all the files that change every day, such as word-processing files, database files, spreadsheets files, media files, graphics files, and configuration files (like the registry, DHCP, WINS, DNS, and the Active Directory databases). Depending on your business, data files can change from 2 percent a day on the low side to 80 percent a day on the high side. The average in many of the businesses for which we have consulted is around 20 percent of the files changing every day. And, you must also consider the new files that arrive.

Understanding the requirements will make your life in the admin seat easier, because this is one of the most critical of all IT or network admin jobs. One person's slip-up can cause millions of dollars in data loss. How often have you backed up an entire system that was lost for some reason, only to find that to restore it, you had to reinstall from scratch? "So why was I backing up the system," you might have asked yourself. And how often have your restored a file for a user who then complained he or she lost five days' worth of work on the file because the restore was so outdated. It's happened to us on many occasions and is very disheartening if you are trying so hard to keep your people productive.

There is nothing worse than trying to recover lost data, knowing that all on Mahogany Row are sitting idle, with the IT director standing behind you in the server room, and discovering you cannot recover. The thought of your employment record being pulled should make you realize how important it is to pay attention to this function.

We will delve into these two subjects in more depth in this chapter and explore how Windows 2000 helps us better manage our recovery and record-keeping processes. We will start by focusing on the data side of the backup equation and finally lead this discussion into system backup/restore.

Understanding Backup

Before you can get started using Windows 2000 Backup, or any other backup program, you need to know how backing up works and have a basic backup strategy in mind.

Archive Bits

The archive bit is a *flag,* or a unit of data, indicating that the file has been modified. When we refer to the *setting* of the archive bit, we mean that we have turned it on, or we have set it to "1." Turning it off means we set it to zero or "0." If the archive bit is turned on since we last backed up the file, it means that the file has been modified since it was last backed up.

Trusting the state of the archive bit, however, is not an exact science by any means, because it is not unusual for other applications (and developers) and processes to mess with the archive bit. This is the reason we recommend that a full backup be performed on all data at least once a week.

What Is a Backup?

A *backup* is an exact copy of a file (including documentation) that is stored on a storage media (usually in a compressed state) and kept in a safe place (usually at a remote location) for use in the event the working copy is destroyed. Notice that we placed emphasis on "including documentation," because with every media holding backups, you need to maintain a history or documentation of the files on the media. This is usually in the form of labels and identification data on the media itself, on the outside casing, and in spreadsheets, hard catalogs, or data ledgers in some form or another. Without history data, restore media will be unable to locate your files and the backup will be useless. This is why it is possible to prepare a tape for overwriting by merely formatting the label so that the magnetic head thinks the media is blank.

There are various types of backups, depending on what you back up and how often you back it up:

✦ **Archived backup:** A backup that documents (in header files, labels, and backup records) the state of the archive bit at the time of copy. The state (on-off) of the bit indicates to the backup software that the file has been changed since the last backup. When Windows 2000 Backup does an archived backup, it sets the archive bit accordingly.

✦ **Copy backup:** An ad-hoc "raw" copy that ignores the archive bit state. It also does not set the archive bit after the copy. A copy backup is useful for quick copies between DR processes and rotations, or to pull an "annual" during the monthly rotation (we discuss this later).

✦ **Daily backup:** This does not form part of any rotation scheme (in our book anyway). It is just a backup of files that have been changed on the day of the backup. We question the usefulness of the daily backup in Backup, because mission-critical DR practice dictates the deployment of a manual or auto-mated rotation scheme (described later). Also, Backup does not offer a sum-mary or history of the files that have changed during the day. If you were responsible for backing up a couple of million files a day . . . well, this just would not fly.

✦ **Normal backup:** A complete backup of all files (that can be backed up), period. The term "normal" is more a Windows 2000 term because this backup is more commonly called a "full" backup in DR circles. The full backup copies all files and then sets the archive bit to indicate (to Backup) that the files have been backed up. You would do a full backup at the start of any backup scheme. You would also have to do a full backup after making changes to any scheme. A full backup, and documentation or history drawn from it, is the only means of per-forming later incremental backups. Otherwise, the system would not know what has or has not changed since the last backup.

✦ **Incremental backup:** A backup of all files that have changed since the last full or incremental backup. The backup software sets the archive bit, which thereby denotes that the files have been backed up. Under a rotation scheme, a full restore would require you to have all the incremental media used in the media pool, all the way back to the first media, which contains the full backup. You would then have the media containing all the files that have changed (and versions thereof) at the time of the last backup.

✦ **Differential backup:** This works exactly as the incremental, except that it does not do anything to the archive bit. In other words, it does not mark the files as having been backed up. When the system comes around to do a differential backup, it will rely on comparison of the files to be backed up with the original catalog. Differential backups are best done on a weekly basis, along with a full or normal backup, so as to keep differentials comparing against recently backed up files.

What Is a Restore?

A *restore* is the procedure you perform to replace a working copy of a file or collection of files to a computer's hard disks in the event they are lost or destroyed. You will often perform a restore for no reason other than to return files to a former state (such as when a file gets mangled, truncated, corrupted, or infected with a virus).

Restore management is crucial in the DR process. If you lose a hard disk or the entire machine (for example, it is trashed, stolen, lost, or fried in a fire), you will need to rebuild the machine and have it running in almost the same state (if not exactly) as its predecessor was in at the time of the loss. How you manage your DR process will determine how much downtime you experience or the missing generation of information between the last backup and the disaster — a period we call *void recovery time*.

Understanding How Backup Works

A collection of media, such as tapes or disks, is known as a *backup set* (this is different from a *media pool,* which we will discuss in a bit). The backup set is the backup media containing all the files that were backed up during the backup operation. Backup uses the name and date of the backup set as the default set name. Backup allows you to either append to a backup set in future operations or replace or overwrite the files in the media set. It allows you to name your backup set according to your scheme or regimen.

Backup also completes a summary or histories catalog of the backed-up files, which is called a backup set catalog. If your backup set contains several media, then the catalog is stored on the last medium in the set, at the end of the file backup. The backup catalog is loaded when you begin a restore operation. You will be able to select the files and folders you need to restore from the backup catalog.

Removable Storage and Media Pools

Removable Storage (RS) is a new service in Windows 2000 that takes away a lot of the complexity of managing backup systems. This service also brings network support to Windows for a wider range of backup and storage devices.

Microsoft took the responsibility of setting up backup devices and management of media away from the old Backup application and created a central authority for such tasks. This central authority is known as Removable Storage and is one of the largest and most sophisticated additions to the operating system, worth the price of the OS license alone, and a welcome member on any network. If you are not ready to convert to a Windows 2000 network, you might consider raising a Windows 2000 "Backup" server just to obtain the services of Removable Storage.

But Removable Storage is like an iceberg. In this chapter and in other parts of the book, we can only show you the tip. Exposing the rest of this monster service, and everything you can do with it, is beyond the scope of this treatise, and a full treatment of the subject would run into several chapters. To fully appreciate this service, and if you need to get into some serious disaster recovery strategies, possibly even custom backup and media handling algorithms, you should refer to the Microsoft documentation covering both the Removable Storage Service and its API and the Tape/Disk API. A good starting place is the Windows 2000 Server Operations Guide, which is part of the Resource Kit, discussed in Appendix B. We will, however, provide you with an introduction to the service, coming up next.

The Removable Storage Service

Removable Storage comprises several components. But the central nervous system of this technology is the Removable Storage Service and the Win32 Tape/Disk API. These two components, respectively, expose two application programming interfaces (APIs) that any third party can access to obtain removable storage functionality and gain access to removable storage media and devices. The Backup program that ships with the OS makes use of both APIs to provide a usable, but not too sophisticated, backup service.

By using the two services, applications do not need to concern themselves with the specifics of media management, such as identifying cartridges, changing them in backup devices, cataloging, numbering, and so on. This is all left to the Removable Storage Service. All the application requires is access to a media pool created and managed by Removable Storage. The backup application's responsibility is identifying what needs to be backed up or restored, and the source and destination of data; Removable Storage's responsibility deals with where to store it, what to store it on, and how to retrieve it. Essentially, the marriage of backup-restore applications and Removable Storage has been consummated along client/server principles.

The Removable Storage Service can be accessed directly by programming against the API. You can also work with it interactively (albeit not as completely as programming against the API) in the Removable Storage node found in the Computer Management snap-in (`compmgmt.msc`). The Removable Storage node is also present in the Remote Storage snap-in, shown in Figure 17-1, and discussed in Chapter 21. Before we begin with any hard-core backup practice, let's look at Removable Storage and how it relates to backup and disaster recovery. Removable Storage is also briefly discussed in Chapter 16.

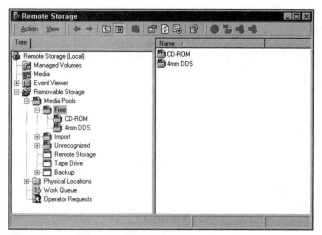

Figure 17-1: The Removable Storage Snap-in

The service provides the following functionality to backup applications, also known as backup or data moving and fetching clients:

✦ Management of hardware, such as drive operations, drive health and status, and drive head cleaning

✦ Mounting and dismounting of cartridges and disks (media)

✦ Media inventory

✦ Library inventory

✦ Access to media and their properties

Access to the actual hardware is hidden from client applications. But the central component exposed to all clients is the *media pool.* To better understand the media pool concept in Removable Storage, let's first discuss *media.*

Backup media ranges from traditional tape cartridges (discussed at the end of this chapter) to magnetic disk, optical disk CD-ROM, DVD, and so on. More types of media are becoming available, such as "sticks" and "cards" that you can pop into cameras and pocket-sized PCs, but these are not traditional backup media formats, nor can they hold the amount of data you would wish to store. DVD, a digital video standard, however, is a good choice for backing up data because so much can be stored on a single DVD disk.

Like the dynamic disk management technology discussed in Chapter 16, Removable Storage hides the physical media from the clients. Instead, media is presented as a logical unit, which is assigned a logical identifier or ID. When a client needs to store or retrieve data from media, it does not deal with the physical media, but rather with that media's logical ID. The logical ID can thus encapsulate any physical media, the format of which is of no concern to the client application.

Note Although the client need not be concerned about the actual media, you, the backup administrator, have the power, by configuring media pools, to dictate onto which format or media type your backups should be placed. If this is confusing to you, it will become clearer when you understand media pools, discussed shortly.

The benefit of the logical ID is patent, but a good example of its application is that the service is able to move data, represented by its logical ID, from one physical medium to another. This would be desirable if media is approaching the end of its life and the data needs to be moved to new cartridges.

Media formats can be extremely complex. Some media allow you to write and read to both sides; others only allow access to one side. How media is written to and read from differs from format to format. Removable Storage handles all those peculiarities for you. Just like the Print Spooler service, which can expose the various features of thousands of different print devices, so can Removable Storage identify many storage devices and expose their capabilities to you and the application. (The pros and cons of each of the popular backup media formats are discussed at the end of this chapter).

Finally, and most important from the cost/benefit aspect, Removable Storage allows media to be shared by various applications. This ensures maximum use of your media asset.

The Removable Storage Database

Removable Storage stores all the information it needs about the hardware, media pools, work lists, and more in its own database. This database is not accessible to clients and is not a catalog of which files have been backed up and when. Everything that Removable Storage is asked to do, or does, is automatically saved in this database.

Physical Locations

Removable Storage also completely handles the burden of managing media location, a chore once shared between the client applications and the administrator. But the physical location service deals with more than knowing in which cupboard, shoebox, vault, or offsite dungeon you prefer your media stored in; it is also responsible for the physical attributes of the hardware devices used for backing up and restoring data. It is worthwhile to understand this section, because you will need such knowledge to perform high-end backup services that protect a company's data.

Removable storage splits the location services into two tiers: libraries and offline locations. If a media is online, then it is inside a tape device of some kind that can at any time be fired up to allow data to be accessed or backed up. If media is offline, then it means that you have taken it out of its drive or slot and sent it somewhere.

As soon as you remove media from a device, Removable Storage makes a note in its database that the media is offline.

Libraries can be single tape drives or highly sophisticated and very expensive robotic storage silos comprising hundreds of drive bays. A CD-R/W tower, with 12 drives, is also an example of a library. Media in these devices or so-called libraries are always considered online, and are marked as such in the database. Removable Storage also understands the physical components that make up these devices.

Library components comprise the following:

✦ **Drives:** All backup devices are equipped with drives. The drive machinery consists of the recording heads, drums, motors, and other electronics. To qualify as a library, a device requires at least one drive.

✦ **Slots:** Slots are pigeonholes, pits, or holding pens in which online media is placed, in an online state. When media is needed for a backup, a restore, or a read, the cartridge or disk is pulled out of the slot and inserted into the drive. When the media is no longer needed, the cartridge is removed from the drive and returned to its slot. The average tape drive does not come equipped with a slot, but all high-end, multi-drive robotic systems do. The basic slot-equipped machine typically comes equipped with two drives and 15 slots. Slots are typically grouped into collections called magazines. Each magazine holds about five cartridges, and one magazine maintains a cleaning cartridge in one of the slots. You typically have access to magazines so that you can populate them with the cartridges you fetched from offline locations.

✦ **Transports:** These are the robotic machines in high-end libraries that move cartridges and disks from slots to drives and back again.

✦ **Bar Code Readers:** Bar coding is discussed later in this chapter. It is a means by which the cartridges can be identified in their slots. You do not require a bar code reader-equipped system to use a multi-drive or multi-slot system because media identifiers can also be written to the media. But bar code reading allows for much faster access to the cartridges, because the system does not need to read information off the actual media, which requires every cartridge to be pulled from a slot and inserted into a drive, a process that could take as long as five minutes for every cartridge.

✦ **Doors:** Doors differ from device to device and from library system to library system. In some cases, the door looks like the door to a safe, which is released by Removable Storage when you need to gain access to slots or magazines. Many systems have doors that only authorized users can access. Some doors are built so strong that you would need a blowtorch to open them. On many cheaper devices, especially single drive-no slot hardware, the door is a small lever that Removable Storage will release so that you can extract the cartridge. Other devices have no doors at all, but when Removable Storage sends an "open sesame" command to the "door," the cartridge is ejected out of the drive bay.

✦ **Insert/Eject Ports:** The IE ports are not supported on all devices. IE ports provide a high degree of controlled access to the unit in a multi-slot library system. In other words, you insert media into the port, and the transport goes and finds a free slot for it. Another way to comprehend the IE port function is to compare it to a valet service. You hand your car keys to the valet, and he or she goes and finds a free parking space for you.

If the hardware you attach supports any or all of these sophisticated features, Removable Storage will be able to "discover it" and use it appropriately.

There are dozens, if not hundreds, of devices from which to choose for backing up and storing data. Removable Storage, as we discussed, can handle not only traditional tape backup systems, but also CD silos, changers, and huge multi-disk readers. If you wish to check if Removable Storage supports a particular device, follow the steps to create a media pool discussed in the section "Performing a Backup" later in this chapter.

Media Pools

A new term in the Windows operating system is the *media pool*. If you are planning to do a lot of backing up or have been delegated the job of backup operator or administrator, you will have a lot to do with media pools in your future backup-restore career.

A media pool in the general sense of the term is a collection of media organized as a logical unit. Conceptually speaking, the media pool contains media that belong to any defined storage or backup device, format, or technology assigned to your hardware, be it a server in the office or one located out on the WAN somewhere, 15,000 miles away. However, each media pool can only represent media of one type. You cannot have a media pool that combines DVD, DAT, and ZIP technology. But you can back up your data to multiple media pools of different types if the client application or function so requires it.

It may be easier to think of the media pool in terms of the hardware devices that are available to your system (such as a CD-R/W or a DLT tape drive). You should strive not to work with media pools from dissimilar devices, especially when backing up zillions of files. For example, you should stay away from creating media pools that consist of Zip drives, DLT tape drives, and a CDR-R/W changer. It would make managing your media, such as offsite storage, boxing, and labeling, very difficult, much like wearing a sneaker on one foot and a hiking boot on the other and then justifying walking with both at the same time because they both represent "pools" of walking attire.

Removable Storage separates media pools into two classes: *system pools* and *application pools*. The Removable Storage Service creates system pools when it is first installed. By default, the Removable Storage Service is enabled and starts up when you boot your system. If you disable it or remove it from installation, any devices installed in your servers — or attached on external busses — will be ignored by Windows 2000, as if they did not exist. When Removable Storage is activated, it will detect your equipment, and if compliant, they will be used in media pools automatically created by the service or applications.

System pools

System pools hold the media that are not being used by any application. When you install new media into your system, the first action that Removable Storage takes is to place the media into a pool for unrecognized media. Then, when you have identified the media, you can make it available to applications by moving it to the free pools group. The system pools are built according to the following groups:

✦ **Free pools:** Free pools allow any application to access the media pools in this group. In other words, these media pools can be made available to any application requiring free media. Applications can draw on these media pools when they need to back up data. When media pools are no longer required, they can be returned to this group.

✦ **Unrecognized pools:** Media in these pools are not known to Removable Storage. If the service cannot read information on a cartridge, or if the cartridge is blank, the media pool supporting it is placed into this grouping.

✦ **Import pools:** This group is for media pools that were used in other Removable Storage systems, on other servers, or by applications that are compatible with Removable Storage or that can be read by Removable Storage. Media written to by the Microsoft Tape Format (MTF) can thus be imported into the local Removable Storage system.

Application pools

When an application is given access to a free media pool, either it will create a special pool into which the media can be placed or you can create pools manually for the application using the Removable Storage snap-in.

A very useful and highly sought after feature of Windows 2000 media pools is that permissions can be assigned to pools to allow other applications to use the pools or to protect the pools in their own sets.

Multi-level media pools

It might astonish you to find out that media pools can be organized into hierarchies or nests. In other words, you can create media pools that hold several other media pools. An application can then use the root media pool and gain access to the different data storage formats in the nested media pools. Expect to see sophisticated document storage, backup, and management applications using such media pools.

An example of using such a hierarchy of media pools can be drawn from a near disaster that was averted during the writing of this chapter. One of our 15-tape DLT changers went nuts and began reporting that our tapes were not really DLT tapes but alien devices it was unable to identify. The only way to continue backing up our server farm was to enlist every SCSI tape and disk device on the network into one large pool. Once the DLT library recovered, we could go back to business as usual.

Work Queue and Operator Requests

You will notice nodes for both Work Queue and Operator Requests in the Removable Storage tree. These services provide a communications and information exchange function between the operator (the backup operator or administrator or the backup operator group) and Removable Storage, respectively.

Work queue

Working backup applications and the HRS/RSS service post work requests to the Removable Storage service. To manage the multitude of requests that can come from applications and services, each request for work from the Removable Storage service is placed into the work queue. The work queue is very similar in concept to a print queue discussed in Chapter 23.

The work queue provides information on queue states on a continual basis, and these are reported to the details pane in the Work Queue node. For example, if an application is busy backing up data, an "In Process" state will be posted to the details pane identifying the work request and the state it is in. Table 17-1 describes the work queue states reported to the Work Queue details pane.

Table 17-1 Work Queue States	
State	**Explanation**
Queued	The work item has been queued. It is waiting for the RS service to examine the request.
In Process	RS is working on the work item.
Waiting	The request is waiting for a resource, currently being used by another service, before work on the item can continue.
Completed	RS has handled the work item successfully. The request has been satisfied.
Failed	RS has failed to complete the work item. The request did not obtain the desired service.

Operator requests

No matter how sophisticated Removable Storage is, there are some things it just will not do. These items will be marked for the "human" work queue. For example, Removable Storage will not go and fetch cartridges from the cabinet or the storeroom. This is something you have to do. The details pane in the Operator Requests node is where Removable Storage posts its request states for you, the operator. Removable Storage can also send you a message via the messenger service or the system tray, just in case you have the habit of pretending the Operator Requests node does not exist. Table 17-2 lists the possible Operator Request States.

Table 17-2 Operator Request States	
State	**Explanation**
Submitted	The described request has been submitted, and the system is waiting for the operator's input.
Refused	The operator has refused to perform the described request.
Completed	The operator has complied and has completed the described request.

Labeling Media

Removable Storage can read data written to the labels on the actual tape or magnetic disk as well as external information supplied in bar code format. The identification service is robust and highly sophisticated and will ensure that your media does not get overwritten or modified by other applications.

You need to provide names for your media pools, and you should also, if you can afford a bar code reader, organize them according to serial numbers (represented as bar codes) for more accurate handling. If you are planning to install a library system, make sure you get one that can read the bar codes from the physical labels on the cartridge casing. This information will be critical when it comes to locating a few files that need restoring from five million files stored on 120 30GB tapes (the bigger the enterprise, the more complex the backup and restore regimen and management).

Another reason we prefer a numbering or bar code scheme for identifying media, as opposed to labeling it according to the day of the week, is that often a cartridge can get inadvertently written to on the wrong day. If that happens, you may have a cart named Wednesday, but with Tuesday data on it, which can get confusing and create unnecessary concern. With a bar code or serial number, you can simply make sure that the cart gets put back into the Wednesday box without having to scratch out or change the label.

Practicing Scratch and Save

Although Windows 2000 does not cater to the concept of *scratch and save* sets, it is worth a mention because you should understand the terms for more advanced backup procedures. Simply put, a *save* set is a set of media in the media pool that cannot be overwritten for a certain period of time. A *scratch* set is a set of media that is safe to overwrite. A backup set should be stored and cataloged in a save set for any period of time during which the media should not be used for backup. You can create your own spreadsheet or table of media rotating in and out of scratch and save sets.

The principal behind scratch and save is to protect data from being overwritten for pre-determined periods. We have included a scratch and save utility on the CD accompanying this book; it is called *Scratch n' Save* and can be found in the SNS folder. Although this little utility does not prevent you from overwriting data, it will assist you in organizing your media pools.

For example, a monthly save set is saved for a month, while a yearly is saved for a year. After a "safe" period of time has elapsed, you can move the save set to the scratch set. In other words, once a set is moved out of the save status into the scratch status, you are tacitly allowing the files on it to be destroyed. A save set becomes a scratch set when you are sure, through proper media pool management, that other media in the pool contain both full and modified, and current and past files of your data, and that it is safe to destroy the data on the scratch media.

It is important to fully understand the concept of save and scratch sets because it is the only way you will be able to ensure your media can be safely recycled. The alternative is to make every set a save set, which means you never recycle the tapes . . . making your DR project a very costly and risky venture because tapes that are being constantly used will stretch and wear out sooner.

Establishing Quality of Support Baselines for Data Backup/Restore

Windows 2000 provides the administrator with backup and recovery tools seen before only on midrange and mainframe technology (such as the ability to mark files for archiving). For the first time, Windows network administrators are in a much better position to commit to service level agreements and quality of service or support levels than before. Unfortunately, the new tools and technologies result in a higher and more critical administrative burden (the service level shifts to the Windows administrator as opposed to being usually the domain of the midrange, UNIX, or mainframe administrative team). Let's consider some of the abstract issues related to backups before we get into procedures.

No matter how regularly you back up the data on your network, you can only restore up to the point of your last complete backup. Unless you are backing up every second of the day, which is highly unlikely and impractical, you can never fully recover the latest data up to the point of meltdown (unless you had a crash immediately after you backed up). You need to decide how critical it is that your business cannot afford to lose even one hour of data. For many companies, any loss could mean serious setback and costly recovery, often lasting long after the disaster occurs.

It is important, therefore, that you consider the numerous alternatives for backup procedures and various strategies if out-of-date data is considered inadequate recovery. You need to decide on a baseline for backup/restores: What is the least acceptable recovery situation? You will also need to take into account the quality of support promised to staff and the departments and divisions that depend on your systems, and the service level agreements (SLA) in place with the customers.

Note   Service level and quality of support are discussed fully in Chapters 1, 4, and 5.

First, before we consider other factors, let's decide what we would consider adequate in terms of the currency of backed-up data. Then, once we have established our tolerance level, we need to work out how to cater to it, and at what cost. Starting with currency, consider this list:

1. Data restored is one month or more old.

2. Data restored is between one and four weeks old.

3. Data restored is between four and seven days old.

4. Data restored is between one and three days old.

5. Data restored is between six and twelve hours old.

6. Data restored is between two and five hours old.

7. Data restored is between one and sixty minutes old.

Now, depending on how the backups were done and the nature of your backup technology, just starting up the recovery process could take anywhere up to ten minutes (such as reading the catalog), depending on the technology. So, level 7 would be out of the picture for you as a tape backup proposition. In cases where backup media is off-site, you would need to take into consideration how long it takes after placing a call to the backup bank for the media to arrive at the data center. This could be anything from 30 minutes to 6 hours. And you may be charged for "rush" delivery.

Now look back at the list and consider your options. How important (mission-critical) is it that data is restored, if not in real-time, almost in real-time? There are many situations requiring immediate restoration of data. Many applications in banking, finance, business, science, engineering, medicine, and so on require real-time recovery of data in the event of a crash, corruption of data, deleted data, and so on.

You could and should be exploring or installing clustered systems, mirrors, replication sets, and RAID-5 level and higher storage arrays, as described in the previous chapter. But these so-called fault-tolerant and redundant systems typically share a common hard-disk array or a central storage facility. Loss of data is thus system-wide and mirrored across the entire array. A mirror is a reflection: no more, no less.

This brings us to another factor to consider: the flawed backup. You bring this factor into consideration if your data is continuously changing. The question to ask is, "How soon after the update of data should I make a backup?" You may decide, based on the previous list, that data even five minutes out of date is damaging to system integrity or the business objectives. A good example is online real-time order or delivery tracking. But backing up data with such narrow intervals between versions brings us to the subject of quality and integrity of backed-up data. (Later in this chapter, we will discuss versioning and how new technology in Windows 2000 facilitates it.) What if the file that just got hit by a killer virus is quarantined and you go to the backup only to find it is also infected or corrupt? What if all the previous files are infected, and now just opening the file renders it useless? It's something to think about.

Earlier this year, we rushed to the aid of our main SQL Server group, which had lost a valuable database on the customer ordering system (on our extranet). Every hour offline was costing the company six figures as customers went elsewhere to place their orders. Four-letter words were flying around the server room. We had to go back three days to find a clean backup of the database that showed no evidence of corrupt metadata.

Figure 17-2 illustrates data backed up on a daily basis, and in this case, bad data is backed up for three days in a row. You may consider some of the gray area as safe, where backup data is bound to have all the flaws of its source (corruption, viruses, lack of integrity, and so forth), if you have other means of assuring quality or data integrity. Such assurances may be provided by means of highly sophisticated anti-virus software, quality of data routines and algorithms, versioning, and just making sure people check their data themselves. Backing up bad data every ten minutes may be a futile exercise depending on the tools you have to recover or rebuild the integrity of the data.

Most companies back up data to a tape drive (we discuss the formats later). The initial cost is really insignificant in relation to the benefit: the ability to back up and recover large amounts of data. A good tape drive can run anywhere from $500 for good Quarter-inch Cartridge (QIC) systems to $3,000 to $4,000 for the high-speed, high-capacity Digital Linear Tape (DLT) systems, and a robotic library system can cost as much as $30,000. Let's now consider minimum restore levels, keeping the quality of backup factors described earlier in mind:

1. Restore is required in real-time (now) or close to it. Data must be no longer than a few seconds old and immediately accessible by users and systems even in the event the primary source is offline. In the case of industrial or medical systems, the secondary source of data must be up-to-date, and the latency might be measured in milliseconds and not seconds. Your SLAs may dictate that 24-7 customers can fine you if data is offline longer than x seconds or minutes. Let's call this the *critical restore* level.

■ = data integrity

A

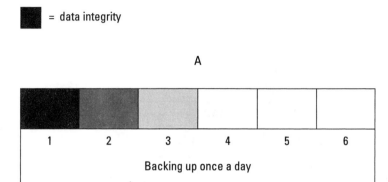

Backing up once a day

B

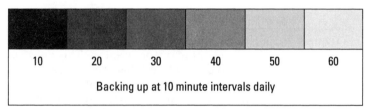

Backing up at 10 minute intervals daily

Figure 17-2: The narrower the interval between backups, the more chance that backed up data is also corrupted, infected, or lacks integrity.

2. Restore is required within ten minutes of the primary source going offline. Let's call this *emergency restore*.

3. Restore is required within one hour of the primary source going offline. Let's call this *urgent restore*.

4. Restore is required within one to four hours of the primary source going offline. Let's call this *important restore*.

5. All other restores that can occur later than the previous can be considered *casual restores*.

Figure 17-3 shows this in a visual hierarchy.

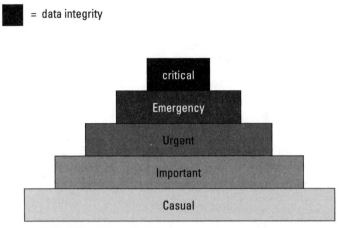

Figure 17-3: The data restoration pyramid

The pyramid in Figure 17-3 illustrates that the faster the response to a restore or recall of data request, the higher the chance of retrieving poor data. Each layer of the pyramid covers the critical level of the restore request. This does not mean that critical restores are always going to be a risk and that the restored data is flawed. It means that the data backed up closest to the point of failure is more likely to be at risk compared to data that was backed up hours or even days before the failure. If a hard disk crashes, the data on the backup tapes is probably sound, but if the crash is due to corrupt data or virus infection, the likelihood of recent data being infected is high.

Another factor to consider is that often you'll find that the "cleanest" backup data is the furthest away from the point of restoration, or the most out-of-date.

If the level of restore you need is not as critical or the quality of the backup not too important, you could consider a tape drive system either to a backup server or local to the hosting machine. You could then set up a scheme of continuous or hourly backup routines. In the event data is lost (usually because someone deletes a file or folder), you would be able to restore the file. The worst-case scenario is that the data restored is one hour out of date, and at such a wide interval, that a replacement of a corrupt file with another corrupt file is unlikely. Consider the following anecdote: We recently lost a very important Exchange-based e-mail system. Many accounts on the server could be considered extremely mission critical. Thousands of dollars were lost every minute the server was down. (The fallout from downed systems compounds damages at an incredible rate. The longer a system is down, the worse it becomes.)

The last full backup of the server was performed on the weekend. The system went down on Wednesday. Since we were backing up only the files that changed on Monday and Tuesday, we would be able to restore the e-mail server to the state it was the night before. This was good news to the MIS director, but not very good news to people who felt that losing six to eight hours of e-mail was unacceptable (for many that would mean losing an entire day of work and a lot of wasted time rewriting and resending e-mail).

But the good news was short-lived when we discovered that the transaction logs covering the Monday and Tuesday backups were corrupt on the system and on the tapes. The result was that we were able to restore the entire system to the state it was on Friday, essentially losing everything between Friday night and Wednesday afternoon. For backup administrators, this was an unacceptable event. Later in the chapter, we discuss how to prevent this from happening.

If you have several servers that need this level of protection, you will have to install some expensive backup equipment and advanced third-party software. Having a hot "clone" mirroring the entire system would be the way to go. Both disk and system mirroring, striping, and redundancy are discussed in Chapters 16 and 21. Full-blown redundant systems are required if applications need to continue oblivious of the switch to alternative media and hardware. To summarize: Looking back at our checklists and matrices for a restore service level of five and up, you would be looking at regular tape backup systems. Anything more critical would require online libraries and a hierarchical storage management system—and yes, we will look into this new service provided by Remote Storage Services (RSS) in Chapter 21.

Establishing Quality of Capture

In planning backup procedures and establishing quality of support levels for backups, and considering what we have discussed previously, it is vital you consider the quality of your backups before you begin designing rotation schedules and schemes and backup/restore procedures. Every business is different. Even businesses in like industries do things differently, so what you work out may work for you, but not for anyone else. What we suggest here are guidelines for establishing procedures. Before you get stuck in here, remember this: Devise a plan, and if it works (after tests work under strict analysis), stick to it. When backup media gets out of sync or gets lost or damaged, you may have a disaster when trying to restore critical data.

Best Backup Time-of-Day

Let's say that you decide to back up your data every night. One of the first items to consider is when you start your backups. If staff work late or your systems are accessed late into the night, you might wait until the early hours of the morning to begin backing up. In other words, the best time to start doing backups is when the files are least likely to be open and changing, or when you feel you are getting the last possible version change before people go home for the night and systems become idle again.

You may run into problems backing up earlier in the evening or even late at night when, for example, a process or department swings around at near midnight and updates 20 percent of the critical data you need to back up (like night order processing). It can be especially tough to decide when to start backing up e-mail systems and database management systems, because they typically are in use around the clock, especially if your organization is a national or global entity.

Some organizations restrict access to systems at certain times to ensure that the best backups are achieved at that certain time. This would naturally have to be coordinated with other departments and change control because making a system unavailable could crash other processes that may be running at the same time, or they may need access to the data. We believe systems should never be taken off line even for backups. Also, in the age of the Internet, who would want to restrict access to systems? That's tantamount to closing shop in the middle of the day for international Web sites that view "after hours" as an obsolete term in the Information Age.

Length of Backup

You should also work out how long your backups take. It may be prudent to start your backups at one minute to midnight, but if morning swings around and your backups are still churning away, you will have hardly performed a backup and the file may become locked or substantially changed when systems and people log in and seize control again.

If your backup devices are backing up multiple servers, you may not get to the last machines until the next day. There's not much sense in a Thursday incremental backup that is part of a rotation scheme, and that only takes place on Saturday.

There are a number of options to consider when striving to ensure that the best quality backups take place in as quick a time as possible.

✦ **Files that do not change:** Repeatedly backing up system and application files is a waste of time. Many administrators, from either lack of time to plan their backups or ignorance, waste an incredible amount of time and resources backing up files that seldom change. System files are a good example, as are temp files and non-critical log files. You could consider dividing your backups into the categories described next.

✦ **Long-term system and system state files:** These files include program files and system state files that never change or change very seldom. As explained later, incremental and differential backup functions ignore these files once a full backup has occurred, but it still makes no sense tying up time and media even on a weekly or monthly full routine that can often run into two or more days of continuous backup.

✦ **Short-term state files:** These files include system or application state files that do change often. Such files include configuration files, registry files, the Active Directory files, and so on. On servers, both registry and Active Directory files can change every day, when new users or resources are added or changed. So if short-term state files change daily on your servers, then they will need to be included in backups. Non-critical short-term state files, including .pagesys files, event log files, and temp files (.tmp), are not needed to restore downed systems, nor are they critical or useful to data.

✦ **Data and resource files:** These files include word-processing files, graphics-related files, database files, transaction logs, e-mails and other communications files, spreadsheets, voice and audio recordings, and so on. These files (and they can often be listed or categorized by their extensions) change often, are almost always critical, and should always be backed up or included in all backup routines.

If you intelligently include or exclude certain groups of files, you can control and keep backup times to a minimum. You will also save on media (at $30 to $50 a pop for DLTs and not much less for small packs of DAT cartridges); you can save a lot of money and wear and tear on systems, media, and backup devices.

Note Redundant systems that use replication services in products like Active Directory, SQL Server 2000, Exchange 2000, and so on, are more effective, in many cases, than fancy backup technology for high-availability initiatives.

Backup of Servers and Workstations

If you have not by now separated your backup procedures into backup of systems and backup of data, now is the time to do it. Often, system administrators repeatedly back up Windows servers and workstations in their entirety for absolutely no reason. We cannot count how many full versions or backups of our systems we have in storage. This has a lot to do with the lack of thought that goes into backup practice and little to do with the inflexible backup technology of earlier versions of the Windows server platform.

In some cases, we have several years of system backups where the only files on the media that are different are the data files. From the get-go, you could probably recover 10 to 20 cartridges and put them back into the rotation without impacting your quality of service and backup integrity levels (that could be worth a lot of money to you in media costs and time).

How do you then deal with the backup of systems? If you have not already done so, you should consider taking an "image" of the system and saving it either on tape media, compact disk, DVD, or on a remote storage volume. We recommend against storing images on any remote storage volume or disk because the hardware could fail or someone else might delete the file, even if you secure it (although Windows 2000 security provides more protection than Windows NT 4.0).

Instead, burn the system image onto a CD, or use a product that specializes in so-called "bare metal" capture of all data. There are several popular products that specialize in bare metal recovery. The Stac Replica system, for example, boasts the ability to back up a server and then restore it to any another machine with zero reinstallation required.

Workstations are viable candidates for image storage because they usually never get backed up. Most system administrators tell their users to stick their data into server share-points where (1) they are accessible to the groups that have interests in the files, and (2) the data gets backed up every day when the rotation sweeps around. Windows 2000 now offers such advanced control over the user's workspace that policy dictating the storage of user's files on a server share is entirely enforceable. See Chapter 11 for information on how to redirect user's data folders to backup share-points.

Many users lose a considerable amount of computing time and inconvenience when they lose a workstation and there is no backup for it. Getting such a system back to what it was before a hard disk crash, fire, or theft can take more than a day. Many critical processes also take place from workstations.

To restore a system from an image is relatively simple, and in many cases, recovery can take place in a morning. Images can also be kept in a safe place at work for quick access.

The upshot of this method is that if a system is blown away, you need only to set up identical or very similar hardware and restore from the image to get back a machine that is at the same state as when the image was burned. You would then restore the data and any files that have changed since the image was burned.

Naturally, you need to ensure that you install the necessary service packs that were installed on the system from the time of the last image burning. Or you should re-burn the image after a new service pack, application software, or new system libraries have been applied.

The best candidates for the image burning and bare metal backup techniques are servers where the majority of files on the system are static system files. A print server is a good example, and the Windows 2000 Resource Kit includes such a utility (`printmig`) to back up logical printer shares. It may not be much of a savings to burn an image of a server where 89 percent of the storage space is dedicated to databases or e-mail files. On the other hand, a Remote Access Server, one of a group of WINS servers, and volumes that have no changing data on them are ideal candidates for image burns.

The Open Files Dilemma

Open files have always been the backup administrator's nightmare on Windows NT Server, and this is still very much the case on Windows 2000 volumes. What are these open files? Any resource file on a system needs to be opened for exclusive or shared use by a user or device that is exploiting or updating its contents. Backup software, backup schemes and rotations, and backup administrators hate open files because:

✦ Open files cannot be backed up.

✦ Open files trash automated backup jobs.

✦ Open files cause the backup schedules to slow down, even grind to a halt.

✦ Forcing open files closed or shutting down services and systems causes headaches, inconveniences, missed deadlines, crashes and, worse, the Blue Screen of Death (although the latter is the least likely to occur).

Many relational database applications, for example, place "locks" on files while they are in use. The system also places locks on files. These files can range from simple configuration files, the registry and Active Directory files (their databases, for example), SQL servers, WINS servers, DHCP servers, and so on. E-mail applications are a good example of an open-files nightmare. These files are often huge and are almost always open and in use by the applications. Microsoft Exchange is a good case in point.

If a file is open or there is an exclusive lock on the file, your backups are in trouble. On a mail server like Exchange, the result of the open files problem could be catastrophic for you. The information stores, the registry, the Exchange directory, the Active Directory, WINS, DNS, DHCP, and so on, are always open. If the backup fails because these huge files could not be backed up, you might be talking about hundreds if not thousands of users inconvenienced, at incredible cost.

Let's suppose a disaster: You do a full backup of Microsoft Exchange every weekend. Then one day your silent pager vibrates your hip joints with the message that the Exchange server crashed. When you try to revive the system, guess what, it does not want to be revived. But that's okay because you have been diligently making full backups of Exchange every weekend. Only, when you go and do your backup, you find that the backup software was skipping exactly those files you need to do the backup from. Career killer?

Database servers can cause even bigger headaches. Many, such as SQL Server, are self-contained domains of users and login mechanisms. From the outside world, you only see a huge database blob. In the case of SQL Server, it's the files with the `.dat` extension, such as `msdb.dat`. In fact, any huge file that has a `.dat` or a `.?db` extension is likely to be a database.

Note Many high-end systems, such as SQL Server 2000, now ship with their own built-in backup services.

There are several ways to deal with this bugbear, from the cheapest to the most expensive solution:

First, you can shut down the open application's services prior to backup, or force closure of the files by requesting users to close applications and even log off (incidentally, any restore of SQL Server requires the database to be placed into single user mode, so that the restore agent gets unrestricted access to the databases). This is by far the cheapest method (software cost), and you can force closure of services and files prior to backup with several batch files and scripts. (We will look at scripts shortly.)

The second solution is to install an open-files utility that provides the backup software with a "window" to the data in the open files. The plus in this solution is that your backup software gets access to open files across the board. One such product is the Open Files Manager (OFM) from St. Bernard software (www.stbernard.com). You can install this tool on your systems and never need to worry about open files not getting backed up. So important to backup and recovery is this utility, that it is worth a special mention here. But you should thoroughly test it on your systems before going live. As important as it is, the product tinkers with files deep into the abyss of the file system, as does anti-virus software. OFM and NetShield from Network Associates have been known to collide, so test your implementation before going into production.

The third and most expensive solution is an agent that works with the backup software you are using. Products like Backup Exec and ARCserve provide their own open-files agents and agents that allow the Microsoft BackOffice products to be backed-up while they are on line with files in use. We'll deal with these agents a little more in this chapter.

Notice that in this short list, we listed the solutions in order of cheapest to most expensive solution. But that expense is only in terms of what it costs to buy the solution. In other words, if you think you are saving money going for the option to shut down services, think again. This could be your most expensive solution. For example: Just when you think you're being clever and shutting down services with the nifty little batch files and scripts we are about to create, the batch file breaks. For some reason, the service does not shut down, and the next day your system crashes and you don't have a backup.

The agents are also not airtight technology. We run nightly backups of several huge SQL Server databases, Oracle, Lotus Notes, and more. Often, we'll notice that the open-files agent stopped for some reason and the backup of critical data did not go through. You have to watch the services like a cat sitting between a mouse and a hole in the wall.

It is worth mentioning that Microsoft provides some limited open-file support for Exchange on NT 4.0. When you install Exchange on NT 4.0, the installation updates the NT Backup utility to allow it to back up Exchange's directory and information store. No doubt, the new version of Exchange for Windows 2000 will similarly update Windows 2000 Backup.

 Caution Never, ever, mix backup technologies on the same files. For starters, each backup job changes the state of the files to some degree, from changing the archive bit on one end to causing the applications to do housekeeping on the other end. Your restores may not work when a second backup application has altered the file system. Also, if a restore job fails, you can forget about getting support from a vendor if another product has interfered.

Backup Procedure

The Windows 2000 Server team can be credited for making backup and restore the lead member of its DR group, at least as far as classification goes. But consistency is not one of their credits: Why they moved the menu item for Backup from Administrative Tools in Windows NT4 to Accessories ➪ System Tools on Windows 2000 is uncertain. An "accessory" is certainly not what a backup application should be to such a high-end operating system. Anyway, under the aforementioned tab is exactly where you'll find it. The path to Backup's door is Start ➪ Programs ➪ Accessories ➪ System Tools ➪ Backup. Or just run the command line shortcut ntbackup.exe.

For most uses of your computer, the Backup utility is sufficient to archive and store data, and to recover it in the event of a disaster. However, that's as far as it goes. Microsoft has again chosen a custom-made version of Veritas Software, Inc.'s BackupExec product. You will certainly want to stick with the likes of ARCserve for enterprise-wide disaster recovery and data protection.

Before we get into the highs and lows of backup and restore, let's first look at the limitations of the utility that ships with Windows 2000 Backup. For starters, it's a vast improvement over the Backup that is bundled with NT4, but it still has limitations. Naturally, Veritas will want you to come and pay extra for a pro version of this product, better known as BackupExec. In our book, Microsoft should either have paid them a higher royalty and put in features more in line with the advanced nature of the OS, or left it out completely. We have several hundred servers in our server portfolio, and we don't use the NT4 version of NTBackup; there have just been too many disasters with it. And after reviewing the new Backup, we are not likely to replace the third-party stuff we are using when we migrate to Windows 2000, although our small clients are using Backup just fine. Let's look at these limitations.

Backup does not allow you to attach to other machines and perform backup and restores of state-related data, such as registries, directories, and system files. You can only attach to the drives and share on the remote computers. In short, it is not a network backup/restore solution. If you are trying to locate and back up domain controllers (especially pre-2000 servers), don't even try. Windows 2000 Backup refuses to even allow them a visitor's visa onto the source list.

Sure, you can attach with the appropriate permissions and pull over user files, but that's about it. This means that Backup is not really useful for managing a mission-critical DR project from a single server devoted to DR. If you manage a server farm, performing backups on each machine is a huge waste of time and resources and a drain on IT budget. The only advantage is better bandwidth, as we will later discuss. You would have to upgrade to a third-party suite if you want to devote to one server the job of being the backup system.

On the other hand, the Removable Storage Service is a great addition to Windows 2000. Earlier versions of Windows provided no professional means of managing complex and sophisticated storage media devices, such as DLT Libraries that automatically change out tape cartridges, read bar codes, and the like. We had to rely on third-party tools for these, which was a bit limiting. This is one area that belongs to the operating system. When we switched from one vendor to another, we would lose the entire storage setup. Now the storage device is managed and controlled at the OS level, just like a hard disk or CD-R or a printer.

The most that Backup promises you is the ability to back up Exchange's system and data files, and the tape drive must be local to the Exchange server. Many mail and group-ware administrators want to be able to back up multiple Exchange servers across the enterprise from a single DR location. If you use good equipment and sensibly manage an Exchange server, it is unlikely you'll ever need to restore the machine and the databases in their entirety.

Any good Exchange administrator will confirm that 99 percent of all requests for restores to Exchange come from whining users who stand in your doorway drooping like basset-hound ears and dribbling out sentences like, "I can't find my Inbox folder. I think it got deleted somehow."

The pro-backup utilities allow you to expand and collapse a mailbox tree in the backup software like an unfolding deck of cards. Trust us, when you have more than a handful of users (we manage about 3,000 on just one of our 67 domains), your Exchange DR will be mostly about restoring a folder. Backing up and restoring folders piecemeal is often referred to as a "brick level" or "object level" backup and recovery.

Database servers are also an example of specialist applications where machines are almost entirely devoted to the database. It is virtually impossible to back up a SQL server, such as Oracle or SQL Server, while it is in use. The leading backup vendors have special agents that can attach to these servers as actual "users" (not domain accounts) created inside the database environment. If you only have a handful of users on a server, or there are times at night when there is no chance anyone will be using the server, then you would probably get away with shutting down the database and all related services and backing up the closed files. In an enterprise level DR project, this would be a practice unbecoming of the backup administrator, unless the entire domain was offline for maintenance.

Some advanced software suites come with "push" agents that send the files to the backup server. ARCServe, for example, provides backup agents that pump files to the server. The agents connect to the servers over IP or IPX, and any open files that could not be pushed, or that were in use, are marked for later transmission when they are no longer being used.

And we have only really discussed backups. Restoring files on running systems can be even trickier because you are attempting to replace a file, not make a copy of it. High-end software suites allow you to restore by session, media, object in a tree, and so on.

As a rule of thumb, you will need something a little more robust than Backup in a heterogeneous, mixed version, multi-vendor/OEM, chock-full-of-nuts environment. However, there will always be a need to use Backup. We even know of one sad case where the Exchange administrator of a Fortune 500 company got so tired of waiting for the backup operator to get around to doing an open files/brick level system on her server that she went with Backup and "the heck with mailboxes." Next day, the CIO came over to whine about recovering his deleted mailbox, which he swore was more valuable than his 401K. It was the Backup administrator who was relocated to an oilrig in the North Sea, not the Exchange administrator.

Performing a Backup

In this section, we'll show you how to actually perform a backup using the Backup utility. The whole thing starts with creating a media pool. Throughout this example, we'll assume that you're using a simple media pool composed of 4mm DAT cartridges.

 Note   You also use Backup to create an emergency repair disk (ERD). This is covered in Appendix B, which covers Resource Kit utilities.

Creating a Media Pool

Attach your DAT drive, or whatever removable storage device you have, to the computer. If you have not already done so, go to Add/Remove New Hardware in the Control Panel and install the device. If the device was installed at the time you installed Windows 2000, the Backup media pool will probably be using it already. If not, you will have to manually create the pool and allocate it to Backup, or nest the new pool in the Backup media pool.

In Computer Management or Remote Storage, expand the Removable Storage option and select Media Pools. Right-click Media Pool and select Create Media Pool from the pop-up list that appears. The Properties page for the media pool is presented, allowing you to select from dozens of supported media formats and technologies. This is illustrated in Figure 17-4.

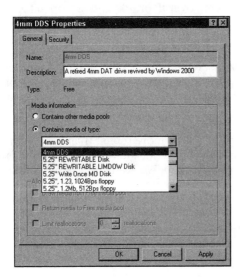

Figure 17-4: The Removable Storage Tape Drive Properties media selection list

Rights and Permissions

As with all Windows server platforms, you need certain rights and privileges to work with files. Windows 2000 will not allow you to back up or restore files for which you cannot claim rights to by virtue of your membership in a group, or ownership.

Here are the rules: If you are the owner of a file or folder, you can back up and restore the file on your domain or local computer, as long as you have logged on at the machine or have direct ownership. You must have access to the files in the form of one or more user permissions, such as read, write, or full access. There is no way to back up files if they are not yours.

Backup software services must use the account of a backup operator to access and back up files regardless of the rights associated with these files. If you are the administrator or you are a member of the Backup Operators group in a local group, you can sign on and perform backup and restores to the local machine.

To perform backup and restores from and to any machine on the network, you must be either the administrator (signed on as) or be a member of the domain's Backup Operator's group. As a domain Backup Operator, you can also do backups and restores in another domain if there is a trust between the domains.

Remember, you cannot back up the system-state of another computer even if you are the Angel of Administration, which is obnoxious to say the least. The advanced evolution of the Windows 2000 sub system must have a lot to do with such a restriction. We will later demonstrate a neat workaround that makes full use of Backup on every server and computer on the network while performing the backups from a single backup server, running any choice of backup software.

Source and Destination

We refer to sources and destinations when talking about backing up . . . on any system. So, open Backup and click the Backup tab. In the left pane—your backup source—click the + box to expand your Desktop, as illustrated in Figure 17-5. You may have to also expand My Computer to expose the System State node of the source tree. In the Backup destination field, select your tape drive. Notice that if a tape drive is not installed, you can back up to a file. You can also back up to the media pool you created, but we will save that for a command line batch example.

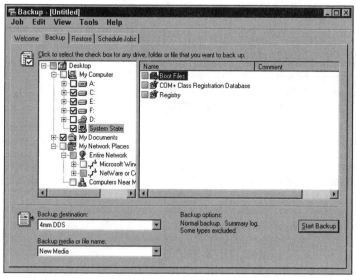

Figure 17-5: Selecting source and destination in Backup

Now click the Start Backup button to open the Backup Job Information dialog box. In this dialog box, you have the option to describe the backup. Windows 2000 inserts the time and date as the description. It also selects the time and date as the default label information.

The Advanced button allows you to select the backup type, as we discussed earlier. Select Normal, which you would do for any first full backup. You can also select Verify after backup, which means that Backup will compare the files backed up with the source data.

Verifying backups is not a bad idea, but you must understand that it adds a lot of time to the length of a backup; in many cases, it can take almost as long to verify a backup as the backup itself. If you have a lot of files and servers to back up, by the time you get to verify a file (compare the original against the backup), the original may have changed. This is a problem in many data centers where about 30 percent of the files backed up (usually over a 15-hour process) are changed before the verification starts. Many professional packages give you various levels of verification. You can on several, for example, check that the label and catalog information is intact or reliable and then make the assumption that the rest of the tape is okay.

We have had to forgo all forms of verification (except for small jobs) because we back up so much data that there is not much interval time between backups. We have new backups starting back-to-back against old backups, and jobs collide and run into the following day's schedules.

Tip   If you have the time to verify your backups, then by all means do it. But backup algorithms are so advanced today it is highly unlikely that a target file on the tape may not be the same as the source. Rather, set aside a day every so often (we do this once a month) to test restore the most critical data to a development server (even a special folder). You should also run disaster simulations, testing the restoration of the most valuable servers and their data.

Setting Up Schedules

Your next option will be to start the backup now or schedule it to run at a later time. A later time might be when the computer is sure to be idle with no one logged on. On a Windows 2000 server, users can be logged on via terminals, shares, RAS, or via some network connection, like FTP. You might consider shutting down certain services or denying access for the time the backup is running, as earlier discussed.

Notice that the Schedule Jobs option tab is a new addition to Backup. The earlier version on NT4 Backup could only be scheduled to run at a later time as part of a batch job triggered by the Task Scheduler; even that provided only the ability to repeat the process at various intervals. The Schedule Jobs tab on Backup provides a quasi-Backup wizard to achieve the manual task we just performed. There are some useful options in the Scheduler, so take some time to step through it and understand all the features.

To edit the job schedule, you can click on the Schedule Jobs tab at any time and load the Schedule Jobs calendar. You can then double-click on any day of the month to start the Backup Wizard, or you can click a previously defined Job and load the Scheduler dialog boxes.

Once in the Scheduled Job Options dialog box, click the Properties button to open the Schedule Job dialog box. The specifics of your task can now be edited or set in these dialog boxes.

That's really all there is to using Backup. Notice how everything we did here was very GUI-oriented. Now we'll look at how you can use media pools and command line batch switches to run Backup as a covert scheduled backup operation. Later, we'll look into advanced DR backup rotation schemes before getting to Restore operations.

Backup Batch files and Backup Scripts

Backup is accessible at the command line just as its predecessor on Windows NT, and if running `backup` from the command line does not solicit a response from the server, try `NTbackup`. You still call the software using NTBackup, so your NT 4.0 backup scripts can be easily ported. You can type in the command line parameters and switches at the command line or prompt, and the OS will load and run the backup routines (or you can just use the "Run" service).

This is a complex and cryptic way of performing backups, but it has its uses. You can, for example, enter the commands into a batch file and have Windows run the batch file at a future date and time. Let's look at a few parameters and switches briefly; you can find details on all the parameters in the Windows 2000 online help. You will recognize concepts and terms from our earlier discussions. Realize that the command parameters are the same ones set by the GUI, and that there is no different or alternative Backup application at work under the hood.

You begin your command line statement with the words `Ntbackup` backup. The first exercise at this point is to clone the job we had earlier set up in Backup, that of backing up the system-state. But as we earlier promised, we are going to use this backup in conjunction with a remote backup server. Open the command console (what we once called the MS-DOS prompt) and type the following:

```
ntbackup backup systemstate /f  x:\st_w2K001.bkf
```

If you cannot find the command prompt option on your menus, do this:

1. Click Start ⇨ Run.

2. Add the run command path as follows: `cmd.exe`.

3. Click OK.

If you use the command console often, put the path into an icon and stick it on your desktop or in the menus. The .bkf file is the backup script file that was created in our earlier interactive example.

You do not need to enter zillions of parameters to see the backup launch from the command file. In your own time, now open the Help File and search for NTBackup. From here, you can study the parameters and determine how they come together to perform a backup process from a batch file.

Notice that we have made a backup of the system-state in the previous command line example. And as we do not have a backup device defined or installed on the local machine, we have commanded NTBackup to back the system-state into a file named st_w2K001.bkf, which would identify this file as the system-state of Windows 2000 machine number 001. We can now back up this file to a remote system of choice.

Another NTBackup Backup Script

Although Backup is a greatly improved application over its predecessor, there will still be times when you will need to run a backup from a script. Remember, you can only run the script against a local tape or backup device.

Make sure you meet all the previously discussed parameters to perform backups and gain access to shares and drives, such as a capable User ID and login password. You can use the Administrator account, although we don't recommend active use of this account, or you can use an account that is a member of the Administrator Group or Backup Operator group. Before you create your script, you should create a source list of the shares and devices (and all subfolders) you intend to map to and back up. Each source operating system or environment will require peculiar login parameters. You may also need additional protocols and libraries to make the connection, such as Pathworks for a VAX share. To back up a Windows server, you will need NTFS-level access, thus:

```
Domain Name\Administrator (or Backup User ID)
```

The script we will create here will let us connect to a local share. We use the command line Net Use option to map to the data or backup source. Then we use the NTBackup commands to perform the backup. After the backup and any post-processing is done, we will again use the Net Use command to disconnect from the source.

The following script lets us back up a group of files to a Zip drive. Let's go through this step by step:

The following parameters will be used in conjunction with NTBackup:

✦ /D Add a comment

✦ /HC:ON Use hardware compression if possible

✦ /T Backup Type

✦ /L Backup Log (path to the log file)

✦ /TAPE The tape drive identified by a zero-based index item (0 through X)

To check the full list of parameters, open a console and type Ntbackup /? | More.

Tip Wherever possible, use the environment variable enclosed between percent symbols %windir% so that the script can be used on other machines.

The finished script should look like this:

```
NET USE <new map>: \\<Server name>\<share name> <password> or
NET USE K:\\MCDC01\MYBACKUPS\ *******
NTBACKUP BACKUP K: /D "MY WORD FILES" /HC:ON /T NORMAL /L
"WINDIR% \LOGFILES\MYBULOG.LOG" /TAPE:0
NET USE K: /DELETE /Y
```

The script can be thrown into a batch file and run from the task scheduler or the command scheduler. This script is very basic, and you should be able to expand it from here or concoct something for yourself . . . you could create quite an elaborate process.

Tip Always disconnect a share you no longer need so that another process can use it. *Delete* prompts for a final Yes or No, so provide the /Y switch as needed.

You can now schedule this script to run at certain intervals. The Command Scheduler is discussed in Appendix A, and the Task Scheduler is discussed in Appendix B.

Rotation Schemes

A rotation scheme is a plan or system by which you rotate the media you use in your backup sets. At the most basic level, a rotation scheme might be a daily backup using one media. You would not have much of a DR scheme because you would be writing over the media every day; but this is a rotation scheme nonetheless. Another consideration in a rotation scheme is the dividing lines between what you consider archiving: data backup, version control, system-state, and recovery.

Figure 17-6 is one way to look at your data's value from a chronological point of view. The scale is a simple one, but it demonstrates the various stages of usefulness that backups go through, starting from the left. Data in the archival period need not be located on-site and is kept for record-keeping (annual backups), and data in the version control period is stored off- and on-site for access to full weekly generations of the data. Data in the recovery period is stored both on-site and off-site and (depending on the critical nature of the data) is either online or within "arm's length" of recovery.

Figure 17-6: The stages of a backup's life

Let us now expand our rotation scheme. The first option would be to rotate the media every other day, so that you could be backing up to one tape while the alternate is in safekeeping somewhere. If the worst were to happen — a tape gets eaten by the device or something less common — you would still have a backup from the previous day. If the machine were stolen, you would be able to restore it. But rotating every other day is only useful in terms of total data loss. So, you have a full backup of all your files, every day. What about wear and tear? A tape or a platter is a delicate device. Inserting it, removing it every other day, and writing to it over and over can put your data at risk. Tapes do stretch, and they do get stuck in tape drives. Tapes should be saved according to the scratch and save discussion earlier in this chapter.

And then what about version control? Rotating with multiple media, say a week's worth, would ensure that you could roll back to previous states of a file. We could refer to such a concept of versioning as a "generation system" of rotation (not sufficient for critical restore, however). In fact, one such standard generation scheme is widely used by the most seasoned of backup administrators to achieve both these ideals — versioning and protecting media from wear and tear and loss. It is known as the GFS system, or Grandfather, Father, Son system.

Let's create a GFS scheme to run under Backup. Most high-end backup software can create and manage a rotation scheme for you, but for now and always with Backup you will need a legal pad. So now let's put a label on one of our tapes or disks and call it Full, or First Backup or Normal # 1 — whatever designates a complete backup of the system and collection of files and folders.

The first backup of any system is always a full backup, and the reason is simple. Backup, and you, need a catalog or history of all the files in the backup list so that you can access every file for a restore and so that Backup can perform incremental or differential analysis on the media. Do your backup according to the procedures we earlier discussed. You should have had enough practice by now. And you are ready to go from a development or trial backup to a production rotation scheme.

As soon as you have made a full backup set, label the members as discussed and then perform a second full backup (or copy the first). On the first backup set, add the following information to the label:

✦ Full_First: January 2000

✦ Retention: G (for Grandfather) or one year, dd-January-2001

✦ Serial number: Your choosing, or automatically generated

On the second set, add the following information to your labels:

✦ Full_First: Week1-January 2000

✦ Retention: F (for Father) or one month, Week1-February-2000

✦ Serial number: Your choosing, or automatically generated

The next day, choose a second set of media, but this time only the files that have been changed will be backed up using differential or incremental options. Let's say we are doing incrementals for example's sake.

On the incremental set, add the following information to the label:

✦ I_First (or a day of the week): Mon, or First

✦ Retention: Seven days or every Monday

✦ Serial number: Your choosing, or automatically generated

The next day, put in a new backup set and perform the next day's incremental. This time, the label information is Tues or "Second;" retain these media in a seven-day save set and store them in a safe place. On Wednesday, perform the third incremental, and on Thursday, perform the fourth incremental. Let's now look at what we are achieving.

We have created a Grandfather set that we store for a year. If we started this system in January 2000, we will not reuse these tapes until January 2001; the retention period is one year, the oldest saved data you will have.

The second copy set is the Father set of the scheme, and this set gets reused in four weeks' time. In other words, every four weeks the set can be overwritten. This does not mean that we only make a full backup once a month. On the contrary: Notice that we made one full set and four incremental sets, so we are making a full backup once a week and four incremental backups Monday to Thursday. We only retain the weekly set for a month, meaning that at the end of each month you will have five full backup sets, one set for each week, retained for a month, and one set for each month retained for a year.

What about the incremental sets? These sets are the grandchildren of our rotation scheme. We save them for seven days and return them for scratching on the same day the following week. So what we back up on Monday gets written over next Monday, Tuesday gets written over on Tuesday, and so on. This also means that at any given time, your people can access the previous day's data, the previous week's data, the previous month's data, and the previous year's data. What we have created here is a traditional rotation scheme for performing safe and accessible backups of data.

There are variations on this theme, and you will need more than just seven of whatever media you are using. For example, for the full GFS rotation, you would need the following for a single server that used one DLT tape drive:

✦ Daily backups (incremental, rotated weekly): 4+

✦ Weekly Full (rotated monthly): 4+

✦ Monthly Full (rotated annually): 12+

✦ Total tapes: 20+

The best days for such a rotation scheme are Monday-Thursday for incremental and Friday for full. Even on big systems, you're unlikely to be doing an incremental into the following day. And on Friday you have the whole day and the weekend to do the full backup, at a time when the system is most idle. You could start after the last person leaves on a Friday, and you would still have about 48 hours of backup time to play with.

Restoring Data

We left the subject of data restoring until later because it is usually the least time-intensive task to perform, and hopefully you will not be asked to restore data too often. Backup has a restore option that lets you select the files you need to restore from the source (the catalog or Backup history), as illustrated in Figure 17-7. You also have the option of restoring some or all of the files to original location or an alternative. Backup, NTBackup, and all third-party software restores are handled in the same way. The following checklist thus applies to any restore you are doing.

✦ Always make sure that restoring files to their original locations will not result in loss of data. While it seems illogical to make such a consideration, it often happens that restoring files results in further damage. For example, if a file is corrupt but up to date, and you restore a file that is not corrupt but out of date, how much better off are you? It may be better to investigate saving the contents of the file you want to replace or salvaging what you can before overwriting the file. You could restore to an alternative location or rename the corrupt file. Better to check if a "corrupt" file is recoverable before you blow it away.

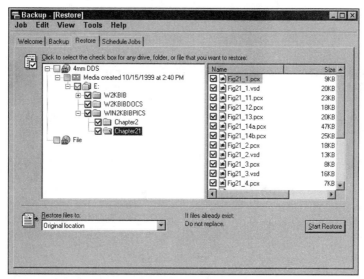

Figure 17-7: Selecting files to restore in Backup

✦ Also, consider the consequences of restoring. Windows 2000 stores all manner of information about a file, the folder it's in, the volume, EFS, DFS, RFS, quota information, share-points, archive information, and so on. Restoring a file restores not only the contents but also any attributes and information known about the file at the time it was backed up. Anything new applied to the file and its relationship with the rest of the universe will not be recorded in the restore. A good example is restoring a folder that several new groups and users were given access to after the last backup. The restore will now block these new users, and a critical process might bring things crashing down when you turn your back. Again, restore to an alternate location if you are unsure of the results.

✦ Block user access while performing a restore to original locations. There is nothing that causes more problems than having users trying to open files that have not been completely restored. Blocking access will result in calls to the helpdesk, so make sure customer service or help desk representatives know about the process. And don't waste your time calling people to tell them about the block. If it is a big share-point, you will always have someone messing things up. On the other hand, if you are restoring a share that needs to be accessed by a critical process coming from another machine or software, let the owners of these processes know before their applications crash.

✦ Always check who is connected to the destination computer and what files they have open. If you restore to files that are open, you will at the least get access errors, and at the worst, you could corrupt the files you are restoring. You can check who is connected to the server by opening Computer Management (Server Manager on NT 4.0 and earlier) and drill down to the Sessions information under the Shared Folders leaf. You can also see who is connected to what by running the NET SESSIONS and NET FILE commands at the Command Console. NET SESSIONS and NET FILE work for all versions of Windows Server.

One last item before we leave Restore. We spent a lot of time digging in the Remote Storage Manager looking for a place to erase, format, and catalog media. After all, RSM is where it's all supposed to happen for media. We guess the hacks at Microsoft let this one slip by them, and we let them know. All is not lost. We discovered the missing erase and format utility in Backup. It is on the Restore tab, of all places, as illustrated in Figure 17-8. Just right-click the tape icon and format away your precious media.

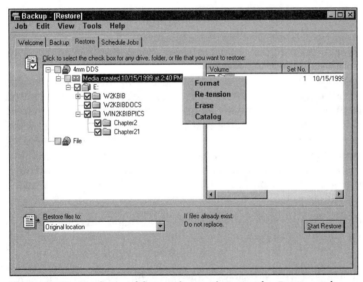

Figure 17-8: Erasing and formatting options on the Restore tab of Backup

Tape Location

It is very important to remove your valuable rotation sets from the premises as soon as the backup job is done, every day, and as long as online media are available. There are many reliable media pick-up companies in all cities in the United States. If you do not have access to a media pick-up firm, find a safe place (like a safe deposit box at a bank) and move your media to this remote location every day. You could also buy a small fireproof safe and keep that on-site.

There are two chief reasons for moving the media off-site: First, if a disaster were to take out your building, it would take out your backups as well. Here in Hurricane Land, Florida, USA, we move backups to a secure location every day.

Second, tapes and backup media grow legs and may walk out of your offices. Worse, someone may access your tapes and steal sensitive information without you knowing it.

We have a very secure computer room, and some time in the latter part of the last millennium, we removed a tape and then left the secure environment to fetch a new label. We were gone two minutes and returned to find the tape gone. We thought we had misplaced it and had to repeat a five-hour backup all over again. Later, we learned that in those two minutes, another administrator had asked the computer room staff for a spare tape and was given our unlabeled tape, thinking it was blank. Lesson learned: Never leave your backup media unattended, even for two minutes.

Backup Bandwidth

Bandwidth is an important item in your Hardware/Media/Support Level equation. From the get-go, you should forget about doing any significant backup over a WAN or Internet connection unless you have upwards of a 1.5Mbit pipe to the source. Anything less (unless it is a very small collection of files) will not provide a suitable facility for backing up. The only time you might try backing up over a low bandwidth connection (and for backup, low bandwidth could be considered anything under 10Mbit) is if you need to grab a handful of important files. To back up a remote registry over a 64Kbit pipe would take several hours.

On the other hand, we routinely back up thousands of server shares over a 10Mbit Ethernet network; if you have a 100Mbit backbone and have servers sitting directly on that, all the better. You need to remember, though, that even a 100Mbit backbone is only as valuable as the speed of the server bus, network links, hard disk I/O, and the abilities of the backup devices.

The minimum rate of backup you can expect over a 10Mbit network is between 15MB and 45MB per minute, depending on the backup device. Local tape drives on fast computers using SCSI technology and high-end hardware can even achieve levels of around 200MB per minute, and even higher on RAID systems and extremely high-speed disk arrays. However, as mentioned earlier, it can be very expensive to place a high-end backup device on every server.

What you then need to do is work out how much data needs to be backed up and then figure out how long it is going to take you to back up all that data. If the data is mission critical, you may want to back it up more often. Remember, data changes every minute of the day. Database applications can see as much as 20 percent of the data changing on the low end and as much as 80 percent changing on the high end. E-mail systems are changing just about every second of the day in busy organizations.

Here is a very simple formula to work out how long it will take to back up your data. Let's say we want to back up X amount of data to a certain device in Y time. Starting with the desired unknown Y, we would want to first figure out how much data we are going to try to back up on the local machine or over the network. After you have calculated this, your equation will resemble the following:

$$Y = S/T$$

Here, Y = time, S = amount of data in megabytes, and T = transfer time in minutes of hardware (locally or over the network). The data transfer or backup rate of the DLT 7000 is around 300MB per minute (hauling data off the local hard drives). Thus, your equation would be $Y = 2000/300$, and 2GB would thus take just over six minutes to back up. Factor in another two minutes or more per 100MB for latency, cataloging, files in use, database updating, and so on. You would be safe to say that 2GB of data could get backed up in less than ten minutes. Over the local area network, you would be safe to divide the transfer rate by a factor of ten. The same 2GB over the network would take over an hour to back up.

Hardware and Media Formats

Choosing hardware and media depends on the applications, size of the data pool or resources, size of the network (number of servers), number of users, critical nature of the data, and so on. In multi-server environments, you would be best off looking to invest in a tape library system. These sophisticated devices cost an arm and a leg (anywhere from $6,000 to $35,000), but what you will save in time and frustration, as well as speed of restore, is worth it. Other choices of backup media include writeable compact discs, remote storage volumes, removable disks such as zip disks and flopticals, and DVD.

Earlier in this chapter, we discussed Quality of Service and Service Level. Now comes the time to consider what we discussed when planning hardware purchase.

4mm Digital Audiotape

Still one of the most popular technologies, 4mm Digital Audiotape (DAT) is widely used in all business sizes. It now comes in three formats: DDS-1, DDS-2, and DDS-3 — holding 2GB, 8GB, and 12GB, respectively. A single DDS-3 tape can thus hold as much as 24GB with high-end hardware compression.

The only major drawback of the DAT format is that the header is read every time the tape is used for backups or restores. This makes the format less hardy than its competitors (even though a single tape will likely live to 300 or more runs). Another problem with DAT is that the cartridge is not hardy and it does not take much to damage it. We have seen several situations where a DAT was taken out of the drive and the media got caught up inside the system . . . unknown to the operator who would then walk away leaving a trail of black tape streaming out behind him or her.

8mm Digital Audiotape

An improvement over its 4mm sibling, the 8mm format can hold up to 40GB of data with hardware compression running at 2:1. Another major advantage is the speed of 8mm DAT. It can typically back up 40GB of data in less than five hours. The Sony AME tapes are the most popular on the market and offer improved performance and reliability.

The 8mm cartridge is also dinky, however, and needs to be handled with care in busy server room environments. Dropping them onto the floor or stepping on them can ruin the tape. The hardware, like the 4mm hosts, can also be unkind to the media. We have had several situations where tapes got stuck inside the drives.

Digital Linear Tape

Digital Linear Tape (DLT) has become one of the most popular tape formats in high-end server operations for several reasons. It is fast, reliable, hardy, and you can store a lot of data on a single high-end version of the format. DLT is a Quantum format, which was introduced mostly to compete against DAT in the mainframe, midrange, and UNIX platform arena. The adoption of DLT in the Windows and NetWare server environments has accelerated the success of the media.

DLT comes in several versions: DLT 2000, DLT 4000, DLT5000, and DLT 7000. Capacity is 10GB on the low-end format (2000), to as much as 70GB compressed on the 7000 format. While DAT tends to be a faster technology, many manufacturers have introduced high-speed SCSI interface library systems capable of holding many drives and providing technology to deliver backup/restore on a continual basis.

The DLT cartridge is very sturdy, which makes it ideal in busy environments where tapes are moved around in robotic library systems all the time. Dropping a DLT cartridge or sending it flying across the server room floor (which often happens when the off-site delivery arrives and the backup admin has forgotten to remove the nightly backups from the system) will not make the slightest dent. You can also keep a DLT tape in service for a year or more, which makes it easy on the budget. DLT hardware is pretty sturdy; we have opened units in-house to reconnect slipped leader bands and to clean simple mechanical components that get clogged with dust and debris.

DAT and DLT technology differ in that DAT stores data in diagonal stripes across the media. The data is laid down using helical scan technology. Helical scanning is achieved by rotating a drumhead across the media surface. DLT on the other hand lays down its data horizontally along the tape in tracks, by running the tape across the stationary head, much like the recording technology in four- and eight-track audiocassettes.

DLT also travels well, which is an important consideration if you manage a number of remote sites and they depend on you for supplies. We typically use retired DLT media, which might have another 50 runs of life left, to make a final annual backup of a system. This tape is then sent off-site into storage forever, only called into service on the remote chance that reference to old data is needed.

Advanced Intelligent Tape

For extremely large quantities of data and backup environments that never rest, the Advanced Intelligent Tape, or AIT, is another format from the Exabyte-Sony alliance. AIT tapes can typically stay in service for as many as 400 runs or backups per cartridge. Sony created a backup technology format for this media called Advanced Metal Evaporated (AME). The material is tough and comprises a carbon protective coating that keeps the tapes from "burning up" in the high-speed drives.

Tape libraries can support up to eight terabytes of data. So for speed and volume, this format is ideal for an online system for backup QoS levels 3 and lower. An advanced version of AME consists of a small EEPROM chip that is housed in the cartridge. This chip holds backup information, cataloging, and backup restore logs. The downside of AIT is that it is more expensive than the tape formats earlier discussed.

QIC

QIC is the acronym for Quarter-inch Cartridge and represents the most popular format for small business. The latest Travan cartridges (the T-series) can now back up as much as 8GB of data per cartridge. The casings are sturdy, making the format durable and easy to handle in situations where company servers are usually behind closets, in office corners, or on factory floors.

Unfortunately, QIC does not scale to large systems of magazine-loaded changers and robotic library systems. This also makes the format less than an ideal partner for RSS solutions. On the other hand, QIC hardware is also very affordable, costing $400 or less for top-of-the-line models.

Disaster Recovery

Data loss and disaster recovery cost us billions every year. In 1998 alone, U.S. companies spent almost $12 billion just *recovering* data from downed systems. According to David Smith, economics professor at Pepperdine University, every incident of data loss on a single PC costs about $2,557 to fix. According to Smith's research, six percent of PCs will lose data in any given year. Smith's figures do not include the costs of lost business and opportunity from crashes, nor the cost of replacing data that could not be recovered.

According to Smith's findings, hardware failure, human error, software corruption, and viruses are the leading causes of data loss. Now you know why we place so much effort on our backup strategy. However, just having a backup available isn't enough. You need to plan for disasters before they occur, and have a system set up to deal with both large and small catastrophes.

DR Planning

The backup administration team should take disaster recovery planning seriously. Unfortunately, this is not always the case, and when disaster strikes, the administrators are less than prepared and leave their companies unnecessarily exposed. There are a number of items that should be on the Backup Administrator's checklist. If you do not have a checklist, or you are new not only to DR-Backup-Restore but also to Windows 2000, the following checklist will become a working draft for your own situation:

✦ Understand the needs of the departments that rely on your systems. These people take it for granted you understand their needs. So if you don't meet with them to discuss special requirements, service level, quality of service, restore levels, and so on, they won't tell you.

✦ Understand the systems that apply to the departments in the previous item. If you are backing up SQL servers, take a course in management or administration of the products you are covering. You should make it your business to know how data is stored, recovered, moved, and manipulated around your network. If you don't understand the architecture, security requirements, storage requirements, versions, service packs, and, well, just about everything else about the system, you can't provide a reliable service. If you are backing up Exchange, for example, you should at least understand its critical components, such as the information store, mailbox structure, directory, and so on.

✦ Make it your business to understand everything you need to about storage systems, media formats, software, scheduling, and more. You should also understand the various bussing architectures, like SCSI and SCSI-2, and how hardware co-exists with the Windows 2000 operating system.

✦ Establish policy and protocol with respect to backup and recovery. Let staff know what to expect from you in the event of a restore requirement, system recovery, and so on.

✦ Establish parameters for Quality of Service and ensure these parameters are published and circulated. If you believe your backup equipment is providing a less-than-reliable service to your organization, make sure your superiors understand this.

✦ Document all the time. Create a backup and restore manual and keep it up to date. This will ensure that your systems and procedures are secure in the event of your absence.

✦ Using the techniques and procedures discussed previously, establish backup-restore procedures for systems and system-states, data and data recovery, and archiving and remote storage. Keep trying to improve your procedures. If you feel your backup procedures need improving, and they always do, keep trying new things (but do not go to production until you are satisfied with your switch to the new methods).

✦ Perform disaster recovery trials, train, and perform weekly or monthly DR drills. This is extremely important, and we discuss it in more depth than any item on this list.

Policy and Protocol

Establishing policy and protocol is a vital aspect of disaster recovery planning. Policy might include how you perform rotation, the level of restore (agreeing that a critical restore will take place within x minutes or hours of a request), establishing rules for requesting restores, and so on.

On our policy document, we set fines for restores that are required on the same day from the off-site depot, because the depot charges us $40 to bring media to the site that is outside the regular pickup and drop-off hours. This charge should not come out of the Backup Administration or MIS budget, but from the department requesting the restore.

Protocol includes the formalities you establish that govern backup and restore procedures. Although it is policy to send data off-site and charge departments for screwing up their data, it is protocol that requires them to first open a ticket with the help desk or customer support center before a restore job can be started up.

When we get calls to restore data from faceless names out of thousands of users, the first thing we do is send them packing to the help desk. Help desk explains the protocol that requires them to go through the formality of opening the ticket. Help desk explains the policies that require the callers to clear restore requests with supervisors, determines why the restore has been ordered, takes names and contact information, and makes sure that chargeable restores get debited to the accounts of the correct departments.

Documentation

Keep a working document explaining all policy and protocol, backup procedures, rotation schemes, restore procedures, passwords, locations of media, types of media, types of hardware, service agreements, media inventory, locations of server images, and more. You should, as best as you can, provide illustrations that identify the locations of backup hardware on server room racks, media, backup server equipment, and so on.

A good backup manual can go very far and be a godsend many times over. The document will also ensure that future generations of backup administrators can step into your shoes when you get promoted to CTO; or that the company is not left standing in quicksand when you get hit by a bus. The manual ensures that at all times there is reliable information pertaining to the setup and configuration of backup software and routines.

Some months ago, our company said goodbye to the backup administrator who left us without any documentation whatsoever. It has taken us several months to get on top of his legacy, and the effort has not been disaster-free. For example: Administrators cleaning up dead accounts came across a user ID that was not clearly marked as having anything to do with backups. So after no one owned up to the account, it was deleted. The following morning, all SQL Server and MS Exchange backups crashed. The deleted account belonged to the push agents, who used the facility for local and domain logon.

Trials, Training, DR Drills, and Action Planning

Trials and DR drills are perhaps the most important disaster recovery prepared-ness exercises you can perform. No matter how well you are doing backups and data archiving, no matter how scientific your restore procedures, or how smooth your deleted file recovery efforts, nothing can prepare you better for meeting a disaster head-on than experience.

Network administrators often use the cliché that "there is no substitute for baptism by fire." But why get thrown into a disaster completely green? Losing a database server or a mail server can be extremely traumatic, especially if a lot of people, and in many cases, the whole company and Service Level, depend on you getting the services back up as quickly as possible.

Make it policy to regularly practice the recovery of systems and data as if a real disaster was in the making. Of course, such drills have to be taken offline and per-formed in safe environments. If your systems are reliable, you probably will not have to perform a real delicate disaster recovery often. But when it happens and you are faced with unexpected items that stymie you along the way, the process can be very unnerving.

Performing a mock disaster or system recovery drill will bring to the surface criti-cal items that could impair a safe return to service of your systems. Also, knowing in advance to what degree you can get things back to normal is very important.

Finally, when disaster does strike, the following policy and protocol comes from valuable experience.

✦ Immediately form a disaster recovery team and appoint a "PR" person who will be responsible for keeping staff updated. There is nothing worse than hav-ing to repeat to hundreds of people when you expect things to return to nor-mal. If you are dealing with huge system crashes, establish a hotline your people can call into for updates.

✦ Advise supervisors and staff that you will report the situation to them on an hourly or half-hourly basis, and request they refrain from hanging over your shoulders in the computer rooms. Assure them that you will keep them posted and that they will get first-hand information should the situation change for the better or worse.

✦ Make sure your help desk has the correct answers and has the latest information as well. Help desk can save you from continuous requests for updates. Once users learn they can get reliable information from the help desk, they will not bother you during trying times.

✦ Meet with the members of the disaster recovery team and forbid anyone from trying anything until you have unanimously decided on procedure. Nothing is more damaging than having staff running around like headless chickens trying to get things back to normal as soon as possible and making things much worse in the process. Make sure every member of the team understands his or her role and has the right tools and information. Include only technical staff that can contribute directly to the problem at hand.

Summary

This chapter dealt more with backup practice and protocol than actual software or technology. Most applications perform backups and restores in the same way. And the Microsoft tape and media APIs ensure that at the file backup level the data state resulting (integrity) from all backup technology is no better or worse from vendor to vendor.

However, some third-party vendors do have software that better manages the backup process. Backup is a useful utility, but in many respects, you will likely use it for quick and dirty work or for recovery disks and ASR media. It is not a high-end utility for the application and data services that Windows 2000 is cut out to provide.

In addition, we stressed how important it is to understand the difference between data backup and system backup. We also gave you food for thought needed to allow you to manage backup procedure (QOST and SL) at the level becoming of a professional administrator.

✦　　✦　　✦

The Registry

The registry is the core repository of configuration information in Windows 2000, storing information about the operating system, applications, and user environment on standalone workstations and member servers (non-domain controllers).

The Purpose of the Registry

Early versions of the Windows operating system family, such as Windows 3.x, stored most of their configuration information in *initialization,* or .ini files. These files were text files containing various sections that stored settings for a variety of properties such as device drivers, application and document associations, user environment settings, and so on. Windows applications used .ini files as well to store their configuration settings. Even today in Windows 2000 and applications, .ini files are still a widely used mechanism for storing user, application, and operating system settings. A quick search of your hard drive for .ini files will illustrate that fact.

Although they provide a simple means of storing and retrieving settings, .ini files offer some disadvantages, particularly for storing important OS settings such as device drivers, configuration data, user environment settings, and so on. First, Windows 2000 needs a fault tolerant system for maintaining its settings to avoid the problem of an unbootable system due to a corrupt or missing .ini file. This information also needs to be secure, something .ini files can't really provide. Finally, managing all the settings needed to keep a Windows 2000 system up and running, plus applications and user-related settings, would be overwhelming if .ini files were the only solution. The registry comes to the rescue.

In Windows 2000, like Windows NT before it, the registry stores configuration information about the system's hardware and software, both operating system- and application-related. The registry also stores information about users, including security settings and rights, working environment (desktop properties, folders, and so on), and much more. However, unlike Windows NT, it no longer stores domain user and computer accounts or information related to "network" objects; this job now belongs to the Active Directory, as explained in Chapter 2 and the chapters in Part III.

Caution   When you promote a member server to a domain controller, all registry settings that also apply to a domain controller server, such as the desktop settings, are absorbed into Active Directory. But when you demote the server, the original registry settings are not restored, and you are returned to a clean registry. (The demotion wizard even asks you for a new Administrator password because the original account is lost.) Keep this in mind when you demote a domain controller, because Active Directory can easily outgrow the host machine it was originally installed on.

The following list explains some of the ways certain components make use of the registry:

✦ **Setup:** When you install Windows 2000, Setup builds the registry based on your selections (or automated selections) during installation. Setup also modifies the registry when you add or remove hardware from the system.

✦ **Application setup:** The Setup program for an application typically will modify the registry to store the application's settings at installation. It also will typically read the registry to determine which components, if any, are already installed.

✦ **Applications:** Most applications that store their settings in the registry modify those settings during program startup, shutdown, or general operation to store changes made to application settings both by the application or the user.

✦ **Ntdetect:** The `Ntdetect.com` program executes at system startup to detect hardware and attached peripherals, and it stores information in the registry about those items for use in subsequent boot steps to initialize device drivers for identified devices.

✦ **The kernel:** The Windows 2000 kernel reads the registry at startup to determine which device drivers to load and in which order, along with other driver initialization parameters.

✦ **Device drivers:** Most device drivers store their configuration and operating settings in the registry, reading the registry at initialization to determine how to load and function.

✦ **System:** The Windows 2000 operating system as a whole uses the registry to store information about services, installed applications, document and OLE (Object Linking and Embedding) associations, networking, user settings, and other properties.

✦ **Administrative tools:** One of the main functions of utilities such as the Control Panel, the various MMC consoles, and standalone administration utilities is typically to modify the registry. In this context, these utilities provide a user interface for registry modification.

✦ **The Registry Editors:** Windows 2000 provides two utilities, `regedit.exe` and `regedt32.exe`, that enable you to view and modify the registry directly. While you'll want to perform most modification tasks using other utilities, the Registry Editors make possible tasks such as direct modification, selected registry backup, and others.

The registry is in many ways the "brain" of the Windows 2000 OS. Nearly everything the OS does is affected by or affects the registry. For that reason, it's important to not only understand the registry's function and how to modify it, but also how to protect it from catastrophe or unauthorized access. The following sections explain the structure of the registry and how to manage it.

The Registry Structure

The registry forms a hierarchical (tree) database with five primary branches called *subtrees.* A subtree can contain *keys,* which function as containers within the subtree for *subkeys* and *values.* Subkeys are sub-branches within a key. Values are the individual settings within a key or subkey. Perhaps the best way to understand the registry structure is to view it through one of the Registry Editors, as shown in Figure 18-1. (You'll find detailed information about the Registry Editors later in this chapter.)

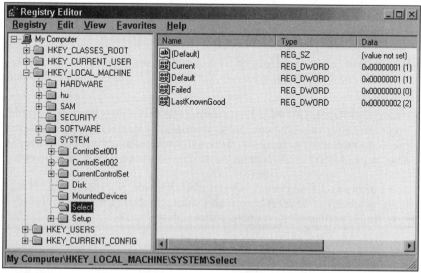

Figure 18-1: The Registry Editors show the structure of the registry — a hierarchical tree, with each subtree serving as a primary branch.

There are two physical subtrees in the Windows 2000 registry: HKEY_LOCAL_ MACHINE and HKEY_USERS, the former containing system- and hardware-related settings and the latter containing user-related settings. These two physical subtrees are divided into the five logical subtrees you see in the Registry Editors. Organizing the registry into five logical subtrees makes it easier to navigate and understand the logical structure of the registry. The five logical subtrees are as follows:

✦ **HKEY_LOCAL_MACHINE:** This subtree, often abbreviated as HKLM, stores settings that apply to the local machine, defining hardware and operating system settings that are the same regardless of which user is logged on. The settings in HKLM, for example, define device drivers, memory, installed hardware, and startup properties.

✦ **HKEY_CLASSES_ROOT:** Abbreviated HKCR, this subtree contains file association data, such as associating a document file type with its parent application and defining the actions taken on a given document type for various tasks (open, play, edit, and so on). This subtree is built from HKLM\SOFTWARE\ Classes and HKEY_CURRENT_USER\SOFTWARE\Classes, with the value in HKCU taking precedence. HKCR provides user- and computer-specific class registration, providing different class registrations for each user. This per-user class registration is different from previous versions of Windows that provided the same registration data for all users.

✦ **HKEY_CURRENT_USER:** This subtree (HKCU) stores the user profile for the user who is currently logged on to the system locally. Settings include desktop configuration and folders, network and printer connections, environment variables, Start menu and applications, and other settings that define the user operating environment and UI. This subtree is actually an alias of HKEY_USERS\ *SID,* where *SID* is the security ID of the current user.

✦ **HKEY_USERS:** This subtree (HKU) stores user profile data for users who log on to the computer locally, as well as the default user profile for the local computer.

✦ **HKEY_CURRENT_CONFIG:** This subtree (HKCC) stores hardware configuration data about the local computer identified at startup and includes settings relating to device assignments, device drivers, and so on. This subtree is an alias of HKLM\SYSTEM\CurrentControlSet\Hardware Profiles\Current.

Each of the subtrees listed previously represents a *hive.* Microsoft defines a hive as describing a body of keys, subkeys, and values rooted at the top of the registry hierarchy. An individual hive comprises three files:

✦ A registry file, in most cases stored in `systemroot\System32\Config`. This file contains the registry structure and settings for the given hive.

✦ A log file, stored in `systemroot\System32\Config`. This file serves as a transaction log for modifications to the hive registry file.

✦ A repair (backup) file, located in `systemroot\System32\Repair`. This is a backup copy of the registry file.

Table 18-1 lists the registry hives and their corresponding file names.

Table 18-1 Registry Hive Files	
Hive	**Files**
HKEY_LOCAL_MACHINE\SAM	`Sam` and `Sam.log`
HKEY_LOCAL_MACHINE\SECURITY	`Security` and `Security.log`
HKEY_LOCAL_MACHINE\SOFTWARE	`Software` and `Software.log`
HKEY_LOCAL_MACHINE\SYSTEM	`System` and `System.alt`
HKEY_CURRENT_CONFIG	`System` and `System.log`
HKEY_CURRENT_USER	`Ntuser.dat` and `Ntuser.dat.log`
HKEY_USERS\DEFAULT	`Default` and `Default.log`

With the exception of `Ntuser.dat` and `Ntuser.data.log`, the hive files are stored in `systemroot\System32\Config`. The `Ntuser.dat` and `Ntuser.dat.log` files are stored in `\Documents` and `Settings\user` for systems with clean Windows 2000 installations or upgrades from Windows 9x. Systems upgraded from Windows NT store the `Ntuser.dat` and `Ntuser.dat.log` files in `systemroot\Profiles\user`.

Windows 2000 uses a process know as *flushing* to ensure a reliable, working copy of the registry at all times, guarding against attempted registry changes not being completed. Attempted changes to the registry, when a given number of seconds has passed or the modifying application explicitly requests it, are flushed or saved to disk. The following explains how flushing occurs for all but the SYSTEM hive (`HKLM\SYSTEM`):

1. Modified data is written to the hive log file so that the data can be reconstructed if the system halts or fails before the data is written to the registry file.

2. The log file is flushed upon completion of a successful update to the log file.

3. Windows 2000 marks the first sector of the registry file to indicate that it is in the process of being modified (dirty).

4. The changes are written to the registry file.

5. Upon successful completion of the write operation, the first sector is modified to indicate successful completion (clean).

When Windows 2000 reads the hive files to construct the registry, it checks the status of each file. If the system failed during a previous registry update operation, the registry file will still be marked as dirty. In that situation, Windows 2000 attempts to recover the registry file using the log file. The changes identified in the log file are applied to the registry file, and if successful, the file is marked as clean.

The SYSTEM hive behaves a little differently from the others in terms of fault tolerance. The `systemroot\System32\Config` folder includes a file named `System.alt`, which is a clean copy of the current System registry file. After a successful modification of the System file, it is copied to `System.alt` for use as a backup. If a problem occurs with the System hive file during boot, Windows 2000 switches to `System.alt`.

Having a backup of the registry is critical to being able to recover a failed system. Although Windows 2000 provides fault-tolerant management of the registry hive files, you should employ some additional procedures to ensure a valid, working copy of the registry. See the section "Backing Up and Securing the Registry" later in this chapter for detailed information. You'll also find coverage of backup procedures in Chapter 17.

Registry Hive Files

As we mentioned earlier, the registry is divided into five logical hives. This section looks at each hive in a bit more detail.

HKEY_LOCAL_MACHINE

As explained earlier, the HKEY_LOCAL_MACHINE (HKLM) root key contains hardware and operating system settings for the local computer. HKLM contains the following subkeys:

- ✦ **HARDWARE:** This key stores the physical hardware configuration for the computer. Windows 2000 recreates this key each time the system boots successfully, ensuring up-to-date hardware detection/configuration.

- ✦ **SAM:** The Security Account Manager key contains security data for users and groups for the local machine.

- ✦ **SECURITY:** This key contains data that defines the local security policy.

- ✦ **SOFTWARE:** This key stores data about installed software.

- ✦ **SYSTEM:** This key stores data about startup parameters, device drivers, services, and other system-wide properties.

When corresponding settings are found in the HKCU key, those settings override settings in HKLM for the current user for certain data. If no corresponding settings exist, those in HKLM are used. For certain items such as device drivers, the data in HKLM is always used regardless of whether the data also resides in HKCU.

HKEY_USERS

The HKEY_USERS (HKU) key stores user profile data for users who log on to the computer locally, as well as the default user profile for the local computer. It contains a subkey for each user whose profile is stored on the computer, in addition to a key for the default user (.DEFAULT). It's virtually impossible to identify a given user from the SID, but you wouldn't want to try to modify settings in this key anyway except through the administrative tools that modify the registry. If you do need to modify settings directly, use the HKCU key instead.

HKEY_CURRENT_USER

As explained previously, the HKCU key is an alias for the KHC*SID* key, where *SID* is the SID for the current local user. In other words, HKCU points to the registry key in HKU where the currently logged-on user's registry data is stored. It contains the following subkeys:

✦ **AppEvents:** This key contains data about application and event associations such as sounds associated to specific events. Use the Sounds and Multimedia object in the Control Panel to modify settings in this key.

✦ **Console:** This key contains data that defines the appearance and behavior of the Windows 2000 command console (command prompt) and character-mode applications. Use the application or command console's Control menu to define settings in this key.

✦ **Control Panel:** This key contains data normally set through the Control Panel applets.

✦ **Environment:** This key contains environment variable assignments for the current user.

✦ **Identities:** This key contains user-specific identity information such as last user ID, last user name, and software-related identity settings for Outlook Express, the address book, and so on.

✦ **Keyboard Layout:** This key stores information about the user's keyboard layout and key mapping for international settings. Use the Regional Options object in the Control Panel to modify these settings.

✦ **Network:** This key stores data about the user's network connections.

✦ **Printers:** This key stores data about the user's printer connections.

✦ **RemoteAccess:** This key stores data about the user's Internet profile and dial-up connection settings.

✦ **Software:** This key stores data about the user's installed applications.

✦ **UNICODE Program Groups:** This key stores data about the user's UNICODE Program Groups and is usually empty unless the system has migrated to Windows 2000 from an original Windows 3.1 installation (unlikely in most cases).

✦ **Volatile Environment:** This key stores volatile operating environment data such as the user's application directory (usually `\Documents` and `Settings\ user\Application Data`) and logon server.

HKEY_CLASSES_ROOT

The HKCR key stores data about file associations and is built from HKLM\SOFTWARE\ Classes and HKEY_CURRENT_USER\SOFTWARE\Classes, with the value in HKCU taking precedence. It contains numerous keys, one for each file/document type. Use the File Types tab of the Folder Options object in the Control Panel to modify file associations. See Chapter 5 for more information about the Control Panel applets.

HKEY_CURRENT_CONFIG

The HKCC key is an alias of HKLM\SYSTEM\CurrentControlSet\Hardware Profiles\ Current, and it stores hardware configuration data about the local computer relating to device assignments, device drivers, and so on. It contains two keys: Software and System. The Software key stores settings for system fonts and a handful of application settings. The System key stores a partial copy of the CurrentControlSet key in HKLM\SYSTEM\CurrentControlSet.

Keys and Values

As you've read up to this point, *keys* serve as containers in the registry. Keys can contain other keys (subkeys). Keys can also contain *value entries,* or simply, *values.* These are the "substance" of the registry. Values comprise three parts: the name, data type, and value. The name identifies the setting. The data type describes the item's data format. The value is the actual data. The following list summarizes data types currently defined and used by the system:

✦ **REG_BINARY:** This data type stores the data in raw binary format, one value per entry. The Registry Editors display this data type using hexadecimal format.

✦ **REG_DWORD:** This data type stores data as a four-byte number, one value per entry. The Registry Editors can display this data type in binary, hexadecimal, or decimal formats.

✦ **REG_EXPAND_SZ:** This is a variable-length string that includes variables expanded when the data is read by a program, service, and so on. The variables are represented by % signs, and an example is the use of the %systemroot% variable to identify the root location of the Windows 2000 folder, such as a path entry to a file stored in `systemroot\System32`. One value is allowed per entry.

✦ **REG_MULTI_SZ:** This data type stores multiple string values in a single entry. String values within an item are separated by spaces, commas, or other such delimiters.

✦ **REG_SZ:** This data type stores a single, fixed-length string, and is the most common data type used in the registry.

✦ **REG_FULL_RESOURCE_DESCRIPTOR:** This data type stores a series of nested arrays such as a resource list for a device driver or hardware component.

Registry Size

As you install additional services, hardware devices, and applications, as well as add local user profiles, the registry grows. The registry is stored in a portion of the system's virtual memory called the *paged pool*. Windows 2000 needs a mechanism to prevent the registry from growing to fill the paged pool with registry data. The default minimum size for the registry is 16MB, or a third of the size of the default paged pool (48MB). You can increase the registry maximum size in situations where the registry needs to grow larger than the minimum size of 16MB. Increasing the maximum size of the registry doesn't actually allocate that much disk space to the registry, but simply sets the maximum size the registry can reach. The maximum size also has no bearing on whether the disk space is available to contain the registry. Windows 2000 doesn't check the registry size against the maximum size until after the system boots. This ensures that the system can boot even when the maximum size is reached.

You can set the maximum size of the registry by modifying the registry directly. However, you should preferably use the System object in the Control Panel to modify the maximum registry size.

 Cross-Reference   See Chapters 1 and 6 for detailed information on using the System object to configure virtual memory settings.

The Registry Editors

Windows 2000 provides two Registry Editors, `regedit.exe` and `regedt32.exe`, for viewing and modifying the registry. Both enable you to connect to, view, and modify a registry on a remote computer. Before you go tromping through the registry, however, keep two things in mind: 1) you need to have a good backup copy of the registry, and 2) you need to be careful with changes you make, as you could introduce changes that might potentially prevent the system from booting. That's why a backup copy is so important. Make sure you read the section, "Backing Up the Registry," in Chapter 17.

Also, before you start playing with the Registry Editors, keep in mind that most changes, whether for the system, user, service, application, or other object, should be made with the administration tools for that object. You should only use the Registry Editors to make changes not available through other administration tools.

Both Registry Editors provide much the same capabilities for viewing and editing the registry. Each has a few features that make it more useful in a given situation. The following sections explain each of the editors and explore the situations in which one is preferable to the other.

Regedit.exe

The first of the Registry Editors is Regedit.exe, which Setup places by default in the systemroot folder. Regedit displays the registry in a single, two-pane window. The registry tree appears in the left pane, and the results pane on the right shows the object currently selected in the tree (Figure 18-2). To view a particular key or setting, expand the tree and select the object you want to view.

Note   Click Start ➪ Run, type **regedit** in the Run dialog box, and click OK to start Regedit.

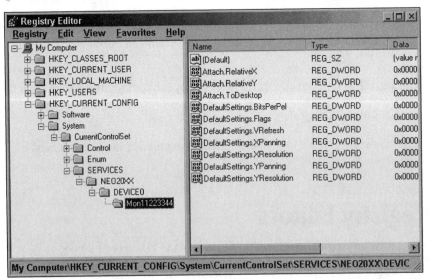

Figure 18-2: Regedit displays the registry as a hierarchical tree in a single window.

The following list summarizes the features unique to Regedit and situations in which you might use those features:

✦ **Search:** You can choose Edit ➪ Find to search through the registry for a given value. The registry is a big place, and having the ability to search for a key or value name helps you quickly locate the data you need to view or modify. Regedt32 only provides the ability to search for a key, not a value.

✦ **Single tree display:** Regedit displays the registry as a single hierarchical tree, bringing all the keys together in one structure. This eliminates the need to switch between different windows to work with different keys.

Regedt32.exe

Regedt32 also lets you view and modify the registry, but it provides a slightly different user interface. Regedt32 separates each root key into its own document window (Figure 18-3). To work with a specific key, you switch to its window. Select the window containing the key you want to view, then expand the necessary subkey(s) to locate and manage the subkey or value in question.

Note   Click Start ➪ Run, type **regedt32** in the Run dialog box, and click OK to start Regedt32.

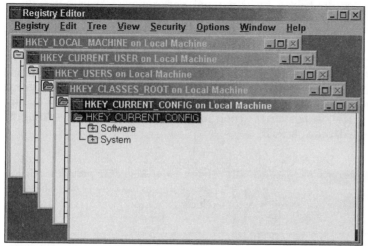

Figure 18-3: Regedt32 provides a multiple document interface (MDI) for managing the registry.

Regedt32 offers the following advantages:

✦ **Ability to load and unload individual hives:** Use this feature when you need to work on a specific hive for a computer that is having problems (can't connect to the network, for example) to repair that specific hive. You also can use this feature to view and modify a user's registry file (Ntuser.dat) even when the user isn't logged on.

✦ **Read-only mode:** Regedt32 offers a read-only mode for viewing the registry, preventing you from making changes. This serves as a safeguard against accidental changes while you're working with the registry.

✦ **Support for five of the six default data types:** Although you can view all of the registry in Regedit, only Regedt32 lets you create these five data types and modify those data types using their native format. Neither editor provides a means of creating the REG_FULL_RESOURCE_DESCRIPTOR data type, although Regedt32 fully supports displaying and modifying it.

✦ **Ability to modify the SECURITY and SAM hives:** Regedt32 lets you directly modify these two security hives, but you should only do so if you have considerable experience with Windows 2000 security and the registry.

✦ **Security:** You can set permissions on individual keys to control and restrict access as well as audit access to the keys.

Modifying the Registry

You can use either Regedit or Regedt32 to modify the registry; your selection of editor depends on which you prefer and whether you need any of the specific features offered by a particular editor. The following sections explain common registry editing tasks using Regedt32. Except where noted, performing tasks with Regedit is very similar, if not identical, to performing those tasks with Regedt32.

Creating and modifying values

You're most likely to modify the registry to change existing values rather than create new ones or modify keys. To change the value of a registry entry, first locate the value in the editor and then double-click the value. Regedt32 displays a dialog box, shown in Figure 18-4, which varies according to the data type you're editing. Modify the data as needed, then click OK.

Figure 18-4: Regedt32 provides a dialog box tailored to the type of data value selected.

You can create a new value in an existing key. You might need to do this, for example, if a given application feature or property defaults to a hard-coded value in the absence of a registry value. Creating the value in the registry lets you control the application's behavior for that feature. To create a value, first locate and select the key in which you want to create the value. Click Edit ⇨ Add Value. In the Add Value dialog box, specify the value name and data type and click OK. Regedt32 displays a subsequent dialog box to prompt for the data.

One advantage in using Regedt32 to create values is that Regedt32 supports five of the six default registry data types. With Regedit, you can only create REG_SZ, REG_DWORD, and REG_BINARY data types. Neither editor provides a means to directly create REG_FULL_RESOURCE_DESCRIPTOR values.

Creating and deleting keys

Although you'll usually be creating and modifying values, you might come across a situation where you need to create a new key. As you do when creating a value item, first locate the key in which you want the new key created. Select Edit ➪ Add Key. Specify the key name and class if needed (REG_SZ, and so on), and click OK.

Deleting a key is even easier than creating one, which in a way is dangerous. When you delete a key, all of its contents are deleted as well. There is no undo feature, so make very sure you've selected the right key and really want to delete it before proceeding. Then, choose Edit ➪ Delete. Click Yes to confirm the deletion or No to cancel it.

Importing and Exporting Keys

On occasion, you might find it useful or necessary to copy all or part of the registry to a file. For example, say you've gone through the trouble of installing an application that created its own registry section to store its settings. Now you want to move the application to a different computer but don't want to go through the whole installation process. Instead, you'd rather just copy the files over to the other computer. In this case, you can export the application's portion of the registry to a text-based registry file. After you copy the application's files to the other system, you can import the registry file into the other computer's registry. A similar example would be installing an application on several systems remotely. You copy the files to the computer, then edit each computer's registry remotely to add the application settings.

With Regedt32, you can save a key and its contents to a binary file that you can later restore to (load into) a registry. To do so, select the key and choose Registry ➪ Save Key. Regedt32 prompts you for a file name. Include a file extension if desired, as Regedt32 doesn't include one automatically. To restore a key from a file, choose Registry ➪ Restore, select the file, and click Open.

You can also export a key to a registry script, which is a text-formatted file and is useful if you want to modify the file before importing it or want a readable copy of the key for archival purposes. To save a key as a text file, select the key and choose Registry ➪ Save Subtree As. Specify a file name and extension (if desired) or select a file type from the drop-down list, and click Save. The same key saved in text format will take up more disk space than when saved in binary format.

You also can use Regedit to export a selected branch or export the entire registry to a registry script. There are other ways to back up the registry, so let's assume you want to export only a single branch (you use the same process either way). Locate and select the branch of the registry you want to export. Choose Registry ➪ Export Registry File. Regedit displays the Export Registry File dialog box shown in Figure 18-5. Specify a file name for the registry file and select either All or Selected branch, depending on how much of the registry you want to export. Then click Save to create the file, which will have a `.reg` extension by default.

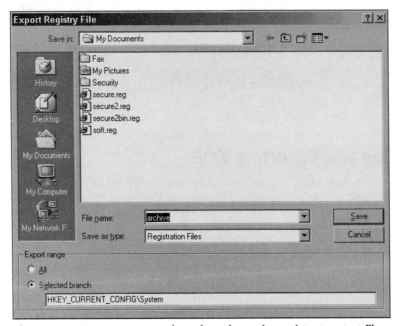

Figure 18-5: You can export a branch or the entire registry to a text file.

Tip

You can use any text editor to view and, if necessary, modify the registry file.

Importing a registry script adds the contents of the file to the registry, creating or replacing keys and values with the imported values. Using the program installation example described previously, you'd import the registry values for the program you want to add to the computer without running the program's Setup program.

You have two ways to import a registry file: Use one of the Registry Editors or simply double-click a registry script. To import a key in Regedt32, choose Registry ➪ Restore and select a binary registry file. To import a registry key in Regedit, choose Registry ➪ Import Registry File. Locate and select the text file, then click Open. Regedit loads the registry file and applies its settings. With either tool, changes take effect immediately. In addition, double-clicking a registry script file causes Windows 2000 to incorporate into the registry the settings stored in the file (after prompting you to confirm).

Note   You also can choose Start ⇨ Run and enter the name of the registry file to import the file's settings into the registry.

Editing a Remote Registry

You can edit the registry of a remote computer subject to your permissions and rights on the remote computer, as well as how the remote system is configured. To open the registry from another computer in Regedit, click Registry ⇨ Connect Network Registry and specify the computer name or browse for it. The registry for the remote computer appears as a separate branch in the tree pane. You can view and modify settings just as you would for the local computer, although the tree includes only the HKCR, HCLM, and HKU keys for the remote computer; the HKCU and HKCC keys are not displayed. When you're finished, click Registry ⇨ Disconnect Network Registry, and the computer's registry disappears from the tree. You can connect to multiple remote systems concurrently, if needed.

You can connect to a remote registry using Regedt32 as well. Click Registry ⇨ Select Computer and enter the name of the remote computer or browse for it. The remote computer's registry appears in two additional windows, one for HKLM and the other for HKU.

Loading and Unloading Hives

Regedt32 provides the ability to load and unload individual hives, which is useful for managing individual hives from another system or managing user registries. For example, you might use Regedt32 to edit the hive of a system that won't boot, repairing the damage so you can replace the hive on the target system and get it running again. You also can load a user's copy of `Ntuser.dat` to modify the user's registry settings.

Loading a hive affects only the HKLM or HKU keys, so you must first select one of those keys before loading the hive. The hive comes in as a subkey of the selected hive rather than replacing the existing key of the same name (you specify the name for the new hive). You can modify the settings in the key, then unload the hive and copy it to the target system, if necessary.

To load a hive, open Regedt32 and choose Registry ⇨ Load Hive. Regedg32 prompts you for the location and name of the previously saved hive. Select the file and click Open. Specify a name for the key under which the hive will reside and click OK. To unload a hive, select Registry ⇨ Unload Hive.

Securing the Registry

As you've probably surmised at this point, the registry is a critical part of the Windows 2000 operating system. It also can present a security risk since virtually every setting for the OS and applications resides in the registry. For that reason, you might want to apply tighter security to certain keys in the registry to prevent unauthorized access that could potentially give a remote user or hacker the ability to change settings that would grant him or her access or cause damage. You also can prevent remote administration of a registry and protect the registry in other ways. This section of the chapter explains your options.

Preventing Access to the Registry

Perhaps the best way to protect the registry from unauthorized changes is to keep users out of it altogether. In the case of a server, keeping the server physically secure and granting only administrators the right to log on locally is the first step. For other systems, or where that isn't practical for a given server, you can secure the Registry Editors. Either remove both Registry Editors from the target system or configure the permissions on Regedit.exe and Regedt32.exe to deny permission to execute for all except those who should have access. If you've removed the Registry Editors from a system and need to modify its registry, you can do so remotely from another computer that does contain a Registry Editor. See the section, "Securing Remote Registry Access," later in this chapter if you want to prevent remote editing of the registry.

Applying Permissions to Registry Keys

Another way to protect the registry or portions thereof is to apply permissions on individual keys to restrict access to those keys. In this way, you can allow access to certain users or groups to certain parts of the registry and deny access to others. However, you should use this capability sparingly. Changing the Access Control List (ACL) for a registry key incorrectly could prevent the system from booting. Either avoid configuring the ACL for pre-existing keys and change only those keys you cre- ate yourself, or tread lightly and be very careful with the changes you make to ensure you won't wreck the system.

Regedit doesn't enable you to modify the ACL for a registry key to set permissions, but Regedt32 does. In Regedt32, select the key or subkey on which you want to set permissions. Choose Security ⇨ Permissions to access the Permissions dialog box (Figure 18-6). Add and remove users and groups as needed, then set permissions for each as needed. For more information about setting permissions, see Chapter 22.

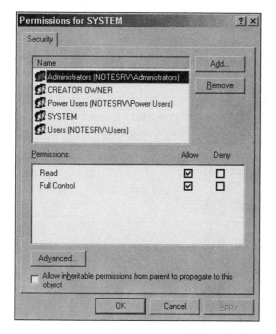

Figure 18-6: Use the Permissions dialog box to configure access permissions on registry keys.

Auditing Registry Access

If you do allow access to a system's registry, you might consider auditing registry access to track who is accessing the registry and what they're doing. Although you could audit all access to the registry, that would generate a potentially huge amount of load on the server. So, consider auditing only success or failure in modifying a key or value.

To enable auditing of the registry, you first have to enable auditing on the target system. You can do this either through the local security policy or through group policy. Here, we will assume you're doing so through the local security policy. To enable auditing, click Start ➪ Programs ➪ Administrative Tools ➪ Local Security Policy. Open the branch Security Settings\Local Policies\Audit Policy. Double-click the policy Audit object access and select Success and/or Failure, depending on which events you want to track.

Enabling auditing of object access doesn't configure auditing for a particular object, but instead simply makes it possible (that is, turns on the ability to audit object access). You then need to configure auditing for each object you want to audit. In the case of the registry, this means you need to configure auditing for each key you want to track. To do so, open Regedt32. Locate and select the key you want to configure and choose Security ⇨ Permissions. Click Advanced, click the Auditing tab, click Add to select the user or group whose access you want to audit for the selected key, and click OK. Regedt32 displays the Auditing Entry dialog box shown in Figure 18-7. Select Successful/Failed as desired. Table 18-2 lists audit events you can configure for registry access.

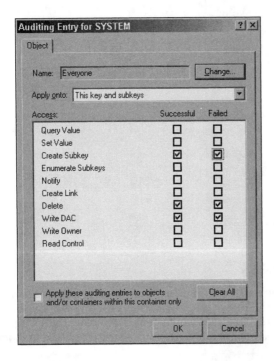

Figure 18-7: Use the Auditing Entry dialog box to configure auditing of the selected key.

Table 18-2
Registry Access Audit Events

Audit Event	Explanation
Query Value	Log attempts to view the key.
Set Value	Log attempts to set values.
Create Subkey	Log attempts to create subkeys.
Enumerate Subkeys	Log attempts to list subkeys.
Notify	Log attempts to open the key with Notify access.

Audit Event	Explanation
Create Link	Log attempts to create links to the key.
Delete	Log attempts to delete a key.
Write DAC	Log attempts to determine who has access to a key.
Writer Owner	Log attempts to determine who owns a key.
Read Control	Log attempts to remotely access registry objects.

Securing Remote Registry Access

A good security step to take to prevent hackers and others from making unauthorized changes to a system's registry is to prevent remote access to a system's registry. When a user attempts to connect to a registry remotely, Windows 2000 checks the ACL for the following registry key:

KHLM\System\CurrentControlSet\Control\SecurePipeServers\winreg

If this key is missing, all users can access the registry subject to the permissions assigned to individual keys. If the key exists, Windows 2000 checks the permissions on the key to determine whether or not the remote user can gain access to the registry (and levels of access). Individual keys then determine what these remote users can do with a given key. So, winreg is the first line of defense, and individual key ACLs are the second line of defense. If you want to prevent all remote access to the registry, make sure you set the permissions on the winreg key accordingly.

Summary

Despite the towering authority of Active Directory at the domain level, the registry still forms the repository of essentially all data that determines the Windows 2000 configuration for hardware, the operating system, and applications. Although you can modify the registry directly, most changes can and should be accomplished through the Control Panel or other administration tools for OS- and hardware-related settings, and through applications for each application's registry settings.

When you do need to modify the registry, you can use one of two Registry Editors: Regedit or Regedt32. Each offers certain advantages, with Regedt32 offering the broadest control and Regedit offering the best view of the registry. Regedt32 lets you perform additional tasks such as loading an individual hive from another computer and opening the registry in read-only mode to prevent accidental changes.

Security on the registry is also important. Restricting registry access is important to secure a system from local and remote viewing and modification of the registry. You can apply permissions on individual keys through Regedt32 and apply permissions to KHLM\System\CurrentControlSet\Control\SecurePipeServers\ winreg to prevent unauthorized remote access to a system's registry. Auditing of registry access lets you track who is accessing the registry and the tasks they're performing on it.

✦   ✦   ✦

Auditing Windows 2000

Auditing provides a means of tracking all events in Windows 2000 to monitor system access and ensure system security.

Auditing Overview

In Windows 2000, *auditing* provides a means of tracking events and is an important facet of security for individual computers as well as the enterprise. As described in other chapters (notably Chapter 6, which covers the Event Viewer), Microsoft defines an *event* as any significant occurrence in the operating system or an application that requires users (particularly administrators) to be notified. Events are recorded in *event logs* that you can manage with the Event Viewer console snap-in.

Auditing enables you to track specific events. More specifically, auditing enables you to track the *success* or *failure* of specific events. For example, you might audit logon attempts, tracking who succeeds in logging on (and when) and who fails at logging on. Or, you might audit object access on a given folder or file, tracking who uses it and the tasks they perform on it. You can track an overwhelming variety of events in Windows 2000, as you'll learn a little later in the chapter.

Windows 2000 provides several categories of events you can audit. The following list describes these event categories:

✦ **Account Logon Events:** Track user logon and logoff via a user account.

✦ **Account Management:** Track when a user account or group is created, changed, or deleted; a user account is renamed, enabled, or disabled; or a password is set or changed.

✦ **Directory Service Access:** Track access to the Active Directory.

✦ **Logon Events:** Track non-local authentication events such as network use of a resource or a remote service logging on using the local System account.

✦ **Object Access:** Track when objects are accessed and the type of access performed. For example, track use of a folder, file, printer, and so on. Configure auditing of specific events through the object's properties (such as the Security tab for a folder or file).

✦ **Policy Change:** Track changes to user rights or audit policies.

✦ **Privilege Use:** Track when a user exercises a right other than those associated with logon and logoff.

✦ **Process Tracking:** Track events related to process execution such as program execution.

✦ **System Events:** Track such system events as restart, startup, shutdown, or events that affect system security or the security log.

Within each category, you'll find several different types of events — some common and some specific to the objects or events being edited. For example, when you audit registry access, the events are very specific to the registry. So rather than cover every possible event that can be audited, this chapter explains how to enable and configure auditing, and looks at specific cases and how auditing improves security and monitoring in those cases.

Configuring Auditing

Configuring auditing can be either a one- or two-step process, depending on the type of events for which you're configuring auditing. For all but object access, enabling auditing simply requires that you define the audit policy for the given audit category. You have an additional step for object access auditing, however, that is configuring auditing of specific objects. For example, enabling auditing for the policy *Audit object access* doesn't actually cause any folders or files to be audited. Instead, you have to configure each folder or file individually for auditing.

Enabling Audit Policies

Before you begin auditing specific events, you need to enable auditing of that event's category. You configure auditing through the computer's local security policy, group policy, or both. If domain audit policies are defined, they override local audit policies. This chapter assumes you're configuring auditing through the local security policy. If you need to configure auditing through group policies, use the Domain Security Policy console to enable auditing.

To configure auditing through the local security policy, open the Security Policy console snap-in by choosing Start ➪ Programs ➪ Administrative Tools ➪ Local Security Policy. Open the Security Settings/Local Policies/Audit Policy branch. As Figure 19-1 illustrates, each audit policy category appears with its local setting and effective setting. The effective setting reflects the application of group policies, if any.

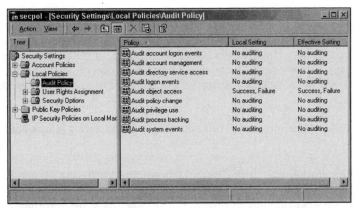

Figure 19-1: Use either the local security policy or domain policy to enable auditing.

Double-click a policy to display its settings (Figure 19-2). You can enable auditing of both success and failure of events in the selected category. Using the logon example given previously, for example, you might audit successful logon to track who is using a given system and when. You might track unsuccessful logon to track attempts at unauthorized use of a system. Select Success, Failure, or both, as desired, and then click OK.

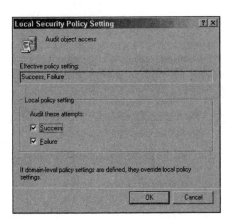

Figure 19-2: Select the types of events (success or failure) for which you want to enable auditing.

After you configure each category as desired, close the Security Policy console. See the next section if you're configuring auditing of object access. Otherwise, audit events will begin appearing in the Security log. Make sure you configure the Security log's size and overflow behavior to accommodate the audit events.

Auditing Object Access

The second step in configuring object access auditing is to enable auditing on the individual objects you want to monitor, such as folders, files, registry keys, and so on. You typically configure the objects where you find them in the UI, such as Explorer for folders and files, the Printers folder for printers, and Regedt32 for the registry keys. The types of events you can audit for a given object depend on the object itself. Events for file access, for example, are different to events for registry key access.

Note   See Chapter 23 for more information on controlling and monitoring printer access.

To configure auditing for a folder or file, open Explorer and locate the object. Right-click the object and choose Properties to view its property sheet. Click Security ➪ Advanced to open the Access Control Settings dialog box. Click the Auditing tab to show the Auditing page, then click Add. Select a user, computer, or group that you want to audit, and click OK. Windows 2000 displays an object dialog box that lists the events you can audit for the selected object (Figure 19-3).

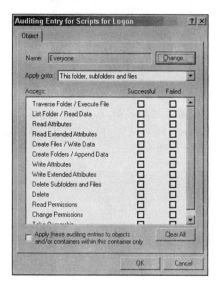

Figure 19-3: Select Successful or Failed as desired to configure auditing for each event type.

Select Successful for a given event if you want to record successful completion of the event. Select Failed to monitor failed attempts. The option "Apply these auditing entries to objects and/or containers within this container only" applies auditing to only the contents of the selected container (such as the files in the selected folder). The contents of subfolders are audited unless this option is selected.

Caution   As you're defining the audit policy for a selected object, keep in mind that you could potentially generate a huge number of events in the Security log. Unless you have a specific reason to audit success on a given event, you should consider only auditing failure to reduce traffic to the log and load on the computer. Auditing failed access is typically most useful for tracking attempts at unauthorized access.

After you're satisfied with the audit event selections, click OK. Repeat the process to add other users, groups, or computers to the list. On the Access Control Settings dialog box (Figure 19-4), you'll find two options that control how auditing entries are affected by the parent object and affect child objects:

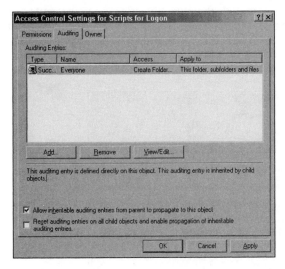

Figure 19-4: Use the Auditing page of the Access Control Settings dialog box to configure auditing for a selected object.

✦ **Allow inheritable auditing entries from parent to propagate to this object.** Select this option if you want auditing properties to be inherited by the current object from its parent object. Deselect this option to prevent audit properties from being inherited.

✦ **Reset auditing entries on all child objects and enable propagation of inheritable auditing entries.** Select this option to clear and audit properties configured within child objects (such as subfolders) and to allow the audit properties for the current object to propagate to child objects.

Close the object's property sheets when you've finished defining the audit policy for the object. Auditing will begin immediately.

Examining the Audit Reports

As explained previously, Windows 2000 records audited events to the Windows 2000 Security log. You can use the Event Viewer console snap-in to view the event logs, save logs as log files for future viewing, and save the logs in either tab- or comma-delimited formats.

Using the Event Viewer

You can use the Event Viewer console snap-in to view and manage the event logs. In addition to the Security log, you can manage the Application and System logs, as well as any additional logs created by Windows 2000 services or applications. By default, the Event Viewer displays the logs dynamically, meaning new events are added to a log as you're viewing it. You also can save a log to disk to use as a bench-mark or simply to archive a log before clearing it. Figure 19-5 shows the Security log in the Event Viewer.

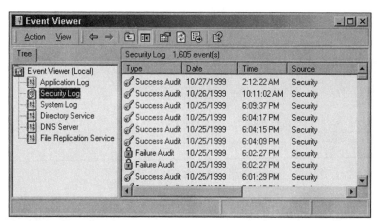

Figure 19-5: You can browse the Security log (and others) using the Event Viewer.

For detailed information on the Event Viewer console snap-in, including how to save logs and configure log behavior, see Chapter 5.

Using Other Tools

The Event Viewer provides the means through which you configure the event logs as well as view them. Because you can save a log to a text file, however, you can use other applications to view a log. For example, you might save a log to a comma-delimited file so you can import the file into Microsoft Access or other database application to create a database you can easily organize by event ID, source, and so on. Or, you might export the data to a text file, and import it into a word processor to create a report. Just make sure you pick an application that can import tab- or comma-delimited files and export the log files in the appropriate format. See also Chapter 20 for information on using the Alert services of the Performance Logs and Alerts console.

A handful of other third-party tools exist for viewing a system's log files. One in particular worth considering is RippleTech's LogCaster. Providing a mechanism to manage the event logs is just a small part of what LogCaster does. It not only provides a unified interface for viewing the event logs, but it also serves as an excellent warning system for administrators. LogCaster provides real-time monitoring of the event logs, services, TCP/IP devices, performance counters, and ASCII logs. It provides automatic delivery of alerts through a variety of mechanisms including paging, e-mail, ODBC, SNMP, and others. When a given event occurs, you can have LogCaster automatically notify you regardless of where you are. Whether you're tracking system performance, want to be notified of audit events, or want to be warned of a possible system intrusion, you'll find LogCaster an excellent resource. You can locate RippleTech on the Internet at `www.rippletech.com`.

Enabling Auditing

Although you could audit every event, doing so wouldn't be practical because you'd place an undue load on the system and either end up with an enormous log file or spend all your time worrying about archiving the logs. The following sections examine some specific situations and how you might employ auditing.

Leaving Auditing Off

The first option is to leave auditing off altogether, and this is not a bad option in some situations. If you're not concerned with security, there's no real reason to enable or perform auditing. Turning off auditing reduces system overhead and helps simplify log management. However, most organizations will or should be concerned with security at least to some degree, so this option might not fit your needs.

Turning All Auditing On

At the other end of the auditing spectrum is complete auditing. If you're very concerned about security or shooting for C2 security certification, this might be an option. However, bear in mind that your system will probably generate a huge number of events requiring very active management of the security log. As an alternative to full logging, consider logging only failure events and not success events.

Auditing Problem Users

Certain users, for one reason or another, can become an administrator's worst nightmare. In some cases, it's through no fault of the user, but is instead due to problems with the user's profile, account, and so on. In other cases, the user can be at fault, frequently using the wrong password, incorrectly typing the account name, trying to log on during periods when they are not allowed to, or even trying to access resources for which they have no permissions (or need). In these situations, you'll want to monitor events associated with the given user and might even need to retain the information for counseling or termination purposes.

Which types of events you audit for a given user or group depends on the problem area. For example, audit account logon events if the user has trouble logging on or attempts to log on during unauthorized hours. Track object access to determine when a user or group is attempting to access a given resource such as a folder or file. Tailor other auditing to specific tasks and events generated by the user or group.

Auditing Administrators

Auditing administrators is a good idea, not only to keep track of what administrators are doing, but also to detect unauthorized use of administrative privileges. Keep in mind, however, that auditing impacts system performance. In particular, you should consider auditing account logon events, account management, policy change, and privilege use of an administrator only if you suspect an individual. Rather, control administrators by delegating through the wise use of groups and organizational units.

Auditing Critical Files and Folders

One very common use for auditing is to track access to important folders and files. In addition to tracking simple access, you probably will want to track when users make or attempt to make specific types of changes to the object such as Change Permissions and Take Ownership. This helps you monitor changes to a folder or file that could affect security.

Summary

Auditing enables you to monitor events associated with specific users, groups, services, and so on. These events are recorded to the Security log. The ability to monitor these events is not only useful for troubleshooting, but also is an important tool for monitoring and managing security. You can keep tabs on the actions of specific users or groups and monitor attempts at unauthorized access to the system or its resources.

Configuring auditing for most types of events is a one-step process. You configure the policy for Success, Failure, or both in the local or group security policy under Security Settings\Local Policies\Audit Policy. Configuring auditing of object access, such as monitoring access to folders/files, printers, or the registry, requires the additional step of configuring auditing on each object to be monitored.

✦   ✦   ✦

Service Level and Performance Monitoring

Windows 2000 Server is being widely considered as an alternative to mainframe-type systems for high-end computing requirements. This will place tremendous burden and responsibility on Windows 2000 administrators to ensure maximum availability of systems. This chapter thus discusses service level and provides an introduction to Windows 2000 Server performance monitoring.

What Is Service Level?

If there is anything you have learned in this book, it is this: Windows 2000 is a major-league operating system. In our opinion, it is the most powerful operating system in existence . . . for the majority of needs of all enterprises. Only time and service packs will tell if Windows 2000 can go up against the big irons such as AS/400, Solaris, S/390, and the like.

Microsoft has aimed Windows 2000 Server squarely at all levels of business and industry and at all business sizes. You will no doubt feel the rush of diatribe in the industry: 99.9 this, 10,000 concurrent hits that, clustering and load balancing, and more. But every system, server or OS, has its meltdown point, weak links, single point of failure (SPOF), "tensile strength," and so on. Knowing, or at least predicting, the meltdown "event horizon" is more important than availability claims. Trust us, poor management will turn any system or service into a service level nightmare.

Note   One of the first things you need to ignore in the press from the get-go is the crazy comparisons of Windows 2000 to $75 operating systems, and so on. If your business is worth your life to you and your staff, you need to invest in performance and monitoring tools, disaster recovery, Quality of Service tools, service level tools, and more. Take a survey of what these tools can cost you. Windows 2000 Server out of the box has more built in to it than anything else, as this chapter will illustrate. On our calculators, Windows 2000 Server is the cheapest system going on performance-monitoring tools alone.

Windows 2000 is no doubt going to be adopted by many organizations; it will certainly replace Windows NT over the next few years and will probably become the leading server operating system on the Internet. With application service providing (ASP), thin-client, Quality of Service, e-commerce, distributed networking architecture (DNA), and the like becoming implementations everywhere as opposed to being new buzzwords, you, the server or network administrator, are going to find yourself dealing with a new animal in your server room. This animal is known as the *service level agreement* (SLA).

Before we discuss the SLA further, we should first define service level and, second, how Windows 2000 addresses it.

Service Level (SL) is simply the ability of IT management or MIS to maintain a consistent, maximum level of system uptime and availability. Many companies may understand SL as quality assurance and quality control (QA/QC). Examples will better explain it, as follows.

Service Level: Example 1

Management comes to MIS with a business plan for application services providing (ASP). If certain customers can lease applications online, over reliable Internet connections, for *x* rate per month, they will forgo expensive in-house IT budgets and outsource instead. An ASP can, therefore, make its highly advanced network operations center and a farm of servers available to these businesses. If enough customers lease applications, the ASP will make a profit.

The business plan flies if ASP servers and applications are available to customers all the time from at least 7 a.m. to 9 p.m. The business plan will only tolerate a .09 percent downtime during the day. Any more and customers will lose respect for the business and rather bring resources back in house. This means that IT or MIS must support the business plan by ensuring that systems are never offline for more than .09 percent of the business day. Response, as opposed to availability, is also a critical factor. And Quality of Service, or QoS, addresses this in SL. This will be discussed shortly in this chapter.

Service Level: Example 2

Management asks MIS to take its order-placing system, typically fax-based and processed by representatives in the field, to the extranet. Current practice involves a representative going to a customer, taking an order for stock, and then faxing the order to the company's fax system, where the orders are manually entered into the system. The new system proposes that customers be equipped with an inexpensive terminal or terminal software and place the orders directly against their accounts on a Web server.

MIS has to ensure that the Web servers and the backend systems, SQL Server 2000, Windows 2000 Server, the WAN, and so on, are available all the time. If customers find the systems offline, they will swamp the phones and fax machines, or simply place their orders with the competition. The system must also be reliable, informative, and responsive to the customers' needs.

The Service Level Agreement

The first example may require a formal service level agreement. In other words, the SLA will be a written contract signed between the client and the provider. The customer demands that the ASP provide written — signed — guarantees that the systems will be available 99.9 percent of the time. The customer demands such an SLA, because it cannot afford to be in the middle of an order-processing application, or sales letter, and then have the ASP suddenly disappear.

The customer may be able to tolerate a certain level of unavailability, but if SL drops beyond what's tolerable, the customer needs a way to obtain redress from the ASP. This redress could be the ability to cancel the contract, or the ability to hold the ASP accountable with penalties, such as fines, discount on service costs, waiver of monthly fees, and so on. Whatever the terms of the SLA, if the ASP cannot meet it, then MIS gets the blame.

In the second example, there is unlikely to be a formal SLA between a customer and the supplier. Service level agreements will be in the form of memos between MIS and other areas of management. MIS will agree to provide a certain level of availability to the business model or plan. These SLAs are put in writing and usually favored by the MIS, who will take the SLA to budget and request money for systems and software to meet the SLA.

However, the SLA can work to the disadvantage of MIS, too. If SL is not met, the MIS staff or CTO may get fired, demoted, or reassigned. The CEO may also decide to outsource or force MIS to bring in expensive consultants (which may help or hurt MIS).

In IT shops that now support SL for mission-critical applications, there are no margins for tolerating error. Engineers who cannot help MIS meet SL do not survive long. Education and experience are likely to be high on the list of employment requirements.

Service Level Management

Understanding Service Level Management (SLM) is an essential requirement for MIS in almost all companies today. This section examines critical SLM factors that have to be addressed.

Problem Detection

This factor requires IT to be constantly monitoring systems for advanced warnings of system failure. You use whatever tools you can obtain to monitor systems and focus on all the possible points of failure. For example, you will need to monitor storage, networks, memory, processors, power, and so on.

Problem detection is a lot like earthquake detection. You spend all of your time listening to the earth, and the quake comes when you least expect it and where you least expect it. Then, 100 percent of your effort is spent on disaster recovery (DR). Your DR systems then need to kick in to recover. According to research from the likes of Forrester Research, close to 40 percent of IT management resources are spent on problem detection.

Performance Management

Performance Management accounts for about 20 percent of MIS resources. This factor is closely related to problem detection. You can hope that poor performance in areas such as networking, access times, transfer rates, restore or recover performance, and so on, will point to problems that can be fixed before they turn into disasters. However, most of the time a failure is usually caused by failures in another part of the system. For example, if you get a flood of continuous writes to a hard disk that does not let up until the hard disk crashes, is the hard disk at fault or should you be looking for better firewall software?

The right answer is a combination of both factors. The fault is caused by the poor quality of firewall software that gives passage to a denial-of-service attack. But in the event this happens again, we need hard disks that can stand the attack a lot longer.

Availability

Availability, for the most part, is a post-operative factor. In other words, availability management covers redundancy, mirrored or duplexed systems, *fail-overs,* and so on. Note that *fail-over* is emphasized because the term itself denotes taking over from a system that has failed.

Clustering of systems or load balancing, on the other hand, is also as much disaster prevention as it is a performance-level maintenance practice. Using performance management, you would take systems to a performance point that is nearing threshold or maximum level, then you switch additional requests for service to other resources. A fail-over, on the other hand, is a machine or process that picks up the users and processes that were on a system that has just failed, and it is supposed to allow the workload to continue uninterrupted on the fail-over systems. A good example of fail-over is a mirrored disk, or a RAID-5 storage set: The failure of one disk does not interrupt the processing, which carries on oblivious to the failure on the remaining disks, giving management time to replace the defective components.

Note   There are several other SL-related areas that IT spends time on and which impact SLM. These include change management and control, software distribution, and systems management. See Chapter 11 for an extensive discussion of Change Management.

SLM by Design

SLM combines tools and metrics or analysis to meet the objectives of SL and Service Level Agreements. The SLM model is a three-legged stool, as illustrated in Figure 20-1.

The *availability* leg supports the model by guaranteeing availability of critical systems. The *administration* leg ensures 24 × 7 operations and administrative housekeeping. The *performance* leg supports the model by assuring that systems are able to service the business and keep systems operating at threshold points considered safely below bottleneck and failure levels. If one of the legs fails or becomes weak, the stool may falter or collapse, which puts the business at risk.

When managing for availability, the enterprise will ensure it has the resources to recover from disasters as soon as possible. This usually means hiring gurus or experts to be available on-site to fix problems as quickly as possible. Often, management will pay a guru who does nothing for 95 percent of his or her time, which seems a waste. But if they can fix a problem in record time, they will have earned their keep several times over.

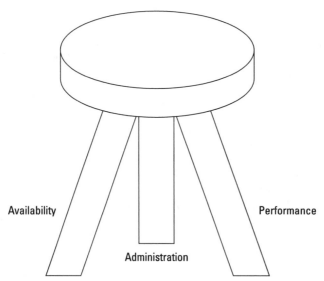

Figure 20-1: The SLM model is a three-legged stool.

Often, a guru will restore a system that, had it stayed offline a few days longer, would have cost the company much more than the salary of the guru. However, it goes without saying that the enterprise will save a lot of money and effort if it can obtain gurus who are also qualified to monitor for performance and problems, and who do not just excel at recovery. This should be worth 50 percent more salary to the guru.

Administration is the effort of technicians to keep systems backed up, keep power supplies on line, monitor servers for error messages, ensure server rooms remain at safe temperatures and air circulation, and so on. The administrative leg manages the SL budget, hires and fires, maintains and reports on service level achievement, and reports to management or the CEO.

The performance leg is usually carried out by analysts who know what to look for in a system. These analysts get paid the big bucks to help management decide how to support business initiatives and how to exploit opportunity. They need to know everything there is about the technology and its capabilities. For example, they need to know which databases should be used, how RAID works and the level required, and so on. They are able to collect data, interpret data, and forecast needs.

SLM and Windows 2000 Server

Key to meeting the objective of SLM is the acquisition of SL tools and technology. This is where Windows 2000 Server comes in. While clustering and load balancing are included in Advanced Server and Datacenter Server, the performance and system monitoring tools and disaster recovery tools are available to all versions of the OS.

These tools are essential to SL. Acquired independently of the operating systems, they can cost an arm and a leg, and they might not integrate at the same level. These tools on Windows NT 4.0 were seriously lacking. On Windows 2000, however, they raise the bar for all operating systems. Many competitive products unfortunately just do not compete when it comes to SLM. The costs of third-party tools and integration for some operating systems are so prohibitive that they cannot be considered of any use to SLM whatsoever.

The Windows 2000 monitoring tools are complex, and continued ignorance of them will not be tolerated by management as more and more customers demand SL compliance and service level agreements. The monitoring and performance tools on Windows 2000 include the following:

✦ System Monitor

✦ Task Manager

✦ Event Viewer

✦ Quality of Service

✦ Windows Management Interface

✦ SNMP

We are not going to provide an exhaustive investigation into the SLM tools that ship with Windows 2000, or how to use each and every one. Such an advanced level of analysis would take several hundred pages, and it is thus beyond the scope of this book. Performance monitoring is also one of the services and support infrastructures that ships with Windows 2000 but takes some effort to get to know and master. However, the information that follows will be sufficient to get you started.

Windows 2000 System Monitoring Architecture

Windows 2000 monitors or analyzes storage, memory, networks, and processing. This does not sound like a big deal, but the data analysis is not done on these areas per se. In other words, you do not monitor memory itself, or disk usage itself, but rather how software components and functionality use these resources. In short, it is not sufficient to just report that 56MB of RAM were used between time *x* and time *y*. Your investigations need to find out what used the RAM at a certain time and why so much was used.

If a system continues to run out of memory, there is a strong possibility, for example, that an application is stealing the RAM somewhere. In other words, the application or process has a bug and is leaking memory. When we refer to *memory leaks,* this means that software that has used memory has not released it after it is done. Software developers are able to watch their applications on servers to be sure they release all the memory they use.

What if you are losing memory and you do not know which application is responsible? Not too long ago, Windows NT servers used on the Internet and in high-end mail applications (no fewer than 100,000 e-mails per hour) would simply run out of RAM. After extensive system monitoring, we were able to determine that the leak was in the latest release of the Winsock libraries responsible for Internet communications on NT. Another company in Europe found the leak about the same time. Microsoft later released a patch. It turned out that the Winsock functions responsible for releasing memory were not able to cope with the rapid demand on the sockets. They were simply being opened at a rate faster than the Winsock libraries could cope with.

The number of software components, services, and threads of functionality in Windows 2000 are so numerous that it is literally impossible to monitor tens of thousands of instances of storage, memory, network, or processor usage.

To achieve such detailed and varied analysis, Windows 2000 includes built-in software objects, associated with services and applications, which are able to collect data in these critical areas. So when you collect data, the *focus* of your data collection is on the software components, in various services of the operating system, that are associated with these areas. When you perform data collection, the system collects data from the targeted object managers in each monitoring area.

There are two methods of data collection supported in Windows 2000. The first one involves accessing registry pointers to functions in the performance counter DLLs in the operating system. The second supports collecting data through the Windows Management Infrastructure (WMI). WMI is an object-oriented framework that allows you to instantiate (create instances of) performance objects that wrap the performance functionality in the operating system.

The OS installs a new technology for recovering data through WMI. These are known as managed object files (MOFs). These MOFs correspond to or are associated with resources in a system. The number of objects that are the subject of performance monitoring are too numerous to list here, but they can be looked up in the Windows 2000 Performance Counters Reference, which is on the Windows 2000

Resource Kit CD (see Appendix B). However, they include the operating system's base services, such as the services that report on the RAM, Paging File functionality, and Physical Disk usage, and the operating system's advanced services, such as Active Directory, Active Server Pages, the FTP service, DNS, WINS, and so on.

To understand the scope and usage of the objects, it helps to first understand some performance data and analysis terms. There are three essential concepts to understanding performance monitoring. These are *throughput, queues,* and *response time.* From these terms, and once you fully understand them, you can broaden your scope of analysis and perform calculations to report transfer rate, access time, latency, tolerance, thresholds, bottlenecks, and so on.

What is Rate and Throughput?

Throughput is the amount of work done in a unit of time. If your child is able to construct 100 pieces of Lego bricks per hour, you could say that his or her assemblage rate is 100 pieces per hour, assessed over a period of x hours, as long as the rate remains constant. However, if the rate of assemblage varies, through fatigue, hunger, thirst, and so on, we can calculate the throughput.

Throughput increases as the number of components increases, or the available time to complete a job is reduced. Throughput depends on resources, and time and space are examples of resources. The slowest point in the system sets the throughput for the system as a whole. Throughput is the true indicator of performance. Memory is a resource, the space in which to carry out instructions. It makes little sense to rate a system by millions of instructions per second, when insufficient memory is not available to hold the instruction information.

What Is a Queue?

If you give your child too many Lego bricks to assemble, or reduce the available time in which he or she has to perform the calculation and assemblage, the number of pieces will begin to pile up. This happens too in software and IS terms, where the number of threads can begin to back up, one behind the other, in a queue. When a queue develops, we say that a *bottleneck* has occurred. Looking for bottlenecks in the system is key to monitoring for performance and troubleshooting or problem detection. If there are no bottlenecks, the system might be considered healthy, but a bottleneck might soon start to develop.

Queues can also form if requests for resources are not evenly spread over the unit of time. If your child assembles one piece per minute evenly every minute, he or she will get through 60 pieces in an hour. But if the child does nothing for 45 minutes and then suddenly gets inspired, a bottleneck will occur in the final 15 minutes because there are more pieces than the child can process in the remaining time. On computer systems when queues and bottlenecks develop, systems become unresponsive. Additional requests for processor or disk resources are stalled. When requesting services are not satisfied, the system begins to break down. In this respect, we reference the response time of a system.

What Is Response Time?

Response time is the measure of how much time elapses between the firing of a computer event, such as a read request, and the system's response to the request. Response time will increase as the load increases because the system is still responding to other events and does not have enough resources to handle new requests. A system that has insufficient memory and/or processing ability will process a huge database sort a lot slower than a better-endowed system with faster hard disks and CPUs. If response time is not satisfactory, you will either have to work with less data or increase the resources.

Response time is typically measured by dividing the queue length over the resource throughput. Response time, queues, and throughput are reported and calculated by the Windows 2000 reporting tools.

How Performance Objects Work

Windows 2000 performance monitoring objects contain functionality known as *performance counters*. These so-called counters perform the actual analysis. For example, a hard disk object is able to calculate transfer rate, while a processor-associated object is able to calculate processor time.

To gain access to the data or to start the data collection, you first have to create the object and gain access to its functionality. This is done by calling a `create` function from a user interface or other process. As soon as the object is created, and its data collection functionality invoked, it begins the data-collection process and stores the data in various properties. Data can be streamed out to disk, in files, RAM, or to other components that assess the data and present it in some meaningful way.

Depending on the object, your analysis software can create at least one copy of the performance object and analyze the counter information it generates. You need to consult Microsoft documentation to "expose" the objects to determine if the object can be created more than once concurrently. If it can be created more than once, you will have to associate your application with the data the object collects by referencing the object's instance counter. Windows 2000 allows you to instantiate an object for a local computer's services, or you can create an object that collects data from a remote computer.

There are two methods of data collection and reporting made possible using performance objects. First, the objects can *sample* data. This means that data is collected periodically rather than when a particular event occurs. All forms of data collection place a burden on resources, which means that monitoring in itself can be a burden to systems. Sampled data has the advantage of being a period-driven load, but the disadvantage is that values may be inaccurate when a certain activity falls outside the sampling period or between events.

The other method of data collection is *event tracing.* Event tracing, new to Windows 2000, is able to collect data as certain events occur. Because there is no sampling window, you can correlate resource usage against events. For example, you can watch an application consume memory when it executes a certain function and monitor how and if it releases that memory when the function completes.

The disadvantage of event tracing is that it consumes more resources than sampling, so you would only want to perform event tracing for short periods where the objective of the trace is to troubleshoot, and not to just monitor.

Counters are able to report their data in one of two ways: instantaneous counting or average counting. An instantaneous counter displays the data as it happens; it is a snapshot. In other words, the counter does not compute the data it receives and just reports it. On the other hand, average counting computes the data for you. For example, it is able to compute bits per second, or pages per second, and so on.

Other counters are able to report percentages, difference, and so on.

System Monitoring Tools

Before you rush out and buy a software development environment to access the performance monitoring routines, you should know that Windows 2000 comes equipped with two primary, ready-to-go monitoring tools: the Performance Console and Task Manager. Task Manager provides an instant view of systems activity such as memory usage, processor activity, process activity, and resource consumption. Task Manager is very helpful for an immediate detection of system problems. The Performance Console is used to provide performance analysis and information that can be used for troubleshooting and bottleneck analysis. It can also be used to establish regular monitoring regimens such as ongoing server health analysis.

Performance Console comes with two tools built in: System Monitor and Performance Logs and Alerts . . . but more about them later. The first tool, due to its immediacy and as a troubleshooting and information tool, is the Task Manager.

Task Manager

Task Manager provides quick information on applications and services currently running on your server. It provides information such as processor usage in percentage terms, memory usage, task priority, response, and some statistics about memory and processor performance.

Task Manager is very useful as a quick system sanity check, and it is usually evoked as a troubleshooting tool when a system indicates slow response times, lockups or errors, or messages pointing to lack of system resources, and so on.

Task Manager, illustrated in Figure 20-2, is started in several ways:

1. Right-click the taskbar (the bottom-right area where the time is usually displayed) and select Task Manager from the Context menu.

2. Select Ctrl+Shift and hit the Esc key.

3. Select Ctrl+Alt and hit the Del key. The Windows Security dialog box loads. Click Task Manager.

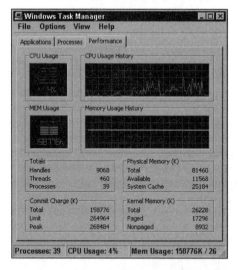

Figure 20-2: The Task Manager opened to the Performance tab

When Task Manager loads, you will notice that the dialog box has three tabs: Applications, Processes, and Performance. There are a number of useful tricks with the Task Manager:

✦ The columns can be sorted in ascending or descending order by clicking the column heads. The columns can also be resized.

✦ When the Task Manager is running, a CPU gauge icon displaying accurate information is placed into the system tray on the bottom-right of the screen. If you drag your mouse cursor over this area, you will obtain a pop-up menu of current CPU usage.

✦ It is also possible to keep the Task Manager button off the system tray if you use it a lot. This is done by selecting the Options menu and then checking the Hide When Minimized option. The CPU icon next to the system time remains, however.

✦ You can control the rate of Refresh or Update from the View ➪ Update Speed menu. You can also pause the update to preserve resources and click Refresh Now to update the display at any time.

The *Process* tab is the most useful and provides a list of running processes on the system. It measures their performance in simple data. These include CPU percent used, the CPU time allocated to a resource, and memory usage.

There are a number of additional performance or process measures that can be added to or removed from the list on the Processes page. Select View ➪ Select Columns. This will show the Select Columns dialog box that will allow you to add or subtract Process counters to the Processes list.

A description of each process counter is available in Windows 2000 Help.

It is also possible to terminate a process by selecting the process in the list and then clicking the End Process button. Some processes are protected, but you can terminate them using the kill or remote kill utilities that are included in the operating system (see Appendix B for more information on `kill` and `rkill`). You will need authority to kill processes, and before you do, you should fully understand the ramifications of terminating a process.

The *Performance* tab (shown in Figure 20-2) allows you to graph the percentage of processor time in kernel mode. To show this, select the View menu and check the Show Kernel Times option. The Kernel Times is the measure of time that applications are using operating system services. The remaining time, known as User mode, is spent in threads that are spawned by applications.

If your server supports multiple processes, you can click CPU History on the View menu and graph each processor in a single graph pane or in separate graph panes.

The *Application* tab lists running applications and allows you to terminate an application that has become unresponsive or that you determine is in trouble or is the cause of trouble on the server.

Performance Console

Performance Console includes the System Monitor, discussed first, and Performance Logs and Alerts, which is discussed next. System Monitor is really a new version of Performance Monitor (known as *perfmon* on Windows NT). It can be opened from Administrative Tools ➪ Performance ➪ System Monitor. Performance Console can be loaded like all MMC snap-ins from the Run console, Task Manager, or command line as `perfmon.msc`.

When the Performance Console starts, it loads a blank System Monitor graph into the console tree.

System Monitor

System Monitor allows you to analyze system data and research performance and bottlenecks. The utility allows you to create graphs, histograms (bar charts), and textual reports of performance counter data. System Monitor is ideal for short-term viewing of data and for diagnostics.

System Monitor is illustrated in Figure 20-3 and includes the following features:

✦ System Monitor is hosted in MMC, which makes it portable. The snap-in can take aim at any computer and monitor remote processing on that computer.

✦ It provides a toolbar that can be used to copy and paste counters, purge or clear counters, add counters, and so on.

✦ You have extensive control on how counter values are displayed. For example, you can vary the line style and width and change the color of the lines. You can also change the color of the chart and then manipulate the chart window.

✦ Legends indicate selected counters and associated data such as the name of the computer, the objects, and object instances.

✦ System Monitor is an ActiveX control named `sysmon.ocx`. You can load the OCX into any OLE-compliant application, such as Microsoft Word or Visio, and even an HTML page on a Web site. The OCX is also useful in applications that can be specifically created for performance monitoring and analysis.

Firstly, the monitor can be configured using the toolbar or the Shortcut menu. The Shortcut menu is loaded by right-clicking in the blank-graph area and selecting the appropriate option. The toolbar is available by default.

Using the toolbar, you can configure the type of display to view by clicking the View Chart, View Histogram, or View Report buttons. In other words, the same information can be viewed in chart, histogram, or report format.

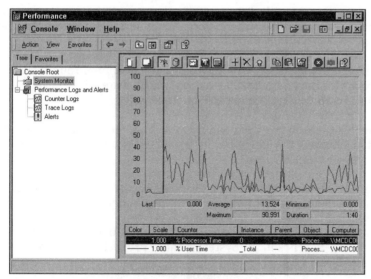

Figure 20-3: The Performance Console

The differences in the view formats should be noted. The histograms and charts can be used to view multiple counters. However, each counter only displays a single value. You use these to track current activity, and view the graphs as they change. The report is more suited to multiple values.

Your data source is obtained by clicking the View Current Activity button for real-time data. You can also select the View Log File Data button, which will allow you to obtain data from completed or running logs.

Of course, you first have to select counters. The counter buttons in the middle of the toolbar include Add, Delete, and the New Counter Set button. The latter resets the display and allows you to select new counters. When you click the Add Counters button, the dialog box, illustrated in Figure 20-4, is shown.

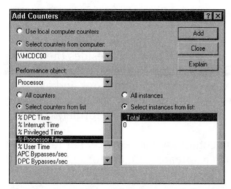

Figure 20-4: The Add Counters dialog box

This dialog box allows you to select the computer you are aiming to monitor, and to select performance objects and counters. Notice also the Explain button. You can click this to learn more about the individual counters you select.

In addition, you update the display with the Clear Display option. You can also freeze the display with the Freeze Display button, which suspends data collection. Click the Update Data button to resume collection.

Clicking the Highlight button lets you highlight chart or histogram data. This serves the purpose of highlighting the line or bar for a selected counter with a white or black background.

The display can also be exported. You can, for example, save it to the Clipboard. Conversely, a saved display can be imported into the running display.

Finally, the Properties button allows you access to settings that control fonts, colors, and so on. When you click it, the System Monitor Properties dialog box loads, as shown in Figure 20-5.

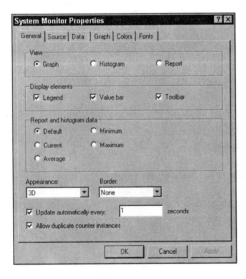

Figure 20-5: The System Monitor Properties dialog box

There are several ways you can save data from the monitor. Besides the clipboard option described previously, you can add the control to a host application, as discussed earlier. But by far the easiest means of preserving the look and feel of the display is to save the control as an HTML file. Right-clicking the pane and saving the display as an HTML file does this, and it is the default Save As format.

Alternately, you can import the log file in comma-separated (CSV) or tab-separated (.tsv) format and then import the data in a spreadsheet, database, or report program such as Crystal Reports.

Working with the Add Counters dialog box, you can select all counters and instances or specific counters and instances to monitor from the list. Keep in mind that the more you monitor, the more system resources you will use. If you monitor a large amount of monitors and counters, consider redirecting the data to log files and then reading the log file data in the display. It makes more sense, however, to work with fewer counters and instances.

Note
It is possible to run two instances of System Monitor (in two performance consoles). This may make it easier to compare data from different sources.

In the instances list box, the first value, _Total, allows you to add all the instance values and report them in the display.

The lines in the display can also be matched with their respective counters by selecting the line in the display.

Performance Logs and Alerts

The Windows 2000 Performance utilities can produce two types of performance-related logs: counter logs and trace logs. These logs are useful for advanced performance analysis and record-keeping that can be done over a period of time. There is also an alerting mechanism. The Performance Logs and Alerts tree is shown in Figure 20-6. The tool is part of the Performance console snap-in and is thus started as described earlier.

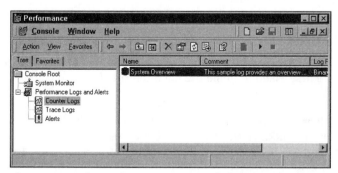

Figure 20-6: The Performance Logs and Alerts tree

The Counter Logs record sampled data about hardware resources and system services based on the performance objects described earlier. It works with counters in the same manner as System Monitor. The Performance Logs and Alert Service obtains data from the operating system when the update interval has elapsed.

Trace logs collect event traces. With trace logs, you can measure performance associated with events related to memory, storage file I/O, and so on. As soon as the event occurs, the data is sent to the logs. The data is measured continuously from the start of the event to the end of the event, as opposed to the sampling that is performed by the System Monitor.

The Performance Logs data is obtained by the default Windows 2000 kernel trace provider. You can analyze the data using a data-parsing tool.

The alerting function is used to define a counter value that will trigger an alert that can send a network message, execute a program, or start a log. This is useful for maintaining a close watch on systems. You can, for example, monitor unusual activity that does not occur consistently and define an alert to let you know when the event has been triggered. Security-related events are good candidates for the alert service. When you are trying to catch a hacker, there is no better time than when he or she is in the act.

You can also configure the alert service to notify you when a particular resource drops below or exceeds certain values, thresholds, or baselines that you establish.

Counter Logs can also be viewed in System Monitor, and the Counter Log data can be saved to CSV and TSV files and viewed in a spreadsheet, or report software. You can configure the logs to be circular, which means that when the log file reaches a predetermined size, it will be overwritten. Logs can be linear, and you can collect data for predefined lengths of time. Logs can be stopped and restarted based on parameters you set.

Like the System Monitor, you can save files to various formats, such as HTML, or import the entire control OCX into an OLE container.

Using Logs and Alerts

To start using Logs and Alerts, right-click the details pane and select the New Log Settings option. You are first asked to name the log or alert before you can define its properties.

> **Note**
>
> To use Logs and Alerts, you need to have Full Control access to the following registry subkey: HKEY_CURRENT_MACHINE\SYSTEM\CurrentControlSet\Services\ SysmonLog\Log_Queries. This key is open to administrators by default, but access can also be given by way of the Security menu in Regedt32. Also, to run or configure the service, you will need the right to start or configure services on the system. Again, administrators have this right by default, but it can be conveyed through security group membership and Group Policy.

Upon choosing the Properties option, the Counter Log Properties or Trace Log Properties dialog box loads, as illustrated in Figures 20-7 and 20-8, respectively. The Log and Alert properties are configured, as demonstrated next.

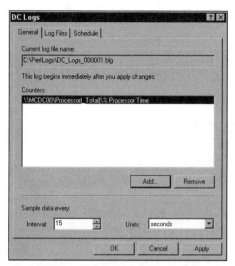

Figure 20-7: Counter Log properties

To configure alerts, you first need to configure counters for the alerts, the sample interval, and the alert threshold. Then you need to configure an action to take when an event occurs. These can include running a program, sending a message, triggering a counter log, or writing to the event log.

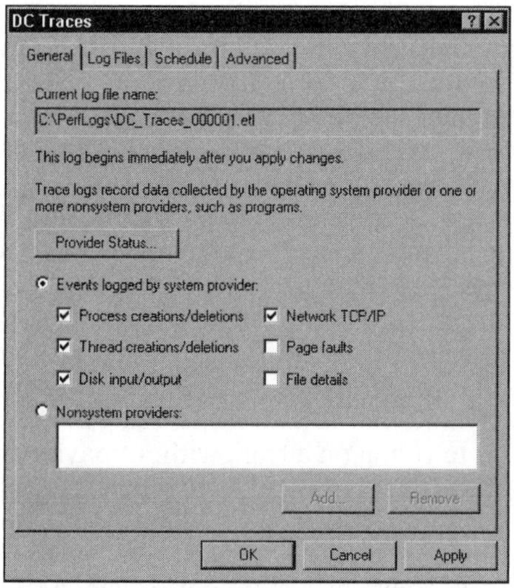

Figure 20-8: The Trace Log properties

Alert startup can also be configured by providing Start and Stop parameters.

To configure Counter Logs, you need to set the Counter Log counters and provide a sample interval. To write to log files, you need to provide a file type, size, path, and any automatic naming parameters needed. The Counter Logs should be defined as SCV files or TSV files, text files, or binary linear or circular files.

Counter Logs can also be scheduled to start automatically, but you cannot configure the service to automatically restart if a log file is configured to stop manually. The same criteria apply to Trace Logs.

Getting to Know Your Servers

To maintain service level and keep servers and applications available, you need to become familiar with each of your machines, the applications running on them, and the resources they use. But it is insufficient to maintain a subjective feel for how a server is "supposed" to operate. Mission-critical applications, server attacks, and system failures can happen suddenly. System monitoring is thus a chore in which you should be engaged continuously.

When you first begin to monitor a system, you basically have nothing to compare it against. After a considerable amount of data has been collected, you will have a data set to work with. You will need to collect data over several weeks, possibly even months, and then based on the assessment of that data, you need to establish baselines against which to base future observation. Normal for some machines may be aggressive CPU usage, while other machines may sit idle for most of their lives.

Tip If a system is unstable collecting data, setting alerts like crazy is only going to compound the problem. Your first option will be to determine the cause of the instability and then set up monitoring and alerts to determine the cause of the instability in the first place. In the event of an unresponsive system, your first option will be to run Task Manager and attempt to end the tasks, applications, and processes that are causing the problems.

With a baseline in hand, you will quickly be alerted to performance that is out of the ordinary. For example, if you notice that at night your mail server's responsiveness begins to diminish suddenly, you may find that the server is being hacked for its relay services, which can be compared to riding on a train without paying the fare. A memory counter would be the object that alerts you as to when this is taking place.

Your information should also reflect various points in system performance. You should note what constitutes normal on a server. For example, we noticed that a client's mail server was low on RAM and had begun to page out to disk excessively.

When we queried this with the MIS, he advised it was "normal" for this time of the day due to replication services.

It is thus important to note periods of low usage, average usage, and high or peak usage. Systems that provide real-time communications are good examples of servers that should be monitored continuously for this type of information.

Tip Make baseline performance information available within an arm's reach of your server. This can be in the form of clipboards or journals into which you can paste data. This will allow other system operators to look up a server and determine what might be considered normal.

Do not expect to obtain any meaningful insight into system performance from the get-go, because the baselines you develop will establish typical values to expect when your system is not experiencing problems.

Monitoring for Bottlenecks

As described previously, when the system performance deviates from your established baselines, bottlenecks occur. It helps to have some guidelines, so the following table suggests thresholds for a minimum set of system counters.

Table 20-1 Suggested System Counter Thresholds				
Item	**Resource**	**Object**	**Counter**	**Threshold**
1	Disk	LogicalDisk	%Free Space	15%
2	Disk	LogicalDisk	%Disk Time	80%
3	Disk	PhysicalDisk	Disk Reads/sec Disk Writes/sec	Check the manufacturer's specifications
4	Disk	PhysicalDisk	Current Disk Queue Length	Number of spindles plus 2
5	Memory	Memory	Available Bytes	4MB, best not to go below 16MB
6	Memory	Memory	Pages/sec	20 per second
7	Network	Network Segment	% Net Utilization	30%

Continued

			Table 20-1 (continued)	
Item	**Resource**	**Object**	**Counter**	**Threshold**
8	Paging File	Paging File	% Usage	Above 70%
9	Processor	Processor	% Processor Time	85%
10	Processor	Processor	Interrupts/sec	1,500 per second
11	Server	Server	Bytes Total/sec	N/A
12	Server	Server	Work Item Shortages	3
13	Server	Server Work Queues	Queue Length	4
14	Multiple Processors	System	Processor Queue Length	2

These values are recommended for a minimum performance monitoring set. Some of these options may vary and still be satisfactory for your server. The following list of notes provides some additional guidance (the notes are numbered according to the table):

1. A threshold of 15 percent free space may be too low depending on the purpose of the machine. You can also ensure the threshold is never suddenly exceeded with disk quotas. Although not all processes can be blocked from using disk space, it is a good idea to configure alerts to signal you when the threshold is exceeded.

2. The value given for Disk Time is a usage period. We are saying that the disk should not be used more than 80 percent of the time. You need to check this value against the advice of the manufacturer. Disks that exceed this usage may not last long. We have seen disks easily overheat and crash when the threshold scaled to 100 percent.

3. The transfer rate information of your disk is usually printed on the disk. Program alerts you if the monitor reports that your rates are exceeding this. If the applications are hammering your disks, you should upgrade to faster technology, such as Ultra Wide SCSI.

4. The number of spindles is a snapshot; you should observe this value over several intervals. You can also use the Avg. Disk Queue Length counter.

5. If memory drops below 4MB, paging activity will begin to increase and system response will begin to wane. If the condition continues, you will get an error message advising that system resources are getting low.

6. If memory use increases, watch that this threshold does not exceed your baselines.

7. This value depends on the type of network you are running. For an Ethernet network, your typical threshold will be around 30 percent.

8. You should fully understand how paging works before trying to make sense of this counter, because the threshold varies according to the nature of the hardware and the number of applications you have running (see Chapter 1 for some guidelines).

9. The Processor Time can be easily observed in the Task Manager, as described earlier. Any processor usage at the 85 percent and higher mark is cause for concern. You can also use Task Manager to identify the process that is using up your CPU's bandwidth. If it is a critical function, like Exchange or SQL Server, you might need to add another processor or upgrade to a faster CPU. On stable or inactive machines, you will notice that the System Idle Process uses the CPU most of the time.

10. This counter can be used to signal hardware problems. If the counter increases dramatically without a corresponding increase in server activity, a piece of hardware is responsible for the flood in interrupts. The hardware could be a disk controller, a network interface card, or something similar.

11. Using the server counter, you can sum the total Bytes Total/sec for all servers, and if the value is equal to the maximum transfer rate for the network, you may have some segmenting to do.

12. If the value exceeds three, you may have to change parameters in the registry. Look up information on WorkItems in the Microsoft knowledge base for a complete discussion of the Work Item Shortages counter.

13. Server work queues is another snapshot counter that may signify a processor bottleneck. You should observe this counter over several intervals.

14. The processor queue length is also a snapshot, and you should monitor the counter over several intervals. A value higher than two over several intervals requires investigation.

Understanding Server Workload

In addition to the starting points just described, you might find useful the following monitoring suggestions for workload monitoring on some standard server configurations. The following list provides a short description of objects to monitor by the server role:

✦ **Application Servers:** These include standard application servers and Terminal Services, or application, servers. Terminal Services are more demanding and require constant performance monitoring. The heaviest resource usage on these servers is memory and CPU. Objects to monitor include Cache, Memory, Processors, and System.

✦ **Backup Servers:** These servers can create bottlenecks on the network and suffer from extensive CPU usage. They may also place a burden on the remote computer they connect to. Consider monitoring the System, Server, Processor, and Network Segment objects.

✦ **Database Server:** Disks and CPU are the most taxed resources on database servers. You would think that available memory is a taxed resource, but most advanced database server technologies, such as SQL Server 2000, only keep a small amount of "hot" data in memory (by caching records) for the majority of queries. You particularly need fast hard disks for database servers, like SQL 2000 or Oracle. Objects you should monitor include the PhysicalDisk, LogicalDisk, Processor, and System.

✦ **Domain Controllers:** Domain controllers can eat up a lot of different resources, including CPUs, disks, memory, and networks. You should monitor Memory, CPU, System, Network Segment, Network Interface, and the protocol counter objects, such as TCP, UDP, IP, NBT, connection, NetBEUI, NetBIOS, and so on. You can also monitor Active Directory's NTDS service objects and the Site Server LDAP service objects. WINS and DNS also have applicable objects that can be observed.

✦ **File and Print Servers:** These servers consume a lot of hard disk space and network resources. Intensive color and graphics rendering (see Chapter 23) can tax a CPU. Monitor here for CPU, Memory, Network Segment, Physical Disk, and Logical Disk. You can also monitor the PrintQueue object to troubleshoot spooling, and so on.

✦ **Mail Servers:** Mail servers, such as Exchange, use CPU, disks, and memory the heaviest. You can monitor the memory collection, Cache, Processor, System, PhsysicalDisk, and LogicalDisk objects. Exchange also ships with specialized counters.

✦ **Web/Internet Information Server:** These servers consume extensive disk, cache, and network components. Consider monitoring the Cache, Network Segment, PhysicalDisk, and LogicalDisk objects.

Performance Monitoring Overhead

Monitoring performance requires resources, which can adversely affect the data you're trying to gather. Therefore, you need to decrease the impact of your performance monitoring activities. There are several techniques you can use to ensure that performance monitoring overhead is kept to a minimum on any server you are monitoring.

✦ The System Monitor application can be demanding on resources. You can use logs instead of displaying a graph, and then import the data into report programs and databases. Save logs to storage that are not being monitored, or to a hard disk that is not the object of analysis. Also, make sure the logs are not growing too big. You should set a quota and alert on the disk space, or make sure to keep your eye on the disks.

✦ Do not use many counters at the same time. Some counters are costly and can increase overhead, which will be counterproductive, and besides, it is hard to monitor too many things at once. What each counter consumes in overhead is available on the Windows 2000 Resource Kit.

✦ Tight collection intervals can also be costly. Microsoft recommends a ten-minute interval for data collection.

✦ While taking care not to impact available resources, you should continue monitoring during peak usage periods to obtain the best assessment of resource usage. It makes no sense to monitor a system that is idle.

✦ Consider monitoring remotely. Remote monitoring allows for a centralized data collection. You can also collect data from several servers and save the data to the local machine. You must be aware, though, that what you save on the swings, you might lose on the roundabout. Network bandwidth increases with the more data you are collecting and the more often you collect. Consider keeping the number of servers in a monitored group to no more than about 10 or 15. To increase network bandwidth, consider saving the remote data to log files on the remote servers and then either copy the data to the local computer or view it remotely.

Summary

This chapter introduced Service Level and Service Level Management. More and more companies and business plans are demanding that MIS maintain SL standards. To ensure that MIS or IT and IS managers adhere to the performance requirements of the business, the Service Level Agreement, or SLA, is going to be seen a lot more often in many enterprises.

As the e-commerce phenomenon continues to explode, so too will the number of applications and business processes that demand SL adherence. The customer will be more and more directly involved in the health of your systems. These include data interchange systems, Web servers, applications servers, ISP equipment, and so on.

SL and SLM have, for the past few years, been the domain mainly of mid-range and legacy systems. SL tools have been lacking on server operating systems for years. Now Windows 2000 rises to the challenge by providing an extensive performance monitoring and reporting architecture that will allow you to monitor systems' health in the ongoing effort to support SL, methodically troubleshoot problems, and maintain server and service health. These tools will also allow you to plan capacity and provide feedback to management to ensure that IT continues to support the business models and marketing plans being adopted.

We have discussed the Performance Console, System Monitor, Log and Alerts, and Task Manager in very loose terms. Our definitions have also been very broad. The number of monitoring objects is so extensive that you need to fully understand what they collect and how they impact the available resources. The Windows 2000 Resource Kit includes a number of tools that can be added to your SLM arsenal. See Appendix B for a brief discussion of these tools.

✦   ✦   ✦

File, Print, and Web Services

◆ ◆ ◆ ◆

◆ ◆ ◆ ◆

The NTFS file system has been substantially enhanced in Windows 2000 with a myriad of sophisticated services found in no other operating system. In Chapter 21, you will learn about the support for compression, encryption, hierarchical storage management, and more.

Chapter 22 takes you into the world of folders and share-points, setting up a shared folder namespace, and permissions and rights for groups of users and computers. We also investigate the new NTFS file and folder encryption services and show you how to configure these for the ultimate in data protection.

Chapter 23 provides a thorough treatise on Windows 2000 printing services, a critical demand in every organization.

The Internet Information Services (IIS) are now part and parcel of the operating system, as they should be. Chapter 24 shows you how to setup services for multiple Web sites, how to configure the FTP services, Web shares, and other topics.

Windows 2000 File Systems

This chapter explores the many aspects of the Windows 2000 file system, including file system structure, the Distributed File System, auditing, and system repair and recovery.

An Overview of Disk Structure

In order to understand the file system options in Windows 2000, you first need to understand some basic physical disk concepts and terms. This section covers concepts and terms that will help you understand file system structure in Windows 2000. This chapter does not cover basic hardware storage concepts such as heads and head gap, as these topics aren't germane to an understanding of file systems. This chapter focuses on logical disk structure rather than physical disk structure.

The circular path a head traverses as it sits motionless over a disk platter is called a *track.* The tracks are magnetically encoded on the disk during formatting and define the physical structure of the disk's storage space. The tracks that reside in the same location on each platter form a *cylinder.* Each track is divided into a certain number of *sectors,* the number of which depends on the disk type and location of the track on the disk. Sectors are the smallest physical storage units on a disk, but they are grouped into *clusters,* which are the smallest *logical* storage units on the disk. Figure 21-1 illustrates basic disk structure.

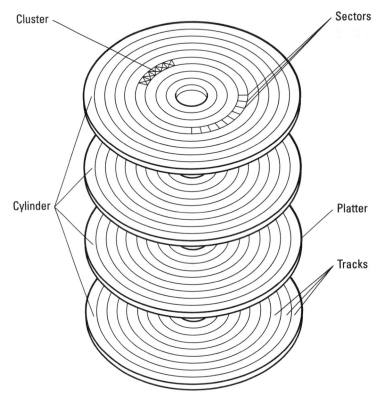

Figure 21-1: Physical disk structure

Each cluster comprises a certain number of sectors. The number of sectors in each cluster depends on the drive type, partition size, and file system (explained in the following sections). When the operating system stores a file, the storage space is allocated not by sector, but by cluster. The cluster size has a significant impact on the amount of free space on a disk, as you'll learn later in the section "Optimizing Storage Capacity."

Basic disks in Windows 2000 contain one or more *partitions* that consist of a series of clusters. A partition has a beginning and an ending sector, and the number of sectors in between determines the partition capacity. Each partition uses a particular file system type (FAT16, FAT32, NTFS, and so on). Each basic disk can contain up to four partitions, all *primary partitions,* or three primary partitions and one *extended partition.* Each primary partition represents a single drive with a single drive ID, while an extended partition can contain multiple logical drives. Each logical drive can be represented by a drive ID, although drive IDs are not required per se. For the sake of simplicity and consistency, the term *volume* refers to a logical drive entity, such as a drive defined by a primary partition or a single logical drive in an extended partition.

Dynamic disks are new in Windows 2000 and overcome the four-partition limitation of basic disks. Dynamic disks don't contain partitions. Instead, they contain *dynamic volumes,* which are a lot like a logical drive within an extended partition in the sense that the disk can contain multiple volumes and each appears as a unique object. However, you can create an unlimited number of volumes in a dynamic disk, subject to disk capacity. As with partitions in a basic disk, each dynamic volume has its own file system (FAT16, FAT32, or NTFS).

Tip   Although you can manage existing fault-tolerant volumes on a basic disk with Windows 2000, you can't create or extend these volumes on basic disks. Full support (creation and modification) for fault-tolerant volumes now requires a dynamic disk. For more information on dynamic disks and volumes, see Chapter 16.

Whether you choose to use basic disks with primary or extended partitions, or dynamic disks with dynamic volumes, each volume requires a file system. You can choose among three in Windows 2000: FAT16, FAT32, or NTFS. Each offers certain advantages and disadvantages. The following section explains the structure, advantages, and disadvantages of the FAT16 and FAT32 file systems.

FAT16 and FAT32

The FAT file system originated with DOS and is supported by DOS, all versions of Windows, Windows NT, Windows 2000, UNIX, Linux, and OS/2. Because of that wide support, it is the most compatible between operating platforms (one of its advantages). FAT stands for File Allocation Table, which is the structure in a FAT volume that stores information about disk space allocation.

A disk formatted with the FAT file system contains five control areas. The first is the *reserve area,* which comprises one or more sectors depending on disk type. The first sector in the reserve area is the *boot sector,* which contains the partition table and bootstrap program. The partition table stores information about the disk's partitions including type, starting and ending sectors, and which partition is active. The bootstrap program executes at startup and boots the operating system or boot loader in the active partition. The boot sector is always located at cylinder 0, head 0, track 1 (the first sector on the disk).

The *File Allocation Table (FAT)* is the second control area and serves as a reference table of the clusters in the volume. Each cluster's entry contains a value defined by those listed in Table 21-1. The value defines the cluster's status, indicating if the cluster is available, in use, bad, or reserved. A *backup copy* of the FAT makes up the third control area and can be used by utility applications to restore the file system when the primary FAT becomes corrupted.

Table 21-1
FAT Cluster Entries

Entry	Meaning
0	Cluster is available.
BAD	Cluster contains bad sector and is unusable.
Reserved	Cluster is reserved for use by the operating system.
EOF	End of File; marks the last cluster of a file.
nnn	Number of the next cluster in the file.

The fourth control area is the *root directory table,* which works in conjunction with the FAT to define files in the root directory, subdirectories (which are really just files in the root directory), and the starting cluster of each file. The fifth control area is the area in which file data is actually stored in the volume. When applications request a file read operation, the OS reads the FAT to locate the beginning cluster for the file. It then uses the FAT as a sort of road map to locate the other clusters for the file, using the FAT as a lookup table to determine which clusters to read and in which order to put a file back together.

Windows 2000 automatically determines the number of sectors per cluster for a volume based on the volume size. Table 21-2 lists the default cluster size for FAT volumes. The sizes listed apply to disks consisting of a single partition and to logical drives in an extended partition. Floppy disks are not included. Cluster size is an important consideration when formatting a disk to optimize disk capacity.

Table 21-2
Default FAT Cluster Size

Volume Size	Cluster Size	Sectors per Cluster
Less than 32MB	512 bytes	1
33 to 64MB	1K	2
65 to 128MB	2K	4

Volume Size	Cluster Size	Sectors per Cluster
129 to 255MB	4K	8
256 to 511MB	8K	16
512MB to 1GB	16K	32
1GB to 2GB	32K	64
2GB to 4GB	64K	128

The FAT file system originally used 12 bits to define the FAT entries. A 16-bit FAT, called FAT16, was introduced in DOS 4.0 to accommodate larger cluster values and therefore larger disks. FAT16 supports a maximum of 65,526 clusters, which limits FAT volumes to 4GB ($clustersize_{max} \times clusters_{max} = bytes$).

Windows 95 OSR2 introduced FAT32, which allocates 32 bits to the FAT, increasing the maximum number of clusters to 268,435,446. The maximum cluster size of 32,768 bytes means that FAT32 volumes can theoretically be up to 8TB (one terabyte equals 1,024 gigabytes), although the current hardware limitation of 512-byte sectors limits the actual size to 2TB. Windows 2000 limits the size of the FAT32 partition you can create within Windows 2000 to 32GB. However, it does support mounting any size FAT32 volume, including those larger than 32GB. The capability enables you to mount FAT32 volumes larger than 32GB created with another operating system or a third-party partitioning utility. Table 21-3 lists the default cluster sizes for FAT32 volumes of a given size.

Note   Microsoft reserves the top four bits of each cluster in a FAT32 volume, so there are only 28 bits for the cluster number, not 32, and therefore the maximum number of clusters totals 268,435,446. In addition, BIOS limitations can limit volume size on any given system. Finally, the 512-byte sector size is also a limiting factor.

Table 21-3
Default FAT32 Cluster Size

Volume Size	Cluster Size	Sectors per Cluster
Less than 512MB	Not supported	N/A
512MB to 8GB	4K	8
8GB to 16GB	8K	16
16GB to 32GB	16K	32
More than 32GB	32K	64

NTFS 5.0

NTFS stands for NT File System, and NTFS is the third file system supported by Windows 2000. It offers several advantages over the FAT16 and FAT32 file systems, although NTFS is not the optimum choice in all situations, as you'll learn shortly.

One primary difference from FAT16 is that NTFS is a recoverable file system. If a failure occurs that affects an NTFS volume, Windows 2000 reconstructs the volume automatically when the system restarts. Another important distinction is security. FAT16 and FAT32 allow you to apply limited share permissions to control access to resources shared from a FAT16 folder. The share permissions apply to all subfolders and files within the share. NTFS, however, allows you to apply not only share permissions, but *object permissions,* as well. Object permissions provide a much more granular control over folder and file access, controlling access on a folder-by-folder and file-by-file basis. Object permissions apply not only to remote connections across the network, but also to local connections. NTFS, therefore, is the only Windows 2000 file system that provides adequate security for folders and files for users who log on locally. NTFS also allows object access auditing, something that is not supported for FAT16/FAT32 volumes.

Note   See Chapter 19 for a detailed description of auditing.

Like FAT32, NTFS supports larger volumes than FAT volumes, with a maximum of 2TB per NTFS volume. Also, like FAT16 and FAT32, NTFS provides for a variable cluster size that adjusts automatically according to volume size. Table 21-4 lists the default NTFS cluster sizes for volumes of a given size.

Table 21-4
Default NTFS Cluster Size

Volume Size	Cluster Size	Sectors per Cluster
512MB or less	512 bytes	1
513MB to 1GB	1K	2
1GB to 2GB	2K	4
2GB to 4GB	4K	8
4GB to 8GB	8K	16
8GB to 16GB	16K	32
16GB to 32GB	32K	16
More than 32GB	64K	128

As with FAT16 and FAT32, you can change the cluster size for an NTFS volume when you format the volume to optimize storage capacity. The cluster sizes identified in Table 21-4 are the default sizes Windows 2000 uses unless you specify otherwise. See the section "Optimizing Storage Capacity" later in this chapter for an explanation of why you would choose a cluster size different from the default values.

NTFS Structure

The structure of an NTFS volume is considerably different from that of the FAT16 and FAT32 file systems. The boot sector, located at sector 0 in the volume, can be up to 16 sectors in size and comprises two structures: the BIOS Parameter Block (BPB) and the bootstrap program. The BPB stores information about the volume's layout. The bootstrap program loads the file NTLDR, which boots the system. NTFS stores a duplicate copy of the boot sector at the end of the volume for redundancy and fault tolerance.

How NTFS stores volume data also differs from FAT. NTFS uses a relational database called the *master file table* (MFT) to manage the contents of a volume. The MFT serves much the same purpose in the NTFS file system that the FAT serves in the FAT file systems. The MFT stores a record for each file and directory, including the MFT itself. Each entry includes the name, security descriptor, and other attributes. The MFT is an array of data with rows representing file records and columns representing attribute fields for each record, as shown in Figure 21-2. The size of each MFT record is constant and determined when the volume is formatted. MFT record size can be 1K, 2K, or 4K, depending on disk size.

The Data field for each record stores the file's data. With very small files, the data is contained completely within the Data field of one MFT record. When all of a file's attributes — including its data — reside in a single MFT record, the attributes are called *resident attributes*.

As a file increases in size or becomes fragmented, however, it requires multiple records to store its data. The primary record in the MFT for a file that spans multiple records is called the *base file record*. The base file record serves as the starting point in the file's data chain. NTFS creates additional areas called *runs* on the disk to store the additional file data. With volumes that have a cluster size of 2K or smaller, the runs are 2K in size. Volumes with 4K or larger clusters use 4K-sized runs. Attributes that don't reside in the MFT but instead reside in runs are called *non-resident attributes*. NTFS adds additional runs as needed when the file size increases.

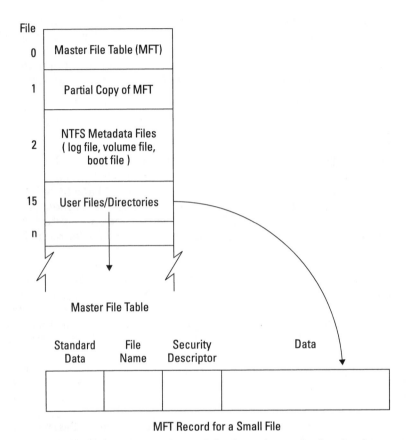

Figure 21-2: The MFT is a relational database that maintains the data on an NTFS volume.

If you compare the way NTFS and FAT store information about data in the volume, you'll see that the MFT is like the FAT. Windows 2000 uses the cluster entries in the FAT to locate the clusters in a file's data chain. Windows 2000 uses the records in the MFT to locate the data in a file's data chain. The clusters belonging to a file are referenced in the MFT using virtual cluster numbers (VCNs). Each file starts with VCN 0, and additional clusters are numbered sequentially up to the last cluster in the file. The Data attribute for the file contains information that maps the VCNs to the logical cluster numbers (LCN) on the disk. When there are too many VCN-to-LCN mappings to store in a single MFT record, NTFS adds additional records to store the additional mappings. Figure 21-3 illustrates VCN-to-LCN mapping in the MFT.

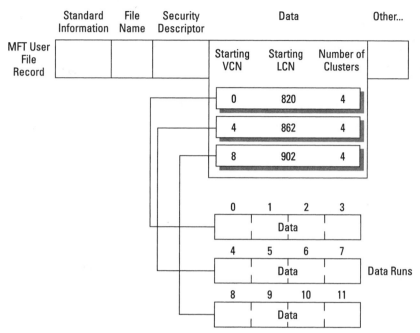

Figure 21-3: The MFT record for a file stores its LCN-to-VCN mapping, using multiple runs if necessary.

The first 16 records in the MFT are reserved by NTFS for *metadata,* which are the files NTFS uses to define the file system structure. Table 21-5 describes the metadata stored in the MFT.

	Table 21-5 NTFS Metadata		
MFT Record	*Description*	*File Name*	*Purpose*
0	Master file table (MFT)	$Mft	Stores base file record for each file and folder in the volume. Additional records are used when the number or size of files and folders exceeds the space available.
1	Master file table 2	$MftMirr	This duplicate MFT stores the first four records of the MFT to ensure access to the MFT in case of a failure. The boot sector stores the data segment locations for both $Mft and $MftMirr for recoverability.

Continued

Table 21-5 *(continued)*

MFT Record	Description	File Name	Purpose
2	Log file	$LogFile	Stores transaction history enabling NTFS to perform a recovery of the file system if an error occurs. The log can be up to 4MB in size.
3	Volume	$Volume	Stores volume data such as the volume version and volume label.
4	Attribute definitions	$AttrDef	Comprises a table of attribute names, numbers, and descriptions.
5	Root file name index	$	The volume's root directory.
6	Cluster bitmap	$Bitmap	Clusters-in-use table.
7	Partition boot sector	$Boot	Contains bootstrap program on bootable volume.
8	Bad cluster file	$BadClus	Bad cluster map.
9	Security file	$Secure	Stores unique security descriptors for all files in the volume.
10	Upcase table	$Upcase	Converts lowercase characters to uppercase Unicode characters.
11	NTFS extension file	$Extend	Enables file system extensions such as reparse points, quotas, and so on.
12-15			Reserved for future use.

While the MFT performs a similar function to the FAT, the similarities between the two file systems stop there. NTFS provides considerably more features than FAT because of the differences in structure. As mentioned previously, NTFS provides much better security and recoverability than FAT. NTFS also provides built-in compression capability, enabling you to compress files on a file-by-file basis. The NTFS driver handles decompression on the fly, making compression transparent to the user.

Note   For detailed information on using compression on NTFS volumes, see Chapter 16.

NTFS' structure also makes it an extensible file system, which means that new features can be added without completely redesigning the file system. Several new features have been added to NTFS version 5 in Windows 2000. The following sections explain the most pertinent changes.

Disk Quotas

NTFS 5.0 in Windows 2000 introduces *disk quotas,* which enable you to restrict the amount of disk space a given account can use. Quotas enable you to more effectively manage storage space, since you can parcel out storage space on an as-needed basis. Quotas also force users to be conservative with their designated storage space, compelling them to delete files when no longer needed. You can configure how quotas are enforced when a given user's quota is reached, either denying additional space to the user or simply displaying a warning message to the user (Figure 21-4).

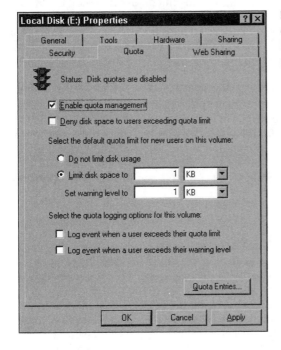

Figure 21-4: You configure quota settings on a per-volume basis through the volume's property sheet.

You assign quotas on a per-volume basis, which means that the entire volume shares the same quota properties. However, you can assign quota limits on a per-user basis, which means that each user can have a different quota limit, if necessary. You can also apply quotas on a per-group basis through the use of group policies. This flexibility enables you to tailor disk quotas to each user's or group's needs.

Although quotas apply to an entire volume rather than a single folder, there is a way around the per-volume nature of quotas. For example, assume you want to apply quotas only to C:\Users but not to the rest of drive C. *Mounted volumes,* new in Windows 2000, let you mount a physical volume to an NTFS folder. The mounted volume appears to both local and remote users as the contents of the host folder. In this situation, you can apply quotas to the mounted volume but not to the volume where it is hosted (drive C in this case). The net effect is that to the user, quotas only apply in the folder C:\Users.

Note For more information regarding quotas and quota assignment, see Chapter 16. See the section "Mounted Volumes" later in this chapter for a discussion of mounted volumes.

Reparse Points

Reparse points are a new feature in NTFS 5.0 through which Windows 2000 implements a handful of other new features (described in the following sections). Reparse points are NTFS objects that carry special attribute tags. They are used to trigger additional functionality in the file system, working in conjunction with file system filters to extend the capability of the NTFS file system. The combination of reparse points and these additional file system filters enables features and functions to be added to the file system by both Microsoft and third parties without the need to redesign or restructure the file system.

In effect, reparse points are like red flags in the file system. When Windows 2000 encounters a reparse point during pathname parsing, it passes the reparse attribute tag (which uniquely defines the purpose of the reparse point) back up the I/O stack. Each installable file system filter in the I/O stack examines the reparse tag. When a match occurs, the driver executes the feature associated with the reparse point. So, this "red flag" tells Windows 2000 that a driver other than the standard NTFS file system driver needs to process the file I/O to accommodate the added functionality made possible by that other driver.

Encrypting File System

The Encrypting File System (EFS) is a new feature made possible by reparse points in Windows 2000 that enhances security for local files on NTFS volumes. EFS is useful for securing files on any system, but it is most useful on systems that can easily be stolen or physically comprised, such as notebook PCs. EFS is integrated within NTFS 5.0 and therefore is applicable only to files on NTFS volumes. FAT16 and FAT32 volumes do not support EFS. Only files can be encrypted; folders cannot, even on NTFS volumes. However, folders are marked to indicate that they contain encrypted data. EFS is designed to protect files locally and therefore doesn't support sharing of encrypted files. You can store your own encrypted files on a remote server and access those files yourself. The data is not encrypted during transmission across the network, however, unless you use Internet Protocol Security (IPSec) to encrypt IP traffic (and assuming you are using TCP/IP as the network protocol for transferring the file).

Note For a detailed discussion of EFS and how to implement it, see the section "Securing Files with the Encrypting File System" in Chapter 22.

Hierarchical Storage Management

Hierarchical Storage Management (HSM) is another new feature in Windows 2000 made possible by reparse points. HSM allows some or all of a file to be stored remotely, and reparse points mark these files accordingly. The reparse point data stores the location of the remote data and allows NTFS to retrieve the data when needed. HSM works in conjunction with Remote Storage Services (RSS) and Removable Storage to enable files to be archived to tape or disk and automatically restored when requested by a user or process.

Note For more information on Removable Storage, see chapters 16 and 17. Configuring the file system to support Remote Storage Services and HSM is discussed later in this chapter.

Directory Junctions

Directory junctions are another feature of NTFS 5.0. Directory junctions mark NTFS directories with a surrogate name. When the reparse point causes the path name to be reparsed, the surrogate name is grafted onto the original name. Directory junctions enable local volumes to be mapped to local NTFS folders, and also allow remote network shares to be mapped to local NTFS folders, thereby integrating these local and remote elements into a single local namespace. Directory junctions offer functions similar to the Distributed File System (Dfs, explained later in the section "Managing the Windows 2000 Distributed File System"). Unlike Dfs, however, directory junctions work solely within the file system and don't require a client-side driver.

The primary purpose of directory junctions is to enable you to create a single local namespace using local folders, other local volumes, and network shares. All of these appear within the local namespace and appear to the local user as part of the local volume. Figure 21-5 illustrates the use of directory junctions to map local volumes and network shares into a local namespace.

Mounted Volumes

Another reparse point feature, *volume mount points* (mounted volumes), brings to Windows 2000 the same advantages for local file systems that the UNIX operating system offers through its distributed file system. In effect, this capability enables you to mount a volume to an NTFS folder on a different volume, making the mounted volume appear as if it were physically contained on the host volume. You can mount multiple volumes within a file system namespace, creating a homogenous file system from disparate physical volumes on the local computer. A single volume can be mounted to multiple NTFS folders if needed.

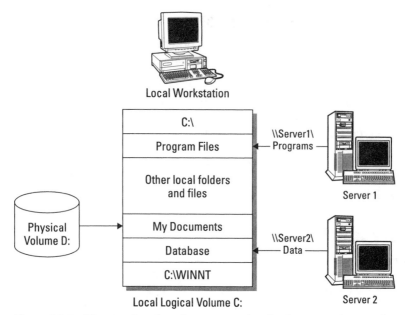

Local Workstation

Physical Volume D:

Local Logical Volume C:

\\Server1\ Programs

Server 1

\\Server2\ Data

Server 2

Figure 21-5: Directory junctions let you map local volumes and network shares into a single local namespace.

Note For a detailed discussion of mounted volumes, see the section "Working with Mounted Volumes" later in this chapter.

NTFS 5.0 Compatibility with Windows NT 4.0

In order to add the new features described previously to NTFS, Microsoft had to modify NTFS' structure. On single-boot systems where Windows 2000 is the only OS, compatibility isn't an issue. On systems that multi-boot between NT and Windows 2000, however, compatibility is an important issue.

The NTFS driver provided with Windows NT Service Pack 4 gives NT systems the ability to mount NTFS 5.0 volumes and read and write to them. However, NT can't take advantage of the new features in NTFS 5.0 described previously. Reparse points, quotas, and encryption are all ignored by NT 4. In addition, NT versions of file system utilities such as Chkdsk and Autochk will not work properly on NTFS volumes created with Windows 2000. For that reason, Microsoft doesn't recommend dual-booting between the two in a production environment.

Choosing a File System

FAT offers a handful of advantages. First, it is compatible with nearly every PC operating system, which is useful for systems that must boot multiple operating systems and enable all (or multiple) operating systems to see a common FAT volume. FAT is also very recoverable because you can boot the system from a DOS diskette in the event of a failure and run one of many third-part FAT recovery utilities to repair and recover a volume. Finally, FAT offers better efficiency than NTFS for volumes smaller than 256MB (FAT32 does not support volumes smaller than 512M).

FAT also has some disadvantages. The fact that the boot sector is stored in a fixed location (first track on the disk) makes it more susceptible to failure. If that track goes, the drive goes. Also, the root directory structure in a FAT volume is limited by design to 512 entries, which limits the number of files in the root folder to 512, but more important, limits the number of folders under the root.

Another disadvantage of FAT16 is the 4GB limit it imposes on volume size, although in reality this isn't a true disadvantage as the overhead imposed by FAT16 on large volumes makes them undesirable. Also, the relatively large default cluster size in a FAT16 volume also makes FAT volumes less efficient in their use of storage space (see "Optimizing Storage Capacity" later in this chapter).

FAT32 offers its own advantages. The 32-bit FAT increases the storage capacity to 2TB, considerably higher than the 4GB supported by FAT16. The smaller default cluster size for a FAT32 volume means that FAT32 volumes store data more efficiently than similarly sized FAT16 volumes.

Aside from different default cluster sizes and maximum capacities, there are a few key differences between FAT32 and FAT16. First, FAT32 offers better performance than FAT16. In addition, FAT32 is more fault-tolerant than FAT16 because Windows 2000 can automatically use the backup copy of the FAT32 if the primary becomes corrupted. The boot record on a FAT32 volume also contains backup data necessary to recreate the volume in the event the boot record becomes damaged.

NTFS offers several advantages over the FAT file systems. In terms of speed, NTFS is not always the fastest of the three. With many mitigating factors on either side (structure, cluster size, fragmentation, number of files) and the fact that today's hardware makes for quick file system performance regardless of the file system type, however, speed is not a factor in most situations. Choosing the right underlying disk subsystem is often more important (SCSI versus other interfaces).

One of the primary advantages offered by NTFS is security. Neither FAT16 nor FAT32 provides any local security for files. The security you can apply to FAT volumes is very limited for shared network access. Only NTFS enables you to assign permissions on a file-by-file basis with a high degree of granularity. Support for compression is another advantage offered by NTFS that you won't find in FAT16 or FAT32 under Windows 2000.

Because you can control cluster size for FAT volumes under Windows 2000, as you can for NTFS, cluster size is not an advantage per se, but NTFS will always use a smaller default cluster size for a volume of a given size. Reducing cluster size improves storage efficiency by reducing sector slack (see "Optimizing Storage Capacity" later in this chapter), but it can also increase file fragmentation, which can reduce performance. Because of the difference in structure between FAT and NTFS, NTFS is more efficient at retrieving a fragmented file, which mitigates fragmentation as a factor in deciding on cluster size.

So, the primary advantages offered by NTFS are those that pertain to functionality and security rather than performance. Consider choosing NTFS for all new installations and converting existing FAT16 and FAT32 partitions to NTFS for upgrades. You'll not only gain the security advantages offered by NTFS' object permissions, but also, you will be able to take advantage of Dfs, EFS, mounted volumes, disk quotas, and the other features discussed previously. The primary reason for retaining a FAT file system is to enable other operating systems on a dual-boot system to see the volume. While the additional overhead imposed by NTFS could be considered a disadvantage, most systems are so fast today that the overhead is transparent or negligible.

Optimizing Storage Capacity

Although quotas offer a means to help you manage storage capacity on NTFS volumes, there are also other issues to consider, including some that apply to FAT16 and FAT32 file systems. This section covers two topics that will help you optimize storage capacity: cluster size and compression.

Optimizing Cluster Size

As explained earlier in this chapter, a sector is the smallest unit of physical storage space on a disk. The smallest *allocation* unit, however, is the cluster. When Windows 2000 parcels out storage space, it does so by cluster. The significance of this is that cluster size has a direct impact on how efficiently the file system stores data. Take this example: Assume a volume uses a cluster size of 64K. You store several files, each 32K in size. Although two files could possibly fit in one cluster, that's not how Windows 2000 allocates the space. Instead, each file resides completely in its own cluster. That means that each file takes up just half of its allocated space, with the rest being unused. This is often called *sector slack.* Take it to the extreme in this example and assume that all your files are like this, and you'll waste half of the space on the volume. A 32GB volume would only hold 16GB of data.

In reality, most files are much larger than 32K, so the amount of wasted space is reduced. Overall, however, sector slack can have a significant impact on storage capacity, leaving as much as 25 percent or more of a disk unusable. You can reduce cluster size to reduce sector slack and make the most of the storage space you have. This has the net effect of increasing file fragmentation (see the next section), but a policy of frequently defragmenting the drive and the fact that NTFS efficiently retrieves even highly fragmented files can eliminate performance as an issue.

You can define the cluster size for a volume when you format the volume. To specify a non-default cluster size for an NTFS volume, simply choose the desired cluster size from the Allocation unit size drop-down list on the Format dialog box (see Figure 21-6). There is no way to change cluster size on an existing volume without reformatting the volume in Windows 2000, although you can use a third-party utility such as Symantec's Quarterdeck Partition-It (http://www.quarterdeck.com) or PowerQuest's PartitionMagic (http://www.powerquest.com) to dynamically modify cluster size without reformatting a disk.

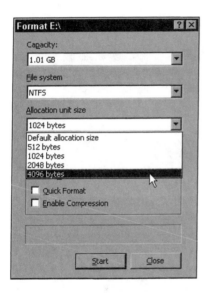

Figure 21-6: Use the Allocation unit size drop-down list to choose the cluster size when formatting a disk with NTFS.

The Format dialog box doesn't give you any options for using a non-default cluster size for FAT16 and FAT32 volumes, however. You must format these volumes using the FORMAT command from a console prompt and specify the desired cluster size as a parameter of the FORMAT command. You can choose any of the cluster sizes defined in Tables 21-2, 21-3, and 21-4 for the respective file systems. In addition, FAT32 and NTFS support cluster sizes of 128K and 256K for volumes with a physical sector size greater than 512 bytes. For a description of the FORMAT command's syntax, open a command console and type **format /?**.

Defragmenting Volumes

Windows 2000 allocates storage space in contiguous clusters whenever possible. This improves file system I/O performance because the disk heads don't have to move much to read or write a file. As files are added and modified, however, the amount of available space changes and files become *fragmented,* or stored in

non-contiguous sectors. The more fragmented a volume, the poorer the performance because the drive heads have to move more to piece together the file.
Even drives that use an efficient cluster size for the size of volume and size of
files on the volume can suffer from fragmentation that reduces performance.

Windows 2000 includes a defragmentation utility called Disk Defragmenter that
you can use to defragment a volume. Disk Defragmenter analyzes disk fragmentation and provides a means to defragment drives that require it. It also provides a
detailed fragmentation analysis report.

To defragment a volume, right-click the volume in My Computer and choose
Properties. Click the Tools tab, then click Defragment Now to open Disk
Defragmenter (Figure 21-7).

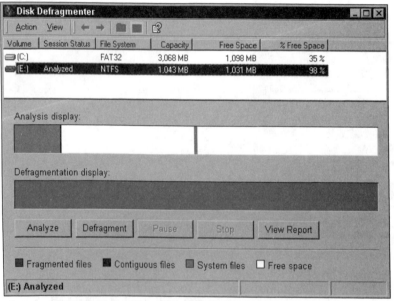

Figure 21-7: Use Disk Defragmenter to optimize storage space by
defragmenting a drive.

Note   You also can access Disk Defragmenter through the Disk Defragmenter node in the
Computer Management console (right-click My Computer and choose Manage).

Disk Defragmenter requires no user-specified parameters or other input. Simply
right-click a volume and choose Analyze to analyze fragmentation or Defragment to
start the defragmentation process. The length of time required to complete an analysis or defragmentation depends on the size and fragmentation of the volume. To
view a report from a previous analysis, right-click a volume and choose View Report
(Figure 21-8).

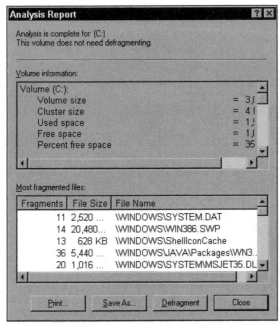

Figure 21-8: Disk Defragmenter provides a detailed analysis report on disk fragmentation.

Using Disk Compression in NTFS

Another means of optimizing storage capacity on NTFS volumes is to use compression. You can enable compression of an entire NTFS volume or configure individual folders and files for compression. Compression is not supported on volumes with a cluster size greater than 4K, however, because the tradeoff between storage capacity and performance degradation isn't worthwhile. The amount of storage increase achieved depends on the types of files being compressed.

Enabling and disabling compression

You can enable compression when you format a volume or turn on compression at any time for an entire volume, a folder, or an individual file. To enable compression for a volume when you format the volume, select the option Enable Compression on the Format dialog box. Use the /C switch if formatting a volume with the FORMAT command from the console prompt. In either case, folders and files added to the volume will be compressed by default.

You also can enable or disable compression for a previously formatted volume. Right-click the volume and choose Properties. On the General page, select the option Compress drive to save disk space, then click OK or Apply. Windows 2000 asks if you want to compress only the root folder or all folders and files. Select as desired and click OK. To turn off compression, deselect the option Compress drive to save disk space. Again, Windows 2000 asks if you want to apply the change to only the root folder or to subfolders and files.

To compress or uncompress a single file, right-click the file and choose Properties. On the General property page, click Advanced to display the Advanced Attributed dialog box. Select or deselect the option Compress contents to save disk space, click OK, and then click OK or Apply.

 Tip
You can use the COMPACT command to compress or decompress a folder or file from the command console. Issue the command **compact /?** to view the syntax and usage for the COMPACT command. Use COMPACT with no command line parameters to view the compression attribute of a folder or file.

Moving and copying files affects their compression attributes:

✦ **Moving an uncompressed file to any folder:** The file remains uncompressed, regardless of the compression attribute of the destination folder.

✦ **Moving a compressed file to any folder:** The file remains compressed, regardless of the compression attribute of the destination folder.

✦ **Copying a file:** The file takes on the compression attribute of the destination folder. A compressed file copied to an uncompressed folder, for example, is uncompressed at the destination.

✦ **Replacing a file:** If you copy a file to a folder that already contains a file by that name (and you replace the original), the file takes on the compression attribute of the file it replaced.

✦ **Copy or move from FAT16/FAT32 to NTFS:** The file assumes the compression attribute of the destination folder. Note that FAT16 and FAT32 do not support compression, so all files start out uncompressed and either remain that way if copied or moved to an uncompressed folder or are compressed if copied or moved to a compressed folder.

✦ **Copy or move from NTFS to FAT16/FAT32 or to floppy:** Files are uncompressed, as neither FAT16/FAT32 nor floppy drives support compression.

Performance considerations

Compression does affect performance, and the degree depends on a handful of factors. As files are moved or copied, even on the same volume, the file has to be uncompressed, then recompressed. Files are uncompressed for transfer across the LAN, so you don't get any benefit from compression in reducing network bandwidth use.

Windows 2000 Professional does not suffer from significant performance degradation when using compression in most cases. Windows 2000 Server, however, can experience significant performance degradation when compression is used, depending on the server's function and load. In general, lightly loaded servers or those that are primarily read-only or read-mostly do not suffer from compression degradation as much as heavily loaded servers or those with a lot of write traffic. In addition, compressing certain types of files (jpg, zip, and so on) is counterproductive and can actually result in larger file sizes rather than smaller. The only real way to determine if compression will have an impact on a given system is to test it. If you find that you don't get the capacity savings you expected or if performance drops significantly, simply uncompress the volume or folders.

Managing the Distributed File System

Windows 2000 includes an extremely useful feature called the Distributed File System (Dfs) that enables you to simplify a user's view of the LAN and its resources. In essence, Dfs lets you bring local volumes, network shares, and entire multiple servers under a common file system namespace. Rather than require users to browse several different servers on the network for resources, those resources can all appear under the same namespace (such as a single drive letter). In other words, these distributed resources all appear to be located in the same place as far as the user is concerned, although they could actually be separated by continents.

Dfs provides other benefits in addition to providing a unified view of a distributed file system and simplifying access to the file system by users. First, Dfs uses link tracking to keep track of objects within the Dfs namespace, which makes it possible for folders and their contents to move without breaking the logical link and structure within Dfs. Because the users see the logical location for a given folder rather than the physical location, you can move a folder from one location to another, whether on the same server or to another server. The user sees no difference and can still access the folders from the same logical location even though they may have moved physically. In the case of a Web server, Dfs enables you to move portions of a given Web site without affecting availability of the site or breaking any links in the site. In the case of an enterprise, Dfs' link-tracking enables you to restructure storage as needs change without affecting users' access to the shared data or the way they access it.

Availability is another benefit to using Dfs when integrated with Active Directory (AD). Dfs publishes the Dfs topology to the AD, making it visible to all users in the domain. You also can replicate the Dfs namespace through AD-integrated replication, making the folders in a given Dfs namespace available even when a particular server is down or unavailable.

Load balancing is the third benefit offered by Dfs. You can bring multiple replicas of a share under a common share point, associating multiple identical shares with a single share name. While each user thinks he is accessing the folder or file from a specific location each time, it can actually be pulled from a different server based on load.

Dfs Structure and Terminology

Essentially, a Dfs namespace is a share of network shares residing under a *Dfs root,* which serves as a container for the namespace and performs much the same function for the distributed file system that a root folder serves for a physical volume. In other words, the Dfs root serves as the share point for the distributed file system. Rather than containing subfolders like a root directory does, the Dfs root contains links to the shares (local and remote) that form the distributed file system. Each link appears as a subfolder of the root share.

A server that hosts a Dfs root is called a *host server.* You can create *root replicas* on other servers to replicate a Dfs namespace and provide redundancy in the event the host server becomes unavailable. A user can access the Dfs root using a UNC pathname in the form *host server**root name*, where *host server* is the network name for the server hosting the Dfs root and *root name* is the root's name. For example, if you created a root named Shares on a server name FileServer, users would access the Dfs namespace from their computers using the UNC pathname \\FileServer\Shares. What they see when they get there is a function of the Dfs itself and might include shares local to that server, shares on other servers, or even shares on the clients' own computers. Users can also specify more defined paths, such as \\FileServer\Shares\George\Files\Somefile.doc.

Note   A host server can host only one Dfs root in the current implementation of Dfs in Windows 2000 Server for both standalone and domain-based Dfs.

Figure 21-9 illustrates a sample Dfs structure. The Dfs root is called \\SRV1\root and contains SQL data in shares from SRV2 and SRV3, program files in a share from APPSRV1, and data from a Windows 98 workstation computer.

As illustrated in Figure 21-9, *Dfs links* connect a name in the root to one or more shared folders called *replicas,* or simply *Dfs shared folders.* The links are essentially sub-containers within the root and serve much the same purpose as subdirectories in the root of a physical volume. Within the link object are one or more replicas (pointers to shared folders) that define the share that a user sees when he or she opens the link. The ability to define multiple replicas in a given link is what gives Dfs its failover capability. Dfs responds to a client request with the list of all replicas in a requested link. The client then decides which one to use. If any particular replica (share) referenced in a link is unavailable (the server sharing it is offline or times out, for example), the client can use a different one.

Tip   Although you may assume that each replica associated with a particular link will be a copy of the same folder, that assumption is wrong. Dfs does not provide any replication of data between replicas by default. There is nothing to prevent you from defining multiple replicas in a Dfs link, each pointing to completely different content. This presents interesting options for creating dynamic content on Web sites that use Dfs in their underlying structure. Provide a means of replication and synchronization if you need to ensure that the content in the multiple replicas is identical. See "Replication" later in this chapter for more information.

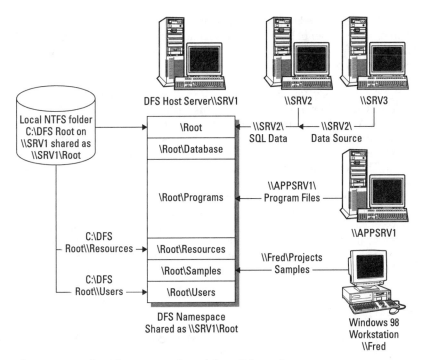

Figure 21-9: The Dfs structure (standalone Dfs root)

Domain-Based Versus Standalone Dfs Roots

Dfs supports two types of Dfs roots: standalone and domain-based. Domain-based Dfs roots integrate with the Active Directory and provide replication of the Dfs topology across the domain (but not replication of folders unless you specifically configure them for replication). A domain-based Dfs root must be hosted on a domain member server. The Dfs' topology is automatically published to the AD to provide access to all users in the domain (and in trusted domains).

Standalone Dfs roots do not integrate with the AD and therefore do not provide the replication offered by domain-based Dfs. Although the Help documentation for Dfs indicates that you can create multiple levels of structure within the Dfs namespace for domain-based roots but not for standalone roots, you can only create a single level in each. In other words, each Dfs link can contain only replicas; they cannot contain other Dfs links. This provides for a single-level implementation of Dfs. This might change in future releases of Dfs, as it is an implementation limitation, not a physical or technical limitation.

Note Although Dfs links are limited to a single level, there is no explicit or implicit limitation on the number of levels that each replica can have within its host share. The link really only contains pointers to the shares, and those shares can contain essentially any number of subfolders.

As mentioned previously, you can create *root replicas* to replicate a Dfs root from one computer to another. You can only do this within the framework of a domain-based Dfs root. You cannot create root replicas of standalone Dfs roots. Because each server can host only one Dfs root, a server hosting a replica cannot host its own root. However, you can create a domain-based Dfs root on any member server in a domain. The server need not be a domain controller.

As with replicas in a Dfs link, there is no guarantee that a given root replica is an exact copy of another. Creating a root replica does not provide any means of folder replication or synchronization—it simply creates a logical relationship between roots on two or more servers that are referenced by the same name in the Dfs namespace. You must configure that replication and synchronization separately to ensure that users see the same content regardless of the server to which they connect.

Client Support

Dfs provides full support for clients to access shared resources through a Dfs root share point, as long as those clients support the underlying network structure and protocol and are Dfs-aware. These clients can browse both standalone and domain-based Dfs roots on the network. Windows 98 and Windows NT 4.0 with Service Pack 4 both include built-in support for browsing standalone and domain-based roots. Windows 95 does not include any built-in Dfs support, so you need to install the Dfs service to enable Windows 95 clients to browse Dfs roots. You'll find the Dfs client for Windows 95 at `http://www.microsoft.com/NTServer/nts/downloads/winfeatures/NTSDistrFile/download.asp`. With this client installed, Windows 95 clients can browse both standalone and domain-based roots.

Windows 95, Windows 98, and Windows NT clients all can host a replica (even Windows 95 clients without the Dfs service installed) because at that level Dfs simply represents a share-redirection mechanism. As long as the folder is shared on the client computer, any Dfs-aware client can be redirected to that share. In addition, the clients don't even have to be in the same domain (or in a domain at all) to host a shared folder, even with a domain-based Dfs root.

Replication

As mentioned briefly earlier in this chapter, Dfs can provide a level of redundancy to ensure that shares within a given Dfs namespace are available even if a server or share becomes unavailable for some reason. Dfs does this through replication, which copies the root or link (and underlying data) to one or more other servers. Because Dfs returns the complete list of root replicas or share replicas in response to a query, a client can try each one in the list to find one that functions if a particular server or share is offline.

While Dfs by default does not provide replication of a Dfs root or any replicas associated with a given Dfs link, you can configure Dfs to replicate entire Dfs roots or individual shared folders (Dfs links). Dfs relies on the File Replication Service (FRS) included with Windows 2000 to perform automatic replication. After you create a root replica or a share replica, you can configure the *replication policy* for that object, which defines how the object is replicated. Automatic replication is only available for domain-based Dfs roots and can only replicate data stored on NTFS volumes. By default, FRS replicates the data every 15 minutes.

Automatic replication is not available for data stored on FAT volumes or for standalone Dfs roots or replicas. In these situations, you need to use manual replication. Manual replication is just what its name implies. You have to replicate the data manually by copying the data periodically through drag-and-drop or a similar method as you would manually copy any file from one place to another. Although you could automate the manual replication through the use of AT commands and batch files, that solution is something of an awkward solution. Automatic replication through the use of domain-based Dfs is by far the best method for sheer simplicity and low administration. Although you could configure a mix of automated and manual replication within a domain-based Dfs root, it's best to use one or the other to make sure that copies remain synchronized.

You can configure your replication scheme such that one copy serves as a master and the other copies serve as read-only copies. To do so, first create the folder and share on the servers that will host the read-only copies. Set NTFS permissions on the main share folder to grant users read-only access but still allow FRS the control necessary to write changes to the share's child folders. Then set the replication policy for the root replica or folder replica to initiate the replication, specifying the dynamic source root or folder as the initial master.

See the section "Configuring Replication" later in this chapter for more detailed information on configuring Dfs replication. See Chapter 9 for detailed information on managing replication within the Active Directory.

Client-Side Caching

Dfs provides for client-side caching of requests to improve performance and reduce network traffic. When a client issues a query to a Dfs host server, the host returns the requested information along with a cache value. The client caches the returned results for the specified period of time. If the client makes another request for the same information within the cache period, the data comes from the client's cache rather than the host. If the cache period has lapsed, the cached data is purged and the host server provides the data, which again is stored in the cache during the next cache period.

You can configure cache values for an entire root or for individual folder replicas. You configure the cache value when you create the root or link. Figure 21-10 shows the dialog box for creating a link, which includes a cache setting. You can also modify the cache value at any time through the object's properties. Right-click a root or link and choose Properties to view its property sheet, then change the cache value on the General page and click Apply or OK.

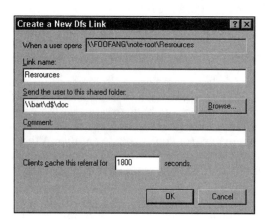

Figure 21-10: You can specify cache time when you create the root or link.

Working with the Distributed File System Console

As with most other administrative functions, Windows 2000 provides an MMC console for managing Dfs. To open the Distributed File System console, choose Start ➪ Programs ➪ Administrative Tools ➪ Distributed File System, or execute the console file Dfsgui.msc. Figure 21-11 shows the Dfs console.

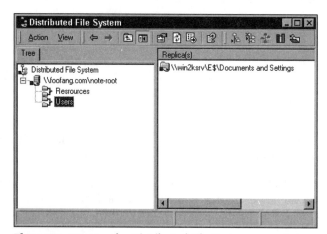

Figure 21-11: Use the Distributed File System console to manage Dfs roots and replicas.

Although each server can only host a single Dfs root, the Dfs console lets you manage multiple Dfs roots across the network. So, the Dfs console provides a single point of management for all Dfs roots in your enterprise, subject to your access permissions within the enterprise. To view another Dfs root, right-click Distributed File System and choose Display an Existing Dfs Root. Specify the Dfs root name or server hosting according to the three naming formats described on the resulting dialog box. To remove a Dfs root from the console display but not delete the root, right-click the root and choose Remove Display of Dfs Root.

You can use the Dfs console to perform the following actions on roots, links, and replicas: create and delete, set properties, check status, and make offline or online. The following sections explain how to use the Dfs console for specific tasks. See Chapter 6 to learn more about general MMC console operations.

Creating and Deleting Dfs Roots

You can create a standalone or domain-based root using the Dfs console. You can create either type on a member server or domain controller. You are not restricted to creating domain-based Dfs roots only on domain controllers. In addition, you can use the Dfs console to create a Dfs root on any appropriate target server in the network; you are not restricted to creating a Dfs root only on the local computer. However, a server can host only one Dfs root, so you must delete any existing root prior to creating a new one.

To create a Dfs root, open the Dfs console, right-click the Distributed File System node, and choose New Dfs Root to start the New Dfs Root Wizard. The wizard prompts you for the following information throughout the process:

✦ **Create a domain Dfs root or a standalone root:** Select the type of Dfs root you want to create. As explained previously, you can create either type of Dfs root on a member server or domain controller.

✦ **Domain name:** Specify the domain name if you are creating a domain-based root.

✦ **Server name:** The wizard prompts you for the name of the server on which the Dfs root will be hosted. Specify the server's UNC name (such as `\\someserver`) or the fully qualified domain name (such as `someserver.somedomain.com`).

✦ **Root share:** Specify the share point on the host server where the Dfs root will be anchored. You can use an existing share or create a new share through the wizard.

✦ **Comment:** You can include an optional comment for the root that identifies its function or provides other information about the root. This information appears when you view the root's properties (right-click the root and choose Properties).

To delete a Dfs root, right-click the root and choose Delete Dfs Root. Windows 2000 will prompt you to verify the deletion. Note that deleting a Dfs root prevents clients from accessing that root, although it does not delete the underlying folders or their contents.

Creating Dfs Links

The share you specify as a Dfs root's share point can contain subfolders and files, which users see when they connect to the Dfs root. The Dfs root can also contain Dfs links that point to shares on the local computer or other computers on the network. Dfs links are the mechanism that lets you bring shares from other computers into the file system defined by the Dfs root.

To create a Dfs link, open the Dfs console, right-click the root where you want to create the link, and choose New Dfs Link. The console displays the Create a New Dfs Link dialog box, shown in Figure 21-12.

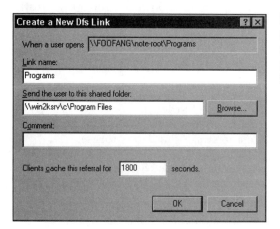

Figure 21-12: Dfs links serve as redirection pointers that associate a share point in the root with a physical share on the network.

The following list summarizes the options on the Create a New Dfs Link dialog box:

✦ **Link name:** This is the virtual folder name the client sees within the Dfs structure.

✦ **Send the user to this shared folder:** Specify the UNC pathname for the local or network share to which the client should be redirected when accessing the folder defined by Link name.

✦ **Comment:** This option appears when you display the link's properties.

✦ **Clients cache this referral for:** Specify the cache-aging period for the link. Clients will cache the referral for the specified time, retrieving the data from their cache until the cache period expires.

Working with Replicas

The previous section explained how to create a single replica associated with a Dfs link. However, you can associate multiple replicas (copies of a share) with a given link. This provides failover so that if the server hosting a particular replica is offline or the share is unavailable, users can still access the data in the share. This failover process happens transparently to the user, who sees a single share under a given Dfs link, even though there might be several.

To create a new replica of a share (create multiple replicas in a link, defining a *replica set*), right-click the link and choose New Replica. Windows 2000 displays the Add a New Replica dialog box, shown in Figure 21-13. The following list summarizes the options:

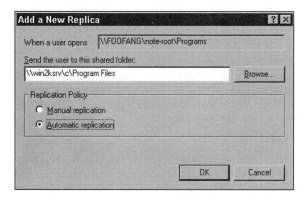

Figure 21-13: Specify the share name and replication type when creating a new replica.

✦ **When a user opens:** Read-only; specify the Dfs link name under which the replica is being created

✦ **Send the user to this shared folder:** Specify the UNC pathname for the local or network share to which the client should be redirected when accessing the folder defined by Link name

✦ **Manual replication:** Do not replicate the folder through FRS

✦ **Automatic replication:** Replicate the folder through FRS

You can only specify a replication method when creating replicas within a domain-based Dfs root. The replication options are dimmed when creating replicas in a standalone root. After you create the replica, you can modify its properties to define its replication policy. See the section later in this chapter, "Configuring Replication," for more information on configuring a replica's replication policy.

Creating Root Replicas

A root replica is a copy of a Dfs root's structure hosted on another server. When you create a root replica, you copy the Dfs structure to the other server but you do not copy any physical folders associated with links in the structure. You can create a root replica from any server in the network on any other server on the network (or the local server), subject to your access permissions. After you create a root replica, you can set its replication policy to define how it replicates (explained in the next section).

To create a root replica, open the Dfs console, right-click the root you want to make a replica of, and choose New Root Replica. The New Dfs Root Wizard prompts you for the following information:

✦ **Server name:** Specify the name of the server or browse the network for the server that will host the root replica. You must choose a server that does not already host a root or root replica, as each server can host only one.

✦ **Share name and path:** Specify the name of the share and the path to the share that will serve as the share point for the Dfs root replica on the new replica server. You can specify an existing share or create a new one.

Configuring Replication

You can replicate roots and shares in domain-based Dfs roots. When you create a root replica, you don't have the option of specifying a replication policy, but you can modify the properties after the root replica is created. When you create a share replica, you can specify either manual or automatic replication. If you specify automatic replication, Windows 2000 prompts you to specify the settings that make up the object's replication policy. Windows 2000 uses the same replication settings and dialog box for root replication and share replication, as shown in Figure 21-14. To modify a share's replication policy, right-click the share and choose Replication Policy to display the Replication Policy dialog box.

The Replication Policy dialog box lists all replicas in the selected object (root or share). The list includes the name of the share, replication status (Yes or No), domain, and site. The first time you define the policy to set up replication, you have the option of specifying which share serves as the initial master, or the one from which replication starts. You don't have this option when modifying an existing replication policy, as it no longer applies (because replication has already started).

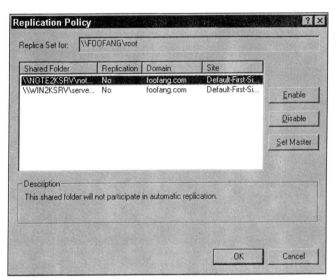

Figure 21-14: The Replication Policy dialog box lets you define replication settings for a root or share replica, including which serves as the initial master.

Configuring replication is fairly easy. You select each replica in the list and either enable or disable it using the Enable or Disable button. Enabling a share turns replication on and means that the replica will participate in the replication process. Disabling a share turns off replication. To specify the share that will serve as the initial master, click the share to select it, then click Set Master. Click OK to apply the replication policy.

Note   See Chapter 9 for more information on FRS and replication within domains.

Working with Mounted Volumes

The previous section discussed the Distributed File System (Dfs), which enables you to create a file system namespace using shares from multiple computers in the enterprise. Windows 2000 provides a new feature called *mounted volumes* that does the same thing for the local file system that Dfs does for the enterprise. Mounted volumes, which rely on NTFS' new reparse points, provide a means for you to mount local volumes under NTFS folders on the local computer. This enables you to create a homogenous file system from multiple volumes so that volumes D:, E:, and F:, for example, can all show up as folders under volume C:. Figure 21-15 illustrates how mounted volumes work.

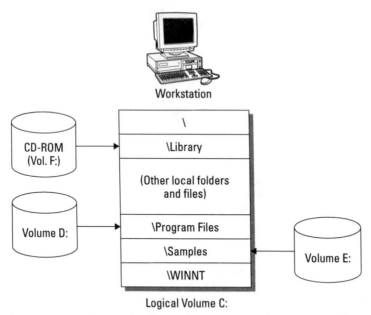

Figure 21-15: Mounted volumes let you create a homogenous file system namespace from multiple local volumes.

The primary benefit to mounted volumes is that they enable you to create a single file system namespace on the local computer that integrates multiple physical or logical volumes. This simplifies the user's view of disk resources and offers the following key advantages:

✦ **Selectively apply disk quotas:** As discussed in a previous section, you can apply quotas to a mounted volume to effectively apply quotas to a single folder within the logical namespace. This capability enables you to apply different quotas to different folders within a single logical volume. For example, you might apply different quotas to C:\Users\Documents and C:\Users\Programs to grant users different quota levels within each folder. (This example assumes that two different local volumes are mounted, one under each folder.) Because quotas apply to an entire physical volume, the only way to achieve different quota values is to mount separate physical volumes with different quota values to each folder.

✦ **Increase apparent volume size without hardware changes:** You'll probably find that in many situations, user storage-space requirements will surpass physical storage capacity over time, even when you apply quotas. Mounted volumes enable you to accommodate increasing storage requirements without replacing existing hardware. Instead, you add additional storage space locally and mount the new space to the existing volume. With servers that support hot-swapping of drives and the ability to add new drives without taking down the system, the volume capacity increase can be accomplished without taking down the host server or affecting the services it provides.

✦ **Create a homogenous file system namespace from disparate volumes:** One of the chief benefits of mounted volumes is the ability they give you to create a single, homogenous file system namespace from various physical volumes.

✦ **Overcome the 26-letter drive ID limitation:** Mounted volumes do not require a drive ID, which overcomes the 26-volume limitation imposed by using letters for drive IDs. Rather than map local volumes to individual drive IDs, you can simply mount each one under its own NTFS folder on a host volume.

Although using a mounted volume can give you much the same effect as extending a volume, mounted volumes offer the advantages of selective quotas and can be used on basic disks. Extending a volume is supported only on dynamic disks.

Mounting a Volume

You use the Disk Management MMC console to mount volumes to NTFS folders. You can only mount a volume to an empty, local NTFS folder. The volume being mounted must also be local. To create a mounted volume, open the Computer Management MMC console and open the Disk Management node. Right-click the volume you want to mount and choose Change Drive Letter and Path from the context menu. Click Add to display the Add New Drive Letter or Path dialog box, as shown in Figure 21-16. Specify the path to the local NTFS folder in which you want to mount the volume and click OK.

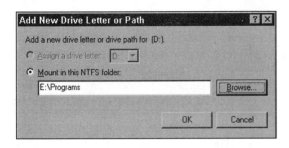

Figure 21-16: Specify the local NTFS folder to which you want to mount the volume.

The way a mounted volume appears in Explorer depends on the volume type. Hard disk volumes appear as drive icons instead of folder icons. CD-ROM volumes appear with a CD icon.

Note You can browse only when creating a mounted volume on the local computer. You must specify the path in the text box if using Disk Management to manage a remote computer.

Unmounting a Volume

Unmounting a volume is equally easy. Open the Disk Management node, right-click the volume you want to unmount, and choose Change Drive Letter and Path. Select the path you want to remove and click Remove. Click Yes to verify the operation or No to cancel it.

Hierarchical Storage Management

Windows 2000's version of Hierarchical Storage Management (HSM) is a service named Remote Storage or Remote Storage Services (RSS). If the term is new to you, it means this: HSM is a service that *relocates* data that is *idle* or inactive to a *cheaper* storage location in order to keep *valuable hard disk space* from getting full.

Notice the italics in the preceding definition of HSM. First, the idea of relocation is important. The data is not backed up, nor is HSM a substitute for the disaster recovery procedures discussed in Chapter 17, even though the data is stored on tape. Candidate data is migrated to a storage medium that should always be available to a user, so if the house burns down, the HSM data is lost.

To further qualify the relocation of data, if the user requires access to the data, the data should be made available as if it were in online files, requiring no extra step to access it. The only difference the user might notice is the lag time between the application issuing a file manipulation command (such as Open, Copy, or Delete or execution) to the file system and the recalling of the file from remote storage.

Second, HSM is applied to files that are idle or stale (excluding system files or similarly flagged files). In other words, idle files become candidates for relocation when they have not been accessed for a predetermined period of time. The terms *data* and *file* are often used interchangeably with respect to HSM. In reality, the contents of the file, the data, are what are relocated. The file remains behind, like an empty envelope, which acts as a marker.

Third, *cheaper* is a key term in defining HSM, because the storage medium chosen as the target location should be cheaper than your average hard disk drive. The concept is worthwhile: Why store unused files on expensive hard disks? The problem with this tenet, however, is that hard disks are getting cheaper all the time, and their capacity is almost doubling every few months. They may soon become cheaper than so-called cheaper storage media, such as tapes. We will return to cost after a full discussion of Remote Storage.

 Disk Management and Removable Storage services are discussed in Chapters 16 and 17.

Finally, the most important component in the definition of HSM is *valuable hard disk space*. Without the component that frees up hard disk space, HSM would be, in many respects, worthless. As with disk quotas (see Chapter 16), HSM can be used to effectively maintain and manage hard disks and prevent them from exceeding certain usage levels. This service applies to the need to make hard disk resources available to users for online storage, as well as the maintenance of applications.

To understand the service and its benefits, let's look at an example. Take a busy newsroom at the local newspaper publisher, which represents an extreme case of file turnover. A group of reporters and editors generates a lot of files every day. Stories are written, then edited, and then imported into layout and production systems before being sent to the printers.

Most of the files will be used and then abandoned on the same day they are created; many of them will be accessed over a course of several days, perhaps to earmark the stories for weekend editions or to refer to for follow-up reports and articles. About 80 percent of the files will become idle after the first day following their creation; by the third day after the files are created, about 95 percent of them will be idle; and by the following week, almost all the files created will be idle. Does it then make sense to keep them lying around taking up hard disk space?

Using Remote Storage, you can configure the file system to relocate the files to removable storage. If a file needs to be accessed, it can be recalled from the library at any time. By the time the files are relocated, they will not be needed as urgently as they were on the day they were created, so the few seconds it takes to retrieve a file's data is not a critical factor. The Remote Storage thus makes for a very effective electronic newspaper morgue.

How HSM Works

HSM is made possible by the new technology of *reparse points* and other components in the Windows 2000 NTFS file system, discussed earlier in this chapter. It is provided by a combination of services derived from the file system, fixed storage, and the removable storage technology owned by Veritas Software Corporation. HSM is managed by the MMC snap-in called Remote Storage.

HSM is split between two tiers of storage. The first tier comprises local storage, the volumes supported on the local machine under the control of the local operating system. *Local* is the key term here because, currently, Windows 2000's HSM does not extend to storage area network (SAN) volumes, paths to remote volumes, or storage anywhere other than in the local machine. And there is currently nothing "remote" about the service.

The second tier comprises removable storage. Removable storage can consist of any local removable media technology, such as a tape drive library. (The Removable Storage service, which configures removable storage hardware and creates and manages media pools, is discussed in Chapters 16 and 17.) The idle data is transferred to and from the aforementioned tiers.

You configure the Remote Storage service to maintain your hard disk at a certain level of "free space." You also need to identify for how long files should be idle and how often and when relocation should occur. The Remote Storage service handles everything automatically.

Installing and Configuring Remote Storage

As mentioned earlier, HSM is installed and managed on the local machine by way of the Remote Storage snap-in. The service is not installed on your server by default. To install the service and MMC snap-in, open the Control Panel and double-click the Add/Remove Programs icon. Click the Add/Remove Windows Components option in the dialog box that loads, then click the Components button. Select Remote Storage and then proceed to install the service. Restart the server if prompted.

As soon as Remote Storage is installed, you can run it from the Administrative Tools menu by choosing Start ➪ Programs ➪ Administrative Tools ➪ Remote Storage, or by running RSADMIN.MSC from the command line or the Run menu.

Unless you have the supported removable storage media already configured (see Chapters 16 and 17), you should not run Remote Storage. As soon as the snap-in runs, Remote Storage starts a wizard that checks to see if supported removable media is available. If you do not have supported media and hardware installed, Remote Storage will report an error. The snap-in will still open, but the Remote Storage options will be disabled.

Managed Volumes

Configuring a volume for HSM using Remote Storage puts it under Managed Volume status. To manage a volume, you need to open the Remote Storage snap-in and perform the following steps:

1. Add a Managed Volume and configure it for Remote Storage.

2. Configure the Managed Volume properties.

3. Configure the Remote Storage service.

Add a Managed Volume and configure it for Remote Storage

Select the Managed Volumes folder in the Remote Storage tree. Right-click it and then select New ➪ Managed Volume(s). This action launches the Add Volume Management Wizard. Click Next to proceed with the wizard. If the wizard finds volumes that can be managed, it will list them in the next page of the wizard. If no volumes are found, the wizard will not proceed further.

There could be a number or reasons why the wizard would fail to detect a volume suitable for management. First, the volumes may not be formatted with the NTFS 5.0 file system. Second, the underlying hardware supporting the hard disks might not be compatible with Windows 2000. Third, all volumes in the system may already be under Remote Storage management.

We found that a simple volume in a Compaq hard disk array (excluded from any RAID level) had to be reformatted twice before Remote Storage noticed it. This points to a likely hardware compatibility problem.

If one or more volumes are listed, select the volume to manage and click Next. The Volume Settings dialog box, illustrated in Figure 21-17, enables you to set the desired amount of free space and the file relocation parameters according to your application, circumstances, or needs. Make the changes or leave the defaults intact, and click Next. You will be asked to confirm the configuration before committing the changes. Click Finish to commit the configuration.

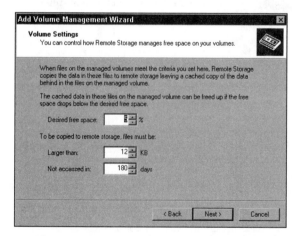

Figure 21-17: The Volume Settings dialog box

Configure the Managed Volume properties

After you have added the volume, you will notice the managed volume listed in the Remote Storage snap-in, as illustrated in Figure 21-18. You can change the configuration of the volume at any time. Double-click the volume in the list, and the volume's property pages will appear.

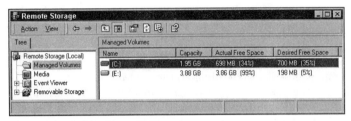

Figure 21-18: The Remote Storage snap-in

In addition to the remote storage options, a third tab on the property page enables you to exclude or include files in the relocation process. You will notice that all system files are automatically excluded from relocation.

Configure the Remote Storage service

Your final step in configuring HSM is to configure the Remote Storage service. Select Remote Storage at the top of the tree and right-click it. Select Properties from the pop-up menu. The Remote Storage (Local) Properties dialog box appears. This collection of property pages, illustrated in Figure 21-19, lets you configure a schedule for the relocation of data, lets you set a recall limit, and gives you the ability to make copies of the removable media holding the relocated data.

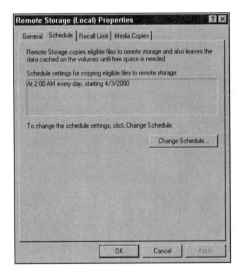

Figure 21-19: The Remote Storage (Local) Properties Settings dialog box

The recall limit, which is set to 60 recalls by default, lets you specify how many times a file can be recalled from storage within a certain Registry defined timeframe. When the limit is reached, all additional recall attempts are refused. In other words, the request is not passed to the Remote Storage service. There is a good reason for this property, and we will discuss it shortly.

You can also configure Remote Storage to make duplicate copies of the removable media on which relocated media is stored. To use the copy service, you need two tape drives supporting identical media. The copy service is disabled if a second drive is unavailable.

Limitations of Remote Storage

HSM is not a new concept; it has been available on legacy systems for many years. The ideal server-based HSM system should conform to several wishes before it can be classified as a true HSM system, the dream of every network administrator. The most important of these wishes, according to our vision of the ideal HSM system, are as follows:

✦ The HSM system must be a network service, able to coexist with any distributed file system.

✦ The HSM system must support a recall override or recall prevention option.

✦ The HSM system must coexist with standard backup and restore procedures and technology.

✦ The HSM system must support all forms of removable or remote media, on any server on the network (running on Windows 2000, of course).

The HSM system made possible by the Remote Storage service has several limitations. First, the Remote Storage service is currently available only to the server on which it is installed. This means that you have to install the service and compliant hardware on every server you wish to place under HSM or Managed Volume status. This is clearly a lot more expensive than disk quota management.

Many companies spend a lot of money investing in a good tape library system for the benefit of all servers. To replicate the investment on each server on which you need HSM would wipe out the cost benefit; sticking in new hard disks would be cheaper. A good tape system starts at about $4,000 and runs to more than $20,000 for a good DLT or DAT library system (see Chapter 17 for details on DLT and DAT systems). But you can pick up a single 70GB hard disk for under $500. Double this for the media duplication feature discussed earlier. Incidentally, the cheaper tape backup hardware discussed in Chapter 17, like QIC, is not supported by Remote Storage.

Second, the current version of Remote Storage does not support the ability to override recalls. This means that all software that attempts to read a file will inadvertently recall it from the library or tape drive system, unless the software has been built with Remote Storage support (such as the Backup utility that ships with Windows 2000).

Granted, software will have to become Remote Storage aware, but this will be a problem for many applications, such as third-party backup software, antivirus software, indexing software, document management systems, and so on. It will take a while before all software is endowed with the ability to work on managed volumes, but it would be nice to set times or other parameters that would cause the recall not to fire. As mentioned earlier, the recall limit is a step in this direction, but it would have been better to program the service to recognize who is reading a file marker before recalling the file. The operating system knows which service or user account is accessing a file.

HSM might save you time and money managing a hard disk, but you could lose that benefit with the added diligence required in the backing up and restoring of data. Once the data has been relocated, Remote Storage leaves a file marker or placeholder on the media. (The marker is represented by the same icon owned by the file, but superimposed with a small clock.) So, what does your backup program back up . . . a placeholder, a token of what was once valuable data? And what do you restore in the event of a hard disk crash . . . the version in the backup or the version on the Remote Storage folder?

Also, Remote Storage brings with it the possibility of losing relocated data. Placeholders and caching data can get deleted and corrupted, possibly even becoming the target of e-terror. The media used to store the data is not impervious to damage or loss. The additional brain strain is not what many Windows server administrators would like. The ideal HSM system should be fully integrated with a backup program.

Note   Some third-party HSM products have catered to many of the above limitations, including Veritas, which contributed much of the backup, remote, and removable storage applications in Windows 2000.

Despite these reservations, we are referring to the first version of what is clearly a valuable addition to the operating system. As the previous example in the newsroom demonstrated, it can be put to good use, and it works very well. If you wish to investigate the Remote Storage Service further, go to Microsoft's Web site and search there using the keyword RSS.

Summary

The topic of file systems in Windows 2000 covers a very broad range of technologies and features. Choosing the best file system naturally depends on several factors, but in most cases, the best choice for providing the broadest range of features and the best security is NTFS.

NTFS not only provides enhanced security through NTFS object permissions, but also, the fact that it can be extended through the use of file system filters from Microsoft and third parties enables certain capabilities not offered by FAT16 or

FAT32. These additional capabilities include the Distributed File System (Dfs), which enables you to create a single, homogenous file system namespace from shares on multiple computers across the enterprise. This homogenous file system simplifies administration, improves availability and failover capability, and most important, greatly simplifies user access to shared resources.

Another feature made possible by NTFS in Windows 2000 is mounted volumes, which bring the same concept to the local file system that Dfs brings to the enterprise. You can use mounted volumes to create a homogenous file system namespace from multiple physical and logical volumes on the local computer, making those volumes appear as an integral part of a single logical volume.

Two mutually exclusive features made possible with NTFS are compression and encryption — you can use one or the other, but not both. NTFS can provide on-the-fly compression and decompression of files to increase storage capacity by as much as 80-90 percent, with the process remaining completely transparent to the user. The Encrypting File System (EFS), which is discussed in the next chapter, functions as an installable file system filter that performs encryption and decryption on-the-fly and transparently to the user. EFS provides a high degree of security for sensitive data that could be susceptible to theft, such as in notebook computers.

Finally, we talked about the Windows 2000 HSM system known as Remote Storage, a useful tool that adds to the suite of volume management tools that comes with the operating system.

✦   ✦   ✦

Sharing and Securing Files and Folders

This chapter provides an understanding of access control to network file and folder resources. Chapter 21 provided an in-depth review of the Windows 2000 file systems, especially NTFS. Now, let's look at the file systems from other viewpoints: users and applications and, of course, administrators.

Most data is generated and stored on computer systems, using the file and folder metaphors inherited from our three-dimensional world. However, since the advent of local and wide area networks, particularly the Internet, your files and folders (directories) are accessible to anyone with a computer and a network connection unless you secure them. You need to secure the data within their files, and the folders that contain those files, while at the same time providing controlled access to authorized users. The NT File System (NTFS) lets you do that on three security access levels:

✦ Shares

✦ Folder permissions and file permissions
  (called NTFS permissions)

✦ Encryption

Note   NTFS creates a hierarchy of folders in a volume, all starting from a root folder (see also Dfs and mounted volumes in Chapter 21). The earlier versions of NTFS could only store a single folder hierarchy on a single hard drive or volume, maintained on a single computer. As we stated in Chapter 21, the folder hierarchy (or folder namespace) can traverse or span hard disk volumes on any computer on the network. To keep things simple in this chapter, we'll discuss folder and files independently of where they may be located on the network.

Sharing and Securing Your Data

Windows 2000, like all modern graphically managed operating systems, allows you to manage your files and folders in the same way as your hardcopy filing systems: in folders and filing cabinets. Think about the file room in a law firm or a newspaper morgue. It is unlikely you would be allowed to just walk into this room: It is usually locked or guarded, and you would need authority to enter, but you know it's there. The company does not hide it away from you, because it is a shared resource, and they usually want you to know about it because you might need data in it to do your work.

Shares are the clubhouses of the network. A share is where users and groups of users go to share resources. You enable folder-sharing for your users and applications by creating a share, or in the lingo of mainframes, midrange, and legacy systems, a *share-point*. By owning the files and folders on your own machine (and we discuss ownership next), you automatically have full access and control over your folders and their contents. Administrators own all the folders they create anywhere on the network, and can thus share them.

> **Note**   Over the years, we have found that most calls to the support desk originate because a user or a group cannot connect to shared resources, such as folders, files, and printers. When users cannot connect, and get the "access denied" message, they assume the world has ended, such is the extent of their panic. Usually, it is a simple case of an incorrect permission. However, we have seen how permission misadventure causes much consternation and is a waste of time, so we stress that every administrator should become an expert in this subject.

Getting back to our brick and mahogany file room: By having access to the file room, you do not necessarily have access to every file or folder it contains. Depending on your rank in the company, the department you work for, and the work you do, you may or may not be allowed to open a file cabinet, read a file, check it out, change its contents, or add data to it. Likewise, by being a member of a group of users or by having individual authority, you may gain access to the NTFS share, but some files will not be for your eyes. Others will be accessible for reading only—you might not be allowed to change, delete, copy, or move them. The levels of access you have to the folders and files are called permissions. Administrators, members of Administrator groups, and the owners of objects can assign permissions and control access to these objects, and they can also encrypt the files.

Folder and file encryption is the third mechanism you can now use for protecting your files and folders. It has been added to the Windows 2000 file system and is only supported under NTFS. When you add Windows 2000's support for cryptography and distributed security services, such as Kerberos and digital certificates, to the file system, you have what is known as the encrypting file system or EFS. The EFS is fully discussed later in this chapter.

Ownership

Another means of understanding shares or share-points is by understanding *ownership*. Ownership is not a configuration setting, or a mere value in the registry or Active Directory; it derives from the security services of the NTFS and the Win32 security system (this is discussed in more detail in Chapters 3 and 10).

It helps to understand ownership if you've done some Windows programming. The Win32 API has a `Create` or `CreateFile` function that creates objects such as folders and files. If the `Create` function you are calling can take a security parameter, you can lock the object (pass a security descriptor) and keep other processes from accessing it. The lock is like a key that you, the owner, get to keep when you create the object. That is the essence of ownership. Of course, the whole process is managed by the OS and requires no user actions.

When a process creates a file or a folder — objects — the file system assigns that process the rights of ownership, and passes it a key. The process created it, so that process owns it . . . and it can do whatever it likes with that object. If *you* create a folder on the computer you are logged onto, or within a folder namespace to which you have access, you own the folder. Only you and the processes that operate within your security context (activated by the validation of your password) can access that folder.

Now, when other users or processes need access to the folder you just created, do you allow them to take ownership, hand them the key? No, not normally, because if you did, you would be losing your right to the object. By creating a share, you are essentially inviting others to access the folder (with restrictions, of course), but you don't give them the key. If someone else with bad intentions got hold of your keys, they might come back after dark and destroy your network. Remember the old adage: Possession is nine-tenths of the law. And remember what we said about safeguarding the Administrator account back in Chapter 10. You can do tremendous damage with 50 lines of code and access to the Administrator account.

The owner of an object can actually allow a specified user or a group to take over the ownership of the object (we'll get to that shortly). Taking ownership is a one-way action. You can take ownership, but you cannot bestow it or return it. You can allow someone else to take ownership; you assign them this permission. Ownership can only be transferred if the would-be benefactor is willing to take it. By not being able to transfer ownership unilaterally, NTFS prevents users from hiding dirty work. In other words, you cannot go and lock up a folder and throw away the key, and then make it look like someone else did the damage.

Publishing Shares in Active Directory

The idea of *published shares* is new to the Windows networking environment, and it begins with Active Directory, as discussed in the previous chapter. Windows 2000 users connect to shared resources on a Windows 2000 domain by looking them up in the Active Directory. You can still connect to shares on the browse list and from the command line, as described later in this chapter.

Creating shares on Windows 2000 is really easy, and if you have Windows experience, you will only need to read the next section as a refresher and to pick up subtle yet important differences. Establishing shares on remote computers is another story, however, and the process is handled in the new Computer Management snap-in described later in this chapter.

Creating a Share

When you first create a share, the file system automatically gives access to the *Everyone* group, unless you have taken steps to prevent that, discussed later. If the contents of the files are sensitive, you need to remove the Everyone group and assign access only to authorized users or groups.

Note   Back in Chapter 10, we encouraged you to use common sense management practices and avoid assigning rights to individual users. The same advice applies to shares. Share folders with groups, not individuals. One of the only times you should circumvent this advice is when you need to audit individuals.

Sharing a Local Folder

If you are the owner of the folder or the folders within the local folder namespace, then sharing a folder involves little more than right-clicking the new or existing folder and selecting Sharing from the Context menu. Select the option Share this folder in the dialog box. The share name field is enabled. This is demonstrated in Figure 22-1.

As soon as the dialog box is enabled, you can enter the following share data:

✦ **Share name:** The actual folder name is used as the default share name, but you can change this to reflect any name that better suits the application for the share. It is a good idea to use the best share name for the share, possibly one that better informs the user of the purpose of the share or that provides a hint of the share's contents. For example, a folder might be named Y2K, and rather than changing that name (it's been done before), which would impact other applications, it would be better to make the share name "Y2K data files and documents." Share names can be up to 80 characters in length, and they can contain spaces. However, if your users are attaching from the command line or you have applications that might send share attach commands to the system console, you should stick to single names of between 8 and 12 characters (and even 8.3 names for those still using Windows 3.1). The best command-line-compliant substitute for the aforementioned share name is the simple Y2KDATA.

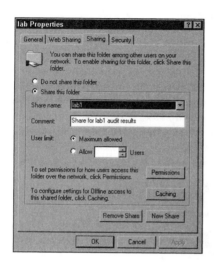

Figure 22-1: The Sharing tab on the folder's Properties dialog box

✦ **Comment:** The comment field will take 100 characters, so you can be creative here. It is a good idea to include the comment field wherever possible because it shows up in Explorer when users browse for a share. Although we said you can be creative, be conservative. A hundred-character comment field forces most users to waste time scrolling to the right.

✦ **User limit:** You will ignore this most of the time, allowing the client access licensing to monitor the number of connections. On server shares there is no maximum limit, but you can restrict connections for application-specific purposes or licensing. Windows 2000 Professional prohibits more than ten concurrent connections and several other exclusions you will discover . . . so forget about using it as a substitute for a server.

✦ **Caching:** The cache settings allow you to configure offline access to the shared folder. Offline folder and file access is touched upon later in this chapter, and explained in the context of Group Policy and change control in Chapter 11.

As soon as you enter the share name and comment, you can click the Permissions button to admit users to the share and set the desired access types.

Once you have created a share, you will notice, as shown in Figure 22-1, that you now have the option of creating another share. The New Share button does not replace the old share; you can share a folder as many times as you like, each time with different access clients and permissions. At any time you need to end a share, just select the share name from the drop-down list and click Remove Share.

Establishing Shares on Remote Computers

There are two ways to connect to a remote computer and create a share-point on it. The first and hardest way is by using the NET SHARE command at the command prompt. This is explained in Appendix A. The second, and by far the easiest way, is by opening the Computer Management snap-in (`compmgmt.msc`).

Once you are in Computer Management, select the first option, Computer Management (Local). Right-click it and select Connect to another computer from the Context menu. This is illustrated in Figure 22-2. You can connect to a computer listed in the Active Directory (the best way), or you can connect to a computer listed in the domain. Once you have opened the remote computer into the snap-in, you will be able to expand the System Tools tree and select the remote computer Shared Folders option. From here on, the process of creating the share-point is no different from creating shares on the local machine.

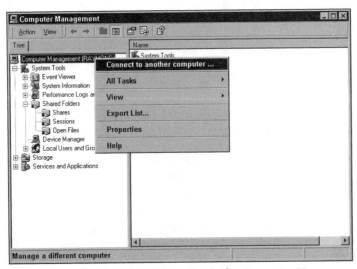

Figure 22-2: The Shared Folders option in the Computer Management snap-in

Share Attributes

Share access can be given directly to users or processes, or implicitly through group membership. Shared folders possess the following attributes:

✦ Shares only work on folder objects, and not on files that folders contain. You cannot select a file, *x-file,* and share it as *x-file* on the network. But you can share a folder called *thexfiles* and allow users to access the files in that folder.

✦ The default access permission on a share is *Full Control*. This permission is assigned to the Everyone group. So, if you create such a share, and have your Guest account enabled and not governed by any domain policy, every computer user has access to it. But you are a common-sense administrator, and you will follow our advice and make sure that your network is locked down.

✦ Shares can be established on most file systems, including FAT. But NTFS permissions, discussed later in this chapter, are peculiar to the Windows NT and Windows 2000 operating systems.

✦ Shares are visible to you (if they are not hidden) when you are trying to connect over the network. Share access also applies to the local user logged onto the computer that is hosting the shared folder. This feature is extremely important because it means you can prevent users who log on locally from accessing folders. And it's a surefire way of protecting your data on a notebook computer.

✦ A shared folder on your machine is represented as an icon with a hand holding the folder. But across the network, the icon does not include the hand.

✦ Shares can be hidden, a very valuable security and administration tool that we will discuss later in this chapter.

Table 22-1 lists the folder permissions that apply to Windows 2000 shares. Remember that the access level is at the share only; NTFS permissions provide the "second line of defense" to locked-down resources. You set these permissions through the Share Permissions properties, which you can access by clicking Permissions on the Sharing page of the shared folder's property sheet, as shown in Figure 22-3.

Table 22-1
Shared Folder Permission Types

Permission	Privilege
Read	The user can see the entire shared folder tree (root shared folder and subfolders). The user can also see all the files in the folder tree (traversing) and open them for reading. The user can execute applications in the shared folder hierarchy.
Change	This privilege inherits the Read privileges and also allows the user to change the folders and the data in the files within the shared folder's namespace. The user can also change file attributes, and can copy, move, and delete files and folders. The user cannot change the actual share.
Full Control	This privilege allows the user to take ownership of the files and folders, within the shared folder's namespace. It inherits the privileges of the Read and Change permissions. Under NTFS, only Full Control allows a user to change permissions and take ownership of a file or folder.

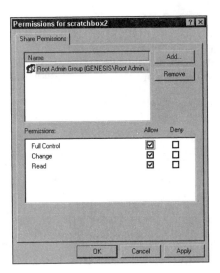

Figure 22-3: The Share Permissions dialog box

Deny

You can deny access to any of the above permissions. For example: If you deny Full Control, you drop the privilege level down to Change. Deny is useful if you wish to single out a user and deny him or her access (the same applies to groups). Deny is the strongest of permission attributes; in other words, it takes precedence over every permission. For example, if a user in a primary group has full access to a share, but you deny access directly or via a secondary group, the user is denied despite the access given in the primary group. However, it is better to take the user out of a group rather than keep him or her in the share and specifically deny him or her the access.

Accumulation of Share Permissions

Share permissions accumulate. If a user is a member of one group that is given Read access, but he or she is also a member of another group that is given Change access (to the same share), then the user's cumulative permissions in the share are Read and Change. The user's effective permission is Change, because it includes Read permission.

Moving or Copying Folders

When you move a folder, the shares assigned to it are deleted. The folder is not shared at the new location. If you copy a folder, the new copy is not shared, but the source folder remains shared.

Intra-Domain Shares

Shares are not restricted to the users and groups of the domain in which they were created. If a trust relationship exists between two domains, then a user or group in one domain can be given access to the share in another domain (see Chapters 3, 7, and 10). The administrator of Domain A can provide access to a user or to a global or universal group from Domain B.

Who Can Share Folders

Members of the predefined Administrators, Server Operators, and Power Users groups can share folders. On a member server, in a Windows 2000 domain, the members of the Administrators or Server Operators groups can share folders that exist on any computer on the network. On a standalone computer, only the Administrator and members of the Power Users and local Administrators groups can share a folder.

Workgroups do not make for such flexible sharing. Only members of the local Administrators group and the Power Users group can share folders. Remember that if you own the folder, you can share it. But an administrator can take ownership at any time.

Hidden Shares

The ability to hide shares is a useful feature of the Windows OS. It makes up for the problem of shares being visible to everyone on the network, even to users who do not have access to the shares. Relative hiding of shares is probably a very difficult and cumbersome technology to introduce into the OS, but it makes sense to only expose shares to users who have access to them. To the other users, the shares should just not be visible . . . only available on a need-to-know basis. Active Directory goes a long way to make that possible by locating published shares in organizational units.

It is, however, possible to hide shares by simply ending the share name with the dollar sign ($). You can still connect to the share if you have access to it, but it does not show up on the browse list (as nothing ending with the dollar sign shows in the browse list). You connect to the share using Run, as explained next, or at the command line using NET SHARE (see Appendix A).

Here is a good example of a hidden share in action: A certain company in Florida transmits millions of dollars of direct deposit information to the bank every afternoon. The application resides at the data center in Miami, but it logs into a hidden share on the wide area network, after an application in Los Angeles writes the direct deposit information to a file in the same hidden share. Both applications or processes are members of the Banking group, and they have Read and Write access to the file in the share. No one else can see the share on the network, and the cloaking affords the share a measure of concealment. Of course, it is possible to dig around on computers and look for hidden shares. But did you know that you can hide computers as well? See Chapter 3.

Connecting to Shares

There are several ways to connect to shares. You can connect using interactive tools or at the command line. You can also connect to published shares in Active Directory, which is the preferred way. DNS directs you to the domain controller hosting the Active Directory, so connecting to a share is as simple as browsing for a Web page:

To connect to a share using the Map Network Drive Wizard (this option assigns a drive letter):

1. Right-click the My Network Places on the desktop and select Map Network Drive.

2. Type in the UNC path to the folder if you know it, or click Browse to drill down to the exact folder.

3. Enter a drive letter of your choice or use the default.

4. Check the Reconnect at Logon checkbox if you wish the connection to remain persistent.

5. You can also connect to the share under another user name. All you need is the logon name and password. This is useful if you need to connect to a resource on a domain for which you have not been fully authenticated.

To connect to a share using Run:

1. Select Start ⇨ Run.

2. Type in the UNC path to the folder if you know it, or click Browse to drill down to the exact folder.

To connect to a share from My Network Places:

1. Open My Network Places.

2. Find the computer that contains the share and drill down until you locate the folder in the browse list.

3. When you find the share, double-click it to establish the connection.

To connect to a share in the Active Directory:

1. Open My Network Places.

2. Expand Active Directory until you locate the domain in which you wish to locate a published share.

3. When you find the share, double-click it to establish the connection.

Administrative Shares

When you install Windows 2000, NTFS automatically creates administrative shares on your local volume. These shares are placed in strategic administrative folders, the most important being where you installed the Windows 2000 system files. The administrative shares are listed in Table 22-2.

Table 22-2 Administrative Shares	
Share	*Purpose*
Roots (C$, D$, E$ and so on)	The root of every volume on a Windows 2000 server (and even on NT 4.0 and earlier servers) is shared. This means that if you can map to the share, you have access to the entire volume.
ADMIN$	This share is the system root, the Windows 2000 system folder hierarchy. To map to this share simply use \\SERVERNAME\ADMIN$.
PRINT$	This share is created when you install the first shared printer on the server. This share is established at \\SERVERNAME\SPOOL\DRIVERS, and its purpose is to allow clients to remotely pull printer drivers for installation on their machines. The Everyone group has Read access to this share, and administrators are able to install new drivers to the share as needed, using Full Control.
NETLOGON	This share is used for the net logon service, which is the mechanism to service logon requests to the server. It is also used for locating logon scripts.
IPC$	This is the share for Named Pipes, intra- and inter-process communications between applications.

It is possible to shut off these shares, and doing so might result in unpredictable results. You can, for example, shut down the NETLOGON share to prevent anyone from trying to obtain authentication at your machine—and you may have legitimate reasons for doing so—but the correct way is to stop the NETLOGON service.

We have found that you can delete the share, if you are an administrator or have ownership of the share. However, if you try to change permissions on the share, Windows 2000 denies access with a nasty message saying that built-in shares cannot be modified—absurd in light of the fact that you can delete the administrative shares at any time after you unseat the ownership.

Incidentally, if you delete an administrative share, it will return when you reboot the computer. The administrative shares are controlled by the server service. Anytime that you restart this service, such as reboot time, the shares are reestablished and reset to the factory default.

You might be concerned that the administrative shares pose a potential danger, and they do. In fact, all shares are dangerous if not managed with common sense. It is feasible, if you know Windows NT or Windows 2000, to map to the shared roots on each drive. If you are able to connect, you get total access to the drive and the entire folder hierarchy within.

You would be right to say that these shares are the equivalent of leaving the hen-house door open for the fox to walk right in. However, only administrators have access to these shares. That, however, is still not comforting, and the whole administrative share quirk is another reason why we lock up the Administrator account. As long as the Administrator account's identity and password are locked away, and security policy is in force, you will not experience hacking of these shares.

Common-Sense Strategies for Sharing Folders

The following sections include strategies for closing holes in your network with respect to shares.

Restricting Shares

Many administrators prefer to keep shares wide open by leaving the Everyone group in the share with full access. Instead, they control access to subfolders via folder and file permissions. We understand this policy, and the reason is the effort to relieve the administrative burden (one less thing to worry about). But is this common-sense management? Not if it means you are leaving doors unlocked on your network.

The problem is that the subfolders below the share become accessible to the users given access at the share-point. And if the Everyone group has access to the root, then it has access to all the subfolders. So by not restricting the share, you are in effect giving yourself more work to do because you have to go to every subfolder and apply NTFS permissions. On a complex folder hierarchy, the task of locking up all the subfolders could be next to impossible. If you want to keep shares (and your network) secure, it is best to remove the Everyone group from the share and admit only the groups that require the access to the folder namespace. Further security can be applied with the file and folder permissions.

Tip   Limiting use of the Everyone group makes it easier to troubleshoot user- related problems. The Everyone group forces you to be cognizant of every user account in your domain and every domain with which you share trusts.

Setting Up Application Share-points

When users need to access a remote application, shortcuts are created on their systems (manually or via profiles, logon scripts, and Group Policy). The users run the applications from the network shares, and the applications run in the local memory space on the client computer. Most well-designed Win32 applications can be executed multiple times in this fashion. And you will often be asked to install an application on the applications server and then share that folder. The following strategies are suggested for creating application shares:

✦ Create a root "application share-point." On our servers, we call these shares the "Apps" share-points.

✦ Under the Apps share-point, you can create a share for each application you are installing, and then share each respective install folder. It might not be necessary, however, because the subfolders are accessible to those given access to the share-point. If you need to restrict access to a subfolder, simply ensure only that the authorized group has access, through folder permissions, which are discussed in the latter part of this chapter.

✦ Provide access to an administrators group (or whatever suits your purpose) for the root (Apps) share and make sure the group has the Full Control privilege assigned. This allows application administrators only to manage the applications, such as patches and upgrades. You might also add a special "applications admins" group with Change control enabled to allow technicians or consultants to troubleshoot the applications.

✦ Remove the Everyone group from the share and provide access to either the Users group or a specific group that requires the access. Make sure these groups have only the Read privilege assigned.

Setting Up Data Share-points

Data shares contain files that users or applications need to share. Users mostly share spreadsheet and document files, while applications (clients) need access to databases. It is common-sense practice to keep the data share-points separate from application share-points because data shares require more that just Read access.

Data backup is another good reason for separate data share-points. Your backups should not be repetitively backing up application files (see Chapter 17), and the share is easy to identify and backup.

✦ Create a root "data" share-point for applications. Name the shares after the groups or projects that require them. For example: Y2K compliance docs or materials management. Naming the shares after the application name is confusing, and you may have many shares that contain data generated by the same application. A share named Microsoft Access Files would be a bad idea. For example, we manage several hundred servers, and they all contain Microsoft Access files.

✦ Give your users Change access so that their applications can update files and save the data. Administrative groups should be given Change or Full Control as needed.

Offline Access

It is possible on Windows 2000 to configure shared folders and their contents for offline access. This means that the contents of these shares can be "seconded" to the target computer. The remote or standalone computer disconnects from the network and maintains a mirror or shadow copy of the folder and files. You continue to work with the offline resource as if you are connected to it on the server.

To mark a file or folder for offline access, do the following: Right-click the shared folder and select the Caching option. The Caching Settings dialog box appears. All shares are cached for offline use by default, so you can clear the "Allow caching of files in this shared folder" checkbox if you do not need to cache the contents of the folder.

If you do want to keep caching for offline access, you can choose one of the options illustrated in Figure 22-4 and outlined in Table 22-3.

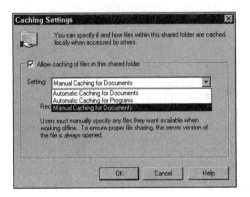

Figure 22-4: The Caching Settings dialog box

Table 22-3
Caching Settings

Caching Option	Purpose
Manual caching for documents	This option lets users select the files to be cached. This is the default setting for all shares, but only files marked for offline use will be cached. Every file marked for caching is cached, regardless of whether the file was opened or not.
Automatic caching for documents	This option allows every file in the folder that is opened to be automatically cached. This option saves on bandwidth because only files actually used are cached.
Automatic caching for programs	This option provides for unilateral caching of program files and applications. The file is cached for offline use, but when the user reconnects to the network, no synchronization is required.

Caching Attributes

The following are attributes of the offline access features of Windows 2000:

✦ When a computer connects to the share on the network, any files marked for caching on the server are copied to the client computer's hard disk.

✦ When a computer connects back to the share on the network, any files that have been updated on the client computer are copied to the server.

✦ When the user logs off the network, the server and the client synchronize the files automatically.

Synchronizing Cached Resources

To manage the synchronization between offline files and folders and their sources on the server clients, you need to open Windows Explorer and select Tools ⇨ Synchronize from the menus. In the Items to Synchronize dialog box, first select the items in the list to synchronize, and then click the Synchronize button.

The synchronization management options, as shown in Figure 22-5, can be used to determine when offline files are synchronized with the versions on the servers. You can do either a quick or full synchronization. The latter takes longer but ensures that the current versions are saved to the network and copied to the client.

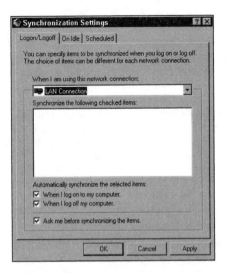

Figure 22-5: The Synchronization Settings dialog box

Securing Files and Folders with Permissions

As you learned in Chapter 3, permissions are the means by which you control access to network objects. After shares, they are the second and third lines of defense in protecting data and network resources. File and folder permissions are controlled by NTFS. This section deals specifically with the permissions that control access to volumes, folders, and files, as opposed to permissions that control access to share-points.

Permissions kick in as soon as you format a volume to NTFS. Volumes are protected with NTFS permissions, just as are folders and files. As soon as you have formatted a volume to NTFS 5.0, right-click the volume in Windows Explorer and select the Properties option on the ensuing Context menu. Click the Security tab. You will now notice that the Everyone group has default access to the drive, and thus any new folder or file you create will allow Everyone access. We advise that you change that as follows (please proceed with caution; this can be done on a drive in service but is safest and most easily done on a new volume):

1. Click Advanced.

2. Make sure the Reset permissions checkbox is unchecked (this avoids resetting permissions on all child objects, and we'll explain why later).

3. Click Add, and add the Administrators group or any special administration group or account you have created. We always create a root admin group and often use this group instead of the built-in one for tighter security.

4. Assign Full Control to the Administrators group.

5. Remove the Everyone group. Click Apply.

Now, only your select administrators can create and manage new folders on the volume. The default allows anyone to create a folder on the volume. Also, each time that you create a folder, you automatically assign your administrators group to the folder and nothing else. This makes for good security practice and keeps the doors locked until the folder is ready for group access. Remember that the Everyone group is automatically given carte blanche access to any share you create, and there is currently no way to override that because the volume's administrative share is inaccessible at the user level.

Caution We strongly recommend that you remove the Everyone group's Full Control permissions. If you don't, you're creating a security risk.

The Permission Types

Table 22-4 lists the folder permissions you can apply. Folder and file permissions are accessible from the Security tab of the Folder Properties dialog box. To access properties, right-click the folder and select the Properties option. Then select the Security tab, as shown in Figure 22-6.

Table 22-4	
Folder Permissions	
Permission	**Purpose**
Read	This permission is the first that provides access to the folder's contents. Without this permission, the user would get the dreaded "Access Denied" message. This permission allows the user to see ownership, permissions, and file attributes. All Write permissions are grayed out.
Write	This permission allows you to authorize the user to create files and folders with the folder under management. You can also permit the ability to change file attributes and view ownership and permissions.
List Folder Contents	This permission allows you to let the users see files and subfolders in the folder under management.
Read & Execute	This permission allows you to authorize the user to traverse the folders from the root folder down. It also lets the user read the files and execute applications in the folder under management and all subfolders.
Modify	This permission lets you authorize users to delete the folder under management and all earlier permissions.
Full Control	This permission allows the user to take ownership and perform all the actions of the previous permissions.
Deny	You can deny the user the permissions at any time. If you deny Full Control, you effectively deny all sub-permissions as well.

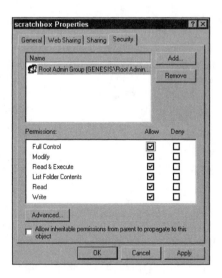

Figure 22-6: The Security tab on the Properties dialog box

Table 22-5 lists the permissions possible on files.

	Table 22-5 **File Permissions**	
Permission	**Purpose**	
Read	This permission permits the user to read the files and view their attributes, ownership, and permissions.	
Write	This permission permits the user to change the files' contents and attributes, and to view ownership and permissions.	
Read & Execute	This permission permits the user to run applications and also applies the Read permissions to the file.	
Modify	This permission permits the user to delete and perform all the actions permitted by the previous permissions.	
Full Control	This permission allows the user to take ownership and perform all the actions of the previous permissions.	
Deny	You can deny the user the permissions at any time. If you deny Full Control, you effectively deny all sub-permissions as well.	

NTFS 5.0 also lets you assign advanced versions of the permissions we just described. These permissions, shown in Figure 22-7, are more specific versions of the general permissions. In other words, they allow you to pinpoint the level of access you wish to provide to the user, such as *only* read a file or *only* execute an application . . . as opposed to the Read and Execute options in the basic permissions.

To assign Advanced permissions, click the Advanced button on the Security page of the Properties dialog box. Then click the View/Edit button on the dialog box that appears.

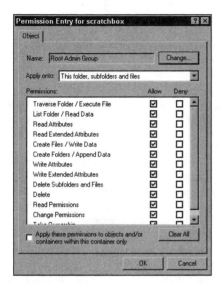

Figure 22-7: The Permission Entry dialog box

Permissions Attributes

You can assign multiple permission types to users, groups, and computer accounts, for tighter control of access to folders and files. As with shares, you need to understand the attributes of permissions to more effectively achieve your objectives. Permissions possess the following attributes:

✦ Permissions are cumulative. A user's total authority is the sum of all permissions granted to him or her over the use or access of an object. For example: If a user is granted Read permission by virtue of his or her membership in the Readers Group, and is a member of an Application Access Group that bestows the Execute permission, then the user's total access is Read and Execute.

✦ The Deny permission option overrides any and all permissions granted to a user over the specific object. If a user has Full Control of an object by virtue of membership in several groups, it only takes the Deny option in one group to lock the user out of the file or folder completely.

✦ File permissions are *not* stronger than folder permissions. This means that any file permission bestowed to a user does not override or supercede any permission granted at the folder level. In other words, if you give a user access to a file (even Full Control), but deny the user access at the folder level, the user cannot access the file. This mechanism prevents the user from connecting to the file from the command line by specifying a UNC path to the file.

Inheritance

The permissions that you assign to a given folder or file can, by default, propagate down to the child folders and files. In other words, if the Everyone group is given access to a folder and inheritance is turned on for all the subfolders in the hierarchy, they will also allow the Everyone group to have access, as will the files. We recommend you keep inheritance turned off by default or via domain policy so that you do not leave doors open by acts of omission or by failure to keep an eye on the propagation chain reaction.

Of course, the inheritance option is useful when you have to build a huge folder hierarchy and automatically provide one group with specific permission access to the entire folder and file namespace.

To prevent or allow permission inheritance, simply uncheck or check the Allow inheritable permissions option on the Security tab. You will be prompted to Copy or Remove the inherited permissions every time you elect to uncheck the checkbox. By turning inheritance off for a folder, you make the folder the new parent, and if subfolders have inheritance turned on, they become children.

Earlier, when we advised you to knock out the Everyone group from the volume access control list, we made special note to ensure you kept the "Reset permissions on all child objects and enable propagation of inheritable permissions" checkbox unchecked. The option can be selected from any level in the folder hierarchy. The option brings back not-too-fond memories of the "Replace permissions on subfolders and files. . ." option on NT 4.0 and earlier versions of NTFS.

By running this option, you are replacing, not merging, the permissions on all child folders and files on the volume. This means that any permissions applied to subfolders and files will be lost. If that is not your desired end, you could end up losing weeks of work restoring permissions so that users and applications can operate. And it gets worse: The action cannot be undone. You will only be able to rebuild what you had from backups and documentation. Proceed with care here, as it could cost you dearly.

Taking Ownership

Administrators, owners, or users with Full Control of an object can set up a user or a group to take ownership of the object. This is done by first admitting the user or group to the access control list (ACL), and checking the Take Ownership option on the Permission Entry list as described previously, or by giving the potential owner Full Control (which is a security risk). See Figure 22-8.

Figure 22-8: The Ownership tab on the Permissions Entry dialog box

Administrators, as long as they inherit their power from an administrator's group, can take ownership of objects regardless of the permissions in the object's ACL.

To take ownership of the object, you do the following:

1. Open the Access Control Settings dialog box for the object in question (see Navigating the Security Tab discussed earlier). Select the Owner tab.

2. In the Change owner to list box, select the user or group account name that will be taking ownership. Highlight the account and click Apply.

3. Check the Replace owner on subcontainers and objects to take ownership of all child subfolders and files contained by the parent folder.

Copying and Moving

Often, you may need to move or copy folders and their contents to other volumes or containers on the network. You cannot do this, even as an administrator, if you do not have ownership or the permission to do so. But you can take ownership and then assign yourself the necessary permissions.

Before you move a folder or a file, you should check and document the ownership and rights before the actual copy or move. Once you have successfully completed the process, you can reapply any permissions along the way.

The following security behavior applies to copying, moving, and ownership of files and folders:

✦ When you copy a file or a folder to a container within the same volume, the permissions assigned to the object are dropped, and the object and its contents and children inherit the permissions assigned to the destination container.

✦ When you move a file or a folder to a container within the same volume, the permissions assigned to the object are kept, and the object's permissions remain independent of the destination container.

✦ When you copy a file or a folder to a container on another volume, the permissions assigned to the object are dropped, and the object and its contents and children inherit the permissions assigned to the destination container.

✦ When you move a file or a folder to a container on another volume, the permissions assigned to the object are dropped, and the object and its contents and children inherit the permissions assigned to the destination container.

✦ You cannot copy or move a folder or a file to the destination container if the destination container has not given you Write access, regardless of which volume you are moving or copying to.

✦ The user account that performs the actual copy or move becomes the owner of the objects when they reach their destination, usually the administrator.

✦ Permissions and ownership do not change at the source objects.

Strategies for Managing Permissions

Assigning permissions is not a complex art, but you need to be orderly and consistent about the process. It looks easy, but on a big network with a lot of resources, thousands of users, and mission critical applications, you cannot afford to drop the ball.

Here's a good example: Every night at a certain company, a process on an AS/400 connects to a share on a Windows network, opens a file, and writes a million dollars worth of business to the file. As soon as the file is closed and saved, another process connects to the same file and performs special functions on the data. What would happen if by some mistake on the part of the administrator, the permission on that file was changed, by some oversight, and the file could not be opened? It's possible that a million dollars worth of business could be lost. In our case, we had alerts on the AS400 that raised an alarm when the process failed. And the only damage done was the administrator was beeped at three in the morning to fix the problem.

everything in the folder where the temporary files are created. EFS addresses this potential problem, as well as other disadvantages of some other file encryption mechanisms.

EFS supports encryption of folders and files on NTFS volumes but does not support encryption on FAT volumes (because encryption is integrated with the NTFS file system, it relies on NTFS reparse points and an installable NTFS file system filter). You can use encryption on folders and files stored locally as well as on remote servers. However, encryption doesn't protect file data as it moves from the remote server to your workstation across the network (or vice-versa) because the network traffic is unencrypted. If you need to ensure security throughout the entire process, use IPSec to encrypt network traffic.

How EFS Works

EFS employs public key encryption and the Windows 2000 CryptoAPI architecture to encrypt and protect files. Windows 2000 encrypts each file with a unique, randomly generated file encryption key. These keys are independent of the user's public/private key pair. By using a different key for each file, Windows 2000 provides a very secure encryption method that is difficult to compromise at all, much less on a widespread basis (decrypting an entire volume of encrypted files, for example). The current implementation of EFS uses the Data Encryption Standard X (DESX), which provides 128-bit encryption, which was until recently only available in North America (see Chapter 3).

As an administrator, there is very little, if anything, you need to do to enable users to encrypt and decrypt files. EFS automatically creates a public key pair and a file encryption certificate for a user the first time he or she attempts to encrypt a file. This eliminates the need for you to create a certificate or key pair for each user who needs or wants to use EFS. The users' encryption certificates and keys are stored in their profiles, so they are available each time a user logs on.

When a user encrypts a file, EFS automatically generates a bulk symmetric encryption key and then encrypts the file using the bulk encryption key. EFS then uses the user's public key to encrypt the bulk encryption key (called a *File Encryption Key,* or FEK). EFS stores the FEK for an encrypted file within an attribute called the *Data Decryption Field* (DDF) within the file itself. In addition, EFS also encrypts the bulk encryption key using the recovery agent's public key. This FEK is stored in the *Data Recovery Field* (DRF) of the file. The DRF can contain data for multiple recovery agents. Each time EFS saves the file, it generates a new DRF using the current recovery agent list, which is based on the recovery policy (explained later). Figure 22-9 illustrates the encryption process.

Encryption and decryption happens transparently to the user as the file is read from and written to the disk. So, a user can simply open an encrypted document using the document's parent application without any special procedures. The application doesn't have to be EFS-aware since the encryption/decryption happens at the file-system level independent of the application. EFS uses the private portion of the user's key pair to decrypt the FEK and enable the user to view the data. If the user doesn't supply the necessary private key required by the file (which happens automatically through the user's certificate store), he or she receives an "Access Denied" message. Figure 22-10 illustrates the decryption process.

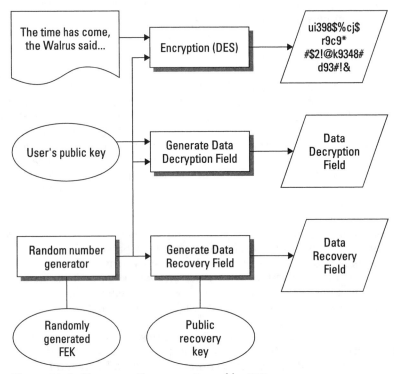

Figure 22-9: The encryption process used by EFS

 Note   EFS does not require an entire file to be decrypted as it is being read. Instead, decryption occurs on a block-by-block basis, so only those portions of the file actually read are decrypted.

Although the current implementation of EFS isn't designed to share data among users, you can enable multiple users to access and work with encrypted folders and files. The users simply need to share the same encryption keys. For more information, see the section "Sharing Encrypted Data" later in this chapter.

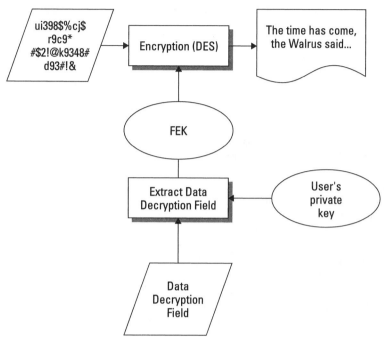

Figure 22-10: The decryption process used by EFS

Recoverability and the Encryption Recovery Policy

In most situations, you'll want to be able to recover encrypted data if a user leaves the organization or loses his or her encryption certificate and keys. EFS ensures recoverability of encrypted files by administrators by requiring that at least one data recovery key be present on the system. These recovery keys enable a *recovery agent* who has the necessary public key to decrypt a file's FEK and thereby is able to decrypt a file. The recovery key doesn't allow the recovery agent to retrieve any other information such as the user's private key, ensuring continued security for the user while still enabling the agent to recover data. By default, the Domain Administrators account is configured automatically as the recovery agent in a domain. The local Administrator account is defined as the recovery agent on stan-dalone computers and those participating in a workgroup. The recovery process is identical to the decryption process illustrated in Figure 22-10, except that the EFS uses the recovery agent's private key instead of the user's private key to decrypt the data.

You can define an encryption recovery policy at the domain level and enforce that policy on all computers in the domain through domain/group policies. Administra-tors can delegate recovery policies to specific security administration accounts through the delegation features inherent in the Active Directory (AD). This capabil-ity enables administrators to delegate authority for encrypted data recovery to one or more security administrators. EFS also allows for multiple recovery key configurations, which provides redundancy and greater flexibility in configuring and implementing the encryption policy.

When there is no domain (such as in a standalone, workgroup, or home office environment), EFS automatically creates recovery keys and saves them as machine keys, enabling the local Administrator account to perform encryption recovery.

The EFS recovery policy is part of the domain security policy for computers participating in a domain and part of the local security policy for computers in a workgroup or for standalone computers. In each case, the security policy is applied through Security Settings\Public Key Policies\Encrypted Data Recovery Agents. You can use the Local Security Policy or Domain Security Policy MMC consoles, as appropriate, to add and configure recovery agents and their certificates. This includes importing and exporting certificates. By implementing the recovery policy in the system security policy, Windows 2000 provides centralized replication, enforcement, and caching of the policy. Because the user's security credentials are cached, he or she can continue to work with encrypted files even when his or her system is not connected to the network.

See the section "Configuring and Using a Recovery Policy" later in this chapter for information on configuring the security policy and performing recovery operations.

Using EFS

Because EFS is integrated with NTFS 5.0 and installed automatically, there is no installation or configuration required for a user to begin encrypting folders and files. As long as a recovery agent is defined, the user can encrypt files. If no recovery agent is defined, EFS is disabled. Since Windows 2000 by default creates the recovery certificate and installs it in the domain or local security policy as appropriate to the system, users can begin using encryption with Windows 2000 out of the box.

Although you can encrypt individual files, it's best to instead apply encryption on a folder-by-folder basis (or in cases requiring extreme security, on a volume-by-volume basis). The main reason for not applying encryption to individual files is that many programs create temporary files when you work with a document (Microsoft Word is a good example), and EFS does not automatically encrypt these temporary files. In order to do so, the application would have to be EFS-aware and notify Windows 2000 that the temporary file needs to be encrypted. By encrypting a folder, you effectively encrypt the contents of the folder. As you create new files in the folder (including automatically created temporary files), those new files are encrypted and enjoy the same security as the other files in the folder.

Tip   When you encrypt a folder, you aren't actually encrypting the NTFS field that defines the folder, but rather setting the folder's encryption attribute. EFS uses this attribute to determine how to handle file creation and modification operations in the folder.

Encrypting and decrypting through Explorer

Encrypting a folder or file is easy. Just right-click the object and choose Properties to display its property sheet. On the object's General property page, click Advanced to access the object's Advanced Attributes dialog box (Figure 22-11). Select the Encrypt contents to secure data check box, click OK, and then click OK again to close the object's property sheet.

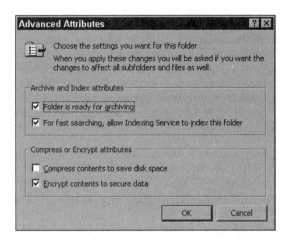

Figure 22-11: The Advanced Attributes dialog box

Note NTFS compression and encryption are mutually exclusive, so encryption is not supported for compressed folders or files or vice versa. If you enable encryption of a compressed folder or file, the file is decompressed. If you compress an encrypted folder or file, it is decrypted. This decryption doesn't happen automatically per se, but when you select the Compress option on the Advanced Attributes dialog box, the Encrypt option is automatically deselected.

When you encrypt a folder, Windows 2000 displays the Confirm Attribute Changes dialog box, as shown in Figure 22-12. If you select Apply changes to this folder only, EFS encrypts the folder but not any of its contents, including subfolders or files. Any new objects that you create in the folder, however, will be encrypted. If instead you choose Apply changes to this folder, subfolders, and files, EFS encrypts not only the folder, but also all of its child objects.

Reversing the attribute has similar implications. If you open the Advanced Attributes dialog box and deselect the Encrypt option, Windows 2000 displays the same Confirm Attribute Changes dialog box. If you apply the changes to the folder only, child objects, including subfolders and files, are unaffected, and if they were encrypted, remain so. When you create new objects in the folder, those objects will not be encrypted, even though previously existing objects might be. If you apply the changes to child objects, all child objects in the folder are decrypted.

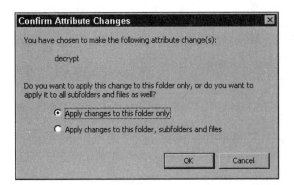

Figure 22-12: The Confirm Attribute Changes dialog box

Encrypting and decrypting through the command prompt

If you work substantially in a command console or need to integrate encryption processes in batch files, you can use the CIPHER command to encrypt and decrypt folders and files. Following is the syntax for the command:

```
CIPHER [/E | /D] [/S:dir] [/A] [/I] [/F] [/Q] [/H] [/K] [pathname [...]]
```

The following list summarizes the command options for CIPHER:

+ /E Encrypts the specified directories. New files added will be encrypted.

+ /D Decrypts the specified directories. New files will not be encrypted; does not affect existing encrypted child objects.

+ /S Performs the specified operation on directories in the given directory and all subdirectories.

+ /A Performs the specified operation for files as well as directories.

+ /I Continues the specified operation even if errors occur. By default, CIPHER stops when an error is encountered.

+ /F Forces the encryption operation on all specified objects, including those already encrypted. Objects already encrypted are skipped by default.

+ /Q Reports only essential information.

+ /H Displays files with hidden or system attributes; these files are omitted by default.

+ /K Creates new file encryption key for the user running CIPHER. All the other options are ignored if this option is used.

+ pathname Specifies a file, or directory.

When used without parameters, CIPHER displays the encryption state of the current directory and any files contained in the folder. You can use multiple directory names and wildcards. Use spaces between multiple parameters.

Copying, Moving, or Renaming Encrypted Files

As with compression, a folder's encryption attribute also has an effect on files you copy or move between encrypted and non-encrypted folders, or files and folders you rename. The following list summarizes the effect of the encryption attribute when copying, moving, and renaming objects:

✦ **Copying and moving encrypted folders or files to unencrypted folders (NTFS volumes):** The copies are encrypted regardless of the encryption attribute of the destination folder. If you are copying to another computer, the objects are encrypted only if the destination computer allows encryption. In a domain environment, the destination computer must be trusted for delegation — remote encryption is not enabled by default.

✦ **Copying and moving unencrypted folders or files to encrypted folders (NTFS volumes):** The folders or files are encrypted. This applies to copies on the same computer and to a remote computer that supports encryption.

✦ **Copying and moving encrypted or unencrypted files to FAT volumes:** The folders or files are decrypted. An exception to this is if you use the Backup utility to back up the files to a Backup file (BKF) on a FAT volume. In this case, the file remains encrypted in the backup set.

The COPY command used in a command console has been modified to support encryption. The following is the syntax of the COPY command:

```
COPY [/E | /I] sourcefile destinationfile
```

The following summarizes the /E and /I switches:

✦ /E Exports an encrypted file (`sourcefile`) as an opaque encrypted stream of bits to `destinationfile`. The destination file need not be on an NTFS volume, but it can be a FAT file on a floppy disk.

✦ /I Imports an opaque encrypted stream of bits from `sourcefile` as an EFS encrypted file on an NTFS volume. The source file need not be an NTFS file, but the destination file must be.

When you rename a folder or file, the encryption attribute is unaffected. So, you can rename an encrypted folder or file in place, and it remains encrypted. In addition, you can rename a folder or file to a different location (essentially a move operation), and the folder or file will remain encrypted, even if renamed to an NTFS folder that is not encrypted.

Accessing Encrypted Data Remotely

In order to access encrypted data, you must have the necessary security certificate and key. If you're logging on from the computer where you encrypted the files, you'll have that certificate and associated private key in your local certificate store, provided you log on using the same account as when you encrypted the files. In order to access the encrypted data remotely from another computer, you must do one of two things: Use a roaming profile or import the certificate to the computer. When you use a roaming profile, your security certificates follow your logon, making them available regardless of your logon location.

If you're not using a roaming profile, you need to import the certificate used when the files were encrypted. You also can share a security certificate to enable multiple users to access the same set of encrypted folders and files. The following section explains how to share a security certificate.

Sharing Encrypted Data

In order to use files on a computer other than the one where they were encrypted, you must have the required certificate and its associated private key on the computer at which you're logged on. This is true whether you're accessing data that you or someone else encrypted. So, you need to install the certificate and its associated key on your computer. You do this with the Certificate Manager. First, you export the certificate and its key on the computer where the files were encrypted, and then you import the key to the other computer(s) where you want to access those files.

Note   Using certificate services to share encrypted data requires you to install a public key infrastructure (PKI) and establish a Windows 2000 network as a local or private certificate authority (CA). Although we introduce Windows 2000 PKI in Chapter 3, installing and setting up certificate services and a PKI is beyond the scope of this book.

To export the certificate and key, follow these steps:

1. Log on with the account that was used to encrypt the files, then open the Certificates MMC console snap-in focused on the user account.

2. Open the Personal folder, then open the Certificates folder and locate the certificate issued for EFS (check the Intended Purpose column for Encrypting File System).

3. Right-click the certificate and choose All Tasks ➪ Export to start the Certificate Export Wizard.

4. In the wizard, choose the option to export the private key.

5. The PKCS format option will automatically be selected (Figure 22-13). Choose options from the dialog box based on the following list:

- **Include all certificates in the certification path if possible:** Select this option if you need to export multiple certificates from the selected store. In most cases, you will not need to select this option, as there will probably only be one EFS certificate in your personal store.

- **Enable strong protection (requires Internet Explorer 5.0, NT 4.0 SP4 or above):** This option enables *iteration count,* which provides stronger security. This option is compatible with Internet Explorer 5.0 and NT 4.0 Service Pack 4 or higher. If you are exporting the key to systems that don't fit those criteria, deselect this option.

- **Delete the private key if the export is successful:** This option, if selected, deletes the private key associated with the certificate. In most cases, you probably will not want to delete the private key so you can continue to use the certificate on the originating system.

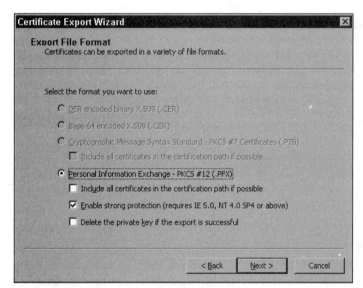

Figure 22-13: Use the Certificate Export Wizard to export the EFS certificate to other computers.

6. Specify and confirm a password for the private key being exported. This ensures that only those persons who have the password can import and use the certificate. Note that you can export the key with a blank password, but doing so reduces security for the key and allows anyone with access to the export file to import and use the certificate to decrypt the files.

7. Specify a file name for the file and click Next, then click Finish to create the file.

After you have exported the certificate file, you need to import the file on the computer(s) and accounts from which you want to access the encrypted files. Follow these steps to import the certificate:

1. Log on at the computer where you want to use the certificate, or in the case of a roaming profile, simply log on at any computer in the domain using the account through which you want to access the encrypted data.

2. Open the Certificate Manager MMC console, then open the Personal folder.

3. Right-click the Personal folder and choose All Tasks ➪ Import to start the Certificate Import Wizard.

4. Within the wizard, locate the file created previously and click Next to display the dialog box shown in Figure 22-14.

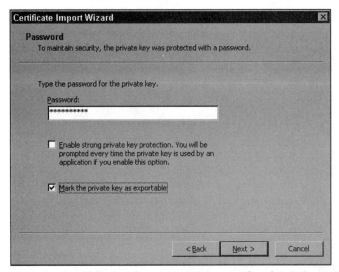

Figure 22-14: The wizard prompts for password and security options.

5. Specify the password for the private key in the certificate, then select options based on the following list:

- **Enable strong private key protection:** Select this option if you want Windows 2000 to prompt you each time the private key is used by an application. This helps you track when the key is used.

- **Mark the private key as exportable:** Select this option if you want to be able to export the key in the future. If you don't select this option, you won't be able to export the key.

6. Specify that you want to place the certificate in the Personal store, and follow the prompts to complete the wizard and the import process.

You can provide the exported certificate to other users who need to access the encrypted data. You can distribute the file as you would any other, such as by e-mail attachment or by placing the file in a network share. Because both methods make the file publicly available, you should make sure you use a password when exporting the certificate, and only give the password to those users who need to import and use the certificate.

Backing Up and Recovering Encrypted Data

The Windows 2000 Backup program can back up and restore files for which the backup operator (or account) doesn't have adequate permissions to actually view the data. The same is true for encrypted data. Backup can back up and restore encrypted data regardless of whether the backup account has the EFS certificate necessary to decrypt the data. The backup and restore operations also have no effect on the encryption state of the files — the files remain encrypted and secure.

Note Even when encrypted files are backed up to media that doesn't support encryption (such as FAT volumes or floppies), Backup maintains the encryption on the files. If an unauthorized user gains access to the backup set and restores it — whether to FAT or NTFS volumes — the encrypted data is not restored. Backup creates the target files, but the files are empty.

Situations might arise where you need to recover encrypted data as a recovery agent. For example, a user who has encrypted data on his or her computer might leave the organization or lose his or her certificate. In this situation, any recovery agent who has the appropriate recovery certificate, which Windows 2000 creates automatically as previously explained, can recover the encrypted data.

Follow this procedure to restore encrypted files:

1. Back up the encrypted files to a BKF on a floppy disk or hard disk accessible from the recovery agent's computer.

2. Log on to the recovery agent's computer and restore the files from the backup set to a secure NTFS folder.

3. If you don't already have the required certificate, use the Certificates console to import the recovery key and certificate to the recovery agent's computer.

4. Open the property sheet for each file and deselect the encryption option to turn off the file's encryption attribute (decrypting the file). You can now send the decrypted files to any user who needs them. If the data needs to be re-encrypted, do so using a certificate shared by those users who need to access the data.

Configuring and Using a Recovery Policy

As mentioned earlier, EFS requires that a recovery agent be designated before encryption can occur. On a standalone computer or those in a workgroup, the local Administrator account is designated as a recovery agent by default, and the appropriate recovery key is placed in the Administrator's personal certificate store. In a domain, the Domain Administrator account is designated as the default recovery agent. You can continue to use the default recovery agents, if desired, or modify the recovery policy to accommodate specific security needs, such as redefining the role of recovery agents within the domain or disabling EFS on certain computers. The following sections examine several administrative issues related to configuring and using a recovery policy.

Securing the default recovery key—workgroup/standalone computer

At the initial logon with the Administrator account on a standalone computer or a computer in a workgroup, Windows 2000 creates a default recovery policy on the computer that makes the local Administrator account the recovery agent for EFS. Windows 2000 does this by creating a recovery certificate for the administrator and placing it in the administrator's personal store.

In some situations, you might wish to secure the local recovery key to prevent the local administrator account from being used to recover encrypted data. You might instead want to delegate this capability to a specific user. To secure the recovery key you need to export the key to a file, then remove the certificate from the local computer. Give the key to the designated recovery agent for import on the agent's computer, or place the certificate file in a secure location for import when it is needed.

See the previous section, "Sharing Encrypted Data," if you're not sure how to export the recovery certificate. After you successfully export the certificate, remove the certificate from the local computer to prevent it from being used for EFS recovery.

Securing the default recovery key—domain

You might want to secure the default recovery key in a domain environment, as well. For example, you might want to create a group of administrators specifically for the purpose of EFS recovery rather than allow any domain administrator to perform recovery. To secure the default recovery key in a domain, log on as Administrator on the first domain controller in the domain. Then use the procedure described in the previous section to export the certificate to a file and delete the certificate from the domain administrator account's certificate store.

Obtaining a file recovery certificate

When you are using the default recovery policy in a domain, it isn't necessary to request recovery certificates since the necessary certificates are already in place in the domain administrator's certificate store. If you are instead delegating recovery responsibility to a specific group of users or to individual accounts, you might want to use a Certificate Authority (CA) to generate recovery certificates when requested by recovery agents.

Note   You don't specifically need to use a CA to distribute recovery certificates. You can simply export the default domain recovery certificate from the domain administrator's certificate store, then give the certificate to individual users designated as recovery agents for import on their computers. Using multiple certificates, however, can increase security by not putting all your recovery eggs in one basket. Instead, you can rely on the CA to issue a unique recovery certificate to each recovery agent.

Since this chapter focuses on file systems, it does not cover how to set up a CA. Instead, the following explains the general steps for providing a means for recovery agents to request recovery certificates:

1. If no CA is currently installed, log on to a domain controller and run the Add/ Remove Programs object in the Control Panel. Install Certificate Services.

2. Create a group called Domain Recovery Agents in the domain and add the appropriate users to the group. Configure policies on the CA to allow the designated users or group to request recovery certificates from the CA.

3. Have each recovery agent request a recovery certificate from the CA. To start this process, the agents open the Certificates MMC console, right-click their Personal store, and choose All Tasks ➪ Request New Certificate to start the Certificate Request Wizard.

4. The wizard will automatically locate a CA in the domain, but the agent can choose a specific CA if needed. Through the wizard, the agent specifies that he or she wants to obtain an EFS Recovery Agent certificate and follows the wizard's prompts to obtain the certificate.

5. Next, if the certificate is not automatically published to the AD, the agent needs to copy the certificate without the private key to a CER file. The domain administrator then uses this file to add the certificate to the domain recovery policy. Use the Certificates console to copy the certificate to the CER file (export the certificate to the file).

6. Finally, the agent exports the certificate to a secure PFX file using the Certificates console and places the PFX in a secure archive. Then, the agent deletes the certificate from the local computer, again through the Certificates console. This ensures that the certificate is applied through the domain policy rather than through the local policy.

Defining a domain-wide recovery policy

After you set up a CA and the designated recovery agents have their certificates exported to CER files, you need to set up the domain-wide recovery policy. You do this by adding the recovery agents and their respective certificates to the default domain policy. The presence of the certificates in the Security Settings\Public Key Policies\Encrypted Data Recovery Agents container implicitly defines the domain recovery policy. Follow these steps to define the domain recovery policy:

1. Use the steps in the previous section to set up a CA and a recovery agents group, and have the agents request certificates and export them to CER files.

2. Collect the CER files into a common secure location on your local computer or on the domain controller.

3. Open the Domain Security Policy console by choosing Start ➪ Programs, Administrative Tools ➪ Domain Security Policy.

4. In the Domain Security Policy console, open Public Key Policies\Encrypted Data Recovery Agents.

5. Right-click the Encrypted Data Recovery Agents folder and choose Add to start the Add Recovery Agent Wizard.

6. If the certificates are already published in the AD, browse the AD to locate them (Figure 22-15). Otherwise, browse to the folder containing the CER files. Follow the wizard's prompts to complete the installation. Repeat the process to add any additional certificates.

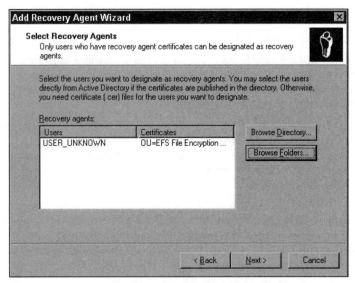

Figure 22-15: Browse either the AD or folders to locate the CER file to import.

Defining a recovery policy for an organizational unit

You define a recovery policy for an OU in essentially the same way you define the domain-wide recovery policy. Rather than working at the domain level, however, you work at the level of the OU. Follow the same steps in the OU as those described previously for the domain, adding recovery agent certificates at the appropriate container in the OU.

Forcing EFS use

In some situations, particularly with notebook computers that contain sensitive data, you might want to force the use of EFS. Because encryption and decryption happens transparently to the user, forcing the use of EFS doesn't impact the user in any way and ensures that if a notebook is stolen, the files on it will be relatively safe from compromise.

To force EFS use, format the drives on the computer using NTFS. Apply object permissions to folders to prevent the user from storing documents in any folder other than those you configure for encryption. For example, you might restrict the user to only working within the My Documents folder, setting permissions on all other folders to prevent the user from creating documents in them. Then, configure My Documents for encryption. Secure the default recovery key if present on the computer by exporting it and then removing the certificate from the computer.

Disabling EFS

In some situations, you might want to disable EFS for specific standalone computers or certain computers in an OU. You can disable EFS by applying an empty recovery policy to the computer — one that contains no recovery certificates and therefore disables EFS. If the user tries to create an encrypted folder or file, he or she will receive an Access Denied message.

An empty recovery policy is different from no recovery policy in a domain. With no recovery policy in place, the recovery policies defined at higher levels in the AD are inherited by the local computer. If no policy exists at a higher level, the local policy applies.

On a standalone computer or one in a workgroup, simply export the recovery certificate from the local Administrator's personal certificate store, then remove the certificate from the computer (along with any other recovery certificates, if installed). This defines an empty local policy, effectively disabling EFS. In a domain, define the empty policy at the OU level.

Summary

You share folders to allow users to access shared or network applications and to provide access to shared data. Shares should not be left wide open by admitting the Everyone group to the share with Full Control. Users should be admitted to shares as members of groups and not individually.

Folder and file permissions are the domain of the NTFS. The permissions provide true network security and access control. Permissions can be complex and cumbersome to manage on a large network with many users, groups, and network resources. We stress strong documentation, change control record keeping, and tracking as common-sense practice in providing access and security to network files and folders.

In situations where physical security of a server is critical, the Encrypting File System (EFS) provides an excellent means of securing files on the server, preventing unauthorized access through file copy to a diskette or backup to offline storage. If you intend to implement EFS, keep in mind that encryption and compression are mutually exclusive, so if you're going to use EFS, it will have to be on an uncompressed volume.

✦   ✦   ✦

Print Services

This chapter covers everything you need to know about the Windows 2000 printing service. Despite all of our efforts to create a paperless office, printers are not going away. And for all intents and purposes, for good or for evil, printers are becoming more sophisticated, cheaper, and easier to use every day.

New technologies like e-mail and the World Wide Web have not done much to alleviate the need for printers. Instead they have often succeeded in shifting the burden of hardcopy output from the sender to the receiver. These days, even attorneys e-mail you contracts — and then ask you to print them out, sign, and return them.

The network operating system lives and dies by its ability to host access to printers. The print service is the third leg of the "stool" that makes up a network operating system. Without it, a network OS simply falls over. Windows 2000 has inherited a rich and robust printing service, culled from years of R&D and the experiences of over a hundred million users.

It may seem like installing printers and printing is a no-brainer. For the large part it is — until the printer stops printing. You need to have a good understanding of the elements and components of Windows networking services to troubleshoot this vital facility.

As an administrator, you need to understand the logical environment in order to troubleshoot printer problems effectively. Therefore, we'll start by introducing the components that make printing actually happen. Later, we'll discuss installing printers, and you'll find that the properties and parameters you set up will mean more to you. Finally, you'll be able to explore print service troubleshooting, once you're equipped with the fundamentals.

You should understand that the components we'll discuss now are extremely complex objects and APIs that make up the Windows 2000 (actually, it's still NT) print service. In this book, our purpose is to provide you with enough information to visualize the components, and therefore be able to solve printing problems in Windows 2000 environments in an effective manner.

Understanding Windows 2000 Printer Services

To help you avoid getting hung up on terminology and concepts later, you should probably look at the printer services from two different points of view — the logical environment and the physical environment. The logical environment is an abstraction of the physical device that the user sees. It includes the software required to interface to the physical environment. The physical environment represents the devices out of which the final printed medium (usually paper) emerges.

Printer Services: The Logical Environment

First of all, printers have no user interface other than a cryptic keypad and a small LCD screen. Their job is to receive data and to convert the data into information that a printer's electronics understands. The printer language or software lays out the page according to specifications in the data and goes about the task of sending this information out to the physical parts that print the images onto a hard medium.

So if you are not able to print, and all the logical printer components check out, the only course of action, once a faulty printer has been detected, is to ship it back to the factory or call a service technician (assuming you know little about corona wires, drums, and hoppers). For the most part, you need only know how to turn the printer or plotter on and off, change toner and paper, connect its interface cables, and clean it.

Windows 2000, on the other hand, is both printer-aware and user-aware. Its task is to provide a logical printer interface that users can see and managers can manage and troubleshoot, as well as a holistic printer spooling and pooling environment. The logical printer, represented by the printer object, its icons, and properties, is representative of the hardware. The printer icon, or the printer share, is all knowledge workers need to know about printing.

You can install logical printers on your client computers (*local printers*), but most of the time the logical printers are installed on servers dedicated to hosting logical printers (*network printers*).

The following list describes the basic user procedure to connect to and use a printer:

1. Install a logical local or remote printer you have access to (the installation is persistent).

2. Once connected, you can manage certain properties of the logical printer, such as paper size and layout, bins and trays, resolution and color, number of pages and copies, and so on.

3. You, or at least your users, then print documents and graphics to the logical printer. The action of printing is often called a *job*. The job encapsulates printing instructions for the printer service, telling the logical printer how the job should be printed to the physical printer. When a client application prints a document or image, the application calls the Windows graphic device interface (GDI), which loads the driver for the target printer. (The driver is downloaded from the server if it does not exist on the client machine. On Windows 2000 clients, the drivers get downloaded at every print job.)

   Using the driver for the target printer, the GDI renders the document in the printer language of the physical printer. Once complete, the GDI then calls the local spooler, hands off the jobs, and closes. At this point, the GDI's work is done, and the client computer sends the job to the print server, via a routing service. The routing service transports the print job over the network using the remote procedure call service, the NetBIOS redirector, or other service (in the case of Unix ,OS/2, and so on).

4. The logical printer, also called the printer service or client spooler, once it has received the job from a print router or other interface, also loads the necessary driver, which tells it how to interface to the physical printer and how to send it the document. This is done via the services of print providers and processors.

5. The print processor checks the job's data types and alters them or leaves them alone depending on the requirements and the data types received. The print processor makes sure the jobs print correctly.

6. If the data types call for separator page processing, the jobs are handed off to the separator page processor. The separator page is added to the front of the job.

7. Meanwhile, as the printer administrator, you'll manage the logical printer's properties (the logical printer is an object), such as where it resides on the network, who has access to it, when they can use it, and so on.

The printer service, illustrated in Figure 23-1, includes several components and concepts, which are described in the following sections.

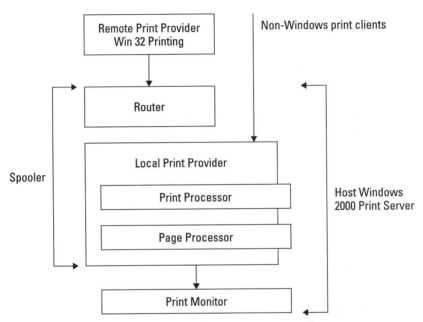

Figure 23-1: The Windows 2000 Print Service represented as a stack of services

Print routers

Print routers sit between the client application and the print server (which can also be on the local machine, if printing to the parallel or serial port). The first job of the router is to route print jobs to the correct servers and print services. The second job of the router, once the target server is found, is to make sure the client has the correct driver for the job. The router will check the target server's driver with the client's, and if the client's driver is older or absent, the router will update the driver on the client machine.

Note   Routers are usually Win32 services. In other words, they cater to Windows printing. All other network clients, such as UNIX, OS/2, Midrange systems, and the Mac environment, get their jobs to the Windows 2000 print service via APIs that interface directly with the server service stack.

Printer drivers

These are the first variable components you are asked to provide when setting up logical printers. Printer drivers are the software components that are sent to the user's software to allow it to create print jobs according to the capabilities of the target printers.

Printer drivers are built for specific printers or printer families. For example, you need a printer driver for jobs printed to the Hewlett Packard LaserJet III printers and different drivers for jobs printed to LaserJet 4 and LaserJet 5 printers respectively. However, LaserJet 4 and 5 drivers will be able to print standard jobs printed to the LaserJet III printers, but the older LaserJet III printers may not print a complex job generated by the LaserJet 4 or 5 driver.

Printer drivers are installed when you install and configure logical printing devices. You can also select alternative drivers after the logical printer has been installed. This is discussed later in this chapter.

Printer drivers are stored in the `\system32\spool\drivers\` folder. Information about the drivers is stored in the Registry of the hosting machine.

The drivers are grouped into raster printer drivers, which include the PCL standard and dot matrix printers and PostScript printer drivers, which are typically used for high-end graphics and publishing applications, the domain of the Apple/Mac computers and printers.

The spooler service stack

The spooler service is an engine — a collection of libraries — that controls each and every print job on a machine. It's best described as a stack starting with a router service that can receive jobs handed off from client processes (see Figure 23-1). Once into the stack, the job is passed down to the print processor for rendering and then finally passed down to the Print Monitor for transmission to the I/O ports on the physical interfaces at either local or remote ports.

The spooler is also the service that controls client and server printer management, installation and administration of logical printers, and more. From the user's point of view, and for all intents and purposes, it's the functionality that exists behind the icons to which users send their print jobs. Each Windows 2000 machine has one spooler service.

The spooler lives under the control of the service control manager. It can be stopped and started at any time. You need only shut down the spooler service (using the `net stop spooler` command) to stop all printing services on a machine. The spooler is part of the Win32 subsystem and is never deleted or relocated. It's owned by the local system account, and a number of child processes and services depend on it.

The spooler service is also responsible for client-side printer management. In fact, when you stop the service, the machine can't request or send print jobs to the logical shared printers on a server machine. In other words, the spooler service acts as both a client or server service as needed.

The spooler service creates the files (spool jobs or files) in the directory where it resides. The service and files are installed by default in the \winnt\system32\ spool\printers folder. So if your server hosts a large number of print jobs, you should consider redirecting the print jobs to a volume dedicated to servicing printers. Changing the path value in the printer's Registry key does this. The key in question is:

```
HKEY_LOCAL_MACHINE\SYSTEM\CurrentControlSet\Control\Print\Printers
```

And the value is a drive letter and subfolder path, not the UNC path. Once the value has changed, you need to stop and restart the print service. You can also set up separate folders for each printer's job, and this is discussed next.

The spooler output files

These are the files that are generated by the spooler service (specifically the print provider component) for each job it handles. Once the job has been sent to the printer successfully, the spooler files are deleted. The spooler output files consist of two types of files: the spool file and the shadow file. They serve the following purpose:

+ **Spool file:** This file has the .spl extension and is the print job — what gets sent to the printer.

+ **Shadow file:** This file has the .shd extension. It contains the information needed for the print job, and is useful only to the print service components. It contains information related to the job's position in the queue, the owner of the job, the destination printer, and so on.

To redirect the spool files for each printer to a separate volume or folder, change the target printer's default spool directory key. The key in question is:

```
HKEY_LOCAL_MACHINE\SYSTEM\CurrentControlSet\Control\Print\Printers
```

Drill down to the printer in question and then look for the SpoolDirectory data item. You can then change the value (the default is blank). Remember that the value must be a drive letter and folder, not UNC. This is demonstrated in Figure 23-2. One reason for redirecting these spool files to custom directories is explained next.

Print queues

Windows print queues are the aforementioned print files (the collection of .spl files) waiting in the spool folder to be printed. Each spooled job prints in the order it was received. You can use the net print command at the command line to manage a job (see Appendix A), or you can work with the document interactively via the respective printer's management interface (accessing the printer management interface for both local and remote computers is discussed later in this chapter).

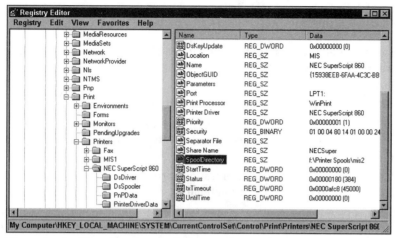

Figure 23-2: Changing the spool directory for a printer

If you manage a lot of printers, redirecting each printer's spool files to a separate folder can make it easier to manage the printer queue from the command line. It may happen that a print job hangs for some reason, and one of the first places to begin your diagnostics is in the print queue. If the queue receives the file from the user, you can be sure that part of the process, the client spooler service, is not the problem. Your next job would be to figure out why the job is sitting in the queue going nowhere.

The print processor

The print processor is the `winprint.dll` file that resides in the `\system32\ spool\prtprocs\w3286` folder. The job of this library of functions is to take the print job data sent by the spooler and render it into data the printer can understand (or not render, if it already is in a format the printer can understand). Most print jobs won't require any intervention by the print processor, unless you have peculiar output requirements.

The default data type spooled to printers by the processor is NT EMF, which can be handled by most printers. EMF stands for Enhanced Metafile Format, and most printers can read it. You won't have to intervene and change the print processor libraries very often because, firstly, the client applications decide the data type to be sent to the processor and, secondly, you can't choose or force a job to be handled by any particular print processor. This work is handled automatically.

Windows 2000 comes with built-in print processors. The one installed by default is known as Winprint, and it handles the standard data types printed by Windows applications. Another important print processor is SFMPSPRT, which is the Macintosh print processor, which handles jobs sent to PostScript printers. The Macintosh print processor is installed when you install Macintosh services on the host machine. Winprint can handle the following data types.

✦ **NT EMF ver 1.00x.** EMF stands for Enhanced Metafile Format. These files can be printed to most printers.

✦ **RAW.** Any job that comes out as this data type indicates to the print processor that nothing further need be done to print the document.

✦ **RAW (FF appended).** This type forces the print processor to check if a form feed has been added to the end of the job — to ensure that the last page exits the printer.

✦ **RAW (FF auto).** This type does not issue a form feed, and the print processor adds it to the end of the job automatically.

✦ **TEXT.** This data type is usually issued for printers that do not accept direct text. The print processor will render the text to meet the needs of the target printer.

Note   The Macintosh print processor, SFMPSPRT, renders jobs to non-postscript printers for the benefit of Mac clients. However, the output is limited to the very basic "playout" (to use a Mac-DTP phrase for sending a job to the printer). The default data type is PSCRIPT1, which is a Windows bitmap format that will print to the non-postscript printers. The best you can do for Mac clients is to install PostScript printers (or face the wrath of the Mac maniacs), which will provide the high resolution and graphics capabilities DTP publishers will require, regardless if the client is Mac or Windows or Linux.

Ports

The term *port* is loosely used to refer to the hardware connections that allow a data stream to flow from one device or media to another. Print servers and printer interface equipment use ports to represent network and cable connections. Ports are assigned network addresses and sit between the printer and the spooler service. We will deal with server ports later in the chapter.

Print monitors

Print monitors are important components to understand. They are soft devices that control the transmission process of the print jobs to the I/O ports on the devices that interface with the physical printer. Windows 2000 supports several standard print monitors. Print monitors perform the following tasks in the print service:

✦ They open up a connection between the print processor and the port. The connection is then used to transfer the data to the I/O ports of the physical printer or remote printer interface. In essence, they touch the actual ports at the interfaces on the remote print servers or printer interface devices.

✦ They monitor the print job for error messages, progress, and completion.

The print monitor essentially monitors the entire print job and reports status back to the spooler. If a print job times out, for whatever reason, the monitor notifies the spooler, and the spooler sends a message to the client.

Several print monitors are built into Windows 2000. You can see the list when attempting to create a new port for the job data connection. Unfortunately, Windows 2000, like its predecessor, tends to create confusion between the monitor type and the actual I/O port, as illustrated in Figure 23-3.

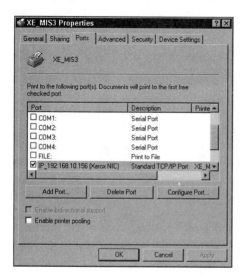

Figure 23-3: The Ports tab on the Properties dialog box

Why is it so important to understand the role of the monitor? It's usually the first component in the print service stack that alerts you to a frequent reason for print problems — inability to communicate with the local or remote port. If the print monitor reports a problem connecting to a remote port, then you have a network problem (IP, IPX/SPX, or lower on the network stack). Usually, a trip to the printer will find the network cable kicked out of the network drop or the interface unit.

The following monitors come bundled with Windows 2000.

Local print monitor

The local print monitor (`localmon.dll`) manages the following ports:

✦ **Parallel Interface:** This interface caters to print jobs that are sent to the parallel port on the computer initiating the job. Every machine supports parallel port printing. You choose this monitor when you set up a *local* printer connected directly to the host. The local printer can also be shared, which makes it a network printer.

✦ **Serial Interface:** This interface provides the same service as the parallel interface. The data, however, is transmitted through the serial interface, a communications port (such as COM1 or COM2), instead of the parallel interface. Serial interfacing is not common on printers.

✦ **File:** This interface allows you to spool the job to a file name. The job is identical to jobs that are spooled directly to print interfaces, local or network. The option of wrapping up the data into a file allows you to relocate the file to another system for printing. In other words, the physical printer does not have to be present or locatable on your network to be of service.

This option is convenient if you do not actually own or have access to the target physical printer. If you need to print to very expensive printers, such as the Linotronic typesetters and heavy-duty PostScript printers run by service bureaus and printing companies, you can print the job to a file and then send the file to the service via the Internet or on a disk. All you need to do is install the driver for the target printer. (By the way, PostScript print files are binary.)

LPR print monitor (TCP/IP printing)

As soon as you put some distance between the physical printers and the computers from which you are requesting the print service, you establish a network-printing environment. The protocol suite of choice for a heterogeneous computing/printing environment is TCP/IP, and you would be well advised to aim for a homogenous TCP/IP printer network. In particular, the LPR and LPD (Line Printer Daemon) service is used as a standard for TCP/IP printing. It was derived from the Berkley UNIX standards.

Windows 2000 supports LPR/LPD printing with the services of the LPR/LPD environment (`lpd.exe`) and the LPR print monitor (`lprmon.dll`). The LPR monitor is installed by default when you install Windows 2000. If you install Services for UNIX, additional TCP/IP printing support is added to the printing system to support printers connected to Unix servers.

The LPR port can be used for all TCP/IP printing environments, especially for connecting to remote printer interface devices that do not support a custom TCP/IP daemon or service. You can also use the LPR service to connect to printers hanging off the local ports of UNIX computers and big iron, like VAX, MVS, and AS/400.

The LPR/LPD facilities are provided by the TCP/IP Print Server service, which is installed when you install Windows 2000. Typing **LPR** at the Command Prompt will return several Command Line commands for LPR printing.

Standard TCP/IP print monitor

Windows 2000 also installs a standard TCP/IP print monitor that will let you create a port to any network interface device or printer that supports IP.

Third-party print monitors

Third-party monitors may need to be loaded when you install printers that require custom or proprietary print monitors. All printer manufacturers create print monitors that can be installed into the printer service at any time, post-installation of Windows 2000. These include the following legacy print monitors:

✦ **Digital's Print Monitor:** Note the apostrophe after Digital. The possessive denotes that the monitor is technology belonging to Digital Equipment Corporation (or DEC, which is now part of Compaq, Inc.) and not "digital" as in binary, which is a common presumption.

The Digital print monitor is not installed as a default monitor and ships with DEC products, such as the DEColorwriter. It requires the DECnet protocol from Digital, which runs atop TCP/IP, typical of the network protocol tomfoolery of the last century.

✦ **Hewlett Packard's Print Monitors:** The older Hewlett Packard monitor talks to HP's printers and plotters and JetDirect devices. This monitor requires the DLC protocol be added to the network services. The old HP monitor is essentially useless because it does not support TCP/IP. In the event you need to install it, possibly to allow the server to cater to printing from the mainframe and mid-range environments, you need to remember that DLC is not a routable protocol. The server and printer will need to be on the same network segment.

The JetDirect print monitor is a new technology that can use several protocols, including TCP/IP and IPX/SPX. The JetDirect print monitor is installed during installation of the JetDirect printer drivers and management software. You can route IP print job packets to a JetDirect card anywhere on the planet.

✦ **Lexmark Print Monitor:** Another big printer manufacturer is Lexmark. Windows 2000 supports both Lexmark DLC and TCP/IP print monitors.

✦ **Macintosh Print Monitor:** This monitor (SFMMON) is installed automatically when you install Services for Macintosh and the AppleTalk protocol. AppleTalk is all you need to print to Apple printers and other PostScript printers. And you get the full features of the PostScript printer environments, including high resolution, color, separations, and more.

Printer Services: The Physical Environment

To use Windows 2000 printer services, you need a computer that can act as a host for the services. If you support a large network, it would be a good idea to dedicate a server to the role of printer server.

All of the Windows 2000 operating systems support printer server services. The only difference is the degree of availability. The servers (Standard, Advanced, and Data Center) are designed to host a large amount of connections, while Windows

2000 Professional is restricted to no more than ten concurrent connections (as was its predecessor, Windows NT Workstation 4). Advanced Server and Data Center Server allow you to cluster the printer service for maximum availability.

Here's a good rule of thumb for determining the hardware resources you'll need for a print server. Experience has shown us over the years that the size of the company or group has little to do with how much hardware you need to throw at print services. For instance, we manage small insurance companies that print five times the amount of documents that the big departments at our larger clients do. However, you should consider the following "street" rules:

✦ If you can determine that RAM will hold 10MB of print data at any given time, provide at least 30MB for expansion.

✦ Provide three to five times more hard disk space for print spools and queues or allow the volumes to be easily extended (see Chapter 16). This might be hard for you to determine when first setting up the print service on a server, but you can easily predict your needs. If all your users are printing concurrently — or at least within a few minutes of each other — total up the size of all their documents in the spool folders. These documents sit in the spooler on the hard disk until the service sends them to the printer, so provide at least three times more hard disk space than the total of all document sizes sent to the printer. You never know when someone will decide to send the entire tax rulebook of the Internal Revenue Service to the printer, over the weekend.

✦ Printing is also a demanding service. At one of our clients, we have as many as 40 printers on one server alone, so it makes sense to make sure the print server machine has a processor to be proud of.

✦ Color printing or printing complicated graphics needs a lot of processor bandwidth. A dedicated server should service these needs, especially in terminal environments.

Print servers

Several hardware components combine to complete the printing system. Unfortunately, the names of the components do not always mean the same thing to everyone. The print server, in our book, is a computer that "serves" printer interfaces to users on the network as earlier discussed. Printer interfaces (logical printers) are established on the server and act as representatives or portals to the printers either on the network or attached directly to the parallel ports of the computer.

Print devices

A *print device* is what Microsoft calls the physical printer hardware. If you ask your user where his or her print device is, he or she will probably draw a blank, but the term seems to have become a Microsoft standard. To stay on the same page as your customers, you should stick with *printer* and forget trying to overcomplicate things with redundant phrases.

Local printers are connected directly to the parallel or serial ports of computers, while network printers can interface directly to the network with the help of network interface components. The components can be network interface devices or network interface cards (NICs) built directly into the printer.

Network interface devices

The makers of these interface boxes say they have a claim to the term *print server,* and some even stamp "print server" on their product. Rather, refer to them by their brand names, such as Lantronix box or JetDirect card — it will result in less explaining.

These guys are very useful and exist for several reasons:

✦ They obviate the need to hook up a computer parallel port to every printer in the office. Instead, the printer cable is attached to a parallel port on the box, which attaches to the network via a network interface port.

✦ In large companies, the print servers (computers) are locked away in cooled server rooms, and the printers are either located near their users or in printing rooms. The interface device allows the printer and the print server computer to co-exist some distance away from each other. At one of our clients, we support label printers in many distribution centers that are installed at loading docks and bays where food is packed and shipped. We would not want to locate an expensive Pentium or AS/400 at every dock just to print labels.

✦ They provide a network interface to the printer, allowing you to place a printer at any convenient location where you have a network drop.

✦ They support a variety of networks, such as Token Ring and Ethernet, and also support all the most popular protocols, especially TCP/IP.

✦ They come packed with smart electronics and embedded software that will allow you to manage their network protocols, such as assigning network addresses, printing capability, and communications with the printer. They come equipped with terminal access and daemons for remote management. You can telnet into them or even access their internals from a Web browser.

✦ They allow you to connect more than one printer to the network at a single network drop and address (many printers on one IP or IPX address). The interface directs the inbound job to an IP port assigned to the printer. (Remember that standard TCP/IP supports up to 65,536 ports.)

✦ They come with built-in memory to further queue documents sent by the server.

These interfaces are very useful, inexpensive, and compact. Keep them hidden out of harm's way, such as under the printer, in a printer cabinet, or behind the printer stand. We have a collection of dead Lantronix boxes, each no bigger than a pack of West Virginia's filtered finest, which have been tortured with butts, coffee, kicking, and electric shock. They also have a habit of going into indefinite seclusion, never to be seen or heard of again.

Print Services Strategy

Providing print services to the enterprise should be a well-planned exercise. Although it appears easy enough to install printers, it makes sense to create blueprints or policy governing printer installation, usage, access, naming, administration, and more.

Often, you will arrive at a company only to find that your predecessor knew his or her printing environment like a palm tree knows where its coconuts fall. Troubleshooting such environments is almost impossible, and you would be best to scrap what you inherited and start all over again. Your best course of action would be to create a new logical printer environment and then move users to the new environment in phases.

The following guidelines for setting up a strategic print service plan are a start.

Printer Taxonomy

Recall earlier that the printers that users print to are not the actual printer devices, but logical printers set up in Windows 2000, and these printers can thus go by several aliases. You will learn later that one physical print device can be used by several groups that will "map" to the printer as different shares, targeting different aliases. You need to set up a consistent and practical naming scheme or convention to cater to a varied user environment.

It's not important if you already have hundreds of printers set up all over the place or if the job of printer admin recently became your responsibility; if you do not have a naming scheme for your printers, now is the time to create one. A large company might have as many as 1,000 physical printers plugged in all over the place, and their logical printer namespace may contain as many as 1,500 names.

The scheme should be simple. Put *HP* in all Hewlett Packard printer names, *Xe* in all Xerox printer names, *Ne* in NEC printer names, and so on. For example: HP5LSI_MIS1 is the share name for the main MIS Hewlett Packard 5LSI printer. And the name HP5LSI_MIS2 might be the same printer shared for after-hour use.

Keep the names simple and try not to leave blank spaces, such as HP MIS1b. Blank spaces make it difficult for advanced users or administrators to map to printers from the command line using the `net use` command. Names with spaces need to be enclosed between quotes and that wastes time. Rather, use underscores to represent spaces in the name.

Also try to keep the name as short as possible. The name does not need to explain life itself. You can be as descriptive as you need in the description fields and in the Active Directory, as we'll soon discover. We have seen printer names you need a cipher to read. If the admin can't shout the name across the room or over the telephone — "you need to map to HP_MIS1b" — then the name is too complex. Consider this e-mail recently received from an associate in a sister company: "You can send the reports to $_IKY14_T_MAT_MGT5." This "fifth" printer allegedly belonged to the materials management group on the 14th floor of the "Tier" building somewhere in Kentucky.

Easy share names also work well for users. In our accounting department, we named all our printers HP_ACT1 to HP_ACT12. The ACT is short for accounting, but it did not take long before our users associated the printers with Shakespeare.

Create Print Groups

Here we go again reminding you not to give share access or permissions to individuals (in permissions and access control), but rather to work with groups. Even if the printer belongs to a group of one person, you never know when someone else needs to print to the same printer. A good example is an executive who has a personal printer in his or her office. So, you create the logical printer in Windows 2000 and add only the name of the executive to the printer object's access control list. But what happens when the assistant needs to print to that printer? If a group has access, then the assistant can be added to the group.

Using groups in access control and permissions makes for effective printer management. Under our corporate policy of controlled access, groups are given only the access they need to certain printers at certain times and for certain jobs. We believe it wise to resist giving the Everyone group access to all the printers they can find on the network. That could lead to many disasters. We've seen stuff like a user sending ten copies of a 1,500-page report to a small printer that could not handle the job, and thus causing urgent smaller documents to wait indefinitely for a chance to get to the printer. If you plan this well, you won't have to spend half your life deleting and purging failed jobs from print queues.

Not too long ago, we received a call from the CEO's assistant saying he sent a highly secret document to the wrong printer, which he couldn't find — anxiety was mounting. We found the document before it printed by tracing the queues and looking for his call sign (ownership). Now the CEO can only print to a printer that does not specifically deny him access.

Controlling access to printers is discussed later in this chapter.

Create a Print Network

Creating a print network, used exclusively for printers, is a worthwhile exercise. It helps keep other devices and machines from invading the printer's address space and makes it easier to manage the printer requirement. Here are some points to consider:

✦ **TCP/IP:** The protocol of choice for most printer networks is TCP/IP. If possible, you should stick to one network protocol. Managing a network of more than one protocol will add dollars to your total cost of ownership. Most models and makes support TCP/IP. Even modern PostScript printers can be assigned an IP address, even though AppleTalk drives them. Older printers and environments (like VMS, MVS, NetWare, and so on) prefer to talk LAT, IPX, Pathworks, and so on, but for a Windows 2000 print network, you may as well introduce Klingon into the school syllabus.

✦ **Subnet:** Organizations with a large amount of printers would do well creating one or more subnets exclusively for printers. One Class C subnet would cater to 254 printers or more on printer interface devices, which would probably be more than enough addresses for a company of 3,000 paper monkeys. If you manage a number of interconnected offices or sites on a WAN, then reserving a block of addresses out of the Class C (say 10 or 20) on the site should suffice. You don't need to add a second subnet to the site just for a bushel of printers; it will only add stress to the routing and replication bandwidth on which DNS and Active Directory depend.

✦ **DHCP:** Make sure the printer IP address range does not get used by DHCP. This is easily handled by reserving the block of addresses in the DHCP service (see Chapter 11).

Keep Drivers Current

The print routers in Windows 95, 98 (with the latest service packs), NT, and 2000 clients are able to receive the printer driver from the server every time they make a connection. Make sure that you keep current and available the printer drivers for every make and model of printer you deploy. Windows 2000 ships with more than 2,500 drivers, so the library on the disk is more than sufficient (although there were no drivers for our Zebra printers, as discussed later).

There are two good reasons why this is an important task:

✦ **Staying current:** By regularly updating the drivers, you ensure that users always have access to the latest feature the drivers publish and that you have maintenance releases that fix earlier release defects. Printer drivers become out-of-date very quickly. You can keep drivers current by downloading them from the Internet using the Windows Update service, explained in the first chapter.

✦ **Availability:** Making sure servers hold and keep current printer drivers for every printer you deploy will ensure that whenever a client connects to a printer (an old or new logical printer) the latest driver will be available. This keeps printing delays to a minimum and the volume of support calls down.

Installing and Setting up Printers

When you install printers on a server, they will usually be installed as local printers printing to remote TCP/IP ports. Local printers, by definition, are printers that coexist with a server, which acts as its proxy. Local printers are shared like files and folders so that groups of users may map to them and use their services.

Just because the physical printer is established out on the network somewhere does not make it a network printer; it must still be installed as a local printer (remember, you are installing a logical printer). Installing the network printer option does not make your server a proxy for the printer. It only gives you the ability to connect to and print from the remote network printer. Installing a network printer only makes you another client, and that is not our objective.

Before you begin installing a new local printer, there are a number of parameters and data you will need handy:

1. If you have a TCP/IP printer network, as most organizations now have, assign the new IP address for the remote port, be it on a printer interface device or on the printer itself. Make sure the DHCP server reserves the IP address and mark the IP address as assigned on an IP address allocation list or database you keep.

2. If you are setting up a port on a remote printer interface device, make up a network name for the device. The name can be derived from the name of the device given by the manufacturer, a serial number, and even a MAC (hardware) address.

3. Have all printer drivers handy. If you do not maintain an install directory on the server, as explained in Chapter 5, you may need your Windows 2000 Server install CDs within arm's reach.

Installing the Local Printer

Follow these steps to install a local printer:

1. Log on to the Print Server computer as a member of the Administrators group. You can do this from the console or log on over a terminal session.

2. Select ➪ Start ➪ Settings ➪ Printers. The Printers folder loads, as illustrated in Figure 23-4.

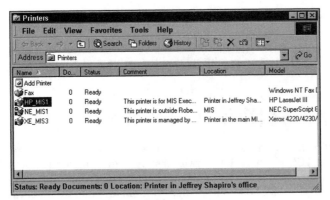

Figure 23-4: The Printers folder

3. Double-click the Add Printer icon. This will launch the Add Printer Wizard. Click Next to arrive at your first totally confusing screen. The Wizard asks you to install a local or network printer, but describes the "Local printer" as being directly connected to the computer. Forget that useless advice. The printer server can be connected directly to your server, or your server can be in Little Rock, Arkansas, USA, and the printer can be in Zululand, Natal, South Africa. As mentioned earlier, only choose Network Printer if the printer you are installing is not going to be serviced by the local computer as its printer server, host, or proxy.

4. Choose the Plug and Play option if you are setting up a PnP printer for the first time. Choosing this option for a printer that is already installed wastes time because PnP discovery takes longer than you knowing what driver is on the system or on the CD in your hand.

5. Next, we come to the Port Selection page. If the printer is indeed installed in Zululand, you will need an IP address for the port on the printer or on the print device interface box to which your Zulu printer is connected. Note that you can also choose a parallel port (the LPT port) or a COM port if the printer actually is connected to the server computer with a data cable.

   For demo purposes, let's assume the printer is a Zebra printer located 9,000 miles away in Zululand. In this case, we need to create an LPR port and assign it the IP address you have handy. (If you do not have the IP address handy, you will have to stop everything and go and get it.)

6. Click Next, and the LPR-compatible printer dialog box loads. You are prompted to provide a name or IP address for the port. If at all possible, provide the IP address, because name resolution just slows things down (the IP address should be permanently assigned to this port in any event).

Also provide the name, as we also requested you do earlier. The far-away Zebra printer is hanging off a Lantronix computer, so the typical name we'll use identifies the port as being on a Lantronix printer "server." This is illustrated in Figure 23-5.

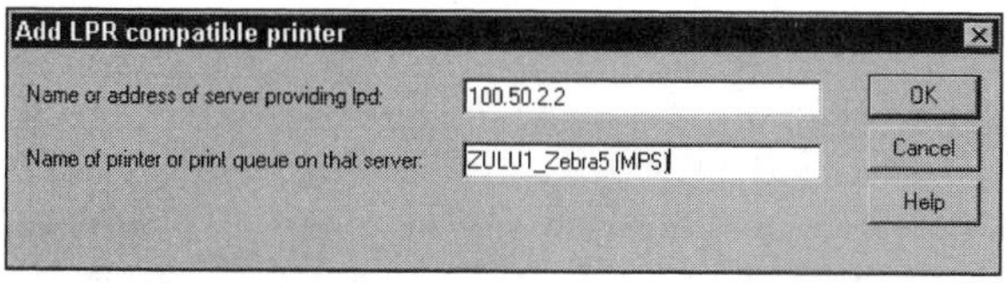

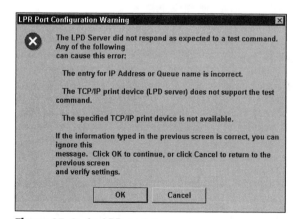

Figure 23-5: Adding an LPR port

7. Because we discussed the function of the print monitor earlier, you will note here that the LPR print monitor immediately tries to touch the remote IP address. The message illustrated in Figure 23-6 pops up if the IP address or remote server does not respond to a test packet sent by the monitor. At this point, you can choose to abandon the installation in order to test the IP address or the remote device, or you can carry on regardless with the setup and return to the troubleshooting later. Either option will get you back to the same point. It's not much of a deal to return later to change the IP address or other settings, as demonstrated later.

Figure 23-6: An LPR port error

There could be several reasons for this message.

a. The IP address might be bad, or unreachable. You should troubleshoot the address (using `ping`, `tracert`, and other TCP/IP tools described in Chapter 12).

b. If the address is valid, then the interface device may not be working properly. You will need to diagnose that problem with the tools that ship with the device.

c. The device may not be connected to the network. Or it may be connected but not have power. Whatever the reason, you will need to have someone at the remote site troubleshoot the device. Many interface devices allow you to connect to the printer and dump, or print setup and diagnostics information to the printer. This will tell you if the device has the correct IP address installed and if the device is working properly. Many modern printers also have the ability to print out configuration and address information. If the device is set up with the wrong IP address, as is usually the case, then a simple change will get your device installed and working.

8. Click Next to load the printer driver for the printer from the manufacturer list, illustrated in Figure 23-7. If the printer you are installing is not in the list (Figure 23-7 indicates the absence of Zebra printers), you will need to get the driver from the Internet or from a CD that ships with the printer. Click Next after you have selected the driver. If the driver is already installed on the system, Windows will prompt you accordingly to replace or use the existing driver.

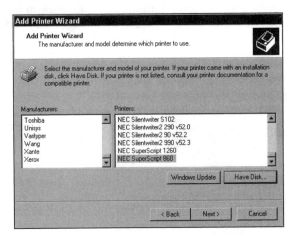

Figure 23-7: The manufacturer's list of printers

9. Click Next to name the printer, as illustrated in Figure 23-8. Remember what we said earlier about name consistency. In the illustration, the name denotes a Zebra printer for the "shipping" group.

10. Click Next to share the printer; then click Next to provide information about the location and use of the printer. This is demonstrated in Figure 23-9.

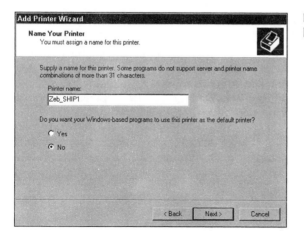

Figure 23-8: Naming the logical printer

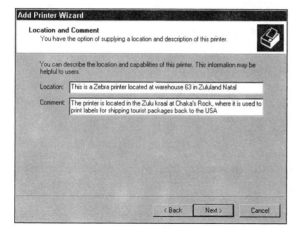

Figure 23-9: Location and Comment information

11. Finally, you can choose to print a test page. Do it. Click the test page but do not use the troubleshooter. In other words, respond YES to the prompt asking if the test page printed correctly, even if you have no idea what came out at the other side, halfway across the planet. It's not that we don't trust the troubleshooter. If we agreed that the test page did not print, we would not be wasting time hyperlinking our way around the help system. After you've troubleshot several printer problems, the troubleshooter becomes a waste of time. The test page is more useful as a means of sending a document to the printer without having to leave the printer configuration to send a page. You can then check the queue of the printer. if the test page has not printed after a few minutes, you need to troubleshoot. Meanwhile, your new printer service is installed.

A local printer has now been installed. Before we allow access to it, we need to still do some fine-tuning.

Publishing Printers

Printers are a resource, but you can either make them available to users or you can hide them. When printers are made available—when they can be found on the network—users will try to connect to them and print, oblivious to any permissions or policy you may have set. If you don't want certain printers used by various groups, you have to lock them down, even hide them away.

Conversely, if you are going to make a printer share available, you should make it easily locatable, not only to ease your work load, but also so that the user or the administrator installing the printer as a network printer can find it. This is what we call *publishing printers*.

Locating Printers

Printers can easily be located by browsing the printer servers, as is the case with legacy Windows NT printer servers. The printer can then be installed on a client machine for printing—using the Add Printer Wizard or via the net use command.

Locating the printer in Active Directory

You can also publish printers in Active Directory. Figure 23-10 illustrates printers listed in the directory. You can search an enterprise for a printer that serves your purpose. Let's say you are looking for a printer that is able to print color separations to 1200 DPI resolution.

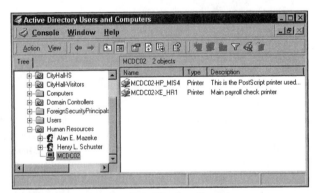

Figure 23-10: Printers listed in the directory

If the printer has been published in Active Directory, you will be able to find it by asking the directory to search for printers matching your specifications, as illustrated in Figure 23-11. You can then look up the printer's manager or contact person and request access to the printer. This is a boon for large or widely dispersed organizations, where machine count can run into the hundreds and thousands.

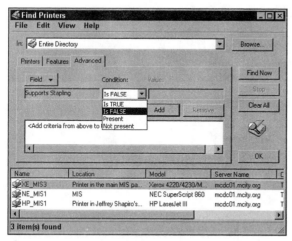

Figure 23-11: Searching for a printer in the directory

So how do you publish or list the printer in Active Directory? You don't have to do anything other than make sure the server is an active member of a domain. When a server is authenticated as a member of a domain, Windows 2000 allows the server to publish its shares in the directory. You can also expressly refuse to publish the shares by unchecking the "List in the Directory" checkbox found on the Shares tab or the printer properties.

However, the print server need not be a domain member to make its print shares available. You can map to the printer share of a standalone machine in the directory as follows:

1. Select the OU in which to publish the share. Right-click the OU, select New, and then choose printer.

2. Enter a UNC name to the share name, as illustrated in Figure 23-12. Although the dialog box makes reference to pre-Windows 2000 print shares, this is how you list standalone Windows 2000 print server shares in the directory. You can also map to the IP address used by the server as follows: \\192.168.10.57\HP1.

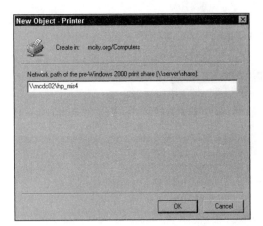

Figure 23-12: Manually listing a printer in Active Directory

Locating printers over the Web

With the Internet Information Server fully integrated into the Windows 2000 Server operating systems, clients running Windows 2000 Professional can connect to the print server's printers via the HTTP protocol. Upon connecting to a logical printer share on the server, the server will automatically update the client with the necessary printer driver.

This service is a boon for large intranets and service bureaus, where a print manager with a flare for HTML can customize the pages for each printer, publishing its features, connection parameters, usage requests, and so on.

Clients connect to the printer using their Web browsers as follows:

✦ **HTTP//*servername*/printers:** This Web page lists all the logical printers hosted by the server identified in the URL. The information entered when the printer was first installed is listed on the page, as well as status information, and so on.

✦ **HTTP//*servername/logicalprinter_share:*** This URL connects you directly to the logical printer.

Hiding Printers

You can hide print shares the same way you hide folders (Chapter 22) — by appending the dollar sign ($) onto the end of the share name like this: HP_MIS8$. You can still map to the share from the command line, using the NET USE command, but you would need to know the exact printer share name.

If you want to hide the share, remember not to list it in the directory when you first install it as a local printer.

Printer Pools

Pooling is another means of publishing printers. Several printers can be grouped together to form a contiguous print resource. Note the checkbox on the Port tab that is checked, as illustrated in Figure 23-13.

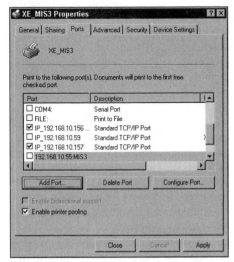

Figure 23-13: Pooling logical printers

Printer pooling is ideal for a shop that is printing a high volume of documents. Print jobs do not have to wait for a job on one printer to finish. If another printer is free, then the jobs automatically route to the first free printer.

To create a pool of printers, do the following:

1. First, install your group of identical printers as local printers. Create as many ports as printers to be added to the pool.

2. Check the Enable Printer Pooling check box.

3. Check all the ports on which a member of the pool is installed. This is illustrated in Figure 23-13. It's important to ensure that each port has an identical printer connected to it.

Loading Printer Ports

Windows 2000 lets you create multiple logical printers and assign them to the same port. We coined the term "loading the ports" to describe this technique. Another way to look at this is as a many-to-one printer setup: many logical printers to one physical printer or port. Each logical printer is a separate instance of the printer object. In other words, you can create several logical printers, all printing to the same physical device and the same physical port.

The following list describes the benefits of loading printer ports:

✦ **Printer Configuration:** Each logical printer can be configured differently for various reasons. Availability, sharing, permissions, and device settings can be different for each logical printer. On one printer, you might provide access to group A to print certain jobs, while on another logical printer you might provide access to a totally different group running other jobs. One printer might be available at night, while another is only available during the day (when the office is busier).

✦ **Job Prioritizing:** Certain logical printers can be given priority over print jobs. Setting the priority property of the logical printer achieves this as described next. One printer can be set up under a high priority to only allow access to users who can justify high-priority printing privileges.

✦ **Delegating Admin Functions:** Each logical printer has its own Print manager and queue. Document administrators can be assigned to manage the documents in the queues belonging to the logical printers installed in their OUs.

✦ **Sharing Physical Printers:** Several organizational units, or departments, might share a single printer. Instead of lumping all the users into one group, it would make better sense to create a logical printer for each group. Separator pages identify each group's job, as described shortly.

Prioritizing jobs can't be done automatically on the same logical printer. If one job requires priority over another job, you can pause the lesser priority job and allow the urgent job to "jump the queue." This becomes tricky and tiresome when there are a lot of documents in the queue. It would be better to create another logical printer on the same port and then set a higher print priority for the latter logical printer. How can this be done?

The logical printer has a priority property that can be set from the lowest value of 1 to the highest value of 99. Jobs that are sent to the printer with the higher priority setting will print before the lower priority jobs.

This is achieved as follows:

1. Create a second logical printer on the same port (loading) as the regular printer.

2. Select the printer in the Printer manager and right-click its icon. Select properties and zero in on the Advanced tab. In the priority setting box, select the priority (you can make it the highest if this printer is the most important) and then click OK. (See Figure 23-14, which illustrates the Advanced tab.)

Now when users need to print urgent jobs, they can print to the second printer. You should create a special group for the latter printer, which can be used for people who need priority over other jobs. Whenever someone needs to print a job urgently, you can temporarily admit him or her to the group.

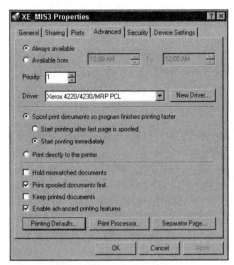

Figure 23-14: The Advanced tab on the Properties dialog box

Printer Administration

Long gone are the days when the only printers we set up in the average office were simple laser printers and dot matrix printers. Today, there are so many brands and so many models around that it would be ridiculous to expect the OS to cater to all the features of the printer. Instead, Microsoft publishes APIs that allow the printer manufacturer to hook into system management facilities to manage and configure the printer. Still, a number of common features are accessible from the printer configuration dialog boxes.

There are three tiers of Windows 2000 administration of printers. First, we can control how and what printers print, and when they can print it. This is printer-centric management. Second, we can control which jobs print; we can delete them, pause them, redirect them, and cancel them. This is job-centric management. Finally, we can publish printer shares and control who has access to the printer, when they have that access, and what they can print. This is printer access control. Let's first deal with printer management functions.

Printer Management

The job of the printer manager requires strong organizational skills. Using the techniques provided in this chapter, you will have to create logical printers, install network interface devices, install physical printers onto the network interface devices, provide access to the printers, delegate administration, and more. In essence, you will have to do everything this chapter covers, including the following chores:

Setting separator pages

Setting separator pages, or banners if you prefer NetWare terminology, can be tedious work, but in very busy printing environments producing substantial documents, they are essential.

Separator pages separate jobs. They also can be used to provide information about jobs and can print at the beginning of each print job, in front of the first page. They do not affect the printing order of the jobs, nor the pagination. Consider the following key reasons for using separator pages:

✦ **Tracking down job owners:** We have several high-end printers to which many people print every day. At the end of each day, there were hundreds of documents that were forgotten by their owners. At the end of the week, a huge pile of uncollected documents was getting thrown out (Web pages, white papers, press releases, e-mail, and so on). The situation got worse by the day, and it did not take long to recognize the waste of time and materials. The situation called for separator pages, to allow a printer administrator to collect the jobs, identify the owners, and threaten them with disciplinary action if they did not collect their output. Habitual offenders were told they needed to clean up their acts or they would lose their printing privileges.

✦ **Separating the print jobs in long runs:** If your printer is receiving large volumes of print runs, or continuous reports, the only way to pull complete jobs from the run or sort them easily is with separator pages. We have several printers that typically print reports on a round-the-clock basis, and all the jobs are separated by separator pages.

✦ **Organizing chaos at high-traffic printers:** Many job owners do run after their print jobs. After printing, they dash off to the printer and wait for the paper to slide out of the hopper. If the printer is busy, hands are grabbing at every page that comes out. It does not take much effort for some job slugs to grab pages and even whole jobs before other users can get to them. Uncollected jobs get stored in the pickup tray as mentioned in option one, but without separator pages, it does not take long to create job spaghetti.

✦ **Job information:** Separator pages can be used with sophisticated printers to print job information, such as the owner, language used (if the printer supports language changing on the fly), and so on.

Windows 2000 provides four types of separator page files. They are stored in the `systemroot\System32` folder. Table 23-1 describes these pages.

Table 23-1	
Separator Pages	
Separator File	**Purpose**
PCL.SEP	Switches a dual-language HP Printer to PCL mode printing
PSCRIPT.SEP	Switches a dual-language HP Printer to PostScript mode printing
SYSPRINT.SEP	Used for PostScript printers
SYSPRTJ.SEP	Same as SYSPRINT.SEP but uses Japanese characters

The pages described in the Table 23-1 are not actually printed. They are script files that contain codes to instruct the print provider to print a separator page, and what to print on it. You can open and edit these files and customize them for your purpose. By default, the separator file instructs the printer to print the job owner's name, date, and job number.

To create your own separator file, copy the existing one (so you have an original to go back to) and modify the copy as needed. You can rename the file whatever you like, but give it the .sep extension. The contents of the Windows 2000 PCL file are as follows:

```
\
\H1B\L%-12345X@PJL ENTER LANGUAGE=PCL
\H1B\L&11T\0
\M\B\S\N\U
\U\LJob : \I
\U\LDate: \D
\U\LTime: \T
\E
```

Note that the first character in each line of code is the backslash (\). This is the character that denotes or signifies that the character following a \ *is* the escape code. You could use a character like the @ sign as the escape code signifier (such as @E). The Windows 2000 Escape codes are as follows:

✦ \B\M Text is printed in double-width blocks until \U.

✦ \B\S Text is printed in single-width blocks until \U.

✦ \E Page eject.

✦ \H*n* Initiates a control sequence where *n* is a hex code for the target printer (see printer manual).

✦ \F*path* Prints the contents of a file at *path*.

✦ \I Job number.

✦ \L*xxx* Prints the characters in *x* following the escape code.

✦ \n Skips *n* lines (zero moves to the next line).

✦ \N Switches a dual-language HP Printer to PCL mode printing.

✦ \T Time the job was printed.

✦ \U Turns off block character printing.

✦ \W*nn* Width of the separator page in characters.

Separator pages are set up on the print server computer as follows:

1. Select the printer from the Print manager dialog box. Right-click and select Properties. Then go to the Advanced tab, as illustrated in Figure 23-14.

2. Click Separator Page. You can type the name and path of the separator page, or you can browse for it. OK your way out of the Properties dialog box. The print provider will now print the separator page.

Some last advice about separator pages: They work well in high-print or high-job volume situations but are annoying on the small stuff. For every single sheet you print, out pops a separator page you have to throw away. To save the forests and your sanity, keep separator pages off the small jobs. The best way of switching separators off small jobs is to have the small-stuff printers print to an alternative logical printer, as described in the previous section, "Publishing Printers."

Mixing and matching forms and trays

Most printers today come with multiple trays, for labels, paper and form sizes, envelopes, and more. And single-tray printers offer the ability to manually feed a form or allow the physical printer to automatically feed the form. You can configure your printer to allow application users to select the paper or form size they need right from their applications.

To assign a form to a particular tray or form feeder, do the following:

1. Select the printer from the Print manager dialog box. Right-click and select Properties. Then go to the Device Settings tab.

2. Click the tray you wish to assign paper sizes to. A drop-down menu appears allowing you to select from the list of standards-based paper sizes. Select a size and then click OK. The tab is illustrated in Figure 23-15.

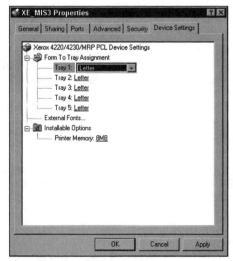

Figure 23-15: Device Settings

Job Management

Server and printer administrators frequently get called to manage print jobs or documents. Windows 2000 lets you delegate the job management function on an OU-to-OU basis. The following task list describes the job management functions that can be assigned to job management administrators. The job management options are accessible from the context menu (right-clicking), the Printer menu, and the Document menu in the respective print queues dialog box, as illustrated in figure 23-16.

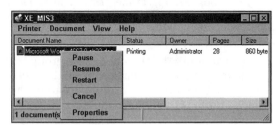

Figure 23-16: The print queue dialog box for printer XE_MIS3

✦ **To pause a job:** Double-click the printer to open the queue or print job manager. Then select a printing document and right-click or click the Document menu. Select the pause option. A check mark appears next to the document to indicate that it's paused.

✦ **To pause all jobs:** Right-click the printer queue and select the option Use Printer Offline. All jobs are suspended.

✦ **To resume a job:** There are two ways to resume a job. You can either pull down the Document menu again and select the Resume option, or you can right-click the job again and re-click the pause option to clear the check mark.

✦ **To cancel all jobs:** Right-click the queue window on any job and select the option to Cancel all Documents.

✦ **To delete a single job:** Select the document and hit the delete key.

You can redirect stalled jobs to another physical printer rather than delete them and have to resubmit them. The logical printer remains the same — all you have to do is change the port and physical printer.

Open the properties of the logical printer, go to the Ports tab, and select a new port. As long as you know that the printer on the new port is the same as the one you are redirecting from, is working, and uses the same driver, your documents will print.

Advanced Spool Options

The default options on the Advanced tab work for the majority of printing environments. But the tab has a number of options available that are useful for troubleshooting and managing printers. The Advanced tab is illustrated in Figure 23-14.

Available time

A logical printer is usually always available, but there might be times during the day when it should be shut down for any number reasons. Some printers are so large and complex that refilling their trays can take up a lot of time, hoppers and bins may need to be cleaned, toner may need to be refilled, and so on.

You also may desire to shut down a logical printer to prevent certain groups from using it at a certain time of day. For example, you might have a group that needs exclusive access to the printer at a certain time, and they can't afford to have other users printing at the same time (check printing is a good example).

To shut down the logical share at a certain time, toggle to the Time available option to enable the option and set the time range.

 Note Remember that setting an available time for a logical printer does not shut down the physical printer at the time range you set. If other logical printers point to the same physical printer and availability is set to Always, the other users will be able to print. If you need to shut down the printer completely at a certain time, make sure all logical printers have the same available time range set.

To spool or not to spool

As mentioned earlier, you can opt to send print jobs directly to the printer. All you need to do is toggle the options to use the spooler or to print directly to the printer. If you choose the latter, the print job bypasses the spooler and prints directly to the printer.

You would choose the latter option only in the rarest of situations, such as a broken spooler, because you lose the benefits of spooler-managed printing. For starters, print jobs will complete much faster at the application level if they are sent to the spooler. A large document could tie up your application for hours as it prints directly to the printer because you are waiting for each printed page to emerge from the printer before the next page is sent.

Still, you might have a special reason to print directly to the printer, and you should explore the use of a sophisticated printer interface device that has sufficient memory to act as a buffer.

Most of the time, however, all logical printers make use of the spooler. But you can toggle between printing immediately when the spooler receives a page or waiting until it has received the entire document before it starts sending the job.

Choosing the latter delays printing, but it ensures that the entire job spools correctly before the printing process starts. You would do this if you had a large job to print and the application that produced the job was no longer available. Such a situation is encountered at print service bureaus where customers bring in print files for processing.

Holding mismatched documents

Check this option for most of your logical printers, especially if they represent sophisticated devices with multiple feeders and hoppers. This option instructs the spooler to examine the codes in the print document and check them against the setup of the physical printer. For example, let's say you print to a bulk cassette or special-size form feeder from the application, but that option has been disabled in the printer's device settings or it's offline for some reason. Instead of throwing an error, the printer will hold the job until the problem has been corrected. This is illustrated in Figure 23-17.

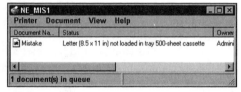

Figure 23-17: Mismatched documents are held.

The spooler does not hold up any valid jobs from printing. While your job is on hold, you can correct the problem at the actual printer, if correctable, or delete the job (Cancel) and reprint with new parameters.

Print spooled documents first

When you tell the spooler to give jobs that have completed spooling priority over jobs that are still spooling, it overrides any priority a job might have. In other words, if you are spooling a job consisting of 1,000 pages, why should all the one-page jobs have to wait in line?

You might turn this feature off in situations where all the jobs are roughly the same size. The spooler then prints the jobs in the order it receives them.

Keep printed documents

This is another feature that at first seems to make no sense — until you get a job to print that takes hours to set up. A good example of such a job is a sheet of labels for ZIP disks, or address labels, or CD labels, or high-resolution color jobs that don't change graphically but need to be reprinted from time to time.

If you have such a need, you can create a logical printer that keeps the documents after they have printed. When you need to reprint the job, right-click the job you need and select Restart from the Context menu. Figure 23-18 illustrates the result.

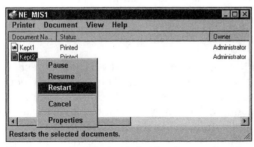

Figure 23-18: Keeping jobs that have printed

Creating a special printer that keeps the jobs makes more sense than toggling this property every time you want to keep the document and running the risk of every user's job having to be manually deleted from the hard disk. Use the techniques described earlier for creating a logical printer that redirects its jobs to a folder you created instead of the default queue folder, so that jobs that should be deleted do not get co-mingled with your persistent jobs.

Tip Another means of keeping the job is to print to a file and then print it from the command line whenever you need it. This might be a better option for you if the environment in which you are working is not sufficiently secure and you run the risk that the queue gets "flushed" and your jobs get lost. The `Copy` command prints documents from the command line (see Appendix A).

Access Control

Providing access to printers is similar to providing access to files and folders. To give users access to the printers on the print server, you first have to share the printer. Sharing also allows the users to browse the network to find the printers. Providing access to printers is almost identical to providing access to share-points. There is only one difference: You can't decide who has access to the print share. Microsoft has hard-coded the share to be open to Everyone. Sounds horrible? Fear not.

The only way to restrict access to printers is via security permissions (access control). Like with file shares, you may be tempted to just leave the Everyone group in the printer access control list. That may be the way to go if you have a huge printer or a collection of printers in a pool that has been set up as a free-for-all, only printing to blank white paper (and you are really sure no one can walk up to the printer and stick a letterhead in the tray). In other situations, especially when it comes to smaller printers, or highly specialized printers (like check and label printers) and plotters, it becomes essential to restrict the printers to only the groups of people who specifically use the printers.

Tip Consider creating groups along application needs and then admitting the application users to these groups. For example, we have a group of users who work with PeopleSoft applications all day long, and we installed a special Xerox system that prints payroll checks. To prevent people from printing to the checks in the tray, only members of the PeopleSoft-Check Printers group have access to this printer.

You can also provide access to — and information about — all printers in the organization by publishing the printers in the Active Directory (which is done automatically when you install printers on any server that is a domain member). And you can delegate the administration task to printer administrators in any groups established on an OU-per-OU basis. We will deal with that later in this chapter.

Assigning permissions according to role

Windows 2000 separates access to printers into three roles or classes of users: People who print, people who manage the documents or jobs, and people who manage the printers. Incidentally, users can be assigned all the permissions. Table 23-2 summarizes the printer permissions.

Table 23-2
Printer Permission Types

Access	Print	Manage Documents	Manage Printers
Print	Yes	Yes	Yes
Manage own job	Yes	Yes	Yes
Manage other's job	No	Yes	Yes
Connect	Yes	Yes	Yes
Control Print Jobs	No	Yes	Yes
Delete all Jobs	No	No	Yes
Share Printers	No	No	Yes
Configure Printers	No	No	Yes
Delete Printers	No	No	Yes
Change Permissions	No	No	Yes

The Manage own job permission allows the user to pause jobs, resume jobs, restart jobs, and cancel any job he or she owns. Users have no access to documents in the queue over which they have no ownership. Administrators, however, have the ability to take ownership of documents.

The printer object is similar to the file object. You can assign the above permissions, and you can also specifically deny any of them. Be careful though — denying some permissions may affect other weaker permissions. For example, if you deny Connect, you might as well remove the group from the access control list. Deny is stronger than the "allow" permissions of any other group and will override other permissions granted.

Permissions have been fully outlined in Chapter 22. Refer to this chapter for techniques and suggestions.

Delegating printer and document administration

Delegating responsibility for the management of print jobs and printers is important, especially in large organizations. Instead of sending all the problems that users get from printers to one person, you should set up two printer groups per OU and assign people from the OU to deal with the OU's printer problems and needs, assuming you have the staff. The following list is a suggestion for the two groups.

✦ **Print Job Admins:** The members of this group are allowed to manage print jobs. They can pause, restart, redirect, and cancel jobs. This group is not allowed to delete jobs, nor are they allowed to change printer properties.

✦ **Printer Admins:** The members of this group can perform print job management, install printers, configure printers, and delete printers. They should also be allowed to change permissions, take ownership, and publish printers in the directory.

Creating groups and delegating administrative control is discussed in Chapters 8, 9, and 10.

Taking ownership

You can take ownership of a logical printer in the same way you take ownership of a file or folder. Ownership rules for printers are no different than the ownership rules for files and folders. For example: The person who created the logical printer owns it; the users own the print jobs they create. Ownership is discussed in Chapter 3 and Chapter 22.

To take ownership of a printer, perform the following:

1. Open the logical printer's properties and then select the Security tab. Click the Advanced button.

2. The Access Control Setting dialog box appears. Click the Owner tab. Your user account (who you are signed on as) and the Administrators group appear in the list of owners. Select the account and click Apply or OK. Click OK again to close the Properties dialog box.

It's important to remember that you can't take ownership if you are not a member of an administrators group that has been assigned the Manage Printers permission.

Troubleshooting

Now that you understand the Windows 2000 printing services, you'll be better equipped to troubleshoot printer problems when they occur, and they will occur. Out of all the services the mighty Windows 2000 networking environment has to offer, the printer services generate the most support calls, behind resource access issues. The following troubleshooting suggestions and tips are a place to start to resolve printing problems as quickly as possible.

Server-Side Print Problems

We like to refer to jobs that do not print as being *blocked*. Blocked jobs arrive at the queues and just sit there, or they time-out with an error. Most calls to a support or help desk are complaints that jobs have spooled to the logical printer but are not emerging from the physical printer.

If a job is sitting in the queue and not indicating an error, it might be possible that a mismatched document has been trapped by the printing service. Mismatch problems are easily corrected, as explained earlier.

Jobs that throw an error indicate they were unable to print to the physical printer. If the job can't print and an error is reported, the following steps should be taken to alleviate the situation and correct the problem:

1. **Check the port assigned to the logical printer:** If the port is an IP address, then ping it. If you get a reply from the port, you have connectivity to the network components involved in the printing process. In other words, jobs can get to the server and the server can see the port, or at least the print monitor can. (If you are some distance away from the print server, open a terminal session to the server and ping the port from the session.) If the IP address is correct and you get a reply from the port, you can check the IP port off your list. If the port is a parallel or serial cable connected directly to the server, you'll need to perform specific diagnostics there as well.

Note   Network addressing is seldom the problem, especially if you maintain your IP printing network as suggested earlier (and if your printer has been printing before and no IP address conflicts appear in the event logs).

2. **Check the hard disk space, memory and event logs:** Resource starvation is one of the biggest causes of printer spooler service shutdown. (With Windows 2000, you can set and enforce disk quotas — as described in Chapter 16 — to help prevent your print server from running out of hard disk space.) Freeing up space or shutting down memory hogs may be all it takes to get printing again. The event logs can tell you when the first jobs failed. These events may tie in with other errors that could point to a reason for the sterile jobs.

   You can also check the driver. Although this is an unlikely point of failure with a printer that has been printing with no problems to date, the driver may have been changed or deleted by another administrator.

   If you can't get the print service printing to the physical printer within, say, five minutes of getting a call for help, go to step 3.

3. **Attempt to redirect the jobs:** Redirect the jobs to another port and physical printing device as described earlier in this chapter under the Publishing section. This is a quick fix that does not impact users and will alleviate the pressure stemming from impatient users. They will still print to the same logical printer.

If the new target physical printer is located somewhere else in your offices, you'll need to notify users where they can collect their jobs. Please don't redirect the jobs to another city in another state as one CNE once did. And make sure you are redirecting the jobs to another printer of the same type and using the same driver.

If you can't redirect the jobs and the other port is printing—and the blocked jobs are not—you most likely have a problem with the spooler and spooler files. This could have been caused by the lack of resources. You need to act fast and proceed to step 4.

4. **Stop and restart the spooler service on the print server computer:** If resources starvation was the problem or the spooler was down for some other reason, the spool files can become corrupted. In fact, you might consider giving the spooler a sharp crack on the head when everything else seems to check out. Restart the spooler and then stop and restart it again. If the spooler starts up normally and responds quickly to the restart command, but the jobs are still not printing, it's likely that they are corrupt. Delete the jobs—kill the spool files and the shadow files. (You may have to take ownership to delete the files. If new jobs are still not printing, things have to get drastic.) The files to delete are the SPL file and SHD files, discussed very early in this chapter.

5. **Take the logical printer offline:** The best way to do this is to prevent access to the logical printer completely. Selecting the option to "Use the printer offline" does nothing but cause the queues to fill up with more sterile print jobs. Your users print and then rush to the printers to stare at empty hoppers like deer in bright lights. It's better to tell them they have been denied access, and they will know why. We prefer to remove access from the printer completely. Go to the Security tab on the Properties dialog box and uncheck the permissions assigned to the groups using the printer. You may have to perform this exercise with several logical printers all using the port on which there is an error.

6. **Notify users there is a problem and notify your help or service desk:** When users discover they can't access a printer, they will call for help. It's better to preempt the calls.

7. **If you can see the port, attempt to log in:** Some ports allow you to telnet into the interface box. If you can log in to the port, you'll be able to get diagnostics from the port. Many manufacturers now ship software that can query the printer for errors and diagnostics. If the printer reports errors, you may have to call in a service technician. If the printer is checking out, you may have a problem with the printer interface device—such as the JetDirect card or the Lantronix device. Often, we have found these to be problem children that were fixed when we downloaded new versions of their firmware.

8. **Check for problems on the client:** If clients are printing and you are not seeing the jobs in the queues, then check the client. Odds are it's not a server-related problem. The spooler service on the client may be stopped.

Client-side Print Problems

Client-side printing problems are very different from server-side problems, although they are certainly interrelated and may stem from the server. The following list represents the most "popular" client-side print problems you will encounter:

1. **Pages print incorrectly or are garbled:** The cause of this problem is usually that the client has received the wrong printer driver. Check the server configuration and make sure the client is getting the correct driver. Remember, you may need drivers for all versions and types of operating systems running on your clients, possibly one for every version of Windows too.

   The clients may also generate error messages saying that they need to install a printer driver when connecting to a specific printer on a Windows 2000 printer server. This means that the correct drivers are installed on the Windows 2000 server, but they are not automatically sent to the legacy client every time the client prints.

   Finally, another cause of garbled text could be related to the physical printer. It may have special font requirements, it may be set to print only PostScript when the job you're sending is PCL (which could happen when you print to a file or restart a job from some time back), or the printer may be low on memory or faulty.

2. **Only some clients print:** This means the client has been misconfigured. Chances are the client has printed — but to the wrong printer. You can minimize this problem by providing adequate information about the location of printers.

Enable Bi-directional Printing

Enabling bi-directional printing allows smart printers equipped with the ability to transmit data to the printing service to talk to the server in real-time. It also makes it easier to find out why a printer is not printing when all else checks out. This means that the physical printer has the ability to report to the server that it's out of paper, requires servicing, toner, its overall status, and more.

The default operation is bi-directional printing disabled. The option is found on the Ports tab of the printer properties. It's grayed out if the port selected does not support bi-directional printing. This does not mean you won't get sufficient status information from the printer, because Windows polls the printer for information. But Windows only polls for standard information (out of paper, and so on), and the messages are not as detailed.

Auditing Printer Usage and Management

Windows 2000 allows you to track print job success and failure on a logical printer. Check out Chapter 19 on auditing Windows objects, if you have not already done so, and how to prepare the system for auditing.

You can audit access and usage to a logical printer as follows:

1. Select the printer you wish to audit for printing and management. Right-click and select Properties, then select the Security tab.

2. On the Security tab, click the Advanced button, which launches the Access Control Setting dialog box for the logical printer. Click the Auditing tab.

3. On the Auditing tab, click Add and select the group or groups you wish to access. Choose the Success or Failure audits you want to trap and press Apply.

That's all there is to auditing printer usage. To check the audits, refer to the System log in Event Viewer.

Summary

This chapter was designed to first get you up to speed on the elements of the Windows 2000 print services. We believe it's important to understand the service — from the manager or administrator perspective — in order to correctly troubleshoot printing problems.

Print services are a vital function of the network; they represent an important part of a network operating system. It's also important to build a blueprint or comprehensive plan of your printing environment or service, and to set down policy and procedures for using printers. If you establish a printing network and manage it correctly (such as reserving a specific range of network addresses and establishing printer user groups), you should not have many problems and be able to boast high availability of printing services.

✦   ✦   ✦

Web and FTP Services

This chapter covers configuring and managing an Internet or intranet server for HTTP, FTP, SMTP, and NNTP services and security. You'll learn how to set up a Windows 2000-based Web server to host Web and FTP sites, act as an e-mail server, and host newsgroups.

Overview of Web and FTP Server Administration

Windows NT provided an extensive range of services for configuring and managing an Internet or intranet server based on Windows NT. Windows 2000 Server expands those services, making Windows 2000 an even better platform for distributing Web-based content. This chapter explains each of the services and also examines global issues such as building a management team to manage your servers and the services they provide.

Note   Because designing and implementing an Internet or intranet server is a complex task that would take its own book to cover in depth, this chapter can't cover every facet of IIS. Instead, you'll examine the most common issues and learn the procedures you should follow in order to accomplish various tasks. In some cases, we'll refer you to other sources of information where you can get more details if you need them.

Web-Related Services

Windows 2000 Server incorporates several services geared toward Internet and intranet clients, collectively know as Internet Information Services (IIS):

✦ **World Wide Web Server:** This service enables you to configure Windows 2000 to function as an HTTP server for the World Wide Web (WWW). Through this service, a Windows 2000 Server computer can host multiple Web sites. The World Wide Web Server is also required by certain other services, primarily to provide remote administrative access to the server and those dependent services.

✦ **File Transfer Protocol (FTP) Server:** The FTP protocol provides for file transfer between computers. Although many sites now provide their file distribution efforts with the HTTP server, FTP is still the most widely used mechanism for serving files for upload and download via the Internet or an intranet. Through the FTP service, a Windows 2000 Server computer can host multiple FTP sites.

✦ **Simple Mail Transport Protocol (SMTP) Service:** The SMTP protocol and service enable you to configure a Windows 2000 Server as an SMTP e-mail server.

✦ **Network News Transfer Protocol (NNTP) Service:** The NNTP protocol and service enable you to configure a Windows 2000 Server to act as a news server. You can host public, private, read-only, moderated, and authenticated newsgroups, and take news feeds from other NNTP servers on the Internet to create a public news server.

✦ **FrontPage Server Extensions:** FrontPage Server Extensions enable the HTTP service in Windows 2000 Server to support FrontPage Webs, which are Web sites developed with Microsoft FrontPage. In general, the FrontPage Server Extensions allow for remote authoring and management of FrontPage sites.

✦ **Visual InterDev RAD Remote Deployment Support:** This service enables developers using Visual InterDev RAD (a development environment authored by Microsoft) to publish and manage sites created with that development platform.

If you are building a public Web server to provide extensive client support, e-commerce, and other Internet services (if you're an ISP, for example), you'll probably want to look at solutions other than just the services built into Windows 2000 Server. For example, Microsoft Commercial Internet Server brings together all the services mentioned so far plus additional ones (SQL Server, Site Server) to enable you to create a full-service Web server. However, the services included with Windows 2000 Server offer a solid platform for developing an intranet server or a public Internet server geared toward hosting your own company or organization site.

Web Services Checklist

Before beginning the process of installing and configuring IIS and related services, you should plan the server implementation and make sure the server is ready for IIS. The following serves as a checklist for planning and preparing for IIS installation and configuration:

✦ **Define the server mission:** By knowing what you expect the server to provide to clients, you can determine which IIS services and related services are required for installation. The role the server will play has a bearing on the server's hardware and connection requirements, as well as how you configure security. Know ahead of time exactly what functions you want the server to perform and whether those functions will be made available to anonymous users or restricted to specific groups or individuals. If you're setting up a Web server to host several sites for your company or for your clients, for example, you'll probably want to invest in a high-performance server with RAID, high-capacity backup hardware, and at a minimum a T1 Internet connection.

✦ **Establish the Internet connection for a public server and acquire IP addresses:** If your server will be connected to the Internet, contact your ISP to establish the connection (if one isn't already in place) and acquire the necessary IP addresses for the server to support its mission.

✦ **Implement network protection:** If your server will be or is connected to the Internet, implement a firewall (or at the very least a proxy server) to secure the server and its content against malicious attacks.

✦ **Prepare the hardware, OS, and file system:** Based on the server's mission, determine the type of hardware required to adequately support the mission. Install Windows 2000 Server and test the server. Then, determine where you will store IIS services and content and convert those volumes to NTFS (not required but highly recommended for security).

✦ **Secure the server's non-IIS services and files:** Review the server's other services and files and secure them with object permissions and account restrictions to prevent unauthorized access to these services and files.

✦ **Install and configure TCP/IP:** IIS services require TCP/IP whether you are installing an Internet or intranet server. Install TCP/IP and configure the server's settings according to the server's mission. If the server will host multiple sites, bind multiple IP addresses (as many as required) to the TCP/IP protocol.

Note See Chapter 12 for detailed information on installing and configuring TCP/IP.

✦ **Install and configure DNS to support your domain(s):** If you are providing your own Domain Name Service (DNS) namespace resolution, set up and configure the DNS service, either on the IIS server or on a different server. Create the initial zones to be hosted by the IIS server and create resource records as needed. If an ISP or other organization will be providing DNS services, ensure that those services are in place and the necessary zones and records are ready.

✦ **Install IIS services:** Install the IIS services necessary to support the server's mission.

✦ **Secure directories and develop user access permissions and policies:** After setting up the IIS services, review the object permissions for content folders and for user accounts and groups to ensure adequate security for the server and its content.

✦ **Create and test sites:** Create sites that support the server's mission, then test those sites for functionality. Configure the sites to accommodate specific resource needs, such as throttling bandwidth or limiting connections.

The process described in the preceding checklist can take several weeks of careful study, planning, and implementation. Each step is critical to successful implementation of an IIS server. Many of these topics are covered elsewhere in this book. Part IV, for example, covers TCP/IP configuration, DNS, DHCP, remote access, and related topics. See Chapter 3 for a discussion of local and network security issues relevant to IIS. See chapter 22 for information on how to use object permissions to restrict access to files and folders, which will help control IIS content access.

Installing IIS 5.0

It's a relatively simple process to install IIS through the Add/Remove Programs wizard in the Control Panel. Follow these steps to install IIS:

1. Install, configure, and test any required non-IIS services according to the server function (DHCP, DNS, TCP/IP, Index Server, and so on).

2. Open the Control Panel and double-click the Add/Remove Programs icon.

3. In the wizard, click Add/Remove Windows Components.

4. After Windows 2000 scans the server for installed components, it displays a component list (Figure 24-1). To install all IIS services, select the check box beside the Internet Information Services (IIS) item. Or, click an item and click Details to select an individual IIS component.

5. After selecting the desired services, click OK. Follow the remaining prompts to complete the installation process. Windows 2000 should require no additional input other than you providing the Windows 2000 Server CD for Setup to copy the required files to the system.

6. Reboot the server after installation is complete.

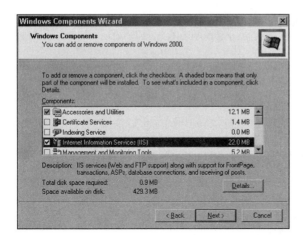

Figure 24-1: Use Add/Remove Programs to add IIS service components to the server.

Configuring and Managing HTTP Services

The World Wide Web Server component of IIS enables a Windows 2000 Server computer to function as a Web server for HTTP content. The Web service offers several features that provide considerable control over content, security, and bandwidth, making IIS a good option for Windows 2000 Server-based Web servers. The following sections explain the Web service's features and how to configure and manage Web sites under IIS.

The Default Site

When you install the Web service, IIS creates a default Web site shown in the Internet Information Services MMC console. This default site provides certain underlying services that the server performs through the following functions:

✦ **IIS administration:** The default site provides a means of managing the Web server through a browser. Administrative content is placed by default in the virtual folder IISAdmin, which you can access in a browser with the URL http://localhost/iisadmin. (See the following section for a discussion of *virtual folders.*) IIS administration through HTML is restricted by default to localhost. You can, however, configure the IISAdmin virtual directory to allow access from other IPs, including those on the LAN as well as on the Internet. For more information on configuring remote administration, see the section "Remote Administration" later in this chapter.

✦ **IIS Help:** The IISHelp virtual folder contains documents in HTML format that provide detailed information about IIS and its services. View the documents by pointing your browser on the server to http://localhost/iishelp.

✦ **IIS Samples:** This virtual folder contains several sample scripts in Java and Visual Basic for administration and in Active Server Pages for several different task categories.

✦ **Internet-based printing:** IIS Setup creates a Printers virtual folder and populates it with the files necessary to support Internet Printing Protocol (IPP), which enables clients to print to the server across the Internet.

Note See Chapter 23 for a detailed discussion of IPP and how to configure Windows 2000 Server to support IPP printing from Internet and intranet clients.

The default site is bound to all unassigned IP addresses. This means that the site responds to all IP addresses bound to the server that are not assigned to other sites. The default site has other implications, particularly on a server hosting multiple sites. For example, assume that all sites on the server use the same IP address and employ host headers to direct incoming client requests to a specific site. If a particular site is not available (because it is stopped, for example), IIS serves the default site to the client. So, you should take the time to develop a default Web site that accommodates situations in which a client will "accidentally" be directed to the site. Think of the default as your "error handler" for incoming Web requests. Design the default site to redirect the clients back to the correct site.

Configuring Web Sites

Setting up a Web site under IIS is not a difficult task, but it takes several steps to accomplish it. This section explains how to set up new sites and configure existing sites.

Preparing the server

The first step in setting up a site is to prepare the site's folders. Often, the simplest approach is to place all of a site's files within a single physical folder structure with all content residing in that folder and its physical subfolders. However, IIS doesn't impose a single folder structure. You can create a virtual structure using a folder on the local server, a share on another server, and virtual folders. All of these appear as a single, logical folder structure to the client and function accordingly within the site content. At this stage, determine how you will store the site files, whether they'll be on a single server or multiple servers, and what NTFS permissions you need to apply to the folders to control access if not using anonymous access or using a combination of anonymous and authenticated access. Create the folders on the target computer(s) and configure permissions as required.

Next, verify that you have the necessary IP address bound to the server. If the server will only host one site, you only need one IP address. You'll need to bind multiple IP addresses to the server, use multiple TCP ports, or use host headers to host multiple sites (explained in the following section). Use the TCP/IP protocol properties in the network connection's settings to view and add IP addresses.

Finally, verify that the necessary DNS zone is created for the domain on the site's designated name server(s) and that the zone is populated with the appropriate resource records. For example, assume you're setting up a Web and FTP server for the mcity.org domain. Create a DNS zone on your DNS server for mcity.org with the appropriate Start of Authority (SOA) and Name Server (NS) records for the zone. Then, create A records (or CNAME records) for www and ftp that point to the appropriate IP addresses for those services on your IIS server. Lastly, make sure that the domain is registered with the root servers and that the root servers' records point to your DNS server for name resolution.

Note See Chapter 14 for detailed information on configuring DNS zones and records.

Creating and configuring the site in IIS

There are several steps to create and configure a Web site in IIS, although the process of simply putting up a site is relatively simple. Applying advanced properties can take a little longer if you have special needs for the site or want to provide additional customization of properties or behavior. The first step is to run the Web Site creation Wizard.

Running the site wizard

To add a site, open the IIS console (Start ⇨ Programs ⇨ Administrative Tools ⇨ Internet Services Manager). Right-click the server where you want to add the site and choose New ⇨ Web Site to start the Web Site Creation Wizard. The wizard prompts you for the following information:

✦ **Description:** This is the description that appears in the IIS console to identify the site.

✦ **IP Address:** Select the IP address for the site from the drop-down list. Each site needs a unique IP address unless you use host headers, as described shortly.

✦ **TCP port:** The default HTTP port is 80, but you can specify any valid port that doesn't conflict with other services on the server. Specifying a non-default port adds a bit of security because the clients will need to know the port number to connect and specify it in the URL, as in http://www.mcity.org:8080, using port 8080 as an example. See http://www.isi.edu/in-notes/iana/assignments/port-numbers for an up-to-date list of registered well-known TCP port numbers.

✦ **Host Header:** The host header is the domain name requested by the client's URL, such as support.mcity.org in the URL http://support.mcity.org/contacts. The host name is passed by the client's browser to the server, and IIS can use that host name to determine which site to serve up on a multi-site server. See the section "Configuring Multiple Sites with a Single IP" later in this chapter for more information.

✦ **SSL port:** If you are using Secure Socket Layer (SSL) to create a secure Web site, specify the SSL port number. The default port number is 443.

✦ **Path to the home directory:** Type or browse to the path that will serve as the site's primary folder. You can specify a local folder, network share, or URL.

✦ **Allow anonymous access:** Select this option to allow anonymous connections to the site. Deselect this option to use Windows 2000 accounts to authenticate within the site.

✦ **Access permissions:** Configure the type of access permissions you want clients to have to the site. Available options include the following:

- **Read:** Enable clients to read the site's content.

- **Run Scripts:** Allow clients to run scripts such as ASP, Java, and so on.

- **Execute:** Allow clients to execute applications such as ISAPI, CGI, and so on.

- **Write:** Allow clients to post content to the site.

- **Browse:** Allow clients to browse the directory structure for the site.

After you create the site through the wizard, you need to set some additional properties to define the site's content, permissions, and so on. The following sections explain these steps.

Configuring default documents

Most sites incorporate at least one *default document*. This is the HTML or ASP document presented to the client if no document is submitted in the URL. For example, browsing to http://www.mcity.org would display whatever default document is configured for the www.mcity.org site (such as default.htm, or default.asp). However, the client could also request a specific document, such as http://www.mcity.org/contacts.htm. In this case, IIS would serve up the document Contacts.htm, assuming it existed within the site's root folder.

You can configure multiple default documents. If one specified in the list is not available, IIS serves the next document in the list. You configure the document priority when you assign the default documents. To do so, open the IIS console, right-click the Web site you want to modify, and choose Properties. On the Documents property page, select Enable Default Document, then either verify that you're using one of the default document names (Default.htm or Default.asp) for the primary document in the target folder, or click Add to add the document name you want to use. After adding all appropriate names, use the up and down arrows to change document order.

Configuring the Home Directory

When you add the site through the wizard, you specify the local folder, network share, or URL to serve as the home directory for the site. Another step in configuring the site is to fine-tune the home directory properties. To do so, right-click the site in the IIS console, choose Properties, and click the Home Directory tab to display the Home Directory page shown in Figure 24-2.

As Figure 24-2 illustrates, you can change the home directory location if needed. Use the check boxes on the dialog box to define access permissions and enable logging and indexing. You also can apply a fine degree of control over application execution and debugging through the Application Settings group of controls. Fine-tune the settings based on the site's function, intended clients, and your security needs.

Figure 24-2: Use the Home Directory page to fine-tune permissions or redirect the site to a different home directory.

Configuring security

A site's Directory Security property page enables you to configure access and security for the site. Through the Directory Security page, you can enable or disable anonymous access and specify authentication options (clear text, digest authentication, or integrated Windows authentication). You also can specify a range of IP addresses that will be either granted or denied access, giving you a means of restricting access to a specific subnet. This is particularly useful for allowing access only to intranet users in a specific physical location, such as a department or throughout the entire organization (to prevent outside connections to the site).

You also can use the Directory Security page to configure certificates and enable SSL. See the section "Enabling Secure Sockets Layer" later in this chapter for more information.

Configuring other site settings

You can get most sites up and running through the tasks and options covered to this point. However, each site provides several other property pages you can use to configure a wide variety of site properties to control performance, configure additional security options, and so on. While this chapter can't cover them all in detail, the following list summarizes the types of tasks you can accomplish through each of the other property pages:

✦ **Operators:** Use the Operators page to specify users and groups that have operator privileges to the site. Operators have limited administrative privileges over the site. Operators can configure and modify a site but can't control site aspects such as anonymous user name and password, bandwidth throttling, virtual directory creation, path changes, or certain other tasks that are limited to the Administrator.

✦ **Performance:** The Performance page provides a means for controlling site performance. You can set the site priority by specifying a range of the number of hits expected per day. The Performance page also lets you enable and configure bandwidth and CPU throttling, which limit the load on the server imposed by the site.

✦ **ISAPI Filters:** ISAPI filters respond to events during processing of HTTP requests and can provide background processing for site traffic. Use the ISAPI Filters page to install and enable or disable ISAPI filters.

✦ **HTTP Headers:** This property page controls several features related to HTTP headers for the site, including the following:

- **Content expiration:** Use this feature to specify when content expires to enable clients and scripts that test for content expiration and automatically refresh content from the site.

- **Custom HTTP headers:** Add custom HTTP headers to the site to enable custom processing within scripts/browsers.

- **Content rating:** Enable and configure the site's content rating to enable rating filters to identify and potentially block the content from the client based on its rating values.

- **MIME mapping for the site:** Configure new file type associations for content on the site.

✦ **Custom Errors:** Defines the error messages received by clients, such as the page that appears when the client requests a page that doesn't exist (the Not Found error). The error pages by default are stored in `systemroot\help\ iishelp\common`. You can edit the files with any HTML or text editor to customize the pages.

✦ **Server Extensions:** The Server Extensions page enables you to configure Server Extensions (also referred to as FrontPage Server Extensions), which control options for Web authoring through FrontPage and related applications. See the section "Configuring Server Extensions" later in this chapter for additional information.

Configuring multiple sites with a single IP address

Although you can configure multiple Web sites on a single server using unique IP addresses for each one, this can pose a problem in cases where only a limited number of addresses are available (if your ISP only gave you a small subnet, for example). The IP address is just one of three properties that define the site. The other two are the TCP port and *host header*. The TCP port is the port through which the site communicates, and the host header is (usually) the site's domain name. Our example `mcity.org` main site uses an internal address of 192.168.0.3, the default TCP port 80, and the host header `www.mcity.org`. The support site could use

192.168.0.3, port 80, and a host header of `support.mcity.org`. Sites on the same server can share any two of these properties, but one must be different. In this case, the host header for each site is unique.

Host headers enable you to share an IP address with multiple sites because most browsers (Internet Explorer 3.0 and Netscape 2.0 and later) support the use of host headers. These browsers pass the host header information to the server, and the server directs traffic to the appropriate site based on that header. Figure 24-3 illustrates how host headers help direct traffic to the correct site.

Note Browsers that support HTTP 1.1 support host headers. Certain other older browsers also support host headers even though they don't support HTTP 1.1. In addition, sites configured for SSL cannot use host headers, since the header information is encrypted. SSL sites must use a unique IP address.

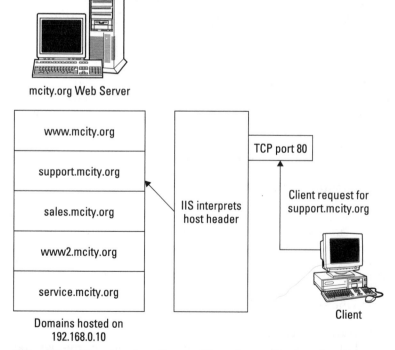

Figure 24-3: Host headers direct traffic to the appropriate site when a single IP is used for multiple sites.

To configure the host header for a site, right-click the site in the IIS console and choose Properties. Click Advanced on the Web Site property page. In the Advanced Multiple Web Site Configuration dialog box, select the site identity you want to modify and click Edit. Specify the domain portion of the site's URL (`www.mcity.org` or `support.mcity.org`, for example) as the host header, then close the site's property sheet. Finally, make sure you modify the DNS records for each domain to point the host (`www`, `support`) to the appropriate IP address.

Note Although you can direct traffic to a specific site with a non-unique IP address by specifying a different port number for each site, that typically requires that the client know the port number ahead of time. You can develop a primary site using port 80 that serves as a jumping-off point to these other non-default port sites, but you would need to incorporate the appropriate port value in all hyperlinks within each site. The better, cleaner solution is to use host headers.

You have two options for supporting client browsers that do not support host headers: cookies or URL-munging (embedding the host name in the URL). Because these topics apply in a limited number of situations (most browsers in use support host headers), they are not covered in this chapter. See the topic "Supporting Host Header Names in Older Browsers" in the IIS online Help documentation to learn how to enable support for browsers that don't support host headers.

Configuring server extensions

Microsoft FrontPage is an HTTP publishing application that lets you create, modify, and publish Web sites to a server that supports FrontPage Server Extensions. While few Web development companies consider FrontPage a viable tool for professional Web development, many companies or organizations use it to enable end-users to create and update their own areas of a site or departmental sites. This section covers the FrontPage Server Extensions in the event you need to install them on a Web server to allow users to manage sites on the server.

Installing FrontPage Server Extensions is really a two-step process. First, you need to install the extensions on the server. Then you install the extensions to each Web site that requires them. To install FrontPage Server Extensions on the server, open the Control Panel and run the Add/Remove Programs object. Click Add/Remove Windows Components, double-click Internet Information Services, and select FrontPage 2000 Server Extensions. Click OK and follow the prompts to complete the installation to the server.

Next, you need to install Server Extensions on each site for which FrontPage is used. You do so through the IIS console. Open the IIS console, right-click the site, and choose All Tasks ⇨ Configure Server Extensions. IIS starts the Server Extensions Configuration Wizard, which prompts you for the following information:

✦ **Create local machine groups:** Select this option to have Windows 2000 automatically create local groups for management purposes. These groups include Admins, Authors, and Browsers. Deselect this option if you already have one or more groups created for grouping site managers.

✦ **Begin the Group names with this distinguishing label:** If creating local machine groups, you can specify a unique label to begin each group name. If you specify Mcity, for example, IIS creates three groups named Mcity Admins, Mcity Authors, and Mcity Browsers. Omit the label to create the groups Admins, Authors, and Browsers.

✦ **Group or user account to be Web Administrator for the site:** Specify the account that will serve as the administrator for the site.

✦ **Mail server settings:** Specify the mail settings for the site, including author for outgoing mail, contact address, and SMTP mail server.

After you configure server extensions on a site, you can manage extension settings through the site's property sheet. Right-click the site, choose Properties, and then click Server Extensions to display the Server Extensions page shown in Figure 24-4.

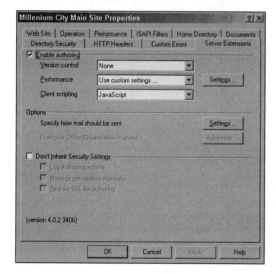

Figure 24-4: FrontPage extension options on the Server Extensions page

The Enable Authoring group of controls determines whether authors can use FrontPage to access and modify the content of the root web for the selected site. Controls in this group configure version control, performance (caching), and scripting options. The Options group lets you configure e-mail settings and Office Collaboration features (which are available only if Office Web Server — OWS — is installed on the server). Use the Don't Inherit Security Settings option and associated controls to determine whether or not the site inherits global security settings from IIS. Deselect this option to override global settings with individual settings to config-ure the site differently from other sites on the server.

Enabling secure socket layer

IIS fully supports Secure Socket Layer (SSL) connections to provide secured trans-actions between the client browser and the server. SSL is typically used to provide secure credit card transactions and other e-commerce functions, but SSL can be used in any situation in which you want the traffic flowing between the client and server to be encrypted and secure from outside tampering or hijackers. For exam-ple, you might want to use SSL for site authoring.

Enabling SSL requires several steps:

1. Obtain a certificate from a Certificate Authority (CA) for the server. If you have Certificate Services installed on a Windows 2000 Server in your enter-prise, you can obtain a certificate from that CA. Otherwise, you'll need to obtain a certificate from another CA, such as Thawte or VeriSign. See Chapter 3 for additional information on certificates and CAs. The following steps assume you're using a Windows 2000 Server running Certificate Services either on the local computer or a computer in your enterprise to generate certificates for you.

2. Open the IIS console, then open the properties for the site for which you want to obtain a certificate to enable SSL. Open the Directory Security page.

3. Click Server Certificate to start the Web Server Certificate Wizard. Within the wizard, select the option to create a new certificate. (You have the option of assigning an existing certificate and importing a certificate from a Key Manager backup file, but this procedure assumes you're requesting a new certificate.)

4. Complete the wizard to create the request. You can submit the request imme-diately if an Enterprise CA is available on the network. IIS will not recognize a standalone CA server on the same computer or detect one on the network. In this situation, you need to create the request using the wizard, which creates an encrypted text file. You then run the wizard again to submit the encrypted request to the CA. The remaining steps assume you'll be creating the file and submitting later. Use the following list as a guide to respond to the wizard's prompts:

   • **Prepare the request now, but send it later:** Use this option if you have no enterprise CA in your enterprise, or wish to submit to a standalone CA.

   • **Send the request immediately to an online certification authority:** Use this option to submit the request immediately to an enterprise CA (dimmed if IIS doesn't detect an available CA).

- **Name:** Friendly name for the certificate.

- **Bit length:** A longer bit length increases security but can decrease performance. The default is 512.

- **Server Gated Cryptography certificate:** Select this option to request an SGC certificate.

- **Organization:** Specify the name of your organization (typically, the business name).

- **Organizational Unit:** Specify a department or other OU to further define the certificate.

- **Common name:** Specify the domain name (such as `www.mcity.org`) for a site hosted on the Internet. You can specify a DNS name or NetBIOS name for a site hosted on your intranet.

- **Regional information:** Specify country, state, city, or other regional information for your organization.

- **File name:** Specify a file name under which the certificate request will be saved.

5. With a Web browser, connect to the CA using `http://ServerCA/CertSrv`, where `ServerCA` is the DNS name or IP address of the certification server. Choose Request a certificate and click Next.

6. Select Advanced Request and click Next.

7. Choose Submit a certificate request using a base64 encoded PKCS #10 file, then click Next.

8. Click Browse and browse for the file created in Step 4, then click Read to read the file into the form. Or, open Notepad and then open the certificate request created in step 4. Copy the text from the file and paste the text into the Saved Request text box on the form. Make sure to select Web Server from the Certificate Template drop-down list. Then click Submit.

9. Follow the prompts provided by the CA to complete the request. Depending on how the certificate server is configured, you'll either be granted the certificate immediately or will have to return to the page after an Administrator has issued the certificate. In either case, you'll have the option of downloading the certificate in DER or Base 64 encoded formats. Either format is acceptable.

10. Open the IIS console and open the property sheet for the site, then open the Directory Security page. Click Server Certificate to run the wizard again, which will recognize that a certificate request is pending for the site. Through the wizard, specify the location of the certificate file provided by the CA in step 9 and then complete the wizard to install the certificate.

11. On the Directory Security page, click Edit to display the Secure Communications page (Figure 24-5). Configure options based on the following list, then close the property sheet and stop/start the site in preparation for testing the site:

- **Require Secure Channel:** Select this option to require the client to use SSL to connect to the site. Deselect the option to allow unencrypted access to the site.

- **Require 128-bit encryption:** Select this option to require the client to use 128-bit encryption.

- **Client certificates:** Specify how client certificates are treated. For a public Web site, choose Ignore client certificates. Select Accept client certificates to allow clients to optionally use client-side certificates to authenticate on the site. Select Require client certificates to force clients to use a certificate.

- **Enable client certificate mapping:** Use this option to allow clients to use their client-side certificates to authenticate against user accounts on the server. This enables you to integrate client logon with your Windows 2000 user accounts and groups.

- **Enable certificate trust list:** Select this option and use the associated controls to define a list of CAs that are trusted for the site.

Figure 24-5: The Secure Communications page

After you configure the site, you should test it to make sure it functions properly. Open a browser on another system and connect to `https://site name`, where `site name` is the Web site's DNS name or the NetBIOS server name (intranet). If you receive an error that the site can't be displayed, open the Directory Security properties for the site and view the certificate. Make sure the Issued To field for the certificate matches the name of the site (www.mcity.org, for example) or the NetBIOS name of the server (for an intranet site). If it does not, you need to remove the certificate and request a new certificate with the correct name.

Tip If the certificate's Issued To field shows a user name or Administrator, you probably neglected to select Web Server from the Certificate Template drop-down list when you requested the certificate. Resubmit the request with the correct template.

Managing the Web Server

The Internet Information Services MMC console provides the primary means through which you manage IIS Web sites. You can use the console to set site properties; stop, pause, and start a site; set properties on documents within a site; configure FrontPage Server Extensions; define custom headers and error pages; and all other management tasks.

You can use the IIS console to manage IIS services and sites locally or to connect to other servers on your network. To connect to another server, right-click on Internet Information Services in the console tree and chose Connect from the context menu. Or, choose Action ⇨ Connect from the console menu. Specify the name of the computer to manage and click OK. You also can connect to systems on a remote network if you first establish a VPN connection to the network. After establishing the VPN connection, connect with the IIS console to the remote server as you would for a local server.

IIS also provides a means of managing Web sites remotely through a browser. The Administration Web Site, which Setup creates automatically when you install IIS, enables you to initially connect on the server locally with a browser to perform limited administration tasks on the default Web site. Connect to http://localhost/iisadmin to manage the server locally through a browser.

You also can configure the IISADMIN site to allow management from other computers, including across the Internet. To do so, open the properties for the Administration Web Site and click the Directory Security tab. Click Edit in the IP address and domain name restrictions group, then specify the individual computers, group of computers, or domain from which the server can be managed. If you prefer, you can grant all computers access to the server, but this isn't recommended for security reasons.

The IISADMIN site lets you manage the Default Web Site, including setting its properties and creating and deleting folders. You also can configure IIS to enable browser-based management of other sites. To do so, add the IISADMIN folder as a virtual folder to those sites you wish to manage through a browser. Right-click the site to which you want to add the folder and choose New ⇨ Virtual Directory. Create a virtual directory with an alias of your choosing (such as admin) that points to *systemroot*\System32\inetsrv\iisadmin. Configure the server and the new virtual directory to allow access by the desired computers or domains, then point a browser to http://*site*/*alias*, where *site* is the DNS name or IP address of the site and *alias* is the alias you assigned to the IISADMIN folder.

Unfortunately, you can't manage FTP, SMTP, or NNTP services through a browser. If you need to administer these remotely, connect to the network with a VPN and use the IIS console instead.

Tip You can stop and start the WWW service remotely by connecting to the server through a Telnet session and issuing the commands NET STOP W3SVC or NET START W3SVC, respectively. This requires that the Telnet service be running and configured to allow you to log on through Telnet.

Configuring and Managing FTP Services

FTP stands for File Transfer Protocol. FTP enables users to upload and download files to and from the server. While HTTP is becoming more common as a means for file transfer, FTP still serves an important role in providing file transfer services. While HTTP restricts clients to a browser for uploading and downloading files, FTP enables clients to use a browser, FTP command line, or third-party FTP utility to transfer files. IIS provides the ability to restart failed FTP transfers, enabling a client to reconnect to the server and restart the transfer from the point of failure rather than transferring the entire file again.

Setting up an FTP site is much like setting up a Web site. The following section explains the process.

Creating and Configuring FTP Sites

As with HTTP, IIS creates a Default FTP Site that responds to FTP requests on all unassigned IP addresses. You can configure this site to use as your only FTP site, or you might prefer to create other FTP sites, particularly if you are hosting multiple domains on a particular server.

Either before or after setting up the FTP site on the server, make sure you create the necessary DNS zone and records to accommodate the site. If you don't already have a DNS zone set up to accommodate the FTP site, create the zone on your DNS server with the appropriate SOA and NS records. Then, create A or CNAME records that define the host portion of the site name. For example, in the zone mcity.org, you might create an A or CNAME record for FTP that points to the IP address assigned in IIS for the FTP site, enabling clients to connect to the site using the URL ftp://ftp.mcity.org. After you've configured the appropriate DNS records, you're ready to begin creating the site.

Creating an FTP site

To create a new site, open the IIS console, right-click the server in the tree, and choose New ➪ FTP Site to start the FTP Site Creation Wizard. The wizard prompts you for the following information:

✦ **Description:** This is the friendly name for the site that appears in the IIS console.

✦ **IP address:** Specify the IP address for the FTP server or choose All Unassigned to have the FTP server respond to all requests for which an IP is not specified or not available.

✦ **TCP port:** Specify the TCP port to be used by the FTP site. The default is 21. You can use a different port to increase security, but clients will have to know beforehand what port to use to connect to the server.

✦ **Path:** Specify the path to the folder that will serve as the FTP site's root folder.

✦ **Read/Write:** Choose Read to enable download and Write to enable upload (subject to NTFS permissions you apply to the site's folders, if applicable).

Configuring site properties

After you create a site, you can configure its properties to fine-tune its function. Right-click the site in the IIS console and choose Properties to display its property sheet (Figure 24-6). You'll find that the properties for an FTP site are similar to those for a Web site, although there are fewer properties.

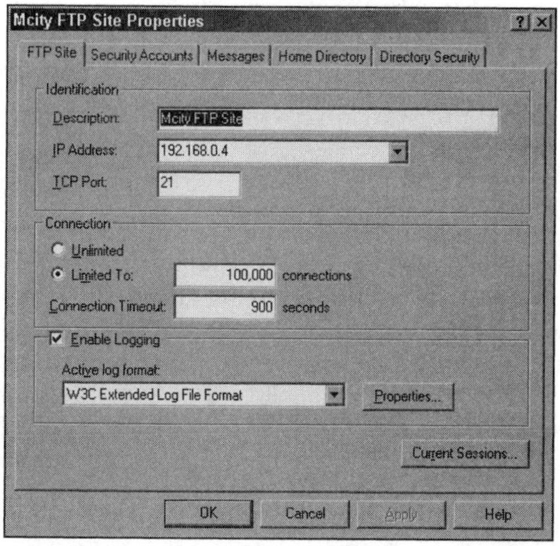

Figure 24-6: The property sheet for an FTP site

The Connection group on the FTP Site page lets you configure the number of concurrent connections allowed to the site and the connection timeout period. You might wish to limit the number of connections for sites with high traffic or low bandwidth to improve performance for connected users. Increase the connection timeout value if clients are experiencing difficulty in maintaining a connection during large transfers or times when there is significant traffic on the site.

The Enable Logging option lets you turn on connection logging and specify the log file format. Use the Current Sessions button to view a list of currently connected users and, if desired, disconnect one or more users.

Setting security

The Security Accounts page of the FTP site's properties lets you configure how IIS grants access to the FTP site. The Allow Anonymous Connections option, when selected, allows users to connect to the site with the user name *anonymous*. If you deselect this option, users must specify a valid user account and password on the server or within the domain in order to authenticate and log on to the FTP site. When anonymous connections are enabled, IIS uses the user account and password specified in the Username and Password fields of the Security Accounts page. By default, the account is IUSR_*server,* where *server* is the name of the computer. In general, you shouldn't change this account, but you can if you prefer to make it more difficult for hackers to guess the default anonymous account. If you specify a different account, make sure you configure the account's rights and permissions on folders accordingly to enable the account be used successfully for anonymous logon.

In order to log on for FTP, an account must have the right to log on locally. The IUSR account by default has this right. To enable other user accounts to log on for FTP, however, you need to grant those accounts the right to log on locally. Although you can do this on an account-by-account basis, it's best to create an FTP group, grant the group the right to log on locally, and then place in the group any users who need authenticated (non-anonymous) FTP access.

Tip   If a virtual folder with the same name as a user exists within the FTP site, IIS automatically connects the user to that virtual folder when he or she logs on, making the virtual folder the user's home folder. For example, assume the site contains a virtual folder by the name jboyce. When jboyce logs on to the FTP site, he or she is automatically placed in the folder pointed to by the jboyce virtual folder. An added benefit is that other users don't see the virtual folders, regardless of their logon accounts. They can, however, change to them manually if they know the virtual folder name. Their access to the folder is subject to its NTFS permissions. See the section "Configuring the Site's Directory Structure" later in this chapter for additional information.

The FTP Site Operators control group on the Security Accounts page defines the accounts or groups that are designated as site operators. A site operator has limited administrative privileges within the site and can configure properties that affect the site. Site operators do not have the ability to modify global IIS properties or properties for other sites unless their accounts are designated within that site as a site operator account or group.

Configuring logon and logoff messages

In most cases, you probably will want to define messages that appear when the user logs on or off the FTP site or when the maximum number of connections is reached for the site. You configure these messages through the Messages property page for the site. In particular, consider posting a welcome message that adequately addresses your company's legal rights should the site be misused by unauthorized personnel (typically applies to a private FTP site rather than a public site). The following is a sample of such a message, although you should consult with the company's legal counsel to be certain the message addresses your needs:

WARNING: Access to this system by authorized personnel only. All users will be monitored for security purposes and potential law enforcement. Unauthorized use will be subject to criminal and civil prosecution and penalties.

Configuring the site's directory structure

You define an FTP site's home directory when you create the site, but you can modify the directory through the Home Directory page of the site's properties in the IIS console. The site's home directory can be a folder on the local computer or a share on the network. Subfolders of the home directory appear within the site's folder structure just as they do on the local computer or network share.

You can configure a site's home directory for Read, Write, and Log Visits. Read enables users to download from the site, and Write enables them to upload to the site, subject to any NTFS permissions you might apply to the folder and its contents. The Log Visits option turns on logging of access to the selected folder if logging is enabled for the site in the FTP Site property page.

In addition to defining the home directory, you also can configure *virtual folders* for the FTP site. A virtual folder functions as a part of the site's directory structure but is effectively hidden from users — it doesn't show up when users browse the site or issue a DIR command from an FTP prompt. However, users can connect to the folder in one of two ways: specify the folder explicitly in the browser or FTP prompt, or connect with a user account that matches the virtual folder's alias name.

To create a new virtual folder, open the IIS console, right-click the FTP site where you want to create the folder, and choose New ⇨ Virtual Directory. A wizard prompts you for the folder's alias name, path, and Read/Write properties. After you create the folder, right-click the folder in the IIS console and choose Properties to set its properties, which are similar to those for a home directory but more limited.

Note As with a home directory and its child objects, a virtual folder's NTFS permissions control access to the folder and its contents in conjunction with the Read and Write properties you set for the folder when you create it in IIS.

Configuring directory security

By default, all FTP users are granted access to all folders in a site. You can, however, restrict access to individual computers and groups of computers, just as you can with a Web site's folders. You configure access through the Directory Security page of the site's or folder's property sheet, configuring them differently if needed.

Managing the FTP Server

The primary tool you'll use to manage the FTP service is the IIS console. As with Web sites, you can connect with a VPN to the network where the server is located and use the IIS console remotely to administer FTP sites on the server. However, you can't use the HTML version of the Internet Services Manager to manage FTP sites or services, because it restricts you to managing only the default Web site.

Tip   You can stop and start the FTP service from a command prompt (including through a Telnet session to a server) using the NET STOP MSFTPSVC and NET START MSFTPSVC commands from the command prompt.

FTP Client Access

Clients can connect to an FTP site using a Web browser, FTP command-line utility (included with Windows 9x, Windows NT, Windows 2000, UNIX, and other platforms), or third-party FTP utility. When connecting from Internet Explorer 5.0, clients can specify the user account for the connection within the URL if using an account other than anonymous to access the site. Enter the URL in the form ftp://user@site, where user is the account name and site is the FTP site name. Logging on as user jboyce to the site ftp.mcity.org, for example, would require a URL of ftp://jboyce@ftp.mcity.org. Internet Explorer will prompt for the password. To log on using the anonymous account, specify anonymous in the URL or choose File ⇨ Login As to display a login dialog box in which you can specify the account to use.

Note   For information on using the FTP command, open a console prompt and enter **ftp /?** to view a description of the FTP command's options. The advantage to using a command prompt is its support for scripting and several other features not offered by Internet Explorer.

Configuring and Managing SMTP Services

SMTP stands for Simple Mail Transport Protocol. SMTP is the primary protocol for transferring e-mail on the Internet. The SMTP Service included with IIS doesn't turn a server running IIS into a full-blow e-mail server, but instead it provides a means for you to create *virtual e-mail servers* that forward their mail to designated full-featured e-mail servers that provide client support (POP3, for example). In effect, the SMTP service is primarily a message-forwarding service. Its benefit is that you can create multiple e-mail identities and servers to go along with each domain hosted on the server. The SMTP service can handle mail coming in from clients on the Internet or mail generated within a Web site.

The SMTP Service included with Windows 2000 offers several key features:

✦ **Integrated Management:** The SMTP service uses the same IIS console for management as Web, FTP, and NNTP services, providing a single point for management of all services. You also can use SNMP, the Windows 2000 event logs (and Event Viewer), and SMTP transaction logs to monitor the service.

✦ **Directed mail drop and delivery:** The SMTP service can be configured to drop all incoming mail into a drop directory on the server, enabling other applications on the server to use the SMTP service as a mail receiver. Applications also can use a pickup directory to send messages — properly formatted messages placed in the pickup directory are delivered automatically by the SMTP service. Applications can also send messages via the SMTP server's TCP port(s).

✦ **Ability to restrict messages:** You can configure each SMTP server for a variety of restrictions that limit message size, number of recipients, and so on. You also can restrict message relay to prevent a server from being used as a relay for spamming.

✦ **Routing options:** The SMTP Service provides several options to control message routing and delivery. You can route messages directly, use a smart host as an interim relay agent, and configure other settings to fine-tune message routing.

✦ **Secure transmission:** The SMTP Service supports anonymous as well as authenticated access to each virtual server, and it also supports Transport Layer Security (TLS) for encryption of incoming messages.

✦ **Transaction logging:** You can perform extensive logging of SMTP transactions for troubleshooting and tracking server usage.

Overview of the SMTP Service

The SMTP Service included with IIS enables a Windows 2000 Server computer to function as an SMTP mail server (e-mail delivery agent). The SMTP service does not provide for mailboxes on the server or client support for POP3, so it isn't really designed to function as a full-featured mail server like Microsoft Exchange or other e-mail server applications. However, you can use the SMTP service to process messages coming from clients on the Internet, from the local LAN, or from applications on the server itself.

The SMTP services work essentially as a file transfer agent. When you create a virtual SMTP server, you define the server's home directory. IIS creates the specified folder and creates four subfolders by default:

✦ **Badmail:** This folder stores undeliverable messages that can't be returned to the sender.

✦ **Drop:** This folder stores all incoming messages for the domains handled by the virtual server.

✦ **Pickup:** This folder stores all outgoing messages. The SMTP service monitors the Pickup folder, and as soon as a properly formatted message is placed in the folder, the service collects the message and attempts delivery.

✦ **Queue:** This folder holds messages waiting delivery. When a message can't be delivered because of a communications failure or other problem, it leaves the message in the Queue folder for later delivery attempts based on the settings configured for the server (explained in a later section).

Messages can come to the server from the Internet, the LAN, or from an application on the server itself. These messages can arrive at the server through the virtual server's designated TCP port (25 by default), or in the case of LAN or local messages, can also be placed directly in the Pickup folder. The SMTP service processes the message into the Queue folder and initiates delivery. The SMTP service places the message in the Drop folder if the message is for a local recipient, or the service relays the message to the appropriate server if the message is for a remote recipient. Figure 24-7 illustrates the process.

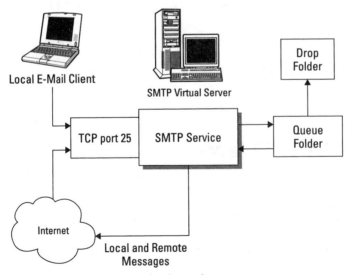

Figure 24-7: SMTP processing incoming messages

For local recipients, delivery ends when the message is placed in the Drop folder. The process for remote delivery is different. SMTP attempts to connect to the receiving mail server, and if the server can't be reached or a communications error occurs, SMTP leaves the message in the queue for later delivery at intervals you designate for the server in its Delivery property page (explained later). Once the receiving server acknowledges the message receipt, SMTP removes the message from the Queue folder, indicating a completed delivery.

Tip SMTP supports Transport Layer Security (TLS) for remove delivery, providing enhanced security by encrypting all outgoing messages. You can enable or disable TLS for individual remote domains, giving you control over the remote domains for which SMTP uses TLS.

If you prefer, you can route outgoing messages from a virtual server to a *smart host*, which essentially serves as an intermediary and takes care of transmitting the messages to their destinations. The primary use of a smart host is to direct messages through a connection that might be faster or less costly than the one the server would otherwise use for a direct delivery. You can specify a smart host in one of two places: for the entire virtual server or for each remote domain hosted on the server. The domain setting overrides the server setting, enabling you to route all outgoing messages through a single smart host except for specific domains, which can be directed to other smart hosts. Figure 24-8 illustrates the use of smart hosts for routing message delivery.

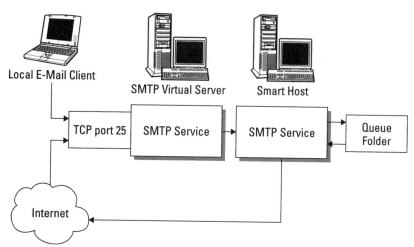

Figure 24-8: Smart hosts act as routing intermediaries.

SMTP offers support for several options for controlling security and connections for both incoming and outgoing messages. For example, you can limit the number of connections for both incoming and outgoing connections, specify timeout for connections, and limit the number of connections per domain (outgoing). To secure both incoming and outgoing access, SMTP supports anonymous authentication, basic (clear text) authentication against Windows 2000 domain accounts, TLS encrypted authentication, and Windows Security Package (WSP) — the authentication mechanism built into Windows 2000. This last option enables clients to use the same single sign-on for mail server authentication as for other enterprise resources, but it requires the use of an e-mail client that supports WSP authentication. The version of Outlook Express included with Windows 2000 supports WSP.

Installing SMTP

Windows 2000 does not install the SMTP service by default, but you can use the Add/Remove Programs object in the Control Panel to add the service. Open the Control Panel, open Add/Remove Programs, and click Add/Remove Windows Components. Double-click Internet Information Services, select SMTP Service, and click OK. Click Next to run the wizard and add the service.

Configuring SMTP

As with the Web and FTP services, IIS automatically creates an SMTP server that by default responds to all unassigned IP addresses. You should configure the default SMTP server to process messages as a backup for any other SMTP virtual server that happens to be offline.

In addition to the default SMTP server, you can create any number of other virtual servers to process messages for specific domains and IP addresses. The following sections explain how to create and configure SMTP virtual servers under IIS.

Creating a virtual SMTP server

To create a new virtual SMTP server, open the IIS console, right-click the server, and choose New ➪ SMTP Virtual Server. The New SMTP Virtual Server Wizard prompts you for the following information:

+ **SMTP virtual server description:** This is the friendly name for the virtual server as it appears in the IIS console.

+ **IP address:** Select the IP address for the server or select All Unassigned to have the server respond to all IP addresses bound to the server that are not assigned to other sites.

+ **Home directory:** This is the root folder under which messages in process are stored. For enhanced security, this should be an NTFS folder. SMTP creates the required folder structure (Badmail, Drop, Pickup, and Queue) automatically.

✦ **Default domain:** Each virtual server has one default domain that is used to stamp messages from addresses that don't have a domain. You can specify the DNS name specified in the server's TCP/IP properties or any unique DNS name. You can create additional domains after the virtual server is created. See the following section for more information on domain settings.

After you create the virtual server, it appears in the IIS console with two child objects: Domains and Current Sessions. The Domains object contains the domains assigned to the server. You can use this object to create and delete domains and configure their properties. Use the Current Sessions object to view current connections to the virtual server and, if needed, disconnect sessions.

Managing SMTP domains

SMTP supports two types of domains: *local* and *remote.* Local domains are hosted on the virtual server, and remote domains are hosted elsewhere. As mentioned previously, each virtual SMTP server has one default local domain that is used to stamp messages from addresses that don't specify a domain. Logically, only one domain can be the default domain, but you can create multiple alias domains that use the same settings as the default domain. Messages that arrive for an alias domain are stamped with the default domain name and placed in the default domain's Drop directory.

When you create an SMTP virtual server, IIS creates a default domain for that server based on your response in the New SMTP Virtual Server Wizard. Use the IIS console to configure the properties for the default domain, create local alias domains and remote domains, and change the default domain.

Creating domains

To create a new domain, open the IIS console and open the virtual server where you want to create the domain. Right-click on the Domains node and choose New ➪ Domain to start the New SMTP Domain Wizard. Because the default domain will already exist, you can only create remote and alias domains. Select the desired type and specify the name for the domain. You can use the computer host name specified on the DNS tab of the server's TCP/IP properties for an alias domain, or you can specify a unique name for the domain that can optionally be supported by valid DNS entries in the domain's DNS server. However, the name specified for the domain in the SMTP service has no bearing on name resolution for incoming messages.

If the default domain uses the DNS name specified in the server's TCP/IP properties and you change the server's host name in its TCP/IP properties, you don't have to change the domain name in the SMTP service. IIS automatically uses the new name at startup.

Note   The options in the wizard are identical regardless of the type of domain you create.

Setting default domain properties

Open the IIS console, open the Domain node for the desired server, right-click the default domain in the list, and choose Properties. You can configure two options for the local default domain:

✦ **Drop directory:** Use this property to specify the location of the Drop directory for the domain. You can specify any local directory other than the Pickup directory.

✦ **Enable drop directory quota:** Select this option to enable quotas to be enforced on the Drop directory.

Note There are no properties you can change for an alias domain, as it is simply an alias for the default local domain.

Changing the default domain

You can't delete the default domain, but you can designate a different local domain as the default, leaving the previous default domain as an alias or deleting it after setting up a new default domain. To change the default domain, first create an alias domain using the properties you want for the new default domain. Then, in the IIS console, right-click the newly created local alias domain and choose Set as default. SMTP designates the domain as the default and sets the old domain as an alias.

Configuring remote domain properties

The properties for a remote domain are different from those of the default local domain. To configure the properties for a remote domain, open the IIS console and locate the remote domain in the appropriate SMTP virtual server. Open the Domains node, right-click the remote domain to modify, and choose Properties. IIS displays a property sheet for the domain similar to the one shown in Figure 24-9.

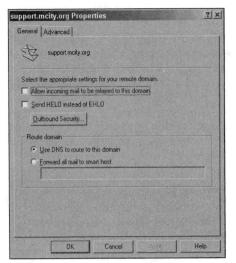

Figure 24-9: Properties for a remote domain

Use the General tab to configure the following options:

✦ **Allow incoming mail to be relayed to this domain:** SMTP by default prevents messages from being relayed to the remote domain unless otherwise specified in the Access property page for the virtual server (covered in the following section). Select this option to override the settings on the Access page and allow message relay to the remote host.

✦ **Send HELO instead of EHLO:** Servers that support ESTMP (Extended SMTP) supply a list of supported extensions when a connection is made using the EHLO command rather than the standard HELO command. Servers that do not support ESMTP generate an error if a connection attempt is made using EHLO instead of HELO. Select this option to have SMTP use standard HELO commands instead of EHLO when connecting to the remote domain.

✦ **Outbound security:** Click this button to configure security options for the outbound connection to the remote domain. Configure the type of authentication (anonymous, basic, WSP, or TLS) and user account or password required by the remote server, if any.

✦ **Use DNS to route to this domain:** Select this option to have SMTP attempt to deliver messages directly to the remote host using DNS lookup rather than forwarding to a smart host for delivery.

✦ **Forward all mail to smart host:** Select this option to forward all messages for the remote domain to the specified smart host. You can enter a Fully Qualified Domain Name (FQDN) or IP address for the smart host. If entering an IP address, enclose the address in brackets to identify the entry to SMTP as an IP address, bypassing DNS lookup and speeding up the connection process. Specifying a smart host in this field overrides the smart host setting, if any, specified in the general properties for the virtual server for the selected remote domain only.

Use the Advanced tab to configure which remote hosts can use remote triggered delivery (ATRN) to pull messages bound for them from the virtual server. Remote triggered delivery enables the remote host to pull messages from the virtual server at its own designated times to reduce network bandwidth utilization at peak times or to accommodate other administrative or performance requirements on the remote host or network. Rather than attempt to deliver messages waiting in the queue to these remote hosts, SMTP simply places the messages in the queue and waits for the remote host to connect and issue an ATRN command to retrieve the messages. The options on the Advanced page are self-explanatory.

Setting general properties

SMTP provides several property pages you can use to configure global options for each virtual server that determine how the virtual server functions. Open the IIS console, right-click the SMTP virtual server you want to manage, and click Properties. The following sections explain the options you can set.

General

The General tab enables you to configure several global properties for the site, which are explained in the following list:

✦ **Name:** This is the friendly name for the virtual server as it appears in the IIS console.

✦ **IP Address:** Select a single IP address or select All unassigned.

✦ **Advanced:** Click to add multiple IP addresses for the server or to change address/port assignments for the server.

✦ **Connection:** Click to configure limit and timeout for incoming and outgoing connections, maximum number of concurrent connections per domain, and TCP port.

✦ **Enable logging:** Select this option to turn on SMTP service logging, then select a log format from the associated drop-down list. Click Properties to configure log properties such as how often a new log is created, size limit for the log, log file directory, and the types of events that are logged.

Access

Use the Access tab to configure properties that control remote server and client access to the virtual server and their ability to relay through the server. The Access control group lets you configure the types of authentication accepted by the server and can include anonymous access, basic authentication against a specified Windows 2000 domain, TLS encryption, and WSP. Selecting the anonymous access option and deselecting all others effectively turn off authentication for the virtual server and allow all clients to access the server.

The Secure Communication group on the Access page lets you request and install a certificate for securing access to the server through TLS encryption. Click Certificate to run the Web Server Certificate Wizard, which enables you to request, install, and configure a certificate for enabling TLS on the virtual server. The process is essentially identical to that for installing a certificate to enable SSL on a Web site. You can request a certificate from a CA in your enterprise or from an outside CA. See the section "Enabling Secure Socket Layer" earlier in this chapter for an explanation of how to request and install a certificate.

Use the Communication button to enable and configure TLS. Select the Require secure channel option on the resulting Security dialog box to require TLS encryption for remote clients to connect to the virtual server. You also can configure the server to require stronger 128-bit encryption if needed.

The Connection Control group on the Access page lets you specify which computers can access the SMTP virtual server, giving you the means to restrict access as needed. As with Web and FTP sites, you can restrict access by allowing or denying access to a specified group. You can add computers to the group to be allowed or denied access by single IP, subnet (group), or domain name.

The last group on the Access tab — Relay restrictions — lets you configure the list of computers that is either allowed or denied the privilege of relaying messages through the server (Figure 24-10). As with connection control, you can specify a single IP, subnet, or domain to allow or deny the privilege. The Allow all computers option at the bottom of the dialog box allows all clients that successfully authenticate to relay messages through the server even if they would otherwise be denied access based on their IP address or domain.

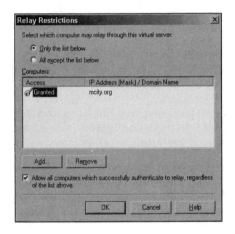

Figure 24-10: The Relay Restrictions dialog box

Messages

The Messages tab for an SMTP virtual server lets you apply limits on message size, session size, number of messages per connection, and number of recipients per message. These options can help reduce spamming and can serve to reduce the load on the server.

The option "Send copy of Non-Delivery report to" lets you specify an e-mail address to which a copy of non-delivery reports (NDRs) are sent. NDRs are generated when SMTP is unable to deliver a message, such as when a bad mailbox or domain is specified in the address. The message is returned to the sender with an NDR, but you might want to also forward a copy to an administrative account for monitoring. Numerous NDRs for messages bound for the same domain can indicate a connectivity, name resolution, or similar problem with a remote host, and receiving the NDRs can be a heads-up alert that a potential problem exists.

The last option on the Messages page lets you change the location of the Badmail folder for the virtual server. By default, bad messages are stored in the Badmail folder under the SMTP mail root folder that you specify when you create the server, but you can redirect the folder if needed through this setting.

Delivery

Except in the case of a remote domain that uses remote triggered delivery to trigger the virtual server to transmit messages to it, SMTP tries to send messages as soon as they are ready. The Outbound group of controls on the Delivery property page lets you specify the frequency of retransmission attempts, when the server sends a delay notification to the sender indicating that the message is delayed in delivery, and period of time at which waiting messages expire and are returned with an NDR. This group controls the delay notification and expiration times for local messages.

You also configure outbound connection security options through the Delivery page. As with incoming connections, you can configure the virtual server to use anonymous access, basic authentication against the remote server's security database, WSP, and enable TLS. Refer to the section "Access" earlier in this chapter if you need more information on configuring these properties.

Clicking the Advanced button on the Delivery page displays the Advanced Delivery dialog box shown in Figure 24-11, which enables you to configure advanced routing options for the virtual server. The following list explains the options:

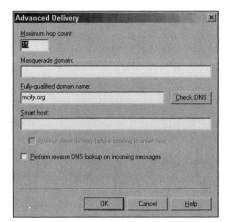

Figure 24-11: The Advanced Delivery dialog box

✦ **Maximum hop count:** Each server that a message passes through on its way to delivery is called a *hop*. The total number of hops is called the *hop count*. The SMTP server counts the number of hops listed in each message's header and compares it with the hop count specified by this setting. SMTP returns the message to the sender with an NDR if the number of hops exceeds this setting. The default value is 15. Decreasing the value can help reduce spamming, since spammed messages often route through multiple servers to reach their final destinations. Increase the value if you're having trouble getting messages delivered because the hop count is exceeding that set for the server.

✦ **Masquerade domain:** This property lets you insert a masquerade domain name in the Mail From lines in each message's protocol for readability or to match an existing domain naming policy. For example, you might replace `mail2.mcity.org` with simply `mcity.org`.

✦ **Fully-qualified domain name:** The SMTP service automatically uses the FQDN derived from the host and domain name properties on the host server's DNS property page (TCP/IP properties) for connectivity. If the host or domain name changes, SMTP adjusts automatically and uses the new name. However, you might want to instead specify an explicit FQDN for each virtual server, particularly when you are hosting multiple virtual domains on a single server. So, the server's native FQDN might be `server1.mcity.org`, but you're hosting the domain `support.mcity.org` and want to differentiate it with its own FQDN. In this case, you might create MX and A resource records in the appropriate DNS server for `mail.support.mcity.org`, and use that as the FQDN for the virtual server that supports that domain.

✦ **Check DNS:** Click this button to perform a name server lookup on the FQDN specified in the Fully-qualified domain name field to verify that it is a valid name. SMTP checks the name servers listed in the host server's DNS properties for a corresponding zone and host record.

✦ **Smart host:** Use this option to direct all outgoing mail to an intermediate host that will handle delivery of the messages. This property applies to all messages coming through the virtual server, regardless of the destination domain. You can configure individual domains within the virtual server to use another smart host, if desired. The smart host setting defined in each remote domain's properties overrides the host setting defined here. Specify the FQDN or IP address of the host that will handle message delivery. If specifying an IP address, enclose the address in brackets, such as [192.168.0.24], to indicate to SMTP that the entry is an IP address and to bypass name resolution.

✦ **Attempt direct delivery before sending to smart host:** Select this option if you want the virtual server to attempt to deliver messages before forwarding them to the smart host. By default, the SMTP service will not attempt delivery if a smart host is specified, but selecting this option causes it to do so.

✦ **Perform reverse DNS lookup on incoming messages:** By default, SMTP does not attempt to verify that the client's IP address matches the DNS name submitted by the client when establishing the connection with the server. It's possible for a client to spoof its DNS name to enable it to relay through your server or otherwise hide its true origin. The only way for the SMTP service to verify the identity of the client is to perform a reverse lookup. If the reverse lookup fails, SMTP inserts "unverified" after the IP address in the message header. No change occurs if the reverse lookup succeeds. For the reverse lookup to succeed, the originating domain's DNS zone must contain a host record for the originating host. With this option enabled, SMTP performs a reverse lookup for every message received by the virtual server, which can negatively impact server performance if the server receives a large number of messages on a regular basis.

LDAP routing

The SMTP service can use Lightweight Directory Access Protocol (LDAP) to resolve sender and recipient addresses. The directory service stores information about clients, including e-mail addresses and other data. By configuring the SMTP service to use LDAP, you enable it to perform such tasks as resolving a distribution list into individual addresses stored on a directory server. The SMTP service can use the Windows 2000 Active Directory, Site Server Membership Directory (MCIS 2.0 or later), or Exchange (Site Server 3.0 or later) LDAP service. Select the option Enable LDAP Routing to configure the virtual server to use LDAP. You specify the LDAP server, schema, authentication settings, and base container in the directory at which to begin the search.

Security

Use the Security tab to grant users Operator status for the SMTP virtual server, giving them the ability to perform limited administrative functions on the virtual server.

Configuring and Managing NNTP Services

NNTP stands for Network News Transport Protocol. NNTP serves as the protocol by which news messages are distributed across the Internet. This chapter assumes you have some familiarity with NNTP and understand its purpose and function. We focus on how to install and configure NNTP under IIS in Windows 2000 Server to create a local news server to host your organization's newsgroups.

Installing NNTP

As with the other IIS services, you add NNTP through the Add/Remove Programs object in the Windows 2000 Control Panel. After you start the Add/Remove Programs object, click Add/Remove Windows Components, double-click Internet Information Services, and select NNTP. Click OK, then click Next and follow the prompts provided to complete the software installation.

Configuring NNTP

As with the other IIS services, IIS sets up a default NNTP virtual server when you install the NNTP service. The default NNTP virtual server is bound to all unassigned IP addresses by default, which causes it to respond to all IP addresses bound on the server that are not assigned to another NNTP virtual server. If another virtual server defined on the server isn't available, the default server will respond to client and server NNTP requests. You can modify the configuration of the default NNTP virtual server and use it as the only one on the server, or you can create multiple virtual servers to accommodate multiple domains or other organization units.

Creating NNTP virtual servers

Creating an NNTP virtual server is relatively simple thanks to the New NNTP Virtual Server Wizard provided by IIS. To run the wizard, open the IIS console, right-click the server where you want to add the virtual server, and choose New ➪ NNTP Virtual Server. You also can right-click an existing NNTP virtual server and choose New ➪ Virtual Server. Specify the following information in the wizard:

✦ **NNTP virtual server description:** This is the friendly name for the virtual server as it appears in the IIS console.

✦ **IP address:** Select a single IP from the drop-down list or select All unassigned to have the server respond to all NNTP requests not serviced by another virtual server on a specific IP.

✦ **TCP port:** Specify the TCP port the virtual server should monitor for NNTP traffic. The default port is 119. For communication using SSL, the default port is 563.

✦ **Path:** Specify the path to the folder the NNTP virtual server should use for its general, non-content files. These include temporary files, drop folder for incoming messages, pickup folder for outgoing messages, and so on.

✦ **File system** or **remote share:** Specify whether the NNTP virtual server will use a local folder or remote share to store news content.

✦ **Path to content folder:** Choose the folder where the NNTP virtual server will store newsgroup folders, messages, and related data. For enhanced security, this should be on an NTFS volume so you can apply additional restrictions if needed through NTFS object permissions.

When you create an NNTP virtual server, IIS creates three newsgroups by default: control.cancel, control.newgroup, and control.rmgroup. These three special newsgroups are used to enable clients to cancel messages, create newsgroups, and remove newsgroups, respectively. If a client posts a message to a newsgroup but then decides he or she wants to cancel the message and remove it from the group, he or she can click the message and choose Message ➪ Cancel Message (using Outlook Express as the example NNTP client). Outlook Express posts a cancel message to the control.cancel newsgroup, and the NNTP virtual server processes the request, removing the selected message if it was posted by the client who requested the cancellation and if the user has access to the control.cancel newsgroup (explained shortly).

The control.newgroup newsgroup processes newgroup messages typically generated by a server to create new newsgroups. The control.rmgroup newsgroup processes messages from servers to remove newsgroups. Generally, NNTP client programs such as Outlook Express don't support the ability to generate newgroup (create a new newsgroup) or rmgroup (remove an existing newsgroup) messages. This feature is generally provided for other servers to be able to create and remove newsgroups from the virtual server.

Applying security through physical and virtual directories

When you create a virtual server, the NNTP service creates a folder structure to contain the newsgroups. For example, create a newsgroup called support.technical, and NNTP creates a folder under the NNTP root folder called `Support\Technical`. Messages for that newsgroup are stored in that folder. However, you can build a distributed file structure for a news server by using virtual directories.

As with Web and FTP sites, an NNTP virtual directory can be located on the server's file system or on a remote share. A virtual directory serves as the root of a portion of the newsgroup hierarchy. Take the mcity.org news server as an example. It contains several newsgroup areas of interest including sales, support, help, and general. The general and sales portions of the newsgroup hierarchy are stored on the server under the NNTP root folder. The support and help portions, however, are stored on a remote share managed by the technical support department. Figure 24-12 illustrates the virtual server structure.

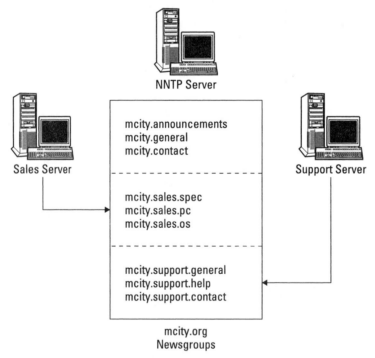

Figure 24-12: A virtual server can use virtual directories to distribute the newsgroup hierarchy on multiple systems.

Virtual directories offer multiple advantages. They enable you to distribute the newsgroup hierarchy onto multiple volumes to accommodate space requirements and improve performance. On a system with several SCSI physical volumes, each volume can be reading or writing concurrently with the others. This improves performance in situations where the newsgroups stored on the individual volumes see a lot of traffic. While the system is posting messages to one volume, it can be retrieving messages from others. If all the newsgroups were stored on a single volume, access would have to be sequential rather than concurrent. Distributing the newsgroup hierarchy to network shares also offers the same advantage but naturally generates additional network traffic. A final advantage to virtual folders is that you can grant administrative access to certain portions of the newsgroup structure. The technical support staff can manage the folders stored on their server, for example.

Whether you're using physical or virtual folders, you can configure security on individual folders, which applies security for the newsgroups stored in those folders. For example, you can protect a private newsgroup by simply applying permissions so that only those persons who should have access to the newsgroup can do so. Assigning permissions in this way requires that the folders be located on NTFS volumes. To restrict access to a newsgroup, simply configure the NTFS object permissions for the newsgroup's folder to allow read and write access for only the individual accounts or groups that should have access. Allow read and deny write permissions for specific users or groups to enable those clients to view messages but not post.

Creating virtual folders

Creating virtual folders is an easy task. First, create the physical folder that will be assigned as the virtual folder. Then, open the IIS console and open the NNTP virtual server under which the virtual folder will be created. Right-click the Virtual Directories node and choose New ➪ Virtual Directory to start the New NNTP Virtual Directory wizard. Specify the root of the newsgroup hierarchy to be stored under the virtual folder. For example, to store all of the support.* newsgroups under the virtual folder, specify support as the subtree. Or, specify a more defined structure to host only a portion of a newsgroup category. For example, specify support.help to host support.help, support.help.self, support.help.pub, and so on.

You must also specify whether to locate the virtual folder on the local file system or on a network share through the wizard. Select the appropriate option and then specify the local folder or remote share to complete the wizard.

Creating a virtual folder does not in itself cause any newsgroups to be created. You still need to create the newsgroups to be hosted in each virtual directory. As you'll learn in the next section, you don't explicitly define where a newsgroup is stored. Instead, the NNTP service creates the folder structure for the newsgroup based on its name and whether or not there is a matching virtual directory. After creating a support subtree virtual folder, for example, creating the newsgroups support.help and support.pubs will cause the NNTP service to create the necessary folders under the support virtual directory. If there is no matching virtual directory for a newsgroup, the NNTP service creates the folder structure for the newsgroup under the NNTP root folder defined in the virtual folder's global properties.

Creating newsgroups

You can create any number of newsgroups on a virtual server to accommodate your needs. Open the IIS console and then open the virtual server where the newsgroups will be hosted. Right-click the Newsgroups node and choose New ➪ Newsgroup. Or, right-click in the Newsgroup pane and choose New ➪ Newsgroup. The NNTP service starts the New Newsgroup Wizard in which you specify the newsgroup name (such as support.help) and optional description and pretty name. Clients can download newsgroup descriptions along with newsgroup names and search by description as well as by name. The client can retrieve the pretty name if the client software is capable of issuing the list prettynames command, and the pretty name serves as an alias for the newsgroup.

By default, NNTP creates non-moderated newsgroups with read and write access. Any client can post messages in a non-moderated newsgroup subject to his or her access to the newsgroup, as defined by its NTFS object permissions. In a moderated newsgroup, however, messages are sent to a moderator who either accepts and posts the message or rejects it.

You can configure a newsgroup's properties to make it read-only, define it as a moderated newsgroup, and change its description or pretty name. To do so, right-click the newsgroup in the IIS console and choose Properties. Except for the Moderated option, the options are self-explanatory. The section "Moderating Newsgroups" later in this chapter offers more information on configuring and managing moderated newsgroups.

Defining expiration policies

If you allow all messages to remain indefinitely on a server with a large number of newsgroups or messages, performance will rapidly deteriorate, users will have difficulty finding messages, and you'll eventually run out of storage space. To overcome those potential problems, you can define *expiration policies* that determine how long a message can reside on the server before it expires and is removed. You can create a single policy to control all newsgroups or create multiple policies to expire only specific newsgroups.

To create an expiration policy, open the IIS console and then open the NNTP virtual server to which you want to apply the policies. Right-click the Expiration Policies node and choose New ➪ Expiration Policy to start the New NNTP Expiration Policy Wizard. Within the wizard, specify the following information:

✦ **Expiration policy description:** This is the friendly name for the policy as it appears in the IIS console.

✦ **Affected newsgroups:** You can apply the policy to all newsgroups on the virtual server or only to selected newsgroups on the server. If you choose to apply the policy selectively, the wizard displays a dialog box you use to add newsgroups to the policy. Add the applicable newsgroup names one at a time. You can use a wildcard to specify all newsgroups within a specific category, such as support.* or alt.*.

✦ **Expiration period:** Specify the number of hours that messages can remain in a newsgroup covered by this policy. The default is 168 hours (7 days).

Moderating newsgroups

As mentioned earlier in this chapter, you can allow anyone to post messages to a newsgroup (subject to their access restrictions) or create a moderated group. In a moderated group, a moderator receives all posted messages and either accepts or rejects them. Accepted messages are posted to the newsgroup, and rejected messages are not (and optionally returned to the sender). Messages can be sent to the moderator either through the SMTP service or placed directly in an SMTP virtual server's Pickup folder. The messages are then forwarded to the specified moderator(s).

Any NNTP client can post to a moderated newsgroup since the client-side process is the same as for a non-moderated newsgroup. However, the moderator needs to use an NNTP client that supports moderator features.

Setting up a moderated newsgroup is a multi-step process:

1. Open the IIS console and right-click the NNTP virtual server you want to configure, then choose Properties.

2. Click the Settings tab and in the field "SMTP server for moderated newsgroups," specify the DNS name or IP address of the SMTP server to which moderated messages are sent, or specify the local Pickup folder for the SMTP virtual folder. The directory for the default SMTP server is \Inetpub\Mailroot\Pickup.

3. In the Default moderator domain field, specify the qualified domain name for the domain that will handle all moderated newsgroups for which there is no specified moderator. These messages are sent to *newsgroup@default_ moderator_domain*, where *newsgroup* is the newsgroup name and *default_ moderator_domain* is the domain specified by this setting. The name you specify must be a valid DNS name.

4. In the Administrator Email Account field, specify the e-mail address to which non-delivery notices should be sent for newsgroup articles that can't be delivered to the designated moderator. To enable sending NDRs, create the DWORD value MailFromHeader in the registry. Use Regedit or Regedt32 to add the DWORD value HKEY_LOCAL_MACHINE\SYSTEM\CurrentControlSet\ Services\NntpSvc\Parameters\MailFromHeader and set the value to 1.

5. The account under which the NNTP service runs needs to be defined as an account on the SMTP server if you use the SMTP service to deliver moderated messages. By default, this is the System account. Verify that this is the case by first verifying the NNTP service's account in the Services console (or Services node of the Computer Management console). Then, verify that the designated account exists on the SMTP server or in the domain.

6. In the IIS console, open the NNTP virtual server, right-click the newsgroup you want to moderate, and choose Properties. On the newsgroup's property sheet, select the Moderated option, and in the Moderator field, specify the e-mail address of the moderator. Or, click Set Default to set the moderator to *newsgroup@default_moderator_domain*, where *newsgroup* is replaced with the name of the newsgroup and *default_moderator_domain* is the domain defined as the default in the virtual server's global properties. Note that only the newsgroup portion of the address appears in the box, and that periods are replaced by dashes (support.help becomes support-help, for example). The domain is appended automatically, which enables the NNTP service to route the messages correctly even if the domain membership of the server changes.

7. Close the newsgroup property sheet and post some test messages to verify that everything works properly.

Indexing the news server

The Indexing Service can index news messages stored in virtual directories. To configure indexing, first verify that Index Server is running on the server. Then open the IIS console and open the NNTP virtual server in question. Open the Virtual Directories node, right-click the virtual directory to index, and choose Properties. On the virtual directory's property sheet, select the Index news content option and click OK.

Using SSL

You can configure an NNTP virtual server to require SSL connections for enhanced security. As with securing a Web server for SSL, you first need to obtain a certificate to install on the server. Follow these steps to enable SSL:

1. Open the IIS console, right-click the NNTP virtual server, and choose Properties.

2. On the Access tab, click Certificate to start the wizard. Prepare a certificate request using the wizard. Make sure to specify the FQDN of the NNTP virtual server as the common name for the certificate if users will be connecting to the server through DNS lookups, or specify the IP address as the common name if users will be using the IP address. If connecting on an intranet, you can specify the NetBIOS name as the common name. See the section "Enabling Secure Sockets Layer" earlier in this chapter if you need additional help creating the certificate request.

3. Open a browser and submit the request to a CA to obtain the certificate. See "Enabling Secure Sockets Layer" earlier in this chapter if you need more detailed information.

4. Open the Access tab for the NNTP virtual server and click Certificate again to process the pending request and install the certificate.

5. Open the Virtual Directories node, right-click the newsgroup subtree for which you want to require SSL, and choose Properties. Apply SSL to the Default subtree to require SSL for all newsgroups.

6. Click Secure on the newsgroup's General property page. Select the option Require secure channel to enable SSL. You can optionally enable 128-bit encryption. Click OK and then close the property sheet for the newsgroup.

7. Configure an NNTP client to access the news server using SSL and test operation of the server.

Controlling access to the server

The Access tab for an NNTP virtual server lets you determine which clients have access to the server and the type of authentication methods employed. To configure access, open the IIS console, right-click the NNTP virtual server, and choose Properties. Click the Access tab, then click Authentication to display the Authentication Methods dialog box shown in Figure 24-13.

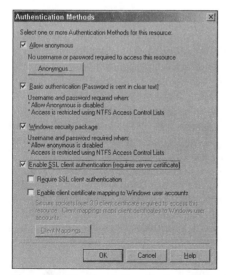

Figure 24-13: The Authentication Methods dialog box

You can configure the server to allow anonymous access, eliminating the need for a client to have or provide a valid user account for authentication. As with the HTTP and FTP services, IIS uses a predefined anonymous account to authenticate the users. Select the option Allow anonymous to enable anonymous access. Click Anonymous if you need to change the user account and password the NNTP server uses to authenticate anonymous access.

You also can disable anonymous access and require clients to log on to the server. This enables you to restrict who can access the server, because only those users with valid accounts will be able to access it. You can use basic clear-text authentication, WSP, or SSL. If you use SSL, you can optionally require the clients to have SSL certificates and enable client certificates to be mapped to Windows 2000 user accounts on the server or in the server's domain.

In addition to defining the authentication options, you also can restrict access to the server to individual computers, subnets, or domains. On the server's Access property page, click Connection to display the Connection dialog box. As with other services, you can allow all except those listed or deny all except those listed. Add computers to the list by their individual IP addresses, specify a group via a subnet entry, or specify a domain name. You can use the DNS Lookup button to look up the IP address of a computer if you know its DNS name.

Summary

Windows 2000 offers a good set of tools in IIS to enable you to build a full-featured Web server for HTTP, FTP, SMTP, and NNTP protocols. You can host multiple Web sites and provide secure access and authentication through SSL and other mechanisms. The FTP server provides a means for serving files throughout your enterprise or to clients on the Internet. The SMTP service makes it possible to create multiple virtual SMTP e-mail servers that can serve as main transfer agents for your company or domains you host for others. The NNTP server lets you set up public and private news servers that support both anonymous or authenticated access, as well as secure access through SSL.

If you're an ISP or company that needs to do e-commerce, however, IIS by itself isn't the solution. Instead, you need to look to Microsoft's MCIS, Site Server, SQL Server 2000, and other Web server applications to provide the types of services you no doubt need to offer your customers. But if you're looking to build an Internet presence for your company, need to do a moderate amount of site hosting, or are looking to build an intranet for your company, IIS is a good choice.

✦   ✦   ✦

Interoperation and Integration Services

P A R T

VII

In This Part

Chapter 25
Terminal Services
and Thin Client
Integration

I n a world of client/server, Terminal Services is perhaps one of the most foreign concepts to understand. Chapter 25 introduces the idea that for most computer tasks, users do not need the power and complexity that comes with their workstations, nor the overhead of the application installed on them. Not only are these workstations expensive, but their management, the administration of the software, and the administration of the user's workspace greatly contribute to the total cost of ownership.

We look at how Terminal Services can reduce, if not eliminate, unauthorized use of software in the enterprise (protection against theft and piracy) and can practically eliminate the virus malady and the technology disease known as obsolescence. We also explore configuration and deployment of Term0inal Services, and investigate the "new" science of thin-client/ server and its application.

Terminal Services and Thin Client Integration

This chapter explores thin-client/server computing and discusses the pros and cons of deploying Terminal Services to support a thin-client/server infrastructure in your enterprise. Thin-client/server technology has been proven to drastically lower total cost of ownership, and it virtually eliminates workstation obsolescence in a vast majority of computer applications. It is also a cost-effective, rapid, and simple means of deploying a native Windows 2000 network, in which all clients connect to Windows 2000 desktops, in a legacy Windows environment.

Thin-Client/Server Computing

No other Windows 2000 architecture causes more anxiety or apprehension than Terminal Services (TS). No other architecture has the power to turn your IT department on its head than Terminal Services. TS represents a major paradigm shift in computing in general and client/server (C/S) computing in particular. As simple as it is, we have found that many administrators shy away from the TS subject (although that is beginning to change with the advent of Windows 2000).

Thin-client services would have been a better description of this service because terminal emulation is a little archaic. Client software, not unlike a Web browser in purpose, is able to receive only the display and user interaction logic — key strokes and mouse clicks at the terminal — while all processing, execution, and storage access takes place on the server. Essentially, this data is miniscule and does not need significant bandwidth (10 to 28Kbps) to travel between the client and the server. This user experience for many applications is sufficient, even over the Internet, to provide enterprise-wide access to computing resources. No application logic travels the network, and no application data needs to be transported from the client to a remote database.

Before you take the plunge into thin-client/server computing, let's look at its foundations.

Refresher: Client/Server Computing Model

A client/server (C/S) example directly drawn from the world of IT is the Internet. Clients connect to it and request information and services, such as news, e-mail, files, information searching and shopping, and so on. The servers handle almost all the data processing; the clients handle the rendering of the images and the user interface.

In other words, the workload or processing is split between a computer on the back end (the server) and a computer on the front end (the client workstation). The server is typically a very powerful computer. The client does not require the processing power, services, memory, and storage of the server.

Since the advent of C/S computing, there have been many variations on the architecture. Today, computing systems are so much more advanced that there is no longer a defining boundary between what represents a server and what represents a client. Both client software and server software can play both roles, to varying degrees. It really boils down to where you place server-centric services.

Windows 2000 Professional, for example, is built on the same operating system as the server. Only, a lot of server-oriented subsystems and services have been left out of or restricted in Professional. For example: Up to ten clients can connect to Professional and use its printers, gain access to its files and hardware, and so on. The limitation has to do more with product line and economics than technological limitations. It would only take a few minutes in source code to change the limitation from 10 to 50 connections.

The C/S concepts extend beyond hardware and processes and into pure software engineering practice. Threads of execution typically operate in a world of processing handoffs, like a relay race, as do the processes in the network protocols and APIs, such as the FTP service, which has two clearly defined C/S components. The FTP service is not flexible; the client cannot turn around and become a server by flipping a switch on or off. They are based on the same underlying technology, the TCP/IP stack. But the client service is imbued with very different attributes, and it has a completely different frame of existence and purpose from the server component.

Over the years, the C/S model has not qualified or defined the weight carried by the clients. An Internet server, such as IIS (see Chapter 24) is packed to the hilt with complex services. The client, your browser, only needs to know how to read HTML, run Java or ActiveX applets, manage URLs, and so on. In fact, the browser can be installed into a very "thin" client device, even a small mobile phone.

But hold that *thin* thought for a moment. While servers have been getting bigger, faster, and fancier, so too have the clients. The average workstation on the market probably carries a more powerful processor and a faster motherboard than the servers that have been faithfully plugging away 24 hours a day, seven days a week for the past five or more years. Is there anything wrong with that? Yes, in an enterprise-computing environment, there is.

While computer prices are coming down all the time, the cost of administration has been going up. Any business that employs more than a handful of computer users and deploys fancy workstations for its people has another cost. This cost is called TCO, which stands for "Total Cost of Ownership." And it is not merely a buzzword. The number of times it is used throughout this book is not coincidental.

The total cost of a computer is more than the total cost of the CPU, monitor, and input devices. It is also the cost of maintaining that equipment so that the users get the best possible service from it, and that the company derives the maximum benefit from its investment. Each workstation also requires software, and there is a cost involved in distributing that software to each workstation, and in keeping the software current, configured, and in service. Further, you need to lock down your workstations so users cannot change settings, fiddle with hardware, save rubbish to the hard disk, or do anything that would put the computer out of commission and pile on your workload. Further, the larger the enterprise, and the more remote offices it has, the harder it is to provide any manner of attention to each workstation. So, you try to get around this by loading remote control products on the workstations, like pcANYWHERE and Carbon Copy. But these solutions are not ideal.

As soon as new workstations are rolled out, at considerable cost, they become obsolete. How many early 486 machines and early Pentiums have you thrown out in recent years, or stashed in your basement?

This is what we call TCO — the true cost of owning technology and the effort to get the most mileage for your investment.

Windows 2000 Server-Windows 2000 Professional goes a long way to reducing the total cost of ownership. It is more client/server than any other OS that has come before it (including non-Windows products). It provides a smooth and very tightly organized integrated, homogenous C/S environment, in which clients and servers cooperate in a well-defined partnership. But, when it comes to TCO, it is far from redeeming. For a lot of companies with huge investments in legacy and homogenous networking environments, upgrading all clients to Windows 2000 Professional may be impractical and very expensive.

What is the solution? Has client/server failed us? What can be done to reduce the cost of technology, of ownership? To find the answer, we had to look in our past . . . to the mainframe computing model.

Total Recall: The Mainframe Computing Model

Before the advent of the PC and graphical user interface systems, knowledge workers, primarily in large organizations, worked at dumb terminals, connected to a behemoth of a mainframe. The only devices at the desktop were the keyboard and a monitor. This model is still in wide use.

The mainframe model is ideal from a client-TCO point of view. Aside from the fact that the mainframe costs a lot of money, there is virtually nothing you need to administer or install at the desktop. The users cannot compromise the system by inserting anything in a floppy disk drive, and there is no local software or hardware to install. The only thing that can fail on the desktop is the terminal or the keyboard, and they rarely do.

When new equipment is needed for a user, it can be shipped to the user who unpacks it and plugs it in . . . no complex installation. All the user has to do is plug the terminal into the power socket and into the network jack. Everyone's computing experience is centrally administered. Before PCs and servers, most large companies employed only a handful of operators on their mainframes.

But these early systems were arcane to use and dumb, and to a large extent nothing has changed in recent years. Everyone has to learn cryptic terminal shortcuts and stare at green or amber characters. The GUI changed everything; it made interacting with the computer much more simple and productive. When the PC and its operating system matured, every small business was able to afford computing power only once available to the multinationals or Fortune 500 companies.

So, what if we can take the C/S model and its graphical user interface and affordable, powerful, and widely used applications, and morph them into the mainframe-computing model? One company decided that it was worth betting the farm to create such a computing environment.

Enter Citrix Systems

Citrix Systems, Inc., came up with the idea of "thin" clients: nothing more than a monitor, a keyboard, and a mouse connecting the user to a server where 100 percent of the graphical user environment and all the user's desktop applications are running. In other words, the user's application processing space (CPU needs, storage needs, memory needs) is on the server. This computing model is identical to the mainframe model. Everything resides on the server, and the server is responsible for 100 percent of the processing. Citrix's main innovation was the Independent Computing Architecture (ICA) protocol, which could run on top of any routable protocol, and on any operating system.

Citrix now concentrates its efforts in extending the Windows 2000 desktop to anything that can load the ICA protocol. Its flagship product line is called MetaFrame, and you can find out more from the Citrix Web site or the Citrix folder on the CD that accompanies this book.

Note It is important to understand that MetaFrame does not ship with Windows 2000. The Windows 2000 Terminal Services Client software that ships with the Server can only be installed on PCs already running a version of Windows (16- or 32-bit). To connect any other device or operating system to Windows 2000 Terminal Services, you need to install MetaFrame from Citrix. This includes MS-DOS, UNIX, the Apple operating systems, and dumb terminals. Also, many advanced features of thin-client/server technology, such as video and audio streaming, require MetaFrame. Additional, more sophisticated features are available as add-ons, and they are often more expensive than the cost of a server license.

Terminal Services in Windows 2000 and MetaFrame have brought us the best of both computing models: a mainframe computing model requiring no PC or computer or administration at the desktop, with the Windows 2000 GUI and Win32 applications running on the server. It is called *thin-client computing* because the client needs nothing more in resources than 4 to 8MB of RAM to load the terminal client and connect to the server.

The Thin-Client/Server Computing Model

Citrix's slogan for thin-client/server computing is availability for "any client over any network connection." The model's simple dictate is this: Any client can connect to the server, which enables 100 percent server-based processing, management, deployment, and support for mission-critical, productivity, Web-based, or legacy applications. In short, just about anything you can do on the workstation can be done at the server.

Note No doubt we have infuriated several camps by making it sound like thin-client/server is a Windows-only thing. You have thin-client/server solutions on other platforms such as Linux, and MetaFrame from Citrix is being aimed at UNIX. And don't get us started on the net-PC debate.

Thin clients now come in many forms. The electronics can fit into a keyboard, and there is no need for a processor, a hard disk, and more than a couple of megabytes of RAM. The terminal makers, such as Wyse, Inc., latched onto the idea like harpoons, channeling their terminal building efforts to terminals running terminal server or Citrix clients and renaming their terminals WBTs, which stands for Windows-based Terminal. Today, they make a variety of thin-client devices, some of them no bigger than a pound of butter. And as flat screens begin to appear and drop in price, eventually the "brick," as Wyse calls its thin-client device, will disappear completely and be merged into the display.

Setting up the client is easy. Like the mainframe terminal, you just switch the client terminal on, and you're at the Windows 2000 logon screen. All client and session administration is done at the server. The only caveat with dumb terminals is the investment in MetaFrame . . . the addition of a third-party product and the loading of new firmware as it becomes available.

The Thin-Client/Server Revolution

Before we dig into Terminal Services (TS) architecture and deployment, let's look at some of the benefits of Terminal Services and circumstances where you would be wise not to deploy thin-client/server. In order to appreciate the discussion, you should first be clear what constitutes a good thin-client or TS candidate and what does not.

To kick off, first consider this bold directive we made to one of our large multinational clients recently: Ninety-five percent of all applications deployed in your enterprise today can and should run on the server, and users should be connected to the servers as TS clients.

To check if such a bold statement applies to your situation or scenario, split the workstation role into two categories: *Data I/O Applications* and *Processor and Graphics Intensive Applications.* You can probably be more specific, but for the majority of companies, these two categories work just fine.

Good Candidates: Data I/O Applications

Data I/O in this case does not only refer to the input or output of data from and to a database, it also embraces word processing, working with spreadsheets, accounting, sending e-mail, browsing the Web, and so on. Data I/O applications are ideal candidates for deployment in the thin-client/server model.

Consider these applications: If all the workers do all day is key information into the applications, create reports, documents, and letters, print, and so on, then they are ideal candidates for Terminal Services. Once the users have logged on and loaded their applications, they do not run any processes that suddenly consume a lot of memory or processing bandwidth, so why do they need the overhead of a fancy workstation?

And what about high-end data I/O applications, the ones that use up memory and processor cycles generating reports, calculating spreadsheets, and re-indexing thousand-page documents? Choosing where to do the processing is relative to the IS environment, user experience, the number of sessions (users) on the servers, the size or quantity of CPUs on the server, and so on. In Chapter 5, we discuss configuring an application server.

Poor Candidates: Processor and Graphics Intensive Applications

Processor- and graphics-intensive applications need and use a lot of memory, the memory consumption is rarely uniform, and they always need dedicated processor time. Such applications are *not always* suitable for deployment in a thin-client/server arrangement. They include graphic design, computer-aided design or engineering, CAD/CAM, software development, desktop publishing applications, drawing applications, and any application that needs to exploit the CPU for intensive computation. Rule of thumb: If the application needs to exploit as much of the machine resources as it can, regardless of what's running in the room next door, it will be better to keep it deployed on a workstation.

Many modern word-processing suites double as desktop publishing (DTP) environments and can command more resources from the server than the average letter writer. Vast repagination, indexing, search and replace, hyphenation and justification, printing, and layout processing may be better served on a dedicated workstation. Conversely, many companies have opted even to keep processor-intensive applications like DTP on the terminal server and have simply added more CPU power and RAM to meet the demand.

Even a small job, like printing a complex document, can consume a lot of RAM and processor bandwidth. And moving the printer server functions away from an application server is more than a worthwhile consideration.

Applications that also need specific hardware loaded on the machine are not candidates for TS or T-C/S deployment. A good example is video editing or graphic design applications that depend on powerful video electronics, sound electronics, or sophisticated digital display and graphics electronics.

Also, we italicized the words *not always* previously because some of these applications will work well on the server and you can cater to specific needs. Again, the key word here is *relative*. For example, we deployed Terminal Services in a call center environment in 1998 (on the NT 4.0 TSE). The call center was located almost 5,000 miles away from our labs. Our software was running on a server, servicing five to six agents concurrently. We even loaded mainframe terminal emulation software (TN3270) on the server to allow the agents to hit the data input screens of the government mainframe systems.

One of our problems was transferring the new software and installing it on the server during the early development days. Our lab was in Florida, and the center was in Idaho. Agents, however, were actually using our beta software in a full production environment. We had read how the University of Idaho installed Visual Basic on WinFrame servers to allow students to complete their projects remotely without requiring a copy of VB or C++ to be loaded on their own machines. We latched onto that idea for our solution.

We installed the complete Visual Java/C/C++ and Delphi software development suites on the server that would allow us to add features or knock out bugs in a production environment as soon as they were reported or soon after. All we would have to do is wait for the customer service representatives to log off, and then we would do a recompile of the application or a component of it and copy the executable to a single location on the same server. All agents got the fix, and we only deployed one file. Of course, we broke all the software development rules in the book and kept the changes marginal, but it demonstrates that we can write software in Florida and compile and deploy it in Idaho, all on one machine.

Poor Candidates: Bad Software

You cannot just load anything on Windows 2000 and expect it to service multiple users in the Terminal Services environment. Check the applications out before purchasing or installing them. There are two criteria to consider:

1. Applications should be multi-user in design or architecture. If your users can load multiple copies of the application from a central location in legacy application server style, meaning that the applications will load across the network but run on the local machine, they will be ideal for Terminal Services.

   This rule is not hard, and you should test the applications. If they are logo-compliant and do not violate multi-user logic (such as writing to a database), they will usually work fine in the multi-user environment.

2. Applications should be Windows 2000 or at least Win32 logo-compliant. Poorly written software that makes no use of the Registry or Active Directory should not be considered.

Note Sometimes, even good or popular software does not work with Terminal Services. QuickBooks 2000 from Intuit, for example, puts up a fight when anyone other than the person who installed it tries to run it. The solution is to download an update and make sure the users are part of a group that has access to that certain registry data.

The Benefits

The following represents the benefits of T-C/S deployment.

Non-Windows workstations

Non-Windows workstations will be one of your first considerations. If you have a number of computers that are not currently running any Windows operating system and you need to extend Windows to these desktops, TS will be ideal. These workstations include MAC, UNIX, DOS, and legacy environments. If the workstation cannot boot to DOS or load TCP/IP, do not worry—MetaFrame from Citrix allows you to connect over protocols like IPX.

No applications on the workstation

If you can boot clients to Windows NT, 9x, or 2000, but do not have specific applications running on the workstations for whatever reason, then TS is your answer. Consider loading the terminal client to give the users access to these applications on the servers in full interactive Windows 2000 sessions.

Phasing out 9x clients, or going native mode

This is related to the prior benefit. If you have seen the Promised Land and have the go-ahead to move to a Windows 2000 native mode environment, you can keep your existing investment and use the TS client to connect users onto the Windows 2000 desktop.

You can, for example, run the parallel environments we discussed in Part II of this book, and you can also put all your 9x clients into a workgroup and not connect them to any domain. They can load without requiring authentication, obtain an IP address from a DHCP Server, and then load the TS client in full-screen mode. The user will not even see the old Windows 9x (or DOS) desktop, and the first logon screen will be the Windows 2000 TS session at the server.

No workstation hardware

If you have to extend the Windows 2000 desktop to a user or location and currently have no PC or workstation in the environment, or cannot put a workstation in the environment, consider TS.

For example, suppose you do not have the budget for another workstation. Thin-client devices are cheaper than PCs. This has been an ongoing debate. PC manufacturers swore the PC would become cheaper than the thin-client device. Guess what? They lost that war. The PC has not only not dropped far enough to compete with thin-clients, it also is showing trends of doing an about-turn and heading the other way again. Computers, dear power user, need RAM. RAM is a commodity; sometimes you can buy it cheaply, and other times shortages occur and the prices rise. The price of about 64MB of RAM on a PC will buy you a nice thin-client TS-compatible keyboard, network card, or brick.

Another secret: TS clients need no hard disks and only a few megabytes of RAM to load. An engineer working for a thin-client hardware manufacturer told us in the strictest confidence (so we won't mention his name) that the $250 device his company was selling cost less than $10 to make. The components are so small they fit inside the average keyboard.

Obsolescence resistance

Yet another secret: The TS client device is obsolescence-resistant. A PC is obsolete the day you buy it. A thin-client device can keep going for five to ten years or more even without a few firmware upgrades. All the TS client needs is enough electronics to load the network interface and enough RAM to hold the terminal client, no more than a few Megabytes. Later, we'll walk you through an experiment to test the obsolescence claim.

A thin-client device is the way to go if the environment is not conducive to workstation deployment. Such an environment can be the loading dock at a factory, the customer service desk at a depot of sorts (such as customs receiving), retail stores, or the beach.

The TS client can now be installed on Windows CE 2.1 or a handheld PC (H/PC) and in other embedded operating systems. And it is a big attraction for PocketPC users. Connected to a mobile or wireless communications network, you can use your handheld to connect to the server while sunning yourself on the beach.

No workstation administration

All administration of the user workspace is done at the server and affects the user's sessions. You no longer need to concern yourself about administration or control of the workspace environment at the machine the user is logging on to. Granted, policies under Windows 2000 are highly advanced, but you might save a lot of time and money relegating desktop or workspace management only on portable or notebook computers, or situations in which the user needs to continue working regardless of the state or severance of the network connection.

Reduced risk of virus infection

By relocating the workspace to the server, you reduce and can completely eliminate the introduction of viruses to the network or servers from the user's machine. It is time-consuming and complex to manage the anti-virus (AV) software on remote computers. In all traditional client/server computing environments we have consulted, anti-virus software on workstations was either disabled or seriously out of date. In a TS environment, you load the AV engine on the server, and protection is extended to every user. You only have to update the AV data files on the server, instead of every machine.

Eliminate the risk of clients introducing illegal software

Clients can be locked down to prevent the user from introducing illegal copies of software into the enterprise. Although you can control this to a fine degree with policies on workstations, a thin-client device would need access to the server's CD or floppy disk drive to install unlicensed or unauthorized software.

Remote access

If you have users working from home or a small remote office, they can connect to RAS and then open a TS session to the server. And to cut the cost of the RAS option further, you can have clients connect to your intranet portal over the Internet and then establish the TS session.

Centralized support environment

User sessions are centrally managed from the server. You can even log on to the server under the user's logon ID to see the exact desktop the user sees without ever having to make a trip to the client's location. Sessions can be managed, users can be sent messages, and you can also shadow the session and monitor the actions of the client as if you are sitting on the other side of the monitor glass.

Despite the flexibility derived from Terminal Services, there are also, naturally, other costs to consider . . . apart from the initial learning curve and deployment. TS is built into the server operating system, but you need to consider and purchase client access licenses (CAL) and applications licenses for a multi-user environment. MetaFrame, as mentioned earlier, is another cost.

Terminal Services Architecture

Windows 2000's Terminal Services comprise a number of components, based in part and concept from the original MultiWin kernel created by Citrix, licensed to Microsoft and now completely integrated into the Win32 subsystem (see Chapter 1):

✦ **Multi-user Kernel:** The multi-user concurrent processing wizardry possible on Windows 2000 is handled by multi-user extensions to the NT kernel. They do not have to be added to the server and are part of the kernel regardless of how the server is being deployed.

✦ **The Remote Desktop Protocol (RDP):** Microsoft uses RDP (instead of Citrix's ICA protocol). The protocol runs on top of TCP/IP and is based on the ITU T.120 protocol, which is used in NetMeeting. RDP supports remote disconnection, routing, network localization, and remote configuration. It also supports three levels of encryption and different bandwidth allocation, an important component in the Microsoft Quality of Service technology described in Chapter 1.

✦ **The Terminal Services Client:** This client is responsible for displaying the 32-bit Windows 2000 user interface on the client device. It is a small application (installed from two floppy disks). The client establishes and maintains a connection to the server and transmits all input/output and screen display logic between the client and the server. The Citrix client, incidentally (also known as the ICA client), already caters to streaming audio and video and can map the client's floppy and hard disk drives to drive letters installed on the server. This functionality requires MetaFrame and the ICA protocol to be supported on the server.

✦ **The Terminal Services Licensing Service:** This service is needed whenever you are running TS in application server mode (discussed next). The service allows TS to obtain licenses for the clients (CALs) that connect to the server. The licenser service can manage unlicensed clients, pre-licensed clients, temporary licenses, and CALs. It also supports the Internet Connector for Terminal Services, which we will discuss shortly.

✦ **Terminal Services Administration Tools:** These tools consist of software for license management, client creation, configuration, and session management.

Note   Terminal service users are *not,* for the most part, managed separately from workstation or local desktop users. The service is so highly integrated into Windows 2000 Server that Microsoft has made a point of making terminal session configuration part of general configuration. Thus, when it comes to user configuration, computer account configuration, or server configuration, the features or parameters that cater to, or are specific to, the terminal service are covered in the chapter that deals with the respective environment or service.

The Microsoft and Citrix partnership splits the client market into two realms. Citrix gets the market to provide clients for anything not running Windows (so small it was embarrassing to express it in percentage terms). Nevertheless, it is a very important segment of the market, which is showing all the signs of growing fast. Citrix also makes its money from advanced server administration and application publishing tools. Microsoft's share is all the Windows clients.

Terminal Services Operation Modes

Terminal Services on Windows 2000 Server can operate in two modes: remote administration and application server.

Remote administration

Say goodbye to pcANYWHERE or Carbon Copy on the server. Under the remote administration mode, any server can be accessed and manipulated as if you are sitting in front of the console. Any administration work that you can do at the console, except for inserting a CD or disk, can be done over the network. Anyone who has suffered working at a server in a cold and cramped server room will appreciate this service.

In remote administration mode, the server only requires the minimal Terminal Services running. Application services need not be installed, and the impact on the machine is negligible. This is ideal for remotely managing a mission-critical machine, such as a database server, that typically does not call for service that requires access to applications or that supports multiple users.

Terminal Services in remote administration mode can support two concurrent users and requires no additional licensing.

Application server

In application server mode, many different types of clients can access applications over any type of network connection. Applications have to be specifically installed for multi-access. Applications can be installed directly on the server or via the Remote Installation Services described in Chapter 5. Terminal Services applications and access policy are managed no differently to regular clients. Therefore, as described in Chapter 11, you can consider targeting policy to workstation clients and extend the policy to terminal server sessions. In fact, it would make sense to enable Terminal Services settings in each user account, so that it is always available if needed (see Chapter 9).

Licensing is an important element with Terminal Services and is discussed in Chapters 4 and 5.

Terminal Services Administration Tools

There are two applications that are used to manage or administer Terminal Services: *Terminal Services Manager* and the *Terminal Services Configuration* utility.

The Terminal Services Manager

This tool, illustrated in Figure 25-1, is used to manage all Windows 2000 servers running Terminal Services. With it you can view user sessions and check the processes they have running, resource consumption, and so on. You can also send messages to individual users or to groups of users.

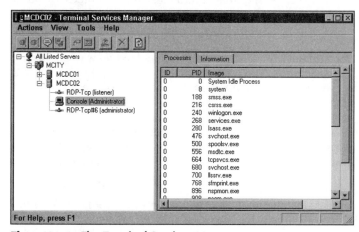

Figure 25-1: The Terminal Services Manager

If you need to shut down the server and you have users connected, you can send a message asking them all to finish what they are doing, save their work, and log off.

A vital feature of the Terminal Services Manager is it enables you to manage each session. You can check what users have running if they have disconnected and cannot log back in, or if their applications have locked up or gone off the deep end. And if the process that is open is safe to close, you can terminate it and reset the session.

Terminal Services Configuration

The Terminal Services Configuration utility, illustrated in Figure 25-2, allows you to globally manage and configure connection protocols, such as RDP. You also use the utility to change the server mode, encryption levels, timeouts, printer mappings, clipboard parameters, and so on. We will discuss this utility later in this chapter.

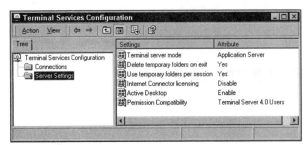

Figure 25-2: The Terminal Services Configuration utility

Enabling Terminal Services

Enabling TS for use on the server requires you to make a few choices. Now that you understand the service from the preceding sections in this chapter, your first task is to decide on the mode TS will run in.

As mentioned earlier, Terminal Services can be deployed in two ways: *application server* and *remote administration*. The remote administration option is really a subset of the complete multi-user environment minus the overhead of the services that support concurrent application access and licensing.

When you installed Windows 2000 server (see Chapter 5), you were given the option of choosing either mode. If the server is not going to be used for application server or publishing purposes, then you probably chose the remote administration mode.

You enable the Terminal Services mode either during installation of the base operating system or post-installation using the Windows Components Wizard (see Chapter 5). Figure 25-3 illustrates the option screen presented to you by the Windows Components Wizard. If you installed or enabled the service, the TS administration tools will be available in the Programs\Administrative Tools folder.

If you are not sure of the mode TS is running in, you can launch the Terminal Services Configuration utility, as illustrated in Figure 25-2, and select the Server Settings option. The mode will be shown in the data panel at the right of the tree.

If you installed in the wrong mode, do the following: Go to Add/Remove Programs in Control Panel. Click Add/Remove Windows Components. The Windows Components Wizard launches. See what the checkbox state for TS is. If it is checked, then the services are installed, so click Next to continue. The ensuing screen will indicate the mode you are in, and you can change it accordingly. If you are not certain how the machine is going to be configured for later use, do not enable TS. This does not mean you will not be able to install TS in the future. The software is machine-resident, and the Components Wizard only enables the software. The changes can also be made from the command line, discussed shortly.

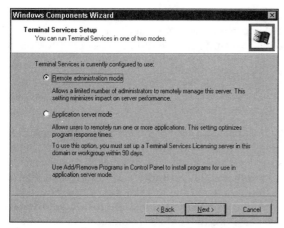

Figure 25-3: The Terminal Services installation screen

If you do plan to install TS, and are not sure if you are going to use it as an application server, then enable remote administration mode. You can always change to application server mode later, but returning from application server mode is more problematic. Any applications that have been installed in application server mode might not work properly after you return the TS to remote administration mode.

And you do not need to enable Terminal Services Licensing unless there are other servers running TS in application mode. The services can also be stopped at any time in the Computer Management snap-in.

Cross-Reference

For further installation options, see Chapter 5.

Remote Administration

In remote administration mode, the server uses minimal resources to support sessions. There is only a 2MB usage of RAM (as opposed to about 4MB that pcANYWHERE uses, not to mention the larger footprint pcANYWHERE or Carbon Copy require on both the server and the client).

This mode provides the most suitable TS configuration for servers running mission-critical applications like SQL Server or Microsoft Exchange where application access would interfere with critical services or use resources required by the niche services.

Also, in remote administration mode, up to two administrators can access the server concurrently. They can collaborate on administering certain aspects on the server, or they can operate independently of each other.

In remote administration mode, you can perform upgrades, install services and additional suites, promote and demote domain controllers, and more. It is thus important to always install the I386 or Alpha source directories from the CDs on the servers when you finish a basic installation. Of course, you can also map a drive on the server to your local CD drive. Both options allow you to access CD builds without needing to insert the actual CD in the server drive during a remote session.

Remote administration mode also allows you to disconnect from the computer instead of logging off, and it leaves your sessions running for later access. This is called roaming disconnect support. But it really has nothing to do with roaming. Often, a complex install (like remotely installing Internet Explorer from a Microsoft Web site) requires a lot of time. You can begin the installation or upgrade, and then leave the session running while you disconnect and head out for a beer. Disconnect leaves your session running (the session's disconnect parameters have to be set, which we will do shortly). When you return to the server, you can simply sign back in as you normally do to find the session still running and open for business.

> **Note**   There are two ways to end a terminal session: Disconnect and Logoff. Disconnect leaves your session running according to predetermined parameters. Logoff shuts down or resets your session, closes any applications that are open, and cleans up resources the session had open or used.

The remote administration option also supports the full RDP feature set. This includes local printing, clipboard mapping, and virtual resource applications such as the ability to map to local drives (the one on the client machine). Automatic drive mapping and audio and video streaming support require the ICA client and MetaFrame installed on the server. If you are not using an ICA connection, the drive mapping and audio support options will be disabled. This limitation in the RDP connection does not prevent you from mapping a drive letter from the server to the local machine, if you have the authority.

Remote administration is an extremely powerful remote access solution for managing Windows 2000 servers remotely. There are, however, a number of important considerations of which to be aware.

> ✦ **Do not use remote administration for application serving.** While you can certainly run administration tools and applications using remote administration, you should not install general multi-user applications for access to the server as a quasi-application server (to circumvent licensing). The remote administration services do not use all the multi-user services that install when you put the server in application server mode.
>
> ✦ **Make sure the TS session is set to Disconnect on Broken.** The Disconnect on Broken option, configured in the User account, ensures that when you suddenly lose a connection to the server, which can easily happen over an unreliable connection, the session is placed into disconnect (Disc) state. In disconnect state, the processes you were running at the time remain running. Thus, if you were performing a delicate operation at the time, such as

defragmenting a disk, the session termination will not kill the processes. If you reset the session on disconnect, you can do some serious damage because reset is akin to killing the process by either ending the task, running the Kill utility, or shutting down the server suddenly, leaving you with possible corrupted data.

✦ **Use Remote Access wisely.** As mentioned earlier, no more than two users can log in to the server at a time, so if your session gets disconnected, there is no way to connect back to the server if another two administrators are logged on under their accounts. How do you get around this dilemma? Enforce a policy of only allowing a special domain "RASADMIN" account to connect to the server. If someone else logs in as RASADMIN, he or she will (you hope) respect the session and leave it in the state he or she found it. You must ensure that your RASADMIN administrator account is configured not to reset after it is disconnected so as not to trash any delicate operation you were performing. Then make sure that any administrative work is performed using this shared account. TS counts the user accounts connecting to the server, so as long as the sessions are running under the same account or user name, you will be able to connect back to the server, end your processes normally, and only then log off and reset the session.

✦ **Coordinate remote administration.** For the reason described previously and many others, you should coordinate remote administration wisely. For starters, only allow remote access to the server for a select experienced group of administrators. Secondly, make sure that you and the other administrators coordinate the work you are doing on the server (such as installing software or configuring storage). You don't want to collide with the other administrators, which could lead to a disaster. When you log in to a server under Terminal Services, you can check to see if anyone else is logged in by running the Terminal Services Manager (which can be cumbersome) or by running the `quser` command from the Command Prompt in the session.

Application Server Mode

Application server mode allows you to install and publish applications and manage as many sessions to the server as resources will allow. Configuring application servers is discussed in Chapter 5. Terminals can connect to the server over any network connection that routes IP. In other words, using RDP, it is essential that the client is able to obtain an IP address and resolve the server in order to connect. Clients that cannot load the IP stack can still connect if they use MetaFrame from Citrix. A good example is clients that load the IPX stack, in which case the server needs to run IPX as well.

Case history: We recently ported an old NetWare 3.11 network direct to Windows 2000 without ever having to open the client workstations. The workstations were MS-DOS machines from the mid-1990s that loaded the IPX protocol and NetWare client software that allowed each user to connect to the old NetWare server (IP was nowhere to be found). We simply installed the MetaFrame client on the old machines and switched them on. The MetaFrame software found the application server running IPX, and, like magic, the client machines were able to connect. Talk about leapfrogging the technology gap. Our customer was able to go from DOS to Windows 2000 on old 486 machines with zero investment in new client hardware. The employees were none the wiser.

As mentioned previously, the application server can be used to cater to several needs. It is an ideal means of deploying the Windows 2000 desktop and Windows applications to legacy hardware that is otherwise incompatible with Windows 2000, running locally. The prior example of the NetWare environment conversion is a case in point.

Other applications or scenarios include general desktop deployment and application publishing. The general desktop deployment is straightforward. Users simply connect to the server and interact with the desktop as if it is local. You can set up the connection to the server using the connection manager and have clients boot directly to the server logon screen after they fire up their machines.

Remote Desktop Deployment

In the remote desktop deployment scenario, configure your Windows client to take one of three routes in providing a session to the client:

1. Configure a connection that allows the user to work in both the local environment and the remote (TS session) environment. This option should be provided to experienced users, possibly only technical personnel, because it can be disconcerting and counter-productive to the users to have them toggling between two desktops. Over a fast intranet, the sessions are so responsive that it is almost impossible to discern the remote desktop from the local desktop. Policy ensures they are set up the same, so the only way to be sure is to click Start and check the logo banner that runs up to the left of the Start menu icons.

2. Configure a connection that is booted to as soon as the local operating system loads. You'll need a script or batch file to process the local logon automatically and then put the user at the TS logon screen. Use the Connection Manager to put the TS screen into Full Screen mode as soon as the user signs in. The local desktop will then be completely hidden from view. Your script can then shut down the local workstation when the user logs off or disconnects from the terminal service.

3. You can also use the Client Connection Manager to provide an automatic logon after local authentication to the domain is obtained. This means that the user is authenticating twice. And yet another option lets the user log on locally and then automatically to the terminal service. As you can see, you have some flexibility in the way you set this all up.

Note Citrix's MetaFrame is an additional cost, so if you can get IP running on client machines that did not need it before, and you use RDP for the connection, you'll be saving a lot of money.

Application Publishing Deployment

In this scenario, your user authenticates to the domain and works on the local machine normally, either on the intranet or via RAS. When he or she needs access to an application on the server, you can configure a connection to take the user directly into a terminal session with automatic logon, and then launch the application he or she needs.

To publish an application, create a connection to the server in the Connection Manager. Configure the connection to run in Full Screen mode and then set it up to automatically log on to the terminal session. You need to provide a user name, password, and domain. Provide the environment settings, such as screen resolution, and provide the program path and file name of the application you wish to start. Finally, you can even change the icon of the connection to reflect the icon of the program you intend to publish.

The connection icon is added to the Terminal Services Client group by default, but you can locate it anywhere on the user desktop. When the user double-clicks the icon, he or she launches the application in the terminal client on the local machine as if it was installed locally.

Deploying Terminal Services

After installing and enabling TS in your mode of choice, there are several items to configure that are peculiar to TS sessions. In this section, we will first deal with session configuration and then with application installation and connection peculiarities.

Session Encryption Levels

As explained in Chapter 3, every portal of access to a Windows 2000 network is protected by one of the many security mechanisms available. TS clients connect using low or medium encryption. If you use low or medium encryption on the connection, it means that any data sent up and down the RDP channels is encrypted using the server's standard 56-bit key strength.

But if you plan to connect to TS from outside the intranet, then you should enable the encryption level to encode at 128-bit, which by early 2000, was still only available in the United States.

You can make the change in the RDP-TCP Properties dialog box in the Terminal Services Configuration snap-in, as shown in Figure 25-2. Launch the utility as described earlier and open the properties dialog box for RDP. The encryption level can be changed from the General tab, as shown in Figure 25-4.

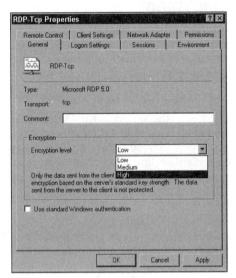

Figure 25-4: Changing the encryption level

Obviously, raising the encryption level increases the CPU bandwidth usage. But remember, every time you connect as an administrator or as a highly enabled user, you take the risk, albeit a very small one, of having your password snatched. While 56-bit is nothing to sneeze at, regular Internet connections to exposed servers warrant the best encryption that money and CPU cycles can buy.

Deploying the Client

Back in Chapter 5, along with the general installation described, we installed TS and also installed the Terminal Services Client Creator Files. Now we can deploy the client to workstations using one of two options:

1. Use the Terminal Services Client Creator.

2. Share the client directory and install over the network.

Option 1: Using the Client Creator

Launch the Terminal Services Client Creator as follows: Go to Programs ⇨ Administrative Tools ⇨ Terminal Services Client Creator. Launch the utility. You can choose to create clients for 16-bit windows or 32-bit windows, as illustrated in Figure 25-5. The 32-bit client installation files will fit on two floppy disks. The 16-bit client will install to four floppy disks (it needs to install 32 files).

Tip   Microsoft employs an irritating habit of preventing the first disk in the client set from being reused by encrypting the user's name and organization into a file on the disk. (The source files on the server are freely distributable so the practice is unnecessary.) To get around this — if connecting over the network is not an option — make a copy of the file `setup.ini` on the first disk. Notice that all the files on this first disk have the same date. Name the copy `setup.bak`. When you install the client, you will notice that the date of this file has changed and the disk cannot be reused. Open to the command line and execute the command **copy setup.bak setup.ini**. If the `setup.ini` file date is the same as the others, you are set to go.

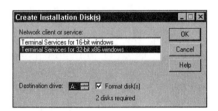

Figure 25-5: The Terminal Services Client Creator utility

Option 2: Connecting to a share-point

The TS client files reside in the `%systemroot%\system32\clients\tsclient` folder. You can share the folder in the usual fashion and publish the share in Active Directory as described in Chapter 22, and as shown in Figure 25-6. Once you have published a shared folder that can be located in the Windows Explorer, you should uninstall the `tsclient` folders in the other Windows 2000 servers you've installed. It is an unnecessary waste of space to have the same files on every server.

To remove the files, open the Windows Components Wizard from Control Panel, select the Terminal Services line, and click the Details button. Clear the Client Creator Files checkbox and then click OK.

You will also notice that the share is open to Everyone with Full Access by default. The Everyone group needs access to this folder to install the software, but you should uncheck all but the Read permission, in case someone deletes the files.

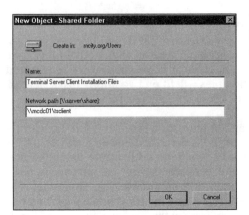

Figure 25-6: Publishing the Terminal Services Client installation folder in Active Directory

To install over the network, drill down into the Net folder. Once installed, the client can run in 8MB of RAM, and the client device or PC does not need to be rebooted after installation.

Connecting to the server

You connect to the server in one of two ways: Run the Terminal Services client or set up a connection in the Connection Manager (CONMAN). Both shortcuts are placed in the `Programs\Terminal Services Client` folder. To connect to the server from the client, you can simply enter the NetBIOS name of the client (its WINS name), a DNS name, or the IP address.

The Connection Manager not only lets you configure a connection that gets installed to the `Programs\Terminal Services Client` folder, but also allows you to run it in full-screen mode. Depending on your screen resolution, you can connect all the way up to 1600 × 1200 resolution. You can also select an option to have the client launch a program on the server as soon as you log in.

Once logged in, you can transfer files between the computers by mapping to the client's shares from the server or by using the files transfer utility that ships with the Windows 2000 Resource Kit. You can also map to the local CD drive share to install applications or transfer files to the server.

Getting the most out of the client connection

Client desktops and sessions should be configured to cater to the worst possible connection to the server. One day, the user might connect to the intranet over a 100Mbit backbone; the next day, he or she may connect via RAS over a 28.8Kbit connection from home or a hotel room. Here are some suggestions to allow the user to get the most out of the client connection:

✦ Keep the use of graphics low. Try to eliminate or disable screen savers (use the power saver features at the local machine), blinking cursors, and animated features, such as the Microsoft Office Assistant.

✦ Try to disable the splash screen of an application. Every time a user loads an application while connected over a low bandwidth connection, the splash screen will take forever to reach the screen. It can be a real pain in the neck. Many applications run really well on the server, but their splash screens are so graphics- and animation-intensive that we have often had to kill the task for an irate user. If the software is saddled with such egotistical grandeur, get with the manufacturer and ask them to disable the splash.

✦ Disable the Active Desktop. It requires more resources than the legacy desktop.

✦ Disable smooth scrolling.

✦ When you set up the user profiles and policies, prevent them from enabling or using animation and graphics features. For example, set the bitmap in the wallpaper to none and then prevent the user from configuring the desktop.

✦ Keep legacy applications (DOS and 16-bit Windows applications) away from the server.

There is no harm in enabling every user account with Terminal Services, even if you run a mixed, as in workstation and terminal, environment. You never know when a user might need access to an application from a remote location, and as mentioned earlier, it can be used to provide access to the Windows 2000 desktop from legacy Windows desktops.

Installing Applications

As discussed earlier, you can operate Terminal Services in two modes: *remote administration mode* and *application server mode*. Installing applications in remote administration mode requires no special installation handling procedures. However, installing applications in application server mode requires you to place the server into an installation mode.

Application servers operate in one of two modes: *install mode* and *execute mode*. When you need to install applications on the server, you need to place the server in the install mode, which you can do from the command line. However, Windows 2000 Server is able to detect an attempt to install software. It will then show a message advising you to first click on the Add/Remove icon in Control Panel. This action automatically puts the server into install mode. It's a good idea to get used to changing the mode without relying on Windows 2000 to detect an installation because Windows may not always detect an installation.

You can also use the command `Change User /Install` to change the modes. `Change User /Execute` changes to the normal operations mode. To view the running modes of the server, run the command `Change User /Query`. You can also install applications from the command line. The Change commands and other Terminal Services utilities are discussed in Appendix B. They can be run from the Run item on the Start menu.

Tip   If you need to install software during normal operational hours and have a number of users online, you will need to request that they save their work and log off. This can be done from the Terminal Services Manager or the NET SEND command discussed in Appendix A. Give your users time to log off, set a deadline at which time you can go into the Manager and reset their connections, and place the server into install mode.

To install interactively, perform the following steps:

1. Click the Add/Remove icon in Control Panel.

2. Click the Add New Programs option and then click CD or Floppy. The install Wizard loads.

3. Add the media into its respective drive and then click Next to locate the install program. This is usually the `setup.exe` file. At the Run Installation Program dialog box, click Next. The installation will now run as it was designed to, with Windows 2000 monitoring the process. The Wizard will also load the Finish Admin Install dialog box that instructs you to click Finish only when the installation has fully completed. Do not click the Finish button on this dialog box until the installation has completed, or your software will not install with the full support of application server services.

4. Now comes the important part. Software installation packages do not know they are being installed on an application server (at least not until Terminal Services becomes more popular). So, when the installation completes and you get the message to reboot, DO NOT REBOOT. Select the option to restart the machine later if it so requires you to reboot. Now click the Finish button as described in the previous step. When the install Wizard closes, you can restart the server.

Configuration

To manage the connection environment on a server, you use the Terminal Services Configuration snap-in. The snap-in is usually placed on the Administrative Tools menu when you install Terminal Services. The snap-in allows you to change server mode type (not install or execution mode) and other global sessions. But the most important settings can be found in the Connections mode.

To open Connections, click the node in the tree to display installed connections. If you have MetaFrame installed on the server, the ICA connection will also show up in the same pane. Double-click the connection to load the properties. For RDP connections, this dialog box is called RDP-TCP Properties.

The property pages in the dialog box allow you to select encryption levels, global logon information, global session information, global environment options, and port and drive mappings with connecting clients.

User Access Tips

Configuring user access to Terminal Services is done at the user account level. Setting up and configuring user accounts is discussed in Chapter 10. Terminal session users should be treated no differently than standard client users. In other words, follow the same group, access rights, permissions, group policy advice, and so on discussed in the earlier chapters. Disk quotas, security, redirected folders, and more all apply to session users. Restrictions that apply at the workstation also apply in a terminal session.

However, there is one very important policy that will no doubt cause you to bang your head against the wall with frustration . . . the right to log on locally. If your users do not have this right, they cannot establish a terminal session and will instead get a message to the effect that local policy does not allow interactive logon. This is caused by not providing local logon rights to Terminal Services users.

Connecting to a member server that has been configured as an application server usually provides this right to the users when they are granted the ability to log on to Terminal Services in the user account fields in Active Directory. The user is given membership in the built-in, out of bounds, TERMINAL SERVICE USER group. But the right (discussed in Chapter 10) can often become negated by an overriding policy, or an undocumented or unauthorized change control activity, or an adventurous administrator. Also, if you plan to use a domain controller as a terminal server as well, which will be the norm for many small companies, this right can be the barrier to logon if not defined in the domain controllers group policy object.

For the record, the right to log on locally can be set at any of the SDOU group policy objects and the target domain controller's GPO. The policy needs to be applied to a user or group before local logon is permitted.

To find the right in the domain controller GPO or any GPO, open to the object as demonstrated in Chapter 11. Expand the tree in the GP Editor and locate the following node: Computer Configuration ➪ Windows Settings ➪ Security Settings ➪ Local Policies ➪ User Rights Assignment ➪ Log on Locally. You need to define (enable) the policy and add the user group to the list of users or groups granted the logon right.

If you plan to use a domain controller as a terminal server, make sure to lock the server down very well, or you risk unauthorized tampering in the Active Directory, registry, and Windows NT folders.

Summary

Windows 2000 Terminal Services and the thin-client/server computer model represent a major paradigm shift in computing. In this chapter, our objective was to introduce you to the services and to present a framework and a holistic overview of the concept and the design objectives. We also talked about total cost of ownership (TCO) and how the thin-client/server can provide a greater return on the cost of technology.

On the technical side, we introduced you to the two operation modes of the server: remote access and application server. In remote access mode, Windows 2000 server provides a very effective mechanism for attaching to the server from a remote location and managing or administering it in a full-blown interactive environment, identical to the console. This is a feature that many have begged for over the years, and it is one reason for you to enable Terminal Services.

✦   ✦   ✦

What's on the CD-ROM

This appendix provides an overview of the software included on the Windows 2000 Server Bible CD and explains how to install the software from the CD.

Aelita Software Group

The Windows 2000 Server Bible CD includes several utilities from Aelita Software Group, described in the following sections. These products are included in the Aelita Enterprise Suite. Aelita's Web site is located at `http://www.aelita.com`.

Delegation Manager

Delegation Manager is targeted at medium- to large-size networks where managing security for domains, member servers, and workstations can be difficult because of the sheer number of accounts involved. Delegation Manager adds access control over user accounts and groups, enabling an administrator to delegate routine administrative tasks with limited permissions to other users. For example, you might delegate the ability to re-enabled locked accounts or change passwords to a specified user or group of users.

Delegation Manager lets you represent any subset of administrative authority as a custom *access template* containing collections of elementary permissions. You can then use the template to easily and quickly grant administrative authority to other users without giving them full administrative rights and permissions.

Delegation Manager uses a client/server architecture to enable this security delegation. The Server component runs as a secure service on a Windows 2000 Server or Professional computer. The Delegation Manager Client runs on the client side and passes administrative requests to the Delegation Server, which controls whether or not the user can perform the specified tasks.

Aelita ERDisk

The Rdisk utility included with Windows NT provided a means of backing up the registry and creating an emergency repair disk (ERD) for NT systems. The Windows 2000 Backup utility provides much the same capability, enabling you to back up the system state data and create an emergency repair disk (though arguably a less useful ERD than that created by NT's Rdisk). Aelita ERDisk utility broadens the ability to create repair disks, enabling you to create disks for remote servers and workstations across the network from a central location, simplifying system administration. ERDisk can store the repair information on a network server for security, and you can use the files for a given server or workstation (or class of computers) to repair the system if it becomes necessary.

Enterprise Directory Reporter

Aelita's Enterprise Directory Reporter (formerly Virtuosity) comprises three tools: the Virtuosity Wizard, Virtuosity Classic, and Domain Migration Wizard. The Virtuosity Wizard puts a more user-friendly face on Virtuosity Classic, both of which enable you to store in an Access or SQL database network-wide information about users, groups, account security configuration, access permissions, password settings, and a wide range of other data collected from the network. In addition to providing a means of collecting and analyzing the data, Virtuosity also enables you to apply changes to settings across the enterprise.

The Domain Migration Wizard is particularly useful for organizations moving from Windows NT domains to Windows 2000 domains and the Active Directory. The wizard is targeted at domain reconfiguration tasks such as domain consolidation, domain split, transition from multi-master model to multi-resource model, and other changes.

ClockWatch

Beagle Software's ClockWatch 1.3.4 enables you to synchronize the time on multiple systems running Windows 2000, Windows NT, and Windows 95/98. The software provides separate server and client components. All clients can synchronize the system time from a ClockWatch server (running the Server component) or communicate with the National Institute of Standards and Technology (NIST) or other Internet time server to synchronize time. Beagle's Web site is located at `http://www.beaglesoft.com`.

Diskeeper Lite

Diskeeper Lite, from Executive Software, Inc., is an advanced disk defragmenter application. It can defragment volumes on remote computers, and can be set to defragment volumes according to a schedule.

Full Armor Zero Administration 2000

The Full Armor Zero Administration kit (FAZAM) enables you to analyze and plan group policy implementation, which helps avoid potential problems in applying group policies that can have an unintended affect on a large number of users. You can use the tool to perform what-if analysis on policies to determine what impact they'll have on users in the enterprise before you apply the policy changes. You also can use FAZAM to analyze existing policies to troubleshoot problems and provide help desk support. Full Armor's Web site is located at http://www.fullarmor.com.

crondSys™

crondSys™, from #ifdef Software, Incorporated, provides a means of scheduling any Windows NT or Windows 2000 application for unattended execution at specified dates and times by Windows 95/98, Windows NT, and Windows 2000 clients. The crondSys™ Scheduling Engine runs as a Windows 2000 service on the target system and uses the security inherent in the network domain/workgroup structure to allow or deny users the ability to execute applications. Administrators can specify which users or groups of users can schedule tasks with crondSys™.

The crondSys' client provides an interface through which users can create, view, and manage tasks on the local or remote systems running the crondSys™ Scheduling Engine. In addition to enabling you to schedule tasks in much the same way that the AT command provides, crondSys™ lets you send keystrokes to applications, develop your own applications through VB, Java, or other scripting languages, generate notifications through SMTP, and much more. The Web site for #ifdef Software Incorporated is located at http://www.ifdef.com.

KeyServer

KeyServer 5.1, from Sassafras Software, Inc., is a software sentry and software asset manager for your network. This product specializes in metering software use throughout the enterprise, which ensures licensing is adhered to, and that software access is not being abused by anyone.

In addition to metering this product offers protection from piracy. Anyone who attempts to steal software from the corporate network will not be able to use his or her loot without the key server in the loop. KeyServer supports both convenient and secure metering choices. KeyServer's auto-discovery tool allows automatic monitoring and/or control of any applications. And KeyServer will continue to add newly installed applications as they are used by end-users

The product is especially useful in the world of thin-client/server and application service providers. It is the only software license metering system that has the capability to simultaneously support thin-client desktops and traditional desktops.

Sassafras' Web site is located at http://www.sassafras.com.

RecoverNT

RecoverNT 3.1, LC Technology International scans a drive sector-by-sector, enabling you to rebuild a drive and recover lost data. RecoverNT enables you to restore delete files and directories. Changes are made in memory, giving you an opportunity to review them before committing them to disk. You can view the recovered data as text or in hex. Because RecoverNT works above the file system driver level it can restore data from stripe sets, RAID volumes, and NTFS volumes.

LC Technology's Web site is located at http://www.lc-tech.com.

Liquid Time

Liquid Time, from Code Blue Technologies, is a utility for Windows NT and Windows 2000 designed for creating and scheduling executable programs, batch files, and scripts. Liquid Time incorporates several features:

- ✦ **Administrator Console**: GUI for creating, editing, and managing batch jobs. You also use the Administrator Console for viewing log files and templates.
- ✦ **GUI Diagramming Editor**: Use this tool to graphically design and view batch jobs using a flow chart analogy.
- ✦ **Server Scripts**: Use server scripts in batch programs to perform higher-level functions such as accessing the file system or databases, generating e-mail, etc.
- ✦ **Server Script Editor**: Use this tool to write and debug server scripts.
- ✦ **Batch Job Triggers**: Triggers let your batch programs watch for events and initiate tasks when the events occur.
- ✦ **Agents**: Use agents to distribute execution of batch programs across the network, using multiple systems to provide increased CPU power for the task.
- ✦ **Navigator**: This folder provides a graphical view of the Liquid Time server and current / pending jobs.

You'll find Code Blue's Web site at http://www.liquidtime.com.

DirectoryAnalyzer Hyperlink

NetPro Computing, Inc. specializes in the health of directory services. Directory Analyzer 1.02, for Active Directory , monitors and troubleshoots all critical components of Active Directory, including domain controllers, domains, sites, and certain DNS functions. DirectoryAnalyzer provides the peace of mind you need to deploy Active Directory in a rapid timeframe.

The product monitors all critical functions of the directory service, from replication latency and replication topology problems to high LDAP loads and DNS inconsistencies. The product also monitors and alerts you immediately to critical infrastructure problems. On the CD is a link that will take you to NetPro's Web site, where you can download DirectoryAnalyzer.

ScriptLogic

ScriptLogic 2.5, from Inteletek, Inc., builds on the KiXtart logon scripting language to enable you to build sophisticated logon scripts that provide validation logic of drive mappings, path control, printer deployment, shell folders, Internet access, service pack installations, anti-virus signature updates, mail profile creation, and many other automated tasks. In addition to providing a GUI for building scripts, ScriptLogic includes a GUI for managing replication of scripts, an important aspect of logon script management. See the company's Web site at http://www.scriptlogic.com.

SiteScope

SiteScope, from Freshwater Software, Inc. provides a sophisticated suite of tools you use to monitor your web server environment. It can work around the clock using over 20 standard monitors.

The product comes with a specialized technology known as *deep monitoring*. This is a process of testing failure points at several levels, providing Web administrators with an accurate and complete picture of the health of their web sites. For example, in addition to confirming that a URL is accessible, SiteScope can verify that the content is correct, the file size hasn't changed, and the graphics are all available. This helps avoid false alarms.

SiteScope offers the following features:

✦ Centralized monitoring of large and small Web server farms

✦ Monitors that watch critical Web environment components

✦ A published API for the creation of custom monitors and integration of home-grown tools

✦ Escalation paths for error and warning notification

✦ Multiple notification methods including e-mail, pager, SNMP trap, or execution of an error recovery script

✦ Scheduled and on-demand management reports for file systems and recovering wasted space.

The program also offers 18 standard reports on wasted space, quotas, disk space usage, and file security.

Support Aide

Support Aide 1.01, from Lakeside Software, Inc., is a system metrics tool that records and analyzes the applications and system resources that are accessed by users as they perform their day-to-day work. It allows a system planner to find out key information such as what applications and application versions each user executes, what system resources these applications consume, what level of service users are receiving, and the effect that users and applications have on overall system performance.

As a system metrics tool, Support Aide aids system administrators in medium and large scale Windows NT/2000 installations. The product is scalable and can provide information on thousands of systems from a single console. It collects data from each system and automatically maintains a hierarchy of databases. Administrators can analyze the entire organization or can drill all the way down to an individual system. You'll find Lakeside Software on the Web at http://www.lakesidesoftware.com.

UltraAdmin

UltraAdmin 1.5, from Dorian Software Creations, Inc., bundles several common administrative tasks into a single GUI, giving you a central point of control over a wide variety of system and network administration tasks. The program automatically shows all systems in a specified workgroup or domain in the main UltraAdmin window. You can right-click on a computer in the list and choose one of several commands on its context menu to view administrative shares, reboot the computer, send a message to it, and manage several other aspects such as file shares, services, connected users, open files, printers, etc. You can use UltraAdmin as a replacement to the Network Neighborhood since it displays all computers in the domain or workgroup and lets you browse to them.

UltraAdmin's SID Wizard is a useful feature, as well. You can use the wizard to view the SIDs of user or computer accounts and export SIDs to an ODBC-compliant database such as Access or SQL Server. You also can export the SIDs to a comma-delimited text file for import into other applications such as Excel or other databases.

Dorian Software Creations' Web site is located at http://www.doriansoft.com.

W. Quinn Associates

The Windows 2000 Server Bible includes four utilities from W. Quinn Associates for managing disks and quotas and preventing unwanted files from being downloaded to a server or workstation. The company's Web site is located at http://www.wquinn.com.

DiskAdvisor 4.1

DiskAdvisor provides a means of monitoring your file systems and recovering wasted space. The program offers 18 standard reports on wasted space, quotas, disk space usage, and file security. You can use the Custom Report Writer to create your own reports, as well. DiskAdvisor can help you identify such things as duplicate files, outdated files, oversized files, insecure files, and view space usage by user, group, share, quota, or directory.

FileScreen 2000

FileScreen 2000 lets you prevent specific types of files from being store on your servers or workstations. The program screens files by type or file name and prevents specified files from being written to the system. For example, you can use FileScreen 2000 to prevent mp3, video, or other types of files from being downloaded to the computer.

QuotaAdvisor 4.1

QuotaAdvisor expands Windows 2000's quota management capabilities for NTFS volumes. The program enables you to define varying levels of quotas for users and groups and supports automatic quota assignment, user disk space management policies, hard and soft quotas, up to five threshold settings, SMTP support, and several other features that make it a solid quota management package.

StorageCeNTral

StorageCeNTral combines the features of the other Quinn tools into one application that provides quota management, disk storage management, disk security, and related features. In addition to Quota Manager and DiskAdvisor, StorageCeNTral includes a copy of Trend Analysis, which provides data collection and reporting capabilities to help you analyze disk storage needs, use, and statistics. Trend Analysis supports ODBC, enabling you to store collected data in any ODBC-compliant database.

NTDMatch

Shareware product NTDMatch (ver 2.0.0.7) is a 32-bit native Windows NT/95/98/2000 program that is supported by Larry Waibel of Leading the Way. Larry can be reached at lwaibel@cwia.com. The product was apparently inspired by the DirMatch utility originally published some time back in PC Magazine. We included it here because despite all the lofty features of Windows 2000 we still found that something as basic as a utility to compare folders and their contents (and be deductive) was absent from the visual applets. The command line programs that support folder compare are cryptic and they are not too informative.

The tool compares directories based on filters which allow it to only show, for example, those files which exist in both, but the file in one has been modified. It allows file manipulations such as copy, delete, edit, and so on, on all or selected files. A useful feature of this product is that it can be used to take a snapshot of the directories, which can be used later to compare to the same directory. This is handy for determining which files were changed when a new software package is installed.

Adobe Acrobat Reader

Adobe's Acrobat Reader is a helpful program that will enable you to view the two bonus appendixes included on this CD-ROM in the same page format as the actual book. To install Adobe Acrobat Reader, follow these steps:

1. Open the Acrobat Reader folder.
2. In the acrobat folder, double-click rs40eng.exe and follow the instructions presented on-screen for installing Adobe Acrobat Reader.

Extras

This folder provides the complete template deployment plan described in Chapter 4. The document provides placeholders for items such IP addresses and subnets, domain names and site specific information to include in the plan. The document is in Word 97 format and is a document template.

Two bonus appendixes are provided on the CD-ROM:

✦ Appendix A: Windows 2000 Command Line Reference
✦ Appendix B: Windows 2000 Resource Kit

These appendixes are provided in PDF format, and can be read using the Adobe Acrobat Reader found on this CD-ROM.

✦   ✦   ✦

Index

Continued

Continued

Continued

IDG Books Worldwide, Inc.
End-User License Agreement

READ THIS. You should carefully read these terms and conditions before opening the software packet(s) included with this book ("Book"). This is a license agreement ("Agreement") between you and IDG Books Worldwide, Inc. ("IDGB"). By opening the accompanying software packet(s), you acknowledge that you have read and accept the following terms and conditions. If you do not agree and do not want to be bound by such terms and conditions, promptly return the Book and the unopened software packet(s) to the place you obtained them for a full refund.

1. **License Grant.** IDGB grants to you (either an individual or entity) a nonexclusive license to use one copy of the enclosed software program(s) (collectively, the "Software") solely for your own personal or business purposes on a single computer (whether a standard computer or a workstation component of a multiuser network). The Software is in use on a computer when it is loaded into temporary memory (RAM) or installed into permanent memory (hard disk, CD-ROM, or other storage device). IDGB reserves all rights not expressly granted herein.

2. **Ownership.** IDGB is the owner of all right, title, and interest, including copyright, in and to the compilation of the Software recorded on the disk(s) or CD-ROM ("Software Media"). Copyright to the individual programs recorded on the Software Media is owned by the author or other authorized copyright owner of each program. Ownership of the Software and all proprietary rights relating thereto remain with IDGB and its licensers.

3. **Restrictions On Use and Transfer.**

    (a) You may only (i) make one copy of the Software for backup or archival purposes, or (ii) transfer the Software to a single hard disk, provided that you keep the original for backup or archival purposes. You may not (i) rent or lease the Software, (ii) copy or reproduce the Software through a LAN or other network system or through any computer subscriber system or bulletin-board system, or (iii) modify, adapt, or create derivative works based on the Software.

    (b) You may not reverse engineer, decompile, or disassemble the Software. You may transfer the Software and user documentation on a permanent basis, provided that the transferee agrees to accept the terms and conditions of this Agreement and you retain no copies. If the Software is an update or has been updated, any transfer must include the most recent update and all prior versions.

4. **Restrictions on Use of Individual Programs.** You must follow the individual requirements and restrictions detailed for each individual program in the "What's on the CD ROM" Appendix of this Book. These limitations are also contained in the individual license agreements recorded on the Software Media. These limitations may include a requirement that after using the program for a specified period of time, the user must pay a registration fee or discontinue use. By opening the Software packet(s), you will be agreeing to abide by the licenses and restrictions for these individual programs that are detailed in the Appendix and on the Software Media. None of the material on this Software Media or listed in this Book may ever be redistributed, in original or modified form, for commercial purposes.

5. **Limited Warranty.**

   (a) IDGB warrants that the Software and Software Media are free from defects in materials and workmanship under normal use for a period of sixty (60) days from the date of purchase of this Book. If IDGB receives notification within the warranty period of defects in materials or workmanship, IDGB will replace the defective Software Media.

   (b) **IDGB AND THE AUTHORS OF THE BOOK DISCLAIM ALL OTHER WARRANTIES, EXPRESS OR IMPLIED, INCLUDING WITHOUT LIMITATION IMPLIED WARRANTIES OF MERCHANTABILITY AND FITNESS FOR A PARTICULAR PURPOSE, WITH RESPECT TO THE SOFTWARE, THE PROGRAMS, THE SOURCE CODE CONTAINED THEREIN, AND/OR THE TECHNIQUES DESCRIBED IN THIS BOOK. IDGB DOES NOT WARRANT THAT THE FUNCTIONS CONTAINED IN THE SOFTWARE WILL MEET YOUR REQUIREMENTS OR THAT THE OPERATION OF THE SOFTWARE WILL BE ERROR FREE.**

   (c) This limited warranty gives you specific legal rights, and you may have other rights that vary from jurisdiction to jurisdiction.

6. **Remedies.**

   (a) IDGB's entire liability and your exclusive remedy for defects in materials and workmanship shall be limited to replacement of the Software Media, which may be returned to IDGB with a copy of your receipt at the following address: Software Media Fulfillment Department, Attn.: *Windows 2000 Server Bible*, IDG Books Worldwide, Inc., 10475 Crosspoint Blvd., Indianapolis, IN 46256, or call 1-800-762-2974. Please allow three to four weeks for delivery. This Limited Warranty is void if failure of the Software Media has resulted from accident, abuse, or misapplication. Any replacement Software Media will be warranted for the remainder of the original warranty period or thirty (30) days, whichever is longer.

   (b) In no event shall IDGB or the authors be liable for any damages whatsoever (including without limitation damages for loss of business profits, business interruption, loss of business information, or any other pecuniary loss) arising from the use of or inability to use the Book or the Software, even if IDGB has been advised of the possibility of such damages.

(c) Because some jurisdictions do not allow the exclusion or limitation of liability for consequential or incidental damages, the above limitation or exclusion may not apply to you.

7. **U.S. Government Restricted Rights.** Use, duplication, or disclosure of the Software by the U.S. Government is subject to restrictions stated in paragraph (c)(1)(ii) of the Rights in Technical Data and Computer Software clause of DFARS 252.227-7013, and in subparagraphs (a) through (d) of the Commercial Computer — Restricted Rights clause at FAR 52.227-19, and in similar clauses in the NASA FAR supplement, when applicable.

8. **General.** This Agreement constitutes the entire understanding of the parties and revokes and supersedes all prior agreements, oral or written, between them and may not be modified or amended except in a writing signed by both parties hereto that specifically refers to this Agreement. This Agreement shall take precedence over any other documents that may be in conflict herewith. If any one or more provisions contained in this Agreement are held by any court or tribunal to be invalid, illegal, or otherwise unenforceable, each and every other provision shall remain in full force and effect.

my2cents.idgbooks.com

Register This Book — And Win!

Visit **http://my2cents.idgbooks.com** to register this book and we'll automatically enter you in our fantastic monthly prize giveaway. It's also your opportunity to give us feedback: let us know what you thought of this book and how you would like to see other topics covered.

Discover IDG Books Online!

The IDG Books Online Web site is your online resource for tackling technology — at home and at the office. Frequently updated, the IDG Books Online Web site features exclusive software, insider information, online books, and live events!

10 Productive & Career-Enhancing Things You Can Do at www.idgbooks.com

- Nab source code for your own programming projects.

- Download software.

- Read Web exclusives: special articles and book excerpts by IDG Books Worldwide authors.

- Take advantage of resources to help you advance your career as a Novell or Microsoft professional.

- Buy IDG Books Worldwide titles or find a convenient bookstore that carries them.

- Register your book and win a prize.

- Chat live online with authors.

- Sign up for regular e-mail updates about our latest books.

- Suggest a book you'd like to read or write.

- Give us your 2¢ about our books and about our Web site.

You say you're not on the Web yet? It's easy to get started with IDG Books' *Discover the Internet*, available at local retailers everywhere.

CD-ROM Installation Instructions

Each software item on the *Windows 2000 Server Bible* CD-ROM is located in its own folder. To install a particular piece of software, open its folder with My Computer or Internet Explorer. What you do next depends on what you find in the software's folder:

1. First, look for a ReadMe.txt file or a .doc or .htm document. If this is present, it should contain installation instructions and other useful information.

2. If the folder contains an executable (.exe) file, this is usually an installation program. Often it will be called Setup.exe or Install.exe, but in some cases the filename reflects an abbreviated version of the software's name and version number. Run the .exe file to start the installation process.

The ReadMe.txt file in the CD-ROM's root directory may contain additional installation information, so be sure to check it.

For a listing of the software on the CD-ROM, see the Appendix.